# PLEROMATICA

GABRIEL CATREN

# Pleromatica

OR
ELSINORE'S TRANCE

*Translated by*
THOMAS MURPHY

*sequence*

Published in 2023 by

URBANOMIC MEDIA LTD
THE OLD LEMONADE FACTORY
WINDSOR QUARRY
FALMOUTH TR11 3EX
UNITED KINGDOM

SEQUENCE PRESS
88 ELDRIDGE STREET
NEW YORK
NY 10002
UNITED STATES



US Library of Congress Control Number: 2022918800

BRITISH LIBRARY CATALOGUING-IN-PUBLICATION DATA

A full catalogue record of this book is available
from the British Library
ISBN 978-1-7336281-4-3

Printed and bound in the UK by
Short Run Press

Distributed by the MIT Press, Cambridge, Massachusetts
and London, England

www.urbanomic.com
www.sequencepress.com

# CONTENTS

Fragments of this text were previously published in the philosophical review *Nombres* 29 (Cordoba: Alción Editora, 2015), 171–208, in S. de Sanctis and A. Longo (eds.), *Breaking the Spell: Contemporary Realism under Discussion* (Mimesis International, 2015), 63–89, in G. Catren, 'The Trans-Umweltic Express', *Glass Bead* 0 (2016) (Portuguese translation: *O Expresso trans-umwéltico,* tr. L. Olimpio [Fortaleza, CE: Raiz Imaginaria, 2022]), in A. Popa and F. Flueras (eds.), *Black Hyperbox* (Berlin: Motto Books, 2017), in G. Catren, *Pleromática o las mareaciones de Elsinor* (Buenos Aires: Hekht Libros, 2017), in G. Catren, 'A Plea for Narcissus: On the Transcendental Reflexion ∧ Refraction Mediation Tandem', in F. Gironi (ed.), *The Legacy of Kant in Sellars and Meillassoux: Analytical and Continental Kantianism* (New York: Routledge, 2018), in G. Catren, 'Le phénoumène', in E. Alloa and E. During (eds.), *Choses en soi* (Paris: PUF, 2018), and in G. Catren, 'Fichte en el Amazonas', postface to J.-C. Goddard, *La filosofía fichteana de la vida. Lo transcendental y lo patológico* (Buenos Aires: Hekht, 2021).

# Acknowledgements

With my deepest gratitude to Aída, Alberto, Pablo, Alianza, Francisco, Enia, Moises, Narcisa, Silvana, Bibi, Adrián, Paulo, Carolina, Lucas, Esteban, Diego, Paula, Tomas, Damián, Analía, Martín, Nadine, Na Kar, Tamar, Ximena, Alfredo, Alain, Laurent, Elie, and Frida for enlivening, supporting, nourishing, embellishing, and challenging this life that is not mine.

I would also like to thank Robin Mackay for his encouragement to publish this text, Robin Mackay, Katherine Pickard, Miguel Abreu, and Maya B. Kronic for welcoming it into the catalogue of Sequence Press and Urbanomic and for their outstanding editorial work, and Thomas Murphy for 'translating' it into English from a patchwork of languages (Spanish, French, English) with such dedication and virtuosity.

# Preamble

> *[...] y en esa noche oscura del fosfeno ver surgir un delfín iridiscente un arco iris de delfines un delfinado aéreo o irisado un arqueado delfín.*
>
> NESTOR PERLONGHER[1]

A suspended scenario: the phantasmal ark, 'between the constellations and the sea'; a senseless task, to sublate chance; and a methodical patience, 'word for word'. This absolutely modern scene will be submerged in the phenoumenodelic solution. Rather than condescending to a catastrophic *pathos,* the shipwreck invoked in Mallarmé's *Coup de dés* shall denote the ship's immersion in an atonal daydream, its transubstantiation into an inebriated vessel. All phenoumena—storms, UFOs, symmetriads—shall form a part of the same impersonal trance. The *Maître*—'standing in the storm'[2] aboard his 'noetic ark', tempering and tanning himself at the top of the mast, vomiting—will have done with all melancholic lethargy, and throw the dice.

---

1 '[...] and on that dark night of the phosphene to see a rainbow of dolphins an aerial or iridescent dolphin an arched dolphin an opalescent dolphin emerging.' N. Perlongher, *Chorreo de las iluminaciones*, in *Poemas completos* (Buenos Aires: La Flauta Mágica, 2002), 231.

2 Plato, *Republic*, 497 d, 9, quoted in M. Heidegger, 'The Self-Assertion of the German University', tr. K Harries, in *Philosophical and Political Writings*, ed. M. Satssen (New York: Continuum, 2003), 2–11: 11.

# Introduction

Let us begin with an irrevocable fact: we have undergone an exquisite and unforgettable crisis in our foundations: *on a touché au sol*—the ground has been compromised, launched into a state of freefall. Beginning with the Copernican decentralisation of the earth on the one hand and the Galilean indiscernibility of uniform motion and rest on the other, we have passed through a multitude of relativisations and ungroundings that continue to undermine pre-modern forms of building, dwelling, and thinking. An abyssal landscape emerges within modern cosmology, that of a centreless, boundless, and groundless universe, characterised by spatial and temporal vastness, darkness, emptiness and silence, harbouring cataclysmic events; stars going supernova, galaxies whirling around supermassive black holes; a universe which itself is the remnant expanding firework of an 'initial' outbursting singularity, displaying a sheer, blind indifference to human values, meanings, and projects. Measured in relation to such cosmic spatiotemporal scales, the emergence and evolution of life and intelligence on Earth seem to be nothing but an insignificant and ephemeral fluctuation emerging out of a ground state of absolute death.

Deepening this first narcissistic wound, Darwinism primatises the human species and initiates the revelation of the chain of natural contingencies leading to the existence of human beings and to their particular psycho-physiological structure. The nineteenth century sees a *crisis in verse*—the shipwreck of *mètre* in favour of free verse—that announces the deconstruction of any *master* signifier, the relativisation of any metrical canon. A little later, music undergoes a crisis in tonality, an invitation to absolve (artistic, scientific, philosophical) composition from tone-centred gravitational constraints. The *ego cogito*—a desperate attempt to regain a ground in the midst of this modern upheaval—clearly exposed its ultimate vocation and the effective modalities of its being-in-the-world, that of becoming an *ego conquero*[1] whose purported 'mastery' over others and over nature led to the massacre of the indigenous populations of a whole 'new' continent, to the transatlantic 'middle passage' and its contemporary Mediterranean reverberations, to a wide spectrum of colonial and postcolonial genocides, ethnocides, epistemicides, and linguicides, and—last but not least—to the extractivist devastation of the earthly Ark and the ravaging of the multifarious forms of life that it carries through the phenoumenodelic deluge. Faithful to the 'puny virile reason' of the *ego conquero*, the techno-'medical nemesis' strives to absolve existence from vulnerability, finitude, and death, and the derisory heroism of capitalistic Prometheanism elicits puerile dreams about colonising space and opening new markets in the 'wide blue yonder'. At the same time, the Cartesian subject becomes *unheimlich* and its alleged mastery is definitively compromised: the conscious *m'être* understood as a self-grounded last instance of experience comprehends its true existential condition, that of having always already embarked on an impersonal unconscious. And what is more, the anarchist and communist traditions obstruct de jure the possibility of withdrawing from the act of existing by means of a reifying identification between the subject and its private properties. In the same vein, the existentialist legacy showed that any form of humanist essentialisation of the subject's existential condition that reifies the continuous process of speculative morphogenesis that is life—i.e. any conception of the subject as a bundle of essential properties—is no longer an 'authentic' option.

On the side of the sciences, mathematics experiences a crisis in its foundations: axiomatic systems proliferate, the inherent limits of proof and computation are formally exposed, and the logical and set-theoretical bases of mathematics are called into question in favour of the structures

1 E. Dussel, *Philosophy of Liberation* (New York: Orbis Books, 1985), 3.

of category theory. In physics, relativity theory dynamises the hitherto fixed spatiotemporal background, quantum mechanics calls into question classical onto-logic and its attendant 'God's-eye view' epistemology, and the theory of nonlinear dynamical systems disentangles scientific intelligibility and nomological determinism from the control-oriented illusion of unlimited predictability. And this is just the beginning: '[T]he things we now esteem fixed shall, one by one, detach themselves like ripe fruit from our experience, and fall. The wind shall blow them none knows whither.'[2]

All of these crises signal, in different ways, the drawing to a close of the same pre-modern scene. In each case, a purported last instance or fixed background that has supposedly subtracted from the dynamics of the corresponding experiential field—an immobile Ur-Arche Earth as the condition of possibility of all rest and movement (be it planetary, subjective, tonal, axiomatic, geometric, set-theoretical, logical, etc.)—or else a supposedly universal perspective or point of reference—a standard metre or privileged perspective—is decentred, dynamised, relativised, repositioned, existentialised, or else suspended between multiple other equally valid grounds or points of view.

Not only have these grounds been launched into orbit, but the heavens themselves have been stormed. The Newtonian fusion of the sublunar and the supralunar—the gravitational synthesis of the falling apple and the orbiting moon—marks the ultimate disastrous disastralisation. Humanity no longer dwells upon a *terra firma* beneath the stars, and the heavens no longer sing the glory of a hypertranscendent God: '[T]he sky, the same sky, suddenly open, absolutely black and absolutely empty, revealing (as though the pane had broken) such an absence that all has since always and forever been lost therein—so lost that therein is affirmed the vertiginous knowledge that nothing is what there is, and first of all nothing beyond.'[3] The sky is no longer a 'great outdoors', a hyper-transcendence beyond any

---

2 R.W. Emerson, 'The Over-Soul', in *The Complete Essays and Other Writings of Ralph Waldo Emerson* (New York: Random House, 1950), 261–78: 265.

3 M. Blanchot, *The Writing of the Disaster*, tr. A. Smock (Lincoln, NE: University of Nebraska Press, 1995), 72.

form of objective transcendence capable of housing the God of ontotheology and the corresponding celestial hierarchies:[4] '[T]here is no doubt that it had been a profanity: the old heaven, the heaven of religions and contemplations, the pure and sublime "up there", had dissolved in a moment, deprived of the privilege of inaccessibility [...].'[5] The sky over modernity is no more than an objective transcendence, a phenomenological horizon for the appearance of stellar phenomena, a lifeless *res extensa* offered up to conquest. As Levinas noted, the sky is no longer the recipient of a devotional gaze that is totally divorced from any possible complicity with the hand, from the subjective capacity to touch, take, use, or appropriate.[6] The sky,

---

4 Following Heidegger, by ontotheology we understand the thesis that God is an *ens supremum* (an entity that superlatively *is*) located in a hyper-transcendence, that is, in a non-objective transcendence.

5 M. Blanchot, 'The Conquest of Space', tr. C.C. Stevens, in M. Holland (ed.), *The Blanchot Reader* (Oxford: Blackwell, 1995), 269. See also E. Levinas, 'Heidegger, Gagarin and Us', in *Difficult Freedom: Essays on Judaism*, tr. S. Hand (Baltimore, MD: The Johns Hopkins University Press, 1990), 231–34.

6 Levinas describes the complicity between the optical and haptic (in)accessibility of the hypertranscendent sky in the following terms: 'In an age in which movement towards the heights is limited by the line of the summits, the heavenly bodies—stars fixed in their positions or traveling along closed trajectories—are intangible. The sky calls for a gaze other than that of a vision that is already an aiming and proceeds from need and to the pursuit of things. It calls for eyes purified of covetousness, a gaze other than that of the hunter with all his ruse, awaiting the capture. Thus the eyes turned towards the sky separate themselves in some fashion from the body in which they are implanted. And in this separation the complicity of the eye and the hand, which is older than the distinction between knowing and doing, is undone. Raising itself towards the sky, the gaze thus encounters the untouchable: the sacred. (The untouchable is the name of an impossibility before being that of a taboo.) The distance thus traversed by the gaze is transcendence. The gaze is not a climbing but a deference. In this way, it is wonder and worship. There is an astonishment before the extraordinary rupture that is height or elevation within a space closed to movement. Height thus takes on the dignity of the superior and becomes divine. [...] Unlike the agitation in which covetousness struggles (*epithemitikon*), and unlike those shifts towards the intended object wherein the eye anticipates the movement of the hand, the heavenly vault confirms the imperturbable repose of

far from being a sheltering sky or a crystal palace of concentric spheres, is an exploding dark abyss in which humanity, like Victor Hugo's Satan, is nothing but an arrogant freefalling splinter. Modernity's tendency to uproot, the 'disenchantment of the world', and the 'death' of the hypertranscendent God—the closure of ontotheology—are concomitant phenomena. The Earth below, the world in which we live, and the sky above are no longer what they used to be.

It could be argued that the anguish elicited by the progressive unfolding of this modern landscape is counteracted by the certainty of having finally found ourselves upon the 'secure path of a science'.[7] Doesn't science provide the canonical model of modern epistemic-political progressivism? Is it not the case that the supposed necessity of scientific rationality allows us to counteract 'the implacable contingency of a world without God'?[8] The greatest hecatomb imaginable, the sacrifice of God itself, has taken place on the altar of truth and progress. Was it not worth having had the courage to finally get rid of obscurantism and superstition? How could we have persisted in sustaining a comforting dogmatic illusion to the detriment of a heartbreaking but enlightening truth?

However, Kantian critique, having raised the Copernican revolution to a transcendental power, seems to have established that even the most exact sciences, such as mechanics, geometry and arithmetic, are relative to the particular transcendental structure of the subject of science. According to Kant, scientific reason is de jure limited by the contingency of our subjective structure—our faculties of sensibility, understanding, imagination, and reason. In spite of the universalist commitment of scientific reason and its unique capacity to progressively construct an accurate objective description of nature, in Kant's view modern science remains all too human.

---

the *terra firma*.' E. Levinas, 'God and Onto-Theo-Logy', in *God, Death and Time*, tr. B. Bergo (Stanford, CA: Stanford University Press, 2000), 121–224: 163–64.

7 I. Kant, *Critique of Pure Reason*, tr. P. Guyer and A.W. Wood (Cambridge and New York: Cambridge University Press, 2000), 107 [Bix–x].

8 Q. Meillassoux, *The Number and the Siren*, tr. R. Mackay (Falmouth and New York: Urbanomic/Sequence Press, 2012), 35.

Its universality is a restricted type of universality, valid only for subjects of a specific transcendental type. In this way, so-called modern universality bears the stigma of transcendental insularity: not only are we now 'lost in this remote corner of nature',[9] but we also find ourselves thrown into a neglected zone of the landscape of possible transcendental types of subjectivity. The realisation of Darwin (and his heirs) that the singular transcendental structure of human subjectivity is the result of a complex evolutionary interplay between chance and necessity, between contingent mutations and self-organising processes, between manducation and procreation, between entropic dissipation and morphogenesis, between organic integrity and technical prothesis, between competition and symbiogenetic cooperation, between natural-cultural selection and artificial plasticity, between phylogenesis and epigenesis, between environmentally-induced alterations and self-modelling interventions, is yet another narcissistic wound which only serves to reinforce the transcendental relativism implicit in the Kantian thesis.[10] The naturalist understanding of the complex process of the institution of human subjectivity demonstrates that no *transcendental deduction* of the supposed a priori structure of our subjectivity (i.e. of our location in the landscape of transcendental subjective types) is in fact possible. This being the case, we would have disenchanted existence and abandoned the garden 'brimming with divinity of the intra-divine [procession]'[11] without even being able to console ourselves with the possession—or at least the promise—of a properly apodeictic, unrestrictedly universal form of knowledge.

---

9 B. Pascal, *Thoughts, Letters and Minor Works*, tr. W.F. Trotter (New York: P.F. Collier & Son, 1910), 27 [§72].

10 Regarding the impact of the theory of evolution on Kant's transcendental idealism, see in particular K. Lorenz, 'Kant's Doctrine of the A Priori in the Light of Contemporary Biology', in M. Ruse (ed.), *Philosophy after Darwin: Classical and Contemporary Readings* (Princeton, NJ: Princeton University Press, 2009), 231–47.

11 J.-C. Goddard, *La philosophie fichtéene de la vie. Le transcendental et le pathologique* (Paris: Vrin, 1999), 206.

This transcendental relativisation of human rationality seems to entail a relativisation of the Principle of Sufficient Reason: human, all too human, reason is no longer capable of founding a universal and necessary order, since every local articulation of the *logos* unveiled by human understanding is contingent upon its particular transcendental structures and existential conditions. The *Maître*'s attempt to produce patterns, redundancy, information, predictability, form, mastery is limited by the fact that every possible form of order—being transcendental-dependent—is undermined by different kinds of anomalies, lapsus, impasses, dissipation, pollution, tropical maladies, and other forms of material resistance. In that 'point of indistinction between entropy and epiphany',[12] 'heat and mosquitos' ferment the *Maître*'s *res cogitans* and dismantle its futile attempt to conquer extension: 'I'm pensive but I'm not being compensated for it: the Sibyl pinches me, the pythoness hypnotises me. [...] Beasts spawned in the most intense fire of the day... Eating these beasts must disturb one's thoughts so uniquely. I spend my days walking among these strange beasts. My dreams are populated by strange fauna and flora: stuff snapping, bugs bursting [...]: the flora shimmers and the fauna flourishes... Singular excesses... [...] To breathe in these herbal fumes, to fill my chest with the breath of this undergrowth [...] fermenting speech [...] The eternal silence of these crazy, twisted beings terrifies me [...] I see things: [...] Plants eating flesh. The utter nonsense of these beasts, so full of shit, victims of the forms in which they are manifest [...] This world is made of the substance that shines out at the beautiful, extreme edges of matter. [...] This world is the seat of madness; here righteous reason tends to delirium. [...] Bugs bow down to one other, salaam-alaikum chameleons turn into Solomons of learned chromaticisms, infinite affinities tune and detune species.'[13] Every thought—every subjective patterning of the pleroma, every umweltisation of the experiential field, every protocol for the rationalisation of the phenoumenodelic stream—emits a throw of the dice that will never completely abolish that real 'swarm of

12 R. Jiménez, 'Del endés y su demasiada', in P. Leminski, *Catatau*, tr. R. Jiménez (Madrid: Libros de la Resistencia, 2019), 284.

13 P. Leminski, *Catatau* (São Paulo: Editora Iluminuras, 2010), 16–17.

suppurations'[14] that ferments, insists, and reveals: 'The real is coming, the real is about to arrive, this is its advent! [...] It comes in the blacks of the Quilombos, in the ships of the Carcamanos, in the faces of creatures. [...] Troy will fall, Vrijburg has fallen. The real, full of decay, is coming. Its like has never been seen before: no swindle can thwart it. Nothing can get in the way of the designs of the prima materia.'[15]

The Kantian critical revolution further intensifies the relativism and the ungrounding inherent to modernity. Modern science produces forms of knowledge that are relative to the transcendental structure of the subject of science, sophisticated rational constructs expounded *more geometrico* but dissociated from all *ethos*, a learned form of ignorance that does not seem to inspire any sort of communal devotion, along with technical forms of mastery and control that seem to deepen the condition of existential shelterlessness. The heavens thus stormed and the earth thus suspended, nothing seems able to pinion the bad infinity of chance, to absolve human experience and reason of transcendental relativism (and of its multiculturalist and multinaturalist avatars), to claim the right to pronounce (theoretical, ethical, aesthetical) judgements of value, to release the subject from being condemned to exert a disligated form of free will, to stop the fall unleashed by the Ur-ungrounding, or to overcome the lack of a transcendent orientation for thought and existence. The crisis in foundations seems to go from the hypertranscendent father to the worst (*du père au pire*), from the immobile Ur-mat(t)er and the standard Ur-pattern to the unrestricted contingency of all order and the unsurpassable hyper-relativism of every possible experience. Worse still, there seems to be no religative principle capable of containing the modern degeneration into *separation* (which accompanies individualisation) and the arche-disease of *disligation* and its various deadly conjugations: the madness of appropriation ('this is mine') and its self-essentialising radicalisation ('this is me'), the uprooting myth of a subjective self-foundation that forecloses the heterinstitution of one's own

14 Na Kar Eliff-ce, 'Apostillas a Lo Real (entre el Eliotrueno y el rayoPaulo)', talk given at the Centro de Estudios Brasilers, Buenos Aires, September 2001.

15 Leminski, *Catatau*, 37.

individuality (i.e. the foreclosure of the fact that every form of subjective a priori is an a posteriori product of nature), the unbound Promethean voluntarism of a presumptuous creature detached from life.

How might it then be possible to bear the hyperbolic ungrounding effected by modern science if such an ungrounding necessarily wipes out all the religative resources of religion? Wasn't the Inquisition right, as the 'little monk' in Brecht's *Life of Galileo*[16] argues, to suggest that humanity does not yet have the necessary existential resources to come to terms with the abyssal domains opened up by modern science? Didn't the dialectic of Enlightenment sufficiently demonstrate how deeply we can delve into the heart of darkness? The *mise en abyme* of the earth and of the life it sustains awakens the spectrum of distinctively modern affects: Pascal's anxiety—'But our whole groundwork cracks, and the earth opens to abysses. Let us therefore not look for certainty and stability [...]. The eternal silence of these infinite spaces frightens me';[17] Hamlet's melancholic paralysis ('tupi or not tupi'),[18] the vacillation of Mallarmé's *Maître* (what's the point of throwing the dice if such a throw will never completely abolish dissipation, unpredictability, stochasticity?), the three narcissistic wounds (Copernican, Darwinian, Freudian) diagnosed by Freud; the Weberian disenchantment of the rationalised world; the Heideggerian horror of uprooting and desecration embodied in the photographs of the

---

16 B. Brecht, *Galileo* (New York: Grove Press 1966), 87–97.

17 Pascal, *Thoughts, Letters and Minor Works*, 30 and 78, respectively. 'When I see the blindness and the wretchedness of man, when I regard the whole silent universe, and man without light, left to himself, and, as it were, lost in this corner of the universe, without knowing who has put him there, what he has come to do, what will become of him at death, and incapable of all knowledge, I become terrified, like a man who should be carried in his sleep to a dreadful desert island, and should awake without knowing where he is, and without means of escape. And thereupon I wonder how people in a condition so wretched do not fall into despair.' Ibid., 233 [§693].

18 O. de Andrade, 'Cannibalistic Manifesto', tr. L. Bary, *Latin American Literary Review* 19:38 (1991): 38–47: 38.

earth taken from the moon;[19] the dessicated eliminativist zombification of existence fostered by certain contemporary forms of melancholic nihilism ('everything is dead already'),[20] as well as (albeit closer to life in its passionate despair) the romantic nightmare of Jean-Paul Nerval-Richter: 'Now a sublime noble figure, bearing an imperishable sorrow, sank down from on high to the altar, and the dead all cried: "Christ! is there no God?" He replied: "There is none." Each whole shadow of the dead, not only their breasts alone, shook, and one by one they were ripped apart by their quaking. Christ went on: "I traversed the worlds, I ascended into the suns, and soared with the Milky Ways through the wastes of heaven; but there is no God. I descended to the last reaches of the shadows of Being, and I looked into the chasm and cried: 'Father, where art thou?' But I heard only the eternal storm ruled by none, and the shimmering rainbow of essence stood without sun to create it, trickling above the abyss. And when I raised my eyes to the boundless world for the divine eye, it stared at me from an empty bottomless socket; and Eternity lay on Chaos and gnawed it and ruminated itself. —Shriek on, discords, rend the shadows; for He is not!" The pallid shadows dispersed just as a white vapor formed by the frost will melt in a warm breath; and all became void. Then came into the temple a heartrending sight, the dead children who had wakened in the churchyard, and now cast themselves before the sublime form on the altar saying: "Jesus! have we no father?" —And he replied with streaming tears: "We are all orphans, I and you, we are without a father." Then the discords screeched more harshly—the quaking temple walls sundered—and temple and children sank—and the entire earth and the sun sank after them—and the whole immeasurable fabric of the universe sank past us, and high on

19 M. Heidegger, 'Only a God Can Save Us: Der Spiegel's Interview with Martin Heidegger (September 23, 1966)', tr. M.P. Alter and J.D. Caputo, in *Philosophical and Political Writings* (New York: Continuum, 2006), 24–48: 37.

20 J.-F. Lyotard, *The Inhuman: Reflections on Time*, tr. G. Bennington and R. Bowlby (Stanford, CA: Stanford University Press, 1991), 9. This is analysed in R. Brassier, *Nihil Unbound: Enlightenment and Extinction* (Basingstoke: Palgrave Macmillan, 2007), 223.

the summit of boundless Nature stood Christ and gazed down into the universe, pierced by a thousand suns, as into a mine dug out of eternal night, where the suns are pit lamps and the Milky Ways the veins of silver core.[21] [...] Abyss! Abyss! Abyss! The god is missing from the altar upon which I'm the victim... [...] All's dead [already]! I've wandered the worlds; I have lost my flight in their Milky Ways, [...] but no spirit exists in these immensities [...].'[22]

In its attempts to cope with the trauma inflicted by modern science, mankind ended up exacerbating the originary arche-disease of disligation, isolation and estrangement. The scientific vocation of orienting ourselves in thinking by following the prescriptions provided by the infinite idea of truth was distorted into the promise of security in the face of abyssal cosmic landscapes: a purported form of protection, obtained through technical mastery of the world, and 'salvation' from death. In an attempt to counteract its cosmic insignificance, mankind gave in to an understanding of freedom as disligated self-sufficiency, to a conception of subjective individuality based on private property, to the horror of appropriation, cumulation, and consumerism ('Mankind has the absolute right to appropriate all that is a thing ["Something not free, impersonal and without rights"]'),[23] to colonial exploitation, to the conception of nature as a 'standing reserve' available to an extractivist technical domination, to the idea that human beings can 'conquer' space and time. The pre-critical conflation of scientific objectivity, which is just a typed form of universality, with unrestricted universality is the condition of possibility for colonialism and imperialism, for the illegitimate hypostasis of a certain transcendental type of subjectivity (that of the white, European, wealthy, neurotypical, able-bodied man, for example), to the detriment of other human and non-human types.

---

21 J.-P. Richter, 'Speech of the Dead Christ from the Universe that There Is No God', in *Jean Paul: A Reader*, tr. E. Casey (Baltimore, MD: Johns Hopkins University Press, 1992), 179–83.

22 G. de Nerval, *Selected Writings* (London: Penguin 1999), 749 [translation modified].

23 G.W.F. Hegel, *Philosophy of Right*, tr. S.W. Dyde (Kitchener, ON: Batoche Books, 2001), 57 [§44] and 56 [§42].

Appropriation as denial of the inappropriable otherness of every other (human, animal, vegetable, mineral) is disligation, isolation: closure of the possibility of a fraternity, absence of an other—of a living sibling (whatever its transcendental type may be)—to be with; the impossibility of an existence oriented by the infinite idea of religating love. As Hegel argued, the position of the master is an 'existential impasse' in so far as it lacks another to recognise it as a master: of what value is the recognition of a slave, someone the master itself does not recognise as a subject? *Techné* (linguistic, conceptual, technological, etc.) as the properly speculative capacity to mediate 'word for word'—patiently, ever failing, trying to fail better—the limits of always finite experience become *potestas*, the will of the human being's verticalist power over nature and over other human and non-human living beings, the illusory possibility of an individual life disligated from life. *Techné* is diverted from its speculative vocation and is converted into a weapon in the service of a tragic hubris that negates finitude, death, and castration, that forecloses the limits of mastery and control. This repression of the real impasses that obstruct the idealist expansion of the *ego conquero* and place limits upon the deepening of the 'colonial difference' is the quintessential modern psychosis, one which makes it impossible to effect a radical synthesis with alterity.

Must the unfolding of modern science and the attendant 'terrible battle against this nasty old [arche-]plumage',[24] the hypertranscendent and arche-feathered God, necessarily lead to a disenchanted, nostalgic or melancholic nihilism and the unbound Promethean hubris of appropriation and voluntarist heroism? Or might it be possible to conceive of and unleash a religating mode of thought and practice synchronic with modern science, that of an absolutely modern religion capable of providing the existential resources that would make it possible to endure the shipwreck of mastery and the intoxicating exposure to the narcotic solution concocted from the force that engenders and the light that reveals, that would make it possible

---

24 S. Mallarmé, Letter to Henri Cazalis (14 May 1867), in B. Marchal (ed.), *Correspondance complète 1862–1871. Lettres sur la poésie 1872–1898* (Paris: Gallimard, 1995), 342.

to be religated to Guaraci, the mat(t)er of the living,[25] to enter into concert with other lifeforms in a trans-species 'tribe of mutants',[26] without possible salvation but with the promise of healing in the immanental warp of life? Is it possible 'to start digging [in a religion, even one long abandoned] in order to exhume ancient and magnificent intentions'?[27] Is it possible to activate existential resources that would enable us to live a life oriented by the infinite ideas of reason (justice, truth, beauty, love), to become finite 'servants of the infinite Life Force',[28] probing tentacles that locally enact 'God's living act of Ex-istence'?[29]

Are melancholy and desperation the only affects that can be associated with modern science? Are the sacrilegious hubris of appropriation and the consequent expansion of the disease of disligation the only possible reactions to the anguish triggered by modern science? Or would it be possible to bring about a distinctly modern synthesis between science and religion, a synthesis faithful to the Enlightenment, one that is post-critical and responsive to the infinite project of finite scientific understanding? Might it be possible to perform a synthesis between the will to know and religion now understood (beyond all dogmatic content, beyond all pre-critical obscurantism, beyond bygone 'mythological world views' as Bultmann would say, and beyond any theology of a purported hypertranscendent 'God') as a practice intended to perform an epiphytic re-implantation of all knowledge and of all practice (whether scientific, artistic or political) into the abyss of the absolute immanental life which institutes, carries, and irrigates every finite being? Is it possible to place the modern *age of rational Enlightenment* in the

25 De Andrade, 'Cannibalistic Manifesto', 42.

26 T. Leary, in D.S. Calonne (ed.), *Conversations with Gary Snyder* (Jackson, MS: University Press of Mississippi, 2017).

27 S. Mallarmé, *Divagations*, tr. B. Johnson (Cambridge, MA and London: Belknap Press, 2007), 251.

28 R.A. Wilson, *Prometheus Rising* (Grand Junction, CO: Hilaritas Press, 2006), 280.

29 J.G. Fichte, *The Way Towards the Blessed Life; Or, The Doctrine of Religion*, tr. W. Smith (London: John Chapman, 1849), 69.

service of a 'spiritual' Enlightenment, of a finite existence suspended within and capable of enhancing the 'Beatific ultra-vision' of life, of enduring the transmutation of 'the daily bread of experience into the radiant [flesh] of everliving[-and-dying] life'?[30] Is it true, as Jung argued, that 'healing' (and no longer salvation) is *the* strictly religious problem?[31] Is it true, as Heidegger maintained, that 'what is distinctive about this world-epoch consists in the closure of the dimension of the hale [*des Heilen*]'?[32] Is it really possible to maintain that we can cure life of the capitalist disease by means of a political 'revolution' without 'spirituality', without the attempt to institute a wholly spiritual trans-species community based on a communism of material, perceptual, affective, and cognitive resources ('That such a programme could seem utopian may simply indicate the degree of "alienation" of [s]he who judges it such, and the force wielded by those who claim themselves to be invincible')?[33] Is it still possible for us to project a new philosophical constellation of (theoretical, aesthetical, political, spiritual) interests of reason designed to heal modernity from its arche-disease? Is it still possible to become 'absolutely modern' by absolving modernity of all those colonial, appropriating, extractivist, and ego-conquering reactions to the anguish elicited by the modern ungrounding? Is it possible to bracket this reaction and respond to the modern ungrounding by means of a speculative enhancement of our existential, political, and spiritual resources? Is it still possible to become 'absolutely modern' by releasing the subject from the myth of a self-sufficient free will and from the attendant melancholic paralysis, by submitting it to a higher form of freedom, by converting it into a local valve which alone would

30 J. Joyce, *A Portrait of the Artist as a Young Man* (Oxford: Oxford University Press, 2000), 196.

31 C.G. Jung, 'Psychotherapists or the Clergy', in *Modern Man in Search of a Soul*, tr. W.S. Dell and C.F. Baynes (New York: Harcourt, 1933), 237.

32 M. Heidegger, 'Letter on Humanism', in D.F. Krell (ed.), *Basic Writings* (New York: HarperCollins, 1993), 254.

33 F. Eboussi Boulaga, *Christianisme sans fétiche. Révélation et domination* (Paris: Éditions Présence Africaine, 1981), 113.

modulate the deterministic flow of the *natura naturans*—the unique and ubiquitous living act of creation—by embedding Elsinore in the 'fulminant order' of a pleromatic trance beyond 'the Judgement of God'?[34] Is it possible to make science, art, politics, and religion something more than (in the best case) mere cultural entertainments in the service of the sickness of capitalism? 'Shall we continue scientific research?'[35] Is it not time once again to take up Alexander Grothendieck's question and then extrapolate it to the various fields of cultural production? In the service of which interests, of what idea of life and death, would we continue working as scientists, as artists, as engineers, as intellectuals, as healers, as educators, if we were to absolve ourselves of capitalistic values (private property, the accumulation of capital—whether monetary or symbolic—the extraction of profit as the regulative idea of all forms of production, unconditional growth, competition, individualistic narcissism, the will to *potestas*, etc.), when the personal pleasure elicited by these activities or the possibility of earning a living are no longer sufficient motivations in the context of a collapsing 'civilisation', at a moment when the house is burning?

Is it possible to place these modes of thought and practice in the service of a 'change of civilisation' oriented toward the creation of 'lifestyles and human relationships that are worth living' (Grothendieck again)? Is it still possible to disentangle science (and truth) from the technical appropriation and exploitation of nature, politics (and justice) from the bureaucratic and police management of private property, art (and beauty) from the capitalist art market and the 'society of the spectacle' that instrumentalises art to produce more commodities and 'adorn our prison walls',[36] religion (and love) from obscurantist and superstitious dogma at the service of a

34 Cf. A. Artaud, 'To Have Done With the Judgement of God', in *Selected Writings*, tr. H. Weaver, ed. S. Sontag (New York: Farrar, Straus and Giroux, 1976), 555–71.

35 A. Grothendieck, 'Allons-nous continuer la recherche scientifique?', *Écologie & politique* 52 (2016): 159–69.

36 J. Morrison, 'The Lords', in *The Collected Works of Jim Morrison: Poetry, Journals, Transcripts, and Lyrics* (New York: Harper Design, 2021).

pre-modern regression?[37] Is it still possible to place science, art, politics, and religion in the service of the infinite regulative ideas of truth, beauty, justice, and love—that is to say, in the service of the imperative not to cede the desire to always want to understand a little more; not to stop expanding our affective and perceptive sensibility; not to stop experimenting with new forms of being-together capable of doing justice to different lifeforms; not to cease deepening our immanental religation with the one absolute life that has been, 'in and for itself, with us, all along;'[38] not to stop 'making kins' of the *n*th kind with the living ones who locally instantiate and potentialise this one immanental life? Is it true that where the danger lies, deeper within the heart of cosmic darkness, at the uttermost extreme of modern disligation, there grows the plant that heals, the pharmakon that re-ligates us to (what James Lispector and Clarice Joyce call) the 'wild heart of life'?

Now, isn't it the case that it is 'the very shipwreck—the very ruin of classical verse—that, for the *Maître*, holds out the promise of the Number'?[39] Isn't the 'Death of God', as Marion has it,[40] the deconstruction of a certain idolatrous reduction of divinity ('science could never destroy a deity, but

---

37 According to Alain Badiou, (what he calls) 'truth procedures' are by their very nature hostile to the contemporary capitalistic world: 'This hostility betrays itself though nominal occlusions: where the name of a truth procedure should obtain, another, which represses it, holds sway. The name "culture" comes to obliterate that of "art." The word "technology" obliterates the word "science." The word "management" obliterates the word "politics." The word "sexuality" obliterates love. The "culture-technology-management-sexuality" system, which has the immense merit of being homogeneous to the market, and all of whose terms designate a category of commercial presentation, constitutes the modern nominal occlusion of the "art-science-politics-love" system, which identifies truth procedures typologically.' A. Badiou, *Saint Paul:The Foundation of Universalism*, tr. R. Brassier (Stanford, CA: Stanford University Press, 2003), 12.

38 G.W.F. Hegel, *Phenomenology of Spirit*, tr. A.V. Miller (Oxford: Oxford University Press, 1977), 47.

39 Meillassoux, *The Number and the Siren*, 37.

40 J.-L. Marion, *God Without Being* (Chicago: University of Chicago Press, 1991), 25–33.

only the earthen feet of a man-made idol')[41] and therefore the condition of possibility for a religion freed from onto-theological idolatry, from the contradictory notion (in Schelling's terms) of an *absolute thing* (an *un*thing*ed thing* [*unbe*dings*tes Ding*])? And—if we take into account that 'It's not just that "God is dead", so is the "Goddess"'[42] (that is, 'the founding myth' of original unity, virginal innocence, and organic wholeness to which we would need to return—or that we would need to restore—in order to achieve 'salvation')—isn't the Copernican launching of the Earth and the zooming out provided by contemporary cosmology the condition of possibility for religating practices released both from the parochial hypostasis of the local and contingent conditions of terrestrial life and from origin myths and their apocalyptic hypertones? Far from sanctioning the transcendental hyper-relativity of modern reason, Mallarmé's *Maître* infers from 'this conflagration at his feet'—from the transmutation of the immobile Ur-Arche Earth into an ark shipwrecreated upon descent into the Maelstrom—the advent of the 'unique Number that cannot be another',[43] the infinite trans(in)substantiation of finite existence, the abolition of a purported 'chainless freewheel'[44] that would allow the subject to choose between several contingent possibilities (Hamlet's 'supreme drama of doubt')[45] in favour of a religated form of freedom that locally channels the unique self-positing act of the insubstance. The supposed implication that from the modern closure of hypertranscendent ontotheology stems the absolutisation of contingency and the insuperability of transcendental relativism is a nonsequitur: transcendental relativism is not (it will be argued

---

41 K. Lorenz, 'Kant's Doctrine of the A Priori', 246.

42 D. Haraway, 'A Cyborg Manifesto: Science, Technology, and Socialist-feminism in the Late Twentieth Century', in R. Latham (ed.), *Science Fiction Criticism:An Anthology of Essential Writings* (New York: Bloomsbury Academic, 2017), 306–29: 317.

43 S. Mallarmé, 'A Throw of the Dice', in *Collected Poems*, tr. H. Weinfield (Berkeley and Los Angeles: University of California Press, 1994), 130.

44 J. Joyce, *Ulysses* (London: Penguin, 2000), 840.

45 H. Miller, *Hamlet's Letters*, ed. M. Hargraves (Santa Barbara, CA: Capra Press, 1988), 19.

here) necessarily incompatible with a speculative (i.e. post-critical and post-foundational) absolutism. Transcendental relativism is not necessarily incompatible with the principle of reason, on account of the fact that forms of rationality can be conceived of which are no longer indissolubly attached to the cognitive, affective, and political apparatus of a single transcendental type. Just as the Copernican democratisation of different empirical frames of reference did not sanction the existence of unsurpassable limits to the scientific processes of objectivation, but rather propelled an enhancement of the objectifying capacities of human understanding, so the Kantian democratisation of transcendental types of subjectivity can also be used to set in motion trans-species and speculative forms of rationality. The infinite turbulence triggered by the modern ungrounding of existence and thought, the Copernican launching into orbit of foundations, the transcendental relativisation of images of the world, far from being definitive obstructions to the legitimacy of the infinite projects of reason, far from leading necessarily to an insurmountable hyper-relativism, open up a suspended site in which all these projects can be raised to new, absolutely modern modalities that remain faithful to the heritage of the Enlightenment. The modern closure of ontotheology—the Newtonian immanentisation of the heavens and the sweeping away of the hypertranscendent Father—does not forestall the possibility of an absolutely modern religion, of a 'civic religion'[46] as Rousseau would say ('if, in future, [...] religion comes back, it will be the amplification of the heaven-instinct in each of us'),[47] of a religating healing process projectively absolved of all dogmatic content and all superstitious drift. Maybe the advent of modern science and the closure of ontotheology make it possible to conceive of religating modes of thought and practice absolved from hypostatised world views, of a healing cult without dogma, of a religion without God: '[Modern] science [might become] a source of the purest and [new]est religion. [...] [T]he [absolutely modern] world [will be] entirely religious and godless. [When human

46 Cf. J.J. Rousseau, *The Social Contract and Other Later Political Essays* (Cambridge: Cambridge University Press, 1997), 141–51 (Chapter 8, Book IV).

47 Mallarmé, *Divagations*, 195.

beings live] in close physical unison, like flocks of birds on the wing, in a close physical oneness, an ancient tribal unison in which the individual [is] hardly [disligated] out [tupi!], then the tribe [lives] breast to breast, as it were, with the [*natura naturans*], in naked contact with [Guaraci], the whole [immanental substance is] alive and in contact with the flesh of [human beings], there [is] no room for the intrusion of the god idea. It was not till the individual began to feel separated off, not till [it] fell into awareness of [it]self, and hence into apartness; not, mythologically, till [it] ate of the Tree of Knowledge instead of the Tree of Life, and knew [it]self apart and separate, that the conception of a God arose [...]. The very oldest ideas of [human beings] are purely religious, and there is no notion of any sort of god or gods. God and gods enter when [human beings have] "fallen" into a sense of [disligation] and loneliness [and they start longing for salvation].'[48]

If one rejects the dubious assumption that proceeds from the closure of ontotheology to the insurmountability of the ensuing groundless hyper-relativism and the supposedly ineluctable character of appropriative isolation, then the launching of the earthly mother into orbit and the sweeping away of the hypertranscendent father present an Elsinorian dilemma. Either one accepts, or even hypostatises, the sovereignty of chance and the undialectisable multiplicity of perspectives and contingent orders—as well as the disenchantment elicited by humanity's fall into the bottomless abysses opened up by modern science (with the consequent nihilistic, melancholic, and paralysing despair)—, or the crisis in foundations is understood as a determinate negation inducing post-critical and post-foundational modalities of experience, of reason, of existence. This dilemma threatens to shut us off as Hamletian 'latent [souls] who cannot become'[49]—as living ghosts detached from the transcendental plasticity of the one life—if we do not force a collapse of the waves of undecidability by means of an ungrounded decision. We cannot refuse this wager. 'It is

48 D.H. Lawrence, 'Apocalypse', in M. Kalnins (ed.), *Apocalypse and the Writings on Revelation* (Cambridge: Cambridge University Press, 1980), 130–31.

49 Mallarmé, *Divagations*, 125.

not optional.' Like Mallarmé's *Maître*, we 'are [always already] embarked'.[50] At this point the second path will be explored, the path of those who—like Spinoza, who was 'drunk with God'[51]—decide to become intoxicated to the breaking point at which scepticism runs out of words, the path of those who throw the dice and do not give up on the attempt to vanquish the contingency of disligated free will, to make themselves available for 'a liberation to a new freedom', for a 'self-imposed [spell]binding [*selbstübernommene Bindung*]'[52] submission to the impersonal living force of the *natura naturans*, those who try in every way possible to stay loyal to the prescription transmitted by the ghosts of those alchimerical ancestors of the Mallarméan *Maître*—those who decide, in the absence of any transcendent decree or guarantee, in the passage opened up by the shipwreck of all master signifiers, to overcome melancholic lethargy and to carry out eidetic acts, acts oriented, in the wilderness of the ungrounding disaster, by regulatory ideas projected by human reason.

German Idealism was the first philosophical movement to address the problem of deciding to what extent and under which conditions it was possible to construct a *philosophy of the absolute* capable of sublating the hyper-relativism of post-critical modernity. Let us then begin with a central question: *What is the philosophical project that we have inherited from German idealism*? And let us resolutely assume the risks of a laconic response: German idealism is the movement that began to develop the project of synthesising *Spinoza with Kant*, that is, *Spinozist immanentism* (the thesis that we are born, live, and die both in and for the absolute, immersed in 'Guaraci or the absolutely immanent Substance')[53] and *Kantian transcendentalism* understood as a philosophy of the finite subject, of the transcendental

50 Pascal, *Thoughts, Letters and Minor Works*, 85 [§233].

51 Novalis, *Fragmente und Studien* 1799/1800, HKA III, no. 562, 651.

52 M. Heidegger, *What Is a Thing?*, tr. W.B. Barton, Jr. and V. Deutsch (Indianapolis: Gateway Editions, 1967), 97.

53 J.-C. Goddard, *Un brésilien noir et crasseux* (São Paulo: n-1 edições, 2017), 17; *A Scabby Black Brazilian*, tr. T. Murphy (Falmouth: Urbanomic, forthcoming 2023).

conditions of possibility of its experience and the resulting limitations of this experience. To synthesise Kant with Spinoza means combining critical ascetism with the capacity to dive into inebriating insubstance until we 'oscillate like beings made of phosphorescent matter';[54] it means articulating a philosophy that seeks the absolute *behind* the phenomena with a philosophy that starts *from* the absolute, it means bringing together two forms of 'experiencing' the absolute: by differentially mediating the transcendental limits of our cognitive, affective, perceptual, and social capacities in an open process oriented by the infinite ideas of reason, and by existing[55] the (f)act that we live, we breathe, we interrelate, we know, we move, and we die in the absolute; it means acknowledging that every unilateral form of finite knowledge is itself a living act through which the absolute substance self-manifests. To synthesise Kant with Spinoza, to devise an immanental transcendentalism, means synthesising a philosophy of the finite subject with a philosophy of the absolute, conceiving of a post-critical non-dogmatic absolutism, an absolutism that does not obliterate the (immanently) instituted and (transcendentally) constitutive finitude of every subject of experience. To synthesise Kant with Spinoza means reaching the point of contact between a *transcendental idealism* and an *immanental realism*; it means putting together the transcendental thesis of a constituting subjectivity with the naturalist assumption of its immanental institution; it means reconciling the rationalising spontaneity of subjectivity with the shock (the *Anstoss*, in Fichte's jargon) of the encounter, of the mat(t)er that resists, of the real that makes ingression into the constituted circumambient worlds, of the others that cannot be reduced, digested, assimilated, conquered. To synthesise Kant with Spinoza means endeavouring to place the weapons of transcendental critique at the service of a post-critical philosophical project that tries to think, to perceive, to feel, to taste (otherwise than in a purely negative manner) the absolute as such, the absolute that is in and for itself 'always already with us'. To synthesise Kant with Spinoza

54 A. Pizarnik, *Diarios*, ed. A. Becciú (Barcelona: Lumen, 2013), 320.

55 I follow Goddard's use of the expression '*exister la vie*' as if existing were a transitive verb—see Goddard, *La philosophie fichtienne de la vie*.

means recognising that the 'co-nascence [*co-naissance*] of subject and world'[56] takes place in the immanental realm of life; it means enriching the analysis of the transcendental conditions of possibility of finite experience with the thesis that the unfolding of knowledge is part of the immanental process of life, of the process through which life ceaselessly awakens and self-posits; it means recognising—against any unidimensional inflation of human rationality to the detriment of other human capacities—that scientific understanding is just a particular mode of thought and practice that aims to tune into a single attribute of substance, the *logos*, among infinitely many others. To synthesise Kant with Spinoza means passing from the *intensity* of the local vibrant modes on the surface of substance to phenomenological *intentionality*, it means recognising beneath the intentional subject-object polarisation the buzzing univocity of a unique phenoumenodelic insubstance: '[I]ntensity becomes intentionality to the extent that it takes as its object another intensity which it comprehends and is itself comprehended, itself taken as its object. [...] As for the passage from intensity to intentionality, it is the passage from sign [as the trace of a fluctuation] to sense.'[57] And yet the project of synthesising Spinozism with Kantianism seems like a contradiction in terms. Isn't Kant's philosophy supposed to be a definitive treatment targeting the metaphysical infirmity of believing that we can have any kind of experience that is not relative to, and limited by, our transcendental faculties—against the belief that we can perceive, think, and speak without submitting to the transcendental conditions of every perception, every thought and every (all too) human language, of believing that we can think *X* without *thinking* X? Doesn't the Kantian autocritique of reason therefore demand a retreat from any more of those transcendental illusions that are native to any absolutist philosophy and dogmatic ontology? Isn't the Enlightenment, of which Kantian critique constitutes the reflexive apogee, meant to have produced

56 J.-C. Goddard, '1804–1805. La désubjectivation du transcendantal', *Archives de Philosophie* 72:3 (2009), 423–41: 424.

57 G. Deleuze, *The Logic of Sense*, tr. M. Lester with C. Stivale (New York: Columbia University Press, 1990), 298.

a definitive closure of any religious obscurantism based around some form of dogmatically positioned 'absolute'? Isn't the very idea of a critical absolutism a triangular circle?

Far from being an outmoded historical artefact, this vast project can still—as long as it is submitted to an anthropophagic trans-substantiation that dissolves its supremacist euro-white-phallo-centric unilaterality—be taken up again and perverted. Such a project consists in deploying a contemporary speculative philosophy strengthened by the armaments of critique provisioned by more than two centuries of deconstructions of various forms of dogmatism, transcendental illusions of reason, and pre-critical naivety. As a result of various updates and revisions of the Kantian a priori (naturalisations, relativisations, historicisations, and decolonisations), the upgraded speculative philosophy fostered here is pressed into the service of an absolutely modern existence in which *I*, far from being the autarkic, self-sufficient and grounding centre of all experience, *is another*: a finite mode, both receptive and expressive, of the infinite (in)substance thrown to a living and dying existence, a fluctuating focus of experience—an eye of the absolute as 'living self-penetration of the absoluteness itself'[58]—by means of which the one life locally diversifies and empowers its own experience, a finite embodiment of the absolute living out its singular determination (its *suchness* as well as its *resolution*, its *vocation*), a living being borne by mat(t)er to the life and death of perceptions, affections, conceptualisations, pleasures and pains, desires and drives, a *Dasein* responsible for tuning its note—for honing its *Da* to such an extent that it distils a vibrant point—within the resonating community of the living.

As we shall see, the project of synthesising Kantianism with Spinozism requires that we define and develop a philosophy *of* life in the double sense (subjective and objective) of the genitive, that we synthesise a transcendental phenomenology of intentional experience (of the transcendental capacity to experience) with an 'ontological psychoanalysis'[59] of the immanental

58 J.G. Fichte, *Doctrine de la science 1801–1802 et textes annexes*, vol. 1, tr. A. Philonenko (Paris: Vrin, 1987), 46.

59 M. Merleau-Ponty, *The Visible and the Invisible: Followed by Working Notes*, ed. C. Lefort, tr. A. Lingis (Evanston, IL: Northwestern University Press, 1968), 270.

vital unconscious beneath the multiplicity of experiencing lifeforms, of the vital intimacy among the living, of the morphogenetic drive that continually institutes new transcendental types of subjectivity, and that we push the diverging lines of natural-cultural-artificial evolution far beyond any form of local equilibrium.[60] It requires us to understand philosophy as an *organon* of the concrete exploration of the living (in)substance which, in the face of the abyssal and trans-planetary landscapes opened up by modern science, does not yield to the Gaia-centric temptation to restrict the notion of life to its terrestrial manifestation.[61] Rather than contributing to the modern tendency to think of life as an improbable contingency in an otherwise dead universe, the synthesis we seek between Kantianism and Spinozism must attempt to reinscribe the notion of life into a 'general economy', one that is transplanetary and, going beyond Bataille's *Accursed Share*, trans-solar and trans-cosmological—a post-critical philosophy in which every 'image of the world' (including those formed by contemporary biology and cosmology) is no more than a local transcendental-dependent mode of pleromatic revelation. Without denying the existential finitude of the human being, the speculative synthesis between Kantianism and Spinozism should continually place itself in the service of a constant refractive mediation of the limits of its experience, should not give up in the attempt to open itself up, 'word for word', to the transmundane, to the

---

60 While on the one hand '[t]he phenomenological tradition, with its fetish of [conscious] awareness, is quite alien to the philosophies of the energetic [living] unconscious' (N. Land, *The Thirst for Annihilation: Georges Bataille and Virulent Nihilism* [London: Routledge, 1992], 11), on the other, the diverse philosophies of unconscious life (at least with the exception of Bergson and Merleau-Ponty) are not necessarily in a better position with respect to the phenomenological-transcendental stance.

61 This means that we shall not assume that it is possible to answer the question *What is life?* by appealing to characteristics of Earth life (e.g., being subject to Darwinian evolution, depending on a carbon-based biochemistry capable of undergoing metabolism, self-maintenance, adaptation, growth, and reproduction, etc.). See C.E. Cleland, *The Quest for a Universal Theory of Life: Searching for Life as We Don't Know It* (Cambridge: Cambridge University Press, 2019).

overflowing impersonal effluvium of phenoumenodelic dilapidation, to the transcendental hyperplasticity of impersonal vitality (to its extravagance, its prodigality, its 'crazy exuberance' as Bataille would have it), should never stop deepening our immersion, theoretically and existentially, in the one life that we are and in which we are, should not cease to resist spiritually and politically (the 'two [vertical and horizontal] battles', as Megafón would say, reunited in the cross)[62] to the reification-profanation of living matter and its consequent transmutation into a stock of usable raw materials, against the malady of appropriation, of disligation. A transcendental immanentism should help us to place our finite lives and their transcendental and speculative capacities—with gratitude, dignity, and humility—in the service of the immanental life, reminding us to honour the prodigality of life in finitude and death. Far from being a flaw or a punishment from which the living must be saved or redeemed, finitude and death are constitutive of the being-*there* of existence, of the fact that every living being instantiates a singular perspective with respect to which the pleroma appears in a unique manner, thereby contributing to the pleroma's self-manifestation. An immanental transcendentalism should help us to open a path of re-ligation with the 'feminine sun [...] from which each is born according to their ability to love all things, whatever their rank in the speculative scale of beings, as so many unique individuals, inimitable essences, and to love themselves, to enjoy themselves through this insatiable and joyful alteration of them by everything that is not their own',[63] with the 'barbaric matriarchy',[64] the *natura naturans*, the Great-Mat(t)er,[65] the 'white sun of the [infinite in]substance'[66] that spurts out of the roach's belly, a religation performed '[i]n the name of Annah the Allmaziful, the

62 Cf. L. Marechal, *Megafón o la guerra* (Barcelona: Seix Barral, 2014) and L. Marechal, *Didáctica de la Patria*, in *Heptamerón* (Buenos Aires: Sudamericana, 1974).

63 Goddard, *Un brésilien noir et crasseux*, 17.

64 Ibid., 23.

65 Ibid. 24.

66 R. Rolland, *L'éclair de Spinoza* (Paris: Éditions Manucius, 2014), 99.

Everliving, the Bringer of Plurabilities, haloed be her eve, her singtime sung, her rill be run, unhemmed as it is uneven!'[67]

On the one side, transcendental philosophy hinges on the term *transcendence*: the transcendence of objective experience with respect to the constituting subject, that of a pleromatic outside that cannot be reduced to a single Umwelt (to use von Uexküll's term), that of the mat(t)er that resists, of the irreducible others, of the real epiphanies that never cease to come and disturb the symbolic order. The term 'transcendence' points to the ek-static character of existence, to the fact that every subject is always already outside of itself ('[o]utside, in the world, among others. It is not in some hiding-place that we will discover ourselves: it is on the road, in the town, in the midst of the crowd, a thing among things, a [human] among [humans]').[68]

On the other side, Spinozism hinges on the term *immanence*: the immanence of subjective finite modes to the infinite insubstance, of the living to the one life, of constituted worlds to the pleroma. The term immanence denotes the *absoluteness* of the insubstantial field of manifestation, that is, its being absolved both with respect to a hypertranscendent God and with respect to the idealist, imperialist or supremacist tendencies of certain transcendental types of subjectivity. Whereas a critical theory of (perceptual, affective, conceptual, social) experience addresses the transcendental conditions of possibility of subjective experience and its limits, an impersonal vitalism deepens the immanental experience of the pre-individual medium—the (in)substance—in which the living subject of objective experience is locally instituted as a finite breathing mode. Whereas Kantianism focussed on the *transcendental constitution* of objects of experience, Spinozism allows for a focus on the *immanental institution* of finite subjects of experience within an (in)substantial medium that can no longer

67 J. Joyce, *Finnegans Wake* (Oxford: Oxford University Press, 2012), 104.

68 J.-P. Sartre, 'Intentionality: A Fundamental Idea of Husserl's Phenomenology', in D. Moran and T. Mooney (eds.), *The Phenomenology Reader* (London: Routledge, 2002), 382–84.

be thought of (without falling into a vicious circle) as a transcendentally constituted objective nature (a *natura naturata*). Whereas Kantianism focused on the subjective constitution of the phenomenal visions deployed in the conscious foreground, Spinozism focused on the immanental experience of 'the push of life which [the subject] feels behind them'.[69] Whereas objects of experience are transcendentally constituted, subjects of experience are immanently instituted. While experience of the finite subject is limited to the *natura naturata* constituted by (or correlative to) its transcendental apparatus, its life is immanently generated within *natura naturans*. Every lifeform experiences a transcendent world and lives in the immanental insubstance. Every lifeform is a finite mode of infinite life, an incarnation that pares that infinite life down into a lifeworld, an Umwelt, a phenomenological horizon correlative to the transcendental structure of the given lifeform. The objective knowledge of life constructed by finite subjects (the *knowledge of being* in Fichte or the *knowledge of life* in Deleuze) ultimately depends upon the lives of the subjects who produce this knowledge (on the *being of the knowledge of being* in Fichte or the *life of knowledge* in Deleuze). What in the last instance drives us to think on (the different manifestations of) life is life itself. Every intellection of life is itself lived ('Life cannot be studied *in vitro*, one has to explore it *in vivo*'),[70] every theorising subject is a finite subject who is born, falls freely through the living insubstance of which the subject itself is a local receptive and expressive mode, feels, perceives, tells stories, breathes, understands how much and how little its science allows it, and dies. Every subject is a local operator of the self-experience of life that induces a singular *factorisation* of life, a unique immanental loop through which life lives itself. Every finite experience provides a concrete proof of the type-theoretic identity *life = life* (life is life), that is, a concrete self-identification of life witnessed by an intentional link

69 H. Bergson, *Creative Evolution*, tr. A. Mitchell (New York: Random House, 1944), xxiii.

70 H. von Foerster, 'Notes on an Epistemology for Living Things', in *Understanding Understanding:Essays in Cybernetics and Cognition* (Berlin: Springer, 2010), 248.

between an *I* and a *not-I*. In Fichtean terms, the material first principle *life = life* denotes the always ongoing original (f)act through which life continually posits itself into existence through the institution of finite experiencing lifeforms. Life is the original act (*Tathandlung*) that underpins every single fact (*Tatsache*) of experience. The phenomenological horizons in which subjective experience unfolds are constituted in the midst of a unique 'preserved night' (*die gerettete Nacht*).[71] The phenomenological clearings (*Lichtungen*) into which the images that make up the experience of the living are poured open up into the darkness of the thicket, within the opacity of the supernatural forest. While the *pater*, the symbolic apparatus epitomised by the 'name of the father', deploys his morality (*Thou shalt not kill!*) within worldly, phenomenological horizons, the *mat(t)er* spans those very horizons and establishes the primordial imperative of a general therapethics, the imperative that precedes all forms of experience and all totem-centred taboos: *thou shalt live!*, thou shalt exist here and now in the revelation of life, thou shalt locally incarnate the Word by using thine singular transcendental and speculative resources to enact the original living act and extract new visions from the living depths of the pleroma.[72] There is no *pattern* (*logos*, structure, information, redundancy, predictability, meaning, morality, law, symbolic order) without *matter*, without the living force that institutes subjects and unfolds the correlated horizons of experience. The are no intra-umweltic forms of order and organisation without the material impasses, noise, accidents, exceptions, heat, and friction that resist, force 'accommodations' (Piaget) of transcendental structures, and

---

71 W. Benjamin, Letter to Florens Christian Rang (December 9, 1923), in G. Scholem and T.W. Adorno (eds.), *The Correspondence of Walter Benjamin, 1910–1940*, tr. M.R. Jacobson and E.M. Jacobson (Chicago: University of Chicago Press, 1994), 224.

72 'Before the paternal *thou shalt not kill* [...] there is another word, denser and more complex, linked to the sensitivity of the mother's body to which it is attached [...] the one that proclaims without fury and without noise the warm *thou shalt live* of the maternal.' L. Rozitchner, 'Primero hay que saber vivir', *El Ojo Mocho. Revista de crítica política y cultural* 20 (2006), reprinted in *No matar. Sobre la responsabilidad* (Cordoba: La intemperie, 2007), 387.

elicit the constitution of new patterns.[73] There is no paternal imperative calling for the regulation and maintenance of a given symbolic order without the material force of the institution and destitution of every symbolic order. The infinite speculative expansion of experience beyond every local Umwelt is rooted in the mat(t)er 'that opens to life but also to death', that teaches the living to live and die.[74] There is no living being that is not born, engendered as a local incarnation of life, as a finite living probe whose experience unfolds within the phenomenological horizon constituted by its transcendental apparatus. In the phenoumenodelic foreground, every finite living being ecstatically transcends toward the worldly horizon in which its transcendentally-dependent experience takes place and time. In the immanental background, every living being is always already implanted into the impersonal and premundane life that engenders it, that bears it, that irrigates it with its strength and impels it to sprout toward the phenoumenodelic clearings. We could understand Fichte's *intellectual intuition* as the umbilical thread that religates the transcendental foreground with the immanental background, that apprehends every fact of experience lived by a finite subject as a local existing mode of the everlasting and omnipresent self-positing act of life. Every living-something (*erleben*) understood as an experience of a phenomenon in a world is rooted in the being alive (*leben*) of the incarnate subject: every experience is lived by a finite living mode of the one life. '[T]he existence of the subject of correlation [...] must be defined as *living*. In French, [the word *vivre*] is used in a twofold sense: *vivre* means to be alive (*leben*) but also to feel, to have the experience of something (*erleben*). The distinction here is between the present participle and the past participle, between the living being and lived experience, as if the action of living [...] always implied being affected by [some other] in an experience, as if vital activity had always as its inverse the passivity of a perceiving. The subject of correlation has this feature

73 'All that is not information, not redundancy, not form and not restraints—[appears as] noise, the only possible source of *new* patterns.' G. Bateson, *Steps to an Ecology of Mind* (Chicago: University of Chicago Press, 2000), 416.

74 Rozitchner, 'Primero hay que saber vivir', 389.

particular to it: that it *lives*: it is at once a living being, and as a result participates in the world, and a subject that lives the world, that is to say for which *there is* this world. To say that it lives is first of all to recognise that its existence in the world envelopes an appearing of the world [...].'[75] The barbarian synthesis between the Kantian *erleben* and the Spinozist *leben* amounts to recognising that the transcendental constitution of a world that appears before the subject and the institution of this very subject are aspects of the same immanental living vortex, that the visions deployed in the experiential foreground are modes of the same insubstance that raises its tide in the unconscious background and informs the subject's life. *Intellectual intuition* grasps the subject's (*er*)*leben*, the immanental-transcendental point of indistinction at which the subject experiences itself as an immanental fold of life, as a singular channel through which life appears to itself: '[A]ssailed by the excess of this vibration and under threat that you will be dissolved into it, you close your eyes, only to rediscover the same force within you, in the deepest hollows of your being there springs forth the impulse that diversifies itself through you and—just as a river, in expending its force, branches off infinitely—here develops an arm, there a leg, an eye, losing itself in the web of speech, engendering the structure of your body in order to find its thunderous way through it. For it is given to us to perceive, we feel it first of all within ourselves [...].'[76]

As we shall see, the reimplantation of the subject's phenomenological life in the immanence of the one life defines a first form of trinitarian religation, that which reconnects the personal to the impersonal, the transcendental-phenomenological to the immanental. But life does not unfold only by instituting separated individuals, but also by concerting them into collective forms of subjectivity. The process of *exteriorisation* associated with the institution of I/not-I polarisations and the concomitant spanning of phenomenological forms of transcendence is counteracted by an *interiorisation* which, by making kin between those separate individuals, institutes transpersonal forms of subjectivity and envelops their

75 R. Barbaras, *Introduction à une phénoménologie de la vie* (Paris: Vrin, 2008), 19–20.

76 M. Henry, *L'amour les yeux fermés* (Paris: Editions Gallimard, 1976), 72.

reciprocal being-out-of-each-other in a common overarching interiority. Every lifeform emerges into the world of its experience from the physical and psychic unconsciousness associated with the one life (Freud) and is also a local component of higher-order forms of subjectivity (Bateson).[77] Every form of personal consciousness is rooted in an impersonal unconsciousness and is holonically inscribed in a transpersonal supraconsciousness. The religation is threefold: with the *impersonal life* that reaches us from the nearest and the farthest confines in dreams, through our breathing, through the water and the winds, through the omens that reach us as propagating vibrations of the *textum*, through the sunlight, through the lapsus that interrupts the continuity of our alleged mastery, through the stellar elements of which we are made, through the imperceptible multidimensional living networks that bathe the salient causal chains and unidimensional narratives, through the cycles of the moon, through unforeseen events that disrupt our plans, through our genetic heritage, through the invisible spirits that populate the 'animic field'; with the *personal life* through which the everlasting creative act of living assumes a singular form—the instrument through which the original Word is modulated into a unique voca(lisa)tion (*Bestimmung*), the living and dying icon through which the desire to live is channelled and manifested in an unrepeatable manner, the breathing mode of the insubstance that deepens its belonging to this univocal 'plane of immanence' by self-positing and affirming its individual freedom—; and finally with the *transpersonal life* that results from the communitarian forms of reciprocity among different lifeforms, from the integration of local individuals into distributed forms of (un)consciousness, from the phenoumenodelics of the Holy Spirit.

---

77 As Bateson writes: 'Freudian psychology expanded the concept of mind in-wards to include the whole communication system within the body—the autonomic, the habitual, and the vast range of unconscious process. What I am saying expands mind out-wards. And both of these changes reduce the scope of the conscious self. A certain humility becomes appropriate, tempered by the dignity or joy of being part of something much bigger. A part—if you will—of God.' Bateson, *Steps to an Ecology of Mind*, 461–62.

Whereas Kant placed philosophy under the sign of an insuperable finitude, Spinoza, in divinising the immanental field into which finite existence dives, transmuted finitude absolutely, making it a local mode of the absolute (in)substance. Whereas Kant held that all experience (even the intersubjective experience of modern science) is relative to the transcendental structure of the corresponding subject, Spinoza maintained that the latter, far from being a self-grounded last instance (a substance *causa sui*) is itself only a finite mode of infinite (in)substance. We shall always be indebted to Kant for having brought to light the transcendental perspectivism of the experience of every finite subject, but it was Spinoza who closed off (*avant la lettre*) the only pre-modern escape route left to reduce this increase in relativism: that of converting transcendental idealism into a subjectivist metaphysics, that of conceiving of the transcendental subject itself as a self-caused substance *qua* absolute ground.[78] If all experience depends upon the transcendental type of the subject of experience, this type, far from being itself a self-grounded and hetero-grounding last instance, is not even master in its own house. Human rationality, rather than providing an ultimate rational ground, is a contingent product of the biomorphogenetic process of the institution of living beings immanent to living (in)substance. Every finite subject is *limited* by the transcendental structure of its subjectivity and *alienated* upon being begotten, instituted as a finite and local mode of infinite (in)substance, estranged in its being rooted in the impersonal life in which it is born, lives, and dies. Every personal act of free will is a local scintillation, a singular refraction, of the immanental *potentia absoluta Dei*, of the living force that continually diverges from itself, traversing bifurcation points, instituting new kinds of receptive-imaginative-expressive modes, breaking causal reactions in favour of subjectified responses, spanning new degrees of freedom, opening zones of indeterminacy that propel its phenoumenodelic effusion. All experience is relative to the transcendental structure of a

78 As Vaysse writes, 'to use substance as the basis for the individuality of the mode is to break with the idea of a grounding subjectivity [...].' J.-M. Vaysse, *Totalité et Finitude. Spinoza et Heidegger* (Paris: Vrin, 2004), 49.

subject which—far from being itself a self-caused ultimate ground—is existentially alienated: 'I is another', 'someone who isn't me'. Every empirical subject as instance of a transcendental type is no more than a receptive and expressive mode, a finite fluctuation of infinite (in)substance, a pneumatic instrument capable of conveying *hic et nunc* a singular modulation of the Word. Reading Kant with Spinoza (and vice versa), we can affirm that the modern subject is a finite subject, contingently localised in spacetime (Copernican empirical perspectivism), contingently localised in the space of possible transcendental types (Kantian transcendental perspectivism) and alienated (ominously cut off from any form of self-grounding immediacy). It is in this way, we shall maintain here that Kantian transcendentalism and Spinozist immanentism ultimately emphasise—beyond any form of subjectivist metaphysics—different aspects of the same, properly modern conception of subjectivity: transcendental perspectivism and immanental alienation, existential finitude (whatever is, is *there*) and zoetic possession ('Whatever is, is in [life]').[79]

This projected synthesis between Kantian transcendental idealism and Spinozist absolutism—the construction of a *philosophy of the finite subject understood as a breathing riddle of the living (in)substance*—cannot merely be understood as a conjunction of separate and self-sufficient terms, indifferent to the opposition into which the very project of a synthesis brings them. In order to avoid a synthesis that is merely a juxtaposition and to prime Kantianism and Spinozism for this alchemical wedding, we need to intervene on either side of the opposition. Synthesising Kant with Spinoza initially requires absolving Spinozism from certain objections formulated within the framework of the post-critical tradition: first, Kant and Fichte charged that, by proposing a system of statements on the nature of substance without taking into account the transcendental conditions of enunciation of the same, Spinozism is culpable of pre-critical dogmatism. Second, Hegel famously charged that Spinoza could not think of 'substance' as living 'subject'. Equally, synthesising Kant with Spinoza requires absolving

79 B. de Spinoza, *Ethics: Proved in Geometrical Order*, tr. M. Silverthorne and M.J. Kisner (Cambridge: Cambridge University Press, 2018), 14 [Book I, Prop. 15].

Kantianism of its possible egotistic, idealist, and claustrophobic derivatives. These mutually reinforcing refinements of Spinozism and Kantianism will be brought about by means of a phenomenological suspension and subjectivation of Spinoza's substance, and a speculative diagonalisation of the Kantian distinction between phenomena and noumena. Far from being incompatible, Kantian transcendentalism and Spinozist immanentism correct one another's errors and counterbalance one another's inherent tendencies to degenerate into, respectively, a claustrophobic idealism and a dogmatic vagary. Whereas the critical tradition permits Spinozism to be released from dogmatic naiveties, Spinozism frees the critical motif from 'Descartes' walled garden', thereby opening it up to 'unlimited [transcendental] perspectives'[80] and to trans-species variations and alliances.

80 Rolland, *L'éclair de Spinoza*, 97.

# PART I

Spinozism enriched the modern philosophical landscape with at least four fundamental gestures: the closure of ontotheology qua science of a hypertranscendent *summum ens* (thereby bringing forth the possibility of conceiving an atheistic religion), the rational critique of the superstitious and intolerant degeneration of the 'true' religion and of the alliance between ecclesiastical authority and political power ('nothing governs the multitude as effectively as superstition'!),[1] the thesis on the concrescence of infinite abstract 'attributes' of experience in a single 'substance' (contra the Cartesian dualism of *res extensa* and *res cogitans*), and the alienating conception of modern subjectivity as a finite mode of infinite substance. Despite this, Spinozism was the object of the two charges mentioned above (among others): that of pre-critical dogmatism and that of not thinking substance as living subject. As we shall see below, these criticisms will lead us to introduce a *suspension*, an *enlivening*, and a *subjectivation* of Spinozist substance. The result of these three operations will be called *pleroma*.

It could be said that the dissolution of the pre-modern boundary between the sublunar earth and the supralunar heavens offers two possibilities for conceiving a religion synchronic with modern science: either hyperbolic hypertranscendence or speculative (post-critical) immanence, either the neo-gnostic route that consists in a further radicalisation of

1 B. de Spinoza, *Theological-Political Treatise*, tr. M. Silverthorne and J. Israel (Cambridge: Cambridge University Press, 2007), 5.

divine hypertranscendence, making of God a *Deus absconditus*,[2] beyond cosmic extension and worldly understanding (e.g. Pascal, Jacobi)—a God who is 'infinitely incomprehensible since [...] he has no affinity to us',[3] or the Spinozist route that consists in making divinity immanent to the whole cosmic field of appearance ('Christianity has had only two dimensions, antinomical to one another: that of the *Deus absconditus*, in which the Western disappearance of the divine is still engulfed, and that of the [...] *Deus communis* [...]', of the conversion into living insubstance 'as the immanence of [cure]').[4] While Pascal confronted the advent of modern rationality by abandoning mediaeval scholasticism's attempt to rationally demonstrate the existence of God, and making it the 'object' of a radically different logic ('the reasons of the heart'), the Spinozist identity Nature = God (*Deus sive natura*) makes modern science as such knowledge of God. The neo-gnostic Pascalian strategy is a sort of *fuite en avant* that confronts the advent of modern science by further intensifying the ontotheological hypertranscendence of God and the corresponding depreciation of human finitude and of nature (both of which are fallen, corrupted, and radically estranged from God). In doing so, Pascal aims to preserve the Christian God from the existential disenchantment elicited by modern science and from the purported silence of an astrophysical sky that no longer sings the glory of God. In Pascal, the death of God is no more than the death of God as creator of the world, which is to say, of a God that would be able to recognise itself in its creation. In short, the death of God can be understood in this context as a gnostic disidentification between God and the Demiurgic creator of the worldly prison. How could one believe in a God who created the desolation described by Pascal, in God as creator of a world that must be redeemed?[5] The modern experience of a world

2 Pascal, *Thoughts, Letters and Minor Works*, 70 [§194].

3 Ibid., 84 [§233].

4 J-L. Nancy, *The Inoperative Community*, tr. P. Connor et al. (Minneapolis and Oxford: University of Minnesota Press, 1991), 10.

5 Cf. H. Blumenberg, *The Legitimacy of the Modern Age* (Cambridge, MA and London: MIT Press, 1999). On the relationship between gnosticism and Pascal's existential

without God can thus be adapted into a neo-gnostic existentialism in which the anguish elicited by being exiled in a universe deserted by divinity can find consolation not in the idea of God the creator, but in that of God the redeemer, the saviour. Existential angst and hope for eternal salvation are therefore the two sides of the Pascalian neo-gnostic means of coping with the expansion of the post-Copernican universe. Pascal's strategy leads to a depreciation of scientific knowledge ('the vanity of the sciences!'),[6] which is posited as nothing more than an attempt to rationally understand a temporal, contingent, and corrupt nature—in the end nothing but a kind of cultural entertainment—incapable of apprehending the hypertranscendent absolute. Ultimately, science is a distraction from the one matter of definitive importance, the problem of salvation. The unique service provided by science (to which Pascal significantly contributed) is that of exhibiting the desolated nature of the physical universe and the misery of human existence, thereby triggering the longing for a trans-worldly eternal salvation. The Pascalian reduction of the domain of science may then be included in the long sequence of 'modern' philosophical attempts to reactively reduce the unbearable impact of the advent of modern science: science has either no soteriological relevance (Pascal), no ontological significance (Heidegger), or no speculative scope (Meillassoux). Regarding religion, the Pascalian elevation of the transcendent God to a new degree of exteriority persists in grounding religion on a 'wager' regarding a hypothetical *summum ens* rooted neither in worldly experience nor in the use of human understanding or reason. It could be said that Pascal's route anticipates Jacobi's criticism of Spinozism as well as certain contemporary forms of 'speculation' which claim to provide direct access to the 'great outdoors', suspending the mediations (the methodical patience, the resistance, the frustration, the slowness) of worldly practices and finite forms of knowledge.

---

nihilism see H. Jonas, *The Phenomenon of Life: Towards a Philosophical Biology* (Evanston, IL: Northwestern University Press, 2001), Chapter 9, 211–34, and D.R. Hiller, 'La dernière crise gnostique: Pascal et le gnosticisme ad hominem', *Philosophiques* 45:1 (2018): 3–20.

6 Pascal, *Thoughts, Letters and Minor Works*, 25 [§67].

On the other hand, Spinozist immanent absolutism leads to the possibility of conceiving, within the bounds of modernity itself, an atheistic religion absolved from the ontotheological conception of a hypertranscendent God. In effect, the immanent thesis—the identity *Nature = God*—ultimately makes both the concept of God and the 'science' of which it is the 'object', theology, superfluous. This thesis also entails an identification between the phenoumenodelic notion of manifestation and the theological notion of revelation. The God of Spinoza, far from being the God of a revealed religion, far from being a hidden and hypertranscendent God that would at best reveal itself partially, locally, at a given site, a given age, a given book, or to a chosen people or that would be the object of a personal faith, belief, or 'wager', is a God whose revelation fully coincides with, and is indeed nothing more than, *the phenoumenodelic field of manifestation*. It is worth emphasising that this identification relies on a phenoumenodelic extension of the concept of manifestation beyond its phenomenological conjugation: as we shall see below, a *phenomenon* (that which appears within a phenomenological horizon correlated to a transcendental type of subjectivity) can be understood as a particular objectivation of an uncorrelated *phenoumenon* that cannot be fully and faithfully embedded in any phenomenological horizon. Far from being a local event, the revelation is coextensive with Being qua (uncorrelated) Appearing.

As Heidegger wrote, '[t]hinking does not overcome metaphysics by climbing still higher, surmounting it, transcending it somehow or other; thinking overcomes metaphysics by climbing back down into the nearness of the nearest'.[7] While the 'nearest' is, for Heidegger, what he calls 'the truth of Being', we shall characterise it here as the 'act of living', in so far as this act holds within it the amphiboly (emphasised by Barbaras) between *experiencing something* (to live through something) and *being alive*, i.e. between *erleben* and *leben*. We could say that Heidegger turns the gaze from the entities that appear toward the phenomenological eclosion of Being as such, but that he does so at the price of a concealment of the living nature of the experiential field, of the fact that the phenoumenodelic pleroma is one life

7 Heidegger, 'Letter on Humanism', *Basic Writings*, 254.

that reveals by engendering, by instituting living forms of finitude. Heidegger's fundamental ontology starts with a Dasein that is already 'thrown' *there* and the analysis of the *sum* of the *cogitare* as existence rather than subsistence to a great extent abstracts from the living character of Dasein's existence.[8] The intraworldliness of the constitutive Dasein emphasised by Heidegger is subtended by Dasein's belonging to the field of life: before being in the constituted world, the subject exists in the instituting life. Maybe the Heideggerian recourse to the term *physis* as one of the names of Being could be understood as a way to compensate for what risks seeming like the ontologically fleshless abstraction of his existential analytic. This precedence of life (the Spinozist *natura naturans*) with respect to the constituted world (the Spinozist *natura naturata*) explains why the immanental stance that we are exploring here is that of a *radical* immanence: Spinozist immanence does not command a return to the 'natural' world but rather, and more radically, to the living field of revelation within which every world grows. In this sense, the Spinozist divinisation of 'nature' cannot be reduced to a 'pantheistic' hypostasis of 'that tiny fragment of nature that we are accustomed to call "nature"'.[9]

Since God-Nature qua *physis* or *natura naturans* is nothing but a continuous living act of self-revelation, we could say, with Spinoza, that God's essence envelops its existence, that there is no hidden essence separated from its existential act of manifestation. The essence of substance envelops its phenoumenodelic ek-sistence since substance is nothing but the continuous living act of self-revelation, the ebb and flow of the institution of finite lifeforms and constitution of phenomenological horizons of experience. *Natura naturans* is, in Christian terms, the Word, pure insubstantial activity that reveals itself, that begets living beings as local resonance chambers, instruments through which life breathes and modulates its *pneuma*. The *natura naturans* is an insubstance *causa sui*, a reflexive phenoumenodelic

8 Cf. Barbaras, *Introduction à une phénoménologie de la vie*, chapter 2.

9 W. Benjamin, 'To the Planetarium', in M.W. Jennings et al. (eds.), *The Work of Art in the Age of Its Technological Reproducibility, and Other Writings on Media* (Cambridge, MA and London: The Belknap Press of Harvard University Press, 2008), 58–59: 59.

self-positing, an uninterrupted process of self-revelation whose being is sustained in and by its own appearance, 'an absolute immediate consciousness [an absolute I] whose very activity no longer refers to a [substantial, subsistent] being but is ceaselessly [actively] posed in a life.[10] [...] [L]ife is [...]: the self-grounded, held and sustained by itself.[11] [...] That life persists in its being is only possible because, given to itself at each point of its being and never faltering in its self-affection, it does not ever fall into nothingness but, supported by itself, so to speak, and extracting its being from the sensation it has of itself, it does not cease to be, and to be life.'[12]

If we maintain the thesis that modern science is the mode of thought appropriate to the construction of a legitimate rational comprehension of God-Nature—if 'the more we understand particular things, the more we understand God'[13]—if there is no revelation outside of the phenoumenal, then Spinozist immanentism renders entirely superfluous the distinction between theo-logy understood as the construction of rational knowledge about God and the naturo-logy deployed by modern science. Scholastic attempts to prove the existence of God give way definitively to modern science as the knowledge of a God-Nature whose existence is now simply manifest. For who could claim that the existence of nature needs to be proved? As Goethe writes in a letter to Jacobi: '[Spinoza] proves not the existence of God, but rather that existence is God'.[14] In this sense, Spinoza's immanentism seems like nothing but a kind of crypto-atheism intended to absolve itself from the accusation of atheism by means of the mere nominal concession of calling nature 'God'. Progressive modern secularisation would then have been characterised by a series of ruses and euphemistic turns of phrase intended to smuggle in a latent atheism

10 G. Deleuze, 'Immanence: A Life', in *Pure Immanence: Essays on a Life*, tr. A. Boyman (New York: Zone Books, 2001), 25–33: 27.

11 J.G. Fichte, *The Science of Knowing: J.G. Fichte's 1804 Lectures on the Wissenschaftslehre*, tr. W. E. White (New York: State University of New York Press, 2005), 91.

12 M. Henry, *La barbarie* (Paris: Presses Universitaires de France, 2004), 169.

13 Spinoza, *Ethics*, 238 [Book V, Prop. 24].

14 Goethe, Letter to F. H. Jacobi, 9 June 1785.

under the guise of a manifest deism. Spinoza's God, Kant's *rational belief* (*Vernunftglaube*),[15] and the Fichtean God as 'moral order of the world'[16] would have been the hallmarks of this modern crypto-atheism. But both the 'pantheism controversy'[17] and the 'atheism controversy'[18] testify to the fact that no euphemism can disguise the violence that Spinozism and its Fichtean conjugation inflict upon the body of ontotheology. Now, as will be argued below, the consequent redundancy of the ontotheological notion of God ('we have no need for that hypothesis', as Laplace would have it), and of the theological science which takes God as its 'object' of study, does not necessarily render void the possibility of a properly modern atheistic religion. But in what sense can the notion of religion be preserved if we dissociate it from the notion of 'God' and a corresponding theology? Without further ado, let us introduce the response that we shall explore in what follows: exploiting the etymological root of the term *religion* (which, according to an interpretation that Benveniste attributes to Lactantius and Tertullian, comes from the Latin *re-ligare*—from *ligare*, to tie, bind),[19] we shall understand by *religion* a human practice oriented by the infinite idea of *love* and intended to perpetuate healing from disligation and the accompanying illnesses of capitalistic and colonial *appropriation* ('This is mine'), humanist *essentialisation* ('This is me'), and idealistic *isolation*

---

15 I. Kant, 'What Does it Mean to Orient Oneself in Thinking?', in *Religion and Rational Theology*, tr. A.W. Wood (Cambridge: Cambridge University Press 1996), 1–18: 13.

16 Cf. J.G. Fichte, 'On the Ground of Our Belief in a Divine World-Governance', in Y. Estes and C. Bowman (eds.), *J.G. Fichte and the Atheism Dispute (1798–1800)* (London: Routledge, 2010), 17–30.

17 Cf. J. Solé (ed.), *Jacobi, Mendelssohn, Wizenmann, Kant, Goethe, Herder. El ocaso de la ilustración. La polémica del Spinozismo* (Bernal and Buenos Aires: Universidad Nacional de Quilmes Editorial/Prometeo 3010, 2013).

18 Cf. J.-C. Goddard, *La Querelle de l'athéisme* (Paris: Vrin, 1993).

19 Cf. E. Benveniste, *Dictionary of Indo-European Concepts and Society* (Chicago, IL: Hau Books, 2016), 528, and J. Derrida, 'Faith and Knowledge: The Two Sources of "Religion" at the Limits of Reason Alone', in G. Anidjar (ed.), *Acts of Religion* (New York and London: Routledge 2002), 70–3 [§33].

('There is no one beside[s] *me*'). Instead of depending on purported theoretical knowledge, doctrinal content, or revealed dogma, religion will be understood in this way as a *practice* of experimentation guided by the idea of re-ligating ourselves with the impersonal life force that engenders lifeforms—with the living mat(t)er, with ourselves qua finite and singular instantiations of life, and with other living beings (with the siblings) and the corresponding emergent forms of trans-species collective subjectivity (with the Holy Spirit).[20]

To understand Spinozism as the closure of ontotheology, it is necessary to rid oneself of both the *onto*theological interpretation of God, that of God as a *summum ens* located in hypertranscendence, and the onto*theological* interpretation of Spinozism as science (presented *more geometrico*) of God. In the present post-critical context, the prospect of proposing a theology seems like a kind of outright *pre-critical dogmatism*. After all, what can we say about infinite and absolute substance as such without transgressing the limits set by transcendental critique, without falling into the transcendental illusions typical of an exercise of the faculty of understanding that does not know its own bounds?[21] In particular, what legitimacy can the

---

20 Concerning the concept of *religation*, see the chapter 'En torno a la idea de Dios' in X. Zubiri, *Naturaleza, Historia, Dios* (Madrid: Alianza Editorial, 1971). According to Zubiri, 'exteriority and religation [...] are of the opposite sign. [Human beings are] open to things; [they find themselves] *among* them and *with them*. That is why [they go] *towards* them, sketching out a world of possibilities of doing something with these things. But in this way [human beings do] not meet God. God is not a thing in this sense. When [human beings are] religated, [they are] not *with* God, but rather *in* God. [...] to *go towards* God is *to be led* by [It]. In openness to things, [human beings *meet*] things and confront them. In the openness that is religation, [human beings *are*] *placed* into existence, implanted in being, as I said at the beginning, and placed in it as if coming "from".' Ibid., 376.

21 Kant emphasised the incompatibility between his critiques of dogmatism and Spinozism in the following terms: 'It is hard to comprehend how [...] scholars could find support for Spinozism in the *Critique of Pure Reason*. The *Critique* completely clips dogmatism's wings in respect of the cognition of supersensible objects, and Spinozism is so dogmatic in this respect that it even competes with the mathematicians in respect of the strictness of its proofs. [...] It is just for this reason that Spinozism

Spinozist thesis of the univocity of substance maintain within the post-critical milieu? In response to this criticism, we shall adopt a Fichtean proposition. Fichte, phenomenologist *avant la lettre*,[22] *suspended* the Spinozist substance in a purely phenomenological *insubstance* (a 'non-substantial absolute', as Sartre says of consciousness)[23] woven from the subtle immateriality of appearing: 'The Science of Knowledge works within appearance as Spinoza did within being.[24] [...] Everything was suspension.[25] [...] The waves of this Sea are faltering, it is impossible to know where they are going, they have no port or course, everything floats, as in a baroque suspension [...][26] Everything goes into suspension, everything takes flight[27] [...]

---

leads directly to enthusiasm. By contrast, there is not a single means more certain to eliminate enthusiasm from the roots up than that determination of the bounds of the pure faculty of understanding.' Kant, 'What Does it Mean to Orient Oneself in Thinking?', 15n. In the *Opus Postumum*, Kant resumes this last characterisation in the following terms: 'Spinoza's concept of God and man, according to which the philosopher intuits all things in God, is enthusiastic [*schwärmerisch*] (*conceptus fanaticus*).' I. Kant, *Opus Postumum*, tr. E. Förster and M. Rosen (Cambridge: Cambridge University Press, 1993), 225. As Heidegger remarked, '[...] Spinoza appeals always afresh to the whole thinking of German Idealism, and at the same time provokes its contradiction, because he lets thinking begin with the absolute.' M. Heidegger, *Identity and Difference* (New York, Evanston, IL, and London: Harper & Row 1969), 47–48.

22 See J. Hyppolite, 'L'idée fichtéenne de la doctrine de la science et le projet husserlien', in J. Hyppolite, *Figures de la pensée philosophique, I* (Paris: PUF, 1971).

23 J.-P. Sartre, *The Transcendence of the Ego*, tr. A. Brown (London and New York: Routledge, 2004), 42.

24 J.G. Fichte, *Doctrine de la science. Exposé de 1812*, tr. I. Thomas Fogiel (Paris: Presses Universitaires de France, 2005), 53.

25 N. Perlongher, *Hule*, in *Poemas Completos*, 131.

26 N. Perlongher, *Sopa Paraguaya*, in W. Bueno, *Mar paraguayo* (Buenos Aires: Interzona, 2020), 9.

27 N. Perlongher, *Caribe Transplatino*, in *Prosa Plebeya. Ensayos 1980–1992* (Buenos Aires: Colihue, 2008), 96.

*Alles Schwebt.*'[28] Following Fichte, we shall not understand Spinozist substance as the global *something*, the '*stuff*' of which every pattern, shape, or structure is a local form. 'For [if] it is common sense that every pattern, shape, or structure is a form *of* something as pots are forms of clay',[29] the Fichtean suspension of univocal substance frees Spinozism from the dogmatic commonsensical presupposition of a unified polymorphic material-energetic background in the last instance. Thanks to the Fichtean *epoché*, 'the burden of stuff drops' and substance acquires the lightness of manifestation. From a strict phenoumenodelic standpoint, this presupposed 'something' 'is as dispensable as the ether in which light was once supposed to travel.[30] [...] What is involved is no longer the affirmation of a single substance, but rather the laying out of a common [phenoumenodelic] plane of immanence on which all bodies, all minds, and all individuals are situated [as 'images', as Bergson puts it]. [...] [To perform the *epoché*] is to install oneself on this plane–which implies a mode of living, a way of life.'[31] Rather than referring to some theoretical proposition about a dubious 'substantial' univocal infrastructure of the real (e.g. a unified quantum field, a cosmic energy, etc.)—which would be pre-critical, dogmatic naivety (How could one pretend to know it? By appealing to contemporary physics or to any other finite form of knowledge?)—the notion of substance then denotes the univocal monism of appearance, the 'original and absolute activity' (Schelling) of manifestation. The *epoché* allows Spinozist immanent monism to be absolved of any suspect *theoretical* thesis regarding the experiential field and that which appears within it. Where the theoretical interpretation of substance as a sort of material or energetic field ultimately laid Spinozism open to the accusation of dogmatism, thus making it impervious to any synthesis with Kantianism, on the contrary, the monism

28 A. Webern, quoted in P. Lacoue-Labarthe, *Typography: Mimesis, Philosophy, Politics* (Cambridge, MA: Harvard University Press, 1989), 208.

29 A. Watts, *The Joyous Cosmology* (Novato, CA: New World Library, 2013), 2.

30 Ibid., 2.

31 G. Deleuze, *Spinoza: Practical Philosophy*, tr. R. Hurley (San Francisco, CA: City Lights Books, 1988), 122.

of appearance as suspended insubstance, far from depending on a consummate and dogmatically employed theoretical corpus, only depends on the phenoumenological description of our existential situation: that of being immersed in an impersonal field of manifestation from which our experience (that of a finite subject always located in a certain empirical state and instantiating a certain type of transcendental subjectivity among others) appears to offer only a partial, pared-down, coarse-grained impression. Rather than relying on any purported theory on the ultimate nature of the real, insubstance is simply a name for the impersonal experiential field of which all phenoumena are local salient forms. In this way, the *absoluteness* of the insubstance makes no reference to an alleged ultimate theoretical truth about its nature and structure, but rather to the fact that it is not correlative to any transcendental type of subjectivity. In a post-Kantian context, the truth is nothing more than the regulative idea that orients the infinite tasks of an always finite understanding, not some specific theoretical content that can be disposed of where convenient. The 'image of the world' constructed by modern science–that of an expanding universe described by relativistic cosmology, that of a 'standard model' of elementary particles and fundamental interactions, that of a terrestrial biosphere in which animal and plant life emerged through an adaptive and evolutionary process—is no more (or less) than the symbolisation of the experiential field that is available at this particular moment in time and in certain regions of planet Earth. And when it comes to the question about the human existential situation (about the 'human place in the cosmos'), absolute modernity is characterised by a radicalisation of the modern transition from the premodern site ('We are inhabitants of a world bounded by the Earth below and the Heavens above') to the cosmological site ('We are inhabitants of a vast expanding universe') into the phenoumenodelic thesis that we live in the immanental pleroma, in the suspended insubstance, in the self-manifestation of life. The 'infinite universe' of the moderns is also a 'closed [circumambient] world' suspended in life, and the unfathomable empirical vastness of cosmic spatiotemporal extension seems parochial compared to the speculative openness of the all-encompassing insubstance: 'Blowing up our environmental space by millions of light-years does not lift us beyond ourselves, but what certainly does is the knowledge that, beyond our personal environment, the environments of our human and animal brethren are secured in an all-encompassing plan.'[32] This recalibration of our existential situation beyond the astrophysical landscape depicted by modern cosmology is not a regression to a pre-scientific stage, but rather a further radicalisation of modernity's ungrounding process, a radicalisation that renders even scientific 'images of the world' hypothetical. The transition from an earth-based description of our existential situation to scientific cosmology and the corresponding zoom-out transformations (from the solar system to the Milky Way to the local group to the Virgo supercluster to Laniakea to the whole universe to the multiverse, and so on and so forth) still belong to (what Spinoza called) the second kind of knowledge. The *epoché* subordinates this second kind of knowledge (namely, scientific understanding) to the third kind, namely to the (intellectual) intuition of the phenoumenodelic living insubstance itself, to the fact that we and our finite understanding and its rational constructs are all local outgrowths of life. 'Images of the world' change, symbolisations follow on from one another, no scientific theory remains unscathed in the face of the will to know guided by the infinite idea of truth. In the end it is always a matter of pushing further our understanding of the rational structure of the experiential field we were thrown into, or, more precisely, the field we were instituted upon. As Husserl already attempted in *The Originary Ark, the Earth, Does Not Move,* the *epoché* performs a sort of phenoumenodelic reduction of the Copernican Revolution: it is not so much the case that planet Earth with its different lifeforms freefalls through the cosmic extensions of a purely objective 'nature in itself', deprived of sensibility and self-awareness, but rather that the 'image of the world' constructed by modern science (that of orbiting celestial bodies, cosmic expanses, ancestral timescales, quantum-scale microscopies) is itself no more than a highly sophisticated and effective symbolisation (a *solaristic* image of the world)

32 J. von Uexküll, *A Foray into the Worlds of Animals and Humans,* with *A Theory of Meaning*, tr. J.D. O'Neil (Minneapolis and London: University of Minnesota Press, 2010), 200.

that *appears* in the living heart of an uninterrupted phenoumenodelic flux in which we are born to the manifestation, to the sensation, to the (un) consciousness that perceives, feels and understands, a living field in which we are immersed and in which we shall die. The *epoché* suspends the apparent 'inescapable presupposition of all science'—that of 'nature in itself' as pure inanimate objectivity—in order to implant science back into the phenoumenodelic maelstrom of life, to make science an infinite project of reason and a singular manifestation of desire deployed collectively by finite subjects who live, exist, and die in the core of the immanent arche-revelation that is life. Strictly speaking, the Husserlian native Ur-instance within which the phenoumenodelic suspension implants the avatars of the Child Yesses—pure immanental flux, from and to itself (rather a tempestuous ocean than an immobile earth: '[W]hat is at the bottom is not the fixed element, but water!')[33]—is not so much a 'lifeworld' as the absolute life in which worlds emerge, coalesce, and disappear: 'The [living Over-Soul] looketh steadily forwards, creating a world before her, leaving worlds behind her. [...] The soul knows only the soul; the web of events [and worlds] is the flowing robe in which she is clothed.'[34] The *epoché* transforms Spinozist substance into 'a free-flowing, undulating, definitively liquid absolute',[35] an absolute without any fixity whatsoever, one that lets go of any fixed point, a living absolute—a singular form that never ceases to inform and deform itself. Insubstance is a narcotic ocean, Solaris, a 'watery world' of 'affluvial flowandflow',[36] 'a pure [lactescent] mat(t)er, a [self-organising] crystal of appearing',[37] a deliquescent plasma, enlightened flesh, an epiphytic informalescence, a stream of imponderable self-experience, the ebb and flow of a vibrant phenoumenodelic dehiscence, an ethereal

33 Henry, *L'amour les yeux fermés*, 52.

34 Emerson, 'The Over-Soul', 265.

35 DenaKmar naKhabra, 'The Undulating Unknown', in J. Ramey and M. Harr Farris (eds.), *The Enigmatic Absolute: Heresy, Gnosis and Speculation in Continental Philosophy of Religion* (London: Rowman and Littlefield International, 2016).

36 Joyce, *Finnegans Wake*, 452, 404.

37 Henry, *Incarnation*, 367.

rubber, liquid sky, 'aerial waters', 'Paraguayan soup' of 'vicissitudinal mutations' (Bruno), *parapeté*, 'liquid florilegium (always flowing)'.[38] Every phenomenon is therefore a finite mode, a local fluctuation of that which we shall call *phenoumenodelic insubstance* or *pleroma*. Spinoza's infinite substance will thus be understood as a dreamlike insubstance woven from the phenoumenodelic immateriality of pure appearance.[39] Before all the theoretical theses that we can construct about the ultimate nature of the 'real'—fundamental particles, unified field, projections immanent to a hallucinating mind, computer simulations, vibrating cosmic energy, etc.—*experience* itself is 'the fundamental given natural [*naturans*] fact [...]'.[40] The ultimate (f)act before any theory, before any science, before any ontology, before any division of Being into ontic regions, before any system of transcendental categories, before any nature-culture, matter-spirit, persons-things, inorganic-organic, physics-metaphysics-pataphysics, existence-subsistence, nature-freedom, illusion-reality, or waking-dreaming divisions, the ultimate (f)act before all of this is experience in its pure phenoumenodelic givenness. The term 'pleroma' is precisely intended to emphasise—before any (meta)physics or any ontology—the impersonal nature of the phenoumenodelic field, the infinite excess of experience with respect to any subject, the fact that phenoumenodelic givenness can be reduced neither to the actual experiences of an empirical subject nor to the phenomenological horizon of possible experiences defined by its transcendental type. The term 'pleroma' denotes the fullness, the exuberance, the prodigality, the ubiquity, the exorbitance of revelation. There is no manifestation besides the manifestation of 'God', there is no 'God' 'before' or 'after' manifestation, and every intra-worldly phenomenalisation is a finite mode of 'God''s revelation. Rather than being the term of a speculative

38 Perlongher, *Caribe Transplatino*, 94.

39 Cf. L. Rozitchner, *Materialismo ensoñado* (Buenos Aires: Tinta Limón Ediciones, 2011), 60.

40 G. Strawson, 'Realistic Monism: Why Physicalism Entails Panpsychism', in D. Skribina (ed.), *Mind that Abides: Panpsychism in the New Millennium* (Amsterdam and Philadelphia, PA: John Benjamins, 2009), 33.

demonstration, the Absolute savours, hears, caresses, thinks, smells, constructs, breathes, cooks, dances, feels, sweats, calculates, sings, lives, bathes 'in itself, for in [itself] alone hath [it] the highest joy' (*Infinita essendi fruitio*).[41]

The pleroma is not something withdrawn from the field of manifestation, a hidden or hypertranscendent God, but an infinite revelation, an absolute phenoumenodelic disclosure that is not relative to any transcendental subject. A finite subject can experience it only at the price of a process of selection, a paring down, an umwelticisation of the pleroma mediated by a transcendental valve ('the vision of an infinite piece of [flesh] is the vision of the mad, but if I cut that [flesh] into pieces and parcel them out over days and over hungers [and over worlds]—then it would no longer be perdition and madness: it would once again be [finitised] life').[42] Rather than being an *idealist production* of phenomenality, every transcendental constitution of a form of experience works by limiting, trimming, editing, ignoring differences and renormalising pleromatic infinitude. The transcendental subject extracts *finite visions* from the constantly metamorphosing *infinite ultra-vision of life: 'voyage en kaleidoscope'*! Every worldly determination is a negation of the insubstance's infinity, a narrowing down of infinite experiential possibilities: 'It is the function of the nervous system to focus, to select, to narrow down; to choose, from an infinity of possibilities, the biochemical imprints which determine the tactics and strategies that ensure survival in one place, status in one tribe. [...] Survival and status mean forfeiting the infinite possibilities of unconditioned consciousness. The domesticated primate, inside the social reality-tunnel, is a trivial fragment of the potentials for experience and intelligence.'[43]

---

41 A. Silesius, *Cherubinischer Wandersmann*, ed. L. Gnädinger (Stuttgart: Reclam, 2006), Book II, §190.

42 C. Lispector, *The Passion According to G.H.*, tr. I. Novey (New York: New Directions, 2012), 6.

43 Wilson, *Prometheus Rising*, 124. Along the same lines, Aldous Huxley writes (partly quoting C.D. Broad): '[T]he function of the brain and nervous system and sense organs is in the main *eliminative* and not productive. [...] The function of the brain and nervous system is to protect us from being overwhelmed and confused by this

Husserl's phenomenological iteration of transcendental philosophy introduces a narcotic operator into the critical tradition that will play a central role in what follows, the *epoché* or *phenomenological reduction.*[44] By *epoché*, we shall understand the existential conversion by which the 'natural attitude' that reifies, normalises, and naturalises what appears—applying the thesis of 'reality' to it—is suspended, substituted by a phenoumenodelic attitude by means of which the experiential field is inhabited *as such*, in the immanence of its pure phenomenological givenness. 'Here I am', says the hanged human, 'in the presence of images',[45] in the most general sense of the term *images* (in the presence of percepts, affects, concepts, sociolepts), and it acknowledges that these images are 'constituted' by a 'transparent'

---

mass of largely useless and irrelevant knowledge, by shutting out most of what we should otherwise perceive or remember at any moment, and leaving only that very small and special selection which is likely to be practically useful. According to such a theory, each one of us is potentially Mind at Large. But in so far as we are animals, our business is at all costs to survive. To make biological survival possible, Mind at Large has to be funneled through the reducing valve of the brain and nervous system. [...] That which, in the language of religion, is called "this world" is the universe of reduced awareness, expressed, and, as it were, petrified by language. The various "other worlds," with which human beings erratically make contact are so many elements in the totality of the awareness belonging to Mind at Large.' A. Huxley, *The Doors of Perception and Heaven and Hell* (New York: Harper and Row, 1954), 22–3. In the same vein, Elie During describes the Bergsonian theory of consciousness in the following terms: 'It [consciousness] is not longer this beam of light travelling through the darkness of the world, it is a filter, a "black screen" offering the light that is infinitely spread out among things the occasion to reveal itself [in the form of transcendental-dependent phenomena].' E. During, 'Présence et répétition: Bergson chez les phénoménologues', *Critique* 678: 11 (2003): 848–64.

44 Cf. E. Husserl, *Cartesian Meditations: An Introduction to Phenomenology*, tr. D. Cairns (The Hague: Martinus Nijhoff, 1960), 18–21 [§8], and 25–26 [§11], and E. Husserl, *Ideas Pertaining to a Pure Phenomenology and to a Phenomenological Philosophy. First Book: General Introduction to a Pure Phenomenology*, tr. F. Kersten (The Hague: Martinus Nijhoff, 1983), 60–62 [§32], and 112–14 [§50].

45 H. Bergson, *Matter and Memory*, tr. N.M. Paul and W.S. Palmer (New York: Zone, 1991), 17.

transcendental frame, that they are phenomena that appear in the limited framework of its transcendental-dependent model-reality, *even if it might not be able to describe and explain* (to make 'opaque', i.e. the object of a reflexive 'attentional availability' in Thomas Metzinger's terms)[46] *the corresponding transcendental portals*. Thanks to the *epoché*, the subject acknowledges the existence of what might still remain 'invisible'. The *epoché* leads us back to our fundamental factual state, that of being thrown into the midst of an experiential field that always exceeds both our actual intra-worldly experience and the transcendental limits of the 'world' associated with our transcendental type. We could say that the phenoumenological suspension brings about what Michel Henry calls the first principle of phenomenology, namely the upholding of the identity between *being* and (transcendental-dependent) *appearing*: before being this or that, before being assigned to an ontic region, before being placed in an ontological hierarchy, before being understood as a perspectival adumbration of an essence, before any classification whatsoever, that which is *appears*.[47] In Heidegger's parlance, the immanental *epoché* redirects the phenomenological gaze from the entity that appears to the *being qua appearing* of the entity within the corresponding phenomenological horizon. The *epoché* is the clash of the gong that suspends every entity in its pure phenoumenodelic insubstance, that turns every 'substantial' entity into a vibrating local mode of a univocal field of manifestation.

The *epoché* suspends what Wilson dubs '*modeltheism*', also known as *naive realism*. This is the dogmatic identification between an Umwelt correlative to a certain transcendental type of subjectivity—a model of the pleroma, a symbolic structure, a 'reality-tunnel'—and the pleromatic real, which is not correlated to any constituting subjectivity. As Husserl already pointed out, the *epoché* brings about the conversion to a new modality of existence, a new

46 See T. Metzinger, *Being No One: The Self-Model Theory of Subjectivity* (Cambridge, MA: MIT Press, 2003), Ch. 3.2.7.

47 M. Henry, 'The Four Principles of Phenomenology', tr. J. Rivera and G.E. Faithful, *Continental Philosophy Review* 48:1 (2015): 1–21 (first published in J.-L. Marion [ed.], *Revue de Métaphysique et de Morale* 96:1 [1991], 3–26).

manner of *being-there*: 'Perhaps it will even become manifest that the total phenomenological attitude and the *epoché* belonging to it are destined in essence to effect, at first, a complete personal transformation, comparable in the beginning to a religious conversion, which then, however, over and above this, bears within itself the significance of the greatest existential transformation which is assigned as a task to mankind as such.'[48] The *epoché* is a conversion to an absolute modernity in which every 'image of the world'—even those provided by the most accurate and sophisticated scientific theories—is understood as a transcendental-dependent construct hovering in the living revelation. This conversion can be understood as a shift in the natural answer to the question *Where am I?* The converted subject no longer understands its existence as a being-there-in-the-world, but rather as a being-there in the midst of a phenoumenodelic dehiscence of which the world is nothing but a singular naturalised model. Through the *epoché*, the subject gets *philosophically stoned*, emplaced within the phenoumenodelic primal scene, suspended within the concrete, ungrounded, and transmundane field of impersonal manifestation.

In Timothy Leary's terms, the *epoché* signals the conversion to a subjective mode of existence in which the degrees of freedom associated with the sixth mini-brain—or the 'meta-programming circuit' (as Wilson would have it)—are activated. The sixth mini-brain is the speculative 'organ' through which it is possible, by deprogramming and reprogramming the other transcendental circuits, by recalibrating the transcendental editor, to bring about speculative variations of one's own transcendental structures. The hanged human suspends the naturality of its Umwelt, thereby becoming available to adopt other transcendental postures. The effective sublation of the transcendental limits of a certain Umwelt presupposes the suspension of its naturality, bracketing the naive realism intrinsic to the natural attitude, the recognition that the transcendental operations which constitute phenomenality are (before the critical reflection that makes them 'attentionally

48 E. Husserl, *The Crisis of European Sciences and Transcendental Phenomenology* (Evanston, IL: Northwestern University Press, 1978), 137 [§35].

available') transparent, 'invisible and imperious circles'[49] which trace the limits of possible experience. In this sense, naive realism is not really a consequence of the fact that the transcendental frame is itself invisible (as Metzinger seems to claim),[50] but rather results from the second-order transparency associated with the fact that this invisibility might itself be invisible. The bracketing of the 'natural attitude' per se entails neither the complete opacification of the frame nor an effective recalibration of the corresponding transcendental filters. All that is suspended is the naturalisation itself: the dogmatic hypothesis that the Umwelt at hand is the unique possible reality-tunnel through which we can auscultate and telescope the pleroma, the conflation between (model-)reality and the real (Lacan), between the map and the territory (Korzybski), between phenomena and (phe)noumena. On its own, the *epoché* raises the possibility, but not necessarily the actuality, of the variation of the corresponding reality-tunnel. The *epoché* is a necessary but not sufficient condition for the sublation of the limits of experience: the effective de- or re- programming of the corresponding reality-tunnel might be the result of a difficult (scientific, artistic, political, existential) process, unfolded patiently, 'word for word'.

The understanding of Spinozist substance in terms of an impersonal field of experience requires a sufficiently general concept of experience and of the subject of experience. For the purposes of the present work, we shall simply understand by *subject* (following thinkers like Kant, James, Whitehead, and Bergson) any *breathing*[51] *local mode* of the phenoumenodelic

---

49 A. Grothendieck, *Recoltes et Semailles I. Reflection et temoignage sur un passé de mathematicien* (Paris: Gallimard, 2022). English translation by R. Lisker available at <https://uberty.org/wp-content/uploads/2015/12/Grothendeick-RetS.pdf>.

50 'Fully transparent phenomenal representations force a conscious system to functionally become a naive realist with regard to their contents: whatever is transparently represented is experienced as real and as undoubtedly existing by this system.' Metzinger, *Being No One*, 167.

51 According to what we could call James's *transcendental principle of pneumatic apperception*: '[T]he stream of thinking (which I recognize emphatically as a phenomenon) is only a careless name for what, when scrutinized, reveals itself to consist chiefly of the stream of my breathing. The "I think" which Kant said must be able

insubstance—that is, any local mode endowed with receptive, retentive (imaginative), and expressive functions. A subject is an invagination of the pleromatic animic field that embodies *pneumatic* cycles of inspirations-interiorisations-receptions and expirations-expressions-responses separated by novelty-creating 'zones of indetermination' that break the continuity of what would otherwise be merely a predictable propagation of 'images', a chain of actions and immediate reactions, of causes and effects. A subject is a local mode of the insubstance characterised by this rhythmic 'alternation between that which returns [it] to [it]self or [the] opening to the world, these tightenings and then this extension, this respiration [which makes of it] a living being [...]'.[52] In cybernetic terms, a subject is a system that transforms an input (stimulus) into an output (response) in such a way that this transformation depends on the subject's dynamical *internal state* (which might change either as a consequence of each input-output transformation, as a result of self-regulatory and self-modelling mechanisms, or under different forms of hetero-modelling external pressure).[53] A subject is a finite mode of the pleroma endowed with patience, imagination, and agency, a mode that produces perspectival representations of the pleroma in a response-able (rather than merely reactive) manner. In something of

---

to accompany all my objects, is the "I breathe" which actually does accompany them.' W. James, 'Does "Consciousness" Exist?', in *Essays in Radical Empiricism* (Lincoln, NE: University of Nebraska Press, 1996), 19.

52 Henry, *L'amour les yeux fermés*, 68.

53 See for instance H. von Foerster, 'Perception of the Future and the Future of Perception', in *Understanding Understanding*, 208: 'Their input-output relationship [that of nontrivial machines] is not invariant, but is determined by the machine's previous output. In other words, its previous steps determine its present reactions. While these machines are again deterministic systems, for all practical reasons they are unpredictable: an output once observed for a given input will most likely be not the same for the same input given later. In order to grasp the profound difference between these two kinds of machines [trivial and nontrivial] it may be helpful to envision "internal states" in these machines. While in the trivial machine only one internal state participates always in its internal operation, in the nontrivial machine it is the shift from one internal state to another that makes it so elusive.'

a *détournement* of Kant's terminology, we could say that a subject is an assemblage of a *receptivity faculty* and a *spontaneity faculty* mediated by a third faculty that he dubbed *imagination*. In Lacan's jargon, a subject is a knot that imagines (that constitutes unprecedented images) by plugging symbolic faculties into real pleromancy, a fisher that uses a symbolic net to extract images or schemes out of the phenoumenodelic stream. The scope of a subject's imagination, of its capacity to span ever wider zones of indeterminacy between stimulus and response, can then be taken as a first measure of its degree of *subjectivation*. At the lower limit, a causal chain of actions and reactions defines the degree zero of subjectivation, its acephalic or imaginationless ground state. At the other extreme, a 'nervous system [...] is a veritable [receptive and responsive] *reservoir of indetermination*'.[54] A second measure of the degree of subjectivation of an individual besides the subject's imaginative depth between receptivity and spontaneity will be given by its degree of transcendental and speculative reflexivity, i.e., by the subjective capacities to support apperceptive forms of experience and/or to intervene and modify its own subjective structures (to self-regulate its own transcendental and speculative regulations). As Whitehead argued, while '[self-]consciousness presupposes experience', experience does not necessarily presuppose [self-]consciousness.[55] A self-conscious subject (for example, a subject of the human type) is only a particular case of this generalised notion of subjectivity characterised by an *apperceptive* or *reflexive* structure, i.e., by the capacity to say 'I am', 'I think', 'I experience',

54 Bergson, *Creative Evolution*, 140.

55 A.N. Whitehead, *Process and Reality* (New York: The Free Press, 1978), 53. He also writes in *Adventures of Ideas* that 'mere knowledge is a high abstraction, and [...] conscious discrimination itself is a variable factor only present in the more elaborate examples of occasions of experience [...]. [A]n occasion of experience which includes a human mentality is an extreme instance, at one end of the scale, of those happenings which constitute nature. [...] But any doctrine which refuses to place human experience outside nature, must find in descriptions of human experience factors which also enter into the description of less specialized natural occurrences.' A.N. Whitehead, *Adventures of Ideas* (New York: The Free Press, 1967), 175–76, 184.

by the ability to have thoughts about its percepts, to be affected by its thoughts, to make jokes about its beliefs. In Metzinger's terms, a world-modelling system does not necessarily include a 'phenomenal self-model'. In turn, the apperceptive structure of a subject can be classified according to the kind of reflexivity it can afford. For instance, a pre-critical subject might be endowed with apperception without being able to focus on the 'transparent' transcendental filters that make its experience (of the world and of itself) possible. In other words, a world-modelling system including a phenomenal self-model is not necessarily equipped with critical tools allowing it to 'opacify' its own transcendental frame. On the next level, a critical-subject might be able to reflect on its own transcendental structures without being able to bring to mind the speculative faculties by means of which it can regulate these structures themselves.

In Fichtean terms, the conceptual understanding proper to human beings fixes and objectifies life in the form of an inanimate *world*: '[B]y the act of Conception, that which, in itself, is the immediate Divine Life in life [...] becomes a fixed [, objective] and abiding substance. [...] [A] fixed and unmoving [dead] substance is the *form* which [the living Divine Life] assumes in that change. [...] This abiding presence is the characteristic of that which we call the World ["Postulate of cognitive homeostasis: The nervous system is organized (or organizes itself) so that it computes a stable reality"];[56] hence Conception is the true World-creator [...] but beyond Conception,—that is truly and in itself,—there is nothing [...] but the Living God in [its] fullness of Life.'[57] In particular, Fichteanism cannot be understood as an *inverted* Spinozism (or materialism) as Jacobi contended (in the sense that it would affirm the ontological privilege of the finite self with respect to the substantial, material, or objective non-self), but instead should be thought of as a *suspended* Spinozism in which all finite selves and all configurations of objective matter become finite modes

56 H. von Foerster, 'On Constructing a Reality', in *Understanding Understanding*, 225.

57 Fichte, *The Way Towards the Blessed Life; Or, The Doctrine of Religion*, 68.

of phenoumenodelic insubstance.[58] The Fichtean *epoché* suspends both the natural attitude that reifies the images that appear in subsistent, substantial things, and also any attempt to distort this suspension in the form of a reduction to a transcendental ego understood as the ultimate ground of appearance. As Sartre posits, the I is also an image for the absolute self-'consciousness' that is the pleroma: 'All the results of phenomenology are in danger of crumbling away if the I is not, every bit as much as the world, a relative existent [a finite and contingent mode of insubstance], i.e. an [image] for [absolute] consciousness.'[59] The phenoumenodelic suspension of Spinozist substance allows Fichte to circumvent one of the principal impasses of Spinozism, its pre-critical dogmatism,[60] while maintaining

58 '[...] I first found entry into the Doctrine of Science through the representation of an inverted Spinozism.' F.H. Jacobi, *Main Philosophical Writings and the Novel Allwill*, tr. G. di Giovanni (Montreal: McGill-Queen's University Press, 1994), 502. This characterisation of the Fichtean system will be taken up again in particular by Schelling in his *On the History of Modern Philosophy*: 'Fichte's idealism thus is the complete opposite of Spinozism or is an *inverted* Spinozism, because it opposes to Spinoza's absolute object, which destroys everything subjective, the subject in its absoluteness, opposes the *deed* to the merely immobile being (*Seyn*) of Spinoza.' F.W.J. von Schelling, *On the History of Modern Philosophy*, tr. A. Bowie (Cambridge: Cambridge University Press, 1994), 108.

59 Sartre, *The Transcendence of the Ego*, 5.

60 In *Foundations of the Science of Knowledge* (1794), Fichte states that '[i]n so far as dogmatism can be consistent, Spinozism is its most logical outcome' (J.G. Fichte, *The Science of Knowledge*, tr. P. Heath and J. Lachs [Cambridge: Cambridge University Press, 1991], 117). Later, in the *The Science of Knowledge* (1812), Fichte describes Spinoza's pre-critical dogmatism as follows: 'In it, the One, everything is; nothing is outside of it [...]. This is what Spinoza says, and so do we. [...] But we, we are in the habit of reflecting at every moment on what we do. [...] We do not consider being as being but as a thought [...]. By means of this reflection, we go beyond this certainty which Spinoza holds to.' Fichte, *Doctrine de la science. Exposé de 1812*, 44. On the relationship between Fichte and Spinoza, see J.-C. Goddard, 'Dans quelle mesure Fichte est-il spinoziste?', in C. Bouton (ed.), *Dieu et la nature. La question du panthéisme dans l'idéalisme allemand* (Zurich: Olms, 2005) and 'Idéalisme et Spinozisme chez Fichte dans les Doctrines de la science de 1811 et 1812', in K.S. Ong Van Cung (ed.), *Idée et Idéalisme: Études sur l'idéalisme et le romantisme allemand II* (Paris: Vrin, 2005), 149–65.

the central thesis that the modern foreclosure of the hypertranscendent ontotheological apparatus—far from leading to atheism—is the gateway to a true absolutism, to a philosophy of the absolute as radical experiential immanence of which every existence, every factual being, every Dasein, every form of knowledge, is an accident, a mode, an image, a local revelation. The 'death of God' is nothing more than the closure of the ontotheological 'infantilism of idolatry'[61] associated with the idea of a hypertranscendent God as a *summum ens* or with any other ontotheological *père-version* (in the sense of an almighty version of the father) in Lacan's terms. The absolute—not some hypertranscendent instance from which we would necessarily be separated—is the one life understood as the field of experience in which we already 'live and we move and have our being' (Acts 17:28), the narcotic ether that pneumatic beings breathe, the solaristic solution wherein the anointed ones bathe: '[T]he Eternal [the impersonal life in which the birth, life, and death of every living thing has its time and place] surrounds us at all times and offers itself incessantly to our regards; we have nothing more to do than to lay hold of it'[62]—that is, to breathe it: to inhale it, hold it in, and exhale it.

The suspension of Spinozist substance in a phenoumenodelic insubstance allows the Fichtean project to converge with the various philosophical attempts (notably in James, Bergson, and Deleuze) to think a field of impersonal or a-subjective experience, that is, a plane of immanental experience not indexed by any transcendental type of subjectivity.[63]

61 E. Levinas, 'Heidegger, Gagarin and Us', in *Difficult Freedom: Essays on Judaism*, tr. S. Hand (Baltimore, MD: Johns Hopkins University Press, 1997), 232.

62 Fichte, *The Way Towards the Blessed Life; Or, The Doctrine of Religion*, 8.

63 Regarding the concept of an *a-subjective* or *impersonal experiential field* see the following texts: Sartre, *The Transcendence of the Ego*; Hyppolite, 'L'idée fichtéenne de la doctrine de la science et le projet husserlien'; James, *Essays in Radical Empiricism*; Bergson, *Matter and Memory*, Chapter 1; B. Prado Jr., *Présence et champ transcendental. Conscience et négativité dans la philosophie de Bergson*, tr. R. Barbaras (Paris: Olms, 2002); Deleuze, 'Immanence: A Life'; G. Deleuze and F. Guattari, *What is Philosophy?*, tr. H. Tomlinson and G. Burchell (New York: Columbia University Press, 1994), 'Example III', 44–49; R. Barbaras, *Dynamique de la manifestation*

By definition this impersonal field of experience is the instance within which I/not-I polarisations—that is, the institution of subjects and the correlative constitution of worlds—take place and time, the 'plane of immanence' that envelops the transcendental constitution of different phenomenological horizons of objective transcendence, the underlying *Band* (Fichte) that makes possible both 'the opening of consciousness to being' and 'the revelation of being to consciousness'.[64] According to Bento Prado's description, '[i]t is not only consciousness that proceeds from an instance that precedes it: it is the very universe of objects that comes from it and finds its origin in it. Ultimately, the proper domain of philosophical experience is this "there is something" anterior to the establishment of the scission between subject and object. The analysis of the transcendental field, in fact, appeared to us as transcendental analysis, that is to say as an analysis of the conditions of possibility of commerce between a subject and an object in general. The domain of the transcendental opened up by the discovery of a primitive and undifferentiated mode of being—image or life—which is at once the root of vision and of the visible, or the indistinction between one and the other. If a relation between beings is possible—on the mode of a consciousness of an object—it is because the Being itself establishes within itself a minimal distance. [...] It is this minimal distance that we call "ipseity of Presence" or Presence (to) self. The transcendental enterprise is possible—or realism and idealism are two erroneous enterprises—because that which is in itself gives itself (to itself) as spectacle [...].'[65] Since the experiential field does not depend on any transcendental type of subjectivity, we prefer to call it *immanental field* rather than *transcendental field* (as Deleuze and Bento Prado do). In order to underline the difference between infinite (in)substance and

---

(Paris: Vrin, 2013), Chapter 4; Goddard, '1804–1805. La désubjectivation du transcendantal'; J.-C. Goddard, 'Croyance et intelligence dans la *Staatslehre* de Fichte', *Carnets du Centre de Philosophie du Droit* 99 (2002); V. Goldschmidt, 'Cours sur le premier chapitre de *Matière et Mémoire* (1960)', in F. Worms (ed.), *Annales bergsoniennes, I. Bergson dans le siècle* (Paris: PUF, 2002), 69–128.

64 Goldschmidt, 'Cours sur le premier chapitre de *Matière et Mémoire* (1960)', 73.

65 B. Prado Jr., *Présence et champ transcendantal*, 169.

its finite subjective modes qua tokens of different transcendental types, we prefer to reserve the term 'transcendental' for the latter and characterise (in)substance as an *immanental field of self-experience*. Whereas this field has the immanental capacity to institute finite lifeforms, the latter have the transcendental capacity to constitute correlative worlds, phenomenological horizons. The immanental field is the flux of self-revelation, a kaleidoscopic profusion of *images of images of images of...* in which images are revealed by other images, an immanental plane that is traversed by propagating modes made of the same immaterial dreaminess, that potentialises itself by splitting into manifold I/not-I polarizations, into dreamers and worldly visions: 'There is nothing enduring, either out of me, or in me, but only a ceaseless change. I know of no being, not even of my own. There is no being. I myself absolutely know not, and am not. Images [*Bilder*] are:—they are the only things which exist, and they know of themselves after the fashion of images:—images which float past without there being anything past which they float; which, by means of like images, are connected with each other:—images without anything which is pictured in them, without significance and without aim. I myself am one of these images;—nay, I am not even this, but merely a confused image of the images. All reality is transformed into a strange dream, without a life which is dreamed of, and without a spirit [*Geist*] which dreams it;—into a dream which is woven together in a dream of itself. Intuition is the dream; thought [...] is the dream of that dream.[66] [...] What the dreamt image with neither dreamer nor dreamt-of world gives to be seen is [...] being-in-itself [...] being-One as unlimited life and activity ["which posits itself absolutely", "absolute self", "of itself, in itself, and by itself", "neither subject nor object"], of which it [the image] is an immanent production. [...] [T]his access to being-One by way of [...] a reduction of the objective, of the separated existence of objects, to a phantomal existence of images, defines [...] an *absolute knowledge* [...].'[67] The pleroma

66 J.G. Fichte, *The Vocation of Man*, tr. W. Smith (LaSalle, IL: Open Court, 1965), 89–90 [translation modified].

67 J.-C. Goddard, 'Croyance et intelligence dans la *Staatslehre* de Fichte'.

qua suspended substance is an impersonal, ungrounded, non-substantial 'field of images'[68] that is not immanent to any transcendental subjectivity, a 'shamanic plane of [phenoumenodelic] immanence',[69] an 'all-encompassing plane' in which the Umwelten correlative to the different forms of life push forth and coalesce, the vibrating continuum of unedited experience, the ocean of unfiltered information out of which different phenomena emerge by means of subjective operations of transcendental constitution, the absolute *Band* (Fichte) which precedes every I/not-I polarisation (every institution of a living being and every constitution of the correlative world), the Rilkean 'pure perception' not yet sieved by a finite lifeform, the absolute of James, 'a "pure" experience on an enormous scale, undifferentiated and indifferentiable in thought and thing'.[70]

The *transcendental epoché* does not just acquit the world of experience from any thesis regarding its 'reality', but also emphasises its dependence upon the 'transparent' operations of transcendental constitution carried out by the subject of experience. In the Husserlian phenomenological tradition, the suspension effectuated by means of the *epoché* is understood as a subjectivation, i.e. as a *reduction* of the experiential field to the constituting subjectivity. Any given worldly transcendence, any phenomenon, is *reduced* to a mere correlate of the subjective apparatus for the transcendental constitution of experience ('By virtue of our present method of *epoché*, everything objective is transformed into something subjective').[71]

---

68 Bergson, *Matter and Memory*, 16.

69 E. Viveiros de Castro, 'The Crystal Forest: Notes on the Ontology of Amazonian Spirits', *Inner Asia* 9:2, 'Special Issue: Perspectivism' (2007): 153–72: 155.

70 W. James, 'How Two Minds Can Know One Thing', in *Essays in Radical Empiricism*, 70–71.

71 Husserl, *The Crisis of European Sciences*, 178 [§53]. In *Cartesian Meditations*, Husserl characterises the *epoché* as a *reduction* in the following terms: 'At this point, following Descartes, we make the great reversal that, if made in the right manner, leads to transcendental subjectivity: the turn to the ego cogito as the ultimate and apodictically certain basis for judgements, the basis on which any radical-philosophy must be grounded.' Husserl, *Cartesian Meditations*, 18 [§8].

The denaturalisation of the world enacted by the *epoché* is understood by Husserl as a tendentially idealistic reduction of worldly experience to subjective constitution, to the immanent life of the constituent ego. Husserl's transcendental reduction therefore transforms the phenomenal world into the property of a transcendental subject and 'immanence becomes immanent "to" a transcendental subjectivity'.[72] In the wake of Descartes, the Husserlian reduction *grounds* appearance in a transcendental ego, and this appropriation tends dangerously toward a 'transcendental solipsism' (at least in the so-called solipsistic or pre-intersubjective stage of Husserlian phenomenology).[73] It is as if the characterisation of subjectivity as 'transcendental' no longer referred to the subjective portals through which a subject can have access to a *transcendent* realm. 'Transcendental subjectivity' is instead understood as an instance that is not itself embedded in an impersonal field of manifestation. The term 'transcendental' no longer denotes the ek-static character of finite subjectivity but rather the alleged omni-grounding exceptional role played by the so-called 'transcendental' subject. As Brassier puts it, transcendental '[c]onsciousness construed as originary condition of givenness becomes an [universal] unexplained explainer', a gesture that makes 'transcendental idealism inimical to naturalism'.[74]

The comprehension of the *epoché* as *egological reduction* in certain phases of the phenomenological tradition is a direct consequence of the inherent difficulties encountered in trying to conceive a field of experience not indexed by (that is, not correlated to or, even worse, not immanent to) a transcendental subjectivity. But the experiential field that the immanental *epoché* suspends us within—being the one life that reveals itself by engendering lifeforms—cannot be affixed to a unique (empirical or transcendental) subject. The vital field of appearance is impersonal in the sense that it is always in excess with regard to both the actual experience of every empirical

72 Deleuze and Guattari, *What is Philosophy?*, 46.

73 Cf. Husserl, *Cartesian Meditations*, 30 [§13].

74 R. Brassier, 'The View from Nowhere', *Identities: Journal for Politics, Gender and Culture* 8:2 (2011): 7–23: 11.

subject (the field constantly overflows every effective subjective experience with new possible adumbrations), and with regard to the circumambient worlds constituted by the framings of the experiential field carried out by different transcendental types of subjectivity. Every Umwelt is a partial cut of the phenoumenodelic pleroma. The experiential field is impersonal or inappropriable since it contains multiple empirical subjects whose transcendental types are not necessarily the same.

Moreover, the transcendental reduction of the phenomenal appearance to the constituting ego abstracts from the fact that every constituting lifeform is begotten—as one form of life among others—at the wild heart of instituting life. The Cartesio-Husserlian reduction to the *ego cogito* makes an abstraction of the impersonal life that reverberates beneath and supports every constituting act, of the fact that thinking—far from being grounded in itself—is physically and psychically rooted in the one life. Every finite subject is a whirling moment in an ongoing process of subjective institution, a breathing fold (receptive, vibrant, and expressive) of the experiential field, a begotten localisation of the ominipresent act of living and revealing. Suspended existence is always already outside, thrown into a transcendent experiential field that continually offers new adumbrations of observed phenomena, presenting real obstacles that resist the advance of the symbolic, haunting wakefulness with oneiric visitations, offering encounters with irreducible human and nonhuman others, spanning horizons that recede under the subject's furtherance, disrupting subjective at-homeness with extimate omens, irrigating its personal life with an impersonal morphogenetic force that recalibrates its transcendental valves, enmeshing the subject in a material background that supports and nourishes its phenomenalising activity, constantly confronting the subject with the narcissistic naivety of any purported form of self-sufficiency or last-instanceness.

In order to avoid this tendentially idealistic use of the concept of *epoché*, we shall hold, following Bergson, Patočka,[75] and Heidegger, and moving

75 See for example his essay 'Epochè et réduction', in *Qu'est-ce que la phénoménologie?*, 249–62. In his own words: 'Thanks to the universalisation of the *epoché*, it will subsequently become clear that, just as the self is the condition of possibility of the

beyond Husserl, that the (immanental rather than transcendental) *epoché* brings every phenomenal world back to their being-constituted and every constituting subject back to their being-instituted. The *epoché* embeds the subject of experience within an experiential field that is not immanent to a transcendental ego, a field endowed with the capacity to span within itself subjective zones of indetermination that provide darkrooms for its self-revelation: '[T]he reduction may avoid the realist perspective, but it does not for all that reduce the universe to a system of appearances posited by a transcendental or absolute consciousness. [...] Here we perceive the peculiar character of the Bergsonian reduction, which distinguishes it radically from the phenomenological reduction. The latter, by transforming the world into a system of phenomena or noema, opens up the field of "transcendental experience" as horizon of a transcendental subjectivity. Although the Bergsonian reduction also opens up [...] a field of transcendental experience, it will not be within a constituting subject. On the contrary, it is on the basis of the notion of indetermination or the introduction of novelty that we will see, within the transcendental field, the birth of subjectivity itself. We may say, in a certain sense, that the system of images corresponds to the idea of a *spectacle without spectator*. More precisely, it is the place where, as the spectacle becomes possible, the conditions of possibility for the spectator in general are created at the same time.'[76] The *epoché* enacts what Kant called Spinoza's 'enormous idea', that 'of intuiting all things, and oneself, in God',[77] that of plunging every thing into turbulent living insubstance. Far from infinitely unbalancing the subject-object correlation in favour of a constituting subjectivity, the immanental *epoché* reimplants the subject-object correlation in the one life that subtends it. 'There is

appearance of the worldly, so the world as the originary horizon (and not as the totality of realities) represents the condition of possibility of the appearance of the self. [...] The self is experienced in the world and on the grounds of the world [...]' (258).

76 B. Prado Jr., *Présence et champ transcendantal*, 114.

77 Kant, *Opus Postumum*, 241.

life beyond the objective/subjective duality',[78] a life that can be explored through infinite attributes besides thought and extension, a life vibrating in myriad subjective modes of different transcendental types. Beneath the representational correlations between subjects and objects, beneath the interpersonal relations between subjects, subjects and objects are always already mutually religated by a living immanental *Band*. Whereas the transcendental reduction grounds experience upon the constituting subject, the immanental *epoché* suspends the subject in ungrounded life. If the experienced objective body (*Körper*) is constituted by the subject of experience, the latter is an instituted living being (*Leib*) as a local mode of the fleshly (f)actuality (*leibhafte Wirklichkeit*). If the phenomenal world is 'in' the subject as a particular model-reality among others, the subject is in life. The absolute last instance in which the immanental *epoché* implants us is no longer the *transcendental ego* but *immanental life*, the phenoumenodelic living field of revelation in which both the institution of different lifeforms and the constitution of their correlative worlds play out. Every act of consciousness—including attempts to prove phenomenological solipsism—stems from and unfolds within a living last instance, mat(t)er: 'The production of ideas, of conceptions, of consciousness, is at first directly interwoven with the material activity and the material intercourse of [humans]—the language of real life. [...] Consciousness [*das Bewusstsein*] can never be anything else than conscious being [*das bewusste Sein*], and the being of [humans] is their actual life-process. [...] Morality, religion, metaphysics [...] as well as the forms of consciousness corresponding to these, thus no longer retain the semblance of independence. [...] It is not consciousness that determines life, but life that determines consciousness.'[79] Through the *epoché*, everything solid—things, worlds, subjects, theories—is suspended in the living pleroma. In gnostico-phenomenological terms, the *epoché* makes of every subject a pneumatic *living one* (a local individual mode of the living insubstance) and of every *world*—of every phenomenological horizon correlative to a

78 F. Varela, 'Neurophenomenology: A Methodological Remedy for the Hard Problem', *Journal of Consciousness Studies* 3:4 (1996): 330–349: 339.

79 K. Marx and F. Engels, *The German Ideology* (New York: Prometheus, 1998), 42.

transcendental type of subjectivity—an *aeon* suspended in the transmundane pleroma.[80] While the transcendental Husserlian *epoché* 'redirects the phenomenological gaze to the transcendental life of consciousness',[81] the Fichtean suspension of Spinozist substance reimplants consciousness in the impersonal immanence of life. This distinction between the *transcendental epoché* of Husserl as radical grounding in a 'transcendental' ego that cannot transcend itself anymore and the *immanental epoché* as suspension in the vital, pre-subjective and pre-mundane pleroma allows the ego to be absolved from the role of absolute constitutive ground, affirming its true nature as existent, finite, living Dasein. The 'experiential "there is"' (the effective occurrence of manifestation) defines a sufficient field for the exercise of an immanental phenoumenodelia: '[A]n ego, a substantial entity to which experience happens, is more of a minus than a plus. It is an estrangement from experience, a lack of participation.[82] [...] [T]he transcendent [ego] must fall under the phenomenological reduction. The Cogito affirms too much. The sure and certain content of the pseudo-"cogito" is not "I am conscious of this chair," but "There is consciousness of this chair." This content is sufficient to constitute an infinite and absolute field for the investigations of phenomenology.[83] [...] I may then indeed say "it is thought,"—and yet I can scarcely say even this;—rather, strictly speaking, I ought to say "the thought appears that I feel, perceive, think,"—but by no means that "I feel, perceive, think." The first only is fact; the second is an imaginary addition to the fact.[84] [...] [This impersonal consciousness is] a *non-substantial* absolute. A pure consciousness is an absolute quite simply because it is consciousness of itself. It thus remains a [phenoumenodelic field of experiential primal

---

80 Regarding the relationship between gnosticism and phenomenology, see N. Depraz, 'Le statut phénoménologique du monde dans la gnose: du dualisme à la non-dualité', *Laval théologique et philosophique* 52:3, 'Foi et Raison' (October 1996).

81 Heidegger, quoted in Patočka, *Qu'est-ce que la phénoménologie?*, 260.

82 Watts, *The Joyous Cosmology*, 72.

83 Sartre, *The Transcendence of the Ego*, 9.

84 Fichte, *The Vocation of Man*, 107.

being] in the highly particular sense in which "to be" and "to appear" are one and the same. It is nothing but lightness and translucency.'[85] Thanks to this conversion into the experiential and genetic insubstance that is life, every entity or event is transmuted into a mere phenoumenodelic datum, drifting through the concrete stream of 'immanent consciousness without object or self', the 'pure plane of immanence of the one, impersonal and yet singular life', of the life that 'is everywhere, in all the moments that a given living subject goes through'.[86] Every subject of experience, far from being the 'ultimate and apodeictic' source of phenoumenalisation, the unconstituted agent of constitution, the 'unexplained explainer', is nothing more than a local subjective vortex within the impersonal field of experience, a living salience drifting through life, a non-substantial 'living and ephemeral superficial form of coherence',[87] a breathing finite mode inducing an unforeseen umweltisation of the pleroma, a transcendental 'capture of the overabundant'.[88] The phenoumenodelic stream, far from being an *ego trip*, is an impersonal deluge carrying the living along with it.

The *epoché* allows the subject to make 'attentionally available' not only the 'transparent' acts of transcendental constitution of objectivity, but also the immanental processes of institution of subjectivity. This means that the field in which the *epoché* suspends us cannot be understood uniquely as a *phenoumenal field*, the finite modes of which are phenoumena. It is also necessary to think of this phenoumenal field as a *vital field* capable of instituting forms of life that constitute different Umwelten out of it. Here the Schellingian and Hegelian project of reconceptualising Spinozist substance as 'living substance' (and, more radically, as a living free subject) assumes

85 Sartre, *The Transcendence of the Ego*, 5.

86 Deleuze, 'Immanence: A Life', 26–29.

87 J.-C. Goddard, 'Autonomie, réduction et réflexivité: la philosophie naturelle de Francisco J. Varela et le projet transcendantal', *Intellectica. Revue de l'Association pour la Recherche Cognitive* 36–37 (2003): 205–25: 208.

88 J. Lezama Lima, *La dignidad de la poesía*, in *Tratados de la Habana* (Buenos Aires: Ediciones de la Flor, 1969), 381.

its full importance.[89] The phenoumenodelic pleroma is not a dead or inert substance but a living insubstance, an infinite and impersonal experiential field that experiences itself—that self-manifests—through the institution of local subjective modes endowed with particular transcendental structures capable of constituting transcendent horizons of experience—worlds of revelation—at the very heart of experiential immanence. It could be said, in Rozitchner's terms, that the immanental *epoché* makes a *dreamlike materialism* possible, a dreamlike *mater*ialism that does not make an abstraction of the living force that begets the living (the pleroma *qua* engendering mat[t]er) and a *dreamlike* materialism absolved of the reality thesis that defines the

89 In Schelling's words: 'The error of [Spinoza's] system lies by no means in his placing things *in God* but in the fact that they are *things*—in the abstract concept of beings in the world, indeed of infinite substance itself, which for him is exactly also a thing. [...] Hence the lifelessness of his system, the sterility of its form [...] hence his mechanistic view of nature follows quite naturally as well. Or does one doubt that the basic views of Spinozism must already be essentially changed by a dynamic notion of nature? If the doctrine that all things are contained in God is the ground of the whole system, then, at the very least, it must first be brought to life and torn from abstraction before it can become the principle of a system of reason. [...] One could look at the rigidity of Spinozism as at Pygmalion's statue that had to be made animate [*beseelt*] through the warm breath of love [...]. In a word, it is a one-sidedly realist system. [...] Spinoza's basic concept, when infused by spirit (and, in one essential point, changed) by the principle of idealism, received a living basis [...]; out of this grew the philosophy of nature, which as pure physics was indeed able to stand for itself, yet at any time in regard to the whole of philosophy was only considered as a part, namely the real part that would be capable of rising up into the genuine system of reason only through completion by the ideal part in which freedom rules. [...] [I]n this rising up (of freedom) the final empowering [*potenzierende*] act was found through which all of nature transfigured itself in feeling, intelligence and, finally, in will. In the final and highest judgement, there is no other Being than will. Will is primal Being [*Ursein*] to which alone all predicates of Being apply: groundlessness [...] self-affirmation. All of philosophy strives only to find this highest expression.' F.W.J. Schelling, *Philosophical Investigations into the Essence of Human Freedom*, tr. J. Love and J. Schmidt (Albany, NY: State University of New York Press, 2006), 20–21.

natural attitude (the pleroma qua phenoumenodelic field).[90] Pleroma is not only the *impersonal field of experience* qua phenoumenodelic absolute, but also the living insubstance that engenders constituting lifeforms, an atonal and impersonal 'animic field' of revelation. The immanental *epoché* suspends both the constituting *lifeforms* and the constituted *lifeworlds* in the immanence of the pre-subjective and pre-mundane field of the one life.

The *immanentisation* of transcendental philosophy stems from the proposition that every transcendental type is instituted at the heart of the immanental experiential field and that the horizon of transcendence correlated to this type also unfolds in the immanence of the field. Following this position, there would be no structure of subjectivity which was not produced by the 'naturalcultural' dynamics of the experiential field itself. 'The nature outside of us is revealed by the nature that we are',[91] and a subject is nothing but a local carrier of a singular factorisation of nature's self-revelation. The correlation between the a priori subjective dimensions of transcendent experience and the constituted phenomenal contents of this experience relies on an underlying phenoumenodelic monism: both the transcendental subject and the objective contents of its experience are modes—cuts—of the same phenoumenal flesh. The *transcendental activity* of the transcending subject, the work of the constitution of objectivity, is always underpinned by an *immanental passivity*.[92] According to this droning animism, 'spirits and animals [imply] a universal animic field in which they

---

90 Cf. Rozitchner, *Materialismo ensoñado.*

91 Cited by R. Vallier, 'Être Sauvage and the Barbaric Principle: Merleau-Ponty's Reading of Schelling', in J.M. Wirth and P. Burke (eds.), *The Barbarian Principle: Merleau-Ponty, Schelling, and the Question of Nature* (New York: State University of New York Press, 2013), 133.

92 In Merleau-Ponty's words: 'Philosophy has never spoken [...] of the passivity of our activity, as Valéry spoke of a *body of the spirit*: new as our initiatives may be, they come to birth at the heart of being, they are connected onto the time that streams forth in us, supported on the pivots or hinges of our life.' Merleau-Ponty, *The Visible and the Invisible*, 221.

are the invisible and visible modes, respectively, of "vibration"'.[93] The active subject of the transcendental constitution of objective experience is itself a passive product of an immanental institution, an 'undulating unknown'. Only the (immanently) instituted can (transcendentally) constitute. Only an incarnated subject endowed with a particular transcendental structure can activate a local process of umweltic phenomenalisation of the experiential field. In *Process and Reality*, Whitehead writes: 'For Kant, the world emerges from the subject; for the philosophy of the organism, the subject emerges from the world—a "superject" rather than a "subject"'.[94] In the context of immanental phenoumenodelia, the medium from which the subject emerges (or is instituted) is not strictly speaking a world but an unworldly experiential field from which a world can be locally constituted. In this way, the two processes of emergence–far from being opposed as seems to be the case in Whitehead–are made compatible: the objective world emerges from the subject (in the sense of being transcendentally *constituted* by it) while the subject 'emerges' from the immanental experiential field (in the sense of being *instituted* upon and by it).

In his late period, around 1935, Husserl himself recognised the limits of his egological idealism, and thematised the pre-subjective substratum or 'lifeworld' (*Lebenswelt*) that underlies every transcendental constitution of objectivity and envelops the corresponding circumambient worlds.[95] The Husserlian notion of the lifeworld plays a doubly essential role in the development of phenomenology. Firstly, it roots the supposedly subjective foundation of all processes of phenomenalisation, the constituting ego, in a mundane, historical, vital, and intersubjective infra-foundation, thereby successfully bypassing the potentially idealistic drift of transcendental egology. Secondly, the notion of lifeworld allows the 'scientific image' of the

---

93 Viveiros de Castro, 'The Crystal Forest', 161.

94 Whitehead, *Process and Reality*, 88.

95 Regarding the characterisation of the lifeworld (*Lebenswelt*) as an *earth* capable of enveloping different surrounding worlds, see E. Husserl, *Experience and Judgment: Investigations in a Genealogy of Logic*, tr. J.S. Churchill and K. Ameriks (Evanston, IL: Northwestern University Press, 1973), 163 [§38].

experiential field to be rooted in a concrete and intersubjective prescientific instance from which the former proceeds by abstraction, idealisation, and objectivation. In this way, the notion of lifeworld reinscribes both the subject of science and the objective world that is correlative to it—both the I and the not-I, as Fichte would have it—into the immanence of the always already given concrete life, into the full concreteness of the living and self-revealing pleroma. Nonetheless, and in order to play such role, the Husserlian notion of lifeworld has to be divested of the undertones that associate it with an alleged immediate 'sense certainty', a given communal historical background, or any other form of purported ultimate unmediated ground. The historico-natural world circumambient to the life of a certain form of subjectivity is also a singular Umwelt among others and enmeshed with others. Every form of concrete historical intraworldliness, every form of sensuous immediacy, every daily life, every community of rational agents, hovers within life. Even every form of concreteness available to a given subject—such as the concrescence of percepts, affects, concepts, and sociolepts accessible to human beings—is a cut from a pleromatic arche-concreteness that includes attributes which the subject in question may not be able to conceive of, and which vibrates at frequencies that the subject cannot tune in to. This all-encompassing life, understood as a generative power that engenders living beings endowed with different transcendental structures, is the ultimate source of all transcendental constitution of circumambient worlds, of the movement by which the pleroma ceaselessly decants itself into new umweltic aeons, of the 'images' (scientific and others) that shine out in these phenomenological horizons. The two successive groundings performed by Husserl—the (potentially idealistic) reduction of phenomenality to the *constituting subject* and the (counter-idealistic) inscription of the latter in a common 'lifeworld'—already point toward the amphibological 'act of living'—that is, to the point of indistinction between (in Barbaras's terms) the act of experiencing (*erleben*) and the act of being alive (*leben*). The immanental *epoché* leads experience back from the realm of substantial realities (including substantial selves) into the immanence of the one phenoumenodelic life and its existing finite tentacles. Following Barbaras, we shall understand life in terms of what life *does*: instituting living beings that constitute phenomenological horizons, worlds of life, circumambient vessels into which revelation flows: '[W]e neutralise the ontology of death from the outset [...], we approach life from within itself rather than from that which negates it. In so doing we ask what it *does* instead of what it struggles against, and discover that its task is nothing less than a phenomenalisation of the world [...].'[96]

The kernel of transcendental philosophy, which still remains latent to a certain extent, is provided by the premise that Copernicanism can and must be raised to a transcendental power. This means that not only the Earth as a physical body, far from defining an immobile centre, is in a state of freefall in cosmic space, but also that every supposedly fundamental tone, every purported Ur-ground, every supposedly 'immediate' form of givenness, every form of historical concreteness, every alleged privileged system of reference (the transcendental subject, a community of rational agents, the spacetime background, the 'immediate' content of sensuous intuition, the images of the world painted onto the umvaults), are all phenoumena adrift in an experiential flow that is unturtled all the way down. The existentialisation of transcendental subjects—the suspension of their essentialisation in the form of fixed transcendental types—must be radicalised by a suspension of the grounds which support and transport them, of the intersubjective 'lifeworlds' in which they live, of the umweltic bubbles which surround them. Every empirical or transcendental basis for an intersubjective process of phenoumenalisation—every empirical or transcendental earth—is not an Ur-Arche, a first principle, an immobile ground, but a drifting *ark* which transports the local subjective vortices of the experiential field across the phenoumenodelic flood: 'The earth as "Noah's Ark" = bearing the living [...] above the Flood.'[97] The *epoché* transmutes every umweltic bubble into an ark descending into the phenoumenodelic Maelstrom. The pleroma is not

---

96 R. Barbaras, *La vie lacunaire* (Paris: Vrin, 2011), 147.

97 M. Merleau-Ponty, *Husserl at the Limits of Phenomenology: Including Texts by Edmund Husserl*, eds. L. Lawlor and B. Bergo (Evanston, IL: Northwestern University Press, 2002), 68.

an 'Ur-Arche Earth that does not move', but an abyssal phenoumenodelic insubstance within which every ground hovers, a flux of manifestation that prodigiously and exuberantly overflows all particular lifeworlds, an engendering force that does not stop at any particular form of life. Pleroma, the 'emerging, abiding sway that reposes in itself',[98] relies neither upon something that appears, a pre-phenomenological noumenon, nor upon a self-grounded transcendental subject. Everything, without exception—even the fatherland at the end of Tarkovsky's *Solaris*—is a phenoumenon suspended within the pleroma. Every lifeworld is a *world in life*, an aeon drifting in the heart of the vital pleroma: 'Then I saw a distant and [reverberating] sea over which the small oval world swam alone, spotted and grey, convulsing fiercely.'[99]

The *natura naturans* of suspended Spinozism should not be conflated with an alleged state of nature, sacred organic whole, lost origin, or idyllic arcadian landscape that should be restored, with the *naturally given* as opposed to the *culturally constructed*, with a passive raw materiality as opposed to the active dominating (male) labour, or with the external and unilateral being-out-of-itself of the Hegelian procession of Spirit. The Spinozist *natura naturans* denotes the barbarian point of indistinction between the experiential field in its infinite phenoumenodelic turbulence and the morphogenetic capacity to excite living modes equipped with transcendental helmets that filter, edit, sieve, and renormalise this very flood. Nature cannot be understood here as a harmonious and bucolic instance that would provide maternal protection, but rather as a material force that informs and irrigates the living and throws them into the risk of the phenoumenodelic deluge: 'Nature risks living beings and "shelters none in particular".'[100] There is 'no hidden plan of nature tailor-made for

98 M. Heidegger, *Introduction to Metaphysics*, tr. G. Fried and R. Polt (New Haven, CT and London: Yale University Press, 2000), 106.

99 J.P.F. Richter, *Sämmtliche Werke* (Paris: Tétot Frères, 65 vols., 1837), vol. 3, 176.

100 M. Heidegger, 'Why Poets?', in *Off the Beaten Track* (Cambridge: Cambridge University Press, 2002), 200–241: 209.

us, [...] [nor is there] a progressive realisation of the Spirit'[101] in which humanity would play a necessary role, nor a lost origin to which we could return. We can either play our instrument with love, respect, and humility and leave the stage with dignity, without leaving a mess behind, or continue the pathetic farce of the capitalist and colonial mode of inexistence and its systematic devastation of human and nonhuman lifeforms.

Confronted with this *sailing-in-the-flood*, we can distinguish two abstract existential archetypes, the first 'nomadic' (one that 'breaches the walls [of Descartes's garden]. [...] I am not your kind, I belong eternally to the inferior race, I am a beast. [...] *withdrawal, freaks*!' drop out!), the second 'segregative' ('a paranoiac fascisizing type [...] that invests the formation of central sovereignty; [...] I am your kind, and I belong to the superior race and class').[102] On the one hand, Noah provides the subjective archetype of the embarked ones, of those who (like Captain Nemo or the Mallarméan *Maître*) do not stand upon *terra firma* but on a swaying ark that could never be mistaken for an arche-ground (the uprising of the *mareação* bears witness to the fact that even the most seemingly immobile ground is in motion, that it is not possible to land or disembark onto any Ur-Arche Earth whatsoever). Noah provides the archetype of those whose conceptual attunement to the *logos* does not take the form of control and exploitation but rather that of an always-subject-to-revision and truth-oriented exercise of reason that makes orientation and navigation possible ('Noah is the concept [...] of noesis':[103] 'noetic arkana!');[104] 'The life of the [chromatic] yachts will be—as the Trances argue—that of *pontiffs of the sea*: bridges passing from one side of the *ocean* to the other, their way of naming the soma among the stars, the *black matter* of the thaumaturgies of Libya. [...]

101 E. Viveiros de Castro, 'For a Strategic Primitivism: A Dialogue between Eduardo Viveiros de Castro and Yuk Hui', *Philosophy Today*, 20 April 2021.

102 G. Deleuze and F. Guattari, *Anti-Oedipus*, tr. R. Hurley, M. Seem, and Helen R. Lane (London: Continuum, 2004), 277.

103 J. Derrida, *Glas* (Paris: Éditions Galilée, 1974), 47.

104 Leminski, *Catatau*, 160.

This ship, whose name is plural because it multiplies in the conductive mirage, is the dimensional switch of a race that comes from inner Africa and yet from outer space, they will unscrupulously say from Sirius-B, like Sun Ra, the preacher.'[105] Now, 'one can respond otherwise [to] the rupture of maternal *Gleichgewicht* [equal equilibrium, original harmony]. Not the calm flanks of a floating dwelling but the erection of a military tower. [...] Rather than opposing to the sea the very thing she bears [...] cradled by her, the ark, [Nimrod] confronts it, attacks it, and parts it with an immense tower.'[106] Nimrod is the subjective archetype that tries to reduce the 'risk into which [he is] let loose'—to stand against the deluge—by extracting himself out of the flowing insubstance in order to dam it up and control it; he is the ideal type of the subjective tendency to confront the impersonal outburst of nature and the emetic deregulation of the subjective faculties by constructing a fixed tower that sinks into the waves and streams, anchors itself in the underwater ground, and gives its tubular form to the male fantasies of conquering outer space. Nimrod 'endeavored so far to master nature that it could no longer be dangerous to men. He put himself in a state of defense against it, "a rash man and one boasting in the strength of his arm. In the event of God's having a mind to overwhelm the world with a flood again, he threatened to neglect no means and no power to make an adequate resistance to Him. For he had resolved to build a tower which was to be far higher than the waves and streams could ever rise and in this way to avenge the downfall of his forefathers."[107] [...] [But] you will fall, tower of Vrijburg, tower of great ruin. I walk, among snakes and scorpions, my Aquinas heel, my Achilles stride. And that tower of Babel, of the pride of Marcgravf and Spix, stone upon stone shall not remain, the weeds will grow upon the stone and the stone awaiting darkness shall

105 Khatarnak & Khabandar, 'Umbanda-Jackson', in *¡Santas incubaciones!* (Buenos Aires: Hekht, 2017), 57–58.

106 Derrida, *Glas*, 47–48.

107 G.W.F. Hegel, *On Christianity: Early Theological Writings*, tr. T.M. Knox (New York: Harper & Brothers, 1961), 184.

rot and turn to ivy the stone that was.... [...][108] Cracks and reforms and bursts in the violet air / Falling towers / Jerusalem Athens Alexandria / Vienna London / Unreal.'[109]

While the corrosive solaristic solution dissolved the foundations of the tower and pulled it down brick by brick, a thunderbolt blasted its outer space-oriented head. The Tower of Babel falls and the linguisticidals are condemned to babble in barbarian languages—'*Raphèl mai amèche zabì almi*'—the existence of which they had not even suspected. Whereas Dante placed Nimrod in the ninth circle of Hell, we prefer to imagine Nimrod managing to reach a tropical island where a single mosquito is more than enough to put him—along with his dominating and conquering vagaries—in his place. We can certainly imagine an ab-original people—an *Urvolk* of Calibans, in Fichte's terms—concocting a brew of plants in an 'orgonic *ambience*'[110] in order to heal Nimrod—of his foreignness (*Auslanderkeit*), of his monolinguistic parochialism, of his monocultural drive to conquer, of his paranoic xenophobia, of his brave unidimensional rationalism, of his unbound Prometheanism, of his reluctance to acknowledge his castration, of his phallocentric dreams of salvation—and serving it with delectation during the anthropophagic carnival.

Nature is the mat(t)er that informs, nourishes, and irrigates the living with its vital force ('I've studied mathematics, which is the madness of reason—["There was a vagueness in my mind [...]. You replaced it with excessive coldness, consummate prudence and implacable logic."][111]—but now I want the plasma—I want to eat straight from the placenta').[112]

---

108 Leminski, *Catatau*, 37.

109 T.S. Eliot, *The Waste Land. Authoritative Text. Contexts. Criticism*, ed. M. North (New York: Norton, 2001). 17–18. Regarding the connection between Leminski's *Catatau* and Eliot's *The Waste Land*, see Na Kar Eliff-ce, *Apostillas a Lo Real (entre el Eliotrueno y el rayoPaulo)*, talk given at the Centro de Estudios Brasileros, Buenos Aires, September 2001.

110 Khatarnak & Khabandar, 'Umbanda-Jackson', 46.

111 Comte de Lautréamont, *Maldoror*, tr. P. Knight (London: Penguin Classics, 1978), 93.

112 C. Lispector, *Agua Viva*, tr. S. Tobler (New York: New Directions, 2012), 3.

And nature is also the *Abgrund* where the Titans dwell and the echo chamber in which the rising percussion of their beating hearts ('the pulse of our slumber')[113] resonates and is amplified. Nature is the cosmic Athanor where the most cataclysmic transubstantiations take place and time, and the horizon of umweltic horizons where heterogeneous life-forms perform the most delicate trans-species choreographies. Nature is '[t]he living thing, lightly dreaming, whose cycle of life reverberates in itself and in its environs, constantly renew[ing] itself, streaming out over itself in ever new forms, and yet [remaining] in its own *single* route'.[114] Nature is the uncanniest because 'it harbours such an inception in which, from overabundance, everything breaks out at once into what is overwhelming'[115] and at the same time it soothes the living with the 'overabundance of its softness', with the extreme lightness of its omnipresent touch. Nature is beautiful and terrible, the exorbitance of procreation and the mercilessness of manducation. Nature is the transvaultic dome, the 'chrysanthemum, [the] swirling floral pattern, infinitely unfolding' (Terence McKenna). Nature is the force of imagination (*Einbildungskraft*) that galvanises the living and impels them to spring forth into the risk of existence, to become visionaries. Nature is the fabric that imbricates incommensurable spatiotemporal scales, from the infinitesimal 'vicinity of vagueness' where even space and time dissolve to the prolific exorbitance of the jungle to the unfathomable vastness of Laniakea and even upstream and beyond. Nature is both the spice and the immanental psychonaut. Nature is the sea ('the wintry swells in which it constantly drags up its own depths and drags itself down into them'),[116] the heavens (the 'preserved night' within which the worldly clearings open up, expand, and implode), and the earth ('Here the overwhelming does not hold sway in self-devouring wildness, but as that which without toil and without tiring, from out of the superiority of the calm of

113 Joyce, *Finnegans Wake*, 428.

114 Heidegger, *Introduction to Metaphysics*, 172.

115 Ibid., 173.

116 Ibid., 171.

great riches, ripens and dispenses what is inexhaustible and rises above all impatience').[117] Nature envelops the infra-naturality of the underlying impersonal background, the natural familiarity of the worldly horizons, and also the overarching transmundane vaults, the supernatural. Nature is the single uninterrupted overwhelming eruption of the *natura naturans* and also the spectrum of landscapes associated with the different *natura naturatae*: '[I]t was the equinox...green spring equal nights...canyons are opening up, at the bottoms are steaming fumaroles, steaming the tropical life there like greens in a pot, rank, dope-perfume, a hood of smell... [...] This is the World just before [humans]. Too violently pitched alive in constant flow ever to be seen by [humans] directly. They are meant only to look at it [filtered and edited], in still strata, transputrefied to oil or coal. Alive, it was a threat: it was Titans, was an overpeaking of life so clangorous and mad, such a green corona about Earth's body [...].'[118]

But at the dawn of European modernity, the gods fled ('the radiance of divinity [was] extinguished in [European] world-history'),[119] Galilean science was born, and some were frightened to death by the 'eternal silence of these infinite spaces' while others reacted to this traumatic event by desperately seeking protection and reterritorialising in the most abject *terra firma*, the *ego conquero*; they betrayed the infinite idea of truth by making science an instrument of domination and massive destruction. We then became the despoilers of creation: 'So we, the crippled keepers, were sent out to multiply, to have dominion. [Life]'s spoilers. Us. Counter-revolutionaries. *It is our mission to promote [the illness of disligation]*. The way we kill, the way we die, being unique among the Creatures. It was something we had to work on, historically and personally. To build from scratch up to its present status as reaction, nearly as strong as life, holding down the green uprising. But only nearly as strong.'[120] And we reached the extreme limit

117 Ibid.

118 T. Pynchon, *Gravity's Rainbow* (New York: Viking, 1973), 720.

119 Heidegger, 'Why Poets?', *Off the Beaten Track*, 200.

120 Pynchon, *Gravity's Rainbow*, 720.

where the ultimate danger is not the danger of collectively disappearing, but the danger of leaving the scene with the certainty that we have done our best to destroy life, that we have systematically enslaved and murdered our human and nonhuman siblings, that we have treated nature as a game reserve, that we destroyed *El Dorado* while greedily looking for gold. At this uttermost extreme of the illness of disligation, shall we dare to follow the Leminiskian Cartesius into the rainforest ('My day is done. I am leaving Europe [...] with its ancient parapets')[121] or Artaud on his voyage to the land of the Tarahumara, to drink the plant that heals ('[Ciguri] is the only barrier holding the disease back'),[122] bear the rising tide of the *miração* and undergo the resulting purge, to channel and modulate the Titan's beats that rise up from the depths of the Earth, to reorient ourselves in existence by projecting a new philosophical constellation of truth, beauty, justice, and love, to reverse 'the turning away against the open', turn down the 'sheltering defenses' and stand firm in the terrible beauty of life? Shall be have the courage to 'drop out', to desert, to defect, to withdraw from an imploding world and step back into the 'preserved night' where everything is always still possible? 'Only nearly [as strong as life], because of the defection rate. A few keep going over to the Titans every day, in their striving subcreation (how can flesh tumble and flow so, and never be any less beautiful?), into the rests of the folksong Death (empty stone rooms), out, and through, and down under the net, down down to the uprising. In harsh-edged echo, Titans stir far below. They are all the presences we are not supposed to be seeing—wind gods, hilltop gods, sunset gods—that we train ourselves away from to keep from looking further even though enough of us do, leave Their electric voices behind in the twilight at the edge of the town and move into the constantly parted cloak of our nightwalk till suddenly, Pan—leaping—its face too beautiful to bear, beautiful Serpent, its coils in rainbow lashings in the sky—into the sure bones of fright—.'[123]

121 A. Rimbaud, *Complete Works, Selected Letters*, tr. W. Fowlie (Chicago: University of Chicago Press, 2005), 135, 269.

122 A. Artaud, *Les Tarahumaras* (Paris: Gallimard, 1971), 38.

123 Pynchon, *Gravity's Rainbow*, 720–21.

If surrounding worlds were 'stopped' (Carlos Castaneda), if the natural attitude was 'bracketed' (Husserl), if 'I [a case of a transcendental type instituted in the wild heart of life] am not of this [constituted] world' (St. John), if—being 'a member of the Angel race'— 'this world is not my home' (Sun Ra),[124] if the immobile Ur-Arche Earth itself is launched into orbit at the gong clash of the phenoumenodelic *epoché*, where do we find ourselves? Where are we? 'Where can I find space for my soul' given that '[f]or me, the world is too narrow'?[125] How might we schematise our existential situation? What type of primordial scene can take the place of the Husserlian pre-given natural-historical lifeworld, the Pascalian disenchanted abyssal locus, the cosmological sublime depicted by contemporary astrophysics, or the Heideggerian pastoral *fourfold* (*Geviert*)? Where is the Ark—containing the chamber with the *grimoire* that prescribes the performance of noetic acts—on board of which Mallarmé's *Maître*, 'threatening a destiny and the winds', perseveres defiantly in the task of stalking the interzones and surveying the pleroma by means of theoretical, aesthetic, political, and liturgical probes? How can we conceive of the worldless milieu in which the phenoumenodelic *epoché* suspends the Ur-Arche Earth? What is the *Stimmung*—the affective tonality—brought about by plunging into the narcotic insubstance?

Let us first point out that the suspension of the Ur-Arche Earth does not necessarily lead to the silent darkness of infinite spaces and their associated *Stimmung*, Pascalian angst: the suspension of all forms of privileged fundamental tonality opens existence up to an *atonal medium* full of unheard-of possibilities. We can imagine Pythagoras and Bruno listening to the skies and wondering, *Is Pascal deaf?* The suspended pleroma is pregnant with chords which—through patient mediation—can be deployed infinitely: 'there is no silence in the universe',[126] only relative thresholds of

124 Sun Ra, *The Immeasurable Equation: The Collected Poetry and Prose*, ed. J.L. Wolf and H. Geerken (Waitawhile, 2005), 381.

125 Silesius, *Cherubinischer Wandersmann*, Book I, §187.

126 P. Valéry, 'Variation sur une Pensée', in P. Valéry, Variété *I et II* (Paris: Gallimard, 1930), 118.

perceptibility, affectability, comprehensibility, sociability. The living pleroma 'surrounds us and offers itself to us incessantly and we only have to take it'.[127] Beyond the anguish occasioned by being thrown out into the cosmic openness and the supposed security that results from the bucolic reterritorialisation in the fatherland, beyond the Weberian disenchantment of nature and the Heideggerian reactive mirage of a pastoral homecoming, beyond the oscillatory tension between movements of modern deterritorialisation and reactive reterritorialisation, the phenoumenodelic *epoché* is a *conversion* that submerges us in the ungrounded phenoumenodelic pleroma and opens up the possibility of a solaristic oceanification of existence. The existential conversion enacted by the *epoché* is a baptism, an immersion into the phenoumenodelic solution, a plunge into the insubstantial daydream within which every world is suspended: 'No feeling is so homogeneous with the desire for the infinite, the longing to merge into the infinite, as the desire to immerse one's self in the [phenoumenodelic] sea. To plunge into it is to be confronted by an alien element which at once flows round us on every side and which is felt at every point of the body. We are taken away from the world and the world from us. We are nothing but felt water which touches us where we are, and we are only where we feel it. In the sea there is no gap, no restriction, no multiplicity, nothing specific. The feeling of it is the simplest, the least broken up. After immersion a [living being] comes up into the air again, separates [it]self from the water [...] So soon as the water leaves [it], the world around [it] takes on specific characteristics again, and [it] comes back strengthened to the consciousness of multiplicity. [...] In immersion there is only one feeling, there is only forgetfulness of the world. [...] The baptism of [Yesses] appears in Mark's account (i. 9 ff.) as such a withdrawal from the entire past, as an inspiring consecration into a new [state of being] in which reality floats before the new spirit in a form in which there is no distinction between reality and dream.'[128] Transplanted into the primal scene of the speculative initiation—the pond of the narcissi—the *epoché* takes the form of a narcissistic

127 Fichte, *The Way Towards the Blessed Life; Or, The Doctrine of Religion, 8.*

128 Hegel, *On Christianity: Early Theological Writings*, 275.

articulation between *transcendental reflection* (the realisation of the fact that every Umwelt results from a transparent subject-dependent framing) and the *refractive mediation* of the swamp's reflective interface. After contemplating himself in the liquid *speculum*, the ichthyfied Narcissus (the baptised Christ) dives into the narcotic solution of the phenoumenodelic stream, articulating the *solaristic* 'doctrine' of the flowing insubstance announced by Spinoza's *Ethics* and the *nautilic* navigational faculties (of which Kant's transcendental idealism provides an initial survey). The 'faucet that does not close' muddies the land with its 'infinite preambles'[129] and the resulting marshes, evaporating without any rain falling to replenish them, are transplanted into *aerial waters*. While terrestrial waters are contained in planetary basins, aerial waters engulf all land and enclose all of the circumambient world. Whereas solaristics understands all (supposedly) firm land as a floating island, a particularly opaque densification of the pleromatic insubstance, nautilics understands all worlds as phenomenological horizons correlative to a particular lifeform, as a transcendental-dependent clearing hovering within the immanental insubstance, as a sheltering vessel that protects the subject from imploding under the phenoumenodelic pressure. The Mallarméan shipwreck, far from implying a disaster, expresses the immersion of the vessel in an atonal daydream in which every possible note is nothing more than a phenoumenodelic datum made up of the same hallucinogenic droplets. By placing the *Maître* under the *influence* of the field, by imbuing his existence with dreaminess ('He is guided, but like a sleeper'),[130] the phenoumenodelic *epoché* suspends the distinction between a supposedly fundamental tone and the excited tones that decay to the fundamental—for instance, the distinction between material infrastructure and superstructural spirits; between wakefulness and sleep; between

129 Perlongher, *Hule*, 127. See the commentary on these Perlonghian themes in denaKmar naKhabra, 'The Undulating Unknown'.

130 W. Benjamin, 'Outline of the Psychophysical Problem', in M. Bullock and M.W. Jennings (eds.), *Selected Writings, Volume 1, 1913–1926* (London and Cambridge, MA: Belknap Press, 2002), 398.

sense-certainty and hallucination.[131] Thanks to the *epoché*, all of these distinctions are flattened onto a univocal phenoumenodelic field: *there is nothing but 'images'*. The absence of a globally valid fundamental tone does not exclude the possibility of multiple and suspended terrestrial densifications, of arks that support navigation, of deserted islands for the shipwrecked, of motherships, of sheltering skies hovering in the insubstance, of freefalling soils to ground oneself in, of local fundamental vacua to which regional excitations and decays may refer, of submarines to delve into the trenches, of drifting homelands to return to. The pleroma is no stationary land or tonal ground state, like some absolute coordinate system with respect to which it would be possible to define all rest and movement, all tension and release. It is not true—as Husserl claimed—that the last instance in relation to which every form of rest and movement (and in particular the movement of the empirical earth) must always be referred to must itself be understood as an Ur-Arche Earth that cannot be either at rest (understood as a particular mode of motion) or in motion. Husserl's attempt to overcome the idealism of monadological egology is marred by the repetition of the same type of argument that he uses to object to all forms of naturalisation of the transcendental subject: just as the conditions of possibility for the constitution of objectivity cannot be naturalised themselves, so the background condition of possibility of dynamics must also be withdrawn from any form of scientific objectivation.[132] The Husserlian field of experience is always

---

131 William James's 'radical empiricism' also proceeds by means of a flattening of perceptual, affective, conceptual, imaginary, oneiric, hallucinatory experiences—as well as of past and future experiences—onto a single plane made up of the 'primal stuff' of 'pure experience' (see James, 'Does "Consciousness" Exist?'). James explicitly insists that this flattening of 'pure experience' must not be understood in terms of 'a universal element of which all things would be made' (Ibid., 14): the *atonal neutrality* of the suspended experiential field means precisely that there is no substantial fundamental state, fundamental tone or immobile Ur-Arche Earth, only an ungrounded and un-hierarchical multiplicity of phenoumenodelic data taking shape in the insubstance of the one life.

132 This point has been clearly laid out by Derrida in the following terms: 'But if an objective science of earthly things is possible, an objective science of the Earth

grounded, either on a transcendental ego or on an immobile Ur-Arche Earth of some sort. But in our post-Galilean and post-Einsteinian modern world, we have understood how to conceive movement (even accelerated movement) without the need to presuppose a fixed a priori absolutely immobile kinematic background, one against which all movement and all rest would take place.[133] What in physics is called the *principle of background*

---

itself, the ground and foundation of these objects, is as radically impossible as that of transcendental subjectivity. The transcendental Earth is not an object and can never become one. And the possibility of a geometry strictly complements the impossibility of what could be called a "geo-logy", the objective science of the Earth itself. [...] [T]he earth in its proto-primordiality does not move. [...] The Earth therefore knows the rest of an absolute *here*; a rest which is not the rest of the object (rest as "mode of motion"), but Rest starting from which motion and rest can appear and be thought as such [...]. There is then a science of space, in so far as its starting point is not in space.' J. Derrida, *Edmund Husserl's Origin of Geometry: An Introduction* (Lincoln, NE and London: University of Nebraska Press: 1989), 83–85.

133 A phenomenologist might argue that it is not legitimate to use scientific theories such as the general theory of relativity (which results from innumerable mediations which foreclose the pre-objective and sedimentary layers of the immediately given) to argue against (purported) phenomenological evidence. As Husserl writes in the famous fragment concerning the immobility of the Ur-arche earth: the phenomenological reduction of the Copernican Revolution *doesn't affect physics* but merely emphasises that 'we must not forget the pre-givenness and constitution belonging to the apodictic Ego or to me, to us, as the source of all actual and possible sense of being, of all possible broadening which can be further constructed in the already constituted world developing historically' (Husserl, 'Foundational Investigations', 230). However, even this proposed phenomenological account according to which all forms of movement and rest appear to take place in relation to a motionless background is phenomenologically problematic, in the sense that it lacks any immediate evidence: uniform movement and rest are phenomenologically indistinguishable. The only type of motion that could be characterised as absolute is accelerated motion. Even so, Einstein showed that accelerated motion can also be conceived as relative motion, in the precise sense that it is relative to the inertial-gravitational field, which is a dynamic physical entity rather than an absolute background. Even if this superior form of relativity is not phenomenologically evident to human beings, there is no in-principle reason to categorically dismiss the possibility of conceiving subjects (or transcendental variations of human subjectivity)

*independence* points toward an understanding of dynamics progressively released from the presupposition of fixed (non-dynamical) a priori structures. Rather than being fixed 'by hand', the geometric background itself (or at least certain geometric structures of such a background—for instance, the spatiotemporal metric in the general theory of relativity) is a solution of the corresponding equations of motion. In less abstract terms, the purported fixed island on which Sinbad the Sailor disembarks on his first voyage reveals itself to be a sleeping whale—that is, another living being.[134] Scientific rationality boosts itself through a gradual process which involves immanentising of its presuppositions: what might at first play the role of a sort of requisite a priori structure of a given scientific theory may, in the framework of a later development of that theory, become a physical structure endowed with degrees of freedom the dynamics of which are described by the theory. The impossibility of definitively ridding phenomenology of the premodern drive toward foundation prevents Husserl from fully installing phenomenology in the ungrounded immanence of the phenoumenodelic experiential field, despite the suspensory dementia of the *epoché*. Husserl's desperate attempt to phenomenologically reduce Copernicanism has the merit of bringing to light the fact that the relationship with the ground as foundation, whose canonical model is our dwelling on the surface of the empirical earth, structures not just the actual experience of surrounding physical space, but also the spatial schematisations of the various modalities of human experience, including, for instance, the foundational proclivities that pervade science and philosophy. The Copernican Revolution itself—Copernicanism of the zeroth order—was not enough to definitively rid us of the foundational motif of an immobile Ur-Arche Earth, a motif that continues to operate across different dimensions of human experience.

---

which, sufficiently sensitive to the dynamics of the inertial-gravitational field, could experience the relativity of accelerated movement as 'immediate' phenomenological evidence.

134 The story of Sinbad is used by Carlo Rovelli to illustrate the principle of background independence in C. Rovelli, *Quantum Gravity* (Cambridge: Cambridge University Press, 2004), 9.

However, this factual limitation on the scope of the Copernican Revolution does not necessarily imply a juridical restriction on the possibility of launching all forms of grounds into orbit (as Husserl seems to believe), but can instead be understood as a call to extend and deepen the Copernican Revolution, until every purported Ur-Arche Earth hovers and drifts in the ungrounded phenoumenodelic insubstance—the pleroma. The pleroma is the phenoumenodelic 'sea of life' upon which every land drifts and within which every phenomenological horizon unfolds. The phenoumenodelic sea carries the arks, surrounds the circumambient worlds, envelops and interconnects the conscious riddles, and deposits oneiric visitations on the shores of finite experience: 'This sea of sleep [...] has its high tide at night; every slumber indicates only that it washes a shore from which it retreats in waking hours.[135] [...] [The sea] is the unconscious milieu that surrounds the specifically conscious or the horizon of the latent unconscious.[136] [...] As sleep [the phenoumenodelic sea] bears the ship of life on its current, which is accompanied from a distance by the wind and the stars; as slumber, it arises at night like the tide breaking on the shores of life, on which it leaves dreams dying the next day. [...] [I]n the "true world", dream and waking as such do not exist [...] the world of truth may well not be the world of any consciousness. [...] [And] for consciousness [...] only the relation to life—not the relation to truth—is relevant. And neither of these two modes of consciousness [dream and waking] is "truer" to life; they merely have different meanings for it.'[137] In the last instance, only the relation to life is relevant. Each alleged site of existence—the Husserlian natural-historical lifeworld, the disenchanted neo-Pascalian abysses, the Heideggerian intrawordly not-at-homeness (*Unzuhause*) and his later fourfoldian reterritorialisation, the contingent and stubborn positivity of the Sartrean in-itself, the Levinasian there-is-ness (*il y a*)—elicits

135 Benjamin, 'Outline of the Psychophysical Problem', 398–99.

136 E. Husserl, *Die Lebenswelt. Auslegungen der vorgegebenen Welt und ihrer Konstitution. Texte aus dem Nachlass (1916–1937), Gesameltte Werke, Band XXXIX*, ed. R. Sowa (Dordrecht: Springer, 2008), 102.

137 Benjamin, 'Outline of the Psychophysical Problem', 399.

a particular kind of affect (e.g. anguish, nausea, vertigo, serenity, insomniac horror). But which are the affects elicited by the phenoumenodelic suspension in the living insubstance? The *epoché* launches existence into a worldless medium which, without offering any salvation whatsoever, all the same provides a manner of cure, an interzonal tempering. The pleroma is the glorious living flesh, the phenoumenodelic insubstance, from which immanentities are extracted, and at the same time the very 'unconscious milieu' upon which they are staked, gambled, and thrown. The pleroma provides the insubstance of the breathing entities, of their absolute environment, and of the pneuma that inter-converts them. In launching entities into insecurity, the pleroma is not abandoning them or driving them out of itself. For 'although the unsheltered are risked' (having been thrown into the vulnerability of separation and exposed to the wilderness of their own autonomous desire), 'they are nevertheless not abandoned. If they were, they would be as little risked as sheltered. Delivered only unto annihilation, they would no longer hang in the balance'.[138] To be unprotected is to be *un-secured*, removed from the *securitas*, from the '*sine cura*', i.e. from the state in which the living is not in the cure.[139] To be unprotected is then to be in the cure, to be exposed, to exist in the unshelteredness of life, to be permeable to the healing forces. The cure is only available where the speculative turbulence elicited by the morphogenetic drives of life, by the will to live, subtracts existence from its essentialisation and brackets the concomitant reification of the reality-models. When it comes to the religating cure, being-on-board is no longer immune to the affect induced by phenoumenodelic turmoil: 'Nausea perhaps? Such melodrama [too Parisian for the high seas] comes rapidly to amuse (although we still vomit, just as we die)'.[140] The unmediated bifurcation between *free subjectivity* (the *res cogitans* for-itself) and *inert, contingent and factic nature* (the *res extensa* in itself) leads necessarily (depending on personal temperament) to Pascalian

138 Heidegger, 'Why Poets?', *Off the Beaten Track*, 210.

139 Ibid., 223.

140 Land, *The Thirst for Annihilation*, xii.

anguish in the face of cosmic lifeless extensions or Sartrean nausea in the face of the opaque and viscous fullness of the in-itself. But the freedom-nature divide can be dialecticised in the direction of the phenoumenodelic imponderable flesh, the living mat(t)er that self-organises in the form of finite free beings, the only concrete *res* that envelops all the infinite attributes, the unique concrescence that enmeshes the *res cogitans* and the *res extensa* in an indissoluble manner. Here we should evoke—rather than Roquentin—Turner, getting tanned and tempered, tied to the top of the mast. If the premodern myth of an Ur-ground works as an antiemetic, the phenoumenodelic *epoché* triggers the *mareação* as a *Stimmung* proper to the cure, the wooziness that makes us vomit, not because of existential nausea but from healing purge. Once freed of all catastrophic pathos, of that 'apocalyptic tone recently adopted in philosophy', and of all hope of salvation too, the cure exposes the subject to 'the binding, the spellbinding powers'[141] of life and transplants it to the 'wild heart' where the material processes of institution of subjectivity and constitution of worlds—their knowledge [*connaissance*], their *co-nascence*—takes place and time. The reification of '[w]hat's in front'—the objectified world correlative to a particular transcendental type of subjectivity—'does not allow the subject to expose itself to the [trans-umweltic] open',[142] to bind itself both with the living mat(t)er in the impersonal background and with the supernatural heavens beyond the sheltering skies. Life is L.I.F.E: Loving Inter(-zonal, -personal, -umweltic, -national, -species, -linguistic, -galactic) Forms of Experience, instituting, launching, and coordinating living tentacles for probing the Epicurean *intermundia* between the constituted worlds. By risking existence with 'one more breath'—by unsettling the fixed system of linguistic and conceptual categories that frame experience, by recalibrating existentials, by disrupting cultural imprints, by confronting the 'poverty in world' that results from the speculative trans-umweltisation of experience, by instituting hetero-chrono-topias in-between the Umwelten (ZADs, TAZs, etc.), by assuming that every constituting subject is an instituted fluctuation in the

141 Benjamin, 'Outline of the Psychophysical Problem', 400.

142 Heidegger, 'Why Poets?', *Off the Beaten Track,* 256.

impersonal animic field—the resulting plastic subjects acquire the possibility of beginning to heal from the arche-disease of disligation. This attunement with the *intermundia* is always already a contemperation—co-'tempering the membranes [tanning them] so they reverberate'[143]—a speculative concertation that integrates different transcendental types of subjectivity into trans-species tribes.

Another of the criticisms directed at Spinozism by the German idealists, in this case Hegel in particular, is his failure to attain a conception of substance as a subject.[144] Now, the proposed conception of substance as one life advances in the direction opened up by the Hegelian criticism. The pleroma will not only be apprehended as impersonal phenoumenodelic insubstance, but also and to the same extent as an absolute living subject, as a singular and purely reflexive form of self-experience. Whereas the pleroma can be characterised as impersonal with respect to the finite subjective modes, we shall understand its immanental unfolding as the one life of a singular (triune) persona. So, how can we conceive of a form of subjectivity 'coextensive to life'?[145] We can initially understand the Hegelian amendment to Spinozist monism on the basis of the thesis that every experience of a finite living subject is by transitivity an experience of the infinite one life the subject locally incarnates. If a subject is a breathing mode of the impersonal insubstance, every subjective experience is, in the last instance, umbilically anchored to the latter. '[E]ach being matters in the fabric of [the pleroma's experiences]. Every sensation[, every emotion, every thought] of every [living] being [...] is a mode through which [life] lives, feels [and thinks] itself, and through which it exists. [...] [The] unique[, sensual, living,

143 NaKh ab Ra, 'Breve Diccionario de Brujería Portátil', in J. Salzano (ed.), *Nosotros, los brujos. Apuntes de arte, poesía y brujería* (Buenos Aires: Santiago Arcos, 2008), 252.

144 'In my view [...] everything turns on grasping and expressing the True, not only as *Substance*, but equally as *Subject*. [...] Further, the living Substance is being which is in truth *Subject*, or, what is the same, is in truth actual only in so far as it is the movement of positing itself, or is the mediation of its self-othering with itself.' Hegel, *Phenomenology of Spirit*, 10.

145 Bergson, *Creative Evolution*, xxiii.

warm, musical, and colourful] point of view [that the Passenger Pigeons embody] brings forth the happiness of being an immense wing traversing infinite spaces; the feeling of being a cloud above Earth and of creating changing shapes on it, flowing and shadowy: the sensation of the fields and the woods that, far below, fly by like the images of an accelerating film[; t]he joy of being innumerable and of forming one perfectly attuned being, and the trust in this attunement, which is the figure of joy that the Passenger Pigeons invented when they learned to rely on the air and the wind.'[146] Every experience of the living, every lived experience, is a self-experience *of* life in the double sense of the genitive, a self-experience of life made possible, factorised, or channelled by the finite being in question. Every interaction between local subjects is a local salience in the monologue of the insubstance, every intentional-transcendent subjective experience of an objective phenomenon is ultimately a reflexive-immanent experience of life itself, a self-revelation of life, a case of what Fichte, in the *Science of Knowing* of 1804, called 'pure knowing' or 'knowing in itself', that is to say an absolute awareness that is not relative (as all finite consciousness is) to a transcendent instance, that does not posit any object or subject outside of itself.[147] The one life as absolute self-awareness is not only the immanental insubstance in which finite subjects are instituted and in which lifeworlds are constituted, but also the supra-subjective and trans-worldly envelopment of the

146 V. Despret, 'It Is an Entire World That Has Disappeared', Afterword to D. Bird Rose, T. van Dooren, and M. Chrulew (eds.), *Extinction Studies: Stories of Time, Death, and Generation* (New York: Columbia University Press, 2017), 219–21.

147 In Fichte's own terms: '[A]bsolute oneness can no more reside in being than in its correlative consciousness; it can as little be posited in the thing as in the representation of the thing. Rather, it resides in the principle, which we have just discovered, of the absolute oneness and indivisibility of both, which is equally, as we have seen, the principle of their disjunction. We will name this principle pure knowing, knowing in itself, and, thus, completely objectless knowing, because otherwise it would not be knowing in itself but would require objectivity for its being. It is distinct from consciousness, which posits a being and is therefore only a half.' Fichte, *The Science of Knowing*, 25–26.

experiences that vibrate in the phenoumenodelic continuum. In his 'dialogue' with Eco, Pasolini excites the following vibrations in the Monologue of Brahma: '"[R]eality is the language of B. [which stands for Brahma]." With whom does B. speak? [...] Let us assume that in this moment B. speaks with Eco, using as sign, as ultimate sign, the hair of Jerry Malanga. But what difference is there between the hair of Jerry Malanga and the eyes of Umberto Eco? They are but two organisms of reality, which is a continuum without any break in continuity; a single body, as far as I know. The hair of Jerry Malanga and the eyes of Umberto Eco therefore belong to the same Body, the physical manifestation of the Real, of the Existing, of Being. [...] [I]t cannot be said that this is a dialogue; [it is] a monologue which the infinite Body of Reality has with itself. [...] "Reality speaks with itself." [...] It is B., it is B., dear Eco, who says to [itself], through the pink [image-sign] of the light [which spreads in the sky] and through your looking eyes, that a new day is breaking.'[148] Life feels, perceives, breathes, and thinks itself. But this self-experience is nothing more than the envelope of the experiences associated with the singular perspectives made possible by the being-there of life in the living: there is thus no absolute consciousness without relative consciousnesses. Thanks to the *epoché*, the finite subject lives its experiencing life as a local transient breathing mode of the immanental insubstance qua subject, of the self-positing and self-revealing original activity of the one life. 'In each individual, Nature beholds itself from a particular point of view. [...] There is an infinite variety of possible individuals, and hence also an infinite variety of possible starting points of consciousness. This consciousness of all individuals taken together, constitutes the complete consciousness of the [immanental one life]; and there is no other.[149] [...] There is [...] such a life imagining itself absolutely [...]. This imagining force takes [...] according to inner [transcendental] laws, the form of such

---

148 P.P. Pasolini, *Heretical Empiricism*, tr. B. Lawton and L.K. Barnett (Washington, D.C.: New Academia Publishing, 2005), 279, 281.

149 Fichte, *The Vocation of Man*, 36.

and such [images-signs]; and the sum of these images is the consciousness of all of us, which just is, immediately, and is encountered as being.'[150]

The thesis that every experience of a living being is by transitivity an experience of the one life is restricted to describing absolute consciousness as a mere 'multiplicity of juxtaposition'[151] of local experiences within which they maintain a relation of reciprocal exteriority. Now, absolute consciousness is 'an ego that is also [an integrated] *we*',[152] a transpersonal concertation of selves, a self-positing process of tribalisation, an autopoietic unfolding of higher forms of collective subjectivity that *integrates* the experiences of all finite subjects into multiplicities 'of interpenetration'[153] and brings about the harmonic counterpoint between their phenomenological worldly horizons. The representational correlations between subjects and objects, the intersubjective relations, the different forms of societal nexus among the living, can be understood as 'synaptic' connections through which local experiences, individual faculties, and different Umwelten are integrated into emergent global experiences, affordances and functionalities of distributed forms of subjectivity, and wider phenoumenodelic horizons. Life exteriorises itself by instituting I/not-I polarisations along divergent lines of naturalcultural evolution and sublates this exteriorisation and the corresponding multiplicity of perspectival viewpoints on itself by means of a 'spiritual' process of progressive reinteriorisation of its divergent expressions: '[T]he line of evolution that ends in [human beings] is not the only one. On other paths, divergent from it, other forms of consciousness have been developed [...]. Suppose these other forms of consciousness brought together and amalgamated with intellect: would not the result be a consciousness as wide as life?[154] [...] [L]ife can be defined [...] as a

150 J.G. Fichte, *La doctrine de l'État (1813). Leçons sur des contenus variés de philosophie pratique*, tr., ed. J.-C. Goddard (Paris: Vrin, 2006), 66.

151 Bergson, *Time and Free Will*, 75.

152 Goddard, 'Autonomie, réduction et réflexivité: la philosophie naturelle de Francisco J. Varela et le projet transcendantal', 211.

153 Bergson, *Time and Free Will*, 162.

154 Bergson, *Creative Evolution*, xxii–xxiii.

continual act of self-creation and a reinteriorisation, also continual, of its 'expressions'. [...] [I]f originary consciousness is 'alienated' or 'divided' [...] it is susceptible to an *Erinnerung*, a reinteriorisation of its forms, and a reconciliation of its divergent tendencies. The end of the series—or the totalising consciousness that becomes coextensive with life—"conserves" all the other particular forms of consciousness, "while surpassing them" [...] [In particular,] it is anthropology itself that is surpassed in the direction of something greater than itself [...] superconsciousness [...]. The emergence of [human] intelligence is not the sound of the trumpets of the Last Judgement; it defines humanity as a *point of passage* [among others], a [local] valve through which passes, finally liberated, Life itself [...].'[155]

According to this phenoumenodelia of spirit, immanent life is one life, transindividual and transmundane; one life which raises its self-experience to new powers through its localisation, its incarnation, its refraction into divergent lines of evolution, through the institution of living probes—receptive, vibrant and expressive vortices swirling in the experiential stream—whose experiences will be enveloped, integrated, interfused with others' experiences. Life is *one*, one life among other possible lives, always singularly determined. Life is the impersonal unity from which the separated living are derived and the morphogenetic force that informs this very centrifugal separation. And life is at the same time the centripetal tendency to interiorise subjective experiences and heterogeneous Umwelten into a transpersonal unfolding subjectivity. Life is the impersonal alpha and the transpersonal omega of the immanental processes of institution of personal lifeforms, of the transcendental acts of constitution of lifeworlds, of the concertations of these lifeforms into collective forms of subjectivity, of the integration of local experiences into global ones, of the coalescence of worlds into wider phenoumenodelic horizons. The divine life—Guaraci, 'the mat(t)er of the living'[156]—is not revealed in a book but incarnated in the living ones, whom it brings together into tribes of higher and higher orders of collective subjectivity. The phenoumenodelic process of manifestation resulting from

155 B. Prado Jr., *Présence et champ transcendantal*, 146, 155–56.

156 De Andrade, 'Cannibalistic Manifesto', 38 [translation modified].

finite incarnation and communitarian integration is the unique revelation. There is no transcendental phenomenology without the *élan vital* that morphs the eye and compels it to open to a world of visions. And there is no phenoumenodelia of spirit without the neurological-communitarian capacity to mine new forms of experiential depth by concertating heterogeneous lifeforms and integrating their singular experiences.

On the one hand, the concept of pleroma retains from Spinozist substance (a) its *immanence*, that is, its capacity to envelop every form of transcendence, (b) its *concreteness*, that is, its antecedence with respect to its refraction into abstract attributes such as the *affectum*, the *sensorium*, the *logos* and the *socius* (or, in more restricted Cartesian terms, *res extensa* and *res cogitans*), and (c) the understanding of finite subjectivity as a mode of infinite substance. On the other hand, the notion of pleroma departs from the Spinozist notion of substance thanks to three operations: its phenoumenodelic *suspension*, its *vivification*—that is, its capacity to institute living beings endowed with transcendental structures that constitute images—, and its *subjectivation* as absolute or purely reflexive consciousness emerging from the progressive interconnection of finite lifeforms and from the integration of their local experiences. Let us now summarise the objections faced by Spinozism from the standpoints provided by the refinements introduced by Fichte, Schelling, and Hegel. Regarding its form, Spinozism seems to be a mere dogmatic system that does not take into account the transcendental limits of the human theoretical faculties. Regarding its content, it might seem to propose a mechanistic, deterministic, and fatalistic conception of nature deprived of freedom, contingency, and purposiveness. The first problem was dissolved by Fichte by means of a phenomenological suspension of substance. This suspension deliquesces substance into a phenoumenodelic insubstance and allows us to understand the Spinozist univocity of being in terms of the univocity of appearing. Spinozist substance becomes a self-revealing phenoumenodelic insubstance or, in more Fichtean terms, the original ongoing act of self-revelation. This revelation should not be understood as an act through which an already existing hidden content would be exposed, unconcealed, or unveiled, but rather as an immanental self-sustained (*causa sui*) phenoumenodelic unfolding that ceaselessly produces new 'images' and broadcasts new signs. The pleroma is the unedited field of impersonal experience, the unfiltered flow of phenoumenodelic information out of which each transcendental type frames an Umwelt. But how does this uninterrupted distillation of unforeseen 'images' proceed? It is here that the suspension of substance needs to be enriched with a central Christian thesis, namely that finite lifeforms play a necessary role in the phenoumenology of insubstance. The finite subjective modes of insubstance umweltify the latter, thereby constituting worldly retorts for the distillation of new images that potentiate its self-revelation. In this way, the (Fichtean) suspension of Spinozist substance is followed by the (Fichtean and Schellingean) vivification of the resulting insubstance: insubstance is a life that reveals or manifests itself by engendering, by producing subjective whirlpools equipped with transcendental faculties, by never arresting the immanental generation of the most improbable lifeforms. The *vivification* of insubstance allows for an account of the immanental institution of constituting subjects of different transcendental types. Phenoumenodelic insubstance is alive since it reveals itself by generating finite lifeforms capable of constituting (filtering, extracting, editing, abstracting, framing, distilling, sieving) perspectival images of the pleroma. Finite subjective modes define a necessary *persona* in the general trinitarian economy of phenoumenodelic revelation: there is no revelation except through the images that appear in the Umwelten constituted by different lifeforms. The pleroma as living insubstance is the *natura naturans* that begets living beings qua local carriers of experience, qua finite modes of the impersonal experiential field. Now, different lifeforms are not only connected by the impersonal underlying *Band* provided by the living insubstance of which they are local modes, but also by the societal relations that they can entertain qua distinct singular individuals. These relations provide the 'synaptic' connexions out of which collective, transpersonal, or distributed forms of spirit gradually emerge. The *subjectivation* of pleroma refers to the immanental self-experience of the pleroma itself and to its gradual progression toward higher and higher forms of collective spirit. The pleroma as absolute subject is a field of purely reflexive immanental experience (i.e. without intentional transcendence, without transcendent objects or subjects), pure experience of itself, one life progressively unfolding from the integration, concertation, and coordination of local lifeforms. This symbiogenetic integration of finite subjects into lifeforms of a higher subjective order transforms the flow of phenoumenodelic information into coherent global intelligence. Whereas the institution of finite lifeforms is tantamount to a process of exteriorisation associated with corresponding I/not-I polarisations, the collectivisation of experience is tantamount to an interiorisation, an immanentisation, a progressive transition from reflexive and intentional forms of subjectivity to purely reflexive forms of the (w)hol(l)y spirit(ual). For instance, the external relation between local subjects such as a wasp and an orchid is an endosemiotic process immanent to the overarching jungle. The jungle is a single persona in the sense that (a) it entertains intentional relations and exchanges with its external environment (with the Spanish conquerors, with the incoming flux of sunlight, with metal and rubber prospectors, with the governments of the countries through which it extends, with the anthropologists, ethnographers, and biologists that study it from their respective standpoints) and (b) in the sense that the jungle itself is a transpersonal reflexive envelope of the different lifeforms it contains. The Hegelian comprehension of Spinozist substance as subject points toward the process through which the impersonal unconscious that religates every personal finite lifeform—the underlying *Band* beneath every subject-object correlation and every interpersonal relation—becomes a transpersonal and purely immanental subjectivity that interiorises the being-out-of-each-other of different local subjects. The ideal accomplishment of this process can be identified with the omega point in which (in Fichte's terms) '[a]ll individuals are included in the one great unity of pure spirit' (albeit understood as an 'unreachable ideal, an ultimate goal which, however, will never be actual').[157] In this sense, the Fichtean suspension and the Fichtean-Schellingean vivification of Spinozist substance is completed by its Fichtean-Hegelian immanental subjectivation. The pleroma is subsequently a life in the trinitarian sense of

157 J.G. Fichte, 'Concerning Human Dignity', in *Fichte: Early Philosophical Writings*, tr., ed. D. Breazeale (New York: Cornell University Press, 1988), 86.

that which engenders lifeforms—the mat(t)er—that which is traversed by finite experiences qua local modes of its living and, finally, in the sense that it integrates these local experiences into global self-experiences that make up the singular determination of its distributed subjectivity. The notion of pleroma qua *living and subjective phenoumenodelic insubstance* then subsumes the double transconsciousness in which all finite subjectivity is inscribed: the *unconsciousness* of impersonal life that begets us and supports us, and the *supraconsciousness* of the emerging collective subjectivity in which every finite holon participates locally. In Christian terms, the concept of life allows us to reinscribe living beings into the *trinity*, occupying the position of the finite persona in their relationship with the impersonal mat(t)er that bears them and with the Holy Spirit qua transpersonal form of subjectivity in which they take part.

In the framework of this 'refined Spinozism'[158] the (Kantian) antinomy between nature and freedom (between a rigid deterministic order that precludes any form of subjective innovation and a free subjectivity whose autonomy relies on its capacity to withdraw from or dominate the mechanistic 'natural' order) is sublated. On the one hand, the freedom of a finite form of subjectivity is not grounded on a purported self-sufficient individual capacity to choose in an autonomous manner between different possibilities, but rather on its ability to channel in a singular and unpredictable manner the force of imagination (*Einbildungskraft*) of impersonal life. 'The individual seems here almost to serve merely as a medium, only as a [singular] channel, through which that organic vibration, the formative force (the spark of life) propagates itself.'[159] Freedom does not mean here 'arbitrariness of intentions and inclinations, lack of restraint in what [is] done and left undone',[160] a causality of the will: 'the self-determination of [the human being is] its making itself unreservedly available to welcome

158 G.C. Lichtenberg, *Philosophical Writings*, tr. S. Tester (Albany, NY: SUNY Press, 2012), 100.

159 Schelling, *First Outline of a System of the Philosophy of Nature*, 41.

160 Heidegger, 'The Self-Assertion of the German University', 7.

life[161] [...] [by actively] refusing to [arbitrarily] intrude into [its] immanent rhythm [...].[162] True freedom in the sense of the most primordial self-determination is found only where a choice is no longer possible and no longer necessary. Whoever must first choose and wants to choose does not yet really know what [it] wants. [It] does not yet will primordially.[163] [...] [In this sense,] decisions are not worked out by merely talking about them but by creating situations and taking positions in which the decision is unavoidable [...].'[164] On the other hand, *natura naturans* potentiates its immanental manifestation by instituting local agents equipped with (empirical, transcendental, and speculative) degrees of freedom. These subjective degrees of freedom bear witness in the last instance to the immanental generativity of *natura naturans*, to its capacity to unpredictably diverge from any of its actual states, to span temporary autonomous zones of undetermination, to blow open imaginative gaps that disturb the sequences of causal reactions. The question of the essence of freedom is strictly speaking a religious question: only a being religated to life can act freely, since there is no freedom other than the creative freedom of life; and only a subject disligated from life can understand its for-itselfness, its capacity to take decisions, its autonomy, its purposiveness, in terms of an alleged essential difference between itself and a supposed deterministic, mechanistic, and dead 'natural' order. Schelling and Heidegger could not have expressed in a clearer manner this spellbinding Spinozist understanding of the essence of human freedom: 'As long as I myself am *identical* with Nature [as a mode of the insubstance], I understand what a living nature is as well as I understand my own life; I comprehend how this universal life of nature reveals itself in the most manifold forms, in measured developments, in gradual approximations to freedom. However, as soon as I separate myself, and with me everything ideal, from nature, nothing remains to me but a dead object, and I cease

161 Eboussi Boulaga, *Christianisme sans fétiche*, 113.

162 Hegel, *Phenomenology of Spirit*, 36.

163 M. Heidegger, *Schelling's Treatise on the Essence of Human Freedom*, tr. J. Stambaugh (Athens, OH: Ohio University Press, 1985), 154.

164 Heidegger, *What is a Thing?*, 10.

to comprehend how a *life outside me* could be possible.[165] [...] [L]anguage, understanding, mood, passion, and building, are no less a part of the overwhelming violence than sea and earth and animal. The difference is only that the latter envelop humans in their sway and sustain, beset, and inflame them, whereas what is to be named now pervades them in its sway as that which they have to take over expressly as the beings that they themselves are. This pervasive sway becomes no less overwhelming because humans take up this sway itself directly into their violence and use this violence as such. This merely conceals the uncanniness of language, of passions, as that into which human beings as historical are disposed, while it seems to them that it is they who have language and passions at their disposal. [...] The extent to which humanity is not at home in its own essence is betrayed by the opinion human beings cherish of themselves as those who have invented and who could have invented language and understanding, building and poetry. How is humanity ever supposed to have invented that which pervades it in its sway, due to which humanity itself can be as humanity in the first place? [...] The violence-doing of poetic saying, of thoughtful projection, of constructive building, of state-creating action, is not an application of faculties that the human being has, but is a disciplining and disposing of the violent forces by virtue of which beings disclose themselves as such, in so far as the human being enters into them.'[166] Finite subjective autonomy is the cunning of infinite life. The freedom and autonomy of the finite living being—far from necessarily assuming the form of an insurrection by which the subject would presume to be a self-sufficient and self-grounded last instance to the detriment of its being a finite lifeform among others and dependent on others (a subject which, 'as the extreme of the negativity that is within itself, asserts its independence to the point of evil')[167]—are the means by which the subject can singularly contribute to the realisation

165 F.W.J. Schelling, *Ideas for a Philosophy of Nature*, quoted in the translator's introduction to *First Outline of a System of the Philosophy of Nature*, tr. K.R. Peterson (Albany, NY: State University of New York Press, 2004), xx.

166 Heidegger, *Introduction to Metaphysics*, 173–75.

167 G.W.F. Hegel, *Philosophy of Mind*, tr. W. Wallace and A.V. Miller (Oxford: Clarendon Press, 2007), 265 [§568].

of the work of life. The institution of autonomous subjects is one of the ways by means of which the *natura naturans* raises its self-revelation to new powers: free autonomous agents bring forth new perspectives and unforeseeable actions. The institution of new planes of autonomy (like the logical space of axiomatic-deductive autonomy or ethico-political forms of self-determination) and the independentising of new types of subjectivity from its naturalcultural conditions of possibility are still part of the immanental naturalcultural process of self-revelation. Even the most autonomous forms of subjectivity are still probes of life and a subject that conflates its autonomy with a self-grounded self-sufficiency, a subject that mistakes its capacity to axiomatically decide the beginning of a dynamical process with a purported causa-suiness, a subject that forecloses the immanental passivity that pulses beneath its self-determined actions, a subject that does not acknowledge the contingent material process of its own institution, such a subject deepens the arche-disease of (its own) life. Any form of opposition between the mechanistic and deterministic order of nature and the purported for-itselfness of subjective autonomy—or between the *order of Being* and the *order of the Event*, or between *mythical* and *divine violence*—betrays Spinozist immanence and perpetuates a sempiternal 'bifurcation of nature'. This bifurcation can only strengthen the idea that freedom is exerted against (or as an state of exception with respect to) the nomological order of nature, thereby fostering a radicalisation of the modern disligation and the ecological crisis that goes along with it. When we open all our perceptual, affective, and conceptual senses to the spectacle of nature, to its unbelievable capacity to create lifeforms, patterns, ever-renewed forms of order, to disrupt every form of equilibrium and throw up improbable Umwelten, when we witness the inexhaustible exuberance of life, its prodigality, it becomes difficult to believe that modern humanity attempted to disentangle subjectivity from the natural order in order to try to explain and exert its alleged freedom and 'cultural' creativity. How was that possible?

Experience is said in many senses: a subject locally immersed in the phenoumenodelic field may have perceptive, affective, conceptual, interpersonal experiences. In actual experience, *percepts*, *affects*, *concepts*, and *intersubjective relations* are entangled: being-there suspended in the experiential field is *perceiving*, *feeling*, *understanding*, *being-with*, all concrescing in an impure *menstruum*. What we shall call an abstract form of experience results from a process of abstraction, i.e., from a process by means of which the subject abstracts from certain dimensions or attributes of experience in order to focus attention on a single one. In other words, a subject can selectively plug in to any of the multiple attributes of insubstance and partially bracket others. The different *abstract dimensions* of experience—abstract cuts of the concrete pleroma—that we can tune in to will be termed *affectum* (the affective field), *sensorium* (the perceptual field), *logos* (the rational field), *socius* (the political field), and *textum* (the field of signification). Speaking like Spinoza, we shall say that the *affectum*, the *sensorium*, the *logos*, the *socius*, and the *textum* are abstract *attributes* of the concrete pleroma. The pleroma is not only framed in the form of circumambient worlds by means of the operations of transcendental constitution associated with the different types of subjectivity, but can also be cut into abstract sections or attributes. In particular, the *res cogitans* (the pleroma *qua logos*) and the *res extensa* (the pleroma *qua sensorium*) are just two abstract attributes of the concrete pleroma among others. But 'why privilege the attribute [thought or extension]? In fact, there would have to be as many [modes of experience] as there are divine attributes, and there would be as many [children] of "God" as there are [modes of insubstance].'[168] The experiential field as such—that is, before its being subjected to the prismatic refraction that separates *après coup* these different dimensions or abstract attributes—is always a concrete insubstance, that is, an emotional-perceptual-conceptual-social-...-∞ concrescence of infinite attributes. The pleroma is a living flesh, the one and only *res* (the carnal 'sea of the ruby'), before its declension in *res cogitans* and *res extensa* or, more generally, before its abstract refraction into infinite attributes. The fluxion of life irrigates and enlivens the pleroma's ultra-concreteness: 'all the [living ones] dance in the red glow [of the

---

168 H. Corbin, 'Conférence de M. Henry Corbin', *École pratique des hautes études, Section des sciences religieuses, Annuaire* 84 (1975–1976), 273–78: 275.

univocal flesh] and live in it. Their blood, their life, everything is [...] in the red, in the colour. This [ocean of insubstance] is the only one. Everything [flows] in this [ocean] and everything is ruby.'[169] The living pleroma is a deliquescent rubber streaming of lights, pulsed by drives, mesmerised by the propagation of iridescent perceptual fields, rationally structured by the innervations of the *logos*, a phenoumenodelic daydream inhabited by a *socius* of experience-able (receptive) and response-able (expressive) subjective modes whose experiences (affects, percepts, concepts) are finite modes of the *affectum*, of the *sensorium*, of the *logos*, and of the other infinite attributes.

Spinoza's hyper-rationalism could not be more distant from the unidimensional forms of rationalism that hypostatise a unique attribute of the insubstance—typically the *logos*—to the detriment of the infinite other attributes. What we have called *logos* is a singular cut in an ultra-concrete experiential field that can also be explored along an infinite number of other sections, including affective strata, political fields, and aesthetic layers. The hypostasis of rational sapience—the capacity to attune to the pleroma qua *logos*—to the detriment of perceptual, affective, and social forms of X-ience lags far behind the egalitarian refraction of the concrete insubstance into infinite abstract attributes postulated by Spinoza. The genius of Spinoza was not only to have bypassed Cartesian dualism, but, more radically, to have postulated that the *res cogitans/res extensa* divide (or the culture-nature bifurcation) is nothing but one possible split of the univocal insubstance among others: 'Not only do my body and my mind [...] bathe in oceans without shores, Extension, Thought, which no caravelle will be able to circumvent. But, in the unfathomable immensity, I hear the murmuring of other seas, to infinity, other unknown seas, unnameable, inconceivable Attributes, to infinity. And all are contained in the Ocean [of Insubstance].'[170] The absolutisation of modernity depends on the recognition that the 'autonomy of reason' should not be conflated with a hypostasis of the *logos* which forgets that rationality is nothing more and nothing less than one possible way of sounding the real, that the *logos* is

169 *Heart of Glass* (1976, dir. Werner Herzog).

170 Rolland, *L'éclair de Spinoza*, 103.

one abstract attribute of the pleroma among infinite others, that science is just one form of knowledge in the generalised sense of this term.

Exploring insubstance amounts to not only mediating the limits of the prevailing Umwelt cognitively, affectively, perceptually, politically—that is, by way of the abstract attributes that are the *logos*, the *affectum*, the *sensorium*, and the *socius*—but also mining transcendental portals to other attributes, to new forms of experience besides perception, affection, cognition, and socialisation. For instance, what we could call the *textum* denotes the pleroma qua readable and writable tissue, the living insubstance experienced as a generalised semiotic process, the droning Word of life channelled and modulated by each living being in a singular manner, the attribute that the anti-Oedipians called the surface of inscription or surface of recording, the section of the experiential field that can be navigated by means of reading and inscription techniques, the abstract cut of the pleroma whose local vibrating modes are propagating 'images-signs', the univocal flow of information that can be filtered, edited, decoded, interpreted, embroidered, encrypted, translated, and broadcast by the different finite lifeforms, the semiorrhagic ocean of 'sangnifiance',[171] the 'Ocean of the Streams of Story', 'made up of a thousand thousand thousand and one different currents, each one a different colour, weaving in and out of one another like a liquid tapestry of breathtaking complexity'.[172] The speculative enhancement of the subjective capacities to attune to the *textum*—by learning new natural and formal languages, by acquiring the ability to receive, interpret, and emit different kinds of signs (symbolic, iconic, indexical, etc.), by trying to open channels of communication with lifeforms of different transcendental types (plants, animals, extraterrestrials), by learning how to knit intertextiles that engage with heterogeneous semiotic process (e.g. the language of the birds, mathematical inscriptions, dune patterns, musical notes, oneiric glyphs, symptoms, smoke wisps), by improving the subject's computational and information processing skills, by elaborating new writing techniques

171 Joyce, *Finnegans Wake*, 357.

172 S. Rushdie, *Haroun and The Sea of Stories* (London: Puffin, 2012). My thanks to Agathe Keller for having brought this text to my attention.

(e.g. choreography, cryptography, holography) and new reading techniques (e.g. deconstruction, astrology, graphology, psychoanalysis, palmistry, hermeneutics, haruspicy, etc.), by developing new communications technologies (e.g. transport and transformation of information by means of letters, chemical signals, pigeons, scents, acoustic, electromagnetic radiation, gravitational waves)—these upgradings of the subjective capacity to plug into the *textum* could be simply called generalized alphabetisation. 'Signatures of all things I am here to read.'[173]

We shall understand by *immanental phenoumenodelia*—or *pleromatica*—the properly philosophical exploration of the pleroma. The notion of *immanental phenoumenodelia* distinguishes itself in three ways from Husserl's concept of transcendental phenomenology: (a) by the incorporation of a noumenal dimension (i.e. one in excess in relation to the transcendentally constituted) in the very insubstance of pheno(u)mena (in contrast to Husserl's elimination of the Kantian concept of noumenon); (b) by its *-delic* nature (in accord with the multiple attributes of manifestation—perceptive, affective, conceptual, social), in contrast to the restrictively *-logical* (focused on the exclusively theoretical-conceptual analysis of manifestation and its conditions of possibility); and (c) by the subordination of the *transcendental constitution* of experience to an *immanental institution* of constituting subjectivity. It is worth noting here that the central concept X of this immanental phenoumenodelia is denoted by means of different expressions (*pleroma*, *phenoumenodelic insubstance*, *impersonal field of experience*, *real*, *natura naturans*, *life*) depending on the aspect that we want to emphasise in the corresponding local context. Each of these denominations is endowed with a particular context-dependent intentional attitude. In Frege's terms, these different 'names of X' emphasise different senses of the same referent. Whereas the term *pleroma* underlines the overwhelming infinite plenitude of X, the locution *phenoumenodelic insubstance* highlights that X is a univocal field of manifestation endowed with attributes (the *logos*, the *sensorium*, the *affectum*, the *socius*, the *textum*) and local modes (the phenoumena), the expression *impersonal field of experience* emphasises that X is a phenoumenodelic field

173 Joyce, *Ulysses*, 45.

not correlated to any transcendental type of subjectivity, the Lacanian denomination *real* puts the accent on the fact that X insists in the form of symptomatic impasses of the worldly 'symbolic orders', the designation *natura naturans* underscores that X envelops the spectrum of *natura naturatae* defined by the different transcendental types, and the name *life* emphasises that X is an engendering force of world-constituting lifeforms.

The task proper to philosophy as we shall understand it here is not that of constructing a theory of appearance (a phenomeno-*logic)*—a definition of philosophy that would irremediably suture it to the *understanding* as a *theoretical* faculty (thus losing the richness of the difference between philosophy and science)—but that of expanding human experience *polyphanically*, it its own concreteness, in the effective entanglement between the various abstract attributes of experience (perceptive, affective, conceptual, social). The tasks of philosophy understood as an aesthetico-politico-epistemo-religious concrescence of the various abstract forms of exploring the living pleroma are oriented by *eidetic constellations*, by dynamic figures inscribed in the supernatural skies and formed by connecting the different infinite ideas (or 'transcendentals') that guide such abstract forms of thought and practice (truth, beauty, justice, love). In the last instance—i.e., from the standpoint of the concrete insubstance—'the transcendentals are inseparable, and [...] neglecting one can only have a devastating effect on the others'.[174] We are concretists[175] and our task as philosophers is to perform (as Lenin puts it) 'concrete analyses' (we would rather say *mediations*) of 'concrete situations'.

Art, science, and politics (among other possible practices for the expansion of experience) operate differential transgressions of the transcendental limits of human experience by stalking the trans-umweltic interzones of the pleroma along the corresponding abstract attributes. Of course, 'there can be no objection to the procedure' of focusing on a single attribute by abstracting from the others, 'provided that we remember

174 H.U. von Balthasar, *The Glory of the Lord: A Theological Aesthetics. I. Seeing the Form*, tr. E. Leiva-Merikakis (San Francisco: Ignatius Press, 2009), 11.

175 De Andrade, 'Cannibalist Manifesto', 43.

what we are doing'.[176] In this sense, 'philosophy is the criticism of abstractions which govern special modes of thought.[177] [...] Its function is the double one, first of harmonising them by assigning to them their right relative status of abstractions, and secondly of completing them by direct comparison with more concrete intuitions of the universe, and thereby promoting the formation of more complete schemes of thought.'[178] We understand here by philosophy a glass-beadic organon of exploration of the experiential field capable of composing the different abstract sounding lines of mediation that are art, science, and politics (among others); for 'is the life of a thinking[, feeling, and perceiving philosopher] anything other than a constant [...] symphilosoph[ical]'[179] activity intended to tune in to, mediate and compose as many attributes of the living insubstance as possible? The concrete character of the experiential field is at the base of the following division of labour among the different forms of thought and practice: whereas the abstract forms of thought and practice such as art, science, and politics focus on a particular abstract attribute of experience in order to sublate the corresponding limits, philosophy aims to overcome the transcendental limits of experience *by addressing experience in its full concreteness* (in its philosophical *stonedness*), i.e. without performing a prismatic decomposition into abstract attributes. The general programme of constructing this concrete organon of mediation is (according to the definition that we are proposing) broader in amplitude than the restricted attempts to perform transversal compositions internal to each abstract form of thought and practice such as, for instance, interdisciplinary collaborations between different sciences, or multimedia integrations of different artistic practices. The concrete symphilosophical organon, far from providing an overarching position capable of totalising the abstract forms of thought and practice, acts horizontally,

176 A.N. Whitehead, *Modes of Thought* (Cambridge: Cambridge University Press, 1938), 10.

177 Ibid., 48–9.

178 A.N. Whitehead, *Science and the Modern World* (London: MacMillan, 1925), 87.

179 F. Schlegel, *Characteristiken und Kritiken I (1796–1801)* (Munich: Ferdinand Schöningh, 1967), [20].

attempting to locally synthetise abstract procedures of exploration into concrete mediators. Far from occupying a position of domination—and far from believing that the multiplicity of abstract forms of thought and practice could be the object of any totalisation whatsoever—philosophy has to defect from its supposed self-sufficiency and humbly submit itself to the irreducible sovereignty and multiplicity of these abstract modes of thought and practice.

The definition of philosophy as an organon of concrete composition requires absolving philosophy from what Badiou called the 'sutures' between philosophy and these abstract forms of exploration, such as for instance the suture between philosophy and science (e.g. Husserl), the suture between philosophy and art (e.g. Heidegger and Henry), or the suture between philosophy and ethics (e.g. Levinas).[180] Philosophy shares with the abstract forms of sounding the pleroma their vocation to transgress the (empirical and transcendental) limits of human experience, but it must counterbalance their inherent tendency to abstraction, to depart from the concreteness of the experiential field in order to focus on a single abstract attribute. By composing affective, conceptual, existential, and political vectors of mediation of the corresponding Umwelt, philosophy can be understood as a higher form of synaesthetic exploration directly plugged into the concrete pleroma as such. Philosophy enriches the trans-umweltic directionality of the different abstract exploratory vectors with degrees of freedom that are transversal to the different attributes. The multi-attribute vocation of such a symphilosophical organon implies that it should not establish any privileged identification with any abstract mode of experience, be it art, science, or politics. No abstract form of exploration can claim to occupy a privileged position in the philosophical space of compossibility, an overarching position from which it could subordinate or dominate the other modes. In particular, science is nothing but one particular modality of experience, a mode of experience which, by being attuned to the *logos*, focuses on the expansion of conceptual and techno-perceptual experience.

---

180 Cf. A. Badiou, *Manifesto for Philosophy*, tr. N. Madarasz (Albany, NY: SUNY Press, 1999).

As such, science is a precious ingredient in philosophical composition. However, any form of identification between science and philosophy, any attempt to understand philosophy as a science of sciences, as a first or 'rigorous' science (Husserl), or any definition of philosophy as a *theoretical* mode of thought that would allow us to sublate the supposed (transcendental, ontic, representational, etc.) limits of science is a betrayal of the trans-attribute nature of philosophical exploration. 'The mystery of life isn't a [theoretical] problem to solve [by biologists or cosmologists], but a [concrete revelation] to experience'—to unfold, to channel, to potentialise, to transmute, to refract, to modulate—by perceiving, feeling, building, playing, understanding, loving, making kin, cooking, breathing.[181] Philosophy moves upstream with respect to the refraction of the concrete pleroma into different abstract attributes in order to address the being-there of humanity in the midst of the phenoumenodelic revelation in its absolute ultra-concreteness. But it is not the task of philosophy to conceptually understand the *logos* that inheres the experiential field or to restrictively expand the scope of human understanding. The task of not ceding the desire to understand the rational structure of the experiential field—whether at the ontic, ontological, or transcendental level—is the defining prerogative of science. Of course, this characterisation of science presupposes an open definition so that it can include among its infinite tasks the reflection on its conditions of possibility, on its transcendental limitations, and on its speculative capacities: we shall understand by science '[T]he projective compactification of the successive [speculative] extensions of [humans' rational capacities (methods, concepts, aprioristic structures)] required by [the] infinite regulative idea [of truth]'.[182]

The philosophical concept of pleroma does not presuppose any theoretical thesis on the ultimate nature of the 'real'. The theoretical study of the experiential field—its conceptualisation, its rationalisation, the

---

181 F. Herbert, *Dune* (London: Penguin, 2003), 35.

182 G. Catren, 'Outland Empire: Prolegomena to Speculative Absolutism', in L. Bryant, N. Srnicek, and G. Harman (eds.), *The Speculative Turn: Continental Materialism and Realism* (Melbourne: Re.press, 2011), 345.

intersubjective attunement to the *logos*, the institution of new transcendental forms of cognition—defines the infinite tasks of science as an abstract mode of thought. The pleroma is a non-theoretical phenoumenodelic concept that subsumes the different ways in which the field of experience overflows the actual and possible experiences of every finite subject: the phenomenological excess of every Umwelt with respect to the effective experience of an empirical subject (always new adumbrations and receding horizons!), the phenoumenodelic excess of experience with respect to any transcendental-dependent Umwelt (always new worlds!), the excess of the concrete pleroma with respect to the limited numbers of attributes that are accessible to a finite lifeform (always new possible ways of plugging into the concrete experiential field!), the underlying impersonality of life that engenders, bears, and irrigates individual persons (always new forms of incorporating and transmuting the narcotic spice, the force of imagination that enlivens!), the overarching transpersonal nature of the higher forms of collective subjectivity we are locally a part of (always new tribes!). The pleroma denotes the experiential field in which impersonal, personal, and transpersonal forms of experience interfuse and through which all local subjective forms navigate, the horizon of experiential horizons in which a finite form of subjectivity can expand its experience, opening the doors of perception, of affection, of conceptualisation, of socialisation, mediating the transcendental limits defined by its transcendental type, deepening its religation with the impersonal life that it incarnates locally, putting its finite life at the service of the tribal concertation of the living, of the wholly spiritual.

Any reduction of the pleroma to one of its abstract attributes to the detriment of the others falls into what Whitehead calls the *fallacy of misplaced concreteness*. In particular, neither phenoumenodelic insubstance in its own concreteness nor its finite modes can be thought of reductively in terms of the purely physical 'mechanics' of a 'material substance'. Only by abstracting from an infinite number of attributes is it possible to understand insubstance in restrictively 'material' terms (in the physicalist sense of the term) and perceptual, affective, intellective and normative dimensions of experience merely as derivative epiphenomenal superstructures. At the same time, being able to relate to the pleroma by means of the scientific mode of thought in no way reduces the possibility of attuning oneself to other attributes of the pleroma and deploying the experience of it through other means, be they artistic, political, or religious. The inability to assert this forcibly concrete character of the experiential field is at the root of most of the so-called 'romantic' critiques of science, according to which science reduces 'the colour and shine of the things themselves, beyond waves of light and nerve currents—the green of the leaf and the gold of the cornfield, the black of the crow and the gray of the sky. The relation to all this is not only there as well but must also constantly be presupposed as that which physiological-physical inquiry immediately shatters and reinterprets [...].[183] [T]hese colours and these forms are constitutive of the being of nature, because real nature is sensible nature and not the universe of idealities that science substitutes for it in its constructions and theories.'[184] This criticism proceeds as if phenoumenodelic insubstance were not capable of manifesting itself according to an open multiplicity of possible attributes, as if the richness of experience were not amplified with the subjective capacity to hold together its multiple attributes, as if it were not possible to inform new organs capable of tuning into new attributes. It is quite true that 'the scientific world is only an abstraction',[185] but this does not make the other modalities of experience (perceptual, affective, political) any less abstract themselves. Concreteness is not the province of a certain mode of experience (theoretical, aesthetic, political), thereby excluding the others: all these modes are only abstract attributes of the concrete phenoumenodelic insubstance. 'The terms *morality*, *logic*, *religion*, *art*, have each of them been claimed as exhausting the whole meaning of importance. Each of them denotes [an abstract attribute]. But the [insubstance] stretches beyond any finite group of [attributes]. There are [attributes] of the [pleroma] to which morality is irrelevant, to which logic

183 Heidegger, *What is a Thing?*, 144.

184 Henry, *La barbarie*, 46.

185 Ibid., 65.

is irrelevant, to which religion is irrelevant, to which art is irrelevant. By this false limitation the activity expressing the ultimate aim infused into the [living] process of nature has been trivialised into the guardianship of mores, or of rules of thought, or of mystic sentiment, or of aesthetic enjoyment. No one of these specialisations exhausts the final unity of purpose in the [immanental life].'[186] The modes of experience associated with the scientific, aesthetic, affective, and political apprehensions of the pleroma, far from competing to name the ultimate essence of the pleroma, can very well coexist, in accordance and harmonious interference, within a projectively concrete experience. Instead of hypostasising one attribute (and the corresponding way of experiencing) at the expense of the others, it is a matter of recognising and exploring the richness of the pleroma in the phenoumenodelic concrescence of its infinite attributes. We could say that 'we are instinctively willing to believe that with due attention, more can be found' in the concrete phenoumenodelic pleroma—more attributes, different objectivations of the same phenoumena, new forms of experiential depth, new empirical and transcendental perspectives, new worlds, new histories—than is experienced at first sight. 'But we shall not be content with less',[187] for example with one-sided scientism to the detriment of aesthetical experience and ethico-political normativity (or any other permutation of this hierarchy), with particular kinds of 'validity claims' to the detriment of others, with a single perspectival vision to the detriment of multi-ocular and synaesthetic experience, with mono-narratives to the detriment of multi-perspectival narratives, with multiversal relativism to the detriment of concrete universality, with X-centric descriptions (where X stands for ego-, ethno-, anthropo-, geo-, world-) to the detriment of integrated standpoints.

In particular, we can provide a new meaning to the expression *philosophy of X* (as in *philosophy of art* or *philosophy of science*): the application of the philosophical organon to any abstract form of exploration requires that the latter be addressed in its full concreteness. Even if a form of exploration is oriented by a particular interest of reason (theoretical, aesthetic, political),

186 Whitehead, *Modes of Thought*, 2.

187 A.N. Whitehead, *The Concept of Nature* (New York: Dover, 2004), 29.

this does not eliminate the fact that it is a concrete human activity endowed with a multi-attribute transversality. For instance, mathematics is oriented by a theoretical goal, namely, to expand our rational comprehension of formal—e.g. geometrical, algebraic, arithmetical, etc.—structures. But mathematics is also a concrete human activity undertaken by concrete human beings embedded in a concrete experiential field, and therefore an activity necessarily endowed with aesthetic, political, and affective dimensions. And these dimensions open communicating vessels that discretely connect mathematics to the other abstract forms of exploration such as arts and politics. Hence the expression *philosophy of X* does not mean that X is itself considered an object of a theoretical meta-discipline—e.g., epistemology, aesthetics, etc. (in this sense, as Althusser claimed, philosophy has no object),[188] but rather an activity intended to reinsert an abstract form of exploration into the concreteness of its effective practice, thereby opening it up to possible alliances with other forms of exploration, alliances that might finally compose concrete mediators of the limits of experience. This philosophical reinsertion of an abstract sounding line of exploration into the concrete experiential field should counteract what we could call the pathologies of abstraction, that is, the tendency to hypostasise or isolate a mode of exploration by forgetting its intertwining and its dependency with respect to the other modalities (e.g., the dependency of scientific inquiry, even in its purest form, upon politics).[189]

---

188 L. Althusser, 'Lenin and Philosophy', in *Lenin and Philosophy and Other Essays*, tr. B. Brewster (New York and London: Monthly Review Press, 2001), 23–70: 34.

189 Describing his career as a mathematician and the associated *pathologies of abstraction*, Grothendieck writes: 'In fact, up until now, the activity, the life that I've lived, I considered it worth living. I had a certain sense of fulfilment which satisfied me. Now, in retrospect, I see my past life in a very different light, in the sense that I realise that this fulfilment was at the same time a mutilation. Indeed, it is an extremely intense activity, but one that is directed excessively narrowly, in such a way that all the other possibilities of a person's development are not affected. [...] [An] integration of our different cognitive faculties, of our faculties of knowledge is truly lacking in the dominant, Western scientific practice. [...] we do our utmost to separate at all costs the purely rational faculties from the rest of our possibilities

Rather than trying to specify its particular tasks (e.g. thinking 'being qua being', performing a transcendental deduction of categories, proposing an ultimate 'theory of everything', circumventing the subject-object correlation, and so on), choosing its favourite attribute (the *logos*, the *socius*) and accordingly selecting a singular regulative idea (e.g. the truth, the good), privileging a national language (English, German, Greek), delimiting its subjective profile (the philosopher, the professor, the thinker, the historian), clarifying its method (e.g. analytic, (de)constructive, *more geometrico*, critically reflexive, hermeneutical), resolving the 'conflict of the faculties' by carefully defining the perimeter of the philosophy department in the architecture of the university, philosophy, as we understand it here, has to indulge in a transversal mixture of rhetorical genres (e.g. argumentative, poetic, formal, imperative, performative), a diagonalisation of subjective profiles (e.g. the scientist, the artist, the militant, the healer, the educator, the monk, the analyst, the student, the historian, the technician), and a patchwork of media and procedures. Philosophy's task is to place itself at the focal point of ultra-concreteness from which human existence radiates, throughout all worldly cultures—their sciences, their mythologies, their religions, their arts, their politics, their metaphysics and their ontologies, their literatures, their social structures, their techniques, their rituals—and to start digging, to perform concrete mediations of human's concrete being-there, in the midst of the phenoumenodelic flood, among other lifeforms. Philosophy, as we understand it here, is the speculative and experimental organon of the concrete mediation of humankind's Umwelt, an organon thanks to which we, human beings, can face and explore the absolute unknown into which we are 'thrown' in the full multi-attribute concreteness of our existence, as a singular sapient, sentient, social, and

---

of knowledge. [...] Among the distinctive features of this scientific practice, there is an initiatory gesture which is the strict separation of our rational faculties from other modes of knowledge. Thus, an instinctive distrust of all that is, let's say, emotional, of all knowledge that is philosophical, religious, of all ethical considerations, of all that is felt, sensory, direct' (Grothendieck, 'Allons-nous continuer la recherche scientifique?').

spiritual form of life that acknowledges and deepens the ultimate living mystery of its existential situation.

Let us now consider in more detail the transcendental motif initiated by Kant. To do so, we shall start with one of the most elementary phenomenological facts, namely that the experience of a finite subject is always *perspectival.* This means that a finite subject only has access to viewpoint-dependent aspects of phenomena. We could then say that experience is always 'correlated' to the state of the subject of experience. This *empirical perspectivism* of experience is closely linked to the fact that the different forms of experience take place in *extensions* with respect to which every possible subject is always in a particular (possibly changing) *state.* In the case of perceptual experience, the state of the perceiving subject is given by its spatiotemporal position and its state of motion; in the case of political experience, we could say following Bourdieu, that the state of the political subject is given by its position in the corresponding political 'field'.[190]

According to the infinite regulative idea of science, scientific knowledge has to be *objective* or *intersubjective*, that is to say valid for any subject, independently of its particular state. Science is supposed to provide *perspectiveless descriptions* and *state-independent* conceptualisations of the field of experience—what we could call a 'view from nowhere' (Nagel), a 'viewpoint of no-one in particular' (Eddington), or an 'absolute conception' (Williams).[191] But how might we venture beyond the empirical perspectivism of experience and construct subject-independent descriptions and explanations of different natural phenomena? Is not the subject of experience condemned to an insurmountable relativism? The answer is (at least formally) simple:

190 Cf. P. Bourdieu, 'The Political Field, the Social Science Field and the Journalistic Field', in R. Benson and E. Neveu (eds.), *Bourdieu and The Journalistic Field* (Cambridge: Polity, 2005), 30.

191 Cf. T. Nagel, *The View From Nowhere* (Oxford: Oxford University Press, 1986), A. Eddington, *Space, Time and Gravitation* (Cambridge: Cambridge University Press, 1921), and B. Williams, *Descartes: The Project of Pure Enquiry* [1978] (Oxford: Routledge, 2005).

there is a well-defined operation that renders the transition from empirical perspectivism to objectivity possible, namely the operation that consists in *performing variations of the empirical standpoint of observation*. According to the *invariantist* conception of *objectivity*, we can call *objective* all the features of the phenomenon at stake that do not change when the subject changes its observational point of view (or the coordinate system used to describe the phenomenon), that is to say the so-called *invariants*.[192] By definition, invariants provide a perspective-independent (or coordinate-independent) description of the corresponding phenomenon. The invariantist conception of scientific objectivity finds its philosophical prehistory in the Aristotelian conception of *substance* understood as the invariant substrate that supports accidental changes (where the transformation of the perspectival standpoint of observation is given by the temporal evolution of the subject's state) and—at the other extreme of Western intellectual history—plays a central role in the post-relativistic description of fundamental physical interactions provided by so-called gauge theories.[193]

The invariantist conception of objectivity—important and useful as it is—is limited by the fact that it discards as inessential everything that changes, that is, all features that are perspective-dependent. In privileging endurance to the detriment of (both spatial and temporal) change, the invariantist stance only half satisfies Whitehead's dictum: 'Every scheme for the analysis of nature has to face these two facts, change and endurance.'[194] Yet those

192 Cf. T. Debs and M. Redhead, *Objectivity, Invariance, and Convention: Symmetry in Physics* (Cambridge, MA: Harvard University Press, 2007) and R. Nozick, 'Invariance and Objectivity', *Proceedings and Addresses of the American Philosophical Association* 72:2 (1998): 21–48.

193 The geometric description of the fundamental forces of nature in contemporary physics (that is, the gravitational, electromagnetic, and nuclear interactions) strongly relies on the notions of *gauge symmetry* and *gauge invariants*. In these theories, the intrinsic properties of the physical system at stake—that is, the so-called *observables*—have to fulfil the constraint of being *gauge invariants* under the so-called gauge transformations that encode the local (that is, spacetime-dependent) symmetries of the theory.

194 Whitehead, *Science and the Modern World*, 88.

aspects that change are not mere discardable perspectival representations: they also form part of the intrinsic structure of the phenomenon in question. The perspectivism inherent to experience is the subjective counterpart of the multifaceted character of the objects of experience, that is, of the fact that the phenomenalisation of an object is always already refracted into a spectrum of profiles, sketches, faces, or adumbrations. The variation of the subjective standpoint of observation gives access to a form of variation—namely, the variation between the object's different adumbrations—that belongs to the intrinsic structure of the object being observed: 'The point will be raised that the object is given to me according to a certain aspect, a certain profile, depending on the point of view it is observed from. But this is not a sign of the object's dependency. On the contrary, it is the manifestation of its total objectivity.[195] [...] Perspectivism, or scientific relativism, is never relative to a subject: it constitutes not a relativity of truth but, on the contrary, a truth of the relative.[196] [...] A needed relation exists between variation and point of view: not simply because of the variety of points of view [...] but in the first place because every point of view is a point of view on variation. The point of view is not what varies with the subject, at least in the first instance; it is, to the contrary, the condition in which an eventual subject apprehends [an intrinsic] variation. [...] [P]erspectivism amounts to a relativism, but not the relativism we take for granted. It is not a variation of truth according to the subject, but the condition in which the truth of a variation appears to the subject.[197] [E]ach Dublin [e.g. Stephen's Dublin, Mr. Bloom's Dublin, Molly's Dublin] is equally [and one-sidedly] real: that is the essence of the Relativity Revolution.'[198] In Fregean terms, we could say that any *referent* (e.g. Venus), far from being given as such

---

195 G. Deleuze, 'Mathesis, Science and Philosophy', in R. Mackay (ed.), *Collapse III: Unknown Deleuze* (Falmouth: Urbanomic, 2007), 141–55.

196 Deleuze and Guattari, *What is Philosophy?*, 130.

197 G. Deleuze, *The Fold: Leibniz and the Baroque*, tr. T. Conley (London: Athlone, 1993), 20.

198 R.A. Wilson, Introduction to I. Regardie, *The Eye in the Triangle: An Interpretation of Aleister Crowley, XII* (Tempe, AZ: New Falcon Publications, 1997).

in the subject's experience, appears under the form of different one-sided *senses* or *modes of presentation* (e.g. the morning star, the evening star) which depend on the subject's state. The existence of a precise correlation between the transformations of the state of the subject and the adumbrations of the object observed by the subject—together with the fact that the same effect can also be obtained by keeping the observer fixed and acting upon the object in a precise manner—undermines the thesis that the variants are merely subjective representations devoid of any relevant information about the object as such.[199] Moreover, the very notion of invariance is always relative to a particular group of variations: what is invariant with respect to a certain group of transformations may vary when considering other transformations.[200]

A *phenomenologically informed conception of objectivity* relies on the definition of an object as a *multifaceted structure* that *integrates* a number of different perspectival or one-sided adumbrations. While the invariantist conception of objectivity proceeds by *neutralising* perspectives, this enhanced conception *integrates* the perspectives. In general, scientific understanding does not uniquely proceed by trying to identify objective invariants, but also by varying the groups of transformations with respect to which these

199 For example, the number observed by a subject looking at a die certainly depends on the relative position between the die and the subject. But one cannot conclude that the observation of such a variant provides only dispensable information about the observed object. Indeed, it is in the very nature of the die to be a multifaceted structure, each side of which presents a certain number that can only be observed from certain relative positions.

200 This point has been emphasised in particular by Merleau-Ponty ('In order to pass [...] to the essences, it is necessary for me to actively intervene, to vary the things [...] It is from this test that the essence emerges—it is therefore not a positive being. It is an in-variant [...] and the solidity, the essentiality of the essence is exactly measured by the power we have to vary the thing.' Merleau-Ponty, *The Visible and the Invisible*, 111) and by Nozick ('The notion of invariance under transformations cannot [without further supplementation] be a complete criterion of the objectivity of facts, for its application depends upon a selection of which transformations something is to be invariant under.' R. Nozick, 'Invariance and Objectivity', *Proceedings and Addresses of the American Philosophical Association* 72: 2 [1998]: 21–48).

invariants are defined (e.g. Klein's Erlangen Program), by integrating variants into multifaceted sheaf-theoretic structures, by exposing the variancy of purported invariants (for instance, the existence and the precise articulation of the nature-culture divide, far from being an ethnological invariant, was shown to be dependent on the ethnological group at stake), by showing that certain features can be both variants—with respect to a slow time scale—and invariants—with respect to a fast time scale—(for instance, forest variables can be treated as constants when studying the fast-time evolution of a population of insects),[201] by exploring the horizon of possible variations, transformations or deformations of a given germinal structure, and (as we shall see) by passing from empirical variations of the subject's state to transcendental variations of its subjective type (that is, by passing from 'variations *in* imagination' to 'variation *of* imagination' as Viveiros de Castro puts it).[202]

As far as human beings are concerned, not only do they have sense organs that allow them to perceive the profiles of an object, along with motor faculties that allow them to vary their empirical state (thereby enabling them to observe different profiles), but they also have a brain allowing them to *integrate* the different profiles into a single multifaceted object. These integrations make it possible to overcome potential incompatibilities between different perspectival experiences by opening up a compatibilising *experiential depth.* For instance, the propositions 'the die is green' and 'the die is red' can be made compatible in the proposition 'the (three-dimensional) die has a red (two-dimensional) side and a green (two-dimensional) side'. By performing variations—by assuming different subjective viewpoints on the object at stake in the corresponding extension—we can *integrate* a multiplicity of adumbrations, *constitute* the corresponding multifaceted

---

201 S.H. Strogatz, *Nonlinear Dynamics and Chaos: With Applications to Physics, Biology, Chemistry, and Engineering* (New York: Perseus Books, 1994), 73 [Sect. 3.7].

202 E. Viveiros de Castro, 'Metaphysics as Mitophysics. Or, Why I Have Always Been an Anthropologist', in P. Charbonnier, G. Salmon, and P. Skafish (eds.), *Comparative Metaphysics: Ontology After Anthropology* (New York: Rowman & Littlefield, 2017), 257.

object, and identify the *objective properties* that remain invariant under these variations (properties that can then be used to describe the object in a subject-independent manner). In this way, what we might term the method of empirical variations of the subjective standpoint of observation allows us (at least projectively) to pass from the perspective-dependence of subjective experience to the multifaceted nature of objective phenomena endowed with invariant properties.

Perspectival and objective experiences are pronominally indexed by the first and the third person respectively, and we could say that these two kinds of experience define the realms of phenomenology and scientific naturalism. Even if—for instance—neurobiology undermined the ontological primacy of first-person experience by showing that selfhood can be reduced to a phenomenal construction resulting from neurocomputational processes (a 'phenomenal self-model' embedded in the wider reality-model, in Metzinger's terms), this uncanny enhancement of scientific objectification would not compromise the phenomenological fact that human experience also continues to take place from an incarnated first-person perspective endowed with different kinds of degrees of freedom and having access to attributes of the pleroma others than the *logos* (for instance, the *affectum*, whose modes are not objective configurations). There is no objective knowledge without an incarnated life that supports it; there is no objective body (*Körper*) without a living flesh (*Leib*); there is no projective 'view from nowhere', no third-person perspective, no intersubjective 'space of reasons' without existing finite subjects embedded in a concrete lifeworld that they can experience through percepts, affects, concepts, sociolepts ; there is no 'scientific image' without the subjective capacity to freely and responsibly subject itself to the prescriptions posited by the infinite regulative idea of truth.[203] Rather than trying to reduce the open multiplicity of forms of

203 In Brassier-with-Sellars's terms, 'The manifest image is indispensable in so far as it provides the structure within which we exercise our capacity for rational thought. [...] The manifest image remains indispensable because it provides us with the necessary conceptual resources we require in order to make sense of ourselves as *persons*, that is to say, concept-governed creatures continually engaged in giving

experience to a purportedly privileged one (first-person perspective for phenomenologists, third-person perspective for neurobiologists), the challenge is for us to acknowledge and to understand both the interdependency and the relative autonomy between these forms of experience and to train our ability to circulate between them and to integrate them into higher forms of personhood. In particular, the sharp opposition between first-person and third-person standpoints has to be dialectically sublated: whereas first-person perspectives are themselves the result of internal integrations (e.g. binocular vision), third-person standpoints (like those produced by scientific intersubjectivity) also define, as Kant pointed out, higher forms of (transcendental) perspectivism. The alleged 'view from nowhere' is at best a regulative idea for scientific inquiry: the concomitant institution of intersubjective, multi-centred, or nemocentric forms of cognition produces new subjective types that can be classified according to the locality that they occupy (and the perspective that they embody) in the speculative landscape. Life does not unfold by simply transcending first-person perspectives, but rather by concertating individuals into higher forms of collective subjectivity *which are themselves endowed with higher first-person perspectives*. Reciprocally, the phenoumenodelia of spirit does not unfold from an purported ultimate ground to which every possible form of spirit should be reconducted (like an intersubjective space of norms and rules, the 'immediate' givenness of

and asking for reasons. [...] [I]t renders us susceptible to the force of reasons. It is the medium for the normative commitments that underwrite our ability to change our minds about things, to revise our beliefs in the face of new evidence and correct our understanding when confronted with a superior argument. In this regard, science itself grows out of the manifest image precisely in so far as it constitutes a *self-correcting* enterprise. [...] The rational compunction enshrined in the manifest image is the source of our ability to continually revise our beliefs, and this revisability has proven crucial in facilitating the ongoing expansion of the scientific image. [...] [S]cience cannot lead us to abandon our manifest self-conception as rationally responsible agents, since to do so would be to abandon the source of the imperative to revise. It is our manifest self-understanding as persons that furnishes us, qua community of rational agents, with the ultimate horizon of rational purposiveness with regard to which we are motivated to try to understand the world.' Brassier, 'The View from Nowhere', 8–9.

sensuous experience, any alleged form of 'immediate intuition', or a given concrete lifeworld). Life continuously takes off from its planes of alleged givenness by instituting new types of subjectivity, new degrees of freedom, new beginnings, new forms of autonomy, new forms of indetermination, new strata regulated by its own rules and norms, new kinds of immanental transcendence.

It is worth noting that integrations similar to those operative in the constitution of an object from its multiple adumbrations are already performed at the level of the perspectival experience of a situated subject. Every perspectival experience, however situated it may be, is already the result of an integration of infra-perspectives. Strictly speaking, perspectives are not indexed by 'viewpoints', but rather by 'viewzones' which, as we shall see, can be subject to a topological calculus (that is, to a calculus based on the operations of intersection and union acting on the different zones and satisfying a distributivity condition). For instance, human visual experience, relying on a binocular optical system, does not take place from a well-defined focal point of observation. The neurological integration of the different signals transmitted by each eye (which are located in slightly different spatial positions) induces a particular form of *depth perception* that yields three-dimensionality. In other words, the three-dimensional nature of human visual experience results from the binocular character of the human visual system, that is, from the integration of different (albeit partially similar) visual perspectives.[204] In this way, every experience is

204 Regarding 'the genesis of information of new logical type out of the juxtaposing of multiple descriptions', Bateson writes: 'The binocular image, which appears to be undivided, is in fact a complex synthesis of information from the left front in the right brain and a corresponding synthesis of material from the right front in the left brain. Later these two synthesized aggregates of information are themselves synthesized into a single subjective picture from which all traces of the vertical boundary have disappeared. From this elaborate arrangement [...] information about depth is created. In more formal language, the *difference* between the information provided by the one retina and that provided by the other is itself information of a *different logical type*. From this new sort of information, the seer adds an extra *dimension* to seeing. [...] In principle, extra "depth" in some metaphoric sense

at the same time the result of an integration of infra-perspectives and a perspectival experience susceptible to being integrated into other experiences of a greater degree of experiential depth.

By changing its state in the corresponding extension and by integrating the resulting multiplicity of perspectival experiences, a subject excavates a particular form of experiential depth, thereby adding another dimension to its phenomenological horizon. In other words, the transition from a multiplicity of situated visions to a single integrated and partially delocalised vision allows the experiential field to be deepened through an increase in dimensionality. In this sense, the experiential field cannot be understood as a sort of space endowed with a well-defined number of dimensions. Empirical subjects instantiating different transcendental types (characterised, for instance, by different perceptual, motor, and neurological capacities) constitute horizons of transcendent experience endowed with different degrees of experiential depth. Depending on its transcendental and speculative resources, a subject can open up ever deeper zones of the experiential field and launch exploratory probes into the corresponding trenches. We can certainly transcend the perspectival limitations associated to the fact that we are always *there* in some form of empirical extension by changing our state. But rather than transporting us out of the experiential field toward a supposed aperspectival outside, these variations bring about a deepening of the field itself, an enhancement of the field through the opening up of new internal dimensions. In this sense, the experiential field can be thought of as an *immanental field*: the vectors of (perceptual,

---

is to be expected whenever the information for the two descriptions is differently collected or differently coded.' G. Bateson, *Mind and Nature: A Necessary Unit* (New York: E.P. Dutton, 1979), 69–70. As Bateson emphasises further on, the translation between different languages (such as the language of *geometry* and language of *algebra* in the example he proposes) also provides a further "enlightenment" of the experiential field (ibid., 73–75). It is worth noting that Bateson's analysis joins Benjamin's conception of translation: the translation between different languages should not be understood as a prosthetic artefact intended to cope with a post-Babelian fall, but rather as an integration of linguistic perspectives by means of which we can mine new forms of linguistic depth.

affective, conceptual, and social) transcendence fired out by the subject's transcendental resources do not transcend the experiential field itself, but rather deepen the subject's immersion in the field. Rather than constituting an 'outside' that stands in a relationship of radical exteriority with respect to the experiential field, all transcendence is a new form of depth internal to the field itself.

Whereas the perspectival differences that yield the three-dimensional character of binocular vision are already embodied in the physiological structure of a single individual, other forms of depth can be mined by using the motor, conceptual, and neurological faculties of the subject to vary its viewpoint and integrate the resulting experiences. In particular, we could understand scientific objectivity as a form of experience characterised by a certain form of depth-perception resulting from the particular kind of variations and intersubjective integrations used in scientific (theoretical and experimental) practice. Rather than leaving behind the effective field of experience in order to reach a supposed realm of abstract idealities, objective knowledge deepens the experiential field itself, enhancing its experiential resources by means of the production of scientific descriptions and conceptualisations. Rather than *diminishing* the experiential field by only retaining the corresponding ideal abstractions, scientific objectivity enriches the field by *adding* scientific experience.[205] Scientific objectivity and the concomitant triggering of modes of the experiential insubstance that underwrite scientific sapience do not introduce a discontinuity with 'immediate' sentience, but simply mine different forms of depth within the experiential field itself. Thinking is also a manner of sinking into the experiential stream.

---

205 As James writes: 'That function [of abstract concepts] is of course to enlarge mentally our momentary experiences by *adding* to them the consequences conceived; but unfortunately, that function is not only too often forgotten by philosophers in their reasonings, but is often converted into its exact opposite, and made a means of diminishing the original experience by *denying* (implicitly or explicitly) all its features save the one specially abstracted to conceive it by.' W. James, *The Meaning of Truth* (New York: Longman Green and Co., 1911), 248.

To summarise, we could say that the constitution of multifaceted phenomena is based on sequences made up of *sensible reception* (of empirical adumbrations), *variation* (of the subjective viewpoint), and *integration* (of the different adumbrations indexed by these viewpoints into a single experience). The subjective capacity to deploy *reception-variation-integration* sequences can be understood as a sort of drilling machine that endows the experiential field with new forms of experiential depth. In particular, the systematic variations of the subjective standpoints of observation (or, equivalently, of the coordinate systems used to describe the corresponding phenomena) makes possible the transition that grounds the objectivity (or the intersubjective character) of scientific representation, namely the transition from (perspectival) *subjective representations* to (multifaceted) *objective phenomena*. Now, as we said before, the notion of invariant is always relative to a particular group of variations. In particular, we could say that the scientific method makes it possible to identify invariants defined in relation to the group of transformations of the empirical state of a subject of human type. But the experience of a phenomenon depends not only on the spatiotemporal position and state of movement of such a subject, but also on what we shall call its *transcendental type of subjectivity*, that is, its physiological, linguistic, conceptual, technological faculties, and so on. In other words, scientific descriptions of natural phenomena, even if they no longer depend upon the contingent spatiotemporal state of the subject of experience, still depend upon the *transcendental structures* that make human experience (and in particular human cognition) possible. Kant's fundamental stance is that the scientific objectivity made possible by the effectuation of variations of the empirical state of a human subject is not universal enough: science remains all too human, and scientific objectivism should not be conflated with unrestricted universality. Far from making possible an unconditioned apprehension of the *logos* that inheres the pleroma, 'science is the scheme of physical laws which, with unexpressed presuppositions, expresses the patterns of perspective as observed by average human beings'[206] that share certain physiological, cognitive, linguistic, and technological resources.

206 Whitehead, *Modes of Thought*, 11.

It follows that '[w]e can get from the thing in itself, the *Ding an sich*, only such information as a few of its immanent differentiations will allow our sense organs[, categories,] and scientific instruments to pick up.'[207]

Here, holding to the spirit rather than the letter of Kant's text—a spirit that has been enriched by more than two centuries of developments, interpretations, refinements, relativisations, naturalisations, and historicisations of his foundational stance—we shall understand by 'transcendental structure' any structure which (while itself, in general, remaining 'invisible') plays a role in the constitution of subjective experience—such as, for instance, the 'genetically-programmed hard wiring' (Wilson)[208] associated with our naturally evolved physiological structures (e.g. the perceptual-motor system, the neurological system), technological prostheses to human physiology (e.g. telescopes, microscopes, computers, etc.),[209] the categorical resources of human understanding, linguistic and discursive frameworks (Carnap)[210] or 'discursive formations' (Foucault), contextual forms of aprioricity (Putnam),[211] statements distant from the 'experiential periphery' of the field of knowledge or beliefs (according to Quine's holistic empiricism),[212] the 'constitutive principles' (Friedman)[213] and paradigmatic contexts (Kuhn) that orient any form of scientific research, the different forms of situatedness, embodiment, and partiality that propel any scientific endeavour that assumes the challenge of overcoming both relativism and pre-critical

207 G. Bateson and M.C. Bateson, *Angels Fear: Towards an Epistemology of the Sacred* (New York: Bantam Books, 1988), 152.

208 Wilson, *Prometheus Rising*, 221.

209 See L. Daston, P. Galison, *Objectivity* (New York: Zone Books, 2007).

210 See R. Carnap, 'Empiricism, Semantics, and Ontology', *Revue Internationale de Philosophie*, 4 (1950), 40–50.

211 See H. Putnam, 'There Is At Least One *A Priori* Truth', in *Realism and Reason: Philosophical Papers, Volume 3* (Cambridge: Cambridge University Press, 1983), 98–114.

212 See W.V.O. Quine, 'Two Dogmas of Empiricism', in *From a Logical Point of View* (New York: Harper & Row, 1963), 20–46.

213 M. Friedman, *Dynamics of Reason* (Stanford, CA: Stanford University Press, 2001), 32.

totalisation (Haraway),[214] the generic structure of human 'existentiality' in the Heideggerian sense of the term,[215] the *habitus* qua implicit structure of human practices associated with the corresponding living conditions of existence (Bourdieu),[216] and, last but not least, all the diverse forms of historical, cultural, political, institutional, and economical imprints, practices, norms, and conditions that predetermine and make possible the experience of the corresponding subjects.[217] A particular assemblage of such transcendental structures defines, in turn, what we shall call a *transcendental type* of subjectivity (or *transcendental subject*). Every subject will be said to be a particular *token* or *instantiation* of a transcendental type (which can change during the individual's life). In this way, the multiple *abstract modalities* (perceptual, conceptual, affective, and so on) of being always already immersed in an experiential field are necessarily predetermined by the *transcendental structures* of the subject of experience, by its transcendental type, by its location in what we shall call the *transcendental landscape* of types of subjectivity. In Kantian jargon, the generic structure of the object in general of human experience depends upon a transcendental *framing*, a 'reducing valve',[218] a filter, an editing-down. This means that the transcendental apparatus that defines the subjective conditions of possibility of every transcendent experience simultaneously determines the generic structure of the intentional objects of this experience.

---

214 D. Haraway, 'Situated Knowledges: The Science Question in Feminism and the Privilege of Partial Perspective', *Feminist Studies* 14:3 (1988): 575–99.

215 M. Heidegger, *Being and Time*, tr. J. Macquarrie and E. Robinson (Oxford: Blackwell, 1962), 33 [§4].

216 Cf. P. Bourdieu, *The Logic of Practice*, tr. R. Nice (Stanford, CA: Stanford University Press, 1990), 53.

217 It is worth noting that this list of 'transcendental' structures—which in the last instance is a list of empirical structures—blurs Kant's rigid boundary between the empirical and the transcendental, thereby setting the transcendental project off on its path toward 'natureculturalisation' (we shall come back to this important point below).

218 Huxley, *The Doors of Perception and Heaven and Hell*, 23.

The framing of the experiential field operated by a subject of transcendental type $\alpha$ gives rise to what we shall call, adopting von Uexküll's term, the $\alpha$–Umwelt. The human transcendental type defines only one particular type—among other nonhuman types (e.g. mineral, vegetable, animal, extraterrestrial)—by means of which the impersonal field of experience locally *umweltifies* its immanental self-experience, its singular one life. The fact that the umweltic—or monadological—spheres constituted by each transcendental type are pared-down versions of the same experiential field explains their pre-established inter-umweltic harmony, the fine tuning of the species, the musaic of reciprocal and contrapuntal chords between Umwelten constituted by subjects of different transcendental types. Even if umweltic monads do not have doors or windows, 'they are not the cells of monks because they include the same—solidary but not solitary—world',[219] for they arise from the same pleroma: they are coordinated, concertated, and mutually attuned.

Taking up Kant's transcendental aesthetic, it could be argued that, while human beings can change their spatiotemporal states and integrate the corresponding experiences, the particular geometric properties of the very spatiotemporal extension in which they perform these variations—for instance its (3+1)-dimensionality and its continuous structure—might depend on their transcendental type $\alpha$.[220] For example, these particular features of spacetime (dimension and continuity) might depend upon the restricted range of scales to which human beings have empirical (either physiological

219 Deleuze, *The Fold*, 132.

220 See also J. von Uexküll, *Theoretical Biology* (London: Kegan Paul, Trench, Trubner and Co., 1926), chapters 1 and 2 ('Space', 'Time'). Stjernfelt paraphrases von Uexküll's thesis about the transcendental dependence of spatial and temporal notions in the following terms: 'Both space and time are subject to a crucial granulation in the Umwelt construction. Umwelt space is constructed—unlike Euclidean geometry—from localities, from *Orte*, just like Umwelt time is constituted not from timeless nows, but from short time bits, from *Momente*. The size of these Umwelt building blocks is of course relative to the senses and the inner life of the animal in question, respectively.' F. Stjernfelt, *Diagrammatology: An Investigation on the Borderlines of Phenomenology, Ontology, and Semiotics* (Dordrecht: Springer, 2007), 236.

or technological) access. After von Uexküll, we could then argue that the experiences of different types of subjects (such as for instance vegetable, animal, and extraterrestrial types, or even human types endowed with different forms of technological resources) take place in Umwelten that are perceptually unfolded in their own kinds of spatiotemporal extensions. We can for instance associate with each transcendental type $\alpha$ an $\alpha$-sensory-motor extension that defines the sensory-motor degrees of freedom of the empirical subjects of type $\alpha$, that is the 'spacetime' constituted by its transcendental affordances. Such an extension parameterises the possible positions that a subject of type $\alpha$ can occupy in order to have perceptual experiences. Since the very extension that defines the possible states of an empirical subject depends on its transcendental type, the objects that this subject can constitute by performing variations in such extension must also depend on this type. In short, different types of subjects inhabit and move in different forms of extensions (and temporalities) and have experiences of different objects. We could say for instance that the difference between a stable object and an ephemeral event is transcendental-dependent: the fact that the Great Pyramid (to use Whitehead's example) is experienced as a stable enduring object depends on the particular temporal window that define the specious present of human beings. We could certainly conceive—following the examples proposed by von Uexküll—lifeforms endowed with specious presents such that a flying arrow seems to be still in the air, such that the growing grass looks like a fountain of a greenish water that sprays from the earth, such that the trajectory of the sun in the sky would be perceived as a brief scintillating ray breaking through a short darkness, such that the seemingly uninhabited vastness of cosmic extensions would be experienced as a thick jungle bursting with the most diverse lifeforms.[221]

It is worth noting that even the notion of a single human transcendental type ('humanity' as such) presupposes a coarse graining that abstracts both from all of the physiological, cultural, linguistic, historical, gender, and social variations of the human motif and from the different forms of

221 Cf. J. von Uexküll, *Biologische Briefe an eine Dame* (Berlin: Verlag von Gebrüder Paetel, 1920).

intricacies between humans and nonhumans: 'The question [...] "Are we really a humanity?" can be understood in two ways depending on which word is emphasized: are we really *a* humanity (and not an irreducible diversity of ways of living in society)? And are we a *humanity* (and not an inextricable network of interdependencies of humans and nonhumans)?'[222] For example, the a priori structures of a child and an adult, of a woman and a man, or of a European and an Asian differ, even though they are all cases of the transcendental human type. The partitioning of the class of empirical subjects into transcendental types—and therefore the demarcation line between transcendental and empirical structures—depends upon the contextual extension given to the notion of transcendental type. If, in a given theoretical context, we understand language as a transcendental structure, then a Japanese person and a French person will be instances of different transcendental types. Whereas the notion of a unique human transcendental type—which abstracts from linguistic, cultural, historical, and other forms of differences in 'type' among human beings—could prove useful to an exobiologist, such a notion will be too coarse-grained for an anthropologist studying the cultural and natural lifeworlds constituted by the Aztec and the European civilisations.[223] Ultimately, every individual defines a transcendental type and lives in a separate (albeit changing) Umwelt. Indeed, 'it is neurologically obvious that no two brains have the same genetically-programmed hard wiring, the same imprints, the same conditioning, the same learning experiences. We are all living in

---

222 E. Viveiros de Castro, 'Le monde a commence sans l'homme et s'achèvera sans lui', Postface to Ailton Krenak, *Idées pour retarder la fin du monde* (France: Éditions Dehors, 2020), 55–56.

223 Bourdieu provides the following example of a classification of types of subjectivity that is relevant in the particular theoretical context provided by sociology: 'Sociology treats as identical all biological individuals who, being the products of the same objective conditions, have the same *habitus*. A social class (in-itself)—a class of identical or similar conditions of existence and conditionings—is at the same time a class of biological individuals having the same *habitus*, understood as a system of dispositions common to all products of the same conditioning.' Bourdieu, *The Logic of Practice*, 59.

separate realities.'[224] Therefore, the concept of a transcendental type relies upon a context-dependent procedure of abstraction that allows us to dialectically sublate the sharp opposition between *mere difference* and *trivial self-identity*: different subjects might be identical *in certain respects*. A transcendental type is an equivalence class of empirical subjects that are *similar* according to a given relevant criterion albeit not identical *strictu sensu*.[225] If we were to maintain the sharp opposition between mere differences and trivial self-identity—in this particular case, if we were to consider that different subjects are simply different, and only identical to themselves—then conceptualisation qua categorisation would be impossible (for example, a butterfly would be considered just as different from another butterfly as to a monkey). To think is to abstract—that is, to methodically 'forget' differences (this explains why Borges's Funes was incapable of thought).[226] Pathologies are liable to arise (and Husserl's 'crisis' begins) only when one forgets that one is forgetting, when abstract entities are hypostasised or reified, and when the operations of abstraction proliferate in an uncontrolled manner. The hypostasis of a particular transcendental type, which forgets that each token of the type is ultimately a singular individual living in a unique Umwelt, gives rise to what we could call a *transcendental stereotype*.[227]

---

224 Wilson, *Prometheus Rising*, 211.

225 In mathematics, the fundamental notion of an *equivalence relation* (that is, a relation $R \subset S \times S$ on a set S that is reflexive, symmetric, and transitive) encodes the classification of *similar* (albeit different) objects in disjoint equivalence classes. By doing so, new abstract notions can be constituted (like the notion of *direction* associated with the equivalence classes of parallel straight lines in Euclidean space).

226 J.L. Borges, 'Funes, His Memory', in *Collected Fictions* (New York: Penguin Books, 1999), 131–37.

227 Regarding the advantages and dangers of the transcendental consideration of subjects in terms of abstract (stereo)types and the consideration of subjects in their unique concrete singularity, see M. Jackson, 'Persons and Types', in *As Wide as the World is Wise: Reinventing Philosophical Anthropology* (New York: Columbia University Press, 2016), 137–52. In *The Meaning of Truth*, William James describes the pathologies of abstraction in the following terms: 'Let me give the name of "vicious abstractionism" to a way of using concepts which may be thus described:

This 'fallacy of misplaced concreteness' can be avoided by methodically keeping a hand on the calibration dial through which one can attune different abstractive resolutions. We shall then endorse Hegel's answer to the question *Who thinks abstractly?*: it is (what Hegel calls) 'uneducated' people—those who do not engage in the *Bildung* that teaches one to recognise and dialectically resolve the abstractions of language, conceptual categories, and sharp oppositions—who think abstractly. In particular, those who acritically reduce the infinite concrete complexity of a human existence to an abstract statement of the form 'This person is a murderer!' hover in the astralised spaces of full-fledged abstraction. In Hegel's own words, '[t]his is abstract thinking: to see nothing in the murderer except the abstract fact that he is a murderer, and to annul all other human essence in him with this simple quality'.[228] Of course, this does not mean that an 'educated' person does not use abstract language, categories, and oppositions. It just means that they make sure neither to forget the abstract nature of the latter, nor to use abstract statements to simply 'cancel out' the infinite concrete complexity of the real. *Bildung* trains the capacity to move along the abstract-concrete axis, that is, to circulate in a context-dependent manner along different degrees of abstraction and concreteness.

In what follows, we shall schematise Kant's stance regarding the transcendental dependency of scientific reason by defining a topological space

---

We conceive a concrete situation by singling out some salient or important feature in it, and classing it under that; then, instead of adding to its previous characters all the positive consequences which the new way of conceiving it may bring, we proceed to use our concept privatively; reducing the originally rich phenomenon to the naked suggestions of that name abstractly taken, treating it as a case of "nothing but" that concept, and acting as if all the other characters from out of which the concept is abstracted were expunged. Abstraction, functioning in this way, becomes a means of arrest far more than a means of advance in thought. It mutilates things [...]. *The viciously privative employment of abstract characters and class names* is, I am persuaded, one of the great original sins of the rationalistic mind.' James, *The Meaning of Truth*, 249–50.

228 G.W.F. Hegel, 'Who Thinks Abstractly?', in W. Kaufmann (ed.), *Hegel: Texts and Commentary* (Garden City, NY: Anchor Books, 1966), 113–18.

of possible transcendental types, which we shall call *transcendental landscape*. By definition, each transcendental type occupies (what we shall call) a *zone* of the transcendental landscape of subjective types.[229] Different from sharp or punctual positions, zones of the transcendental landscape are subject to a topological calculus given by the operations of *union* and *intersection* of zones (satisfying a distributivity relation). This approach will also allow us to consider transcendental types with nontrivial intersections—that is to say, with shared transcendental structures—and 'multiocular' transcendental types resulting from the union of other transcendental types. In particular, if the locality defined by a transcendental type β is included in the locality defined by a transcendental type α (that is, if type α is equipped with at least all the transcendental resources of type β), we shall say that type α is an *extension* of type β. Each transcendental type α frames the experiential field, thus defining a horizon of transcendence that we shall call the α-Umwelt. In other words, each zone in the transcendental landscape defines a *transcendental perspective* or *transcendental viewzone* (which may be more or less punctual) from which the experiential field appears in the form of a horizon of transcendence immanent to the field. A subject of transcendental type α can only have experiences of the objects that appear within the α-Umwelt, while the corresponding α-noumenal 'great outdoors' remains inaccessible for subjects of that transcendental type. We could say that every empirical subject is localised twice: once in the corresponding umweltic extensions, and once in the transcendental landscape. These two forms of localisation—the empirical and the transcendental—entail two forms of perspectivism, namely the *empirical perspectivism* associated with the localisation of the empirical subject in the corresponding umweltic extensions (such as spacetime), and the *transcendental perspectivism*

229 The notion of *fitness landscape* used in evolutionary biology (introduced by the biologist Sewall Wright in the 1930s) is similar in spirit to the notion of transcendental landscape introduced here. Briefly, a fitness landscape is a space that parameterises genotypes such that nearby locations define genotypes related by minimal mutations. See for instance, H. Richter and A.P. Engelbrecht (eds.), *Recent Advances in the Theory and Application of Fitness Landscapes* (Berlin and Heidelberg: Springer-Verlag, 2014).

associated with the localisation of its type in the transcendental landscape. Now, whereas an empirical subject of a fixed transcendental type α can be occupy different states in the α-Umwelt (thereby being able to sublate the empirical perspectivism of its experience), the subject's type itself defines a single viewzone in the transcendental landscape. In short, a subject can be a nomad in the corresponding umweltic extensions while being sedentary in the transcendental landscape. For instance, a subject can turn around an object in order to gain access to and integrate its different adumbrations, but the object thus constituted will still depend on the subject's transcendental type. We can then rephrase Kant's main thesis by stating that sedentarity in the transcendental landscape induces an unmediated form of transcendental perspectivism that limits the scope of experience to a restricted form of transcendence, the *transcendental transcendence* given by the corresponding Umwelt.

While the variations of the state of the subject in the corresponding Umwelt make possible a *typed form of intersubjectivity* only valid for human subjects, an *untyped form of intersubjectivity*—what we could call *unrestricted* or *untyped universality*—remains, according to Kant, beyond the scope of science. According to Kant, the scientific method—as well as the resulting form of restricted universality—relies on empirical variations between different *human* perspectives. This fact entails two limitations. First, the assumed invariants might cease to be invariants if one also considered transcendental variations including nonhuman perspectives. Second, the corresponding pheno(u)mena might radiate adumbrations that cannot be experienced from human perspectives. In order to emphasise that the scientific mediation of empirical perspectivism is still limited by transcendental perspectivism, Kant complexified the pre-critical duality that structures the naive realism of scientific knowledge—the duality between the 'manifest image of the common-sense lifeworld' on the one hand, and a supposed 'reality' faithfully represented (albeit always in a projective manner) by 'scientific images' on the other—by introducing the threefold distinction between actual *subjective representations* (of the 'lifeworld' as it effectively appears to the subject in its perspectival manifestation), *objective phenomena* (constituted by the subject's transcendental resources and studied by the natural sciences), and *noumena* (that is, the hypothetical configurations that inhabit the inaccessible 'great outdoors'). According to Kant, any kind of conflation between the 'scientific images' provided by the descriptive and explanatory resources of modern science and things as they are 'in themselves' belongs to the pre-critical phase of scientific rationality.

We arrive therefore at the question *par excellence* defining the project of speculative thinking: Is it possible to overcome (at least differentially) transcendental perspectivism, to go beyond transcendental transcendence and upgrade the infinite regulative idea of science from human intersubjectivity to an unrestricted (or untyped) form of universality? We shall here endorse an affirmative answer: just as we can sublate empirical perspectivism by performing empirical variations in the corresponding extension (such as spacetime), so we can sublate transcendental perspectivism by performing *speculative variations* in the transcendental landscape of subjective types. In other words, the primary claim is that the upgrading of the regulative idea of scientific research from human intersubjectivity to unrestricted universality requires an extension of the range of possible variations, from variations taking place within the extensions defined by the transcendental type of the subject of science to variations of the transcendental type itself—that is, to variations taking place in the transcendental landscape of subjective types. This stance amounts to the claim that the so-called a priori conditions of possibility of experience—far from being eternal, ahistorical, withdrawn from the morphogenetic evolutionary dynamics of the experiential field itself—can themselves be subjected to variation.[230] The task laid out by

---

230 This *relativisation* of the Kantian *a priori* (and in particular its 'natureculturalisation' [Haraway]) has been proposed in many guises in the history of Kantian exegesis. In his article 'What Has Kant Ever Done for Us? Speculative Realism and Dynamic Kantianism' (in S. de Sanctis, A. Longo [eds.], *Breaking the Spell: Contemporary Realism under Discussion* [Mimesis International, 2015], 89–113), Fabio Gironi analyses several examples of such relativisations, as for instance in Kuhn: 'I am a Kantian with moveable categories' (T. Kuhn, *The Road Since Structure: Philosophical Essays, 1970–1993, with an Autobiographical Interview*, ed. J. Conant and J. Haugeland [Chicago and London: University of Chicago Press, 2000], 64), in Reichenbach: '[T]here exists the possibility of a contradiction between the human system of

Mallarmé's *Maître* (that of abolishing chance) thus acquires a precise definition: it is possible to understand the infinite projects of reason—for example, the project of a post-critical science oriented by the regulative idea of truth as untyped universality—as projects of absolutisation tending toward an overcoming of the transcendental insularity of human experience, thereby extending the scope of human experience beyond the limits prescribed by its contingent transcendental type. To 'abolish chance' here means to overcome the contingency of our transcendental perspective, to venture away from the particular zone in the transcendental landscape into which we have been thrown.

We shall call speculative science a mode of thought oriented by the regulative idea of truth qua unrestricted universality. According to what we have just said, the subject of such a speculative science cannot be a token of a particular transcendental type of subjectivity: in order not to cede its desire to know, the subject of science must be endowed with a transcendental plasticity allowing it to drift in the transcendental landscape of subjective types. The infinite project oriented by the regulative idea of truth cannot proceed solely by means of the acts of objective knowledge implemented by the transcendental subject of science: the representation of nature as objective *natura naturata* as counterposed to the subject of science is the lot of the pre-critical phase of the scientific project. A subject oriented by the infinite idea of truth qua unrestricted universality has to engage in the task of deforming and expanding its linguistic (literary and formal) resources, its stock of conceptual categories, its technological resources, its *habitus*, its capacity to perform and integrate inter-species mutations, its ability to tune in to different scales of the experiential field and to mine

---

concepts and nature. Yet, in such a case, epistemology does not have to fail at all, for *the human being possesses the ability to change his system of concepts and to adapt it to nature*' (H. Reichenbach, *Selected Writings 1909–1953: Volume One*, ed. E.H. Schneewind et al. [Dordrecht: Springer, 1978], 4), and in Lewis: 'The assumption that our categories are fixed for all time by an original human endowment, is a superstition comparable to the belief of primitive peoples that the general features of their life and culture are immemorial and of supernatural origin' (C.I. Lewis, *Mind and the World-Order: Outline of a Theory of Knowledge* [New York: Dover, 1956], 234).

new forms of perceptual and conceptual depth. In this sense, the subject of speculative science is necessarily endowed with a *spiritual* dimension in the Foucauldian sense of the term: '[W]e could call "spirituality" the search, practice, and experience through which the subject carries out the necessary transformations on itself in order to have access to the truth. [...] Spirituality postulates that the truth is never given to the subject by right. [...] [Spirituality] postulates that the truth is not given to the subject by a simple act of knowledge [*connaissance*], which would be founded and justified simply by the fact that [it] is the subject and because [it] possesses this or that structure of subjectivity. It postulates that for the subject to have right of access to the truth it must be changed, transformed, shifted, and become, to some extent and up to a certain point, other than [itself]. The truth is only given to the subject at a price that brings the subject's being into play.'[231]

One might here object to the proposed analysis that the 'spiritual' (or speculative) capacity to modify its own transcendental structure is itself a subjective capacity that should be included as a constitutive part of the subject's typical structure. Indeed, different types of living beings are equipped with different capacities to reflexively change their own transcendental structures (for instance by learning, by developing new technical faculties, by intervening in their own psycho-physiological structures, by 'accommodating' their subjective types to different forms of external pressure, by performing evolutionary leaps at the ontogenetic level, and so on). For example, the fact that human beings can actively modify the conceptual categories by means of which they tune in to the *logos* is itself a typical characteristic of the human 'type'. In order to take into account this important observation, we shall enrich the notion of subjective type by also considering, besides the transcendental faculties, *speculative faculties* of different orders $n$. In order to classify these systems of subjective faculties, we shall introduce a stratified space—which we shall call *speculative landscape*—such that the transcendental landscape introduced before is the 1-stratum of this space.

231 M. Foucault, *Hermeneutics of the Subject: Lectures at the Collège de France 1981–1982*, ed. F. Gros, tr. G. Burchell (New York: Palgrave Macmillan, 2005), 15.

By definition, the speculative landscape has a *n-stratum* for each natural number $n = 0, 1, 2, \ldots$ The $n$-stratum classifies the $n$-type of the subject, that is, the $n$-faculties of its subjective structure. The overall type of a subject is given by its location in the 0-stratum, in the 1-stratum, in the 2-stratum, and so on for every $n$. We shall assume that in each $n$-stratum, there is a location (which we shall denote $0_n$) corresponding to the total absence of subjective resources of order $n$. A subject deprived of $n'$-resources for every $n' > n$ (that is, a subject located at $0_{n'}$ in each $n'$-stratum for every $n' > n$) instantiates what we shall call a *n-type of subjectivity*. An instance of a $n$-type of subjectivity has nontrivial 0-faculties, 1-faculties, 2-faculties, up to $n$-faculties but no nontrivial $n'$-faculties for $n' > n$. The higher the type of a subject, the higher its degree of *reflexive autonomy*, that is, its capacity to self-regulate (modify, deform, enhance) its own subjective structures. As we shall see, a subject can modify its $n$-type (that is, move in the $n$-stratum) either under the effect of an external enforcement (e.g. environmental pressure eliciting mutations or crossovers, developmental 'accommodation' [Piaget], a traumatic encounter, an entheogenic force, the intervention of what we shall call a *n-teacher* or a *n-programmer*) or reflexively by using its $n$+1-faculties. This means in particular that a subject equipped with nontrivial $n$+1-faculties can modify its own $n$-type without requiring any external intervention.

Let us consider this classificatory system of types of subjectivity in more detail. At the bottom level of the speculative landscape, we can consider the informational content possessed by a subject, that is, the data possessed by the subject at a given moment of its life. This *informational capital* defines what we shall call the *0-type* of the subject. A subject endowed with a particular informational capital occupies a particular location in the *0-stratum* of the speculative landscape, that is, in the stratum of the speculative landscape that classifies 0-types. The 0-type of the subject can change owing to some form of external pressure. For instance, what we could call a *0-teacher* might pipe informational content into the subject's head by means of a Nuremberg Funnel, thereby changing the subject's location in the 0-stratum. As von Foerster notes, the flattening of the notion of education to this 0-stratum amounts to conflating the act of learning with the acquisition of 'exchangeable commodities, that is with [informational] substance'.[232]

This externally induced motion of the subject in the 0-stratum is not the only way in which a subject can modify its 0-type. If the subject is equipped with transcendental faculties (e.g. sensibility, understanding, imagination, reason), then it can enrich its informational capital by simply using its own transcendental resources, that is, by observing the world, by reading, by reasoning, by performing computations, by concocting questions and searching for answers. In other words, a subject that instantiates a nontrivial 1-type of subjectivity can move by itself in the 0-stratum without requiring the intervention of a 0-teacher. These transcendental faculties will be called *1-order faculties*. The corresponding arrangement of 1-order faculties defines the locality of the subject in the transcendental landscape, that is, in the 1-stratum of the speculative landscape. In other words, the 1-order faculties of the subject define the subject's 1-type (i.e. what has been hitherto called its transcendental type). Since a token of a 1-type of subjectivity only has nontrivial 1-faculties, it can move in the 0-stratum (i.e. acquire new information) but, in the absence of external pressure, it necessarily remains at a fixed location in the 1-stratum (i.e. it can not self-induce changes of its own 1-type).

Let us consider now the possible (forced as well as self-induced) motions of the subject in the 1-stratum. From an evolutionary perspective, contingent mutations or crossovers can externally induce shifts of a given population in the 1-stratum. From an educational standpoint, what we could call a *1-teacher* might stimulate the development of new transcendental resources (1-faculties) by means of which the subject becomes capable of acquiring new informational content. By doing so, a 1-teacher induces motions of the subject in the 1-stratum, that is, it changes its transcendental type. By teaching a subject to read or to use technological devices (e.g. a telescope, a computer), or by conveying a critical attitude with respect to the inductive biases or implicit assumptions that frame the subject's experience, a

232 H. von Foerster, 'Perception of the Future and the Future of Perception', in *Understanding Understanding*, 200–201.

1-teacher does not directly funnel new informational data into them, but rather *teaches them to learn*. In particular, a 1-teacher can teach to learn what the teacher itself does not necessarily know and in this sense a 1-teacher can be an 'ignorant schoolmaster': 'Teaching is a giving, an offering; but what is offered in teaching is not the learnable [...] [Teaching] does not mean anything else than to let the others learn, i.e., to bring one another to learning.[233] [...] The real teacher, in fact, lets nothing else be learned than learning. [Its] conduct, therefore, often produces the impression that we properly learn nothing from [it], if by "learning" we now suddenly understand merely the procurement of useful information. The teacher is ahead of [its] apprentices in this alone, that [it] has still far more to learn than they–[it] has to learn to let them learn.'[234]

In the framework of artificial intelligence research, artificial neural networks are collections of artificial 'neurons' modelling biological neurons which are interconnected by means of 'synapses' endowed with different weights (in more formal terms, artificial neural networks are *directed weighted graphs*). Artificial neural networks are constructed in such a way that they can (for instance) classify a given input (e.g. decide the truth value of a proposition or recognise an object in a picture). We could say that artificial neural networks are tokens of 1-types of subjectivity, that is, subjects constructed by an external 1-programmer in such a way that they can receive a certain kind of information and process it in a particular way. The task-specific architecture of an artificial neural network (such as the weights of the different 'synaptic' connections) is defined by the external 1-programmer, which means that these 'subjects' occupy a fixed position in the 1-stratum. In other words, these artificial neural networks do not have the capacity to modify their own transcendental structure.

For the moment, we have introduced the two first strata of the speculative landscape: the 1-stratum that defines the possible 0-types of the subject (its informational capital) and the 1-stratum that defines the possible 1-types (its transcendental resources). But '[o]f course we do not want to stop at

233 Heidegger, *What is a Thing?*, 73.

234 Heidegger, *What is Called Thinking?*, 15.

the first meta-level!'[235] We shall now add higher strata that classify higher order faculties, such as the speculative 2-faculties by means of which a subject can self-induce—without the intervention of a 1-teacher or an external 1-programmer—changes of its transcendental type (that is, its location in the 1-stratum), the speculative 3-faculties by means of which the subject can self-induce changes of its 2-type (that is, its location in the 2-stratum) and so on and so forth all the way up.

The next step in this progression is to consider what we shall call the *speculative faculties* of the subject, that is its 2-faculties. These are the faculties that enable the subject to self-induce changes of its 1-order faculties (i.e. of its transcendental type) without necessarily requiring the external intervention of a 1-teacher or a 1-programmer. We could say with Bergson that '[a]n intelligent being [of subjective type 2 or higher] bears within [itself] the means to transcend [its] own [transcendental] nature'.[236] The 2-faculties of a subject are reflexive tools by means of which the subject can regulate its 1-type (i.e. its transcendental capacities) and move in the 1-stratum, that is, intervene in the very structure of its perceptual, linguistic, conceptual, symbolic, schematising, formal, and computational resources. For instance, the capacity of a subject to develop its own technological resources–i.e. the capacity to technologically modify its perceptual, motor, and computational skills–is an example of a 2-faculty.[237] According to the geometric schematisation that we are using here, the speculative 2-faculties of a subject define its location in the 2-stratum of the speculative landscape. A token of a 2-type of subjectivity—that is, a subject endowed with speculative 2-faculties and no higher-order faculties—has a fixed location in the

---

235 J. Schmidhuber, *Evolutionary Principles in Self-Referential Learning*, Diploma Thesis, Tech. Univ. Munich, 1987.

236 Bergson, *Creative Evolution*, 167.

237 It is worth emphasising here the distinction between a subject whose transcendental structure is equipped with a particular technological resource (which contributes to the definition of the subject's 1-type) and the capacity to further develop this technological resource (which contributes to the definition of the subject's 2-type).

2-stratum of the speculative landscape and—thanks to the corresponding speculative faculties—can perform certain motions in the 1-stratum.

In the framework of artificial intelligence research, deep learning methods provide examples of 2-types of subjectivity, that is, of types of subjectivity equipped with nontrivial 2-faculties. Whereas artificial neural networks considered above are constructed in such a way that they can (for instance) recognise shapes, neural networks of type 2 can *learn* to recognise shapes (e.g. Rosenblatt's Perceptron).[238] In other words, neural networks of speculative type 2 are endowed with a (restricted) form of neuroplasticity. By exposing the network to a training dataset, the constraint of minimalising an error function allows the network to intervene in its own structure (typically by changing the weights of the 'synaptic' connections) in order to optimise the task that it is intended to perform (e.g. to classify images). In Matteo Pasquinelli's words, this kind of neural network 'transmutates external information into internal logic', that is, 'it morphs logic itself to new rules and habits'.[239]

We can now consider the possible (forced or self-induced) motions of the subject in the 2-stratum. The artificial neural networks of subjective type 2 considered above can change the parameters that define their internal architecture during the training process (thereby moving in the 1-stratum), but they cannot modify certain hyperparameters or meta-parameters externally fixed by the 2-programmer (such as the error function that defines the learning process). The 2-type of such a subject (its meta-learning capacities) can only be changed by the external intervention of a 2-programmer. Analogously, what we could call a 2-teacher teaches how to *learn to learn*, that

238 Cf. F. Rosenblatt, *Principles of Neurodynamics: Perceptrons and the Theory of Brain Mechanisms* (Buffalo, NY: Cornell Aeronautical Laboratory, 1961). In the simplest example, a change of the so-called threshold in a 'McCulloch formal neuron' with two input fibres can change the logical function computed by the 'neuron' (e.g. from an *and* to an *or* logic gate). See for instance, H. von Foerster, 'Computation in Neural Nets', in *Understanding Understanding*, 39–40.

239 M. Pasquinelli, 'Machines that Morph Logic: Neural Networks and the Distorted Automation of Intelligence as Statistical Inference', *Glass Bead* 1 (2017), <https://www.glass-bead.org/article/machines-that-morph-logic/>.

is, it teaches the subject how to modify its own meta-learning capacities.[240] Hence, a 2-teacher teaches neither informational content nor new learning skills, but rather the speculative capacity to develop new learning skills. An example of a 2-teacher is a PhD advisor. A PhD advisor does not only teach new informational content and how to use existing techniques and procedures (e.g. the use of existing algorithms for extracting information from raw data, the use of existing mathematical techniques, the manipulation of experimental setups, and so on). A PhD advisor teaches the subject to perform research, that is, they teach the capacity to develop new learning techniques adapted to the new phenomena addressed by the researcher.

Once again, we can conceive a type of subjectivity endowed with nontrivial 3-faculties allowing the subject to self-induce motions in the 2-stratum without requiring the external intervention of a 2-teacher or a 2-programmer. Such a subject is equipped with the capacity to perform meta-meta-learning, that is, to learn to learn to learn, to regulate its own learning-to-learn algorithms without the external intervention of a 2-programmer, to learn to do research without a PhD advisor, to reflexively regulate its own speculative capacities.

To summarise, we can say that a subject of subjective type 0 can only store information, a subject of subjective type 1 can use its transcendental resources to acquire new information (without the external intervention of a 0-teacher), a subject of subjective type 2 can learn to learn, that is, it can modify its transcendental or learning capacities (without the external intervention of a 1-teacher or a 1-programmer), a subject of subjective type 3 is equipped with meta-meta-learning capacities, that is, it can self-regulate its learning-to-learn faculties without requiring an external intervention. We can now continue this stratification of the speculative landscape by considering $n$-faculties for every natural number $n$, i.e. faculties by means of which a subject can spontaneously modify its $(n-1)$-type. In principle, the speculative landscape has strata of order $n$ for every natural number $n$,

240 Regarding the notion of meta-learning from an artificial-intelligence-oriented perspective see Schmidhuber, *Evolutionary Principles in Self-Referential Learning*, and T. Schaul and J. Schmidhuber, 'Metalearning', *Scholarpedia* 5:6: 4650 (2010).

that is, it classifies types of subjectivity equipped with meta-meta-...-meta-learning capacities. In the natural-cultural-artificial evolution of life, environmental selective pressure, symbiogenetic processes, spontaneous self-organising dynamics, entheogenic catalysers or other mechanisms for instituting new types of subjectivity might both (a) induce displacements of typical lifeforms within the different strata of the speculative landscape (e.g. natural evolution of a given species in the 1-stratum of transcendental types) and (b) induce the emergence of nontrivial faculties of order *n* (e.g. the emergence of *n*-types of subjectivity endowed with the reflexive capacity to self-regulate their own transcendental and speculative affordances). Human reflexivity—that is, the human capacity to introspect and intervene on its own subjective structure at the lower strata of the speculative landscape—is just a first step in the living exploration of possible subjective meta-meta-...-meta-capacities. Life is a name for the pleroma's capacity to explore the speculative landscape of possible types of subjectivity, to potentialise its self-revelation in ever new unforeseen subjective manners.

An important obstacle for the speculative programme endorsed here is provided by (what we shall call) the *claustrophobic interpretation* of transcendental reflection, an interpretation whose first and most illustrious proponent was Kant himself. Paradoxically, the critical thesis according to which human experience is framed a priori by a transcendental structure induced a pre-modernising counter-revolution that continues to hinder the development of an absolutely modern scenario.[241] This self-enclosing reaction is based on the fallacy according to which transcendental reflection on the typical structures of human subjectivity and the recognition of the concomitant transcendental perspectivism, rather than enabling speculative differential sublations of the corresponding phenomenological horizons, sanctions an unsurpassable limitation of human experience. According to the claustrophobic interpretation, the human transcendental structure would determine once and for all the ultimate and insurmountable limits of human experience, and the only form of transcendence accessible to

241 Cf. Q. Meillassoux, *After Finitude: An Essay on the Necessity of Contingency*, tr. R. Brassier (London: Continuum, 2008), Chapter 5.

human beings would be the transcendental transcendence (the phenomenological horizon) defined by its transcendental type. The claustrophobic interpretation of transcendental reflection therefore maintains that human beings live, think, and die in a phenomenal umweltic prison suspended in a purely inferred, noumenal 'great outdoors' that remains absolutely unthinkable, unspeakable, subtracted from all possible experience. The argument that grounds the claustrophobic interpretation is simply that we cannot jump over our own shadows, that we cannot have experiences that are not predetermined by the transcendental conditions to which we owe the very possibility of experience, that we cannot speak or think about something without subjecting it to the general conditions of possibility of speech and thinking, that we cannot think *X* without *thinking* X. The Kantian concept of the noumenon is then a purely negative, limitative concept, designed merely to police the excesses of pre-critical reason. Following this interpretation, transcendental reflection can play only a critical role in the general economy of thought and existence, its only legitimate task being to limit the illegitimate extrapolations of pre-critical thought, both those of a purported metaphysics pretending to think that which by definition cannot be the object of experience (such as, for example, the constituting and pre-mundane 'soul', 'god' qua immanent life, or 'world' as a phenomenological horizon of possible experience), and those of a science that claims to represent things as they are 'in themselves' instead of limiting itself to its legitimate domain of competence, that of objective phenomena. The theoretical (rather than aesthetic or political) conjugation of this transcendental limitation affirms that the scope of scientific rationality is limited de jure to the *objective nature* constituted by the transcendental structures of the subject of science. In order to overcome this limitation, the subject of science would have to be able to jump over its own shadow, to have experiences that are not predetermined by the very transcendental conditions that make it possible for it to have an experience at all. Since this jumping-over-its-own-shadow is supposed to be impossible, every act performed within the framework of a human mode of thought is only a 'dice throw', an act that is overdetermined by the contingent transcendental structures that at once make possible and set boundaries to human thought and existence. Human thought will never abolish chance; it will never be able to activate speculative degrees of freedom that would make it capable of overcoming the contingency of transcendental perspectivism and the associated form of relativism. The very attempt to perform acts intended to abolish 'the infinite randomness of [phylogenetic and ontogenetic] conjunctions' (Mallarmé) out of which our transcendental type emerged might seem like madness, pure and simple, mere speculation. An impassable frontier is drawn between a phenomenal transcendental transcendence and an inaccessible noumenal realm.

One of the more pernicious consequences of the claustrophobic interpretation of the transcendental motif is the reactivation of the tandem made up of an ontotheological fascination with an inaccessible 'great outdoors' (that is, with the utterly impossible, unthinkable, and unspeakable) and the onset of protocols of transgression that aim to circumvent the Kantian interdiction through different possible shortcuts that could take over where scientific reason finds its supposed transcendental limits. Examples of such forms of transgression of the Kantian interdiction are given by the neo-scholastic arguments of certain contemporary forms of 'speculative philosophy' or the different iterations of a *maniac enthusiasm* (*Schwärmerei*) which—in the wake of Jacobi—would allow us to 'overstep [in a single leap of faith] the bounds of human reason'. Critical self-enclosure sets off the illusion of an immediate transgression of the Kantian interdiction, of a direct communion with the 'great outdoors', of a discontinuous leap out of the Umwelt, of an alleged conclusive argument that (by jumping in a single acrobatic step over the infinite mediations, patience, and frustrations of scientific understanding) would allow us to step out of the transcendental-dependent subject-object correlation. At the point where scientific knowledge ends, faith and 'speculative' enthusiasm begin. While the different modes of thought and practice such as science and art proceed laboriously, 'word for word', 'number by number', patiently working on the affect, the percept, the concept, always failing, always attempting to 'fail better', bringing about transgressions of transcendental limitations that are always differential and local, these *thoughts of the great outdoors* compress the infinite tasks of such modes of thought and practice into finite operations that (pre)tend to apprehend immediately—once and for all, withdrawing from the effort of overcoming local obstructions and bypassing the various forms of 'material' resistance—an alleged absolute. To the 'speculative philosopher', it may misleadingly seem more appealing to think that it has already understood what the absolute is, rather than engaging in the infinite and laborious tasks prescribed by the regulative ideas that orient the different modes of thought and practice (science, arts, politics) only to inevitably fail again. In Hegel's words, 'dogmatism as a way of thinking [...] is nothing else but the opinion that the True consists in a proposition which is a fixed result, or which is immediately known'.[242] In particular, theoretical dogmatism periodically takes the form of the naive pretension (and '[t]he contempt for reality manifested by such pronouncements is unfathomable')[243] to formulate a new definitive scientific or philosophical 'theory of everything'. In contrast, we can now rephrase the question that defines speculative thinking as we understand it here in the following way: Is it possible to remain faithful to the regulative idea of science—to the infinite idea (that we call *truth*) that prescribes an unyielding commitment to push the limits of our rational comprehension of the experiential field further, refusing to accept any form of a priori restriction—without succumbing to the illusions produced by the ontotheological-oriented protocols of immediate and direct transgression of the Kantian interdiction, that is, without giving up human finitude?[244]

---

242 Hegel, *Phenomenology of Spirit*, 23.

243 Land, *The Thirst for Annihilation*, 24.

244 Heidegger defines the project of a speculative absolutism that rejects transcendental claustrophobia without foreclosing human finitude (as Hegel did, according to Heidegger) as follows: 'No one can do this [to jump over one's own shadow]. However, the greatest effort in attempting this impossibility—that is the decisive ground-movement of the action of thought. [...] Hegel alone apparently succeeded in jumping over this shadow, but only in such a way that he eliminated the shadow, i.e. the finiteness of [human beings], and jumped into the sun itself. [...] [E]very philosopher *must* want to do this. This "must" is [its] vocation. The longer the shadow, the wider the jump.' Heidegger, *What is a Thing?*, 150–51.

In order to circumvent the thesis that human thinking is inexorably limited by a transcendental perspectivism, we shall now revisit Kant's characterisation of transcendental critique as a second-order (transcendental rather than astronomical) Copernican Revolution. To do so, let us reconsider the first-order (astronomical) Copernican Revolution. We could say that modern science is essentially Copernican in the following sense. The Ptolemaic geocentric description of the dynamics of celestial bodies with respect to a frame of reference attached to the Earth yields very complicated motions with, for instance, retrograde phases. In a pre-Copernican approach, we could understand these motions as absolute motions of the bodies being observed with respect to an absolute background in which the Earth would be still. This amounts to transforming the fact that this description is relative to the choice of a particular coordinate system attached to the Earth into the stronger proposition that the Earth is still in an absolute sense, and the apparent motions of the heavenly bodies are absolute motions. By choosing an (equally conventional) coordinate system fixed to the Sun, Copernicus found a far simpler description. In particular, apparently retrograde motions are described by Copernicus as a consequence of the relative motions of the Earth and the other planets, all of which are (in this heliocentric description) orbiting around the Sun. Thanks to Copernicus, we understood that the Ptolemaic description of celestial motions depends upon the conventional choice of a particular frame of reference attached to the Earth, and that at least part of the complexity of the apparent motions that earthbound astronomers observe results from this implicit choice.[245]

Here it becomes important to clear up a certain kind of philosophical misunderstanding of the Copernican Revolution. One might argue that the fact that we are physically attached to a particular frame of reference

245 Cf. J.B. Barbour, *The Discovery of Dynamics: A Study from a Machian Point of View of the Discovery and Structure of Dynamical Theories* (New York: Oxford University Press, 2001) and L. Infeld, 'From Copernicus to Einstein', in B. Bienkowska and Z. Kopal (eds.), *The Scientific World of Copernicus: On the Occasion of the 500th Anniversary of his Birth 1473–1973* (Dordrecht: D. Reidel, 1973), 66–83.

(that of the Earth) imposes certain limits upon astronomy which we cannot bypass. Astronomy would then be condemned to an Earth-based perspectivism. But the fact that we dwell on Earth did not prevent astronomy from describing celestial motions from other frames of reference. In particular, the description of the celestial motions with respect to a frame of reference attached to the Sun ended up being much simpler. It would be unreasonable to argue that the Copernican Revolution, in emphasising the correlation between a scientific description and the state of motion of the chosen frame of reference, paves the way toward some kind of unsurpassable epistemic limitation of astronomical knowledge. That is, the existence of multiple possible frames of reference and the possibility of arbitrarily selecting one frame does not imply that scientific descriptions are inherently coordinate-dependent. Scientists have developed techniques by means of which it is possible to analyse the overall group-theoretical structure of the variations among different coordinate systems, extract invariants, and integrate the frame-dependent descriptions into intrinsic (frame-independent) ones. The Copernican reflection on the fact that astronomical data are always 'correlated' to the observer's position and state of motion, far from limiting the scope of astronomy, was on the contrary the condition of possibility for astronomy's overcoming of the empirical perspectivism of human astronomers, allowing them to adopt (without changing de facto humanity's physical location) what Arendt calls a 'centreless world view', a 'cosmic, universal standpoint'.[246] It was not necessary to actually leave Earth and undertake astronomical voyages in order to obtain the current scientific understanding of the movements of the planets around the Sun, the movement of the solar system in one of the outer spiral arms of the Milky Way, the location of the Milky Way within the local group, that of the latter within the Virgo Supercluster, and finally the location of these structures within the Laniakea Supercluster—the incommensurable paradise. The theoretical ability—which belongs de jure to the 'work of the concept'—to methodically sublate the local conditions of its effective embodiment was

246 H. Arendt, *The Human Condition* (Chicago and London: University of Chicago Press, 1998), 263, 270.

more than enough to absolve astronomy from the contingency of the human place in the cosmos.[247] Reflection on the observer's contingent empirical state is the condition of possibility for the production of an objective (i.e. intersubjective) form of scientific knowledge that is not dependent upon that state. The limitations exposed by this reflection are not impassable boundaries but interfaces that can be traversed. The Copernican Revolution was not an *abstract negation* that traced out the ultimate limits of astronomical science, but rather a *determinate negation* by means of which astronomers transgressed the permeable limits revealed through reflection on their own contingent state. In this way, the Copernican Revolution conveys a fundamental principle of modern science: we have to bring the subject of science into focus and reflect upon its possible states in order for knowledge not to be too human.[248] According to the regulative idea of truth which orients the infinite tasks of science, scientific '[t]hinking is true [...] in terms of form only if it is not a particular instance of being or doing of [a situated] subject, but instead is consciousness conducting itself precisely as [higher order] "I", liberated from [any one-sided dependence with respect to] all the particularity that attaches to qualities and conditions otherwise, and only enacting the [concrete] universal through which [...] all individuals [and their singular perspectives are faithfully integrated].'[249]

In order to overcome the claustrophobic interpretation of transcendental reflection, we must start by noting that this interpretation is implicitly

247 As Arendt writes: 'What ushered in the modern age [...] was [...] the discovery [...] of the astounding human capacity to think in terms of the universe while remaining on the earth. [...] [E]arth alienation became and has remained the hallmark of modern science. [...] [W]e no longer feel bound [...]. [W]e move freely in the universe, choosing our point of reference wherever it may be convenient for a specific purpose.' Ibid., 264, 263.

248 As Reichenbach puts it, 'The only path to objective knowledge leads through conscious awareness of the role that subjectivity plays in our method of research.' H. Reichenbach, *The Philosophy of Space and Time* (New York: Dover, 1958), 37.

249 G.W.F. Hegel, *Encyclopedia of the Philosophical Sciences in Basic Outline Part I: Science of Logic*, tr. K. Brinkmann and D.O. Dahlstrom (New York: Cambridge University Press, 2010), 57.

based on *transcendental humanism*, that is, on the thesis that human beings are characterised by a fixed transcendental type, by a supposed transcendental 'essence' of the human, by a static location in the transcendental landscape. Namely, the *claustrophobic* interpretation of transcendental reflection is based on an *essentialisation* of the transcendental structures of human beings, that is, on the hypothesis that the latter are fixed structures that define an impassable boundary between a phenomenal world and the corresponding noumenal realm. Now, this humanist essentialisation of human faculties forecloses all those natural and historical processes that played a role in the institution of the human transcendental type. The humanist essentialisation of the human type also precludes the possibility of a speculative *techné* through which human beings can modify their own transcendental structures and mediate the corresponding limits. The different transcendental types—far from being immutable subjective essences—are always the emergent results of *processes of subjectivation* or, as we shall call them in what follows, *processes of institution* of subjectivity taking place within the impersonal experiential field.[250] This means that every constituting subject is always an instituted entity, that every a priori structure of experience is an a posteriori product,[251] that every 'structuring

250 If it is assumed, following Kant's transcendental aesthetic, that space and time are transcendental conditions of human sensibility, then the very notion of a process of institution (by definition temporal) of the transcendental subject becomes problematic. In this view, the idea of a temporal institution of the transcendental structures that constitute the very spatiotemporal stage of subjective experience is contradictory. However, the fact that the spatialisation and temporalisation of human experience both depend upon the human transcendental type (such as its perceptive faculties and its motor capacities) does not necessarily imply that the pleroma is devoid of all forms of extension and temporality. The transcendental aesthetic simply calls into question the pre-critical extrapolation of the spacetime structure of human experience (continuous 3+1-dimensional spacetime equipped with a local Minkowski structure) to the noumenal realm. The fact that human experience unfolds in a temporal dimension that depends upon the transcendental structures of human beings does not necessarily imply that the impersonal field of experience is void of any form of temporal processuality.

251 In his remarkable essay on Kant's doctrine of the a priori, Lorenz explicitly claims

structure' is a 'structured structure',[252] that every *transcendental constitution* of objectivity presupposes an *immanental institution* of the corresponding subjective transcendental structures. According to Piaget's 'developmental psychology' and 'genetic epistemology', 'the problem of knowledge [...] cannot be considered separately from the problem of the development of intelligence',[253] at both the phylogenetic, ontogenetic, and epigenetic levels. It is not possible to provide a 'transcendental deduction of the categories' of human understanding, but we can study the diachronic naturalcultural processes of institution of the particular subjective structures that define the different transcendental types.

The *transcendental*, a priori structure of human experience is an a posteriori product of the *immanental* dynamics of *natura naturans*: every local subject is an immanent breathing fold of the 'animic field' of experience, a vibrant receptive and expressive local mode of life. According to Schelling's description of the swirling process of the institution of subjective forms, the external transformations that characterise the flux of the universal phenoumenodelic stream are at some points interiorised as self-transformations or automorphisms of local eigen-forms, breathing kernels of stability within the flux endowed with nontrivial forms of self-identity, symmetric ripples in the flowing insubstance enriched with different degrees of reflexivity, enduring

---

that 'the origin of the "a priori" [...] in a certain sense is "a posteriori".' Lorenz, 'Kant's Doctrine of the A Priori', 233.

252 Bourdieu, *The Logic of Practice*, 53. Bourdieu describes the two-sided nature of the 'transcendental' habitus (both instituted and constituting) in the following terms: '[T]he structures characterizing a determinate class of conditions of existence produce the structures of the *habitus*, which in their turn are the basis of the perception and appreciation of all subsequent experiences. The *habitus*, a product of history, produces individual and collective practices–more history [...]. It ensures the active presence of past experiences [...] deposited in each organism in the form of schemes of perception. [...] The *habitus*–embodied history, internalized as a second nature and so forgotten as history–is the active presence of the whole past of which it is the product.' Ibid., 54, 56.

253 J. Piaget, 'Piaget's Theory', in B. Inhelder and H.H. Chipman (eds.), *Piaget and his School: A Reader in Developmental Psychology* (New York: Springer-Verlag, 1976), 13.

local limitations of the 'original and absolute activity' characterised by singular receptive-expressive transcendental structures, propagating local excitations of the stream of experience, transient products of the *natura naturans* endowed with the capacity to momentarily detain its turbulence in the form of an objective *natura naturata*: 'Life is a vortex [of vortices], more or less rapid, more or less complicated, [...] so that the [enduring *trans*]*form* of a living body [of information] is more [existential] to it than its *matter*.[254] [...] One must [...] simply *deny* all *permanence* in Nature itself [...] for Nature the permanent is a limitation of its own activity[, a point of inhibition]. [...] A stream flows in a straight line forward as long as it encounters no resistance. Where there is [material] resistance—a [living] whirlpool forms. Every original product of Nature is such a vortex, every organized being. E.g., the whirlpool is not something immobilized, it is rather something constantly transforming—but reproduced anew at each moment, [...] gripped in continuous evolution, always changeable, appearing only to [experience and channel the flow from its singular perspective and] fade away again.[255] [...] On this stream, one may see an ever-changing pattern of vortices, ripples, waves, splashes, [frogs,] etc., which evidently have no independent existence as such. Rather, they are abstracted from the flowing movement, arising, [turning,] and vanishing in the total process of the [insubstantial] flow. Such transitory [subsistence] as may be possessed by these abstracted [living] forms implies only a relative independence or autonomy of behaviour, rather than absolutely independent existence as ultimate substances.[256] [...] Nature as a whole co-operates in every [living form].'[257]

---

254 G. Cuvier, *Animal Kingdom, Arranged According to its Organization, Forming the Basis for a Natural History of Animals, and An Introduction to Comparative Anatomy* (London: Wm. S. Orr and Co., 1833), 17.

255 Schelling, *First Outline of a System of the Philosophy of Nature*, 17–18.

256 D. Bohm, *Wholeness and the Implicate Order* (London and New York: Routledge, 2005), 62.

257 Schelling, *First Outline of a System of the Philosophy of Nature*, 18.

The absolutely modern future of the transcendental stance is conditional on its *existentialisation*—that is, on acceptance of the fact that the human transcendental type is not a necessary fixed structure but actually emerges from a local and contingent process of naturalcultural and self-positing subjectivation taking place in the immanence of the impersonal experiential stream. As we shall understand it here, the term *existentialisation* subsumes the *naturalisation* of the transcendental subject (e.g. the evolutionary institution of its physiological structures), its *historicisation* and *culturalisation* (e.g. the institution of its linguistic resources, of its behavioural patterns, of its *habitus*), and finally the *metaprogramming*, *self-positing processes* by means of which a subject can partially pilot its own institution. Firstly, the existentialisation of the transcendental takes up those projects aiming to naturalise the transcendental and generalises them to transcendental structures beyond the 'natural' in the restricted sense of the term (that is, as opposed to history and culture).[258] Second, the existentialisation of the transcendental also contemplates the existence of subjects capable of activating metaprogramming or self-positing circuits. By allowing the subject to acknowledge the degree of contingency of its transcendental structures, a diachronic reflection on the naturalcultural process of its own institution opens up the possibility of performing variations, perturbations, or deformations of these structures—augmenting the process of the institution of subjectivity with a self-positing degree of freedom. Thus, the existentialist stance maintains that the transcendental subject is not a sort of pre-phenoumenal essence that would be in a position of exception in relation to the experiential stream, but rather a *phenoumenal existence* resulting from a naturecultural process of subjectivation, a structure *instituted* within the flowing stream of experience and subject to both externally induced

258 Regarding the project of naturalising the transcendental see, for instance, J. Petitot, F.J. Varela, B. Pachoud, and J.M Roy (eds.), *Naturaliser la phénoménologie. Essais sur la phénoménologie contemporaine et les sciences cognitives* (Paris: CNRS Editions, 2002) and H. Carel and D. Meacham (eds.), *Phenomenology and Naturalism: Examining the Relationship between Human Experience and Nature* (Cambridge: Cambridge University Press, 2013).

and deliberate mutations. Every transcendental type of subjectivity is only a moment abstracted from a local process of subjectivation that takes time and place in the immanence of the experiential field. Thanks to this existentialisation, one of the last avatars of the pre-Copernican Ur-Arche Earth, the essentialised transcendental subject, is forced to abandon its pre-phenoumenal domain, its alleged ahistorical and pre-natural essentiality, in order to be incarnated, to drift, and to fall into the ungrounded field of impersonal experience.

We can therefore decompose the process of transcendental reflection into the following synchronic (focused on the *constitution* of objectivity) and diachronic (focused on the *institution* of subjectivity) phases. In a first synchronic phase, transcendental reflection allows the corresponding subject to bring into focus a hitherto invisible transcendental frame, thereby bracketing out the associated form of naive realism or modeltheism. In a second diachronic phase, the critical subject—far from assuming that such a frame is a God-given structure or a necessary condition of experience—can inquire about the naturecultural processes of institution of such a transcendental structure. This diachronic phase of transcendental reflection brings into focus 'the contingency that has made us what we are'[259] and shows us that the transcendental portals that filter and edit the pleroma are not endowed with any form of ahistorical or pre-natural necessity. This permits the subject to natureculturalise the frame unveiled by the synchronic phase, to understand it as the result of a particular process of institution of subjectivity: the a priori conditions of possibility of experience are now exhibited as the a posteriori result of a particular naturalcultural subjectivation process subsequently subject to a self-positing regulation. The corresponding transcendental type becomes an 'empirico-transcendental doublet',[260] what Etienne Balibar calls an ET.[261]

259 M. Foucault, 'What is Enlightenment?', tr. C. Porter, in P. Rabinow (ed.), *The Foucault Reader* (New York: Pantheon Books, 1984), 45.

260 M. Foucault, *The Order of Things* (London and New York: Routledge, 1996), 347.

261 E. Balibar, 'Foucault's Point of Heresy: "Quasi-Transcendentals" and the Transdisciplinary Function of the Episteme', *Theory, Culture & Society* 32:5–6 (2015): 45–77.

As we have suggested, the existentialisation of the Kantian a priori—the thesis that the transcendental subject is the result of a naturecultural institution and subject to self-positing regulations—takes place along different vectors of institution: *phylogenetic* evolution (unfolding, through different generations, at the global level of populations), the *ontogenetic* development of the individual, *epigenetic* adaptive processes, the *speculative* reflexive transformations of the subject's own structure, and finally the spiritual institution of emergent collective forms of subjectivity. According to the phylogenetic-evolutionary declension of the natureculturalisation of the Kantian a priori, 'everything leads to believe that the human psychic [and physiological] structure has changed over the course of time. [Human beings] spring from animal, and yet it would be surprising to attribute to animals the same cognitive capacities as to [human beings]. In this sense, all [transcendental] epistemology must be "genetic": it must take into account the effect of evolutionary transformations to which the human lineage has been subjected for thousands of years.[262] [...] [A]ll our forms of intuition and categories are thoroughly natural. Like every other organ, they are evolutionarily developed receptacles for the reception and retroactive utilization of those lawful consequences of the thing-in-itself with which we have to cope if we want to remain alive and preserve our species. [...] [A]ll laws of "pure reason" are based on highly physical or mechanical structures of the human central nervous system which have developed through many eons like any other organ. [...] [T]hese clumsy categorical boxes into which we have to pack our external world "in order to be able to spell them as experiences" (Kant) can claim no autonomous and absolute validity whatsoever. This is certain for us the moment we conceive them as evolutionary adaptations. [...] [T]he nature of their adaptation shows that the categorical forms of intuition and categories have proved themselves as working hypotheses in the coping of our species with the

262 R. Thom, *Semio Physics: A Sketch*, tr. V. Meyer (Redwood City, CA: Addison-Wesley, 1990), 1.

absolute reality of the environment (in spite of their validity as being only approximate and relative).'[263]

Second, this phylogenetic approach can be enriched with both ontogenetic and epigenetic perspectives. The 'a priori' structures of experience are not invariant throughout the life of the individual and the latter's ontogenetic and epigenetic development do modify them. We might consider for instance the sensorimotor, cognitive, and behavioural self-regulatory adaptation of an individual to its social and natural environment during its growth, the nonhereditary variations arising from different forms of environmental pressure, the learning processes undergone by the individual (learning of languages, of mathematical reasoning, of manual technics, of socialisation skills, and so on), the cultural imprints and the incorporations of different forms of social *habitus*, the traumatic or sublime experiences that the individual might undergo, the encounters with *n*-types of alterities, and the dynamical establishment (in Piaget's terms) of an adaptive equilibrium between *assimilation* (integration of new elements—like food in animals and solar radiation in plants—by means of the already established subject's transcendental structure) and *accommodation* (transformations of the transcendental apparatus itself in order to cope with an input that cannot be directly assimilated by the subject).[264]

---

263 Lorenz, 'Kant's Doctrine of the A Priori', 235.

264 'Generally speaking, this progressive equilibrium between assimilation and accommodation is an instance of a fundamental process in cognitive development which can be expressed in terms of centration and decentration. The systematically distorting assimilations of sensorimotor or initial representative stages, which distort because they are not accompanied by adequate accommodations, mean that the subject remains centered on his own actions and his own viewpoint. On the other hand, the gradually emerging equilibrium between assimilation and accommodation is the result of successive decentrations, which make it possible for the subject to take the points of view of other subjects or objects themselves. We formerly described this process merely in terms of egocentrism and socialization. But it is far more general and more fundamental to knowledge in all its forms. For cognitive progress is not only assimilation of information; it entails a systematic decentration process which is a necessary condition of objectivity itself.' Piaget, 'Piaget's

Third, the generic type of subjectivity that embodies a given subject at a given moment of its life is also the result of the reflexive meta-programming circuits that the subject might be able to activate. The type of subjectivity that a subject instantiates can be transformed by means of speculative interventions in its own transcendental structures as well as on higher-order speculative recalibrations of its own speculative regulators. Briefly, a subject might engage in and be the result of different forms of practices and protocols of self-transformation that reflexively alter its own subjective type at the different strata of the speculative landscape. Finally, a subject can (it always already does) engage in intersubjective, symbiogenetic, and trans-species forms of kinship and enter into emergent collective forms of subjectivity. These forms of transpersonal subjectivity instantiate subjective types that are different from the types of the individual components (for instance, the computational affordances of a neural network differ from those of each neuron in the network). By doing so, an individual can put its transcendental and speculative resources at the service of the institution of collective forms of (cognitive, affective, aesthetical, political, religious) experience that could never be reached by means of extensions of its own individual type at a personal level.

Certain authors have attempted to preserve an invariant empirical-transcendental divide by assuming the existence of an 'irreducible [arche-transcendental] residuum' supposed to resist the historicisations, naturalisations, culturalisations, and relativisations of the Kantian a priori.[265] By definition, such a residuum cannot be

---

Theory', 20. In Schmidhuber's words, '[w]e can regard assimilation as an oppression of the world by the brains, and accommodation as an oppression of the mind by the world.' Schmidhuber, *Evolutionary Principles in Self-Referential Learning*.

265 Foucault understands his own project of historicisation of knowledge as a regressive reduction of the transcendental that does not exclude the possibility of a hypothetical 'irreducible residuum': 'In all of my work I strive instead to avoid any reference to this transcendental as a condition of the possibility for any knowledge. When I say that I strive to avoid it, I do not mean that I am sure of succeeding. My procedure at this moment is of a regressive sort, I would say; I try to assume a greater and greater detachment in order to define the historical conditions and

the object of any possible speculative variation. For example, the subject-predicate structure[266] and the supposedly native, suffering, and mortal nature of every living individual[267] have both been proposed as arche-transcendental structures that could impose an unsurpassable ultimate limit on the project of performing transcendental variations. However, the thesis that all possible types of subjectivity necessarily instantiate such characteristics is void of rational necessity and simply reflects certain factual limits on the capacity to imagine transcendental variations. We must here remain faithful to the following principle of humility: never hypostasise our own limitations into universal principles (such as the limitations to our conceiving of a language that is not based on a subject-object structure, non-linguistic forms of cognition and agency, non-spatiotemporally situated forms of subjectivity, Kaspar-Hauserian forms of sapience unmediated by social practices and public norms, or finite forms of subjectivity that are not

---

transformations of our knowledge. I try to historicise to the utmost to leave as little space as possible to the transcendental. I cannot exclude the possibility that one day I will have to confront an irreducible *residuum* which will be, in fact, the transcendental.' M. Foucault, 'An Historian of Culture', interview with G. Preti, in S. Lotringer (ed.), *Foucault Live: Collected Interviews, 1961–1984* (New York: Semiotext[e], 1996), 95–104: 99.

266 Adrian Piper claims to have found such an arche-transcendental structure in 'the subject-predicate relation, and so [in] the substance-property transcendental category that corresponds to it [as] a necessary condition of experience. [...] [O]nly that transcendent idea of reason which is generated by the subject-predicate relation is similarly rationally inevitable, if any of them are.' A.M.S. Piper, 'Xenophobia and Kantian Rationalism', *Philosophical Forum* 24: 1–3 (Fall-Spring 1992–93), 188–232; reprinted in R.M. Schott (ed.), *Feminist Interpretations of Immanuel Kant* (University Park, PA: Pennsylvania State University Press, 1997), 21–73 and in J.P. Pittman (ed.), *African-American Perspectives and Philosophical Traditions* (New York: Routledge, 1997).

267 A critical discussion of this supposed 'ineliminable constant of the human condition' (according to Illich and Dupuy) and the associated unsurpassable 'pre-determined limits' can be found in R. Brassier, 'Prometheanism and its Critics', in R. Mackay and A. Avanessian (eds.), *#accelerate: The Accelerationist Reader* (Falmouth: Urbanomic, 2014), 467–87.

born, that do not suffer, that do not die). In other words, we must avoid at all costs contracting the 'Philosopher's Syndrome', that of 'mistaking a failure of imagination for an insight into necessity.'[268] Nonhuman (either posthuman or other-than-human) subjective forms of experience might have the capacity to tune in to attributes of the pleromatic insubstance other than the *sensorium*, the *logos*, the *affectum*, the *textum*, and the *socius*, they might be oriented by infinite ideas of reason that we cannot even conceive, they might instate forms of individuality other than organismal, colonial or driven forms,[269] they might be equipped with non-predicative forms of language or even with non-language-mediated forms of cognition, they might be embedded in a 'multi- or even a noncentered behavioral space'[270] (such as 'conscious interestellar gas clouds', solaristic oceans, or swarm-like superorganisms), they might be endowed with nonlinear and non-narrative forms of consciousness, they might not be endowed with sharp boundaries such as cell membranes, they might not be subject to a temporal reidentification, they might be adapted to environments obeying different physical laws, they might instantiate selfless subjective types deprived of a 'phenomenal self-model'[271] and capable of constituting 'nemocentric (i.e. centered on nobody) reality models',[272] they might not be equipped with a 'virtual window of presence'[273] and with retrospective and prospective capacities, they might have access to multi-scale forms of perception, affection, and socialisation, they might instantiate forms of finitude and perspectivism different from those associated with spatiotemporal localisation and to the birth-to-death existential structure, they might have access

268 D.C. Dennett, *Consciousness Explained* (London: Penguin, 1991), 401.

269 Cf. D. Krakauer, N. Bertschinger, E. Olbrich, J.C. Flack, and N. Ay, 'The Information Theory of Individuality', *Theory in Biosciences* 139 (2020), 209–23.

270 Metzinger, *Being No One*, 161.

271 Ibid., Ch. 6.1.

272 R. Grush, 'Self, World and Space: The Meaning and Mechanisms of Ego- and Allocentric Spatial Representation', *Brain and Mind* 1 (2000), 59–92; Metzinger, *Being No One*, 579.

273 Metzinger, *Being No One*, 42.

to nonbinary existential modalities other than being dead or alive, they might be able to navigate states of consciousness other than wakefulness, hallucinatory, or oneiric states, they might have the capacity to activate degrees of freedom in all the infinite strata of the speculative landscape and engage in meta-meta-...-meta-learning processes, they might be able to circulate through inter-versal channels and ride dimensional elevators to non-spatiotemporal axes, and so on and so forth far beyond what we can imagine and conceive. The only arche-transcendental determination of the subject of experience is its existential finitude, the fact that every subject is embedded in an experiential field that the subject can only experience partially, perspectivally, an experiential field on which a renormalising transcendental cut necessarily operates. The unique irreducible arche-transcendental determination of the subject of experience that we shall assume is that it instantiates a transcendental type—that is, that it somehow frames the field of experience and filters its pleromatic infinitude. But this existential finitude does not entail the existence of well-defined and unsurpassable limits to the different modes of thought and practice. In particular, existential finitude does not fix any impermeable epistemological limit to theoretical knowledge, being on the contrary the very condition of possibility of the project of science: scientific knowledge itself is not limited in principle; what is finite is the subject that desires to know. Modes of thought and practice oriented by infinite ideas only make sense for finite beings whose horizons of experience are restricted. In particular, the infinite project of science would not make sense for an infinite being—that is, for a hypothetical form of subjectivity not embedded in an impersonal experiential field that can only experience partially. Only from the cross of existential finitude does the rose of absolute knowledge endlessly blossom.

A serious objection to the project of natureculturalising transcendental philosophy was advanced by Husserl. According to Husserl, transcendental structures cannot be naturalised—i.e. subordinated to nature—since they are themselves the conditions of possibility for what we understand as 'nature'. What we could call the *Husserlian paradox* was posited by Husserl in the following terms: '[This is] the paradox of human subjectivity: being a subject for the world and at the same time being an object in the world.'[274] [...] Thus, *on the one hand consciousness is said to be the absolute* in which everything transcendent, and therefore, ultimately, the whole psychophysical world, becomes constituted; and, *on the other hand*, consciousness is said to be a *subordinate real event within that world*. How can these statements be reconciled?'[275] In other words, a transcendental subject cannot be instituted from and within nature if that nature is constituted by the transcendental subject. If transcendental reflection exhibits the subjective conditions of possibility of the natural sciences, then we cannot use those sciences to study the immanental institution of transcendental subjects as if they were themselves natural entities. According to Husserl, then, '[a] univocal determination of spirit through merely natural dependencies is unthinkable [...] Subjects cannot be dissolved into nature, for in that case what gives nature its sense would be missing'.[276] In a sense, Husserl's interdiction of the naturalisation of transcendental philosophy is the specular image of Kant's interdiction of a science of noumena: natural sciences can neither study the noumena 'beyond' constituted objects nor the process of subjectivation that institutes the constituting subject. What lies beyond the two poles of the subject-object correlation is in principle inaccessible to the natural sciences.

This objection to the naturalisation of transcendental philosophy results from the amphibological character of the term 'nature'. More precisely, it relies on the assumption that the (objective) nature resulting from the process of transcendental constitution coincides with the (absolute) nature within which the corresponding subject is instituted. But we can break this amphibology and proceed with a consistent naturalisation of

---

274 Husserl, *The Crisis of European Sciences and Transcendental Phenomenology*, 178 [§53].

275 Husserl, *Ideas Pertaining to a Pure Phenomenology and to a Phenomenological Philosophy. First Book*, 124 [§53]. See also E. Husserl, 'Philosophy as a Strict Science', tr. Q. Lauer, *CrossCurrents* 6:3 (1956), 227–46.

276 E. Husserl, *Ideas Pertaining to a Pure Phenomenology and to a Phenomenological Philosophy. Second Book: Studies in the Phenomenology of Constitution*, tr. R. Rojcewicz and A. Schuwer (Dordrecht: Kluwer, 1989), 311 [§64].

the transcendental by distinguishing—in the wake of Spinoza—between two senses of the term 'nature', namely the unique *natura naturans* within which the immanental 'natural' processes of institution of different types of transcendental subjectivity take place and the spectrum of *naturae naturatae* constituted by these types. The Spinozist *natura naturans* stands in contrast both to the ontotheological *meta-physics* that betrays the immanence of the experiential pleroma and to the pre-critical *physics* associated with a particular *natura naturata* correlated to a fixed transcendental type of subjectivity. The processes of subjectivation that take place within *natura naturans* induce the constitution of a spectrum of possible *naturae naturatae*, each correlated with a transcendental type of subjectivity. The absolute character of *natura naturans* results from its unframed, unfiltered, or unedited nature, from the fact that it is not relative to any transcendental type of subjectivity. Whereas on the one hand every subject is *instituted* at the heart of *natura naturans*, on the other hand every subject frames this *natura naturans*, thereby *constituting* a *natura naturata*. The subject is a 'subject for the world' in the sense that the environing world is the result of the subjective operations of transcendental constitution. And the subject itself is an 'object in the world' in the sense that the transcendental portals also constitute a 'self-model'—that is, a phenomenal self-representation of the subject itself. However, the ultimate site that defines the *there* of being-there is not the world constituted by the subject's transcendental faculties, but rather the impersonal life (the *natura naturans*) of which the objective world is just a transcendental-dependent renormalised version. Both the subject and the objective world of Husserl's paradox, both the I and the not-I in Fichte's terms, are instituted and constituted respectively within the living pleroma. I am here and now, sitting at a desk in the apartment where I live, writing this text on a computer, hearing the sounds of the city, peripherally perceiving the objects that surround me. But this description depends upon the transcendental filters of my subjectivity and this environing world is just a renormalised version of this pleromatic X in which I am, a transcendental-dependent niche embedded in an X which is framed differently by all other lifeforms, by the cells in my body, by the insects in the room, by the flowers in the vase, by the photons leaving the screen, by the higher multi-agent organisms of which I am a local 'neural' component. We are all together embedded in life, constituting different interfused circumambient worlds out of the same 'primordial being'. Thus the naturalisation of the transcendental cannot rely on a pre-critical form of scientificity that conflates the two Spinozist conjugations of the concept of nature, the objective *naturae naturatae* correlated to the corresponding transcendental types and the absolute *natura naturans* absolved from any form of correlation. The *naturalisation of the transcendental* is the other face of the *speculativisation of nature* that inserts the spectrum of different *naturae naturatae*—each of which is correlated to a particular transcendental type of subjectivity—into the same absolute nature. In short, the naturalisation of the transcendental will be an *absolute naturalisation*—which means that the term *naturalisation* makes reference to *natura naturans*—or it will be condemned to fall under the stroke of Husserl's paradox.

The naturalisation of transcendental structures, then, is not understood here as a simple inversion of transcendental idealism, an inversion that would oust the transcendental subject from the fundamental position and install the *natura naturata* of pre-critical science in its place. In others words, the naturalisation of the transcendental does not imply the unilateral subordination of transcendental philosophy to modern science or to some other kind of 'philosophy of nature'. The theoretical forms of reflection that focus on the *constitution* of a *natura naturata* and on the *institution* of the transcendental subject—that is, the transcendental analysis of constituted visions that unfold in the phenomenal foreground of the subject and the 'ontological psychoanalysis' of the 'unconscious' background that lies beneath instituted subjects—define the two complementary semicircles of a single theoretical movement that is properly speculative. The *imagination* (*Einbildungskraft*) is the stalk that sinks its roots in the immanental background, sucks its living sap, and sprouts in the transcendental foreground, the *visionary force* that institute subjects that constitute visions revealing themselves in umweltic clearings. In Schelling's terms, transcendental *philosophy* (focused on the transcendental constitution of objective nature) and *philosophy of nature* (focused on the natural institution of transcendental subjects) must be synthesised into a *philosophy of identity* that holds fast to the point of circular indistinction between the conscious ideal that projects images in the foreground and the unconscious real that vivifies the subject in the background: 'Since philosophy assumes the unconscious, or [...] the real activity to be identical with the conscious or ideal, its tendency will be to bring back everywhere the real to the ideal—a process which gives rise to what is called transcendental philosophy. [...] [*C*]*onversely, the ideal must arise out of the real and admit of explanation from it.* [...] [I]f it is the task of transcendental philosophy to subordinate the real to the ideal, it is, on the other hand, the task of the philosophy of nature to explain the ideal [i.e. the constituting subjectivity] by the real. The two sciences are therefore but one science, differentiated only in the opposite orientation of their tasks. [...] Philosophy of nature, as the opposite of transcendental philosophy, is distinguished from the latter chiefly by the fact that it posits Nature [...] as the self-existent; therefore it can most concisely be designated the *Spinozism* ['realism in its most sublime and perfect form'][277] *of physics.*[278] [...] I take neither what I term "transcendental philosophy" nor what I term "philosophy of nature", each in isolation, to be the system of philosophy itself, but instead [...] I regard each of them as nothing more than a one-sided presentation of that system.'[279] *Transcendental philosophy* and *philosophy of nature*—or *transcendental idealism* and *immanental realism*—are circularly complementary ('Nature, in other words, is a cultural concept, but culture itself is a natural fact')[280] and the philosophy of identity is the stereoscopic

277 F.W.J. Schelling, 'Presentation of My System of Philosophy', tr. M. Vater, in *The Philosophical Forum* 32:4 (Winter 2001), 339–71.

278 Schelling, *First Outline of a System of the Philosophy of Nature*, 193–94.

279 Schelling, 'Presentation of My System of Philosophy', 390.

280 R. Wagner, 'The Reciprocity of Perspectives', *Social Anthropology* 26:4 (November 2018), 502–10. It is also worth quoting here the following text by Merleau-Ponty: 'It is clear that Nature in itself is not given to us; there is only a human experience of Nature. [...] So 'Nature' is not just the artifact of a disinterested scientific consciousness, but a myth upon which historical subjectivities project and hide their conflicts in each moment. Indeed, to speak of Nature as an object of reflection separable from humanity or history [of a purported Nature in itself] is to subordinate

stance that results from their speculative integration. In James's terms, the philosophy of identity is a 'radical empiricism' or a 'philosophy of pure experience', where 'pure' means unframed, unedited, pleromatic, indifferentiable into I and not-I, uncorrelated to a transcendental type of subjectivity, released from any umweltic context and—by the same token—always offered up to the constituting operations performed by new renormalising valves, to speculative deformations of the transcendental frames, to fusions of

---

human being in advance to an external, unknown principle; to render oneself blind to the negation of nature that is precisely what makes the human capable of conceiving or dreaming a Nature. [...] These are all good arguments, but they do not justify our [idealistically] reducing the concept of nature to a branch of anthropology. If we were to accept this formal demand, and this humanism, then not only Nature but also philosophy would have to be eliminated. [...] Every philosophy of Nature is a philosophy of history in disguise [a philosophy of the historical processes of constitution of a singular image of Nature] [...]. Every proposition that such a philosophy puts forth must be understood as an operation of a subject, translated before the [transcendental] tribunal of the philosophy of spirit or philosophy of history. [...] We admit that the concepts of Nature, history, and humanity form a tangled web, perhaps an endless one. But this is precisely why it is impossible to treat Nature as a detail of human history [as a pure product of a transcendental constitution]; somehow we have to work through the ideologies of Nature and restore the true traits of the 'veiled idol'. Every positing of a Nature implies a subjectivity and even a historical intersubjectivity. Which does not mean that the sense of natural being is exhausted by its symbolic transcriptions, that these transcriptions leave us nothing more to think. It only proves that the being of Nature is to be sought upstream of its being-posited. If a [transcendental] philosophy of reflection is permitted to treat all philosophy of Nature as a disguised philosophy of spirit or of humanity, and to judge it on the basis of the conditions of all possible objects for a spirit or a human, this generalized suspicion, i.e. reflection, must also submit to investigation. It must turn against itself. And, upon having measured what we risk losing if we start with Nature, we must also take account of what we will surely lack if we start from subjectivity: the primordial being against which all reflection institutes itself, and without which, since there is no outside against which it could measure itself, there is no longer any philosophy.' M. Merleau-Ponty, 'La Nature ou le monde du silence', cited in E. de Saint Aubert, *Maurice Merleau-Ponty* (Paris: Hermann, 2008), 41–42.

heterogeneous circumambient bubbles into wider phenomenological horizons.[281] What we shall call *immanental phenoumenodelia* is a 'philosophy of pure experience' that must not lose sight of the totality of the immanental process of self-revelation that is life: the naturalcultural processes of subjectivation by means of which local subjects of different transcendental types are instituted within the experiential field, the subsequent framings of the experiential field carried out by the transcendental structures of those subjects, the concomitant emergence of a myriad of *naturae naturatae* or Umwelten constituted by these framings, the contrapuntal harmonies between heterogeneous Umwelten, and the interfusion of the latter into wider phenomenological horizons correlative to the emergence of collective forms of subjectivity. In this framework, the speculative upgrading of the concept of nature (the integration of the spectrum of *naturae naturatae* into a single *natura naturans*) and the natureculturalisation of transcendental subjects raise both the concept of nature and the concept of the subject to new post-critical, post-foundational powers. The very conception of an immanental phenoumenodelia requires the reciprocal counterbalancing of the congenitally idealistic tendency of transcendental phenomenology (resulting from the foreclosure of naturalcultural processes of the institution of transcendental subjects and the consequent tendency to make the experiential 'plane of immanence' 'immanent 'to' a transcendental subjectivity')[282] and the potential transcendental naivety of a pre-critical philosophy of nature (a naivety resulting from the foreclosure of transcendental overdeterminations of the concept of *nature*).

---

281 'Since the acquisition of conscious quality on the part of an experience depends upon a context [a *framing* in our terminology] coming to it, it follows that the sum total of all experiences, having no context, cannot strictly be called conscious at all. It is a *that*, an Absolute, a "pure" experience on an enormous scale, undifferentiated and indifferentiable into thought and thing. This the post-Kantian idealists have always practically acknowledged by calling their doctrine *Identitätsphilosophie*. [...] [T]he philosophy of pure experience [is] only a more committed *Identitätsphilosophie*.' W. James, 'How Two Minds Can Know One Thing', in *Essays in Radical Empiricism*, 70–71.

282 Deleuze and Guattari, *What is Philosophy?*, 46.

The presupposition of a unique absolute nature (*natura naturans*) enveloping the spectrum of possible framed natures (*naturae naturatae*) would be a vain formal hypothesis without consequences if such an absolute nature could not be the domain of application of a positive scientific inquiry that would give an effective content to the term *naturalisation*. The speculative positing of an absolute nature (*natura naturans*) beyond the subject-object correlation could not be used to legitimate the project of naturalising transcendental philosophy—that is, the project of scientifically addressing the natural institution of transcendental types of subjectivity—if the absolute nature were withdrawn *de jure* from any form of scientific inquiry. But this would be the case if we accepted that the legitimate domain of application of the natural sciences can only be—as Kant maintained—the objective nature (the *natura naturata*) defined by the human transcendental framing. The notion of a science of absolute nature seems to contradict the very critical spirit of transcendental reflection, in a dogmatic manner. Now, this objection may be twisted into a determinate negation by maintaining that a consequent naturalisation of the transcendental types of subjectivity requires embracing the possibility of a *post-critical science of absolute nature*—that is to say, a post-critical conception of scientificity capable of sublating the Kantian interdiction. But how could we overcome the Kantian interdiction while at the same time remaining faithful to the (spirit of the) transcendental project? How could we conceive a doctrine of a post-critical science of absolute nature without falling back into pre-critical dogmatism? The answer to these questions is elegantly circular in form: a doctrine of a post-critical science of absolute nature capable of endowing the project of naturalising the transcendental types of subjectivity with a positive scientific content requires (as we shall see) the presupposition of such a naturalisation. In other words, the *naturalisation of transcendental philosophy* and the idea of a *post-critical science of absolute nature* do indeed presuppose one another. This play of reciprocal presuppositions, far from precipitating us into a vicious circle, is simply consistent: we need only enter, nonchalantly, into the virtuous circle of speculation.

For instance, the diachronic scientific analysis of the institution of certain human transcendental structures through an evolutionary process fosters a critical awareness regarding the transcendental relativity of human intelligence. Far from having been modelled to think the real in itself, human cognitive faculties emerged from a complex evolutionary process partially driven by the constraint of surviving under different forms of external environmental pressure: 'The history of the evolution of life [...] already reveals to us how the intellect has been formed, by an uninterrupted progress, along a line which ascends through the vertebrate series up to [human beings]. It shows us in the faculty of understanding an appendage of the faculty of acting, a more and more precise, more and more complex and supple adaptation of the consciousness of living beings to the conditions of existence that are made for them. [...] [O]ur intellect, in the narrow sense of the word, is intended to secure the perfect fitting of our body to its environment, to represent the relations of external things among themselves, in short, to think matter.[283] [...] The principal function [...] of our cognitive faculties is not that of producing true or verisimilitudinous beliefs, but instead that of contributing to survival [that is, to succeed in the "four Fs": fighting, fleeing, feeding and fornicating] by getting the body parts in the right place.'[284] But if this is the case, why should we believe that human understanding produces (at least projectively) faithful models of the rational structure of the real? And in particular, why should we believe that evolutionary biology produces a faithful description of the natural process through which living beings were instituted? '[With Darwin] the horrid doubt always arises whether the convictions of [the human being's] mind, which has been developed from the mind of the lower animals, are of any value or at all trustworthy.'[285] On the one hand, the scientific results provided by evolutionary biology enrich critical reflection on the typical structure of human subjectivity and its transcendental perspectivism. On the other hand, critical reflection on

283 Bergson, *Creative Evolution*, xix.

284 A. Plantinga, *Warrant and Proper Function* (New York: Oxford University Press, 1993), 218.

285 C. Darwin, Letter to William Graham, Down, July 3, 1881, quoted in Plantinga, *Warrant and Proper Function*, 219.

the transcendental perspectivism of scientific thinking emphasises that this very scientific analysis should not be dogmatically raised to the rank of an absolute knowledge about the evolutionary emergence of human subjectivity. Like any other science, the current state of biology (and of the theory of evolution in particular) relies on a particular system of conceptual categories, paradigmatic frameworks, constitutive principles, discursive formations, scientific habitus, and socio-economico-political conditions that are themselves the result of processes of naturalcultural institution. The only thing that we can do here in order to avoid the risk of surrendering to an unilateral foundation (either on scientific realism or on transcendental idealism) is to helicoidally circulate through this interplay of mutual presuppositions and recalibrations between scientific inquiry and transcendental reflection: 'Thus, the consideration of the biological thesis does not only convince us that intelligence has a history or that it is a dated event. It is the very function of intelligence that only reveals itself to us when we insert it into the real process that produced it. This is the reason for the necessity of the circular reference between the theory of life [(biology)] and the [transcendental] theory of knowledge: it is the very function of intelligence that would remain hidden from us if we renounced the teachings of biology. [...] [T]here must be a double movement from one pole to the other. What is important is to enter into this circular process.'[286]

So, let us consider in detail the reciprocal presupposition between a *doctrine of a post-critical science* (addressing what dwells 'beyond' the object of the correlation) and the *naturalisation of transcendental philosophy* (addressing what dwells upstream of the constituting subject, that is, the processes of institution of the corresponding transcendental structures). We have already argued that a consistent naturalisation of transcendental philosophy requires presupposing a doctrine of a post-critical science of absolute nature capable of absolving the term *naturalisation* from Husserl's paradox. Briefly, the naturalisation of the transcendental subject requires (a) splitting the concept of nature into a unique *natura naturans* and a spectrum of transcendental-dependent *naturae naturatae* and (b) assuming that

286 B. Prado Jr., *Présence et champ transcendental*, 141.

this *natura naturans* can be the 'object' of a (speculative) scientific inquiry, that is, that science is not necessarily restricted to the *natura naturata* correlative to the corresponding subject of science. We shall now argue that such a post-critical form of scientificity is in turn made possible by the naturalisation of the transcendental types.

The naturalising hypothesis states that the transcendental types of subjectivity result from naturalcultural and self-positing processes of immanental institution. It follows that experience does not take place from a *fixed* viewzone in the transcendental landscape. Every transcendental type is just a specious 'instantaneous' abstraction extracted from an ongoing process of immanental institution of subjectivity. The transcendental Copernicanism initiated by Kant is ultimately defined by the thesis that the location in the transcendental landscape that defines the human transcendental perspective (what we could call, inflecting Husserl's expression, the *transcendental Earth*) is also in motion. In Pascal's terms, constituting subjects—being instituted entities—have always already embarked, both into the physical cosmic extensions and into the transcendental landscape. The thesis that experience takes place from the fixed vantage point provided by an immobile transcendental Earth and the rejection of the naturalisation of the transcendental subject are two sides of the same pre-Copernican coin: if we cannot change our location in the transcendental landscape, then transcendental perspectivism remains unsurpassable and the 'nature' studied by science can only be the constituted *natura naturata* correlated to the transcendental type of the subject of science. In turn, this means that the *natura naturans* or absolute nature remains beyond the grasp of scientific inquiry. If this were the case, then we could not endow the naturalising hypothesis with a positive scientific content. On the contrary, the Copernikantian launching of the transcendental Earth—which implies (as we shall now see) that a post-critical science of absolute nature is possible—and the naturalisation of the transcendental subjects are consistent components of the same speculative stance.

If our transcendental type is always already in motion in the transcendental landscape, then surely we can try to direct these transcendental motions, to 'shift the gears' and 'adjust preconceptions',[287] to activate degrees of freedom in the transcendental landscape, to turn on the metaprogramming circuits, to drive our own subjective institution, to understand the transcendental Earth as a pilotable transcendental Pleromaship Earth. The fact that human experience is necessarily framed by a system of transcendental structures (physiological, technological, conceptual, linguistic, cultural, and so on) does not imply that we cannot try to modify, deform, or perturb the corresponding frame. A subject is certainly a mode of the insubstance that determines which differences will (for the subject) make a difference.[288] But the thesis that we cannot recalibrate the resolution of this transcendental determination of relevant differences is just a dogmatic assumption. According to the speculative interpretation of transcendental reflection, the latter must not be understood as an abstract negation demarcating a fixed and uncrossable limit, but as a determinate negation thanks to which the very limit it reveals can be effectively (albeit differentially) overcome. Transcendental critique, far from demarcating the insuperable limits of human experience, should be understood as a reflection upon the contingent transcendental structure of our subjectivity thanks to which it becomes possible to mediate the limits of experience determined by this very transcendental structure: 'We have to move beyond the outside-inside alternative; we have to be at the frontiers. Criticism indeed consists of analysing and reflecting upon limits. But if the Kantian question was that of knowing what limits knowledge has to renounce transgressing, [...] the critical question today has to be turned back into a positive one: in what is given to us as universal, necessary, obligatory, what place is occupied by whatever is singular, contingent, and the product of arbitrary constraints? The point, in brief, is to transform the critique conducted in the form of necessary limitation into a practical critique that takes the form of a possible transgression. This entails an obvious consequence: that critique is no longer going to be practiced in the search for formal structures with universal value, but rather as a historical investigation into the events that

---

287 Bateson and Bateson, *Angels Fear*, 184.

288 Bateson, *Steps to an Ecology of Mind*, 272.

have led us to constitute ourselves and to recognise ourselves as subjects of what we are doing, thinking, saying. [...] And this critique will be genealogical in the sense that it will not deduce from the form of what we are what it is impossible for us to do and to know; but it will separate out, from the contingency that has made us what we are, the possibility of no longer being, doing, or thinking what we are, do, or think.'[289]

The critical line of demarcation between a phenomenal realm and a noumenal domain removed from all experience then becomes dynamic: instead of being deployed in a phenomenal horizon separated de jure from a noumenal beyond—in an umweltic prison hovering in a 'great outdoors'—instead of being governed by the fixed 'outside-inside alternative' native to the claustrophobic interpretations of transcendental critique, experience unfolds in a unique *phenoumenal* field that admits of several phenomenal-noumenal splits. The critical reflection on the transcendental perspectivism of modern science and the consequent relativisation of the resulting scientific world view (or any form of 'reverse anthropology'[290] that pinpoints the parochial character of European civilisation) would be no more than an unproductive abstract negation if they did not make possible a post-critical overcoming of this transcendental perspectivism, if they did not allow the limits of our contingent transcendental structure to be mediated, if they did not allow us to raise the very concept of scientificity to a post-critical power. Instead of restricting its inquiry to the *natura naturata* correlated to the transcendental type of the subject of science, a post-critical science should be able to reflect on the transcendental conditions of possibility of such an objective nature, to effect speculative variations of the corresponding transcendental structures, to integrate the transcendental perspectives swept away by these variations, and to orient its research activities by means of the regulative idea of truth qua untyped universality. The subject of such a post-critical phase of scientificity is necessarily a *speculative subject*, that is, a subject that can perform variations of its transcendental type and

289 Foucault, 'What is Enlightenment?', 45.

290 Cf. R. Wagner, *The Invention of Culture* (Chicago: University of Chicago Press, 1981).

integrate the corresponding transcendental perspectives into experiences endowed with higher forms of speculative depth.

Let us consider now an example of a sequence of *speculative extensions* of a given transcendental structure provided by the history of number systems. This history provides a good example of the context-dependent distinction between empirical and transcendental structures. We shall understand a numerical system as a transcendental structure by means of which it is possible to formulate problems and search for their answers. Now, some might argue that number systems cannot be considered an a priori transcendental structure that frames human experience, since the history of mathematics shows that human intelligence has the capacity to expand its arithmetical resources. However, this long-term variability does not erase the short-term invariance. During important periods of human history (in the periods of 'normal arithmetic' between two 'numerical revolutions'), the numerical resources of mankind (where for simplicity we are disregarding geographic variances) were limited to a particular numerical system. It is therefore legitimate to consider the latter as a transcendental frame that—during the period in question—fixed the arithmetical capacities and limits of mathematical experience, even if this transcendental a priori is a 'relativised a priori' (Friedman) that is not immune to the vicissitudes of the empirical history of ideas.

To begin with, let us assume that we have only access to a natural language arithmetically enriched by the natural numbers $\mathbb{N}=\{0, 1, 2...\}$ (a language that we shall denote $L_{\mathbb{N}}$). We can understand this language as a transcendental structure by means of which we can ask questions and try to answer them. In particular, we can posit the question 'Is there a number x such that x+1=3?' in the language $L_{\mathbb{N}}$. This question admits of an answer within the discursive framework defined by $L_{\mathbb{N}}$, namely 2. Now, human language (and thinking) is characterised by an exorbitant ek-sistential feature, namely that it allows us to posit questions and problems whose answers and solutions cannot be formulated with the linguistic and conceptual resources used to posit them. In particular, we can formulate in the language $L_{\mathbb{N}}$ questions that have no answer in $L_{\mathbb{N}}$, such as the question 'Is there a number x such that x+1=0?' We can rephrase this fact by saying that no natural number witnesses for the truth of the predicate 'There is a number x such that $x+1=0$'. However, to conclude from the absence of a truthmaker the falseness of the predicate is to fall into a pre-critical naivety. Indeed, the impossibility of demonstrating the truth of the predicate at stake in $L_{\mathbb{N}}$ could simply be a consequence of the transcendental limitations of this particular language. We could nonetheless endorse a strong form of idealism and claim that there is no such truthmaker, that is, that what cannot be said in $L_{\mathbb{N}}$ simply does not exist. This amounts to the claim that the predicate is simply and absolutely false. Alternatively, we could endorse a transcendental-idealist position and maintain that what cannot be said in the framework provided by our transcendental linguistic resources nonetheless exists 'in itself'. We could argue that such exorbitant questions are symptoms that force us to acknowledge the ultimate transcendental limits of our language. We could understand such questions as 'mystical' operators which show us that there is an utterly unsayable 'great outdoors' beyond the sayable 'world'. Following this line of reasoning, we could then claim that the limits of the 'world' defined by the language $L_{\mathbb{N}}$ are the ultimate limits of any possible experience. However, there is no need to hypostatise the limitations of the available language and mystify that which exceeds its transcendental resources: we can always patiently work—'word for word', number by number—to enrich our language and sublate its limits. The internal impasses of a symbolic regime—such as well-formulated unanswerable questions—point toward a 'real' beyond this particular regime, a realm in which language can breathe and expand. What we cannot speak about has to be said by forcing speculative extensions of our linguistic resources. We shall not be mesmerised by the transcendental limits of language, we shall not conflate the critical acknowledgement of these limits with a mystical experience: language goes 'through its own lack of answers [...]. It [might give us] no words for what [is] happening, but [goes] through it [...] and [can] resurface, [speculatively] "enriched" by it all.'[291]

291 From the address given by Paul Celan at the reception of the Literature Award of the Free Hanseatic City of Bremen, January 20, 1958, in P. Celan, *Collected Prose*, tr. R. Waldrop (New York: Sheep Meadow Press, 1986), 34.

In the previous example, we can define a speculative extension of the language $L_{\mathbb{N}}$ by substituting for the natural numbers $\mathbb{N}$ the integers $\mathbb{Z} = \{..., -2, -1, 0, 1, 2, ...\}$.The question 'Is there a number x such that $x+1=0$?' now admits of the answer $x=-1$ in the language $L_{\mathbb{Z}}$. This seemingly trivial extension of the natural numbers $\mathbb{N}$ (also called, for obvious reasons, *counting numbers*) entails a highly nontrivial conceptual leap (for instance, whereas an expression of the form 'there are two apples on the table' is straightforwardly understandable, the comprehension of the expression 'there are minus two apples on the table' is more problematic).[292] From this point of view, the limits of a language cannot be understood as the limits *of language*. Indeed, we can continue this narrative and formulate questions of the form 'Is there a number such that $2x+1=0$?' (a question that forces the speculative extension of the language $L_{\mathbb{Z}}$ to the language $L_{\mathbb{Q}}$ defined by the field of rational numbers $\mathbb{Q}$), 'Is there a number x such that $x^2-2=0$?' (a question that points in the direction of an extension of the language $L_{\mathbb{Q}}$ to the language $L_{\mathbb{R}}$ defined by the field of real numbers $\mathbb{R}$), 'Is there a number x such that $x^2+1=0$?' (a question that forces the speculative extension of the language $L_{\mathbb{R}}$ to the language $L_{\mathbb{C}}$ defined by the field of complex numbers $\mathbb{C}$). In general, the speculative dynamic of reason is such that the search for the solutions to a problem formulated within a given transcendental regime of rationality—that is, in the framework of a particular framing of the experiential field defined by the available perceptual, experimental, conceptual, linguistic, and formal (e.g. geometric,

---

292 In Cassirer's words: 'The difficulties encountered in the introduction of every new type of number—of the negatives and the irrationals as well as the imaginaries—are easily explained if we consider that, in all these transformations, the real basis of numerical assertions seems more and more to disappear. Enumeration, in its most fundamental sense, could be immediately shown to be "real" by means of sensible objects and therefore valid.' E. Cassirer, *Substance and Function and Einstein's Theory of Relativity*, tr. W.C. Swabey and M.C. Swabey (Chicago and London: Open Court, 1923), 55. See also the section 'The "Ideal Elements" and their Meaning for the Structure of Mathematics' in E. Cassirer, *Philosophy of Symbolic Forms. Volume Three: The Phenomenology of Knowledge*, tr. R. Manheim (New Haven, CT: Yale University Press, 1957), 389–405 [III.4.4].

algebraic, arithmetic, logical) resources—might require the activation of degrees of freedom in the transcendental landscape and the exploration of different transcendental domains related by speculative extensions: 'Two thoughts assailed [her]. One in the mother tongue, the other in a foreign language. The first asked the question, the other answered. Result: I am the [mother] of my questions and the [daughter] of my answers.'[293] Two comments are here in order. As Lacan pointed out, 'the real doesn't stop not being written',[294] which means that any sublation of the limits of a particular transcendental regime should not be conflated with a definitive capture of the real as such: the real will always continue to insist, to arrive, to tear up the continuity of the *textum*, to make holes in the symbolic orders and elicit further speculative extensions. Second, the notion of *speculative extension*—that is, of an extension of a transcendental regime elicited by certain impasses of the latter—is a particular case of the more general notion of *extension*, where the new 'ideal elements' are not necessarily required by the limits of the original transcendental regime.[295]

The history of number systems provides an example of a series of extensions propelled by the absence of solutions to certain problems that are formulable within the frameworks of the initial transcendental structures.

---

293 Leminski, *Catatau*, 114.

294 J. Lacan, *The Seminar of Jacques Lacan, Book XX: Encore 1972–1973, On Feminine Sexuality, The Limits of Love and Knowledge*, tr. B. Fink, ed. J.-A. Miller (New York and London: Norton), 94.

295 In mathematical algebra, what we have called *speculative extension* is called *algebraic extension*. An algebraic extension of a field of numbers $k$ is an extension $L$ such that every number in $L$ is the solution of a nontrivial polynomial equation defined over $k$. For instance, the extension of the field of rational numbers $\mathbb{Q}$ defined by the new ideal element $\sqrt{2}$ is algebraic since $\sqrt{2}$ is a solution of a polynomial equation defined over $\mathbb{Q}$ (namely, $x^2-2=0$). By contrast, the extension of $x^2-2=0$ defined by the new 'ideal element' $\pi$ is not algebraic since $\pi$ cannot be obtained as a solution of a polynomial equations with coefficients in $\mathbb{Q}$. We could say that the adjunction of the 'ideal element' $\pi$ is not required by the internal impasses of $\mathbb{Q}$. In the sequence of extensions introduced above, the extension from $\mathbb{Q}$ to $\mathbb{R}$ is not algebraic (or speculative), since $\mathbb{R}$ also contains non-algebraic numbers such as $\pi$ and $e$.

Another type of transcendental obstruction to the deployment of a form of experience is given by the concept of *exception*. Let us consider a geometric example given by the set of straight lines in the Euclidean plane. While two points define a single straight line (the line between the two points), two lines define a single point, the point of intersection between them. However, this duality between lines and points admits of exceptions, since two parallel lines do not define any point of intersection. Now, it is possible to eliminate these exceptions and state a general duality between points and lines by means of a speculative extension of the 'transcendental aesthetic' defined by the Euclidean plane, an extension that equips the Euclidean plane with new 'ideal elements'.[296] This speculative extension of the Euclidean plane is obtained by literally adding the points that are missing, the so-called *points at infinity*. These points result from the conversion of the negative statement 'two parallel lines never intersect' into the positive statement 'two parallel lines meet at infinity', that is, at the new 'ideal points' added at infinity. For each equivalence class of parallel lines, a single point at infinity is formally introduced, the point at which any two lines in that class intersect.[297] There will therefore be a point at infinity corresponding to each equivalence class of parallel lines and the set of these points defines the so-called *horizon line*, or *line at infinity*. In this way, the exception to the duality between points and lines given by parallel lines can be removed by means of a projective extension of the Euclidean plane in the most literal sense of the term, namely by formally adding the missing 'ideal points' at infinity where parallel lines do 'cross'. This projective completion of the Euclidean plane defines the

---

296 Cf. D. Hilbert, 'Die Rolle von idealen Gebilden', in D. Rowe (ed.), *Natur und mathematisches Erkennen* (Basel: Birkhäuser, 1992), 90–101; D. Hilbert, 'Über das Unendliche', *Matematische Annalen* 95 (1926): 161–90 ('On the Infinite', in P. Benacerraf and H. Putnam [eds.], *Philosophy of Mathematics: Selected Readings* [Cambridge: Cambridge University Press, 1984], 183–201).

297 Since the property that we want to be fulfilled is that any two lines cross at a *single* point, we shall assume that the point at infinity at which two parallel lines cross is the same when we move in the two possible directions of the parallel lines.

corresponding *projective space*. Beyond allowing for the formulation of a *principle of duality* between points and lines, the projective completion of the Euclidean plane makes it possible to understand different figures in Euclidean space as particular cases of a single type of figure: *ellipses* (and in particular *circles*), *parabolas*, and *hyperbolas* are all cases of the same type of figure—what are called *conic sections*—in the projective plane. In particular, parabolas and hyperbolas are open curves in Euclidean space since the points that would 'close' them are points at infinity (one for the parabola and two for the hyperbola).[298] By adding these missing points, the parabolas and the hyperbolas become, like the ellipses, closed curves. These different figures can be differentiated by the incidence relations they entertain with the line at infinity: while ellipses never touch the horizon line at infinity (fully remaining on one side of the line), parabolas touch it at a single point (touching the horizon at a tangent, only to come back again) and hyperbolas intersect it at two points (where the two 'disconnected'

---

298 Let us consider for instance the parabola equation $y-x^2=0$. As we move to $\pm\infty$ along the $x$ axis, the two branches of the parabola become more and more vertical in such a way that at $x=\pm\infty$ they are parallel to the $y$ axis. By definition, the two parallel straight lines at $x=+\infty$ and $x=-\infty$ cross at a point at infinity. This point at infinity 'closes' the curve so to speak. Let us consider now the hyperbola $x^2-y^2=1$. Each disconnected branch of the hyperbola has two asymptotes at angles of $\pm 45°$ with respect to the $x$-axis. As we move to $x=+\infty$, the upper side of the right branch becomes parallel to the asymptote at +45° and the lower side of the right branch becomes parallel to the asymptote at $-45°$. In turn, as we move to $x=-\infty$, the upper side of the left branch becomes parallel to the asymptote at $-45°$ and the lower side of the left branch becomes parallel to the asymptote at +45°. Now, the 'two' points at infinity along the asymptote at +45° are in fact the same point (and the same is true for the 'two' points at infinity along the asymptote at $-45$ °). It follows that the upper right and the lower left sections of the hyperbola meet at the same a point at infinity. Analogously, the lower right and the upper left sections of the hyperbola also meet at the same point at infinity (which is different from the previous one). All in all, we can circulate along the hyperbola in a closed loop by following the upper right section up to infinity in order to reenter the realm of finitude along the lower left section, then going to the second point at infinity along the upper left section in order to finally reappear along the lower right section.

sheets of the hyperbola correspond to the two sections of the closed curve on either side of the line at infinity).[299] We could say that Newton's enlightenment beneath the Cambridge apple tree enacts in the realms of gravitational physics a similar unification between the conic forms of the fall, that is, between the ellipsoidal orbits that endlessly freefall without ever reaching the ground, without ever touching infinity ('Everything rotates [A Vorticist!] [...] in a slowly [drifting] loop [...] repeating itself—without end',[300] in an elliptical motion in which 'the body has its place in the motion itself.[301] [T]here is no escape 'from this [periodic] place [...] the Laws of Newton and Kepler constraining'[302] the planets to eternally play the same spherical music), the earthbound trajectories of human cannonballs pathetically reenacting over and over again the same parabolic tales of patriarchal savagery ('And he war. And he shall open his mouth and answer: I hear, O Ismael, how they laud is only as my loud is one')[303] and the hyperbolic fly toward grace, finally crossing the horizon at infinity, where 'it is no longer a matter of [Ur-Arche Earth-bounding] gravity—it is an acceptance of [the supernatural sky]. [...] invisible sources of gravity rolling through like storms, making it possible to fall for distances only astronomers are comfortable with—yet, each time, the [noetic Ark] is brought to safety, in the bright, flowerlike heart of a perfect hyper-hyperboloid.'[304]

---

299 See for instance Fig. 9.1 in J. Richter-Gebert, *Perspectives on Projective Geometry: A Guided Tour Through Real and Complex Geometry* (Berlin and Heidelberg: Springer-Verlag, 2011), 149.

300 T. Pynchon, *Mason & Dixon* (New York: Henry Holt, 1997), 555–56.

301 Heidegger, *What is a Thing?*, 84.

302 Pynchon, *Mason & Dixon*, 162.

303 Joyce, *Finnegans Wake*, 258.

304 T. Pynchon, *Against the Day* (New York: Penguin Books, 2007), 1084–85. I borrow this reading of Pynchon's *Gravity's Rainbow*, *Mason & Dixon*, and *Against the Day* in terms of conic sections from M. Harris, *Mathematics without Apologies: Portrait of a Problematic Vocation* (Princeton, NJ: Princeton University Press, 2015).

The speculative extensions of a given domain of rationality by the adjunction of new 'ideal elements' is—as Hilbert writes—'one of the most important mathematical methods, the application of which is always repeated up to the highest parts of mathematics'[305] and physics. Speculative extensions of a given transcendental regime might allow us to find new solutions to a given problem (which, as we have seen, might have no solutions at all in the domain in which it was formulated), to remove exceptions, to regularise pathological situations (like the so-called 'bad intersections' and 'bad quotients'), to enforce the closure of a domain with respect to a given operation (which means that the operation applied to elements in the domain yields an element that also belongs to the domain), or to get rid of purported aprioristic background structures by extending the dynamical degrees of freedom described by the corresponding theory (as in the general-relativistic physicalisation of certain geometric structures of the spatiotemporal background). We could say that these adjunctions elicit an expansion of the different transcendental regimes of 'pure intuition', like for instance the regime provided by the understanding of numbers as formal entities intended to count an aggregate of things (or, as Kant writes in the *Prolegomena*, as concepts formed 'through successive additions of units in time').[306] The possibility of extending a given domain of rationality and enriching the corresponding forms of 'pure intuition' entails a particular form of (what Friedman calls) 'relativisation of the *a priori*'.[307] In the particular cases treated here, this means that the arithmetic and geometric forms of 'pure intuition' (such as the natural numbers or Euclidean space), far from being fixed once and for all (that is, far from being endowed with a perennial form of aprioricity, as seems

---

305 Hilbert, 'Die Rolle von idealen Gebilden', 90.

306 I. Kant, *Prolegomena to Any Future Metaphysics That Will Be Able to Come Forward as Science*, tr. G. Hatfield (Cambridge: Cambridge University Press, 2004).

307 Cf. M. Friedman, *Reconsidering Logical Positivism* (Cambridge: Cambridge University Press, 1999), I.3.

to be the case in Kant),[308] are subjected to speculative extensions elicited by the very evolution of mathematics. The fact that domain extensions force the modification of what, in a given historical context, is regarded as an a priori form of 'pure intuition' explains the difficulties encountered in performing such extensions, difficulties that left their traces in the denominations chosen to design the new elements (e.g., irrational numbers, imaginary numbers, ideal elements). Now, as Hilbert and Bernays note, '[t]he expression "ideal elements" is only justified from the point of view of the original system. In the new system, we no longer distinguish between real [*wirklichen*] and ideal [*idealen*] elements,[309] [...] the sharp distinction between the intuitive [*Anschaulichen*] and the non-intuitive [*Nicht-Anschaulichen*] [...] can apparently not be drawn so strictly [...]'.[310] The foundationalist stances that intend to canonise a particular transcendental regime of rationality and the corresponding forms of pure, immediate, or irreducible intuition just hinder the unfolding of the 'immanent rhythm of the Notion'.[311] As Jean Cavaillès has forcefully argued, speculative extensions of a given transcendental regime of rationality entail concomitant enhancements of the subjective capacity to produce suitable schematisations of the extended conceptual regime in upgraded forms of 'pure intuition': 'intuition in its quiddity progresses in parallel with the dialectical sequence of concepts. [...] [T]here is no absolute transcendental [...]'.[312]

---

308 In a letter to A.W. Rehberg, Kant expresses the 'puzzlement' he feels about an irrational number such as $\sqrt{2}$ : 'The understanding is not even in a position to assume the possibility of such an object , since it cannot adequately present the concept of such a quantity in an intuition of number, and would even less anticipate that such a quantity could be given a priori.' I. Kant, *Philosophical Correspondence, 1759–99*, ed. A. Zweig (Chicago: University of Chicago Press, 1967), 168–69.

309 Hilbert, 'Die Rolle von idealen Gebilden', 91.

310 P. Bernays, *Abhandlungen zur Philosophie der Mathematik* (Darmstadt: WSB, 1976), 61.

311 *Hegel, Phenomenology of Spirit*, 36.

312 It is worth quoting Cavaillès's fragment at length: 'The conditions imposed by the strict observance finitists on mathematical existence show a misunderstanding of what makes the very reality of the object. There is no absolute at the outset: what can

Let us move now from the mathematical examples that we have considered thus far to the realm of aesthetic experience. According to Lyotard, 'modernity unfolds in the retreat of the real and according to the sublime relationship of the presentable with the conceivable.'[313] The modern transition from the closed world to the infinite universe does not mean that the modern world is not transcendentally limited—being in fact nothing but a singular Umwelt among others—but rather that modern reason does conceive the existence of what the human sensibility, the human understanding, or the human imagination cannot 'present', that is, perceive, represent, comprehend, or schematise. The modern world is a limited world that acknowledges (at least in its critical phase) its own transcendental limitations. Confronted to this (merely conceived) 'great outdoors', modernity explored what Lyotard characterises as *allusive strategies*, which are intended

---

be said of the point, the continuum, the integer, except that they are elements and origins of sequences in which they take on their meaning and which exceed them? An irreducible intuition is only a thoughtless halt. The Kantian theory of mathematics still obsesses logicians and mathematicians, but because of its superficiality and its illegitimate interpretation in psychological terms. Taken in its authenticity, it remains inadequate in so far as it confuses the dialectical moment of the position of the concept and the transcendental moment of its schematisation. [...] At each stage of mathematical progress, new concepts are denied their right to exist, because they cannot provide a representation in the pre-existing intuitive system. This was the case for the negative numbers, for the imaginaries, for infinitesimals, and for the infinite at the time of Kant. The solution each time is not, as is superficially believed, the discovery of a translation in an immutable spatial intuition (representation of negative numbers on a straight line, of imaginary numbers in the plane) [...]. The solution consists in a transformation of the intuitive zone, i.e. of the rules which lay down the use of [...] the schematic system. [...] In other words, intuition in its quiddity progresses in parallel with the dialectical sequence of concepts. [...] [T]here is no absolute transcendental [...].' J. Cavaillès, 'Transfini et continu', in *Œuvres Completès de Philosophie des Sciences* (Paris: Hermann, 1994), 271–74.

313 J.-F. Lyotard, *The Postmodern Explained: Correspondence 1982–1985*, tr. B. Don, B. Maher, J. Pefanis, V. Spate, and M. Thomas (Minneapolis: University Of Minnesota Press, 1992), 13.

to somehow *point to* or *show* (in Wittgenstein's terms) what cannot be said, perceived, understood, or represented. This *nostalgic mode* makes allusion to the 'absent content' ('like one of Malevich's squares') without trying to intervene in the corresponding transcendental structures (like Proust, who 'invokes the unpresentable by means of a language which keeps its syntax and lexicon intact').[314] By contrast, what Lyotard calls *postmodern aesthetics* directly intervenes on the very transcendental element of language, transforming it and perverting it.[315] A paradigmatic example of the latter is Joyce, who fought against Ireland's oppressor by dismembering its language, by deconstructing it, infecting it, calibanising it, queering it, by rendering it unrecognisable, by diffusing it in a linguistic magma that echoes back to the British Empire—in a kind of 'reverse anthropology' that vomits after the anthropophagic deglution—the suffocating incestuous closure of the monochrome and monolinguistic 'monologue of colonial reason'.[316] What we shall rather call *absolute modernity* can be defined by the speculative capacity to '(re)present' or to phenomenalise, by means of speculative extensions and variations of our own capacities to perceive, to understand, to feel, to express, what epiphanically announces itself within the umweltic horizons in the guise of the invisible, the unsayable, the inconceivable. Absolute modernity does not point (by means of 'mystical' allusions) toward what dwells beyond the transcendental limits, but rather deforms the transcendental structure in order to differentially displace the limits.

---

314 Ibid., 14.

315 In Lyotard's own words: 'The postmodern would be that which in the modern [...] refuses the consolation of correct forms, refuses the consensus of taste permitting a common experience of nostalgia for the impossible. [...] [T]he text [the postmodern artist or writer] writes or the work [she] creates is not in principle governed by pre-established rules and cannot be judged according to a determinant judgement, by the application of given categories to this text or work. Such rules and categories are what the work or text is investigating.' Ibid., 15.

316 N. Land, 'Kant, Capital, and the Prohibition of Incest: A Polemical Introduction to the Configuration of Philosophy and Modernity', in *Fanged Noumena: Collected Writings 1997–2007* (Falmouth and New York: Urbanomic/Sequence Press, 1994), 74.

We can sublate the sharp Kantian opposition between an *aesthetic of the beautiful* (based on an harmonious consonance among the transcendental faculties and the corresponding parochial and epochal judgements of taste) and the *aesthetic of the sublime* (based on the painful intrusion 'from outside' of a traumatic breach that is 'powerful enough to break through the protective shield',[317] thereby deregulating the system of transcendental faculties that protects the subject by renormalising the real) by means of a properly *speculative aesthetics* that intervenes in the subject's transcendental structure in order to experience the trans-umweltic beauty that outshines the sublime affliction. By varying our transcendental resources and making kin with other lifeforms, it might be possible to differentially open the doors of perception, affection, and conceptualisation, to find joy in the trans-umweltic consonances hidden in the intra-umweltic dissonant, in what seems to resist the subjective attempts to perform a successful geometrico-conceptual schematisation, in the underlying forms of order sedimented beneath seemingly structureless configurations, in the unsuspected ribbings, articulations, channels, and ligaments of the *logos*, in the trans-mundane patterns that connect the crab's Umwelt to the lobster's Umwelt, the orchid's Umwelt to the primrose's Umwelt,[318] in the communicating vessels that articulate seemingly disconnected regimes, zones, scales, and horizons of experience, in the goldstone degrees of freedom that witness for broken symmetries, in the higher forms of collective experience capable of integrating the most disparate and seemingly incongruous transcendental perspectives. Shamanic variations and trans-species alliances might transmute an ontoseismic shock (the sublime!) into a kalonkinesiooptic experience (pleromatic beauty!): sublime affliction—that 'which we are barely able to endure'—might be 'nothing but the beginning of [trans-umweltic beauty].' Whereas the sublime denotes the pleromatic exorbitance of the real with respect to the corresponding Umwelt's limits, the idea of beauty refers to the harmonies, counterpoints, resonances, and 'aparallel evolutions' of 'beings that have absolutely

317 S. Freud, *Beyond the Pleasure Principle*, tr. J. Strachey (New York: Norton, 1961), 23.

318 See Bateson, *Mind and Nature*, 8.

nothing to do with each other'.[319] Whereas the notion of sublime is Umwelt-dependent, the idea of beauty refers to a quality of the inter-umweltic and trans-species mutual attunements between Umwelten constituted by different transcendental types, a quality that necessarily propagates through the supernatural interzones. The infinite regulative idea of beauty as we shall understand it here does not refer to the restricted aesthetical criteria of a certain provincial Umwelt, but rather to the imperative of extending, varying, and increasing the resolution of our perceptual, affective, and conceptual resources in order to deepen and refine our receptive and expressive participation in trans-umweltic harmonies.

The emergence of a higher form of depth experience out of the integration of different transcendental viewzones implies that the intentional pole of a speculative experience cannot be an objective phenomenon. Indeed, objective phenomena are by definition correlated to a single transcendental type of subjectivity. But the fact that noumena are, by definition, outside of any form of experience implies that the intentional pole of a speculative experience cannot be a noumenon either. We can thus conclude that the fixed Kantian distinction between phenomena and noumena is inadequate for articulating the proposed speculative standpoint. But how can we characterise the finite configurations of experience, the local instances of revelation, the modes of the phenoumenodelic insubstance, otherwise than in terms of phenomena and noumena? To address these questions, let us note that the Kantian distinction is dependent upon the transcendental type at stake: what is noumenally inaccessible to an empirical subject of type $\alpha$ might be phenomenally accessible to a subject of type $\beta$.[320]

319 R. Chauvin, *Entretiens sur la sexualité*, quoted in G. Deleuze and F. Guattari, *A Thousand Plateaus: Capitalism and Schizophrenia*, tr. B. Massumi (Minneapolis: University of Minnesota Press, 1987), 10.

320 In Lorenz's words: 'Many aspects of the thing-in-itself which completely escape being experienced by our present-day apparatus of thought and perception may lie within the boundaries of possible experience in the near future, geologically speaking. Many of those aspects which today are within the sphere of the imminent may have still been beyond these boundaries in the recent past of mankind. [...] [T]he boundary separating the experienceable from the [unexperienceable]

It follows that the shamanic drift of a speculative subject in the transcendental landscape induces a concomitant transformation of the boundary between phenomena and noumena. We shall now take into account the plasticity of the phenomena-noumena distinction by proposing a dialectical sublation of their sharp opposition. To do so, we shall introduce a diagonalising notion that we shall call *phenoumenon*.

In order to introduce the notion of phenoumenon, let us consider once more the example given by the history of numerical systems. This example will allow us to introduce a distinction between what we shall term *speculative extensions* and *speculative variations*. The transitions from the natural numbers $\mathbb{N}$ to the ring of integers $\mathbb{Z}$ and then to the fields of rational numbers $\mathbb{Q}$, real numbers $\mathbb{R}$, and complex numbers $\mathbb{C}$ exemplify a sequence of extensions in which each term in the sequence includes the previous one: every natural number is an integer, every integer is rational, every rational number is real, and every real number is complex. Such a sequence of extensions defines the formal structure of what we could call *speculative progress*, in the sense that each extension is elicited by the impasses of the previous transcendental regime.[321] Now, the field $\mathbb{C}$ of complex numbers has a remarkable property of closure—that of being *algebraically closed*—which makes $\mathbb{C}$ a kind of maximal extension of the natural, integer, rational, and real numbers. A field is algebraically closed if and only if it does not admit of an *algebraic extension*, that is, an extension defined by solutions to polynomial equations over $\mathbb{C}$ that are not in $\mathbb{C}$. However, the

---

must vary for each individual type of organism. The location of the boundary has to be investigated separately for each type of organism. It would mean an unjustifiable anthropomorphism to include the purely accidental present-day location of this boundary for the human species in the definition of the thing-in-itself. If, in spite of the indubitable evolutionary modifiability of our apparatus of experience one nevertheless wanted to continue to define the thing-in-itself as that which is uncognisable for this very apparatus, the definition of the absolute would thereby be held to be relative, obviously an absurdity.' Lorenz, 'Kant's Doctrine of the A Priori', 232.

321 With the exception (as we noted before) of the non-speculative extension from the field of rational numbers $\mathbb{Q}$ to the field of real numbers $\mathbb{R}$.

fact that $\mathbb{C}$ cannot be algebraically extended does not imply that all possible solutions necessarily belong to $\mathbb{C}$. Indeed, it might be possible to find solutions to polynomial equations defined over $\mathbb{C}$ in domains of rationality that are not extensions of $\mathbb{C}$. Even if the field $\mathbb{C}$ has the remarkable property of being algebraically closed, it does not contain the totality of the possible solutions to polynomial equations defined over $\mathbb{C}$.[322] In general, a problem formulated using the expressive resources of a certain transcendental domain of rationality defines different sets of solutions in a variety of domains of rationality. But no single domain of rationality can subsume all possible solutions. In particular, there might be solutions that belong neither to the transcendental domain of rationality in which the problem is formulated nor to speculative extensions of that domain.

Faced with the fact that a system of equations formulated in a domain of rationality L might have different solutions in different domains L' (which may or may not be algebraic extensions of L), the mathematician

---

322 Consider for example the equation of a 'circle' of radius 1, namely $x^2+y^2=1$. This equation admits solutions in the integers $\mathbb{Z}$ (the four solutions given by the pairs $(x, y) = (0,1), (0,-1), (1,0)$ and $(-1,0)$, which define an *integer circle* consisting of four points), solutions in the rational numbers $\mathbb{Q}$ (defining the *rational circle* consisting of infinite points), solutions in the real numbers $\mathbb{R}$ (defining the *real circle* consisting of a one-dimensional continuum of points) and solutions in the complex numbers $\mathbb{C}$ (defining the *complex circle* consisting of a two-dimensional continuum of points); see for instance M. Barr, C. McLarty, and C. Wells, *Variable Set Theory* (1986), <http://www.math.mcgill.ca/barr/papers/vst.pdf>, or Section 14.3.2, 'Schemes as Variable Sets of Solutions' of C. McLarty, '"There is No Ontology Here": Visual and Structural Geometry in Arithmetic', in P. Mancosu (ed.), *The Philosophy of Mathematical Practice* (Oxford: Oxford University Press, 2008), 385–87. All the points of the integer circle are in the rational circle, all the points of the rational circle are in the real circle, and so on. So, we might well think that in the last instance the complex circle is *the* ultimate figure that faithfully schematises the circle equation. However, it is not true that all the solutions $(x, y)$ to the circle equation are complex numbers. For instance, the pairs $(0,2)$ and $(2,0)$ are solutions in the finite field $F_3$, that is in the field where $a = b \bmod 3$ if $a = 3n + b$ where $n$ is a natural number. In particular, this relation implies that $2^2 + 0^2 = 0^2 + 2^2 = 4 = 1$ in $F_3$ (which is not true in the complex numbers).

Alexander Grothendieck—working within the field of algebraic geometry—proposed a groundbreaking idea, namely to consider that the 'solution' to such a system is a formal entity (a *functor*)[323] which encodes the different sets of solutions that can be found in different possible domains L'.[324] More precisely, the 'solution' to a system of equations is the functor that assigns to each suitable numerical system L' the set of solutions of E in L'—which we shall denote $S_E(L')$—and to each 'translation' between numerical systems L'→L'' a map between the corresponding sets of solutions.[325] Subsequently, the 'solution' to E—far from being a single set of numbers belonging to a particular number system—is a *variable set*, that is, a collection of sets of solutions $S_E(L')$ indexed by the different number systems L'. In other words, the solution to a system of equations E is *a set that varies* depending on the domain of rationality in which we search for its solutions. In the face of the transcendental relativity given by the existence of different domains of rationality, this functorial definition of the solution

---

323 A *category* is a set of *objects* and *maps* between these objects (called *morphisms*) such that (1) for each pair of composable maps a → b and b → c there exists a map a → c that coincides with their composition and (2) every object is given an identity arrow that acts as a neutral element for the operation given by the composition. A (covariant) *functor* F is a map F:C→D between two categories C and D, that is to say an application that assigns to each object a in C an object F(a) in D and to each morphism g:a→b a morphism F(g): F(a)→F(b) (or a morphism F(g): F(b)→F(a) if the functor is contravariant) in such a way that compositions and identities are preserved. For more details see, e.g., S. Awodey, *Category Theory* (Oxford: Clarendon Press, 2006).

324 See for instance the introduction to A. Grothendieck and J.A. Dieudonné, *Éléments de Géométrie Algébrique I* (Berlin-Heidelberg: Springer-Verlag, 1971). For a conceptual-oriented discussion of Grothendieck's functorial strategy, see G. Catren and F. Cukierman, 'Grothendieck's Theory of Schemes and the Algebra-Geometry Duality', *Synthese* 200:3 (2022).

325 Given a polynomial equation defined over a field $k$, the minimal condition imposed on the possible domains of rationality $k'$ in which we can search for its solutions is that they must be *k-algebras*. This means that the elements of $k'$ can be multiplied, added, and multiplied by numbers in $k$. If this were not the case, we could not evaluate the polynomial over $k$ in numbers belonging to $k'$.

to a system of equations allows Grothendieck to consider all the suitable domains of rationality at once. Far from defining a mere multiplicity of disconnected sets of solutions (each defined in a certain domain of rationality L'), this variable set of solutions is endowed with what we could describe as a *functorial parallax structure*: every transformation of the transcendental perspective from which the problem is approached—every transformation of the domain of rationality—entails a transformation of the 'observed' set of solutions.

We might say that Grothendieck addressed the transcendental relativity resulting from the existence of different sets of solutions to a given problem by acknowledging the limitations of the notion of *speculative progress*, that is, the idea that the limits of a given domain of rationality can be completely sublated by performing speculative extensions of that domain. As we have seen above, a problem formulated in a domain L might have solutions in domains L' that are not speculative extensions of L. The *absolute modernity* of Grothendieck's idea results from the decision to absolve rationality with respect to any particular domain of rationality or linear sequence of domains related by speculative extensions. Unlike the type-centric progressivism that uniquely operates through speculative extensions of a certain given transcendental type, the functorial absolutisation proposed by Grothendieck considers all possible transcendental types (as well as translations or variations between them) at once, thus absolving itself of any attachment to a given transcendental type and the corresponding sequences of speculative extensions: no transcendental type—no matter how powerful its transcendental resources might be—is privileged. In this way, Grothendieck's approach provides an alternative to the dilemma between an alleged *universality* that hypostasises a single (speculatively extensible) 'universal' type on the one hand—like for instance that of an enlightened European white man (e.g. Husserl)[326]—and the surrender to

326 This seems to be the type-centric and parochial form of universalism endorsed by Husserl when he writes: 'There is something unique here [in Europe] that is recognized in us by all other human groups, too, something that, quite apart from all considerations of utility, becomes a motive for them to Europeanise themselves

postmodern *relativism* on the other. The restricted 'universality' advocated by European civilisation proceeds by privileging a singular manner of living, dwelling, thinking, and dying (and the corresponding avenues of speculative extensions of this type) and by consequently reducing the others. Grothendieck's functorial strategy provides the formal key to conceive an absolute modernity absolved both from a type-centric and colonial form of 'universality' and from a mere relativism released from any universalist commitment. No transcendental type has a 'universal' privilege, but the Umwelten constituted by different types (for instance, White Anglo-Saxon Protestants or orchids) can be mutually 'translated' in the framework of an egalitarian cosmopolitan exchange and integrated with the irreplaceable singularity of their transcendental perspectives into higher forms of subjectivity.

We could here distinguish two modalities of exploration of the transcendental landscape, namely 'longitudinal', time-like or progressive speculative extensions of (or regressions with respect to) our current transcendental type, and 'latitudinal' connections with transcendental types that are neither speculative extensions nor subtypes of our own type,[327] that is, space-like connections with types of subjectivity that belong neither to the prehuman nor to the 'posthuman possibility cone'[328] defined by the current human's location in the transcendental landscape. If we call *transcendental Earth* this location (which, unlike the Husserlian Ur-Arche Earth, is always in motion), we can describe these modalities by saying that we can explore this landscape both by extending our transcendental resources (linear, 'time-like', or longitudinal modality defined by the motion of the

---

even in their unbroken will to spiritual self-preservation; whereas we, if we understand ourselves properly, would never Indianise ourselves, for example.' Husserl, *The Crisis of European Sciences and Transcendental Phenomenology*, 275.

327 We borrow the use of the terms *longitudinal* and *latitudinal* from V. Westhelle, *Eschatology and Space: The Lost Dimension of Theology Past and Present* (New York: Palgrave MacMillan, 2012).

328 R. Scott Bakker, *Interview with David Roden*, *Figure/Ground*, 2015, <http://figure-ground.org/interview-with-david-roden/>.

transcendental Earth) and/or by making kin—by constructing com cating vessels, sending and decoding inter-umweltic signals, developi translation operators, and so on—with lifeforms that do not dwell on the transcendental Earth, that is, with beings whose transcendental types cannot be reached by extending the resources of our own current type (multi-dimensional, 'space-like', latitudinal modality). By concocting an original blend of *temporal progressism* and *spatial colonialism*, Eurocentric modernity has privileged the 'progressive' modality to the detriment of the multi-dimensional latitudinal one. This restricted form of modernity relies on the implicit assumption that every possible transcendental framing of the pleroma is (a) 'primitive' with respect to our own transcendental capacities (a 'primitive' subtype included in our own type), (b) reachable by performing speculative extensions of our own transcendental type ('advanced forms of civilization'), or (c) simply conquerable, enslavable, and profitable as raw materials or workforce. According to the longitudinal modality, progressive history is the unique site for further revelations (cf. Pannenberg) and the unique relevant others that we do recognise as others are some*when* else—in our own speculative or posthuman future—but not some*where* else. In particular, gods, extraterrestrial beings, and artificial forms of intelligence are generally schematised as superhuman beings endowed with superhuman powers, that is, as speculative extensions of the human type. Maybe the modern failure to establish contact with extraterrestrial forms of life and to relate to other (human and nonhuman) types on the planet Earth otherwise than in terms of extractivism, colonialism, conquest, expropriation, and updated forms of slavery is, at least partially, a pathological consequence of the pre-Darwinian prejudice according to which life explores its space of subjective possibilities in a linear and progressive manner, that is, along a 'great chain of Being'.

Husserl was perfectly right in asserting that the current 'crisis of European sciences' stems from the foreclosure of the concrete 'lifeworld' (*Lebenswelt*) in which every scientific protocol of theoretical abstraction is ultimately rooted, from the 'astralisation' of scientific knowledge 'out of the muddle' of life, from thc Cartesian capitulation to the 'myth of a pure

ed from [corporeal, affective, communitarian] life',[329] the fact that every form of knowledge *of* life (objective dge *of* life (subjective genitive), a living act of self- sserl does not seem to have understood is that his own narrative is an abstraction that conceals the worldwide concrete entanglement of an irreducible multiplicity of geopolitical areas and subjective types that sustain the infinite project of the more-than-European sciences. Husserl did not realise that he was endorsing 'one of the greatest acts of intellectual theft in human history' as David Graeber puts it.[330] Husserl did not understand that the Eurocentric co-optation of the scientific project, the emplacement of sciences in a linear monohistory that unfolds from a mythical intra-European origin (the so-called 'Greeks') and conceals its colonial inscription in a vast trans-European horizon, is part of the disease that affects what Husserl calls 'European sciences'. Husserl did not suspect that Europe could be 'morally, spiritually indefensible.'[331] The absolutisation of modernity summoned by Rimbaud before leaving Europe might depend upon our capacity to absolve modern science from the European monopoly appropriation of both scientific rationality—based on the euphemisation of the horror of the 'European *ego conquero*' into the metaphysical and ethereal *ego cogito*[332]—and philosophical inquiry—ultimately leading to the 'authentic' thinking of the 'ontological difference' between Being and beings to the detriment of the (too ontic) 'colonial difference' between universal and subaltern types. Scientific rationality will enter into an absolutely modern phase only on condition that it is released from longitudinal unidimensional narratives and latitudinal colonial epistemicides. The absolutisation of modernity requires—we shall maintain here—a sublation of the tension

---

329 J.-C. Goddard, 'La non-existence de l'Occident. Graeber décolonial', *Anthropologie décoloniale*, 2021, <https://anthropodeco.hypotheses.org>.

330 D. Graeber, 'Radical Alterity is Just Another Way of Saying "Reality." A Reply to Eduardo Viveiros de Castro', *Hau: Journal of Ethnographic Theory* 5:2 (2015), 21.

331 A. Césaire, *Discourse on Colonialism*, tr. J. Pinkham (New York: Monthly Review Press), 32.

332 Goddard, *La non-existence de l'Occident.*

between the colonial and extractivist reduction of other lifeforms pr
to a typocentric form of 'universality' and postmodern relativism in
multicultural and multinatural versions into a *functorial pluralism* capable of integrating the open multiplicity of singular transcendental perspectives.

In order to clarify the difference between speculative extensions and speculative absolutions with respect to any given transcendental type, we shall now consider a linguistic example. Adopting a typocentric standpoint, we might believe that a single language (English, for instance) might be enough for any conceivable purpose (a language in which 'everything may be said', in C.K. Ogden's words); we could believe that the factical multiplicity of languages is a mere ethnographic redundancy, and that translation is the prosthetic operation by means of which this redundancy can be kept under control. If needed—if, after all, we became aware of the limitations of the alleged privileged language—we could always proceed to perform speculative extensions of it (such as creating neologisms, extending its grammatical resources, enhancing its expressive means, and so on).[333] But in the last instance (according to this typocentric stance), we would not really lose anything—and we would significantly simplify human communication—if we could just reduce the multiplicity of languages by agreeing to communicate in a single language, performing a systematic linguisticide and putting an end to cumbersome translation problems. In contrast, the strategy of what we have called functorial pluralism consists in accepting at face value the Babelian multiplicity of languages, considering them as 'fragments of a vessel which are to be glued together'[334] and overcoming their dissemination by means of translation (or gluing) operations.

333 As Ogden writes: 'Standard English may be enriched and cosmopolitanised. [...] If so, English will become not only the International Auxiliary Language, but the Universal language of the world.' C.K. Ogden, *Basic English: A General Introduction with Rules and Grammar* (London: Kegan Paul, Trench, Trubner & Co., 3rd ed., 1932).

334 W. Benjamin, 'The Task of the Translator', in H. Arendt (ed.), *Illuminations: Essays and Reflections*, tr. H. Zohn (New York: Schocken, 2007), 78. See also A. Berman, *L'épreuve de l'étranger* (Paris: Gallimard, 1984) and G. Catren, 'La tâche du philosophe. Variation à partir de *Die Aufgabe des Ubersetzers* de Walter Benjamin', *Philo-Fictions. La Revue des non-philosophies* 3 (2010).

hetic conception of translation relies on the notion s, on the presupposition of an invariant kernel that nd reidentified in the different translations in spite of ological, and phonetic variations—the synthetic unity by the translational integration of different languages brings to the fore and articulates their irreducible untranslatable variants. The 'pure language' described by Benjamin in 'The Task of the Translator' (which we shall rather called *absolute language*) is not a particular language endowed with some alleged privilege: 'Languages imperfect in so far as they are many; the [privileged] one is lacking.'[335] Benjamin is at the antipodes of those (such as Ogden and Heidegger) who sought to hypostasise a particular national language to the detriment of others by simply dismissing the untraslatable singularity of other languages, their mutual irreducibility, their irreplaceable richness, or by proceeding, as the history of colonialism shows repeatedly, to a systematic linguisticide. The absolute language is the category of languages, that is, the set of all languages enriched with the categorical structure given by the translational correspondences between them. The translator's intention, oriented by 'the great longing for linguistic complementation',[336] is not to reduce equivocities or untranslatable expressions, but rather—'by *grafting* languages onto one another, by *playing* on the multiplicity of languages and on the multiplicity of codes within every linguistic corpus'[337]—to diffuse the work in question throughout the absolute language, so that, at the projective end of this process of absolution with respect to any alleged privilege language (like the language of the 'original'), the work becomes a functor on the category of languages. In the spirit of Grothendieck, we can define an *absolute work* as a functor defined on the category that we have called absolute language (that is, the category of languages and translational correspondences between them) which assigns to each language L a work $W_L$ written in this language and to each

335 Mallarmé, *Divagations*, 205.

336 Benjamin, 'The Task of the Translator', 79.

337 J. Derrida, *Who's Afraid of Philosophy: Right to Philosophy 1*, tr. J. Plug (Stanford, CA: Stanford University Press, 2002), 105.

correspondence $L \rightarrow L'$ between languages a translation $W_L \rightarrow W_{L'}$ between the corresponding works.[338] In this way, the 'original' loses all privilege, being now understood as a mere phenomenalisation of the 'absolute work' W, as a transcendental framing of W defined by a particular language. By doing so, 'the original and the translation[s] [are] recognizable as fragments of a greater language, just as fragments are part of a vessel.'[339] Rather than reducing the differences that separate the multiple languages, translation connects those languages by performing transports along the differences, by integrating them along local similarities, thereby constructing in a projective manner a unique linguistic network, the absolute language. The differences between languages can be integrated and the different translations of a given piece can be understood as different modes of presentation of a functorial 'original' that cannot be exclusively ascribed to any local language. As Viveiros de Castro emphasises, we can projectively gain access to a functorial work as such by performing what we could call a *multiscopic reading* that integrates the linguistic variants between its different translations along local similarities: 'In this model of translation [...] difference is [...] a condition of signification and not a hindrance. [...] As in stereoscopic vision, it is necessary that the two eyes not see the same given thing in order for another thing (the real thing in the field of vision) to be able to be seen, that is, constructed or counterinvented. In this case, to translate is to presume a difference.'[340] In this way, the task of the translator is to free any (scientific, literary, philosophical) work from its anchorage in its native language in order to unfold it throughout the

---

338 We could for example say that the 'absolute Quixote' is the functor that assigns to each language L the version of the Quixote in L and assigns to each correspondence $L \rightarrow L'$ between languages the translation $Q_L \rightarrow Q_{L'}$ between the corresponding versions of the Quixote (where we are abstracting from the fact that there may be several versions of the Quixote in a given language L).

339 Benjamin, 'The Task of the Translator', 78.

340 E. Viveiros de Castro, 'Perspectival Anthropology and the Method of Controlled Equivocation', *Tipití: Journal of the Society for the Anthropology of Lowland South America* 2:1 (2004).

extended field of absolute language, that is, to elevate it from *intra-linguistic phenomenality* to *inter-linguistic functorial phenoumenality*.

Thanks to the translation operators, the reciprocal exteriority between the different languages is interiorised, enveloped by a purely reflexive immanental structure with (at the limit) no outside. Analogously to Fichte's absolute knowing, Benjamin's absolute language does not relate to a transcendence, and in this sense it cannot itself be translated, transported elsewhere ('And what will it be to translate when what is at stake is a [text] whose language does not have a distancing effect, [a text that is neither localised in the space of languages nor opposed to other languages] [...]: immanence of an [inter-linguistic] gush?').[341] But Benjamin, like Fichte, does not achieve this immanentisation of language by dismissing or eliminating the alleged 'minor' languages, but rather by enveloping them in a purely immanental structure that preserves the irreducible singularity of each local language. By definition, an absolute functorial piece, being already fully spread in the immanental absolute language, cannot be translated. Translations rather define the internal structural consistency that holds the different phenomenalisations of the piece together, where each phenomenalisation is defined with respect to a particular language. This understanding of translation as an operator that makes possible the institution of an immanental absolute language that envelops the different local languages clarifies the possibility of producing untranslatable works that cannot be ascribed to a unique language, like Bueno's *Mar paraguayo*, Joyce's *Finnegans Wake*, or Leminski and Jimenez's Portuñol version of *Catatau*. Since these works are already more or less spread in the pure language (or at least cannot be simply localised in English, Portuguese, Guarani or Spanish), the outside into which they could be translated is correspondingly reduced. Their untranslatability is proportional to their degree of immanence, that is, to the degree in which they envelop their linguistic outsides. In the ideal limit case, a work directly written in the absolute language is just untranslatable since there is no external language into which it could be translated. The imperial enforcement of Basic English as a 'universal' *lingua franca* (as in Wells's *The Shape*

341 Jimenez, 'Del endés y su demasía', in Leminski, *Catatau*, tr. Jiminez, 286.

*of Things to Come*) and the translinguistic drift of *Finnegans Wake* define two antipodal understandings of universality:[342] a colonial typocentric one intended to reduce the post-Babelian multiplicity of languages and one in which the singularity of every local language is preserved and embedded in the universal *riverrun* of the absolute language, in the inter-linguistic dreamsea of sangnifiance. The fall of the Babelian tower makes space for 'a babbling in transit', a 'language in trance', a 'verbal magma', in which the 'voice of the post-Cartesian monologue is not being translated from one language to another, but drifts by means of tonal transparencies of a vast intermediality',[343] reaching 'everything that vibrates and rings [and resonates] below, far below the line of silence', where 'there are no [separate] languages, [...] just the vertigo of'[344] a unique continuous 'lanjaguar',[345] a language that flows, drifts, self-translates, camaleonizes, sings its icaros in every possible human and nonhuman language. Translation is not a prosthetic palliative for the post-Babelian multiplicity of languages, but an essential operation of the trinitarian dialectical process through which the institution of a disconnected multiplicity of finite lifeforms (in this case, subjects equipped with different languages) is superseded by the Pentecostal gift of absolute language. Translation operations are like the synaptic connections that transform a mere set of isolated neurons into the coherent self-reflexive structure of a higher-order form of linguistic subjectivity. This wholly spiritual process of integration of the complementary 'intentions underlying each [local] language' projectively institutes an immanental absolute language with no outside.

The definition of the concept of *phenoumenon* that we shall now propose is inspired by Grothendieck's take on the problem of finding the common

342 Regarding the relation between James Joyce and C.K. Ogden see S.S. Sailer, 'Universalizing Languages: "Finnegans Wake" Meets Basic English', *James Joyce Quarterly* 36:4 (Summer, 1999), 853–68.

343 Translator's note to the second edition of Leminski, *Catatau*, tr. Jimenez, 11.

344 W. Bueno, *Mar paraguayo* (Buenos Aires: Interzona, 2020), 15.

345 E. Viveiros de Castro, 'Rosa e Clarice, a fera e o fora/Rosa and Clarice, the Beast and the Outside', *Revista Letras, Curitiba, UPFR* 98 (2018): 9–30: 26.

solutions of a family of polynomial equations in the field of algebraic geometry. A *phenoumenon* P is defined as a functor that assigns to each transcendental type $\alpha$ an object $P_\alpha$, and to each transformation between type $\alpha$ and type $\beta$ a transformation between the objects $P_\alpha$ and $P_\beta$. Given a phenoumenon P, an empirical subject of transcendental type $\alpha$ can only access the object $P_\alpha$, that is (what we shall without distinction) the *α-objectivation* or *α-phenomenalisation* of P. Object $P_\alpha$ is the object that results from the transcendental framing of P defined by the transcendental type $\alpha$. We shall say that a phenoumenon P is refracted into a *spectrum of objects*, each of which is correlative to a certain transcendental type of subjectivity. We shall therefore distinguish phenoumenon P *as such* from the distinct objects constituted by the possible transcendental framings of P. *Transcendental transcendence*, that is, the α-Umwelt resulting from the framing of the experiential field defined by the transcendental structure $\alpha$, is not sufficiently transcendent, since it only allows access to the α-objectivations of the different phenoumena.

In the same way that an object O defines different profiles or adumbrations (a profile $O_x$ for each spatiotemporal position $x$ of the observer), a phenoumenon P defines different objects (an object $P_\alpha$ for each transcendental type $\alpha$, that is, for each location $\alpha$ in the transcendental landscape); in the same way that an observer can projectively experience an object *as such* by making empirical variations of its position in the corresponding extension and integrating the corresponding profiles, an observer can (at least in principle) projectively experience a phenoumenon *as such* by making transcendental variations of its locality in the transcendental landscape (occupying, for example, the localities $\alpha$, $\beta$, $\gamma$,...) and integrating the corresponding objects (for example the objects $P_\alpha$, $P_\beta$, $P_\gamma$,...). Whereas an object only manifests its intrinsic multifaceted nature to a family of observers placed in different spatial positions (or equivalently, to an observer that moves around the object), a phenoumenon only manifests its intrinsic multi-objective nature to a family of subjects of different transcendental types (or, equivalently, to a subject that can induce variations of its own type). We could rephrase the core of the Kantian exponentiation of the Copernican Revolution by saying that the empirical perspectivism of experience—that is, the fact that the subjective experience of an object is always the experience of a certain adumbration of the object—is no more than the degree zero of the ultra-perspectivist nature of experience. Even when the subject of science overcomes empirical perspectivism (by integrating different profiles into a single object and extracting objective invariants that do not depend on the relative position between the object and the subject), the resulting object, far from coinciding with the corresponding phenoumenon, depends on the transcendental perspective defined by the type of such a subject. Subjects that instantiate other transcendental types will constitute, from the same phenoumenon, other objects.

As we have argued above, modern science relies to a large extent on what we have called the *invariantist stance*, that is, the thesis that all that matters from a scientific standpoint are the objective invariants under a change of perspective, that is, the features of the phenomenon at stake that do not depend on the empirical state of the observer. According to the invariantist stance, it is necessary to vary the perspective on the corresponding phenomenon in order to be able to discard the perspectival variants and identify its truly essential features. Second, modern science depends—as Kant maintained—on a transcendental parochialism that conflates a singular transcendental perspective (let us say that of patriarchal and colonial Eurocentric modernity) with a 'view from nowhere'. But none of these restrictions defines an unsurpassable limit that could not be sublated by a proper revision of what we understand by scientificity. This revision defines one of the vectors that point from the restricted Eurocentric modernity of pre-critical science toward what we have called an *absolute modernity*. First, the limitations associated with the invariantist stance can be overcome by enriching the modern understanding of objectivity. According to the extended definition that we have sketched, the different adumbrations of an object are constitutive components of a multifaceted structure. In this respect, a faithful description of the object requires not only the identification of *objective invariants*, but also the integration of *perspectival variants*. As we have argued, this argument can be reproduced at the transcendental (rather than empirical) level: whereas an object is a mutifaceted structure composed of different adumbrations accessible by varying the empirical state of the observer, a phenoumenon is a multiobjected structure composed of different objects accessible by varying the transcendental type of the observer. Both limitations of (a certain conception of) scientific objectivism can be differentially sublated by engaging in a radical *transcendental reflection* $\wedge$ *speculative refraction* tandem that includes (a) a synchronic transcendental reflection on our actual location in the transcendental landscape, (b) a diachronic-genealogical reflection on the processes of institution of our own transcendental subjectivity, (c) longitudinal variations of the corresponding transcendental structures (e.g., speculative extensions of our conceptual, perceptual, affective, and social resources), and (d) latitudinal integrations with other transcendental forms of subjectivity.

In order to fix ideas, let us consider a simple example of a phenoumenon. Let us suppose a coin D such that one side is painted with a *matte dark green* and the other one with a *glossy bright yellow*. So, each side of the coin is characterised by a particular combination of three properties (colour, lustre, brightness) with two possible values each, namely (green, yellow), (matte, glossy), and (dark, bright) respectively. We shall consider a transcendental landscape (that is, a topological space of transcendental viewzones) given by a set X of sensorial organs endowed with a topological structure $\tau$. Each zone in this topology will define a transcendental type of subjectivity, that is, a transcendental perspective or transcendental viewzone. A topology on a set X can be understood as a collection of subsets of X—including by definition the whole set X and the empty set $\varnothing$—subjected to the closed operations of intersection $\cap$ and union $\cup$ that satisfy a relation of distributivity. In our case, the set X contains three sensorial organs, namely an organ C to recognise colours, an organ L to recognise lustre, and an organ B to recognise brightness. The topology will be given by the collection of transcendental viewzones $\tau = \{\varnothing, \{C\}, \{L, C\}, \{C, B\}, \{L, C, B\}\}$. For instance, $\{C\}$ denotes the transcendental type of the subjects who are equipped with an organ C to recognise colours and $\{L, C\}$ the transcendental type of those subjects equipped with both an organ C to recognize colours and an organ L to recognise lustre values. A given subject will frame the phenoumenal coin D from its particular transcendental viewzone, thereby constituting a particular object. For instance, a subject of type

{C} experiences the phenoumenal coin D as an object (which we shall denote $D_{\{C\}}$) with two coloured sides which we shall denote (green) and (yellow). In turn, a subject of type {L, C} experiences the phenoumenal coin D as an object $D_{\{L, C\}}$ with two sides defined by particular combinations of lustre and colour, namely (matte, green) and (glossy, yellow). The phenomenon-noumenon distinction is clearly transcendental-dependent, where different phenomenon-noumenon divides result from experiencing the same phenoumenon from different transcendental perspectives. Whereas for a subject of type {L, C} lustre and colour are phenomenal properties and brightness is noumenal, for a subject of type {C} colour is a phenomenal property while lustre and brightness are noumenal. By construction, the phenoumenal coin D encodes all these transcendental-dependent phenomenon-noumenon divides. It is worth noting that for a subject of type {L, C, B} (i.e. a subject that can recognise colours, lustre, and brightness), the object $D_{\{L, C, B\}}$ coincides with the phenoumenal coin D. For such a subject there is no phenomenon-noumenon distinction, which means that all the properties of the object are phenomenalised. In other words, a subject of type {L, C, B} can experience coin D in all its phenoumenal multifaceted richness of colour, lustre, and brightness.

The hybrid concept of phenoumenon combines both phenomenal and noumenal dimensions. On the one hand, a phenoumenon is by definition nothing but a (pre-)sheaf of phenomenalisations or objectivations defined with respect to different transcendental types of subjectivity. On the other hand, the noumenality of a phenoumenon results from the fact that a phenoumenon is generally in excess with respect to any of its possible phenomenalisations. However, we cannot deduce the existence of the 'ill-starred thing in itself'[346] from this noumenal excess withdrawn *de jure* from any form of manifestation, deprived of the joy of simultaneously appearing within myriad phenomenological horizons. As the example of the coin shows, properties of a phenoumenon that are noumenal for subjects of a given transcendental type might be phenomenal for subjects of a different type. We can then maintain that a phenoumenon is nothing

346 Fichte, *The Science of Knowing*, 61.

but pure manifestation, but in a manner that overflows any one particular transcendental-dependent phenomenalisation. Even if no phenomenalisation can exhaust the trans-umweltic profusion of phenoumena, nothing in a phenoumenon remains de jure 'in itself'. The functorial notion of phenoumenon has the twofold merit of preserving the ontological scope of the processes of phenomenalisation (in the sense that the very being of a phenoumenon relies on its appearing) while at the same time obstructing any subjectivist appropriation of the notion of manifestation (that is, without succumbing to the siren song of idealism). Along with Teilhard de Chardin we might say, '*solely* as a pheno[u]menon; but [...] the *whole* pheno[u]menon'[347]—solely manifestation, but a phenoumenodelic concept of manifestation that can do justice to the open multiplicity of transcendental types of subjectivity.

Let us now indicate some resonances and convergences between the notion of phenoumenon and certain concepts put forth by other authors. First, we find some hints that point toward the notion of phenoumenon in Sartre's arguments in favour of the phenomenological indistinction between *being* and *appearing*. According to Sartre, 'the dualism of being and [appearing] is no longer entitled to any legal status within philosophy. The [notion of manifestation] refers to the [variable set] of appearances and not to [an absolutely] hidden reality which would drain to itself all the *being* of the existent. [...] To the extent that [human beings] had believed in noumenal realities, they have presented [the act of appearing] as a pure negative. It was "that which is not being"; it had no other being than that of illusion and error. [...] But [...] if we no longer believe in the being-behind-the-[manifestation], then the [manifestation] becomes full positivity [...] The pheno[u]menal being manifests itself [...] and it is nothing but the [variable set of its transcendental-dependent adumbrations].'[348] Being more precise, we would say that there is certainly something 'behind' the particular set of adumbrations through which an object appears to a subject of a given

347 P. Teilhard de Chardin, *The Human Phenomenon* (London: Harper, 1958), 29.

348 J.P. Sartre, *Being and Nothingness*, tr. H.E. Barnes (New York: Washington Square Press, 1984), xlv–xlvi.

transcendental type. But this 'something' is not a non-appearing essence, but rather all the properties of the phenoumenon that were left out of the corresponding transcendental frame of reference. A phenoumenon is nothing but a collection of multifaceted phenomenalisations indexed by the different transcendental types of subjectivity. This definition encodes two (empirical and transcendental) forms of relativity. First, every perspectival representation of a given object is relative to the empirical position of the subject of experience. Second, the object as such—the object in its intrinsic multifaceted nature—is relative to the transcendental type of the subject. Whereas empirical relativity is subsumed in the notion of a multifaceted object, transcendental relativity is subsumed in the notion of a multiobjectivatable phenoumenon. A phenoumenon is a 'relative-absolute' notion as Sartre puts it, since (a) a particular phenomenalisation of a phenoumenon is always relative to a subject of a given transcendental type ('Relative the phenomenon remains, for "to appear" supposes in essence somebody to whom to appear')[349] and (b) the phenoumenon as such—that is, defined as a (pre)sheaf of different multifaceted phenomenalisations—is not correlated to any particular transcendental type of subjectivity.

We also find in Bateson a description of the Kantian *Ding an sich* which emphasises an important aspect of the concept of phenoumenon: '[I]n a piece of chalk there are an infinite number of potential facts. The *Ding an sich*, the piece of chalk, can never enter into communication or mental process because of this infinitude. The sensory receptors cannot accept it; they filter it out. What they do is to select certain facts out of the piece of chalk, which then become, in modern terminology, information.'[350] Far from not appearing, the *Ding an sich* manifests itself with such a phenoumenodelic opulence that it surpasses the transcendental affordances of finite subjects. The initselfness of the *Ding an sich* does not mean that its manifestation is not constitutive of its very being, but rather that its manifestation overflows any possible phenomenological horizon. Therefore, finite subjects renormalise the 'infinite number of potential facts' of the *Ding an sich* by

349 Ibid., xlvi.

350 Bateson, *Steps to an Ecology of Mind*, 459.

filtering it. Moreover, different transcendental types filter the same *Ding an sich* differently, thereby extracting different information out of it and constituting different objects. The key ingredient of this understanding of the Kantian concept of *Ding an sich* is that the subjective constitution of the phenomenal realm does not add features which we should abstract out in order to reach the thing in its unconstituted initselfness, but rather that the subjective constitution only retains a renormalised number of determinations from the thing's pleromatic nature. For the extreme poverty ascribed to the *Ding an sich* by the first interpretation, the phenoumenal reading substitutes an unaffordable abundance of determinations. Whereas the first description leads to the problematic characterisation of the *Ding an sich* as a purely negative concept—'the *complete abstractum*, something entirely *empty*, determined only as a *beyond*', as Hegel puts it[351]—the second makes of the *Ding an sich* an ideal regulator for finite knowledge that prescribes the effectuation of transcendental variations of the subject's transcendental type. By performing such variations, the speculative subject might gain access to determinations of the phenoumenon that were left outside of the subject's previous transcendental frame.

Equally, the 'commonsensical' concept of 'image' proposed by Bergson in *Matter and Memory* has certain similarities with the concept of phenoumenon. On the one hand, like Bergson's images—a 'self-existing [manifestation] [...] placed halfway between the "thing [in itself]" and [a subjective]

351 'The *thing-in-itself* [...] expresses the object in so far as one *abstracts* from everything that it is for consciousness, i.e. from all determinations of sensation [*Gefühlsbestimmungen*] as well as from all determinate thoughts of it. It is easy to see what remains, namely the *complete abstractum*, something entirely *empty*, determined only as a *beyond*; the *negative* of representation, feeling, determinate thinking, and so on. Equally simple, however, is the reflection that this *caput mortuum* is itself merely *the product* of thought, more specifically, [the product] of thought that has progressed to pure abstraction [...] One can only wonder, then, why one sees it repeated so often that one does not know [*wissen*] what the *thing-in-itself* is, when there is nothing easier to know than this.' Hegel, *Encyclopedia of the Philosophical Sciences in Basic Outline Part I: Science of Logic*, 89 [§44].

"representation" [...]'[352]—a phenoumenon 'is more than that which the idealist calls a *representation*', which means that it cannot be reduced to the immanence of a constituting subjectivity. A phenoumenal 'image' P entertains with the subject a relation characterised by a twofold form of exteriority (empirical and transcendental): whereas on the one hand every singular representation of a multifaceted object $P_\alpha$ is always an experience of one of its perspectival adumbrations (which means that there are always other profiles offered to subsequent experiences), on the other hand such a multifaceted object results from one possible transcendental editing of phenoumenon P among others. Whereas every multifaceted object exceeds each one of its perspectival representations, every phenoumenon exceeds each one of its objectivations. On the other hand, a phenoumenal 'image' P is 'less than that which the realist calls a *thing*' because it does not exist beyond its manifestations, that is, because it lacks an unmanifestable residuum. Bergsonian images are finite instances of manifestation (local modes of the phenoumenodelic insubstance), but they cannot be reduced to a subject-dependent appearance. We could say, paraphrasing Bergson, that a phenoumenon is a revelation 'which exists in itself'. That which exists 'in itself' is not an unmanifestable residuum beyond the realm of appearances, but a vibrant mode of the phenoumenodelic field that appears differently in each possible phenomenological horizon. In this sense, we consider the modes of the insubstance 'before the dissociation which idealism and realism have brought about between' their being and their appearing:[353] whereas idealism misses the pleromatic nature of the phenoumenon by reducing the act of appearing to subjective representations (or, in the case of transcendental idealism, to intrawordly objectivations), realism goes too far in disentangling the initselfness of the thing from its manifestation.

The notion of phenoumenon encodes the *parallactic nature* of manifestation: the appearance of a phenoumenon changes both when the subject changes its empirical state (thereby gaining access to different adumbrations of the corresponding objectivation of the phenoumenon) and when

352 Bergson, *Matter and Memory*, 9–10.

353 Ibid., 10.

it changes its transcendental type (thereby gaining access to different objectivations of the phenoumenon). The Lacanian neologism *para-being*, *apbearing beside* or *appbesiding* [*par-être*][354] encodes both the fact that the phenoumenon's being is nothing but a (pre-)sheaf of appearances and that the phenoumenon's appearing is always one-sided, since it depends on the subject's empirical and transcendental localisations: 'What we must get used to is substituting the *para-being* [*par-être*]—the being *para*, being beside—for the being that would take flight. I say the *para-being* [*par-être*], and not the *appearing* [*paraître*] as the phenomenon has always been called—that beyond which there is supposedly that thing, the noumenon. The latter has, in effect, led us, led us to all sorts of opacifications that can be referred to precisely as obscurantism. [...] [B]eing presents itself, always presents itself, by para-being. We should learn to conjugate that appropriately: I par-am, you par-are, he par-is, we par-are, and so on and so forth.'[355]

Here it is also interesting to compare the notion of *phenoumenon* with Graham Harman's understanding of what he calls *real objects*. Roughly speaking, Harman enriches the Kantian notion of 'thing in itself' by adding that the initselfness of the latter does not only characterise what cannot be known in a subject-object cognitive relation, but also what remains withdrawn in every object-object interaction. The common ground of both conceptions is the thesis that phenoumena/real objects 'are never exhausted by any [phenomenal] manifestation'.[356] Whereas *phenoumena* only reveal themselves in the form of those filtered, edited, or coarse-grained versions of themselves that here we have simply called *objects* (which are indexed by the transcendental types that define the corresponding framings), Harman's *real objects* (which 'always withdraw from direct access [...] permanently lost in [their] own depths')[357] indirectly manifest themselves in the form of

354 See translator's footnote 21 in Lacan, *Encore*, 44–45.

355 Ibid., 44–5.

356 G. Harman, 'Zero-person and the Psyche', in D. Skribina (ed.), *Mind that Abides: Panpsychism in the New Millennium* (Philadelphia: John Benjamins, 2009), 254.

357 G. Harman, *Object-Oriented Ontology: A New Theory of Everything* (London: Penguin Random House, 2017), 87, 100.

*intentional objects*. A phenoumenon P as such—that is, in its multiobjective nature—is also generally withdrawn from direct access: a subject of transcendental type $\alpha$ can only have access to the $\alpha$-objectivation of P. The 'critical' point about the functorial definition is that the full-fledged manifestation of a phenoumenon as such cannot take place in the phenomenological horizon defined by a single transcendental type. However, while phenoumena are not exhausted by any particular phenomenal objectivation, they are nothing but pure phenoumenalisation without a recondite ill-starred remainder. The functorial definition of a phenoumenon is a minimalist definition in the sense that it allows us to take into account the intrinsic structure that organises the different modes of presentation of the 'thing' (both with respect to subjects in different empirical states and with respect to subjects of different transcendental types) without presupposing that there is a noumenal remainder withdrawn de jure from any manifestation.

It is also worth emphasising that the notion of phenoumenon only intends to capture the relativity of that which appears (the local saliencies in the field of manifestation) both with respect to the different possible empirical states of a subject of a given type and with respect to different transcendental types of subjectivity. In other words, the notion of phenoumenon is intended to encode the intrinsic perspectival nature of the experiential field at both the empirical and the transcendental level. But a more complete understanding of the local modes of the experiential field would also require us to consider (which we shall not do here) other characteristics of these modes such as their *discontinuity* with respect to the background phenoumenodelic substrate, their *structural stability* under different forms of disturbances, their *self-identity* (the singular manner according to which every thing $a$ makes the identity principle $a = a$ true), their *suchness* (the qualia or properties of every thing), as well as their *thisness* (the irreducible indexicality or haecceity of things that share the same qualia). We have here focused on the *phenoumenality* of the local modes of the insubstance since this is the notion that allows us to sketch a consistent speculative stance that remains faithful to the main insight of Kantian critical philosophy (namely, that every form of experience is made possible and limited by a transcendental frame) without falling either into a claustrophobic idealistic deviation or into a mere relativism that cannot bootstrap itself up to the functorial integration of the phenoumena's multiple objectivations.

Let us consider now the integration of perspectival experiences associated with different transcendental 'viewzones'. For this purpose, we will continue to be guided by the formal thread provided by the category-theoretic revolution in algebraic geometry. From a formal point of view, the operation of *integrating* perspectival or local experiences into global ones is formalised by the mathematical notion of *sheaf*.[358] In our own terms, a phenoumenon (called *pre-sheaf* in mathematics) is a *phenoumenal sheaf* when profiles $x$ and $y$ defined with respect to transcendental types $\alpha$ and $\beta$ that coincide in their intersection $\alpha \cap \beta$ are integrated into a unique profile $z$ defined with respect to the transcendental type $\alpha \cup \beta$ given by the union of the former. It is worth noting that this *sheaf condition* engages the topological structure of the transcendental landscape defined by the operations of *intersection* and *union* of viewzones. The intersection $\alpha \cap \beta$ of two viewzones $\alpha$ and $\beta$ can be understood as the viewzone associated with a transcendental type defined by the transcendental structures *shared* by types $\alpha$ and $\beta$, that is to say by the transcendental structures available to both $\alpha$ and $\beta$. If, for example, zone $\alpha$ defines the transcendental type of a human being and zone $\beta$ the transcendental type of a jaguar, then zone $\alpha \cap \beta$ defines a transcendental type defined by the common transcendental resources shared by both human beings and jaguars. Zones $\alpha$ and $\beta$ also define (via the definition of a topology) a zone $\alpha \cup \beta$ given by their union. Zone $\alpha \cup \beta$ characterises the transcendental type defined by both the

358 For a philosophically oriented approach to the notion of sheaf, see F. Zalamea, *Modelos en haces para el pensamiento matématico* (Bogota: Editorial Universidad Nacional de Colombia, 2021). A take on the notion of sheaf from a standpoint provided by cognitive science can be found in S. Philipps, 'Going Beyond the Data as the Patching (Sheaving) of Local Knowledge', *Frontiers in Psychology* 9 (2008). Technical introductions to the subject can be found in M. Vaquié, 'Sheaves and Functors of Points', in M. Anel and G. Catren (eds.), *New Spaces in Mathematics: Formal and Conceptual Reflections* (Cambridge: Cambridge University Press, 2021), 407–61 and S. Mac Lane and I. Moerdijk, *Sheaves in Geometry and Logic: A First Introduction to Topos Theory* (Springer-Verlag New York Inc., 1992).

transcendental structures of $\alpha$ and the transcendental structures of $\beta$, even if these structures are not shared by both types.[359] In particular, transcendental viewzones might be included in one another, which induces a relation of partial order between the zones. The flexibility of the topological notion of zone—ranging from punctual zones to the zone that coincides with the whole landscape—allows us to consider different degrees of perspectival centredness, going from subjects that occupy punctual 'viewpoints' in the transcendental landscape to distributed forms of subjectivity characterised by wider 'viewzones'. We shall say that the transcendental type $\alpha \cup \beta$ defines a viewzone that is more *global* than those defined by types $\alpha$ and $\beta$ (or, reciprocally, that the latter are more *local* than the former). For instance, the transcendental viewzone of a subject who speaks only Spanish is more local (closer to a parochial view*point*) than the viewzone of a subject who speaks both Spanish and Guarani.

In our framework, each zone of the transcendental landscape defines a type of subjectivity, i.e. a transcendental perspective on the different phenoumena of the experiential field. As we have explained before, each phenoumenon P is characterised by a *spectrum of objectivations* ($P_\alpha$, $P_\beta$,...), where objectivation $P_\alpha$ is constituted by framing P from the transcendental perspective $\alpha$. In turn, each object $P_\alpha$ is defined as a set of profiles, sketches, or adumbrations.[360] Let us now consider a phenoumenon P and the objects $P_\alpha$ and $P_\beta$ defined by two transcendental types $\alpha$ and $\beta$, i.e. by two viewzones in the transcendental landscape. Let us consider two profiles $x \in P_\alpha$ and $y \in P_\beta$ of the objects $P_\alpha$ and $P_\beta$ respectively such that x and y coincide in the zone defined by the intersection $\alpha \cap \beta$ (which might just

359 The logical connectives *and* and *or* correspond to the set-theoretic notions of *intersection* $\cap$ and *union* $\cup$ respectively, according to the following definitions:

$$x \in (A \cap B) \Leftrightarrow x \in A \text{ and } x \in B$$
$$x \in (A \cup B) \Leftrightarrow x \in A \text{ or } x \in B$$

360 Recall that a phenoumenon P is a *set-valued contravariant functor* on the category of transcendental types. This means that the functor P assigns to each transcendental type $\alpha$ a *set* whose elements are the profiles, sketches, or adumbrations of the object (that we have also denoted) $P_\alpha$.

be $\varnothing$),[361] i.e. such that $x_{|\alpha\cap\beta} = y_{|\alpha\cap\beta}$ (where we are assuming that $x \in P_\alpha$ and $y \in P_\alpha$ can be restricted to the zone $\alpha \cap \beta$, which is included in both $\alpha$ and $\beta$). We shall call the profiles $x \in P_\alpha$ and $y \in P_\alpha$ that coincide in $\alpha \cap \beta$ *integrable profiles*.[362] Integrable profiles combine a *difference* (they are defined with respect to different transcendental types $\alpha$ and $\beta$) and a *local similarity* (they coincide when restricted to their common transcendental type $\alpha \cap \beta$). Now, viewzones $\alpha$ and $\beta$ also define (by the definition of a topological space) a zone $\alpha \cup \beta$ given by their union. If a unique profile $z \in P_{\alpha\cup\beta}$ associated with the zone $\alpha \cup \beta$ exists such that the restriction of z to $\alpha$ is x and the restriction of z to $\beta$ is y, then we will say that the integrable profiles $x \in P_\alpha$ and $y \in P_\beta$ are effectively integrated in the (more global) profile z. A phenoumenon is a *phenoumenal sheaf* when all integrable

361 A technical comment is in order here. Two zones $\alpha$ and $\beta$ might be disjoint, i.e. $\alpha \cap \beta = \varnothing$. Since the operation $\cap$ is closed, $\varnothing$ must also be a zone of the topology. In order to evaluate whether or not two profiles $x \in P_\alpha$ and $y \in P_\beta$ coincide in $\alpha \cap \beta = \varnothing$, phenoumenon P must also assign a set of profiles to the zone $\varnothing$. The corresponding object is defined as $P_\varnothing = \{*\}$, i.e. as a set with one (arbitrary) element. The inclusion of $\varnothing$ in any set implies the existence of restriction maps $P_\alpha \to \varnothing$ and $P_\beta \to \varnothing$ which send all the elements of $P_\alpha$ and $P_\beta$ to the element $*$. It follows that two profiles x and y defined with respect to disjoint zones $\alpha$ and $\beta$ necessarily coincide when restricted to their empty intersection $\alpha \cap \beta = \varnothing$, i.e. that they are integrable.

362 From a constructivist standpoint, a proposition is a type whose tokens are the different proofs or witnesses of its truth. In particular, an equality of the form $a = b$ might be concretely proved by constructing an identification between $a$ and $b$. Far from being a mere epistemic remainder of the fact that there is no truth without proofs, this constructivist enhancement of the notion of proposition introduces an intrinsic 'homotopic' structure whose truncation might lead to different forms of pathologies. For example, two triangles in a space are equal if it is possible to displace one of the triangles in space so as to superimpose it onto the other. If the space has holes, there exist non-equivalent identifications between the two triangles. Now, the notion of sheaf can be constructively enhanced by replacing the condition of strict equality $x_{|\alpha\cap\beta} = y_{|\alpha\cap\beta}$ with a condition stating that $x_{|\alpha\cap\beta}$ and $y_{|\alpha\cap\beta}$ can be identified (denoted $x_{|\alpha\cap\beta} \simeq y_{|\alpha\cap\beta}$). This enhancement of the notion of sheaf gives rise to the notion of *stack* (*champ* in French). See for instance N. Mestrano and C. Simpson, 'Stacks', in Anel and Catren (eds.), *New Spaces in Mathematics: Formal and Conceptual Reflections*, 462–504.

profiles are effectively integrated in a unique manner (sheaf condition). In other words, a phenoumenon P is a sheaf when profiles $x \in P_\alpha$ and $y \in P_\beta$ of different objectivations of P that coincide on $\alpha \cap \beta$ are glued together along this local similarity in a unique manner. The result of this gluing operation is a profile of the objectivation $P_{\alpha \cup \beta}$ of P, that is, a profile of the object constituted by framing P from the viewzone given by the 'binocular' union of $\alpha$ and $\beta$. It is worth emphasising that the sheaf condition has two components, namely an *existence condition* stating that integrable profiles are integrated (also called a *gluing condition*) and a *unicity condition* stating that integrable profiles integrate in a unique manner (also called a *separation* or *locality condition*). Whereas the existence condition guarantees that integrable local data do generate global data, the unicity condition guarantees that this global data is completely defined by the local data, that there are no different global profiles which restrict to the same local data.

Combining mathematical terminology (where the integration operation is called *descent*)[363] with phenomenological terminology (where we speak of *depth perception*), we shall understand the operation that consists in gluing together profiles associated with different 'monocular' transcendental perspectives along their local similarities into single profiles defined with respect to a 'multiocular' perspective as a 'descent' into the depths of experience. A phenoumenal sheaf offers an experiential depth that can be experienced by subjects located in wider viewzones of the transcendental landscape, that is, by subjects equipped with 'multiscopic' transcendental structures that integrate local transcendental perspectives. According to the pictorial technique to represent depth, the integration of different local perspectives in a single bidimensional representation yields a three-dimensional depth experience. Analogously, '[w]e shall speak of a fully ["speculative" experience] [...] only when the entire [experience obtained by integrating local transcendental perspectives] has been transformed

363 Cf. C. Simpson, 'Descent', in L. Schneps (ed.), *Alexandre Grothendieck: A Mathematical Portrait* (Somerville, MA: International Press, 2014) 83–141.

[...] into a "window", and when we are meant to [experience] through this window into a space [of a higher phenoumenal depth].'[364]

Let us come back to the example of a coin D with one side painted in a *matt dark green* and a side painted in a *glossy bright yellow*. As we have already explained, coin D can be understood as a functor that assigns to each transcendental type or viewzone $\alpha$ the set of profiles of the object $D_\alpha$. The objects constituted out of the 'phenoumenal' coin D by the different transcendental types in the topology $\tau = \{\varnothing, \{C\}, \{L, C\}, \{C, B\}, \{L, C, B\}\}$ are given by the following sets of profiles:

$$
\begin{aligned}
D_{\varnothing} &= \{*\}, \\
D_{\{C\}} &= \{\text{green, yellow}\}, \\
D_{\{L, C\}} &= \{(\text{matt, green}), (\text{glossy, yellow})\}, \\
D_{\{C, B\}} &= \{(\text{green, dark}), (\text{yellow, bright})\}, \\
D_{\{L, C, B\}} &= \{(\text{matt, green, dark}), (\text{glossy, yellow, bright})\}.
\end{aligned}
$$

In our (Kantian) terms, each set of profiles corresponds to the multifaceted object constituted by framing the phenoumenal coin D from the corresponding transcendental perspective. Now, is this phenoumenon a phenoumenal sheaf? This will be the case if it satisfies the sheaf condition, that is, if all integrable profiles (i.e. profiles that coincide in the overlapping viewzones of the corresponding transcendental types) are amalgamated (in the form of a profile associated to the union of these transcendental types) in a unique manner. Let's consider for instance the profile (matt, green) of object $D_{\{L, C\}}$ and the profile (green, dark) of object $D_{\{C, B\}}$. Transcendental types {L, C} and {C, B} have a nontrivial intersection given by the type {C}. In other words, types {L, C} and {C, B} are not merely different since both of them are equipped with an organ to perceive colours. Moreover, the profiles (matt, green) and (green, dark) coincide when restricted to {C}, i.e. they are locally similar. Indeed, both (matt, green) and (green, dark) are experienced by a subject of type {C} as profiles of the form (green). Hence, the profiles (matt, green) and (green, dark) are

364 E. Panofsky, *Perspective as Symbolic Form*, tr. C. Wood (New York: Zone, 1991), 27.

integrable. In order to check whether they are integrated or not, we have to consider the union of the transcendental types {L, C} and {C, B}, that is the type {L, C, B}. Since the profiles (matt, green) and (green, dark) coincide along the intersection {C} of viewzones {L, C} and {C, B}, the sheaf condition states that there should be a unique global profile associated with the viewzone {L, C, B} which amalgamates the local profiles (matt, green) and (green, dark). Now, object $D_{\{L, C, B\}}$ constituted by the type {L, C, B} does have a profile of the form (matt, green, dark) that integrates the locally similar profiles (green, matt) and (green, dark). We could say that the transcendental type {L, C, B} provides a kind of 'binocular' description that integrates the local descriptions associated to the types {L, C} and {C, B}. The reader can verify that all the integrable profiles are indeed integrated, which means that the phenoumenon D defined by spectrum of the objects described above is indeed a sheaf.

Let's consider now an example of a phenoumenon that is not a phenoumenal sheaf. To do so, imagine a coin D' such that one side is painted with a *matt dark green* and the other with a *glossy bright green*. It is easy to see that this phenoumenon does not fulfil the sheaf condition with respect to the topology $\tau = \{\varnothing, \{C\}, \{L, C\}, \{C, B\}, \{L, C, B\}\}$. The spectrum of objects defined by the transcendental types in this topology is now:

$$
\begin{aligned}
D_{\varnothing} &= \{*\},\\
D_{\{C\}} &= \{\text{green}\},\\
D_{\{L, C\}} &= \{(\text{matt, green}), (\text{glossy, green})\},\\
D_{\{C, B\}} &= \{(\text{green, dark}), (\text{green, bright})\},\\
D_{\{L, C, B\}} &= \{(\text{matt, green, dark}), (\text{glossy, green, bright})\}.
\end{aligned}
$$

The profile (matt, green) of object $D_{\{L, C\}}$ and the profile (green, bright) of object $D_{\{C, B\}}$ coincide on the intersection $\{L, C\} \cap \{C, B\} = \{C\}$. However, object $D_{\{L, C, B\}}$ does not have a side with the combination (matt, green, bright).[365] In other words, subjects of types {L, C} and {C, B} will observe

365 The same can be said of the integrable profiles (glossy, green) $\in D_{\{L, C\}}$ and (green, dark) $\in D_{\{C, B\}}$. Indeed, the object $D_{\{L, C, B\}}$ does not have a profile of the form (glossy, green, dark).

profiles that are locally similar when considered as profiles of the object $D_{\{C\}}$ observed by subjects of their common type $\{C\}$. However, these locally similar profiles do not give rise to an amalgamated global profile of the object $D_{\{L, C, B\}}$ observed by a subject of the type $\{L, C, B\}$ obtained by fusing the transcendental resources of $\{L, C\}$ and $\{C, B\}$. Hence, phenoumenon D' has integrable profiles that are not effectively integrated, which means that it does not fulfil the existence part of the sheaf condition. It follows that this phenoumenon is not a phenoumenal sheaf.

Let us consider a metaphorical example of these ideas. In this essay, we are making intensive use of Benjamin's patchwork method ('Method of this project: literary montage. I needn't *say* anything. Merely [compose and] show').[366] We could indeed say that this text is to a large extent a vast montage of (sometimes ventriloquised) quotations. The philosophers and scientists who are referred to and who guide us through these reflections (notably Spinoza, Kant, Fichte, Hegel, Heidegger, Grothendieck, Deleuze, Henry, and Goddard, among others) have obviously developed very different philosophical stances that cannot simply be superposed or homologated. But there are certain local zones where we have detected local similarities, equivalences, resonances, correspondences, and counterpoints (as well as explicit cross-references and interpretations). By introducing the local twists that we have considered necessary in these local overlapping regions (reinterpretations, *détournements*, smooth deformations, grafts, forced compatibilisations, etc.), we tried to glue together these local data in a coherent manner. Even if the essential differences between their philosophical perspectives cannot be erased, these different perspectives can be integrated along their local similarities. The global picture that emerges from this gluing and twisting of local philosophical data is certainly very different from the philosophical stances that each of these thinkers proposed. However, we have tried to exhibit here the kind of philosophical depth (if any) that is achieved when we think through a multiscopic device constructed out of these local lenses.

366 W. Benjamin, *The Arcades Project*, tr. H. Eiland and K. McLaughlin (Cambridge, MA: The Belknap Press of Harvard University Press, 1999), N1a,8.

In order to enrich the concept of what we have called immanental phenoumenodelia, let us revisit the so-called *principles of phenomenology*.[367] The first principle—'So much appearing, so much Being [*Soviel Schein, soviel Sein*]'[368]—inverts the 'metaphysical' hierarchy between a purported hidden being—the non-appearing essence—and the undulating veil of appearances that conceals the former. By doing so, the first principle subordinates ontology to phenomenology, that is, it suspends (or traninsubstantiates) being in the form of a phenomenological appearing. This principle comes 'first' so to speak, since it encodes the ungrounding act of conversion that activates the phenomenological attitude, the phenomenological *epoché*. The *epoché* resumes and amplifies the radicality of the Cartesian beginning and opens a new absolutely modern sequence for existence, experience, and thinking: it is only by means of a hyperbolic doubt—and in particular through the realisation that every theoretical construction, every form of 'naturality', and every world view are always relative to a transcendental perspective—that it becomes possible to gain access to the phenoumenodelic absolute. It is not by hypostasising the brave new scientific discovery or by concocting a speculative argument intended to bypass the subject-object correlation that we shall access that living absolute that is always already with us, but rather through a *learned ignorance* that suspends in advance every 'image of the world' and every 'natural attitude' and lets life proceed with its labour of subjectivation and worldification. Descartes took the leap of doubt that inaugurated modern times, a leap into an abyssal experiential field made possible by the most hyperbolic radicalisation of the stubborn fact that, in the last instance, we do not know. It is also worth noting that the first principle also points toward a properly modern declension of the religious interest of reason. Condescending for a moment to use ontotheological terminology, we could say that the first principle (pushed to its limit) implies that the supreme being—the *summum ens*—is the 'being' that (self-)reveals itself in the widest possible manner, that is, a *Deus revelatus*, the antithesis

367 Cf. Henry, 'The Four Principles of Phenomenology' and J.-L. Marion, 'The Reduction and the "Fourth Principle"', *Analecta Hermeneutica* 8 (2016), 41–63.

368 Cf. Husserl, *Cartesian Meditations*, 103. See also Heidegger, *Being and Time*, 60.

of the *Deus absconditus*, a thesis that opens a path to an absolutely modern reactivation of the Christian identification God = (self-revealing) life.

The main limitation of this first principle is that it leaves indeterminate the notion of appearing and its (immanental and transcendental) conditions of possibility. Is such an appearing necessarily an appearing for a (finite) subject? So what is the concept of subject presupposed by the principle? What are the conditions of possibility of the existence of such a subject? Now, the second principle (the so-called 'principle of principles', formulated by Husserl in *Ideen I*) states that '[only an] originary presentive intuition is a legitimizing source of cognition.[369] [...] [presentive intuition is] that which makes possible every phenomenon and every experience in any domain whatsoever [...] the universal condition of phenomena.'[370] In Kantian terms, the 'principle of principles' implies that every form of experience is always correlative to a form of intuition associated with a finite subjectivity of a given transcendental type—that is, that there is no appearing without finite living subjects endowed with transcendental receptive faculties. Hence, the notion of appearing mobilised by the first principle is dependent upon both the *transcendental conditions* of possibility of experience given by the receptive-imaginative-spontaneous faculties of the subject of experience and the *immanental conditions* of possibility given by the morphogenetic capacity to institute such living subjects. We could say that the 'principle of principles' encodes the christic moment of phenomenology, the moment in which a finite being-there 'enacts a presence [...] by which and for which meaning is revealed in the present',[371] a presence that locally witnesses, channels, and modulates the revelation. Whereas on the one hand, this principle legitimately underscores the role played by finite subjectivity—thereby filling the gap left open by the first one—it also entails a new danger, namely the idealistic danger of

369 Cf. Husserl, *Ideas Pertaining to a Pure Phenomenology and to a Phenomenological Philosophy: First Book*, 44 [§24].

370 Henry, 'The Four Principles of Phenomenology', 8.

371 H. Corbin, 'From Heidegger to Suhravardi: An Interview with Nemo', tr. M. Evans-Cockle, <https://www.amiscorbin.com/en/>.

understanding the notion of appearing in purely subjectivist terms, that is, the danger of reducing being to appearing *for a subject*. This danger is radically counterbalanced by the third principle, that is by the principle that summons us to 'return to the things themselves [*Zurück zu den Sachen Selbst*]'. By summoning Renatus Cartesius to venture deep into the catatauonic rainforest, the third principle implies that the *ego cogito* cannot be understood as a last instance that could impose a limit to the depth of the Cartesian leap of doubt. Now, this real-oriented principle does so by seemingly reintroducing—in retroactive contradiction with the first principle—a distinction between being (the substantial *that* which appears) and appearing (the act of showing itself), as well as a subordination of the latter to the former. The act of appearing appears now as a mere mean to access the ultimate goal, the 'things in themselves', that is, things considered independently of any appearing. This apparent contradiction between the first and the third principle can be overcome by claiming that the 'things in themselves' also appear, but in a manner that in general cannot be fully captured by a single finite subjectivity. The expression 'in themselves' does not mean here 'considered independently of its appearing' but rather 'considered independently of its appearing for a subject of a given transcendental type, that is, considered independently of its possible transcendental-dependent objectivations'. The fact that a thing can appear as a phenomenon correlative to a given transcendental type of subjectivity is not incompatible with the thesis that the very being of the thing *in itself* is identical to its uncorrelatated (or phenoumenodelic) appearing. In order to emphasise this fact, we have called the appearing thing in itself *phenoumenon* and its uncorrelated mode of manifestation *phenoumenalisation*. This phenoumenodelic move makes the identification between being and appearing compatible with the injunction to 'return to the things themselves' by distinguishing two modalities of appearing, *phenomenal appearing* (always correlated to a particular transcendental type of subjectivity) and uncorrelated *phenoumenal appearing*. The functorial definition of a phenoumenon encodes the relation between these two modalities.

This series of phenomenological principles culminates in Marion's principle 'So much [suspension], so much givenness'.[372] Thanks to this principle, we can understand the *epoché* as a suspension within the impersonal field of experience rather than as an idealistic reduction of the latter to constitutive transcendental subjectivity. Marion's principle establishes a proportional relation between the radicality of the phenomenological suspension and a notion situated at the opposite pole of the transcendental constitution, namely the phenoumenodelic *givenness* of the phenoumena considered 'in themselves'. Whereas the phenomenological reduction reduces experience to phenomena correlated to a transcendental subjectivity, the *epoché* suspends the subject in the realm of the 'in-itself', in the living insubstance that never ceases giving itself, self-revealing, sprouting into the open, in itself and from itself. The 'things' are 'in themselves' as far as they are embedded in the 'original Ipseity' of the immanental self-revealing phenoumenodelic insubstance, in the primordial reflective act of self-givenness (*Selbstgegebenheit*), in the 'self-appearing of the appearing'[373]. The pleromatic life self-gives by remaining in itself, always instituting new living slits that refract its omnipresent act of self-revelation in singular manners. Finite experience is not coextensive with what is experienced, to the phenoumena considered 'in themselves'; finite experience is always the experience of the phenomena constituted out of the phenoumena by the transcendental faculties of the corresponding subject. But ultimately, the transcendental constitution of what is given in itself—the 'intuitive' transformation of uncorrelated phenoumena into correlated phenomena—can be understood as an immanental local modulation of the impersonal act of self-revelation, as a local operator of the self-givenness of life.

We could say that this succession of principles tends toward an asubjective or impersonal declension of phenomenology. Thanks to the work of Heidegger (who emphasised the always-already being-thrown of the

---

372 Cf. J.-L. Marion, *Reduction and Givenness: Investigations of Husserl, Heidegger, and Phenomenology*, tr. T.A. Carlson (Evanston, IL: Northwestern University Press, 1998).

373 M. Henry, *Phénoménologie matérielle* (Paris: PUF, 1990), 75.

constitutive subject and its irredeemable finitude), Patočka (who underscored the role played by the pre-subjective and pre-objective 'non-appearing immensity' that he calls the 'world'),[374] Levinas (who emphasised the irreducibility of the Other in itself to any form of transcendental-dependent objectivity), Merleau-Ponty (who exhibited the fleshy reversibility of the experiencing and experienced phenomenoudelical actuality), Henry (who turned phenomenological attention from worldly visibility to the invisible life that institutes constituting subjects), and Marion (who reconceptualised the notion of phenomenon by shifting the emphasis from subjective constitution to intrinsic givenness), thanks to all these seminal contributions, phenomenology was able to pass through the danger of idealism concomitant with the identification between being and appearing and reach what we could call its phenoumenodelic phase.[375]

If we accept that the transcendental structures that both make human experience possible and trace out its limits are the partial result of an ongoing process of subjectivation, then there is no legitimate reason to decree the impossibility of bringing about *speculative variations* of these structures, that is to say variations of the transcendental type of the subject of experience. In brief, there is no a priori obstruction to the project of piloting, diversifying, and redirecting the immanental institution of subjectivity. If every transcendental type is no more than a moment abstracted from an ongoing process of subjectivation, then nothing de jure forbids the possibility of systematically reorienting this process by means of a speculative self-positing *techné*. 'The brain [of a speculative subject] can be tuned, like a TV, to turn off any channel, and to bring in a new channel',[376] since 'what is tuned in, is a function of how we use our brains habitually, and what is not-tuned-in may, in many cases, become tuned-in, with practice in

374 J. Patočka, *Le monde naturel et le mouvement de l'existence humaine* (Dordrecht: Kluwer, 1988), 5.

375 Cf. Marion, 'The Reduction and the "Fourth Principle"', 62.

376 Wilson, *Prometheus Rising*, 151.

neurological reprogramming'.[377] Instead of mystifying that which exceeds language, perception, or understanding, we can work (linguistically, philosophically, scientifically, technologically, existentially) to patiently shift the relative limits. That the pleroma is always in excess of any given Umwelt does not mean that it is impossible to rework the transcendental structures that define each Umwelt and enrich them by means of speculative extensions and variations capable of turning something of the previously unspeakable, indiscernible, invisible, inaudible, impossible, unthinkable into something sayable, discernible, visible, audible, possible, thinkable. If every impasse of a symbolic order is a symptom of the limited character of the corresponding transcendental structure and therefore annunciates a real beyond, every speculative variation intended to sublate such an impasse effects an incarnation of the infinite in the finite, of the real in the symbolic. Attention to what is annunciated, attention paid to the symptomatic angel that arrives in the form of impossibility (of perceiving, of feeling, of thinking, of proving), opens up a space in which an incarnation capable of rupturing the boundaries of the prevailing Umwelt is possible, an incarnation by means of which, as Bernardino of Siena states, '[t]he unfigurable [comes] into the figure, the untellable into discourse, the inexplicable into language, the uncircumscribable into place, the invisible into vision, the inaudible into sound, [...] the impalpable into the tangible'.[378] The motifs of *annunciation* (the 'real' impasses of every symbolic order) and of *incarnation* (the institution of new forms of subjectivity) on the one hand, and the concern with *perspective* (concomitant to every experience held by a subject that *exists-there*) on the other are intimately linked:[379] only by varying perspective and by developing the subjective capacities to integrate the corresponding perspectival experiences is it possible to institute new lifeforms capable of opening new horizons of immanent transcendence in the heart of the

---

377 R.A. Wilson, 'Creative Agnosticism', *The Journal of Cognitive Liberties* 2:1 (2000), 61–84.

378 Quoted in D. Arasse, *L'Annonciacion italienne. Une histoire de perspective* (Paris: Éditions Hazan, 2010), 10.

379 Ibid.

pleroma—that is to say, new forms of experiential depth. For every impasse of the Umwelt correlative to a particular transcendental perspective is the strait gate through which a new avatar of Yesses, the native and mortal affirmator of life, might enter.[380] This epiphanic mediation of finitude—the introduction of the infinite into the finite by means of the incarnation of new subjective typologies and the concomitant emergence of new worlds of revelation within pleroma—is indissociable from a drift in the transcendental landscape capable of integrating different transcendental perspectives. In this way the syncretic amalgamation between shamanism—the development of the ability to navigate the transcendental landscape of subjective types and make trans-species kin—and trinitarian Christianity—the thesis that the immanental pleroma (the insubstantial mat[t]er), reveals itself by engendering finite forms of subjectivity (the living ones) capable of being integrated into tribes (Holy Spirit)—acquires a properly speculative foundation.

The speculative understanding of the critical motif requires the transplantation of certain central concepts of transcendental philosophy into a new, post-critical context. Firstly, a subject capable of bringing about variations of its own transcendental structures cannot, by definition, be understood as a particular instantiation of any of the local transcendental types of subjectivity enveloped by the variation. A subject capable of critical reflection on its own transcendental structure can activate the speculative, self-positing, or metaprogramming circuits, that is, the circuits by means of which the subject can transmute, deform, disturb or reprogram the a priori structures of its own experience. A subject that instantiates a speculative type of order 2 or higher is endowed with speculative degrees of freedom in the transcendental landscape. We could say that a speculative subject—a subject endowed with a 'trans-species [or rather trans-type] personhood',[381] a subject who 'consciously seeks to edit less and tune in more'[382]—is capable

380 Cf. W. Benjamin, 'Theses on the Philosophy of History', in *Illuminations: Essays and Reflections*, tr. H. Zohn (New York: Shocken, 1969), 254–64: 264.

381 Viveiros de Castro, 'Perspectival Anthropology and the Method of Controlled Equivocation', 3.

382 Wilson, 'Creative Agnosticism'.

of partially piloting its displacements in the transcendental landscape and transgressing the limits thrown into relief by transcendental reflection; capable of embodying forms of self-identity that can envelop variations of its own transcendental structures; capable of unlocking new modalities of action, perception, conceptualisation, affection, and socialisation; capable of engaging into inter-umweltic, inter-model, inter-kingdom, inter-species, inter-cultural, and inter-natural hybridisations. The speculative subject, working patiently to linger in the process of its own gestation, its own institution, its own formation, is, to some extent, a *plastic* or *larval subject*: 'In this sense, it is not even clear that thought, in so far as it constitutes the dynamism peculiar to philosophical[, scientific, artistic, political] systems, may be related to a substantial, completed and well-constituted subject, such as the [Kantian transcendental subject]: thought is, rather, one of those terrible movements which can be sustained only under the conditions of a larval subject.'[383]

Every transcendental framing, filtering, or editing of the pleroma is a process of abstraction by means of which certain differences are forgotten. Such a transcendental sieve is requisite for the constitution of the renormalised forms of experience that finite subjects can afford and for the design of maps and models that allow the pleroma to be probed and navigated. A map that would coincide with the territory (as in Borges's *On Rigour in Science*), or a model that would not filter the experiential field, is neither economically affordable nor useful. One could of course retort that even if it is certainly true that 'everything which is [too] complex is unusable', one must not forget that 'everything simple is [strictly speaking] false'.[384] The way out of this sharp opposition between useless accuracy and useful falsity is to acknowledge that the expansion of rationality goes hand in hand with the construction and utilisation of ideal models that rely on operations of abstraction, filtering, and editing, without losing sight of how these models were constituted.

383 G. Deleuze, *Difference and Repetition*, tr. P. Patton (New York: Columbia University Press, 1994), 313.

384 P. Valéry, *Œuvres II* (Paris: Gallimard, 1960), 864.

'[T]he finite intellect deals with the myth of finite facts. There can be no objection to this procedure, provided that we remember what we are doing.'[385] When the transcendental acts of constitution of ideality are forgotten, then rational thinking is affected by the pathology described by Husserl in *The Crisis of European Sciences and Transcendental Phenomenology*.

385 Whitehead, *Modes of Thought*, 9. Regarding the necessity for and the limits of abstraction see also the following text by Whitehead: 'The advantage of confining attention to a definite group of abstraction, is that you confine your thoughts to clear-cut definite things, with clear-cut definite relations. Accordingly, if you have a logical head, you can deduce a variety of conclusions representing the relationships between these abstract entities. Furthermore, if these abstractions are well-founded, that is to say, if they do not abstract from everything that is important in experience, the scientific thought which confines itself to these abstractions will arrive at a variety of important truths relating to our experience of nature. [...] The disadvantage of exclusive attention to a group of abstractions, however well-founded, is that, by the nature of the case, you have abstracted from the remainder of things. In so far as the excluded things are important in your experience, your modes of thought are not fitted to deal with them. You cannot think without abstractions; accordingly, it is of the utmost importance to be vigilant in critically revising your modes of abstraction' (Whitehead, *Science and the Modern World*, 59). A similar criticism of unchecked abstraction can be found in contemporary debates about constructive mathematics. See for instance the following text: 'To build up an abstract concept from a raw flow of data, one must disregard inessential details; in other words, to simplify the complexity of concrete reality one must idealise over it, and this is obtained by "forgetting" some information. To forget information is the same as to destroy something, in particular if there is no possibility of restoring that information, like when the magnetic memory of a disk is erased. So to abstract involves a certain amount of destruction; our principle is that an abstraction is constructive, that it is a reliable tool in getting knowledge which is faithful to reality, not when information is kept as much as possible, but when it is "forgotten" in such a way that it can be restored at will at any moment. This after all is the test to show that an abstraction does not lead astray from reality; that is, that it preserves truth. [...] [W]hen it is clear which concrete aspects are forgotten and how they can be restored by a suitable method, then that abstract notion can be used freely and safely.' G. Sambin and S. Valentini, 'Building up a Toolbox for Martin-Lof's Type Theory: Subset Theory', in G. Sambin and J.M. Smith (eds.), *Twenty-five Years of Constructive Type Theory: Proceedings of a Congress Held in Venice, October 1995* (Oxford: Oxford University Press, 1998), 224–25.

Rationality becomes pathological when it is astralised out of pleromatic concreteness without keeping track of the operations of abstraction. By abstracting, idealising, and modelling in a controlled manner, one can fine-tune the degree of abstraction required for the goals at stake, and resolve the abstract back into the concrete when necessary. Rational thinking is not a one-way street toward abstraction but a two-way street of abstractions (forgetfulness) and resolutions (memory). We cannot not forget differences, but we can remember that we are forgetting and try to tune the resolution of our memory. Hence, memory should not be contrasted 'with forgetting but with the forgetting of forgetting [...]'.[386]

Transcendental plasticity presupposes—beyond all self-sufficient voluntarism—religation to the impersonal life, to the morphogenetic force that generates new transcendental types by forcing variations of their transcendental affordances. If only life engenders new lifeforms—if '[l]ife [(the "matter, mutter, mother"[387] "of us all!"[388])] is what modifies the transcendental'[389]—it is only by strengthening our religation to life that we can mutate into new lifeforms. In this sense, the project of bringing about speculative variations of one's own subjective structure, of disturbing the supposed essence of the human, far from being a Promethean project, is a project that presupposes a religating interest of reason: while Prometheus radicalises his separation by attempting to appropriate divine force and embody ontotheological patriarchy, any form of speculative exploration of the transcendental landscape requires engagement in a process that involves sublating the illness of disligation, a deconstruction of the hypostasis of the modern subject as a self-grounded willing substance.

In the dialectical triad developed by Saint Paul in the Second Epistle to the Thessalonians—the *katechon* (the Empire that holds the Antichrist

386 Deleuze, *Foucault*, 107.

387 D. Haraway, *Staying With the Trouble: Making Kin in the Chthulucene* (Durham, NC and London: Duke University Press, 2016), 120.

388 Joyce, *Finnegans Wake*, 299.

389 C. Malabou, 'Can We Relinquish the Transcendental?', *Journal of Speculative Philosophy* 28:3 (2014), 242–55.

back by enforcing the Roman law), the Antichrist (the lawless one), and the Parousia (the concrete fulfilment of the law, not by means of the abstract universality of moral precepts but through the pleroma of love)—the Promethean figure of the Antichrist is described as the one that 'will oppose and will exalt himself over everything that is called God or is worshipped, so that he sets himself up in God's temple, proclaiming himself to be God'.[390] We could say, somewhat anachronistically, that Saint Paul proposes a bifurcation point between three subjective typologies: the (neurotic) citizens of the colonial Empire, a Promethean type of (psychotic) subjectivity, and the religated siblings of Yesses, the anointed one. The Empire hypostasises its Umwelt, enforces a colonial reduction of the open multiplicity of modes of life to a unique transcendental type (so-called 'humanity') and the concomitant nomological order, and provides a sheltering sky whose protection can only be accepted at the price of becoming a citizen, that is, an uprooted medicated neurotic consumer. The Promethean 'lawless one' breaks with this Imperial secularised version of the ontotheological Father and affirms its sovereign power to self-posit and to use the power of technics to destroy and create worlds. But the Antichrist mistakes its speculative capacity to sublate the law with a purported self-sufficiency, as if he could own the anomic divine force that alone can constitute and destitute the different aeons. By setting itself up in the place of God and pretending to embody its wrath, the Antichrist forecloses its finitude and claims to master life and death. If the Antichrist does bypass the neurotic submission of the humanist subject, it does so at the price of converting its separation into a disligation with respect to the ultimate divine power that gives birth and gifts death. In this sense, the 'lawless one' is a 'fallen one', someone that fell out of the immanental realm of life, thereby passing from the almighty Father to the worst (*du père au pire*). The existential dilemma is clearly posited: How can we give consistency to a finite existence by relying neither on the protection of the ontotheological Father (or its secular avatars) nor on a Promethean psychosis that denies the crack? Would it be possible to sublate the Promethean disligation without backsliding to the

390 2 Thessalonians 2:4.

transcendental conservatism of the police and colonial humanistic Empire that holds the Antichrist back? 'And then the lawless one [*anomos*] will be revealed [and will affirm its sovereign self-sufficiency and will radicalise its separation], whom the [Child Yesses] will overthrow with the breath of [its] mouth[, blowing the healing insubstance into his nose, calling it back to the realm of life, rebounding it] by the [pleromatic] splendour of [its] coming specious presence [*parousia*].'[391]

In order to understand more precisely the relationship between religion and Prometheanism, it is necessary to take into account the multivalence of the mythical figure of Prometheus. This conceptual character interweaves (1) the necessary deconstruction of the sun-centred verticalist ontotheology which separates the living from the blazing source of life (and in this sense it is true that Prometheanism is opposed to the strictly ontotheological and hypertranscendent distortion of the religious), (2) a technical empowerment of mankind ('every art possessed by [human beings] comes from Prometheus'), and (3) the unbinding of Prometheus, that is to say the hubris that aims to 'cure' the human subject of its finitude by means of techno-scientific progress. The complex entanglement between these heterogeneous themes explains why the figure of Prometheus could provide both the symbol of the techno-scientific mastery of natural forces characteristic of humanist modernity (Frankenstein qua Prometheus definitively unbound)[392] and the *trope* that set off the 'pantheist quarrel'—enacted by the rupture between the immanentist Goethe and the hypertranscendentalist Jacobi—arising from Goethe's poem 'Prometheus', in which the mythical figure of Prometheus incarnates the immanental Spinozist rebellion against the ontotheological gods.[393] But the key conceptual distinction which makes it

391 2 Thessalonians 2:4.

392 Cf. Mary Shelley's *Frankenstein; or, The Modern Prometheus*, Percy Bysshe Shelley's *Prometheus Unbound*, and H. Jonas, *The Imperative of Responsibility: In Search of Ethics for the Technological Age*, tr. H. Jonas and D. Herr (Chicago, IL: University of Chicago Press), 1984.

393 Cf. F.H. Jacobi, 'Concerning the Doctrine of Spinoza in Letters to Herr Moses Mendelssohn', in *Main Philosophical Writings and the Novel All-Will*, 173–252.

possible to untie the Gordian knot between these different strands is given in the contrast between the states of Prometheus defined by the past participles 'bound/unbound'. The (required) deconstruction of ontotheology and the psychotic denegation of subjective finitude are not two sides of the same coin. Spinozism is in fact the ultimate proof that the two can be disentangled, that is, that the immanence of divine insubstance and the understanding of subjectivity as a particular finite local mode of the latter are consistent theses. In brief, the destitution of the hypertranscendent god does not necessarily entail a foreclosure of the crack that splits and limits the subject. The existential impasse that consists in denying human finitude can and should be avoided. In this respect, the problem is not so much the figure of Prometheus himself, but, as Jonas implicitly notes, that of 'Prometheus definitively unbound [*Der endgültig entfesselte Prometheus*]', that is, in our terms, Prometheus disligated. As we shall understand it here, Prometheus unbound is a conceptual character who conflates technical-scientific empowerment and the necessary deconstruction of ontotheology with a denial of subjective finitude. In the wake of the rapprochement proposed by Simone Weil between the figures of Yesses and (a rebounded) Prometheus, we could say that the attempt to unbound Prometheus from his rock would be homologous to the blunder of seeking to save Yesses from the cross.[394] The figure of a bounded Prometheus embodies at the same time the desire, the courage, and the perseverance of (technical) knowledge and the humility proper to one who assumes its finitude and does not forget the ultimate vulnerability of its living and dying existence: 'Here we want to regain two distinguishing properties of [...] science for our being-there. [...] Aeschylus has this Prometheus utter a saying that expresses the essence of knowing: "Knowing, however, is far weaker than necessity" (Prom. 514, ed. Wil). This is

394 'Note that if we put together the perfect righteous one, who is a [human being] and whom the torture of crucifixion causes to die, and Prometheus, who is an immortal god, and whom a tradition recalled by Hesiod regarded as perpetually crucified, we obtain the analogy of the double conception of the sacrifice of Christ, a sacrifice which was consummated once, but which by the mass is perpetually renewed until the end of the world.' S. Weil, *Intimations of Christianity Among the Ancient Greeks* (London: Routledge, 1998), 119.

to say: all knowing about things has always already been delivered up to overpowering fate and fails before it. Just because of this, knowing must develop its highest defiance; called forth by such defiance, all the power of the hiddenness of what is must first arise for knowing really to fail. Just in this way, what is opens itself in its unfathomable inalterability and lends knowing its truth. Encountering the Greek saying about the creative impotence of knowing, one likes to find here all too readily the prototype of a knowing based purely on itself, while in fact such knowing has forgotten its own essence; this knowing is interpreted for us as the 'theoretical attitude'—but what do the Greeks mean by θεωρία? One says: pure contemplation, which remains bound only to the thing in question and to all it is and demands. This contemplative behaviour [...] is said to be pursued for its own sake. But this appeal is mistaken. For one thing, "theory" is not pursued for its own sake, but only in the passion to remain close to and hard pressed by what is as such. [...] Science is the questioning holding one's ground in the midst of the self-concealing totality of what is. This active perseverance knows, as it perseveres, about its impotence before fate.'[395] Along with Prometheus, let us persevere in our attempts to rationally understand the experiential field in which we live, move, and die. Let us have the courage to place ourselves in the service of truth. But we shall not disligate ourselves from the stone that channels the living forces of the pleroma; we shall not refuse to drink the sacramental *lapis* that anchors us back to our condition of begotten finite beings and imposes 'a limit on infinity'; we shall not forget that all finite life pulsates locally in the infinite life; we shall not confuse the strictly speculative possibility of technically mediating the limits of experience with a denial of existential and transcendental finitude; we shall not conflate the immanental closure of ontotheology with a psychotic foreclosure of 'castration'. It is unbound Prometheanism that longs for a 'liberation *from* finite life' (and castration) rather than a 'liberation *of* finite life', that perpetuates the ontotheological denegation of both finitude and freedom and submits finite human practices (and in particular religion) to the idea of a

395 Heidegger, 'The Self-Assertion of the German University', 4–5.

hypertranscendent highest good.[396] We shall then endorse the Promethean deconstruction of ontotheology and the techno-speculative empowerment of mankind, but we shall not pretend to save Prometheus from his rock. In so doing, this rebound Prometheanism ceases to be incompatible with the project of 'starting our own [absolutely modern] religion'.[397]

The *trope* of the *techné* that mediates between the Promethean rebellion against the hypertranscendent gods and the rejection of castration is the key point here: technoscience—far from being necessarily condemned to be used as a weapon in the service of the self-imposition of the human type and the conquest of space, time, and nature—can be understood and utilised as an I-oriented shamanic operator that performs speculative variations among different transcendental types, and correlatively as a not-I-oriented magical operator that mediates worldly naturalism. Science (a mode of thought designed to attune consciousness with *logos* qua attribute of the pleroma) and technics (tasking scientific understanding itself with mediating motor, perceptive, psychotropic, neurocomputational, culinary, oneiric, communicational, architectonic, linguistic, ludic, visionary faculties of the human subjective type) channel in a singular manner the human desire to step into the transmundane open. Far from being necessarily condemned to deepen the disligation of a human subjectivity that imposes itself and desiccates itself, technoscience can be oriented by the infinite idea of truth. In turn, the idea of truth can be inscribed in a philosophical constellation visible in the heights of the supernatural sky, where 'a [worldly] place fuses with the [pleromatic] beyond'. In particular, the idea of truth can be constellated with the infinite idea of justice—the idea that orients political experimentation with possible forms of living and dying together that do not relinquish the desire to do justice to different forms of life. At the same time, such a constellation can be meta-oriented by the quintessentially religating and anti-capitalist prescription of putting every human project at the service of life and its particular affect, love.

396 M. Hägglund, *This Life: Secular Faith and Spiritual Freedom* (New York: Pantheon, 2019).

397 Cf. T. Leary, *Start Your Own Religion* (Berkeley, CA: Ronin Publishing, 2005).

Of course, removing technoscience from the service of the capitalist disease and reorienting it by other ideas of reason and other eidetic constellations, requires the active commitment of the scientists and engineers without whom there would be no technoscience at all. Scientists are accountable for the capitalistic coopting of scientific discourse and the resulting technical devastation of nature. It is not that 'technology betrayed man',[398] but that disligated humanity betrayed this Promethean gift by using it to hypostatise a conquering subjective type that persists in '[t]aking and not giving back, demanding that "productivity" and "earnings" keep on increasing with time, the System removing from the rest of the [human] World these vast quantities of energy to keep its own tiny desperate fraction showing a profit: and not only most of humanity—[other Worlds], animal, vegetable and mineral, [are] laid waste in the process. [...] [S]ooner or later [the System] must crash to its death, when its addiction to energy has become more than the rest of the World can supply, dragging with it innocent souls all along the chain of life. Living inside the System is like riding across the country in a bus driven by a maniac bent on suicide...'.[399] We must ask ourselves honestly whether we are really capable of anchoring technoscience back into the impersonal life of which the living desire to know is a particular manifestation; whether we are capable of proving that it is not necessarily true that 'technical production is the organisation of disligation'[400] and that the imperialist domination of nature is the final and necessary fate of technoscience. We must repeat the Heideggerian-Grothendieckean question: 'Shall we continue scientific research?[401] [...] Should there still *be* science for us in the future, or should we let it drift toward a quick end? That there should be science at all, is never unconditionally necessary.'[402] The problem is not necessarily that humanity will disappear ('We later civilizations [...]

398 Benjamin, 'To the Planetarium', 59.

399 Pynchon, *Gravity's Rainbow*, 412.

400 Heidegger, 'Why Poets?', *Off the Beaten Track*, 220.

401 Grothendieck, 'Allons-nous continuer la recherche scientifique?', 159–69.

402 Heidegger, 'The Self-Assertion of the German University', 3.

we too now know that we are mortal'),[403] but whether it will do so in the midst of disease and the destruction of other lifeforms. Perhaps we shall have to learn once again how to die discreetly, without making a drama out of our disappearance, without dragging others along with us—to retire with humility, gratitude, and dignity, allowing life to continue its course without us. What does the thunder that blasts the towers say? 'The jungle crouched, humped in silence. Then spoke the thunder / DA / *Datta* [/ Daime]: what have we given?'[404]

A speculative subject is a subject capable of developing and utilising a *speculative techné* to extend and/or vary its transcendental affordances. '[W]hy should our bodies end at the skin? [...] [M]achines can be prosthetic devices, intimate components, friendly selves' that deconstruct the essentialist myths of organic wholeness and transcendental fixity.[405] Telescopes, books, microscopes, rockets, turntables, submarines, glasses, computers, entheogens, helmets, talking sticks, telephones, pipes, and other transcendental prosthesis are all products of the speculative *techné*. In this sense, the essence of technics would not so much be the *structure of enframing* (*Gestell*) of nature as a localised stock of reserves ruled by a self-asserting subject (a structure which, according to Heidegger, defines the properly modern framing), but rather the possibility of disturbing every possible transcendental framing. Speculative *techné* does not necessarily 'construct the world as an object',[406] but can be used to deconstruct naturalised worlds and carve portals to the transmundane open, to jack into it. Placed under the aegis of the idea of truth, the ultimate end of technoscience 'is not mastery over nature, but rather mastery over the [transcendental] relation between nature and humanity': thanks to technics we can alter the transcendental structure that constitutes our filtered

---

403 P. Valéry, 'The Crisis of the Mind', tr. D. Folliot and J. Matthews, *Paul Valéry, An Anthology* (London: Routledge, 1977), 94.

404 Eliot, *The Waste Land*, 18.

405 Haraway, 'A Cyborg Manifesto', 326.

406 Heidegger, 'Why Poets?', *Off the Beaten Track*, 220.

relationship with *natura naturans.*[407] Technics calls any idolatry regarding transcendental location into question: the liberatory potential of technics resides in its capacity to shake up transcendentally sedentary civilisations and clear away any separation between natives and foreigners:[408] in the last instance, every subject, regardless of its transcendental type and beyond any naturalcultural/artificial distinction, is a living being and therefore a sibling. Every new speculative *techné* produces effects that are strictly magical, impossible, strange to umweltic naturalism—and in this sense, '[a]ny sufficiently advanced technological is indistinguishable from magic'.[409] In particular, the MEAD principle ('Magic is Empowerment by Attention to Detail')[410] points toward a privileged operator in the practice of trans-umweltic magic: by (microscopically, telescopically, computationally, or entheogenically) increasing the resolution, one can blow up that which appears indecomposable, one can 'see a World in a Grain of Sand',[411] acknowledge that there is always 'a vague beyond, waiting for penetration with respect to its details',[412] that it is always possible to unfold differences that were previously flattened or unresolved, to choose which differences will make a difference in each particular context.[413] More generally, the bio-

407 Benjamin, 'To the Planetarium', 58–59.

408 Cf. Levinas, 'Heidegger, Gagarin and Us', in *Difficult Freedom*, 231.

409 A.C. Clarke, *Profiles of the Future: An Inquiry into the Limits of the Possible* (New York: MacMillan, 1973), 36.

410 D. Pendell, *Pharmako/Gnosis: Plant Teachers and the Poison Path* (Berkeley, CA: North Atlantic Books, 2009), 139.

411 W. Blake, 'Auguries of Innocence', in *The Complete Poetry and Prose of William Blake*, ed. D.V. Erdman (New York: Anchor, 1988), 490.

412 Whitehead, *Modes of Thought*, 6.

413 In Wilson's words, '[t]he human brain [...] appears much like a very unique self-programming computer. It chooses—usually unconsciously and mechanically—the *quality* of consciousness it will experience and the reality-tunnel it will employ to orchestrate the incoming signals from the experienced world. When it becomes more conscious of this programming, its creativeness becomes truly astounding [...]. In meta-programming or neurological self-criticism, the brain becomes ca-

technological expansion of human beings' motor and perceptual functions; the scientific and philosophical reprogramming of the categories of the understanding; literary and philosophical work on linguistic transcendental structures; the mathematical extension of our formal (algebraic, geometric, logical, arithmetical, etc.) resources; psychedelic interventions in the neurochemical structure of the brain; the opening of liberated zones in relation to the demands of survival, fitness, and utility that shape and modulate the socio-evolutionary institution of different lifeforms; the activation of (r)evolutionary drives other than mutation-based natural selection (e.g. collaborative symbiosis, self-organisation, kin-making, etc.); the possibility of tuning the resolution of sensibility (both perceptive and affective) to different temporal and spatial scales; the speculative regulation of the various modes of daily self-care (e.g. gymnastic, dietary, erotic, economic, sartorial, ecological, social); 'disruptions in the habitus'[414] and the disturbance of the existentiales of being-there (by means of practices such as meditation, ingestion, isolation, fasting, liturgy, etc.);[415] biotechnological intervention in the biological framing of human existence (e.g. transsexuality, genetic engineering, reproductive techniques, human life extension, etc.), and the practice of education understood as a formation (*Bildung*) of new forms of life capable of constituting new Umwelten—all of these practices are means of transcendental variation, speculative devices, inducers of phenoumenodelic experiences.

---

pable of deliberately increasing the number of signals consciously apprehended. One looks casually, in the normal way, and then looks *again*, and *again*', Wilson, 'Creative Agnosticism'.

414 M. Jackson, 'Knowledge of the Body', in *Paths Towards a Clearing: Radical Empiricism and Ethnographic Inquiry* (Bloomington and Indianapolis: Indiana University Press, 1989), 129.

415 In *Expérience et Absolu* (Paris: PUF, 1994), J.-Y. Lacoste lays out an analysis of liturgical practices as methods of disrupting the existentiales of *being-there*.

The characterisation of the speculative subject proposed here, as a subject capable of movement through the transcendental landscape—and of integrating corresponding transcendental perspectives—converges with the conceptualisation of (what Hugh-Jones called *horizontal*) *shamanism*. A shaman is a subjective form characterised by the ability to perform a speculative 'switching of [transcendental zones] of view between the different forms of agency [and patience] populating the cosmos',[416] a living (trans-)form that can withstand 'cross-specific ambiguities' and afford inter-species 'mutations',[417] an amphibian probe equipped with the transcendental plasticity that is required to navigate 'the mythical riverrun of fluent metamorphosis [that] continues its turbulent course not too far below the surface discontinuities separating the types and species'.[418] Unlike the intrazone *stalker*, the shaman is a diagonaliser of zones, an inhabitant of the interworlds, a 'neurosomatic technician',[419] a tuner for the supernatural 'Serpent, in the violet splendor of its scales, shining that is definitely not human'.[420] The shaman's capacity to move through the landscape of transcendental types opens up the possibility of making translations between different Umwelten and of synthesising the corresponding transcendental perspectives. 'Any culture can be considered as a set of symbolic systems headed by language, the matrimonial rules, the economic relations, art, science, and religion. [...] So, in any society, it would be inevitable that a percentage (itself variable) of individuals find themselves placed "off system," so to speak, or between two or more irreducible systems. The group seeks and even requires of those individuals that they figuratively represent certain forms of compromise which are not realisable on the collective plane; that they simulate imaginary transitions,

---

416 Viveiros de Castro, 'The Crystal Forest',163.

417 Ibid., 157.

418 Ibid., 159.

419 Wilson, *Prometheus Rising*, 184.

420 Pynchon, *Gravity's Rainbow*, 411.

embody incompatible syntheses.[421] [...] shamanism is essentially a cosmic diplomacy devoted to the translation between [transcendentally] disparate [zones] of view.[422] [...] [T]he sign of a first-rank shamanic intelligence is the capacity to simultaneously hold two incompatible [transcendental] perspectives.'[423] The shamanic task of translation is that of integrating the multiple visions of the pleroma held by different lifeforms into multiscopic visions; that of reinscribing every object into the phenoumenon of which provides a particular transcendental-dependent phenomenalisation among others: 'The task? To see things as they [reveal in themselves, as they blossom in the phenoumenodelic open]. The means: to look through hundreds of eyes, across many peoples.[424] [...] May God us keep From Single vision!'[425] Life proceeds by means of a bidirectional dynamics that engenders singular lifeforms capable of constituting new visions (the centrifugal force of love that institutes individuals) and integrates the latter into forms of experience characterized by enhanced forms of experiential depth (the centripetal force of love that binds individuals). The ultramultiscopic self-vision of life is the projective experience that results from the progressive integration of signals transmitted by eyes placed in different locations (like for instance at each side of the individual's nose) into binocular visions and from these into multiscopic visions supported by multiple individuals in different spatio-temporal states; from the synaesthetic integration of visual experiences with acoustic, haptic, olfactory experiences; from the integration of these synaesthetic perceptual experiences with affective, conceptual, and political experiences; from the integration of the infinite abstract attributes

421 C. Lévi-Strauss, *Introduction to the Work of Marcel Mauss*, tr. F. Baker (London: Routledge & Kegan Paul, 1987), 16, 18.

422 Viveiros de Castro, 'The Crystal Forest', 154.

423 E. Viveiros de Castro, *Cannibal Metaphysics*, tr. P. Skafish (Minneapolis: Univocal, 2014), 71.

424 Nietzsche, quoted in R.A. Wilson, Introduction to Regardie, *The Eye in the Triangle: An Interpretation of Aleister Crowley*.

425 Blake, Letter to Thomas Butts (22 November 1802), in *The Complete Poetry and Prose of William Blake*, 722.

into a concrete self-experiencing insubstance; from the integration of experiences conveyed by subjective tokens of different transcendental types into experiences supported by trans-species forms of subjectivity.

Rather than granting us access to a hypostasised 'great outdoors', variations of our location in the transcendental landscape simply allow us—no more and no less—to absolve experience of any form of fixed transcendental framing. Transcendental variations should not be understood as some sort of definite deliverance of subjective experience with respect to any form of transcendental framing, but rather as successful *differential transgressions* of the prevailing limits associated with the subject's transcendental type.[426] In Piaget's words, 'every new [speculative] accommodation is conditioned by existing [transcendental] assimilations',[427] and proceeds by differentially altering, deforming, enriching, fine-tuning the corresponding transcendental structures. Instead of pretending to purge experience of all transcendental framing, speculative operations only loosen the anchorage of experience to a fixed location in the transcendental landscape, thereby activating phenoumenodelic or trans-umweltic degrees of freedom.

---

426 Analogously, Huxley argues: 'Through these permanent or temporary by-passes [opened up by transcendental variations] there flows, not indeed the [completely de-umwelticised] perception "of everything that is happening everywhere in the universe" (for the by-pass does not abolish the reducing valve, which still excludes the total content of Mind at Large), but something more than, and above all something different from, the carefully selected utilitarian material which our narrowed, individual [i.e. pre-critical] minds regard as a complete, or at least sufficient, picture of reality' (Huxley, *Doors of Perception*, 24). In the same spirit, Foucault writes that 'the historical ontology of ourselves must turn away from all projects that claim to be global or radical [...]. I prefer the very specific transformations that have proved to be possible in the last twenty years in a certain number of areas that concern our ways of being and thinking, relations to authority, relations between the sexes, the way in which we perceive insanity or illness; I prefer even these partial transformations that have been made in the correlation of historical analysis and the practical attitude, to the programs for a new man that the worst political systems have repeated throughout the twentieth century' (Foucault, 'What is Enlightenment?', 46–47).

427 Piaget, 'Piaget's Theory', 20.

In this way, the impossibility of getting rid of the transcendental framing of experience does not entail the existence of ultimate obstacles to the process of trans-umweltic absolutisation. If we believed that an experience freed from all transcendental framing would be closer to the things as they are in themselves, then we would be like the 'light dove, in free flight cutting through the air the resistance of which it feels, [which] could get the idea that it could do even better in airless space'.[428] Even if we cannot have an unframed experience of the phenoumenodelic field, we can always try to modify the transcendental frame, integrate experiences framed from different transcendental viewzones, and identify the corresponding trans-umweltic invariants. Far from absolving the subject of its finitude, speculation dissolves its essentialisation into a unique transcendental form of the finite. The experience of phenoumenal pleroma is necessarily carried out from the interior of an umweltic Nautilus that prevents the pressure of infinite revelation from killing the subject. But unlike the transcendental sedentarism associated with humanist essentialism, the speculative Nautilus can change the frame that tunes, filters, edits, and renormalises the revelation. As developed by Goddard, speculative ethics is based on the dynamic balance between two tendencies of the finite subject: the (Promethean) tendency toward infinity that compels it to overcome the transcendental limits of its ambient world (an overcoming carried out word for word, in a constant struggle against the real resistances and local obstructions of the 'material' world) and the self-positing tendency to care for oneself and the correlative Umwelt, to position oneself as a singular perspective through which life enhances its self-experience.[429] If the balance between speculative 'accommodations' and transcendental 'assimilations' is broken, the subject degenerates into either the neurotic submission to the patriarchal order—to the prevailing symbolic order, to the law—to the detriment of its speculative capacity to mediate the limits of its ambient world or into the psychotic denial of its finitude, of its constitutive castration, of its limits—thus passing from the Father to the worst. Speculative ethics requires

428 Kant, *Critique of Pure Reason*, 140 [A5/B9].

429 Cf. Goddard, *La philosophie fichtéeene de la vie*.

a delicate balancing act between the two extremes given by the dogmatic denial of the subject's capacity to deform its own 'essence' and overcome the transcendental limits of its experience and the psychotic dissolution of the individual's limits and subjective integrity.

We shall call any experience that envelops a modification of the transcendental structures that make subjective experience possible *phenoumenodelic experience*. A phenoumenodelic experience is an experience capable of 'triangulating' a given phenoumenon from a variety of different transcendental perspectives, that is, from multiple viewzones in the transcendental landscape, thus making it possible to experience different objectivations of the phenoumenon and extract trans-umweltic invariants.[430] By definition, the concept of phenoumenodelic experience presupposes an *existential* understanding of the subject of experience: only a subject that is not characterised by a fixed *essential* nature can delve into such a deeper form of transcendence. Given that the modification of the transcendental type of a subject disrupts and deforms the correlative horizon of transcendental transcendence, a phenoumenodelic experience does not necessarily take place within a single phenomenological horizon. A plastic subject capable of drifting through the transcendental landscape can activate and incarnate phenoumenodelic modes of the experiential field that are not necessarily contained within the limits of the Umwelten traversed by the variation. By definition, the rails of the Trans-Umweltic Express are not confined within a unique reality-tunnel. Accordingly, we might say (at least in a first approximation) that a speculative subject is 'poorer in [circumambient]

430 As Lorenz notes, the ethological comparison of 'world views' constituted by means of different transcendental framing points toward a real phenoumenal continuity beneath the diversity of phenomenological horizons: 'One becomes more and more firmly convinced of this entirely real and lawful correlation between the Real and the Apparent, the more one concerns oneself with the comparison of apparatuses for organizing the image of the world of animals as different from one another as possible. The continuity of the thing-in-itself, most convincingly emerging from such comparisons, is completely incompatible with the supposition of an alogical, extrinsically determined relationship between the thing-in-itself and its appearances.' Lorenz, 'Kant's Doctrine of the A Priori', 241.

world' (or poorer in reality) than a transcendentally sedentary subject. In Spinozist terms, the phenoumenodelic experience of a speculative subject does not necessarily take place within a single transcendental 'plane' of nature, that is, within a unique *natura naturata*: 'It could be said that [a speculative subject] is capable of rediscovering all the levels, all the degrees of expansion and contraction that coexist in the [pleroma]. As if [it] were capable of all the frenzies and brought about in [it]self successively everything that, elsewhere, can only be embodied in different species. [...] Whereas the other directions are closed and go round in circles, whereas a distinct "plane" of nature[, a distinct *natura naturata*,] corresponds to each one, the [speculative subject] is capable of scrambling the planes, of going beyond [its] own plane as [its] own [transcendental] condition, in order finally to express naturing Nature.'[431]

While speculative variations allow the subject to travel across different Umwelten, the activation of this speculative degree of freedom does not necessarily imply that the subject is equipped with the 'neurological' faculties required to integrate these experiences into a unique experience taking place in a broader phenomenological horizon endowed with a higher experiential depth. If the subject is indeed capable of such integration, then we shall say that the Umwelten traversed by the variations *coalesce* into a single phenomenological horizon correlative to a more global transcendental type of subjectivity. This more global type of subjectivity can be thought of as the *union* (in the topological sense of the term) of the transcendental faculties of the types of subjectivity enveloped by the speculative variation. In the same way that the experience of an object acquires a certain depth of field when experiences indexed by different empirical states are integrated into a single experience (as happens, for example, in binocular vision or binaural hearing), the experience of a phenoumenon acquires a properly phenoumenodelic depth of field when objectivations of the same phenoumenon indexed by different viewzones in the transcendental landscape are integrated along their local similarities

431 G. Deleuze, *Bergsonism*, tr. H. Tomlinson and B. Habberjam (New York: Zone, 1997), 106–7.

into a single phenoumenodelic experience. At each level of this process of variations and multi-perspective integrations, the experiential depth of field depends on the type of variations made: while three-dimensional depth results from the spatial difference between the positions of each eye (a variation already literally incorporated in the physiological structure of the human subjects), and while objective depth results from the spatial-temporal variations in the subject's state (or in the frame of reference used to describe the corresponding phenomenon), phenoumenodelic depth results from speculative variations carried out within the transcendental landscape. Phenoumenodelic experiences make possible an upgrading of the restricted form of universality given by objectivity to a more general form of universality that takes into account perspectives associated to different transcendental types of subjectivity.

We shall argue that the deepening of experience by means of the integration of different (empirical and transcendental) perspectives goes hand in hand with a progressive *immanentisation* of experience, that is with a gradual reduction of the transcendence-oriented character of experience in favour of more reflexive forms of experience. It is important to emphasise first that even *transcendent experiences* (that is, intentional relationships between local subjects and transcendent objects or subjects) are always in the last instance *immanent self-experiences* of the field itself, processes by means of which the field enriches and deepens its immanent phenoumenalisation, its self-manifestation ('Life is itself the Wine, Music and Feast and Servant too'[432] and those who dine). All intentional experience can be understood as a local polarisation of the impersonal field that points from an *experiencing pole* to an *experienced pole*. The existentialisation of the transcendental subject allows us to understand the subject of experience as a local fluctuation of the experiential field capable of activating particular modes of its self-experience, as a local subjective vortex inducing a particular process of self-phenomenalisation of the field. The vision of the subject 'is not a view upon the *outside*. [...] The world no longer stands before him through representation; rather, it is [the subject] to whom the things of the world

432 Silesius, *Cherubinischer Wandersmann*, Book I, §207.

give birth by a sort of concentration or coming-to-itself of the visible'.[433] Correlatively, the *transcendental conditions* by means of which a subject can have an intentional experience of a *transcendent* object ultimately depend on the *immanental conditions* that make possible the *immanent* polarisations of the self-experiencing field in subjects and objects, that is, the institution of transcendental types of subjectivity and the concomitant opening up of phenomenological horizons of transcendence. Thanks to the institution of multiple finite subjects capable of effecting distinct perspectival framings of the experiential field, this can unfold and deepen its self-experience, the singular life of its impersonal subjectivity. Every finite subject is plerophanic, a local vortex of the living pleroma through which the latter opens a new phenoumenodelic horizon within itself, a new Umwelt containing new forms of its self-revelation: only from the chalice of this community of finite subjects foams forth for the one life its own infinitude.[434]

The experience of a finite subject is necessarily—to a greater or lesser extent—a *perspectival* experience that depends on the subject's empirical localisation. This justifies the characterisation of intentional vectors extended between subjects and objects as gradients of *transcendence*, as arrows pointing toward a counterposed outside. Now, the integration of perspectival experiences induces less localised—and thereby less transcendent—forms of experience. The wider the network of local perspectives integrated into a single experience, the lower the degree of transcendence-orientedness of this experience. At the limit, a hypothetical Ω-experience obtained by integrating the local experiences associated with every possible subjective state in the corresponding empirical extension would be a purely reflexive experience with no objective transcendence. We could for instance conceive a hypothetical brain-like organ capable of integrating the visual experiences of a continuous field of eyes with spherical fields of view (who could dare to image the experiential depth of the resulting immanental

---

433 M. Merleau-Ponty, *The Primacy of Perception* (Evanston, IL: Northwestern University Press, 1964), 181.

434 An adaptation of Schiller's *Die Freundschaft ad fin*, in Hegel, *Phenomenology of Spirit*, 493.

experience?). Such an Ω-experience would not be a 'view from nowhere' or a 'viewpoint of no-one in particular', but rather a single purely reflexive view from everywhere (in the corresponding extension) experienced by someone, the emergent distributed subject. This global integration of local perspectives does not only take place at the empirical level associated with spatiotemporal states (as in binocular vision, in binaural hearing systems, or in scientific objectivism), but also at the transcendental level associated with the different viewzones in the transcendental landscape. This process of the speculative immanentisation of experience can take place either thanks to the speculative ability to integrate experiences indexed by the different transcendental perspectives traversed in a paralactic speculative motion, or by the kin-making capacity to compose itself with other subjects and institute collective symbionts endowed with emergent 'neurological' capacities. The speculative integration of different transcendental perspectives is concomitant with the institution of an emergent form of subjectivity that is distributed among different transcendental types. In the limit, the ultimate subject of the purely reflexive experiences that result from integrating empirical, transcendental, and speculative perspectives at all the *n*-levels of the speculative landscape is the immanental one life that institutes and envelops every possible finite lifeform.

The effective activation of phenoumenodelic degrees of freedom requires mobilising all the art and the resources—as well as the patience—of the corresponding modes of thought and practice. Let us consider the case of Mallarmé's *Maître*. The *Maître* did not just bequeath us the task of sublating chance (that is, the contingency of our transcendental location) but also prescribed a specific attitude, adapted to his field of operation: this task must be patiently carried out, word for word, in the very element of language. In this context, language must be understood as a particular transcendental operator capable of framing and renormalising the experiential field, as one of the organs of the transcendental 'reducing valve' that filters, edits, and rearranges the pleroma into something that is experienceable. As Kant argued—following on from Aristotle in this—language codifies categorical a priori forms that define the possible propositional bonds that structure the human experience of the impersonal field. Language is a symbolic knife capable of inscribing *abstract cuts* in the pleroma, cuts that structure the umweltic modes of sangnifying appearance. All the same, language is (evolutionarily and socially instituted as) operational: the abstract cuts that perform 'the textual work that comes out of the spider's belly, its web'[435] are based on the need for pragmatic efficiency: the web must be able to trap the noematic flies traversing the pleroma.[436] To this effect we can say that the web that filters and edits the pleroma, retaining the nutritious information relevant to it survival, carries the spider's existence: 'Every subject spins out, like the spider's threads, its relations to certain qualities of things and weaves them into a solid web, which carries its existence.'[437] But language is not like Chuang-Tzu's knife: far from sliding without resistance through the joints and interstices of the living flesh, its abstract cuts instead enables a coarse-grained experience of it. Through transcendental framing, living flesh is converted into digestable chopped meat. Thanks to transcendental reflection, we know that the linguistic web, in order to establish points of impasse capable of obstructing the fly's flight, must have its own points of impasse. If the gaps in the net were too small, the web would not be invisible to its potential victims, rendering it ineffective (as well as economically unaffordable to the spider).[438]

435 Lacan, *Encore*, 93.

436 As Bergson writes, 'The things that language describes have been cut out of reality by human perception in view of human work to be done. The properties which it indicates are the calls made by the thing to a human activity.' H. Bergson, *The Creative Mind: An Introduction to Metaphysics*, tr. M.L. Andison (New York: Dover, 2007), 63.

437 Von Uexküll, *A Foray into the Worlds of Animals and Humans*, 53.

438 In the same vein, Metzinger argues that the pre-critical 'transparency' of the transcendental structures that model the self and the world results from a 'computational-informational strategy' intended to economise resources. In other words, the enactment of a critical reflection intended to focus on the transcendental frame itself is, from an evolutionary perspective, a luxury that living beings cannot always afford: 'Any self-modeling system, operating under real-world constraints and evolutionary pressures, will have to constantly minimize the computational resources needed to make system-related information available on the level of conscious

If, on the contrary, the gaps were too large, the flies could pass through without any resistance. Every linguistic web is thus characterised by a certain degree of resolution that establishes a cut-off point demarcating a 'visible', manifest landscape from a background which remains relatively 'invisible'. The very transcendental operators that allow the spider to grasp the phenoumenal field in a digestively effective way weave an umweltic bubble around the spider: every form of phenomenal revelation takes time and place against a foreclosed background: all that is patent breaks apart against the backdrop of the latent. The impasses of every symbolic spider web—its invisibilities and indiscernibilities: infra-insects—signal the trans-umweltic nature of the experiential field itself, the very impossibility of idealistically identifying the phenoumenodelic field with the phenomenal Umwelten defined by different transcendental types. The impasses of the symbolic order are symptoms of 'real' pleromancy, of the excess of the phenoumenodelic field in respect to any local framing; the real resistances are the side-noises 'through which the thing-in-itself peeps into our world of phenomena'.[439] As the case of Funes the Memorious attests, an unrestricted increase in the power of resolution is not necessarily recommended: there is no intelligence without forgetting and abstraction.[440] The finite nature of every transcendental degree of resolution must not be understood as a sort of limitation that can be superseded by a simple (linguistic, perceptive, affective, conceptual) refinement of granularity: every resolution activates

experience. Because [...] self-modeling possesses a potentially infinite and circular logical structure, it has to find an efficient way to break the reflexive loop. [...] [T]he phenomenon of transparent self-modeling developed as an evolutionary viable strategy because it constituted a reliable way of making system-related information available without entangling the system in endless internal loops of higher-order self-modeling. Any biological system on the path to self-awareness must find a solution to this problem, or it will greatly diminish its reproductive success. One reason philosophers do not have many children may be that they think too much about themselves.' Metzinger, *Being No One*, 338.

439 Lorenz, 'Kant's Doctrine of the A Priori', 238.

440 J.L. Borges, 'Funes, His Memory', in *Collected Fictions* (London: Penguin, 1999), 131–37.

specific effective qualities of the field, qualities that would remain invisible at higher and lower degrees of resolution. Even low degrees of resolution activate qualities of the field as legitimate and unique phenoumenodelic data of the experiential stream. A Kantian spider knows that its web is characterised by a certain degree of resolution, that the transcendental net—shaped by the evolutionary processes that instituted it as a local arachnid mode of the impersonal field—is determined by a granularity that leads to the emergence of a particular Umwelt, an ambient bubble endowed with its effective qualities, its spatiotemporal scales, its nomological regularities, its visible flies and its infra-insects. Implementing a transcendental reflection grants the spider the possibility to speculate, to switch on the meta-programming circuit, to activate processes of speculative variations of its transcendental affordances, exploring different types of stitch, varying the edge of the linguistic knife, enhancing or reducing granularity. The field of experience is endowed with multi-scale patterns, and the reflexive capacity to tune the degree of resolution of perception, affection, conceptualisation, and socialisation allows the speculative spider to probe the field at different scales and bear witness to the spectrum of landscapes and communities that are activated and deactivated as it tunes into different resolutions.

The Mallarméan *Maître* knows better than anyone else that we are not obliged to remain within the transcendental limits set by the 'universal reportage' wrought by the need to communicate and act effectively, that we are not condemned to foreclose the 'real' points of impasse that make holes in symbolic orders, that there is no reason to limit experience to the transcendental framework defined by a given system of linguistic categories, that we can always embed 'the words of our tribe' in the *universal menstruum* of the absolute language. The *Maître*'s *grimoire* exhorts us to perturb *grammar*, to 'restore to the word, which can be viciously stereotyped in us, its mobility,[441] to discern again, sedimented within language, the local modulations of the living Word. Any disturbance of the transcendental linguistic structure allows for the mediation of sclerotic modes of expression

441 S. Mallarmé, 'Notes sur le Langage', in B. Marchal (ed.), *Igitur, Divagations, un coup de dés* (Paris: Éditions Gallimard, 2003), 74.

and for the revivification of 'detained words'. The natural attitude's tendency to hypostasise the linguistic cuts of the experiential field cannot be suspended by means of a hypothetical sovereign act capable of definitively transcending the symbolic order and immediately accessing a supposed noumenal real(m) beyond language. Only language, patiently, word for word, in its own domain, can disrupt the abstract cuts it inflicts upon the experiential flesh. We can distinguish, in particular, two privileged human vectors that radically disrupt 'universal reportage': whereas the poeticisation of language deforms grammar, promotes the flux of misunderstandings, deepens the untranslatable singularity of each language, resists colonial monolingualism and, in a Joycean manner, proceeds through the amalgrammation of different languages into a unique '[im]pure language', the mathematical formalisation of language acts in a contrary fashion, reducing misunderstanding and ambiguities by means of rigorous definitions, submitting it to the computational and deductive power of a fully formalised scriptural regime, and reinforcing its integral transmissibility as much as possible.[442] In order to be faithful to its regulative idea, that of concretely mediating the umweltic limitations of experience, philosophy must engage in the concoction of an angelic language intended to synthesise the different abstract gradients of deformation of the 'universal reportage'. Both the poeticisation of language and its mathematical formalisation are necessary (but not sufficient) components of the linguistic organon of a philosophy that does not lose sight of the concrescence of different attributes (the *sensorium*, the *affectum*, the *logos*, the *socius*) into a single phenoumenodelic insubstance inhabited by different transcendental types of subjectivity. The philosophical linguistic organon must also labour to

442 As Badiou writes, 'poem and matheme are the two extremes of language, its two supreme exercises. The poem in the exercise of its absolute singularity and the matheme in the exercise of its total symbolisation. We pass from the quasi-transmission to the integral transmission, from the inexhaustible to the exhausted. It should be noted that the poem essentially concerns the voice, while the matheme is connected to writing, to inscription.' A. Badiou, *Le Séminaire, Heidegger L'être 3—Figure du retrait 1986–1987* (Paris: Fayard, 2015), 33–34.

attune itself to the 'larval semiotics that work the [pleromatic] viscosity',[443] to the modes of the *textum* excited by other-than-human lifeforms, to the language that 'is the very voice of the things, the waves, and the forests',[444] to the multifarious forms of (physical, chemical, mineral, vegetal, animal) signic patterns that propagate in the insubstance, to the language of the birds, to the grammars that articulate different forms of signifying structures—whirling vortices, fractal branchings, (broken) symmetries, tesselations, flocking collective behaviour. Philosophy must progressively construct a linguistic organon intended to tune in to the wholly scripture of the phenoumenodelic revelation.

We have defined speculative philosophy as a twofold extension of transcendental philosophy which addresses what dwells beyond the two poles of the subject-object correlation: both the phenoumena beyond the constituted object and the immanental process of the institution of subjectivity upstream of the constituting subject. According to this twofold pre-subjective and trans-objective extension of transcendental philosophy, reflection on the transcendental structures of the subject of experience—far from being a mere abstract negation that would critically trace the unsurpassable limits of human experience and demarcate the corresponding inaccessible 'great outdoors'—is understood as a determinate negation by means of which the subject can differentially sublate the limits brought to light by reflection. Reflection on the transcendental structure of the subject of experience will not be understood here as an ultimate limitation of possible experience, but as an operation through which it becomes possible to transgress the corresponding transcendental limits of experience, to differentially overcome the transcendental perspectivism exhibited by critical reflection, and to legitimately aspire (albeit projectively, that is, as an infinite idea of reason) to a truly non-typed cosmopolitanism. The essential Copernikantianism of speculative philosophy is based on what we shall call the *reflection* $\wedge$ *refraction* tandem:

443 Khatarnak & Khabandar, 'Estación hueca', in *¡Santas incubaciones!*, 68.

444 Merleau-Ponty, *The Visible and the Invisible*, 155.

a *reflection* on the transcendental type of the subject of experience and a *refractive mediation* of the limits of its possible experience. In order to justify the characterisation of this twofold extension of transcendental philosophy as speculative, it is worth noting that both transcendental reflection and refractive mediation can be subsumed by the dual meaning of the term *speculation*. On the one hand, speculation makes reference to the optical notion of *reflection*, to the *speculum*. On the other hand, speculation is used to characterise both theoretical constructions that are not grounded on a solid and conclusive basis (such as theoretical or empirical evidence) and financial operations that are not underpinned by concrete processes of production. The concept of speculation refers both to reflection and to that which has no foundation, to 'pure speculation' bereft of all roots in *terra firma*. The amphibological nature of the concept of speculation subsumes both *transcendental reflection* (on the subject of experience) and *refractive mediation* (of the limits of experience defined by the corresponding transcendental perspective). The *transcendental reflection* ∧ *refractive mediation* tandem is nothing but an ungrounding *speculum* for the phenoumenodelic potentialisation of experience beyond transcendental sedentarism. Rather than merely acknowledging the existence of an umweltic bubble around subjects of the same transcendental type, reflection on the transcendental structure of the subject of experience allows subjective experience to be released from any transcendental anchor, from any fixed location in the transcendental landscape, from any form of transcendental Earth 'that does not move'. The term speculation thus denotes the use of transcendental reflection on the structure of the subject as a launchpad for a refractive mediation of the limits of its experience; as an operator of absolution with respect to any anchorage on an immobile transcendental Earth.

We shall now place this conception of speculative philosophy under the aegis of what we shall consider its primal scene, the *narcissistic scene*. The two moments enveloped by the term 'speculation' are enacted by the two phases of the narcissistic scene: the *reflexive moment* in which Narcissus contemplates his own transcendental type on the reflective surface of the solution, experiences his own self as a thrown and finite existence, breathing between birth and death, caring for and enjoying its own singular figure, tempering himself in his self-positing affirmation, and the *refractive moment* in which Narcissus acquits himself of terra firma and passes through the liquid mirror, soaking up the narcotic solution, awakening to the phenoumenodelic dreaminess. By reflecting on his own transcendental structures, Narcissus triggers the possibility of continuing his naturalcultural institution by performing speculative variations of its own type, thereby uprooting himself from any form of fixity in the transcendental landscape. The fall of Narcissus denotes the mythic moment of his conversion—his baptism—of the immersion of his existence in the water-lily flotation tank in which the naturality of every environing world is suspended, of his plunge into the insubstantial medium in which every ground is a drifting ark, every umweltic bubble a world-size helmet. Even the paternal house—the solaristic sequence: the oceanic planet, the visions, the gravitational levitation, the cloudy suspension of the myth of homecoming—is suspended in the material solution: 'false manor / immediately / evaporated in mist / which imposed / a limit on'[445] the infinite possibilities of phenoumenodelic experience. The ungrounding *speculum* defined by the *transcendental reflection* ∧ *refraction mediation* tandem is the narcissistic talisman for summoning phenoumenodelic magick.

Now let us consider the evangelion according to Khatarnak and Khabandar.[446] What is the relationship between Narcissus's plunge, his dolphinisation, and the passion of Yesses Splendour—the astronautical uproar of his annunciation ('his star was so far off course that he shrieked for joy')? Is the speculative family enough—the trinity: a *Father* (the allbegetting 'superabundance of his softness'), a *Living One* (a Soul, finite, thrown—through a triple somersault—into the autonomy of its separation), a *Spirit* (a community: *there will be a band!*)—or will not a more numerous, less abstract family be needed (with a cousin and an imponderable twin and... even a mother!), all 'giving birth to one another'—a family endowed with more intercessors (the one who catalyses processes of extra-Earthification,

---

445 Mallarmé, 'A Throw of the Dice', 138.

446 The following two paragraphs are a montage of Khatarnak & Khabandar, 'Peralta Ramos', in *¡Santas incubaciones!*, 29–43.

the one who signals and half-open portals by means of a 'translucency due to the [sustained] effort of birth', the one who will roll out—as if they were carpets—the routes for the 'infra-ships that will produce the vacancy', the one that arrives—mineral and elemental—in the egg of its green stone to ally itself in and with the forest, the one that comes with its tribe, inevitable, with its outdoors, at great speed, introducing itself like one twisted by the edges and slots, from outcast maceration), a family holiday, released from 'domestic judgements', the 'verisimilar sociofamiliar' already imploded, peering nonchalantly out on the coasts of specular silver...and perhaps even two trios, to hexagrammatise the hydrodynamics of the take-off? Wouldn't more kidoids be necessary to extract the flower and fruit of the passion—more rounded and less crossed—more creatures supported and transported in their secondary trio by adults who, at the wheel on the road ('window open, flapping cotton') divert (brandishing their *splendid chromatic varieties*) the police with 'thinned brains' and smuggle Martians, play baccarat in the casino with 'their relaxed, ambiguous poses (the bracketing of their aspects)', reel in Operation 'White Wicker: believe in everything, preparing for boarding at the port of El Bosque', polarise the 'melodic landscapes' with normalising Ray Bans that block the pink beam, filtering the entheogenic dazzle of the solar empire (Soul gets drunk on the breakout of light), and glimpse ('at that point in February they were already very much extraEarth') that religation—the Soul that plugs back into the pleroma (the cure!)—will be umbilicated by these infant ways or will not be at all?

Which alliance between the narcotic sacrament blossoming forth from immersion and the rose on the cross of its present incarnation? The Soul observes itself in the first stage (the reflexive: the *solaristic*: no longer at the edge of the pond but orbiting above—always already falling into—the silver sea)—'it was especially the withheld water that withheld him': the *speculum*—the Soul that cares for and enjoys itself: egophanic narcissism of the finite one that knows that it is a living icon of the allbegetting one (joy and titillation before its own majesty), Soul that enters little by little into 'spatial deafness': *(s)he put the helmet on* to transmit from the infra-language, beginning to embryonise, tuning by means of its Mohawk (dolphin tumescence), opening up 'umbilical hearing' (the yellow petalescence on its fluoral belly, the tattoo of the extraterrestrial reports on its expressive skin), toward the ignition that was vast—awakening to the limbo of the navel—'planetary and unleashed epic', freefall in the heavens of Laniakea. Finally—second stage, the immersive: the *nautilistic*—triggers the shedding process ('animé zoomorphosis'), splicing 'the umbilical spiral of its transformation' toward the living and airborne waters, by switching on 'petal by petal the umbilicus', airing in the coastal breeze the words of the Prophet: 'to see an opalescent dolphin emerge a rainbow of dolphins an aerial or iridescent dolphin an arched dolphin'. And 'jump right in!' or the infant Soul enjoying the Narcissus-dip—'and the dolphin! Letting go'—passing to the other side of the flowing mirror, 'it was a floating, laminated fish, the brightest and most frizzy, itself a ship', soaking up the irreflexive environment—the Soul turned upside down through the *mareaçao*: its entrails exposed in divination—being itself (now) the one who comes with its grace, 'on another beach in that sea', IChThYs (an amphibious Yesses)—that does not come down from the sky: splashes from the sea,—*Slide with its board through mountains of water!* (Matthew 14:22-33)—to anoint with the love that religates 'those who expect the beginning of a cure from this mad [aboriginal] dolphin'. In the Name of the Mat(t)er, the Living, and the Tribes to come. *Haux!*

The *transcendental reflection* ∧ *speculative refraction* tandem finds an anthropological prefiguration in *totemism*. According to the totemic transcendental typology, every individual belongs to a totemic clan, which means (in our own terms) that it instantiates a particular transcendental type. This taxonomy is generally associated with an exogamic prescription of which the incest prohibition is a particular case. Besides the centripetal patri- or matrilinear character of the transmission of membership in a clan, centrifugal exogamous mating (inter-linguistic, inter-species, inter-naturecultural, inter-planetary) produces hybrids or symbionts that live between circumambient worlds. By engendering new transcendental totems, the inter-totemic combinatorial fosters an 'exogamic dissipation' of totemic features.[447] In the same way, the prohibition against eating the totem (according to Freud a sublimated version of the prohibition against eating the father of the primitive horde), far from being a general prohibition against anthropophagy—is a restricted prohibition against *intra-totemic* anthropophagy: eating one's own totem or eating a member of the same clan would be the gastronomic equivalent of incest. Intra-clan anthropophagy is ultimately a transcendental autophagy devoid of any speculative surplus. If we understand the consumption of flesh as a speculative operation by means of which one can adopt the perspective of the other,[448] incorporate some of its signature characteristics ('Indian thinks? Indian eats who thinks—that's right. Indian sucking me, he will think these my thoughts [...]')[449] or create a symbiont (cf. Margulis's explanation of the endosymbiotic origin of certain organelles of the eukaryotic cell), then intra-totemic consumption is a kind of transcendental redundancy. 'Life is pure devouring',[450] a barbaric process through which lifeforms flow—live and die—into one another. Both the prohibition of incest and the prohibition on eating the totem prefigure the speculative imperative to pass between types, that is, the speculative deconstruction of transcendental type-centrism. The incest prohibition should therefore not be understood as the point of discontinuity which, in the form of the first social contract, would mark the transition between nature and culture (cf. Lévi-Strauss), but rather as a strictly human enhancement of natural symbiogenesis and hybridisation. The cannibalistic maxim according to which it is necessary

---

447 Land, 'Kant, Capital, and the Prohibition of Incest', 60.

448 Viveiros de Castro describes Tupi cannibalism as 'a process for the transmutation of perspectives whereby the "I" is determined as other through the act of incorporating this other [...] what was assimilated from the victim was the signs of [its] alterity, the aim being to reach [its] alterity as point of view on the Self.' Viveiros de Castro, *Cannibal Metaphysics*, 142.

449 Leminski, *Catatau*, 50.

450 O. de Andrade, 'A crise da filosofia messiânica', in *Obras Completas VI. Do Pau-Brasil à Antropofagia e às Utopias. Manifestos, teses de concursos e ensaios* (Rio de Janeiro: Civilição Brasileira, 1978), 77.

to carry out 'the permanent transformation of taboo into totem'[451] reminds us of the need to effect a transcendental indexation of every taboo: there are no universal limits of experience, there is no universally valid moral Law; every limit (and in particular any moral taboo) is correlative to a certain transcendental framing of the pleroma. The 'transformation of taboo into totem' can then be understood as a critical de-universalisation of taboo, that is, as a remainder of the fact that every taboo—far from being a universal imperative—depends on a particular transcendental organisation of experience. In this sense, transforming taboo into totem means passing from a singular symbolic order that does not critically acknowledge its transcendental one-sidedness into a totemic system that fosters a speculative exogamy. The exogamic prohibition of incest and of intra-totemic cannibalism can be understood as a sort of speculative prescription that fosters the mediation of every transcendental-dependent taboo. In this sense, totemism calls into question the 'inhibited synthesis' characteristic of capitalist type-centric colonialism: 'Capital is the point at which a culture refuses the possibility [...] of pushing the prohibition of incest [that is, of totemic exogamy] towards its limit'.[452] Capitalism is a social formation based on the xenophobic transgression of the incest prohibition that fosters a relapse into an endogamic transcendental redundancy. Both the principle of capital accumulation and the orientation of the openness toward the other through the imperative to extract maximal profit inhibit the synthesis with the outside, hinder the 'radical form of hospitality' that is inter-totemic cannibalism,[453] and expand 'the absolute

---

451 De Andrade, 'Cannibalistic Manifesto', 40. For an insightful analysis of Andrade's expression, see A. Nodari, '"A transformação do Tabu em totem": notas sobre (um) a fórmula antropofágica', *Das Questões* 2:2 (2015), <https://periodicos.unb.br/index.php/dasquestoes/article/view/18320>.

452 Land, 'Kant, Capital, and the Prohibition of Incest', 62–63.

453 '[Cannibalism] must indeed always be merely an extreme form of the relationship to the other, and this includes [cannibalism] in the relationship of love. [Cannibalism] is a radical form of hospitality.' J. Baudrillard, *The Transparency of Evil*, tr. J. Benedict (London: Verso, 2009), 144.

monologue of colonial [and incestuous] reason':[454] 'I, the wrath of God, [will 'betray everyone. At once—God, the King, men'][455] and I will marry my own daughter and with her I will found the purest dynasty the earth has ever seen. Together we will rule over this entire continent.'[456]

According to Nick Land, Kant provides the philosophical schema of the modernist tendency 'to open itself to the other and to consolidate itself from within, to expand indefinitely whilst reproducing itself as the same [...] to grow whilst remaining identical to what it was, to touch the other without vulnerability. [...] [A] relation that it precariously resolves within itself on the basis of exploitation, or interaction from a position of unilateral mastery. [...] The paradox of enlightenment, then, is an attempt to fix a stable relation with what is radically other, since in so far as the other is rigidly positioned within a relation it is no longer fully other. If before encountering otherness we already know what its relation to us will be, we have obliterated it in advance. And this brutal denial is the effective implication of the thought of the a priori [...]. This aggressive logical absurdity [...] reaches its zenith in the philosophy of Kant. [...] The first Critique [...] transforms the understanding into a form of intellectual capital.'[457] Since it conflates a framing of the other with a complete reduction of its alterity, Land's criticism of Kant is only valid as far as the idealist interpretation of the transcendental motif is concerned. The empirical framing of a landscape provided by a window certainly provides a particular perspective on that landscape—what we could call a *partial* or *perspectival synthesis*—but it cannot be described as a sheer blockage or inhibition of the landscape's otherness. We should rather say the opposite: it is thanks to the filter provided by the transcendental framing that we can gain access to an otherwise overwhelming phenoumenodelic landscape that would

454 Land, 'Kant, Capital, and the Prohibition of Incest', 74.

455 G. Deleuze, *Cinema 1*, tr. H. Tomlinson and B. Habberjam (Minneapolis: University of Minnesota, 1997), 186.

456 *Aguirre, the Wrath of God* (1972, dir. Werner Herzog).

457 Land, 'Kant, Capital, and the Prohibition of Incest', 63–64, 75.

threaten our subjective integrity. For example, it is not the case that solar filters reduce the otherness of the sun, but rather the contrary, it is thanks to the filters that we can safely look at the sun. The vision provided by the filters is certainly partial, since it allows us access only to a restricted window of the sun's emission spectrum. But this limitation can be progressively sublated by reflexively acknowledging the perspectival partiality associated with the particular frame that is being used, and by implementing a speculative protocol of controlled variations and integrations. According to the speculative interpretation of Kantian critique endorsed here, the transcendental framing of experience does not necessarily entail a relation with the other based on exploitation, obliteration, and 'unilateral mastery' since there is no de jure reason that can preclude the effectuation of a speculative parallax leading to a more radical synthesis of the 'outside'.[458] The problem here is not the Kantian thesis that every form of experience takes place through an a priori frame, but the typo-centric interpretation of the transcendental motif—that is, the dogmatic belief in the impossibility of varying the frame. The attempt to disentangle absolute modernity from neo-colonialism and transcendental xenophobia relies on a speculative rather than idealist interpretation of Kantian critique. In order to become

---

458 Relying on a sharp demarcation line between empirical concepts (that might vary among subjects) and transcendental structures shared by every possible conceivable form of subjectivity, Piper argues that 'Kant's conception of reason as theory-construction implies resources within the structure of the self for overcoming xenophobia' (Piper, 'Xenophobia and Kantian Rationalism', 4). Briefly, another subject can be 'anomalous with respect to one's empirical conception of people [...] but be nevertheless recognizable as instantiating one's transcendent concept of personhood' (ibid.). Piper's stance only holds space for a *restricted* synthesis of outsiders (and therefore for a *limited* critique of xenophobia) since it cannot conceive the existence of other transcendental types of subjectivity, of a variety of forms of personhood. The possibility of a radical speculative synthesis of anomalous outsiders that we advocate here relies on the thesis that there is no transcendental 'irreducible residuum' (Foucault) that should be shared by every conceivable form of subjectivity. In the framework of what we could call *speculative xenophilia*, we should be able to accommodate not only different *empirical conceptions of people* but also different *transcendental notions of personhood*.

'absolutely modern', it is necessary to accept the consequences of the Copernican Revolution resumed by Kant without assuming any a priori constraint with respect to the possibility of performing speculative variations of the a priori transcendental frame. In order to circumvent the complete reduction of the other's otherness that haunts every act of transcendental constitution, we must not relapse into pre-critical thinking, foreclose finitude, and fantasise about an aperspectival synthesis of the outside, but should instead perform speculative variations of the frame through which the other is experienced, extract invariants, and integrate all the differently framed experiences. Transcendental philosophy proposes a reflexion on the fact that every form of experience depends on an a priori framework without implying that such a framework is necessarily fixed, without making the claim that transcendental perspectivism is necessarily an obstruction in the path of absolute knowledge. Being 'absolutely modern' means endorsing a form of modernity that speculatively bypasses the 'inhibited synthesis' of type-centrism in the direction of a fully-fledged inter-totemic exogamy that is not restricted by Capital accumulation, unconstrained productivity, and the imperative of profit extraction.

The spiritual dimension of a post-critical science—the fact that it necessarily engages self-transformations of the transcendental type of the subject of science—is the subjective counterpart of what we shall describe as its *materialistic* nature. By materialism we shall understand a thesis regarding the mechanism by means of which the pleromatic real forces the institution of new transcendental types of subjectivity by piercing the 'symbolic orders' and setting the corresponding reality-tunnels aquake. Firstly, it is worth noting that a materialist characterisation of science as such cannot depend on a particular scientific theory of 'matter', since any such theory is always subject to being superseded by scientific progress. Hence, we shall not understand by materialism a theoretical thesis about a supposed last instance or infrastructure of the real, the supposed 'matter' qua ultimate stuff. We are 'decided materialist[s] with regard to natural philosophy, but [we] do not claim to know what matter is'.[459] In order to characterise scientific materialism, we shall instead bracket any scientific theory about the nature of the 'real' and place ourselves in the phenoumenodelic suspended scene opened up by the immanental *epoché*. In this suspended ambience, we shall start by endorsing the phenomenological characterisation of matter as *resistance* set forth by Fichte: '[M]atter, as such, in no way belongs to the senses [...] [I]t is neither seen, nor heard, nor tasted, nor smelt[, nor touched] [...] [Matter] evinces itself only through the [experience] of a resistance, an inability, which is subjective.[460] [...] Matter is that which resists [sensorially, affectively, conceptually]; it carries no positive content in itself.'[461] Here the Fichtean understanding of matter must be enriched with a procreative dimension suggested by its Latin etymology (from *mater*, mother): we shall understand by *matter* the 'real' points of resistance to the unfolding of a form of experience in so far as they enable the subject to perform mutations of its own transcendental structures. In other words, we shall call *matter* that which, by offering 'real' obstructions to the expansion of experience, makes possible the institution of new types of transcendental subjectivity. We arrive in this way at a materialistic conception of the transcendental subject: far from being simply presupposed, as is the case in Kant, the transcendental subject is instituted out of matter, from the material resistances that obstruct the expansion of the subject's percepts, affects, concepts, and sociolepts (resistances such as problems without solutions, exceptions, undecidable statements, walls, indiscernibilities, uncharted phenomena, traumatic holes, reified institutions). A speculative subject, far from occupying a fixed location in the transcendental landscape, is always already in motion, being constantly produced out of matter, always trying to activate new speculative degrees of freedom, patiently working to force mutations of its own transcendental type, to metaprogram its naturecultural imprints. In the absence of material

459 Lorenz, 'Kant's Doctrine of the A Priori', 239.

460 Fichte, *The Science of Knowledge*, 275.

461 E. During and A. Bublex, *Glenn Gould* (Paris: Philharmonie de Paris Éditions, 2021), 24.

points of resistance, the subject's experience would take place and time within the phenomenological horizon defined by a unique transcendental-dependent Umwelt. By contrast, a subject that takes on the task of trying to sublate the transcendental limits exhibited by material resistances may well be rewarded with a ride on the Trans-Umweltic Express. The existence of transcendental limitations is the very material condition of possibility for the differential infinitisation of experience through the institution of new transcendental types of subjectivity. If 'every determination' of a transcendental type 'is a negation' of the pleromatic infinitude—a finite renormalisation of the experiential field that allows the subject to restrictively experience what it can afford at a given moment of its life—the subject's speculative resources allow it to perform differential 'negations of this negation'. Speculative thought as we understand it here does not proceed by trying to immediately leap right into a supposed 'great outdoors', but by patiently attempting to differentially mediate the transcendental limits of its experience, feeling the caress of the real resistances, taking care of and joy in its own finitude. A speculative subject—being born from ma(t)ter and working to potentialise this material institution by piloted acts of self-positing—might have access to phenoumenodelic visions. In *Foundations of the Entire Science of Knowledge* (1794), Fichte provided a brief and categorical characterisation of this materialist and speculative conception of subjectivity: 'The self is finite, because it is to be subjected to limits; but it is infinite within this finitude because the boundary can be posited every farther out, to infinity.'[462] Every real obstacle offered up by mat(t)er to subjective striving provides a local foothold to the reactivation of the vital power of (self-)transformation. The Fichtean I, far from being an I crystallised in the form of a presumed essence (an I that 'de-exists'),[463] is a finite and infinitely transformable self, a self that re-exists, a self that singularly activates and realises in itself the transcendental malleability

462 Fichte, *The Science of Knowledge*, 228.

463 Cf. O. Bonilla, J.-C. Goddard, and G. Sibertin-Blanc, 'L'autre-mental de Pierre Déléage. Figure de l'anthropologue made in France en polygraphe réactionnaire', *lundimatin* 254 (2020), <https://lundi.am/L-autre-mental-de-Pierre-Deleage>.

of life itself. 'To see [and act] differently', in order to be able to constitute different lifeworlds, 'you would first have to become different than what you are',[464] affirms Fichte in the seventh *Address to the German Nation.* To be religated to the material life is to be religated to the power to engender, to morphogenetic plasticity, to the force that institutes new forms of life and—in particular—to the specifically spiritual capacity for self-institution, for being held until death in one's own birth, to take the process of the institution of the self as an existential self-positing beyond any inert essence ever further. Being religated to the material life entails sustaining 'the immanent generation of our finite life in the infinite' turbulence of living insubstance.[465]

464 J.G. Fichte, *Addresses to the German Nation*, ed. G. Moore (Cambridge: Cambridge University Press, 2009), 86.

465 M. Henry, *Paroles de Christ* (Paris: Seuil, 2002), 46.

# PART II

Immanental phenoumenodelia results from a speculative extension of the concept of experience beyond the phenomenological horizon correlated to a particular transcendental type of subjectivity. The speculative exploration of the phenoumenodelic field through the different abstract attributes of experience (*sensorium*, *affectum*, *logos*, *socius*) is the task of the corresponding modes of thought and practice (art, science, politics). In turn, a systematic probing of phenoumenodelic insubstance and its local modes capable of preserving the concrete entanglement between these abstract attributes defines the task proper to philosophy as we understand it here. But why practice art, science, politics, philosophy? Are these different modes of thought and practice not just *entertainment* (intended to foreclose the anguish elicited by our existential condition) and mere *vanity* (intended to conceal our own nullity)? Are not these modes of thought and practice symptoms of a necessarily unfulfilled desire that aggravates the frustration inherent to a finite existence? Would not be better to damp down the affects concomitant to finitude by trying to attain a desireless state of being? Why then bother to activate degrees of freedom in the transcendental landscape and try to expand the phenomenological horizons of our experience? Why orient our finite lives by infinite projects of reason and strive not to give up on the desire for truth, justice, beauty?

The Mallarméan *Maître* admits that the contingency of all human thought—the fact that any human act is ultimately dependent upon the contingent localisation of the subject's type in the transcendental landscape—does not constitute an ultimate obstruction to the project of obtaining a single Number that cannot be another. The *Maître* recognises that the modern ungrounding, far from necessarily implying the hypostasis of contingency and relativism, opens up human experience to a phenoumenodelic field absolved from any privileged transcendental framing. The *Maître* continues to work patiently and laboriously to sublate chance, to inscribe the singularity of any existential clinamen into the vast concertation, to consider everything that happens *sub specie durationis*—as a transient spark of the omnipresent act of awakening into phenoumenodelic dreaminess—to integrate its transcendental-dependent visions into vaster forms of experience. Nonetheless, and in spite of all this, the *Maître* must still be confronted with a final objection that fuels his Hamletian hesitation to carry out eidetic acts, to act in a way that is guided by the infinite ideas of reason, namely the hypothesis that in the last instance nothing will have ever taken time or place, not even the time or the place. The *transcendental contingency* of the particular structure of the human type, its contingent being-thus, emerges from a background of *existential contingency* associated with the very existence of human beings and of life in general. This contingency reels back to its origin and projects itself toward its end: nothing makes the emergence of life on earth and of humanity a necessity, and there is no reason to believe that it will not once against dissolve into nothingness, leaving no trace. If the emergence of life—of its fauna, its flora, and its fruits—is a highly improbable and spatiotemporally insignificant event in an otherwise lifeless universe, how is possible to provide meaning to existence? 'There were eternities when [the human intellect] did not exist; and someday when it is no longer there, not much will have changed'[1] and nothing—whatever we do, whatever we decide—will make any difference. All operations that aim to preserve the meaning of existence beyond personal death, that inscribe the latter into a selective economy of life driven by the death of individuals, or into the open horizon of a

1 F. Nietzsche, 'On Truth and Lying in an Extra-Moral Sense', in *On Rhetoric and Language*, tr. S.L. Gilman, C. Blair and D.J. Parent (Oxford: Oxford University Press, 1989), 246.

transpersonal future (e.g. posthumous glory, offspring, etc.), all these meaning-producing operations collapse in the face of the presumption of an ultimate and irrevocable catastrophe (such as the destruction of the earth, the death of the sun, the gravitational collapse of the universe)—in the face of the katabatic decay that will eventually restore the equilibrium disturbed by an inconsequential excitation. While personal life and death are inscribed within a horizon that precedes them, succeeds them, and gives them meaning, 'with the disappearance of the earth [or the universe] [...] [i]t's the horizon itself that will be abolished. [...] Wars, conflicts, political tensions, shifts in philosophical debates, even passions—everything's dead already [...] the inevitable explosion to come, the one that's always forgotten in your intellectual ploys, can be seen in a certain way to come before the fact to render these ploys posthumous—make them futile. [...] In 4.5 billion years there will arrive the demise of your phenomenology and your utopian politics, and there'll be no one there to toll the death knell or hear it.'[2] Every infinite task is already posthumous, futile, and every project guided by an idea of reason seems to be pure and simple *vanitas*. The (supposed) certainty of a total annihilation to come encrypts existence, places life in a mortuary vacuole from which it cannot be exhumed. Any roll of the dice, even one capable of differentially transcending the transcendental limits of the corresponding subject, is thrown within a crypt, and nothing of what takes place within it will transcend. It is significant, as Brassier argues, that it is science itself (oriented by the regulative idea of truth) that seems to strip existence, in particular the infinite projects of reason such as science itself, of all meaning: it is thanks to science (argues Brassier) that we have finally understood existence's lack of meaning.[3] Rather than revitalising us with its light, modern enlightenment seems to lead inflexibly to a learned nihilism, to an understanding of life as an insignificant, improbable, and local exception lost in the realm of death. Thus the nihilistic melancholy of this alleged intransigent 'realism' seeks to clothe itself in the authority

2 Lyotard, *The Inhuman*, 9–10.

3 Cf. R. Brassier, 'I Am a Nihilist Because I Still Believe in Truth', interview with M. Rychter, *Kronos* 16:1 (2011). See also Brassier, *Nihil Unbound*, Chapter 7.

and prestige provided by modern science. The (at least apparent) isolation of humanity in an unimaginably vast, dark, cold, and silent universe and the dissolution to come—as well as the correlative contingency of the very emergence of life on earth—spreads the influenza of nihilism into every human project regulated by an infinite idea, awakening what Lyotard calls the 'postmodern affect'[4] *par excellence*: melancholy. The scientifically informed anticipation of the ultimate catastrophe announces nothing more or less than the end of human ends, the end of the temporality in which the supposedly infinite projects of human reason can unfold. This affliction forces us to bracket out eidetic vagaries so as to ask ourselves, seriously: What for? Why engage in the infinite projects of reason if ultimately (only) nothing matters? Why pay attention to eidetic prescriptions when one is already under the influence of a melancholy induced by the temporarily retrograde shockwave of a cosmic catastrophe to come? Doesn't the restricted economy defined by the projects of reason sit within a general economy based on the certainty of absolute dissolution, of sovereign expenditure without remainder? In this scenario, what sense can there be in embarking on a project of a cumulative nature intended to enrich the theoretical heritage of mankind, which is by essence the infinite project of knowledge? Don't the infinite ideas of reason reintroduce a form of transcendence that projects us beyond the immediate gift of life, of vital immanence? Or, as Grothendieck asks, simply: Why continue with scientific research? In the absence of the guarantees and prescriptions of the pre-modern era, any action prescribed by the infinite ideas of reason seems to be nothing more than an inveterate anachronism. Evaluated against the background defined by the wave of contingency and relativism triggered by the closure of all hypertranscendent orientations and guarantees, the subjective commitment to the corresponding infinite projects of reason seems like a futile gesticulation of our vanity, a thoughtless perpetuation of an ancestral folly that will ultimately have no consequences. The infinite project of science, developed by 'clever animals' condemned to an anonymous death 'in some remote corner of the universe that is poured out in countless flickering solar

4 J.-F. Lyotard, *Moralités postmodernes* (Paris: Galilée, 1993), 94.

systems',[5] taking time and place in a cosmos condemned to a thermodynamic death or a cosmological collapse 'after' which not even space and time will have taken place, such a project of reason seems to be no more than a 'delirious jolt', nothingness settling once more into nothingness, a rapidly dissolved clot of arrogance.[6]

In order to face this existential demoralisation regarding the possibility of performing acts under the aegis of the infinite ideas of reason, of throwing the dice from the depths of a shipwreck, of not ceding the desire to mediate the transcendental limits of finite existence, let us paraphrase Hölderlin's maxim, already invoked by Heidegger in order to think beyond the nihilistic *enframing* imposed by the essence of modern science: Where the danger lies—in the wilderness of life—there also grows the cure. As we shall understand it here, the cure does not save, but rids existence of the deceit of eschatological narratives and attendant promises of salvation. It is not possible to save oneself, but it is possible to cure oneself of melancholy lethargy and modern disligation: ridding oneself of apocalyptic eschatologies and consequently of the (now unnecessary) hope of a—messianic or technological—salvation. Perhaps the nihilistic panorama described above does not go far enough into the dark heart of the modern abyss; perhaps the incursion 'where there is danger' should be further radicalised, taken to a greater extreme, an extreme where the very (scientifically updated) hypothesis of a coming apocalypse will assume its true tenor, that of being nothing more than an 'image of the world', a scientific narrative, subject to the hyperbolic ungrounding power of modern reason. If the 'open' is

---

5 Nietzsche, 'On Truth and Lying in an Extra-Moral Sense', 246.

6 A contemporary iteration of this nihilistic stance can be found in the work of Land. See for instance the following text: 'Particles decay, molecules disintegrate, cells die, organisms perish, species become extinct, planets are destroyed and stars burn-out, galaxies explode... until the unfathomable thirst of the entire universe collapses into darkness and ruin. Death, glorious and harsh, sprawls vast beyond all suns [...]. Matter signals to its lost voyagers, telling them that their quest is vain, and that their homeland already lies in ashes behind them.' Land, *The Thirst for Annihilation*, 146.

the 'unobjectiveness of full Nature',[7] then the empty spaces of modern cosmology and its cosmogonic and eschatological narratives cannot be pre-critically conflated with the 'full Nature', that is, with the *natura naturans*: the pleromatic openness is infinitely vaster than the cosmological vastness. The hypostasis of all scientific symbolisation falls under the stroke of the generalised transformation—prescribed by science itself—of every theoretic statement into a thesis subjected to revision. The infinite idea that orients modern science—the imperative not to cede the desire always to expand our rational understanding of the experiential field—requires resisting the temptation to turn a partially successful symbolisation into an 'image of the world' painted hypostatically onto the vacant surfaces of the umweltic vaults, into a kind of constellation in which we could read the cipher of our origin and our destiny, in an imaginary 'new paradigm' capable of providing the ultimate key to the true situation of the human being in the cosmos. As Bateson states, '[s]cience probes, it does not prove'.[8] The dogmatic conversion of a partially successful symbolisation into cosmogonic, eschatological, and existential certainties also projects a sheltering sky that plugs up the abyssal uncertainty opened up by modern science: we prefer to embrace the certainty of a (cosmic) death to come—and perhaps fantasise about the idea of a god (or a technological development) capable of saving us—than to face up to the scenario brought on by modern science. The so-called *truth of extinction* is a pre-modern dogmatic thesis which, in claiming to be based in the authority of scientific discourse, actually in a twisted manner hinders the possibility of becoming absolutely modern, of enduring the suspension of the 'closed world' within the infinite pleroma. Who could dare to imagine what the scientific 'image of the world' will be in 10, 100, 1000 years (if there is still something like science and scientists)? Let us be absolutely modern. Let us 'stay with the trouble', the pain, the risk, and the beauty of finite existence, of an existence that cannot be grounded on any ultimate truth whatsoever, even the 'truth of extinction'. Let us bracket

---

7 Heidegger, 'Why Poets?', *Off The Beaten Track*, 217.

8 Bateson, *Mind and Nature*, 30.

out 'the self-indulgent and self-fulfilling myths of apocalypse',[9] 'the sterilising narrative of wiping the world clean by apocalypse or salvation'.[10] The plant that heals, the one that grows where the danger is, does not save us from death (or from a supposed apocalypse to come), but it might help us to die healthy, clear of the arrogance involved in using the certainty of individual or collective death as an argument against the germinal (scientific, artistic, political, religious) possibilities that belong to us, against the manifold forms of desire that constitute our finite existence. From the depths of the shipwreck, the *Maître* does throw the dice; just before the apocalyptic impact with the planet Melancholia—and against the ontotheological deduction that derives from the truth of imminent extinction the meaninglessness of (a disligated) life (based on the imperative of capital accumulation)—Justine constructs the most transient, fragile, and vulnerable 'magic cave' and firmly 'lingers with the negative'. Radicalising the Copernican ungrounding even further, the speculative opening up of a phenoumenodelic field of experience allows us to delve even deeper into where the danger lies. The speculative trans-umwelticisation of experience relieves existence of the eschatological narratives inscribed on the inner surfaces of the sheltering skies: 'mak[ing] a slit in the [umweltic] umbrella, they tear open the firmament itself, to let in a bit of free and windy [pleroma] and to frame in a sudden light a vision that appears through the rent',[11] to decant the mythic cosmodicies drop by drop into the phenoumenodelic solution. To begin to glimpse the true scope of modern katabasis, it is necessary to accept the absolute absence of any global Ur-tone, of any fixed 'image of the world' that could globally orient our acts, of any immobile transcendental Earth that could provide a final foundational instance for our constructions. We can endorse Althusser's definition of *materialism*, '[n]ot to indulge in storytelling',[12] by resisting the temptation to turn the

9 Haraway, *Staying With the Trouble*, 35.

10 Ibid., 150.

11 Deleuze and Guattari, *What is Philosophy?*, 203

12 L. Althusser, *The Future Lasts Forever: A Memoir*, tr. R. Veasey (New York: The New Press, 1992), 221.

stories that we can legitimately tell ourselves, that we need to tell, into (genealogical, eschatological, or salvific) cosmodicies. A rhetorical practice can constitute a legitimate navigational operator to locally pilot a protocol of experience, to give it an imaginary local consistency, to monitor the pleroma by means of narrative probes, without its pretending to give a global meaning to existence. Loyalty to the regulative idea of modern science demands that we abstain from projecting a hypertranscendent meaning onto existence, even the meaning conveyed by eschatological, apocalyptic and salvific narratives. Let us resist the temptation to use science to ground any form of nihilism, the temptation to transform truth qua infinite regulative idea into a dogmatically hypostatised content, the temptation to use this purported ultimate knowledge to 'deduce' the meaninglessness of existence. The generalised suspension of hypostases—the hypostasis of a given tone (like the present, the waking state, or sensory certainty) into a global Ur-tone, the hypostasis of a given theoretical symbolisation into an ultimate 'truth', the hypostasis of a narrative into a mythical cosmodicy—is also a consequence of the phenoumenodelic *epoché*, of the suspension of every phenoumenon (narratives in particular) in their pure appearance. In the mode of experience opened up by this suspension, '[e]verything occurs, in brief, hypothetically; narrative is avoided.[13] [...] Everything is a working hypothesis.'[14] The suspending of worlds, the launching of lands into the open, and the demystifying of narratives all allow for access to an absolute (because cleared of all hypostasis) experiential field in which different phenoumenodelic data are no longer encapsulated by a world, rooted in an immobile transcendental Earth, or aligned to a universal history. The de-canonisation of these different systems of reference (world, earth, history)—the suspension of hypostases—activates a general relativisation of the experiential field: 'every utensil, spoon, fork, knife, plate' in the *Maître*'s Nautilus 'bears a letter circumscribed by a

13 Mallarmé, *Collected Poems*, 122 [translation modified].

14 Lorenz, 'Kant's Doctrine of the A Priori', 239.

motto: *mobilis in mobili*'.[15] In the last instance, and despite all the partially successful symbolisations provided by modern science, despite all the known ontologies, despite all the physics, the metaphysics, and the pataphysics, almost nothing (and even that may be slightly optimistic) is known about the 'ultimate nature' of the experiential field into which we have been 'thrown', nothing is known about the real extent of the assumed human freedom to perform eidetic acts, nothing is known about the hypothetical consequences of such acts, nothing is known about what will or will not have taken time and place. The only phenoumenodelic fact is that we are immersed in an experiential field of which we know almost nothing, in a concrete flux of revelations conjugated into many abstract attributes (percepts, affects, concepts, sociolepts, etc.), to which we only have access through filtered, edited representations. And these renormalised images of the phenoumenodelic pleroma can be deformed and expanded by means of the different modes of thought and practice (science, art, politics): it is always possible to understand, thanks to the patient effort of conceptualisation, more than was previously understood; to widen the doors of affectivity and perception with the aim of extending the spectrum of accessible sensory landscapes; to disrupt existentials, habits, naturecultural imprints; to tune into different durations (historical, biological, geological, astrophysical, cosmological) that pulse beneath and above the timescales inherent to the 'natural attitude', to religate back to the impersonal life that institutes us as finite individuals freefalling into its turbulent self-revelation, that forces us to freely channel its living act of manifestation. We can only witness the self-revelation of life and enhance it by broadening the phenomenological horizons of our experience along its many abstract attributes. Thanks to the conversion enacted by means of the *epoché*, every phenomenon—captains, sirens, storms—is transmuted into a phenoumenodelic datum drifting across the stream of impersonal experience. Infiltrating every garden, infusing every subject, suspending all naturality, existing all substance, the pleromatic ocean always reverberates (Solaris).

15 J. Verne, *Twenty Thousand Leagues Under the Sea*, <https://www.gutenberg.org/ebooks/164>.

And even if we did have the absolute certainty of our collective extinction—as we have of our personal death—this knowledge would not ground in any possible sense the alleged lack of meaning of existence. The stance according to which the 'truth of extinction' deprives existence of meaning seems to presuppose that meaning is a sort of hypertranscendent fact not produced by our finite practices, by the desiring practices made possible by our living and dying finite existence. The idea that the acceptance of finitude implies the absence of an existential meaning constitutes a reactive pre-modern offering to ontotheology, to the thesis that only a hypertranscendent instance beyond finite life can endow existence with some form of meaningful purposiveness, to the thesis that (individual and collective) finitude is in the last instance a flaw from which we should save ourselves by engaging in an unbound form of Prometheanism. The use of personal death or collective extinction to undermine the infinite projects of reason misses a fundamental point, namely that finitude is the prime mover of infinite desire. In particular, only a finite subject—a subject confronting the 'vast ocean of ignorance'—might want to understand. Desire (for truth, beauty, justice, love) forces the finite subject to infinitely transmute its finitude, to place itself in the service of the infinite revelation in which we 'live and move and have our being' (Acts 17:28). 'Not ceding one's desire' means removing oneself from a melancholic paralysis, reimplanting oneself in life, allowing oneself to be irrigated by its transcendental plasticity, by the force of imagination (*Einbildungskraft*) that institutes visionary subjects. And this religation with life has its own affect, that of love.

The existentialisation of absolute life into a finite, autonomous, and desiring being-there—that is, the institution of an individual—implies to a certain extent a separation, a detachment from the immanental field of life, a finite localisation of its absolute self: '[t]he emergence of a [living being] from the [impersonal life] can be seen as a trauma which marks the temporary estrangement of the [person] from the [impersonal], the transient establishment of a zone of interiority excised out of its [impersonal] precursor.'[16] Separation is a necessary moment of a life that unfolds itself by instituting singular individuals; estrangement is concomitant to the living process that 'eternally forms itself by setting up oppositions'.[17] Every institution of a separated subjectivity, every birth of a mortal living being, establishes a traumatic cut in the vital continuum that demarcates a subjective interiority from different forms of exteriority, thereby introducing a tension between the finite living persona and the impersonal life: '[I]n any [living being] the appearance of the absolute has become isolated from the absolute and fixated into independence.[18] [...] It is as a division in unity of the real and as a fractured reality [...] that the self [is instituted] as autonomous individual force. The glory of individual autonomy is indissociable from this fragility and is undermined by it: the finite mind can only set itself up as a force facing the world and its own future by breaking up the same ground of reality that it nevertheless ceaselessly presupposes and strives toward as the ultimate end of all these acts.'[19] The subject separates from an exorbitant background with which it must engage in manifold relations of experience (affective, perceptual, social, etc.), actions (production, predations, transformations, etc.), exchange (in order to guarantee the flux and reflux of nutrients, waste, and information), and protection (in order to preserve its physical and psychic integrity). The transcendental structure of the individual—the frame that makes possible and at the same time limits its experience and its existence (its skin, its sense organs, its motor functions, its conceptual and linguistic resources)—fulfils these multiple roles.

The 'surface' that demarcates subjective interiority from the 'outside' does not have the 'topology' of a sphere. The counterposited 'outside', far from just insisting on the external borders of the subject and being

---

16 R. Negarestani, 'Globe of Revolution: An Afterthought on Geophilosophical Realism', *Identities: Journal for Politics, Gender and Culture* 8:2 (2011), 25–54.

17 G.W.F Hegel, *The Difference Between Fichte and Schelling's Philosophy*, tr. H.S. Harris and W. Cerf (Albany, NY: State University of New York Press, 1977), 91.

18 Ibid., 89.

19 Goddard, *La philosophie fichtéenne de la vie*, 134.

channelled and filtered through sensory orifices and dermic envelopes, admits of multiple declinations. The finite living being, submerged in the pleromatic infinitude with its transcendental diving suit on, feels 'external' pressure in multiple dimensions: as that which threatens its integrity from within the umweltic bubble (e.g. predators, police, publicity), as that which remains outside of the corresponding transcendental frame (the supernatural sky), as the real impasses of the symbolic structure which cannot be bound (at least for the moment) by means of a speculative extension of its transcendental type, as the impersonal vital background with which the subject necessarily continues to be enmeshed in order to persist in living, as traces of the ongoing processes of the immanental institution of its own subjectivity, as that which, incapable of being either digested by the transcendental faculties or vomited back out, dwells within the subjective extimacy in the form of a *(trop/trou)matism* (Lacan). To schematise this, we could say that the intentional relationship $\$_\alpha \rightarrow P_\alpha$ between a subject $\$_\alpha$ (where $\alpha$ denotes its transcendental type) and the objects $P_\alpha$ that appear in the $\alpha$-Umwelt (where $P_\alpha$ denotes the $\alpha$-objectification of a phenoumenon P) is circumscribed, in particular, by a double trans-objective and pre-subjective 'outside'. Firstly, the intentional relation $\$_\alpha \rightarrow P_\alpha$ is limited by that which resides 'beyond' the objects $P_\alpha$ to which the subject has access. This phenoumenal 'beyond' of the objects constituted by the subject's transcendental faculties defines the so-called 'great outdoors' first introduced in the form of the Kantian *thing in itself*. On the other hand, the immanental process of institution and preservation of the subject happens to form part of the invisible background which renders possible phenomenological visibility. We could say that the 'trauma' of birth—or, more generally, of the always ongoing process of the institution of subjectivity—also remains out of the transcendental frame, upstream of the subject's field of conscious 'visibility'. For instance, the violent act of the institution of a particular nomological order (like the killing of the primordial father or revolutionary terror) cannot be rationalised, justified, or grounded on the basis of the symbolic frame instituted by this very act. Briefly, both what dwells beyond the phenomenological horizon (the phenoumena as such) and what insists behind the subject's back (the multifarious modalities through which life institutes and irrigates the subject's life) are subtracted from its 'conscious' experience.[20]

To this twofold limitation of intentional experience we can add the 'extimacies' lodged within the subjective structure. Any traumatic effraction of the transcendental protective shield—for instance, any experience that cannot be inscribed in the symbolic structure (named, objectified, rationalised, digested, remembered) can at least, in order to preserve subjective integrity, be encrypted, vacuolised, tokonomised, imprisoned (e.g. in a jail or a psychiatric hospital), thus becoming part of the 'topological' structure of the subject in question. In all of these cases, 'what is confined is precisely the outside'.[21] We could say with Lacan that what cannot be *intentionally objectified* is *drively object-a-fied*. These (trop/trou)matisms lodged in subjective extimacy structure the psychic dynamics of the subject: its drives, its pleasures, its desires, its phantasms, its dreams, its repetitions, its enjoyment. In this way, the 'outside' has a threefold declination in the form of (i) a phenoumenodelic 'beyond' of the object ('an outside farther

---

20 As Deleuze contends in a comment on Merleau-Ponty, the 'carnal' insubstance within which relationships between subjects and objects are polarised is at the same time *further away* and *deeper* than any intentional vector going from a subject to an object: 'A radical, "vertical" visibility was fold into a Self-seeing, and from that point on made possible the horizontal[-intentional] relation between a seeing and a seen. [A phenoumenal] Outside, more distant than any [phenomenological] exterior, is "twisted", "folded" and "doubled" by [a vital] Inside that is deeper than any [subjective] interior, and alone creates the possibility of the derived relation between the interior and the exterior [i.e. of the I/not-I intentional polarisations]. It is even this twisting which defines "Flesh" beyond the body proper and its objects. In brief, the [transcendental-phenomenological] intentionality of being is surpassed by the [immanental] fold of Being, Being as fold (Sartre, on the other hand, remained at the level of intentionality, because he was content to make "holes" in being, without reaching the fold of Being). Intentionality is still generated in a Euclidean space that prevents it from understanding itself, and must be surpassed by another, "topological", space which establishes contact between the [phenoumenal] Outside and the [vital] Inside, the most distant, the most deep.' G. Deleuze, *Foucault*, tr. S Hand (London and New York: Continuum, 2006), 110.

21 Ibid., 43.

away than any [surrounding] external world');[22] (ii) a living background—the impersonal flesh—that invisibly ferments and operates 'behind' the subject; and (iii) the traumatic extimacies located within the subject ('an inside that lies deeper than any internal world').[23] In pseudo-Lacanian script:

$$\text{Vital impersonal background} \rightarrow (\text{Subject } \$_{\alpha} \rightarrow \text{Object } P_{\alpha}) \rightarrow \text{Phenoumenon } P$$

where the slash / that crosses the barred subject in the sign $ denotes the extimate holes lodged within the subject.

The institution of finite subjectivities introduces folds, cuts, and twists in the univocal experiential fabric provided by the phenoumenodelic insubstance, which produce complex topological structures made up of relative interiors and exteriors, nested holes, 'regional [phenomenological] horizons', intersubjective communicating channels, trans-umweltic bridges, adjacencies of type *n*.[24] By instituting finite forms of subjectivity embodying different transcendental types, the pleroma, far from unfolding in the form of a Euclidean 'plane' of immanence, becomes a sort of dynamical topological foam. The boundary between inside and outside becomes convoluted, twisted, serpentine, floating, 'with no contours',[25] and ultimately untraceable. In the last instance, '[w]e must conjure up illusory interiority in order to restore [subjects] to their constitutive exteriority. [...] It is as if the relations with the outside folded back on themselves to create a doubling, allowing a relation with oneself to emerge, and constituting an inside which is hollowed out and develops its own unique dimension [...][26] [Renatus Cartesius—Here Comes Everybody!—] is less a discretely individualised "solid man" than a knot of modulating attachments that

22 Ibid., 118.

23 Ibid., 96.

24 Cf. Negarestani, 'Globe of Revolution'.

25 Deleuze, *Foucault*, 113.

26 Ibid., 43 and 100 [translation modified].

lead back in time to the era of his wakening.[27] [...] Formelly confounded with amother[28] [...] A ["preadaminant"] fluidity at the roots of [his] nature rebels against the security of *terra firma*' and the self-sufficiency of the *ego conquero*: 'we are [all] amphibians',[29] crawling in a tonal Umwelt and diving in the solaristic insubstance. At the limit, the subject is nothing but a self-aware concentration of immanental flesh, a breathing invagination of living insubstance, 'an inside which is merely [a local] fold of the outside',[30] a fold that is 'responsive to *difference*'.[31] Since 'individualisation does not mean [in]substantial independence',[32] the separation of the individual from the living impersonal background is only a valid description within a certain regime of abstraction. A 'separated' individual is inextricably enmeshed (materially, physiologically, psychically, existentially, spiritually) with the living impersonal background, with other living human and nonhuman personae, and with overarching transpersonal structures. If one forgets that the description of the individual as a separated lifeform is dependent upon such a process of abstraction, then the door is wide open for the pathological hypostasis of the separation that we have called disligation.

Individuation is inseparable from the assumption of the autonomy of desire and the concomitant helplessness: life throws the living 'to the risk of dull desire and shelters none in particular'.[33] But the separation intrinsically associated with the institution of autonomous finite subjects does not necessarily imply disligation. On the contrary, the separation between the one life and multiple living beings—we might say between (impersonal) *being* and (personal) *existence*—opens up the possibility

---

27 J. Bishop, *Joyce's Book of the Dark* (Madison, WI: University of Wisconsin Press, 1986), 366.

28 Joyce, *Finnegans Wake*, 125.

29 Land, *The Thirst for Annihilation*, 75.

30 Deleuze, *Foucault*, 97.

31 Bateson and Bateson, *Angels Fear*, 135, and Bateson, *Steps to an Ecology of Mind*, 315.

32 Whitehead, *Science and the Modern World*, 71.

33 R.M. Rilke, quoted in Heidegger, 'Why Poets?', *Off the Beaten Track*, 206.

of a therapethic degree of freedom that human existence may (or may not) activate. First, we can hypostasise the separation of the living with respect to the absolute life which is lived locally in them, which is to say, we can radicalise the separation between the finite relative modes and the infinite absolute insubstance in the form of a *disligation*. The disligated living being, having been disconnected (at least to a certain extent) from the origin of its life, becomes a stranger (*Äuslander*). This maximal heteronomy between the living and the absolute launches the latter toward an inexistent 'beyond', totally inaccessible (negative theology) or, in the best of cases, only accessible—'transcending all science' (San Juan de la Cruz)—as an 'object of belief' (Jacobi). The Spinozist-Fichtean critique of the corresponding hypertranscendent God—an everlasting God separate from the finite creatures whose transient existence is understood as a fall into worldly temporality—specifically takes the form of an exorcism of the metaphysical phantasm of *creation* that deconstructs the theoretical illusion that the created can subsist disligated from the creator, that creation is a local inextensive act which is not coextensive to existence: 'Away with the perplexing phantasm [...] of a creation from God of something that is not in [it]self [...] an emanation in which [it] is not [it]self present but forsakes [its] work; an expulsion and separation from [it] that casts out into desolate nothingness, and makes [it] our arbitrary and hostile lord!'[34] The thesis that 'what is ultimate' are *self-substances* created ex nihilo by a hypertranscendent or metaphysical Father—rather than enduring transient patterns immanent to the during flowing mat(t)er—condemns the subject to a distressed disligation and transforms philosophy into a purely 'speculative' metaphysics that anxiously ruminates on the questions *Why is there something instead of nothing? How did life locally appear out of a global background of death?* over and over. The comprehension of existence or life as islands that would have appeared—by some kind of miraculous improbable event or by an unfathomable act of divine will—in the midst of

34 Fichte, *The Way Towards the Blessed Life; Or, the Doctrine of Religion*, 102.

nothingness or death can only elicit a feeling of estrangement and despair. Heterousian theology, which maximises the distance between the creator and the creature, tends to be iconoclastic, iconophobic, outlawing any intramundane epiphany that might counteract disligation, proscribing any incarnation or ingression of the divine, any annunciation of the infinite within the finite. Redemption can only take place through a radical negation of—that is, a salvation with respect to—worldly temporality and existential finitude. The ontotheological projection of the absolute into a hyperbolically external realm entails a deglorification of the flesh and a depreciation of the temporal world, a world that becomes a disenchanted and 'desolate nothingness', impervious to epiphany, impermeable to revelation.[35] In this sense, the current ecological crisis can certainly be understood as a 'new episode' of the ontotheological stance and its iconoclastic drives: '[T]here will come a time when [...] the land which was once the home of [religious practices] will be left desolate, bereft of the presence of its deities. This land [...] will be filled with foreigners [...]. And in that day [human beings] will be weary of life, and they will cease to think the universe (*mundus*) worthy of reverent wonder and of worship. And so religion, the greatest of all blessings [...] will be threatened with destruction; [human beings] will think it a burden, and will come to scorn it. They will no longer love this world around us [...] And so the [spirits] will depart from [the forests]—a grievous departure[...]. Then will the earth no longer stand unshaken, and the sea will bear no ships; heaven will not support the stars in their orbits, nor will the stars pursue their constant course in heaven; all [singing] voices of the [spirits] will of necessity be silenced and dumb; the fruits of the earth will rot; the soil will turn barren, and the very air will sicken in

---

35 As Goddard writes, '[o]pposition to God [in the form of disligation] is compounded by an opposition to the world and to the body. [Separated from the Father], the [human being] no longer knows how to recognise a divine universal order in nature. [It] is miserable in the external world.' J.-C. Goddard, 'Incarnation et philosophie dans l'idealisme allemand (Schelling, Hegel)', in J.-C. Goddard (ed.), *Le corps* (Paris: Vrin, 2005), 165.

sullen stagnation.[36] The whole of humanity is on the verge of sinking with its eyes closed, devastating and devastated, leaving behind it, under the glaring neon lights, in place of the earthly paradise that was entrusted to it, a disembowelled, stinking, dead garbage planet.'[37]

In the midst of the utter desolation left behind by the ontotheological projection of God into the beyond, the principal response explored by European modernity was to reterritorialise itself in the castellated abbey of the 'happy and dauntless and sagacious' Prince Prospero, to try at all costs to keep the risk of dying at bay (even at the price of withdrawing from the act of living), to transform the speculative act of individual self-positing into self-sufficiency and imposition of one's own transcendental type, to make oneself into a *terra firma* from which to launch into the conquest, to make the *ego cogito* into an *ego solus* (Leminski) and from this an *ego conquero*. If the universe is devoid of sacrality, if life seems to be no more than a fragile and insignificant exception in an otherwise lifeless backdrop, it might have seemed reasonable to undertake the systematic transformation of these desolate spaces into a human habitat. The *res conquerans* is thus projected with impunity into that which appears as a *res* that is merely *extensa* and, at the limit, as a stock of merchandisable resources: 'Over there, the bird machine is singing, over there, the tapir machine grazes. Over there the bug machine is taking a shit. I am not a machine, I am not a bug, I am René Descartes, by the grace of God. Once I realise this, I will be whole. I made this undergrowth: come off of it, bridges, supplies and developments, savage journeys and batavo villages. I expend Thoughts and I extend Extension! I seek pure Extension, without the farts of your hearts, without the menses of monsters, without the horseshit of worship, without the faeces of theses, without the muck of these beasts. Down with the metamorphoses of bugs—chameleons stealing the stone's colour!'[38]

---

36 The Hermetic treatise known as the 'Asclepius', quoted by J. Assmann in *The Price of Monotheism*, tr. R. Savage (Stanford, CA: Stanford University Press, 2010), 72–73.

37 Grothendieck, *La clef des songes*, 152.

38 Leminski, *Catatau*, 37.

The hypostasis of separation reaches its apogee in *appropriation* and *conquest*: the subject first deepens its disligation by saying 'this is mine' and then—more radically—by identifying itself with its properties and saying, 'this is me'. What belongs to it becomes its property in the ontological sense of the term: that which defines who it is, its *quidditas*, its suchness. The illness of disligation is concomitant with the institution of a dessicated 'people of merchandise':[39] 'Capital ["the Babylon system"] is dead labour, that, vampire-like, only lives by sucking living labour, [thereby disligating the living ones from the immanent source of their lives] and lives the more, the more labour it sucks.'[40] The deadly identification between the subject and its possessions—the conception of the subject as a bundle of properties—essentialises its existence and leads to the belief that possession is a necessary condition guaranteeing the preservation of existence. To be deprived of one's possessions would be equivalent to dying: How could one be detached from that which one is—from one's essential attributes—and at the same time carry on living? How could one claim to enter into the kingdom of life if at the open doorway the doorkeeper says 'Come in, but only if you leave your possessions at the cloakroom'? Who would remain to enter if this self-dissolving request were accepted? The relationship of possession entails a reification of the subject that possesses, the reification of thought into an *I think* first of all, and then into an *I have* thoughts, and more generally the reification of action into an *I act* and then into an *I have* means of action and production.[41] In turn, the relationship of possession entails a transmutation of that which is possessed into a dead object removed from the process of vital activity. The conception of property in terms of a right

39 D. Kopenawa and B. Albert, *The Falling Sky: Words of a Yanomami Shaman*, tr. N. Elliott and A. Dundy (Cambridge, MA: The Belknap Press of Harvard University Press, 2013), 327.

40 K. Marx, *Capital: A Critique of Political Economy, Volume One*, tr. B. Fowkes (London: Penguin, 1990), 342.

41 Cf. M. Hess, 'The Philosophy of the Act', in A. Fried and R. Sanders (eds.), *Socialist Thought: A Documentary History* (New York: Columbia University Press, 1992), 249–76.

over things is part of a 'non-philosophical' conception according to which 'what is ultimate is a substantial being, [...] a dead, fixed and subsisting being, to which [...] properties are attributed as if they were inherent to it', a being which fixes the living activity of forming images [*Bilden*] into inert images. Property relies on an ontological misconception. The subject understood as a reified self-subsistance obstructs 'the striving of the life that is caught up in it as a part to get out of it [by fluidifying its transcendental essence], and raise itself to freedom'.[42] The 'free, living being' becomes an ossified image determined 'by a limitation of the freedom and life within it. The two ways of seeing thus relate to each other as pure death to pure life'.[43] But nothing will remain 'of the old activity of plunder. None of the forms within which this plunder had affixed itself until now can continue in the face of the [living] free spirit, which now manifests itself only as active, and which does not stop with some result that has been won by someone and fix, embody and materialise it in order to store it up as "property"—which rather, as the real power over all things that are finite and determined, ever transcends them, and creates itself anew as an active force [...].'[44]

The transformation of the transcendental framing necessarily associated with every finite lifeform into a type-centric appropriating constitution, into the imposition of a complete objectivation of the pleroma that claims to foreclose any real residue, into a reduction of the 'sovereign inaccessibility of the other', is the hallmark of the idealistic deformation of the transcendental motif and provides the philosophical plot that grounds imperialism and gives shape to the subjectivity of the coloniser. In the framework of this 'carnophallogocentrism',[45] *predation* ceases to be one of the forms of vital breathing—of the inter-typical self-transformation of life, of immanental theophagy—in order to become the condition of possibility of *predication*, of

42 Hegel, *The Difference Between Fichte and Schelling's Philosophy*, 90.

43 Fichte, *La doctrine de l'État (1813)*, 66.

44 Hess, 'The Philosophy of the Act', 264.

45 Cf. D. Birnbaum and A. Olsson, 'An Interview with Jacques Derrida on the Limits of Digestion', *e-flux journal* 2 (January 2009), <https://www.e-flux.com/journal/02/68495/an-interview-with-jacques-derrida-on-the-limits-of-digestion/>.

the reification of the subject into a bundle of properties: that which is incorporated is not transmuted and spontaneously exhaled in the rhythmic act of living, but rather transformed into an accumulable piece of capital. This idealism forecloses finitude, the fact that not everything can be constituted, rationalised, assimilated, digested, incorporated, imagined—the fact that not everything can be appropriated, conquered, or consumed. The idealist distortion of the Kantian transcendental motif could not be more radical: from being a philosophy of the ineradicable—albeit mediatable—finitude of the subject (as Heidegger argues in his reading of Kant, and which he takes up again in his own thesis on the irreducibility of what Oswald de Andrade would call *odontological difference*),[46] becomes a philosophy of the self-grounding, self-sufficient, coloniser, and demiurgic subject. The transcendental motif becomes idealism and the concomitant reduction of the other transforms separation into an isolating disligation. In its tendency toward aloneness, a disligated being-there denies the existential condition of its existence that is being-with; it becomes—as Goddard puts it in his reading of Kopenawa—a *stranger without strangers*, a stranger (in life) that only recognises other instances of its own transcendental type as subjects. Remember that sort of King Ubu, miserably pretending to incarnate the wrath of God, sick to the core on his raft, utterly blind to the omnipresent 'golden' sacrament in which he is actually drifting, completely disligated from the overflowing life that surrounds him, 'discovering' the meanders of the Amazonas (as if they were not already fully exposed to the innumerable forms of life that inhabit them), and declaring pathetically, faced with the

46 'JD: [...] [N]ot everything for him can be assimilated. What Heidegger calls the 'ontological difference' between 'being' (*Sein*) and 'beings' (*Seienden*)—which is of course the very essence of his philosophy—indicates such a limit. Being always remains inaccessible. Being is never given as a being, a thing in the world that can be named and captured with the question *What?* Being transcends beings [...].
DB, AO: So you take Heidegger's ontological difference to be the boundary between what can be eaten and what cannot be eaten?
JD: Yes, exactly. The ontological difference is the boundary between what can be assimilated and what is already presupposed in all assimilation, but which itself is inaccessible.' Birnbaum and Olsson, 'An Interview with Jacques Derrida'.

ever-renewed display of the new 'virgin' lands (of the 'West'), 'I solemnly and formally take possession of all these lands'. This phrase condenses the absolute madness of conquest, of extractivism, of colonialism, of racism, of slavery in all its (pre-capitalist and capitalist) forms, of the reduction of nature to a 'standing reserve' of raw materials; the 'evil'—i.e. the illness—of ethnocides, ecocides, and specicides, the hubris par excellence that is the unconditional 'will to appropriate',[47] the reduction of subjectivity to be a particular instance of a single transcendental type and the concomitant reduction of the pleroma to a single correlative objective world. If the subject is disligated from life—that is, from the force that generates lifeforms, from the power to drive mutations of the transcendental types—then this disligation can only coincide with the hypostasis of its transcendental type, with the crystallisation of its subjective 'essence', with the transformation of the singular symbolic norms of its totemic clan into universal taboos. 'The definitively [disligated] Prometheus' transforms the vital *potentia*, which makes the subject a mutant that channels the self-revelation of life, into *potestas*, into power-over, into the appropriating reduction of other transcendental forms of life.[48]

The psychotic delirium of appropriation reaches its paroxysm in the conception of life itself as a form of property which, since it belongs to us, we could lose: '[W]e humans [...] tend to cling to life because we think it is our private property. This life is mine, and I do not want to lose this property.'[49] The subject acts as though it were not a living being—a local

---

47 Heidegger, 'Why Poets?', *Off the Beaten Track*, 216.

48 Cf. A. Negri, *The Savage Anomaly: The Power of Spinoza's Metaphysics and Politics*, tr. M. Hardt (Minneapolis: University of Minnesota Press, 1991).

49 F. 'Bifo' Berardi, 'Desire, Pleasure, Senility, and Evolution', *e-flux journal* 106 (February 2020), <https://www.e-flux.com/journal/106/312516/desire-pleasure-senility-and-evolution/>. This point has also been emphasised by Illich in the following terms: '[T]he ideology of possessive individualism has shaped the way life could be talked about as a property.' I. Illich, 'The Institutional Construction of a New Fetish: Human Life', in *In the Mirror of the Past: Lectures and Addresses, 1978–1990* (London: Marion Boyars, 1992), 218–32: 229.

mode of life—and instead understands itself as the owner of life, an owner who will fight—by all means provided by the 'medical nemesis', that is, by the capitalist degradation of a medical science that 'manages life from sperm to worm',[50] which is medicine's own disease—not to lose what it considers its own. The preservation (and the concomitant reification) of life as the property of the individual thus becomes an end in itself, to the detriment of the transient act of living: '[a]fter removing [its] act from the spirit and making it into body, into a lifeless corpse, [the ill subject] wants to make this body eternal. [It] represents eternity to [it]self as the continuance through time of an unchanging body.'[51] The living being subjected to private property, like Hegel's slave, is willing to 'subordinate all things to the fear of death',[52] even its health, even its life: 'for whoever would save "its" life will lose the act of living' (Luke, 9:24–25). And if individual death can be subsumed and rationalised in a trans-individual economy (we have to die in order to make place for others or in order for natural selection to proceed), then the disenchanted realists can still make appeal to a purported 'truth of [collective] extinction' in order to be really convinced that life would be meaningful only under the condition of a sempiternal perpetuation of human existence. This opposition between the transient nature of existence and the meaningfulness of life, the thesis that life would be meaningful only under the condition of not being subject to its disappearance, resumes the most reactive ontotheological tension between temporality and eternity. On this point, we shall always remain thankful and faithful to Heidegger's (Christian) *destruktion* of the ontotheological hierarchy of everlasting presence over living and dying finitude. Death—the fact that we shall individually and (probably) collectively disappear—will never be an argument against a meaningful life. Finitude will never be an argument against the possibility of orienting our transient existence by the infinite regulative ideas of truth, beauty, justice, and love. Let us remember

50 Illich, *In the Mirror of the Past*, 223.

51 Hess, 'The Philosophy of the Act', 253.

52 G. Bataille, 'La guerre et la philosophie du sacré', in *Oeuvres Complètes XII. Articles II 1950–1961* (Paris: Gallimard, 1988).

Mallarmé's *Maître* once more, throwing the dice while sinking into the phenoumenodelic Maelstrom, lost in the 'ultimate ocean of immanence, from which nothing can separate itself, and in which everything loses itself irremediably',[53] knowing that he will never abolish the contingency of temporality, the fragility inherent to every act of transient existence, the vulnerability constitutive of any radical synthesis of the phenoumenodelic spice, while screaming—with his gaze fixed in a constellation—'I will Yes'.

Instead of intensifying separation to the point of the rupture that we have termed *disligation* here, we could attempt to completely annul the separation inherent in individuation through a hypothetical mystical dissolution of the individual in the immanence of an absolute now understood as undifferentiated identity. In Bataille (a 'new [and final] mystic', as Sartre called him) 'communication'—far from being understood as a concertation between separate singular individuals—is a dissipative force, an asymptotic tendency toward indistinctness, the 'dissolution of constituted forms',[54] a tendency to desert the realm of discontinuity—'communication should be understood here in the sense of a fusion, a loss of self, the wholeness of which is only realised through death and of which erotic fusion is an image'[55]—a tendency that is thereby exhibited (claims Bataille) in eroticism, in sacrifice, and in war. That is why the sacred in Bataille is opposed to the principle of the institution and preservation of individuality. In Bataille, it is death—and not the mad exuberance of life, the vertigo of procreation, the ability to institute ever new forms of life and the concomitant improbable worlds—that is 'the privileged sign of the sacred'.[56] In a sense, Bataille conjugates in his own way the ontotheological stance according to which the 'sacred' is somehow 'heterogeneous' to the immanental order of manifestation with its individuated and discontinuous forms. This understanding

---

53 Land, *The Thirst for Annihilation*, 67.

54 G. Bataille, *Eroticism: Death and Sensuality*, tr. M. Dalwood (San Francisco: City Lights, 1986), 17.

55 G. Bataille, *Le Coupable*, *Œuvres complètes V* (Paris: Gallimard, 1973), 508.

56 G. Bataille, 'La guerre et la philosophie du sacré', 54.

of the sphere of individuation as profane is inseparable from the critique of the transcendental operations of the individual: the understanding that renormalises and fragments the pleroma, language and its inherent discrete character, the projects deployed in time and oriented by infinite ideas. Words, projects, scientific knowledge, methodical constructions—all these 'separated operations' in the service of 'utility'—are not understood by Bataille as local modulations of the Word, as vibrating forms of the pneumatic revelation. According to Bataille, every project unfolded in time postpones the sacred intensity of our 'instantaneous' existence and holds back the sacred dissolution of one's self. For Bataille, individuation, separation, and temporalisation constitute a *fall* from the sacred continuity into the profane realm of prosaic language and extended projects that defer the communion. On the contrary, loss, ecstasy, agony, laughter, poetry are all redemptive lines of flight. And yet, 'if he also knew that in something like this [mystical] extinction he could be free of his loneliness and his failure, still he wasn't quite convinced. [...] So he hunted, as a servo valve with a noisy input will, across the Zero, between the two'[57] tendencies, personal reterritorialisation and impersonal dissolution. But these two drives are in fact two sides of the same coin: the hypostasis of a self-sufficient *ego conquero* gorged on properties is an existential impasse that can only conceive 'salvation' in the form of a paroxystic dissolution of the 'ego' into the immensity of the undifferentiated one, as an unrestrained 'work of death'. The mystical path converges with the ontotheological path, and in this sense Bataille is our Jacobi. The thesis that individuation—separation, language, knowledge, work, projects unfolded in time—belong to the realm of the profane continues to fuel a hypertranscendent idea of religiosity according to which redemption entails a movement away from finite, individualised, and transient existence, from an existence deployed in the turbulent realm of life, with its innumerable mutant lifeforms (both separated and interrelated), with all its mediations, deferrals, and spatiotemporalisations, with its prosaic languages, with its transcendentally determined forms of knowledge, with its specious presents weighed down with pasts and futures.

57 Pynchon, *Gravity's Rainbow*, 406.

Both the mystical and the ontotheological paths deny—and this is their main difference from trinitarian Christianity—the divinity of finitude, the mystery of incarnation, the possibility for the discontinuous individual to channel egophanies. The mystical heresy, the monstrous coupling of God and humans ('[t]he fearful enormity of God and [humans] uniting [...]'),[58] privileges the first person of the trinity—the pre-individual unity of the mat(t)er—to the detriment of both self-love (love of the finite I in the devotional acceptance of its singular separated individuality) and the concertation between siblings (of the Holy Spirit). Against any Promethean deification of the subject at the cost of its finitude, Christianity finitises divinity at the cost of its hyper-transcendence. The *Stimmung* proper to trinitarian religion is neither a regressive nostalgia for the primordial undifferentiated One nor an aspiration toward a salvation from finitude by means of an infinitisation of the human. Trinitarian Christianity overcomes both the Promethean foreclosure of castration and the ontotheological impasses of a nostalgic profane present that dreams of a lost sacred unity. In trinitarian Christianity, the religated living one—far from seeking return to the undifferentiated one or salvation from finitude (back to the womb or redeemed from the tomb)—roots itself in a material origin in order to propel itself to the communitarian spirit. The religated persona is rooted in the impersonal life, self-posits and takes care of its own singular individuality, and puts its subjective resources at the service of the transpersonal forms of the spirit. The perichoretic coninsubstantiality of the trinitarian hypostases implies in particular that the third hypostasis—the communitarian life—cannot be understood as a sublation of the second hypostasis's finitude, that is, of the living and dying individual: 'In truth, death is not sublated. [...] Community does not sublate the finitude it exposes. Community itself, in sum, is nothing but this exposition. It is the community of finite beings. [...] The genuine community of mortal beings [...] establishes their impossible communion.'[59] More generally, the relation between the three hypostases

58 F. Hölderlin, 'Remarks on the Oedipus', *Essays and Letters*, tr. J. Adler and C. Louth (London: Penguin, 2009), 323.

59 Nancy, *The Inoperative Community*, 13, 26, 15.

should not be understood in linear time-like terms—either as a subordination (as in Arianism) or as a dialectic sublation—but rather in space-like terms, as a perichoresis through which the impersonal, the personal, and the transpersonal, 'without forfeiture or mutual dissolution of independence, reciprocally interpenetrate each other, [...] inexist in one another',[60] and potentialise one another in a circular manner. Religation brings us back by a 'vicus of recirculation'—'the regenerations of the incarnations of the emanations of the apparentations [of the mamafestations]'[61]—to an intra-trinitarian existence in which 'the divine modes of being mutually condition and permeate one another so completely that one is always in the other two and the other two in the one.[62] [...] [W]e, too, may come to the [roadside] picnic [/ after the Visitation] / With nothing to hide, join the [trance] / As it moves in perichoresis, / Turns about the abiding [vine].'[63]

The entheogenic resurrection of Yesses in each subject releases the conception of the religious from the idea that it would be through the sacrifice of a particular being that 'the community of the faithful goes on communicating with the supreme source of its spiritual life.'[64] In this sense, Christianity sublates the sacrificial logic that seduced thinkers like Bataille and brought them into an ambivalent proximity with the 'heterogeneity' of fascism.[65] In Christianity, the portals to the sacred are half-opened by the personal religation that binds the subject to its own finitude, that allows the individual to acknowledge that its 'castration' provides the slit through which the divine life is refracted in a singular manner, that it is 'only by

60 K. Barth, *Church Dogmatics, Vol. 1.1. The Doctrine of the Word of God*, tr. G.W. Bromiley, G.T. Thomson, and H. Knight (London: T&T Clark, 2009), 103 [§8–12].

61 Joyce, *Finnegans Wake*, 600.

62 Barth, *Church Dogmatics, Vol. 1.1*, 77 [§8–12].

63 W.H. Auden, 'Compline' (*Horae Canonicae*), *Selected Poems*, ed. E. Mendelson (New York: Vintage, 1979), 231.

64 E. Durkheim, *The Elementary Forms of Religious Life*, tr. K.E. Fields (New York: The Free Press, 1995), 30.

65 Cf. G. Bataille, 'The Psychological Structure of Fascism', tr. C.R. Lovitt, *New German Critique* 16 (Winter 1979), 64–87.

means of the crack and at its edges that thought occurs, that anything that is good and great in humanity enters and exits through it.'[66] The Bataillean idea that the institution of a community requires us to squint into the realm of continuity by means of the sacrifice of a particular lifeform tends to foreclose the fact that each lifeform already carries the cross of its finitude, that it is thanks to this finitude that the subject is exposed to myriad forms of pleromatic alterity, that this vulnerable exposure makes the subject permeable to the love that institutes communities, that these spiritual communities are the transpersonal partial totalities that resolve the tension between the impersonal one life and personal singularities, between the continuous and the discontinuous. A Christian community is not formed by periodically reenacting a sacrifice, but instead by experimenting around forms of living, enjoying, suffering, and dying together, by enduring finitude (of the individual and of the community) with love, care, and dignity. The Christian religation is not a dissolution into the oceanic magma of immanence or a salvation from finitude but rather the opposite: an umbilical connexion with the impersonal life that channels the morphogenetic force of individuation and impels the subject to self-posit its singular existence and to enter into communitarian forms of subjectivity.

The pre-Christian element in Bataille's declension of mysticism is not so much the 'oceanic feeling' in itself qua possible umbilical cord capable of linking the separate individual to the underlying vital continuum (a licit 'variety of religious experience' described by Rolland and explained away by Freud in *Civilisation and its Discontents*) as Bataille's double association between the *profane* and *discontinuity* on the one hand and between the *sacred* and *continuity* on the other, that is to say, the idea that individuation—as well as the will to self-posit and preserve itself—is located on the profane side of the divide and is antagonistic to all religiosity. The mystical path thus understood seems to confuse the overcoming of isolation—religation—with the dissolution of individuation, as if love were not a possible diagonal alternative to the false dilemma posed by that set of identifications,

66 Deleuze, *The Logic of Sense*, 160.

*individuation* = *isolation* and *communication* = *dissolution*. If the opposition that structures Bataille's (a)theology is the distinction between the *sacred* (continuity) and the *profane* (discontinuity), the distinction that structures trinitarian religion as we understand it here is the distinction between *sickness* (disligation) and *healing* (threefold religation through love). Paraphrasing Lacan and Nancy, we could say that love is precisely what makes up for the lack of mystical fusion, that 'communication' between separate individuals makes up for the lack of communion. Individuation is not necessarily solitude and disligation; and communication is not a fusional communion, a dissolution of individuality. Truly Christian communication is a concertation, a harmonisation, a 'consonance of free beings'[67] as condition of possibility for the emergence of new symbionts of the spirit, the wholly spiritual capacity to compose individuals and integrate their experiences into spiritual communities. Communication relies on the *holonisation* of individuals—that is, on the simultaneous affirmation of both their *singular individuality* and their *partness* with respect to the higher forms of subjectivity in which they participate.[68] As we shall see later, the religation of the autonomous, singular, and separate persona with the one life, with the impersonal mat(t)er, is one (but only one) of the vertices of trinitarian religious practice.

The association of the sacred with the 'frenzy of destruction' (and the concomitant sacrificial logic) results from the fact that, at the dawn of modernity and in certain regions of the planet, humanity lost its capacity to 'live from the powers of the cosmos', the ability to be intoxicated by communal communication with the cosmos.[69] In this context, technics ceased to be a tool for steering the '[transcendental] relation between nature and [humans]'—for allowing the contact between humanity and the pleroma to be mediated by new and different transcendental framings—and became

67 F. Hölderlin, *Hyperion & Selected Poems*, tr. W.R. Trask (New York: Continuum, 1990), 117.

68 Cf. A. Koestler, *The Ghost in the Machine* (London: Pan, 1970), 369.

69 Benjamin, 'To the Planetarium', 59.

a weapon for the extractivist mastery of nature. As Benjamin concludes, '[l]iving substance conquers the frenzy of destruction only in the ecstasy of procreation'. When sacrality ceases to be conveyed by the 'ecstasy of procreation', by the capacity of *natura naturans* to ceaselessly institute new lifeforms and constitute new lifeworlds, by the human capacity to modify the transcendental framing that defines its horizon of experience, and thus to engender new transcendental types of subjectivity, when all of this happens, only the 'frenzy of destruction' can satisfy the drive of the absolute that continues to pulse in humanity. When the paramount religious imperative—*Thou shalt live!*—ceases to be operative, no *Thou shalt not kill* can prevent the release of the death drive and, in particular, the capitalistic thanentropic tendency to always obtain a surplus value of *jouissance* to the detriment of desire.

If, as Benjamin argues in 'To the Planetarium', the 'ecstatic trance' is the only experience in which we 'gain certain knowledge of what is nearest to us and what is remotest from us, and never of one without the other', then the reactivation of the communal contact with the living forces of the cosmos cannot take place within the framework of a unilateral reterritorialisation upon the terrestrial ark, but requires combining 'what is nearest to us', the maximum implantation upon the living mat(t)er, with 'what is remotest from us', the maximal cosmic projection toward the supernatural sky. Taking into account that even the cosmos depicted by contemporary cosmology is also an 'image of the world' correlated to our own transcendental resources, this 'cosmic' projection should be understood—far beyond interstellar voyages and spatiotemporal vastness—as the maximal phenoumenodelic immersion in the trans-mundane pleroma that we can afford. The genius of Christianity lies in maintaining that the tension between divine infinitude and human finitude is not solved by a return toward the original undifferentiated unity but that a third term, the Holy Spirit, is necessary. As we shall see, the third trinitarian hypostasis prescribes neither an unilateral landing that forecloses the trans-mundane beyond nor a launch out of the gravitational field of the terrestrial ark, but rather a 'backtowards' vineal movement (*axis mundi*) which at the same time roots us into the self-secluding earth and projects us toward the supernatural sky: 'In the end, the liana is nothing other than this race toward the light, which rises from the moist and opaque flesh of the undergrowth to reach the emerald drape of the canopy. [...] [T]he lianas teach us not so much to "land" [...] as to stretch the bow: to maintain the tension between earth and sky.'[70] The alternative between a nostalgic primitivism and an accelerating modernity is a false dilemma: it is only by being rooted in the first hypostasis—the mat(t)er—that the living can sprout into the third one (the Holy Spirit); it is not possible 'to go into outer space unless you count down to zero.'[71] The dehiscence of new forms of spirit is an upwards projection propelled by laying down roots: only the aboriginal can become a spiritual absolunaut, only the 'Indian' ('the one who belongs to the land')[72] can become a shaman. The conceptual character of the shaman combines in a singular manner two seemingly contradictory features, that of being *autochthonous*—that is, not alienated or estranged—and that of being released from any form of transcendental anchorage. These two features become consistent if we identify the instance to which the shaman belongs as the first trinitarian hypostasis, that is, as the impersonal force of material life: 'By "autochthony" I do not mean the alleged authentic purity of the first inhabitants of a territory, but the intimate relationship that a human community can establish in any place with the "chthonian" powers, the elemental [morphogenetic] powers of life.'[73] In order to perform phenoumenodelic mutations between transcendental types and integrate different Umwelten, the shaman radicalises its entanglement with the living fabric, with the impersonal flesh, with the vital milieu, thereby enacting in its own existence a materialist critique of alienation. Whereas the originality of the autochthonous is concomitant with its speculative mobility, the non-originality of the foreign is attendant

---

70 D. Touam Bona, *Sagesse des lianes. Cosmopoétique du refuge, 1* (Post-éditions, 2021), 57–58.

71 Sun Ra, quoted in P. Youngquist, *A Pure Solar World: Sun Ra and the Birth of Afrofuturism* (Austin: University of Texas Press, 2016), 215.

72 E. Viveiros de Castro, 'Les involontaires de la patrie', *Multitudes* 69 (2017), 123–28: 125.

73 Touam Bona, *Sagesse des lianes*, 1, 74.

to 'the belief in something final, fixed, immutably permanent; the belief in a limit, on this side of which free life pursues its sport but which life is unable ever to break through, to dissolve and flow into'.[74] The estrangement (*Entfremdung*) of the foreign with respect to the vital milieu that supports and contains its existence reaches its paroxystic expression in the ontology of death, that is, in the thesis that life is a local improbable exception taking place and time in a lifeless background that can be conquered and capitalised with total impunity: '[The outsider] necessarily believes in death as the first and the last, as the original source of all things—even of life. [...] We have called this belief in death, as opposed to an original living people, foreignism. This foreignism [...] will reveal itself in their actual life also, as quiet resignation to the now unalterable necessity of our being, as the abandonment of all hope of improving ourselves or others through freedom, as the propensity to use ourselves and all others as they are, and to draw from their being the greatest possible advantage to ourselves [...].'[75]

The individuation of every living being subsequently seems to lead to a bifurcation point which forks into a radicalisation of separation in the form of disligation on the one hand and the mystical heresy's tendency toward dissolution on the other hand. Both disligation and mystical communion are attempts to unite the human and the divine at the cost of human finitude. In the former, this comes in the form of a projective infinitisation of the detached human subjective type (Prometheus definitively unbound!), while in the latter it comes in the form of a mystical fusion between the human and the divine (the monstrous communion of God and humans!). But in both cases (total disligation or complete indifferentiation) we forfeit the relationship and the tension between the relative and the absolute, between the personal and the impersonal, between the finite and the infinite. We thus lose the possibility of thinking an absolute that only reveals itself in the

74 Fichte, *Addresses to the German Nation*, 86.

75 Ibid., 86. Regarding the sequence Fichte, Hess, Marx see F. Fischbach, '"Possession" versus "expression": Marx, Hess et Fichte', in E. Renault (ed.), *Lire les Manuscrits de 1844* (Paris: PUF, 2008).

phenomenological clearings constituted by the finite living. In Christian terms, 'the threat both of being merged into everything, of being confused, and that of being distinguished, of being set apart from everything'[76] closes off access to the possibility of conceiving a religion articulated around *incarnation*, a religion capable of understanding the finite living subject as a necessary moment of the immanental theogonical procession.

However, there is a third alternative that diagonalises this false dilemma between absolute separation (the ontotheological path) and absolute fusion (the mystical path). This third position consists in trying to sublate (in the strict sense of overcoming by preserving) the abstract opposition between the living and the one life, that is, to religate the individual as a finite and singular living person both to the impersonal one life and to the transpersonal community of the living. According to this conception, the properly religious life consists in sublating disligation while preserving singular individuality, in living 'the intimate union of our [singularly determined, separate, and finite] life with the divine life[77] [that begets us and flows through us]; religion is the inner relationship of the [finite living one] to the [infinite] life that generates it [in its separated individuality] through generating itself.[78] [...] [A]n act of union to unite in bonds of schismacy.'[79] It is precisely through the resolute affirmation of one's separate, finite and singular character—and not through the mystical denial of one's individuality and relative autonomy—that the religated individual can fulfil its function as a local and singular operator of the self-revelation of life. Its determination (*Bestimmung*) coincides with its voca(lisa)tion (*Bestimmung*), with its singular modulation of the pneuma, of the living Word. The incarnation into a finite and singular lifeform that sprouts out of the womb, breathes, and treads into the cold soil of the tomb is thus a

76 Goddard, *La philosophie fichtéenne de la vie*, 100.

77 Ibid., 218.

78 V. Caruana and M. Henry, 'Entretien avec Michel Henry', *Philosophique* 3 (2000): 69–80, <http://journals.openedition.org/philosophique/230>.

79 Joyce, *Finnegans Wake*, 585.

necessary stage in Christian theogenesis.[80] In this context, to be an avatar of the second trinitarian hypostasis means to live one's own finite existence, one's own determinate individuation, as a local singular mode of the divine procession ('none of us can grasp [this revelation, "manifest and dazzling as the unbearable brightness of a thousand suns..."] in its fullness, but at most sense or glimpse it, under the unique bias and illumination provided to each of us by our own existence'):[81] neither the finitude of the separated individual nor the disappropriating death represents a fall from the divine that needs to be redeemed through mystical dissolution or medical salvation. It's only through the tonic affirmation of liberty, of the subject's determined voca(lisa)tion, of its autonomy as a finite, concrete and desiring individual—contracted in its vibrating being-there—that the subject qua singular living being is religated to the impersonal life as something universal. How does love religate to the *universal* life? By exalting the concrete *singularity* of each lifeform beyond *particularities*, that is, beyond transcendental types, beyond totemic clans, beyond species, beyond properties that distinguish and classify (e.g. being an elephant, being pink, having wings), beyond the distinctions introduced by the law (natives and foreigners, innocents and criminals, Greeks and Jews). The free individual is a concrete mode of the universal, a probing tentacle of impersonal life that became so singular in its existential concreteness—so ungraspable when we try to consider it as a mere particular—that it can broadcast unforeseeable visions, actions, and concepts. By stripping the subject from its properties, religation exhibits and exposes the subject as a singular existing mode of the insubstance. To singularly participate in

80 As Goddard writes, commenting on Jakob Böhme, 'Böhme also rejects the mystical path of fusion with the divine, that of the poor Eckhartian man: it is not by absorption of the self into the One, without distinction from the Deity, that [human beings realise their destiny]. It is on the contrary through realising that which is most personal, most determined, that [they fulfil their] essential function which is to incarnate God[, to exist life]. Finitude and determination are not imperfections[, but necessary conditions for the revelation].' Goddard, 'Incarnation et philosophie dans l'idealisme allemand (Schelling, Hegel)', 160.

81 Grothendieck, *La clef des songes*, 152.

the universal is not to situate oneself at 'the point where everyone loves like everyone else, but [at] that point where everyone loves in their own way. It is at the very moment when the living being persists stubbornly in its [singularity] that it affirms itself as universal.[82] [...] Few philosophies have felt this truth better than Spinoza's, whose fundamental assertion is precisely that the singular is not separate from the true [insubstance] of things and that what is most [singular] in it is also what is most universal.'[83]

Religation does not *save* us—from risk, from finitude, from predators, from the pain associated with individuation, from birth and death—it does not promise any sweet hereafter, but it can *cure* the arche-malady that is disligation, reimplanting the finite individual in the abyssal life that exists within and through it, disselving its alleged egocentric self-sufficiency so that the impersonal life can bear it once more, reactivating in its own flesh the dreaming power of morphogenesis, its transcendental plasticity, tempering and tuning the living one out in the open so that it can ring out its singular note, placing it once more at the service of the self-revelation of the infinite life that it locally incarnates. Religion is an experimental practice intended to 'reexist' the arche-disease of 'disexistence'.[84] What the cure reactivates in the ill being are 'the forces of a life that is larger, more active, more affirmative and richer in possibilities [than the life of an essentialised subject that abides in a reified world] [...], the forces that come from [the pleromatic] outside',[85] the living forces that ceaselessly burst through the particular symbolic orders, that continually break through the impermeable membranes of the disligated clots; the forces that awaken the subjects from the intraumweltic forms of neurotic disenchanted 'realism' to the material dreaminess. The religation does not save, but dissolves the commodification associated with every appropriative gesture and reinstates that which has been appropriated to the common realm of life.

---

82 Deleuze, 'Mathesis, Science and Philosophy', 145.

83 M. Henry, *Le bonheur de Spinoza* (Paris: PUF, 2004), 142.

84 Viveiros de Castro, 'Les involontaires de la patrie', 127.

85 Deleuze, *Foucault*, 92.

The idealist foreclosure of the naturalcultural institution of individuals from impersonal living flesh, the canonisation of the subject as a self-grounding and self-sufficient last instance—as substance *causa sui* and not as finite mode of the immanental insubstance—this hypostasis of the ego qua foundation (the unbinding of Prometheus) is the only arche-disease. A living being disligated from life can only aspire to survive by exhausting its life reserves, by living life in the manner of a daily denial of death. This amounts to giving up on living life as a local and polyphanic potentiation of revelation—as 'the yest and the ist'[86] and the willst—in order to live it exclusively as a negation of the negation of life. A society that forces its members to live just to survive is a society that deepens the arche-disease of disligation.[87] A living being disligated from life prefers merely to survive in sickness and face a disenlivened death than to die in health, to preserve its 'bare life' rather than to afford the risk of living a desiring and meaningful life, to become a 'slave' rather than risking its life in a 'fight to death'. But '[p]ersonal life and its preservation can never be an end, but only a means'[88] of affirming life in the interweaving of its impersonal, individual, and collective dimensions. It is not death that opposes life, but disease: 'All [human beings] should die alive', writes Sony Labou Tansi,[89] 'for to be abandoned by [life] is more cruel than death.'[90] What stands in the way of a meaningful life (that is, of a life that can generate a non-preexisting meaning) is not the certainty of death or the 'truth of extinction', but the

86 Joyce, *Finnegans Wake*, 597.

87 '[O]ur society believes in nothing more than bare life. [We] are ready to sacrifice practically everything [...] when faced with the risk of getting sick [...]. Bare life, and the fear of losing it, is not something that unites people: rather, it blinds and separates them. [...] What is a society that values nothing more than survival?' G. Agamben, *Where Are We Now? The Epidemic as Politics*, tr. V. Dani (Lanham, MD: Rowman and Littlefield, 2021).

88 Fichte, *La Doctrine de l'État (1813)*, 96; *Leçons sur des contenus variés de philosophie pratique*, 96.

89 S. Labou Tansi, *Encre, sueur, salive et sang* (Paris: Seuil, 2015).

90 Luther, quoted in H. Corbin, 'A propos de Luther', *Le Semeur*, 1 March 1932, 289.

arche-disease that affects those living ones who strive to save themselves from finitude, from death. The 'salvation' promised by the capitalistic degeneration of medicine is nothing but a techno-pharmacological attempt to fix the psycho-physiological disfunctionalities so that we can continue to feed capitalistic enjoyment and perpetuate the arche-disease of disligation. '[J]ust as the Christian religion [in its ontotheological modality] proposed salvation through the cult, so does medicine target health through therapy. The first is about sin and the other is about illness, but the analogy is clear. Health in this sense is nothing other than a secularisation of that "eternal life" that the Christians hoped to obtain through their cultural practices.'[91] Health in the sense in which we understand it here relies on the acceptance that 'eternal life'—as well as any other declension of the ontotheological 'beyond'—is a myth that aggravates the arche-disease of the immanental life that we effectively embody, here and now. And the only cure for this arche-disease is, by definition, to be religated back to life, to embrace and take care of the crack, the *Spaltung* ('the Grand Canyon of the world, the "crack" of the [finite] self, the dismembering of God'[92] into multifarious forms of life), to dissolve the self-sufficient causa-suiness of the subject so that impersonal life can wash through it once again, resuming control of the living, affirming in and through the individual its impersonal power, its bursting morphogenetical force. To be religated to life requires that we pass through mourning—a purge. As with multiphase rockets that break away from each of their segments when—having run out of fuel—they pass from being propellants to being dead weight, the cure requires a de-identification with that which is already dead in the individual. The living lives by releasing itself from dead weight, letting it all fall freely away, extricating itself from that Etruscan form of torture where the living body is tied to a dead body—face to face, torso to torso—so that the rotting of the dead passes into the living.[93]

---

91 G. Agamben, 'Where is Science Going? An Interview with Professor Giorgio Agamben', by A. Pensotti, *Organisms: Journal of Biological Sciences* 4:2 (2020): 105–9.

92 Deleuze, *The Logic of Sense*, 160.

93 See R. Negarestani, 'The Corpse Bride. Thinking with Nigredo', in R. Mackay (ed.), *Collapse IV: Concept-Horror* (Falmouth: Urbanomic, 2012), 129–61.

The 'great health'—'our own manner of being pious'[94]—relies on the subjective capacity to embrace finitude, that is, to let go, to lose, to endure the work and play of mourning. Instead of remaining a patient, the cure requires a willingness to actively seek out where the risk stalks, to delve into the 'crystal forest', to move toward that temperate zone where the plant that heals grows. The cure entails a 'passession', a subjective destitution by means of which the subject—far from being dissolved into the one life, far from any denial of its finite individuality—allows the impersonal life to pass through it as a singular individual: 'unity comes about at the level of concrete [person]; very far from transcending the human condition, it is its exact description.'[95] To be rebound, to be religated, to be revined, is to 'stitch yourself into the godless [insubstance, the Source, the Dreamer, the Mat(t)er][96] that assimilates and produces you as if you produced yourself'.[97]

Religation is understood by Fichte as a therapethic act of sewing, a suture that binds without effacing the seam (*Kintsugi*). The religation that reimplants the subject in its native life reactivates its birth—bringing about its *resurrection*—in the form of a transmutation of every supposedly subjective essence into living existence: 'Fichte, the son of a merchant, knows that real sewing separates just as much as it unites—that it unites and separates by means of one and the same gesture. [...] The absolute [...] is a *Band* [...]. *Band* designates the narrow band by which pieces are tied, patched, knotted together without making them indistinct. [...] This gesture is the gesture of traditional medicine itself. That which Pierre Fatumbi-Verger translates as "cut to assemble", and which is better written as "*séparassembler*" ["Connecticut, Connect-I-cut"]:[98] the verb of the "ofò"—the active magical formula—of resurrection and transformation.'[99] This clinical act

94 Deleuze, *The Logic of Sense*, 161.

95 Deleuze, 'Mathesis, Science and Philosophy', 146.

96 Cf. Grothendieck, *La clef des songes*, 15.

97 Artaud, *Les Tarahumaras*, 17.

98 Deleuze and Guattari, *Anti-Oedipus*, 37.

99 J.-C. Goddard, 'Fichte. Le hetre et le palmier', in J.-C. Lemaitre (ed.), *Jean-Marie*

of stitching, of religation to the vital power to institute lifeforms, cannot be carried out by the subject alone. It requires an impersonal force (*Kraft*) capable of drawing the subject out of its essentialisation and the attendant reifying naturalisation of its world that is typical of disligated existence. This force that reveals the transmutative power of the impersonal life within the finite person, that sutures the latter and forms a *Band* that anchors the subject without diluting its singular determinacy—this disappropriating force capable of wiping out any assumed self-sufficiency of the finite subject—is incorporated and reactivated in the living by means of that which we shall call *medicine*. Medicine is 'inherently indigestible, "intolerable". A medicine is not digested any better or worse, it is never digested, being an absolute other with respect to the organism.'[100] That is why medicine is a *pharmakon* that might force the subject to vomit. Initially, vomiting externalises the excess that the subject cannot incorporate into its breathing cycle, the real surplus that the subject has ingested but cannot really afford—what the transcendental valve regulating the receptivity-spontaneity conversion cannot assimilate without putting the subject's own integrity at risk. In this regard, vomiting is a coping strategy that allows us to avoid the traumatic vacuolisation of excess, of that which cannot be breathed.[101] Through vomiting, 'the organism recovers, reappropriates itself, initiates a "process" that enables it to regain possession of its "sense of self" and its "subjectivity"'.[102] The remainder, excluded by the transcendental system

---

*Vaysse: cartographies de la pensée à la fin de la metaphysique* (Hildesheim: Georg Olms Verlag, 2015), 254–55.

100 Derrida, *Glas*, 132.

101 What every transcendental system excludes 'is what does not allow itself to be digested, or represented, or stated—does not allow itself to be transformed into auto-affection by exemplorality [exemplary orality or the essence of speech, involving the self-affective structure of hearing oneself speak]. It is an irreducible heterogeneity which cannot be eaten either sensibly or ideally and which—this is the tautology—by never letting itself be swallowed must therefore *cause itself to be vomited*.' J. Derrida, 'Economimesis', tr. R. Klein, *Diacritics* 2:11 (1981), 2–25: 21.

102 Derrida, *Glas*, 133.

(the unspeakable, the impossible, the unthinkable, the indiscernible, the meaningless), beyond any sort of absolute mystification (far from being an 'irreducible heterogeneity' as Derrida proposes), is a remainder only in relation to the transcendental apparatus in question, an outside that might be breathed out by instances of other transcendental types without necessarily calling the integrity of the subject into question ('Would not all ecstasy in one of the worlds be humiliating sobriety in the complementary world?'[103] Would not 'someone's noise' be 'another one's signal'?). However, this 'feeling of self, of one's subjectivity' is the opposite of a reterritorialisation of the subject into a supposed subjective essence or reaffirmation of its self-sufficiency. In fact, more radically, the medicine forces the subject to vomit even on an empty stomach, a process in which vomiting becomes the vomiting of oneself. In this case, the vomit acts as an existentialisation operator which disappropriates the subject, forcing it to detach itself from that which, after having been incorporated, inhaled, or scoffed is not restored—in a transmuted form—to the vital flow, but is fixed, essentialised, reified, appropriated, accumulated, converted into capital. The living spice must continue flowing, inspired and expired by the insubstance's breathing modes, converted by the latter into phenoumenodelic visions—starships, deserts, water—that short-circuit the intra-umweltic extensions. That which does not return to life in the harmonious oscillations of breath enters into a state of cumulative reserve in the form of property, capital, that which is possessed and with which the subject, to a greater or lesser extent, tends to identify. Property is imprisoned life—a detention of the living Word—which vomit restores to its own flow; property burdens the subject—the more you have, the less you express your own life, the less you exist life[104]—pulling it back from the ek-static character of existence into an essentialist inertia. Thanks to the purge, the subject realises that it is possible to exist life beyond

103 W. Benjamin, 'Surrealism: The Last Snapshot of the European Intelligentsia', tr. E. Jephcott, *Selected Writings, Volume 2: Part 1, 1927–1930* (Cambridge, MA: The Belknap Press of Harvard University Press, 2005), 210.

104 Cf. K. Marx, *Economic and Philosophical Manuscripts*, tr. M. Milligan (New York: Prometheus Books, 1988), 119.

the essentialisation of the I and the reification of the not-I. The *pharmakon* is both a remedy and a poison at the same time, since it cures by intoxicating (acting as a toxin from the perspective of the sick person), revealing the disease that afflicts the *ego conquero*, catalysing and amplifying the noxious character of appropriation, allowing the subject to assume his transient being-there in life. Medicine introduces a hiatus between the subject and that which is de-vivifying in it, a hiatus that allows it to externalise both the appropriated and the indigestible, reincorporating them—'feeling like a Great lost Serpent-seraph vomiting in consciousness of the Transfiguration to come'[105]—into the rhythm of its breath. The *pharmakon* cannot be identified with a particular substance;[106] the *pharmakon* is a function, a function which dissolves that which tends to be crystallised in the form of a subjective essence, that which was not reintegrated into the rhythmic helicoids of individual and collective breathing, that which obstructs the existential modulation of the living Word, that which hinders the transmutation of the life that we receive and channel into volatile 'figures of joy'. In the last instance, even the ingestion of a substance becomes unnecessary ('The effect of the priestly act extends beyond the consecrated host to the cosmos itself. The entire realm of matter is slowly but irresistibly affected by this great consecration'):[107] vomiting is already an effect of the visionary trance itself, of the *mareaçao*, of the affect associated with being embarked across pleroma, swallowing (perceiving, feeling, understanding) the deliquescent insubstance. Phenoumenodelic deluge submerges the Cartesian *ego conquero* in the baroquodelic Maelstrom (*Catatau!*). And the incorporation

105 Cf. A. Ginsberg and W. Burroughs, *The Yage Letters* (San Francisco: City Lights Books, 1975), 54.

106 'The "essence" of the *pharmakon* lies in the way in which, having no stable essence, no "proper" characteristics, it is not, in any sense (metaphysical, physical, chemical, alchemical) of the word, a *substance*.' J. Derrida, *Dissemination*, tr. B. Johnson (London: Athlone Press, 1981), 125–26; 'The *pharmakon* would be [...] antisubstance [we would instead say *insubstance*] itself' (ibid., 70).

107 P. Teilhard de Chardin, *Hymn of the Universe*, tr. Gerald Vann (London: Collins, 1970), 6.

of entheogenic modes of insubstance—inspiration, predation, perception, empathy, understanding, hospitality—is a *theophagy*: 'I drink blood and God. [...] The [religated ones] are so much drunk with God's divinity, so much they are lost and sunk in him'.[108] This is why 'Spinoza [—addicted to (in)substance—] is a God-intoxicated man'.[109]

Goddard, in his contemporary revival and continuation of the Fichtean project, argues that the *Doctrine of Science* is nothing more or less than a performative-theoretical concoction of a substitute for actual medicine, for the psychotropic sacrament ('in the sense of that [imaginative force] that is capable of orienting the *psyche* by means of the formation of images and visions') that can convert one to the only religion worthy of the name, the one that effectively brings about a religation with the immanent one life (in which) we are: 'This is why the *Wissenschaftlehre* is without object but consists in a thoroughgoing pre-construction of an active object. [...] The uniqueness of this object is that unlike, for example, the ofò, it doesn't mobilise any plant, animal, or mineral elements. It does not require the grinding of any plant or mineral elements with a stone. The elements it grinds are theoretical. They are the abstract elements of the Western theoretical world. The similarity between Fichtean pragmatic psychiatry and indigenous medicinal pragmatics is perfect. But it is only a similarity. The theory that serves as an inductor and a screen also serves as material. It replaces living matter, absent from the process, whose trituration and ingestion are nevertheless the real conditions of traditional resurrection-metamorphosis. The most flagrant shortage is that of plants. It is well known that Dionysian transformation does not occur without the intoxication prompted by the ingestion of fermented plants. We philosophers can get drunk on wine or, like Schelling, on opium, but this practice remains outside the medicinal process, it is exercised so to speak privately [...]. Europe is seriously lacking in psychotropic plants: barely twenty [...]. However, no transformation is achieved without a psychotropic plant: yakoana, datura,

108 Silesius, *Cherubinischer Wanderer*, Book I, §209 & §210.

109 'Spinoza ist ein gottrunkener Mensch.' Novalis, *Schriften, Dritter Band* (Stuttgart: Kohlhammer Verlag, 1968), HKA 562, 651.

peyote, etc. That is, without a direct, terrifying experience of death [...]. How to proceed without plants?'[110]

Religion thus understood (and not its obscurantist and superstitious degeneration) is the 'opium [the *natem*, the *floripondio*, the *Ciguri*, the *salvia divinorum*] of the masses', a practice of concocting entheogens capable of religating the living to the morphogenetic force of transformation active in every birth, every death, every resurrection. While the first coming of Yesses sanctioned finitude and death as necessary and irredeemable moments of the theogonical procession, its second coming brings forth the religating sacrament by means of which the immanental godhead is resurrected in the atmanic depths of the disligated subject. Yes, the finite existing individual is separate, exposed, vulnerable, thrown into the risk. But this does not necessarily mean that it is condemned to the illness of disligation. By sacralising finitude and by gifting the sacrament that religates the finite subject, the two comings of Yesses ('indead it be!')[111] deconstruct the onto-theological identification between reli(ga)tion and a hypothetical salvation with respect to finitude: '[I]n the Rites of Ciguri [the Tarahumaras] have preserved the organic gate of the ordeal, by which our being, which the impure assembly of [foreign] beings has repelled, knows that it is linked to that [realm beneath the] bodily perceptions where the [wild] Heart [of divine life] is consumed in calling us. [...] The Tarahumaras of Mexico [...] have preserved in themselves the igneous image of this Source which they call the [Daughter] of [Life]. One day, say the priests of the TUTUGURI, the Great Celestial Healer appeared as if born from the open lips of the [female sun], THE DESIRER, [Her Mother in immanence]. And [She Her]self was that sun, with The First [Caravaca] Cross in H[er] hand, and [She] struck; and other Solar Crosses, and Doubles of Suns, were born of H[er], and came forth at every Syllable that this Mouth of Celestial Crosses, in hosts of light, impressed upon the immensity. [...] And this Healer of the Infinite had given them a plant in h[er] Journeys, to reopen to the tempted and weary soul, the gates of [Life]. And this plant is CIGURI.

110 Goddard, 'Fichte. Le hetre et le palmier', 255–56.

111 Joyce, *Finnegans Wake*, 560.

[...] [T]he Peyote given by [Yesses] [...] takes the soul behind its back and rests it in [enlivening force and revealing] light, as it comes [from the very bowels of Life]; and keeping it in this [immanensity] it teaches it to distinguish between itself and that unfathomable energy which is like the infinite manifold of its own capacities and which begins where, billions of billions of so-called beings, we die out and dry up.'[112]

Thanks to its second coming, Yesses can no longer be understood as a determinate historical figure distinct from the rest of the living beings, but must rather be understood as the arche-type of the religating ones, of those who engage in the healing process of transmuting their lives and deaths into transient rubber temples through which life makes ingression and lives, enjoys, thinks, suffers, decides, constructs, loves, and dies. If we amalgamate Fulcanelli's identification *philosopher's stone = universal medicine* (elixir of life or 'drinking Go[l]d')[113] with Jung's identification *philosopher's stone = Yesses*, we can understand the alchemical concoction and ingestion of the living elixir as an entheogenic process by means of which Yesses resurrects in the finite subject. Through this second coming, life reassumes its infinite power over the living ones and reimplants them in its material matrix, in its immanental Yes. The medicine is called universal because is intended to heal from the ultimate arche-disease, that of surviving disligated from life. The synthesis announced by the German idealists between the morphogenetic eruption of the *natura naturans* and the phenomenological clearings constituted by transcendental subjects—the tragic synthesis between Spinozist Dionysus and Kantian Apollo—can be understood as a philosophical conceptualisation of the alchemical brewing of the elixir of life out of the wedding between (living) force and (revealing) light in a Christian athenorial ecclesia.

And Fichte's response to the question *How to proceed without plants?* is Kantian: ultimately the healing plant grows 'in the depths of the human soul' (Kant), where the imagination (*Einbildungskraft*) operates as a faculty

112 Artaud, *Les Tarahumaras*, 111–13.

113 Fulcanelli, *The Dwellings of the Philosophers*, tr. D. Bernardo (Sojourner Books, 2021), 73.

capable of performing the respiratory synthesis between the receptive and spontaneous capacities of the subject of experience. The schematic *Band* of sensible receptivity and conceptual spontaneity—the synthesis made by the transcendental faculty that Kant calls imagination between the capacity to receive what comes and the capacity to give it an experienceable form, to transform it into a new image—can only come from that unity that precedes all polarisation between an I (the subject of experience) and a not-I (offered to experience), from the immanental one that exfoliates—through a great maze of twists, alliances, excitations, intricacies, resonances, symbiosis, predations, bifurcations, and convolutions—in the form of a diversity of interconnected breathing local modes. But 'the principle of the maze is clear. It is the device of something turning back upon itself so as to seem to be other, and the turns have been so many and so dizzyingly complex that I am quite bewildered. The principle is that all dualities and opposites are not disjoined but polar; they do not encounter and confront one another from afar; they exfoliate from a common center. Ordinary thinking conceals polarity and relativity because it employs *terms*, the terminals or ends, the poles, neglecting what lies between them. The difference of front and back, to be and not to be, hides their unity and mutuality.'[114] Now, writes Fichte, 'life is precisely this final unity in which duality [between I and not-I] is not thereby abolished, but instead permanently endures [...]'.[115] Transcendental imagination—that psychedelic flower bud which is planted deep within the living soul and reactivated by the consumption of the *pharmakon*—is the faculty capable of actively constituting 'images' out of the real that comes, for it is coupled to the one life which underlies all polarisation between I and not-I. The pre-individual unity of life is channelled by the imagination and transmuted into a schematic unity between receptivity and spontaneity. Through imagination, the living can

114 Watts, *The Joyous Cosmology*, 48.

115 Fichte, *The Way Towards the Blessed Life; Or, the Doctrine of Religion*, 2 [translation modified]. As Deleuze also states in his Fichtean youth, '[t]he unity, the hierarchy beyond all anarchic duality, is the unity of life itself, which delineates a third order, irreducible to the other two.' Deleuze, 'Mathesis, Science and Philosophy', 143.

plug into the impersonal vital force thanks to which they sprout into the world, to the insubstance that narcotises them, opening themselves up to the real (receptivity) and actively informing it (spontaneity), extracting unique images from the living pleroma. Each scission of the one life into an I and a correlative not-I generates a potential difference through which new images of the pleroma are discharged. This immanental force flooding into the subject causes 'the terms separated in any separation, in any lethal division, to float [*Schweben*]',[116] enabling both (a) the *schematic Band* between the transcendental hospitality of the subject and the arriving other and (b) the *religating Band* that reimplants the subject into the one life. Fichte's sonnet asks, 'Where does this force which fills my eye come from, such that it [instils] deformity [into stable forms], transforms [the dark] night [of the phosphene] into [a rainbow of dolphins],[117] making order from disorder, life from death',[118] reality from dreams? This Fichtean question admits of a univocal response: that imaginary force that springs up within the subject toward new actions and visions is an umbilical tentacle—a kundalinean appendage—of life itself: 'In this indefinite weave of time and space, who leads me to the [living] fountain of the beautiful, true, good, and delightful, into which all my striving is submerged and appeased, [...] I let my gaze fall upon [Guaraci]'s eye, that deep, calm, clear, [green] and pure flame of light, clear unto itself. Since then this eye has remained in my depths and is in my being—the [Living] One lives my life and looks out through my eyes'[119] and through the eyes of the ferns, the shells, the frogs, the nebulas, the stones, the oceans, the stellar dust.

The impersonal life is the first of the three hypostases that regulate the practices of religation. The religation through which the finite and singular individual becomes permeable to the infinite and impersonal

116 Goddard, 'Fichte. Le hêtre et le palmier', 257.

117 Perlongher, *Chorreo de las iluminaciones*, 231.

118 J.G. Fichte, 'Sonnet' (1802), *Doctrine de la science 1801–1802 et textes annexes*, vol. 1, tr. A. Philonenko (Paris: Vrin, 1987), 191, <https://www.jstor.org/stable/40901600>.

119 Ibid., 191.

life, to the immanental mat(t)er, is an initiation, a process by means of which the living being enters into the kingdom of infinite life as a finite being: 'The initiate is the [finite] living [being] in its relationship with the infinite'[120] mat(t)er. Religation as the coalescence of the *unconscious life of experience* and the *conscious experience of life* in the concrete human being is the work of medicine, which reimplants the subject of the experience of life in the impersonal and singular life that it embodies locally. Curative medicine sutures the excision, forms a Möbius *Band* that indiscerns the personal vortices and the impersonal stream, reimplanting the concrete human being in the point of indistinction between objective experience (in particular the experience of its own body qua object or *Körper*) and the experience of living (in particular the experience of its own body qua incarnated life or *Leib*). In concrete existence, the touched (objectivated) hand and the touching (experiencing, living) hand are indissoluble phases of one and the same flesh: 'My hand feels touched as well as it touches. Real [immanence] means that, nothing more.[121] [...] [T]he eye that sees is simultaneously the eye that is seen. Every theophany [...] accomplishes itself simultaneously in these two aspects.'[122] Relig(at)ion 'is therefore neither a science [of constituted objects], nor a [transcendental] philosophy [of the constituting subject]. It is something else, [a living experience] of life'[123] in the amphiboly carried by the double sense of the genitive: an experience of life that is nothing other than a local manifestation of life itself, a fleshy spark of the self-experiencing life.

This rhythmic conversion, mediated by the imagination, between a receptivity (to extraterrestrial signals arriving from the supernatural sky) and an expressive spontaneity (of what is concocted in the intimate bowels of the subject) is—as Lezama Lima instructs us—language qua generalised expressivity, respiration or pneumatic modulation of the living Word: 'So

---

120 Deleuze, 'Mathesis, Science, Philosophy', 146 [translation modified].

121 P. Valéry, 'Mon Faust', *Œuvres Complètes* (Paris: Gallimard, 2 vols., 1960), vol. 2.

122 Corbin, 'From Heidegger to Suhravardi'.

123 Deleuze, 'Mathesis, Science, Philosophy', 147.

in every word I found a seed sprouting from the union of the stellar and the intimate [...]. The stellar, which the Taoists called the silent sky, required transmutations in the [imaginative] entrails of the [living], secret and intimate metamorphoses in the furnace of their entrails [...] which reached its highest expression in the Augustinian *logos spermatikos*, the participation of each word in the universal Word, a participation that treasured breath, [...] a metamorphic digestion and a spermatic procession, turning the seed into [a local modulation of] the universal Word [...].'[124] Breathing keeps the subject on the edge of the harmonic oscillation between the receptivity of that which arises on the horizon of visibility and the expressiveness of the 'invisible', it carries out 'the work of these continual conversions of the [...] visible and tangible into the invisible vibrations and excitation of [the subject's] nature, which introduces new vibration-frequencies into the vibration-spheres of the universe.'[125] The imagination is rooted in 'the depths of the human soul' because it establishes the retentive hiatus—the athanor of their entrails—between the two phases of the breathing process, a hiatus thanks to which the inspiration-expiration tandem is not merely a causal transmission between what is received and what is expressed. A subject is 'an image [a phenoumenon] which acts like other images, receiving and giving back movement, with, perhaps, this difference only, that [the subject's] body appears to choose, within certain limits, the manner in which it shall restore what it receives.'[126] This one 'difference' between mere causal mechanics and living physics—between trivial and nontrivial 'machines'—lies in the *Einbildungskraft*, in the imagination as a force that (trans-)forms images. In a sort of Spinozist diagonalisation of the apparent tension nature-freedom, we could say that it is only through the religation to the impersonal life channelled by the umbilical force of imagination that the subject can self-posit itself, affirm its subjective autonomy, and

124 J. Lezama Lima, *El reino de la imagen* (Caracas: Biblioteca Ayacucho, 1981), 357.

125 R.M. Rilke, Letter to Hulewicz, 13 November 1925, *Letters of Rainer Maria Rilke 1910–1926* (New York: The Norton Library, 1947), 375.

126 Bergson, *Matter and Memory*, 19.

become a nontrivial 'machine' whose responses cannot be predicted as a function of the real inputs.

Let us not deprive ourselves of the pleasure of following Goddard in his catatauic departure from the 'melancholy of colonial Europe': 'If the psychotropic is required, that's only because of its force (*Kraft*): it is the force that strikes or kills, the force that irresistibly delights. Nobody is capable of dying to the [reified] world without the help of this force. [...] The replacement for this vegetal force mobilised by the *Wissenschaftslehre* simply is *Einbildungskraft*. "*Einbildungskraft*", a term that could also be used in botany to designate a psychotropic button. "Button [*bouton*]" in the literal sense of that which has the power to sprout [*bouter*], to grow. "Psychotropic": in the sense in which it is able to orient the *psyche*, inducing modifications of consciousness, above all provoking the formation of new mental images. The decolonial and therapeutic gesture of the *Wissenschaftslehre* carries out the indigenous gesture outside of any indigenous context, and above all outside of the natural conditions specific to traditional medicine, which African or Amerindian botanists express the inconceivable richness of. This particular, specifically European psychotrope, *Einbildungskraft*, will therefore be used. This is explicitly designated by Fichte as the instrument of the *Wissenschaftslehre*, his organon. [...] It is under the effect of its irresistible thrust, pulling away from any fixity, from any ground, that the terms separated in any separation, in any lethal division, are made to float (*Schweben*). It is the force [...] that realises the unity of inseparability and separation, which, independent of all content, is the only thing that counts in the therapeutic act. [...] Herein lies the contribution of the *Wissenschaftslehre* to contemporary anthropology. [...] The psychiatry that it attempts, which it opposes to the melancholy of colonial Europe, is a traditional practice of rebirth for women and men who are lacking in all that which in traditional medicine is indispensable for healing: a people, living matter, psychotropic plants, supernatural beings. All this it must invent, producing the substitutes with the same movement through which the healing gesture is to be carried out. If we want to resume the Fichtean performance, to reopen the space of the Fichtean cure, to attempt a new

*Wissenschaftslehre*, we will have to keep this in mind.'[127] In this sense, the imagination is not so much a faculty belonging to the transcendental structure of a given subjective type, but rather a de-typing force—a line of flight in the transcendental structure—capable of provoking 'modifications of consciousness', mutations of the transcendental structure of the subject of experience, an imaginative 'deregulation of all the senses'. A 'novel mental image' is an image that cannot be contained within the phenomenological horizon constituted by the corresponding transcendental type, appearing instead in a zone of intermundane indetermination—the supernatural sky—to which the subject can gain access by enduring the speculative deformations of its transcendental structure induced by this vital force. Because of this, 'nature as augmented by the image provided by the [visionary subject]' exceeds the mere transcendentally constituted *natura naturata* and 'reaches the new realm of the [supernatural]'.[128] The myriad *naturae naturatae* correlated to various transcendental totems are constantly crystallising, expanding, coalescing, and dissolving within the supernatural sky. The transcendental landscape is a forest of totems and the extraterrestrial visitors continually making ingression into the clearings from the supernatural heights: 'The *xapiripë* descend to us perching on [specula, not intra-umweltic representational devices, but speculative potentiators of luminous experience],[129] which they keep suspended a little bit above the soil [...]. These mirrors come from their dwelling place in the bosom of the [supernatural] sky.[130] [...] [These shamanic images-essences (*utupë*)] surge from the farthest reaches of the [supernatural] sky, carried by a multitude of glittering paths, like a continuous stream of intensity, of primordial vitality, and trigger a kind of "luminous fairyland" saturated with resplendent spectral forms which, strictly speaking, do not make the invisible visible, but [...] "over-visible", raising it to its proper, primordial power, which

127 Goddard, 'Fichte. Le hêtre et le palmier', 256–57.

128 Lezama Lima, *El reino de la imagen*, 359.

129 Viveiros de Castro, 'The Crystal Forest', 165.

130 D. Kopenawa and B. Albert, quoted in Viveiros de Castro, 'The Crystal Forest', 165.

is to radiate with an abnormal, excessive luminosity, to form a kind of purely transparent, translucent and crystalline primordial "Outside".'[131] The psychotropic force orients the *psyche* in the forest of transcendental totems and the imagined visions unfold in fluctuating phenomenological horizons, fuzzy horizons that inform and deform within the horizon of horizons that is the supernatural sky. The stoned subject of experience, the subject that has indigested and vomited the *lapis philosophorum*—far from remaining a case of a fixed transcendental type wrapped up in its umweltic bubble—embodies a speculative type of subjectivity endowed with trans-umweltic degrees of freedom.

Disligation, the radicalisation of the separation between the living being and the one life, leads to what we call, in clinical terms, the *arche-disease*, in moral terms *evil*, in theological terms the *fall*, and in political terms *alienation* or *estrangement* (*Entfremdung*). According to Hegel's reading of the biblical tale of the fall, eating from the tree of knowledge (that is, positing the object in front—*Gegen-stand*—of the subject in order to entertain a theoretical relationship with it) is the ultimate source of evil.[132] More precisely, the separation between the I and the not-I is not itself the

131 J.-C. Goddard, 'Ce sont d'autres gens', in *Anthropologies tropicales du désastre* (Paris: Éditions Dehors, 2023), 42.

132 'The more precise way of representing this evil [condition] is to say that human beings become evil by cognising, or, as the Bible represents it, that they have eaten of the tree of knowledge of good and evil [Gen. 3:5–6]. [...] [I]t is in fact cognition that is the source of all evil, for knowledge or consciousness is the only act through which separation is posited at all [...]. It is cognition that first posits the antithesis in which evil is to be found. Animals, stones, and plants are not evil: evil first occurs within the sphere of rupture or cleavage; it is the consciousness of being-for-myself in opposition to an external nature [...]. It is through this separation that I exist for myself for the first time, and that is where the evil lies. Abstractly, being evil means singularising myself in a way that cuts me off from the universal.' G.W.F. Hegel, *Lectures on the Philosophy of Religion, Volume III, The Consummate Religion*, ed. P.C. Hodgson, tr. R.F. Brown, P.C. Hodgson, and J.M. Stewart (Oxford: Clarendon Press, 2007), 205–6.

disease, but only its condition of possibility; the site where 'evil has its seat', but not the evil itself. Evil is not being-for-itself in opposition to others and to an external nature, but rather the act of 'standing fast in the cleavage involved in being-for-itself'.[133] Separation entails a risk since it makes evil possible, but it is also a necessary condition for the enhancement of phenoumenodelic disclosure. The revelation of life is propelled both by free living beings qua germs of indetermination and sources of novel images and actions and by the collective concertation of these separate beings, by the communitarian reconciliation that overcomes the dissemination of the one life into multiple individuals: 'Spirit is free; freedom has the essential moment of this separation within itself. In this separation being-for-self is posited and evil has its seat; here is the source of all wrong, but also the point where reconciliation has its ultimate source. It is what produces the disease and is at the same time the source of health.'[134] Life reveals itself by undergoing the ordeal of separation, of the distension of its carnal tissue, which, in maximising the sharp singularity of a lifeform (and thus its capacity to reveal life in a free and singular manner) also increases the danger of disligation, the risk of tearing its immanental fabric apart. We can generally call *illness* any partial or local disconnecting 'fall' out of the immanental realm of life. Separation is, in the last instance, an abstract moment that conceals the concrete interconnectivity that supports any lifeform, a moment that must be sublated, that is, preserved and surpassed. Descriptions of the form 'separate lifeforms embedded in an environment' are abstract representations that depend upon resolving powers which, by focusing on certain ranges of scales, provide particular figure-background distinctions that foreclose the impersonal unity of life—the interconnectivity provided by the underlying background between all salient living figures. As science keeps on showing, abstractions are useful and necessary in so far as they correspond to effective articulations or moments of the real, but they become pathological when one forgets that all abstractions are dependent on a particular calibration of the understanding's resolution. Now, if we

133 Ibid., 208.

134 Ibid., 206.

understand by life the ultimate immanental real(m), the Spinozist enlivened insubstance, does not the very notion of disligation introduce some form of transcendence? What does it mean that the living might be 'disligated' from the immanence of life? Are the disligated ones 'outside' of life, floating in some sort of hypotrascendent limbo? Does not this terminology introduce a binary distinction between the religated and the disligated ones, between immanence and transcendence, thereby undermining the very notion of absolute immanence? In order to dissolve this objection, it is important to emphasise that the sharp opposition between disligation and religation is also an abstraction that envelops a concrete continuum of possible relations between the finite living forms and the impersonal fabric of life. The global 'internal' and 'external' network of connections by means of which the impersonal force of life permeates each individual and collective subject might be locally weakened, loosened, damaged, devitalised, etiolated at certain singular points or in certain regions. Even if this distension cannot expel a living being, in so far as it continues to be alive, out of the immanental realm of life, the partial disconnection might be such that the disligated individual can use its autonomy to direct its living force against life itself.

The deconstruction of the ontotheological notion of God must be accompanied by a de-ontotheologisation of the question of evil. The existence of evil neither bears witness to the action of a malignant demiurge, nor makes audible some kind of 'silence of God'. The existence of 'evil' is a properly human existential possibility for which we are wholly responsible, a possibility that stems from a particular way of understanding our individuating separation. Evil arises when the subject 'holds fast to personality as an unresolved [moment] [...]. For the personality that does not [root] itself in the divine [life] is evil.'[135] Is it not a transcendental illusion to confuse our incapacity to listen to the 'word' of 'God' with its silence? Is it not a blasphemy to maintain that we can no longer 'believe' in 'God' after Hiroshima and Nagasaki, after Auschwitz, after Apartheid? Is it not an act of irresponsibility to make 'God' the scapegoat whose 'death'

135 Ibid., 194.

would allow us to absolve ourselves of our responsibility for the crimes committed against both humanity and other lifeforms on this planet? 'How can we believe in God after Auschwitz? So God does not exist. [...] [But] God does not concern itself with human affairs, God speaks [from the depths of the living heart]. [...] [T]o be scandalised [by the existence of evil] means this: [...] by anathematising another and precisely God [...] not to hear its word any more!'[136] The deconstruction of 'metaphysics' requires abandoning the idea of an ineluctable (theoretical, aesthetic, moral, political) progress, the idea that the unfolding of human history—secretly driven by some form of immanent reason—would necessarily lead to an eschatological kingdom based on justice, truth and beauty (and in this sense, '[t]he current amazement that the things we are experiencing are "still" possible in the twentieth century is not philosophical');[137] it requires absolving human existence from the infantile illusion of a protective paternal figure that could soothe our despair, provide a transcendent guarantee that historical progress will not derail, and become the target of our 'atheistic' anathemes when the heart of darkness opens wide its gates. We are fully responsible for our decision on whether or not to cede the desire for truth, beauty, and justice; we are free to imagine new regulative conceptions of an existence worth living and dying for that could meta-orient the corresponding modes of thought and practice (science, arts, politics). And all these forms of desire can be rekindled only by healing from the disease of disligation, from the alienating sickness that makes us believe that responsibility and freedom stem from an alleged self-sufficient sovereignty.

Hegel continues his analysis of the fall by addressing the fundamental distinction between the *tree of knowledge* and the *tree of life*: 'We are also told that Adam and Eve were driven out of Paradise so that they would not also taste of the tree of life [Gen. 3:22–24]. This means that although individuals arrive at cognition, each remains a single [being] and hence a

---

136 Henry, *Paroles du Christ*, 119.

137 Benjamin, 'Theses on the Philosophy of History', 257.

mortal one.'[138] The dendrological distinction between the tree of knowledge and the tree of life is fundamental since it allows us to avoid the pitfall of confusion between the existential and transcendental finitude of the subject of experience and the impossibility of speculatively transgressing the limits of experience, which many of the interpreters of the transcendental motif have fallen prey to (with the exception of Fichte and Heidegger, at least). The differential speculative transgression of a (theoretical, perceptual, affective, social) limit of experience should not be conflated with a transgression of finitude as such. Eating from the tree of knowledge means placing oneself under the aegis of the infinite idea of truth and not accepting the a priori existence of transcendental limits that cannot be overcome by the speculative desire to know. This licit gastronomical desire should be carefully distinguished from the desire to eat from the tree of life, that is, from the creeping temptation to let oneself be dragged down by the hubristic pretension to escape finitude. Any identification between speculation and a denial of finitude must be broken. The fact that every living being is a native and a mortal and that its experience is made possible and limited by a particular transcendental framework does not imply that there are transcendental limits that cannot in principle be mediated. Genuinely speculative transfinitude—the possibility of differentially transgressing the transcendental limits of finite experience—cannot be confused with actual infinity, with the simple absence of limits, with the pretension to exist (that is, to think, to perceive, to feel, to be-with) 'after finitude'. The speculative thesis that every transcendental limit can be differentially overcome by definition presumes the existence of such limits, and these limits are the index of finitude. The speculative transgression of the limits of experience defined by a transcendental type of subjectivity does not eliminate these limits, but displaces them, deforms them, transforms them. The constant and patient effort to say the unspeakable, to think the unthinkable, to perceive the imperceptible, to present the unpresentable, can only stem from an acceptance of finitude, of the fact that every phenomenological horizon of experience is always circumscribed by an

138 Hegel, *Lectures on the Philosophy of Religion, Volume III*, 208.

unspeakable, an unthinkable, an imperceptible, an unpresentable—that is, in short, by a supernatural sky. It is precisely because we are finite that our thought and our praxis can assume the infinite task of mediating the limits of experience defined by our transcendental type. It is because we are finite that we can (desire to) transgress the factual limitations of our understanding, of our perception, of our affectivity, of our capacity to establish contact with other lifeforms.

We could say that Oedipus and Empedocles provide antithetical resolutions of the tragic scene, that is, of the arche-play that posits the existential problem of regulating the relations between the finite and the infinite. Oedipus is a conceptual character whose desire to devour his father before laying with his mother ultimately leads him to lose the speculative organ *par excellence*—the organ that channels and modulates visions—and to resign the burning desire to know. The Oedipus complex entangles an anthropophagic redundancy deprived of any speculative surplus with an incestuous restriction of the exogamous inter-totemic dissipation. By doing so, the Oedipus complex—the 'nuclear complex of neurosis' according to Freud[139]—fosters an intra-umweltic reterritorialisation and forecloses the subject's speculative capacities to mediate the transcendental limits of its phenomenological horizon. At the other extreme of the tragic spectrum, the figure of Empedocles embodies the psychotic resolution to enact a radical deterritoralisation of the realm of transcendental-dependent finitude. Empedocles's hubris is made manifest in particular in his attempt to escape from being-toward-death by freely choosing death, seeking to make death the result of a free choice, to 'master death', 'to make death an act', to be 'the creator of one's own nothingness'.[140] Empedocles 'is here the very figure of [...] nostalgia for the One-Whole, suffering from temporal limitation

139 S. Freud, *Totem and Taboo*, in *The Standard Edition of the Complete Psychological Works of Sigmund Freud, Volume XIII (1913–1914): Totem and Taboo and Other Works*, ed., tr. J. Strachey (London: The Hogarth Press, 1981), 17.

140 M. Blanchot, 'Death as Possibility', in M. Blanchot, *The Space of Literature*, tr. A. Smock (Lincoln, NE and London: University of Nebraska Press, 1982), 87–107: 102.

and wanting to escape finitude.[141] [...] Empedocles [...] represents the will to burst into the world of the Invisible Ones by dying. [...] [T]o be united with the fiery element [...] in order to attain the intimacy of the divine relation.'[142] According to Hölderlin, Empedocles's 'unusual tendency to universality'[143] leads him to a deep dissatisfaction and impatience with everything that is unilateral, particular, singular, finite, 'bound to the law of succession'.[144] Now, we could say that not only should speculation not be conflated with psychotic hubris that pretends to transgress finitude as such (as Lacoue-Labarthe does)[145] but—more radically—that speculation (the transfinite sublation of transcendental limitations) is the truly dialectical solution to the tragic impasse, that is, to the tension between the finite life of the individual and the infinite one life. According to the trinitarian dialectic, religation with the divine life cannot from any perspective be understood as salvation from the cross, as a denial of

141 P. Lacoue-Labarthe, 'The Caesura of the Speculative', in *Typography: Mimesis, Philosophy, Politics*, 208–35: 228.

142 M. Blanchot, 'Hölderlin's Itinerary', *The Space of Literature*, 269–76: 269.

143 F. Hölderlin, *The Death of Empedocles: A Mourning Play*, tr. D.F. Krell (New York: SUNY Press, 2008), 147.

144 In the 'Frankfurt Plan for Empedocles', Hölderlin describes his tragic character in the following terms: 'Empedocles, by temperament and through his philosophy long since destined to despise his culture, to scorn all neatly circumscribed affairs, every interest directed to sundry objects; an enemy to the death of all one-sided existence, and therefore also in actually beautiful relations unsatisfied, restive, suffering, simply because they are special relations, ones that fulfil him utterly only when they are felt in magnificent accord with all living things; simply because he cannot live in them and love them intimately, with omnipresent heart, like a god, and freely and expansively, like a god; simply because as soon as his heart and his thought embrace anything at hand he finds himself bound to the law of succession.' Hölderlin, *The Death of Empedocles*, 29.

145 '[T]he proper of the Greeks is speculation itself, the transgression of the limit that Hölderlin, via Kant, thinks as the limit assigned to a human Reason that is nevertheless condemned to the "metaphysical drive." The transgression of finitude.' P. Lacoue-Labarthe, 'Hölderlin and the Greeks', in *Typography: Mimesis, Philosophy, Politics*, 236–47: 244.

finitude, of being-from-birth-unto-death, of the fragility and vulnerability of existence. 'The essential [religating act] for the human being does not lie in self-annihilation through fusion in the divine, [...] it does not lie in abandoning that which defines one as a [finite] person and instates one in being. On the contrary, it is in the realisation of that which is the most [singular] and the most personal that the [living] being fulfils [its] essential [bio]phanic function: to express [life], to be the [*bio*]*phore*, the life-bearer.'[146] The Christian religation with the divine life is indissociable from a mourning play (*Trauerspiel*) in which the living being accepts and endures with dignity the cross—that is, finitude in all its forms—placing the singular perspective made possible by its finitude in the service of new visions, new acts of manifestation, new spiritual kins. This mourning is not a mourning for a *Deus absconditus*, for an absent God, for a divinity that draws itself away, infinitely distant, for a 'Father [that] turned his face away from people',[147] for a 'limitless separation' which—by undoing the 'becoming-one-unlimited' proper to psychotic hubris—would leave us helpless in the 'night of the world', as Lacoue-Labarthe melancholically maintains.[148] The absolutely modern mourning play grieves over finitude and the corresponding losses and subtracts the subject from the double temptation of mystical fusion with the divine and the Promethean pretention to save the subject from its finitude by appropriating divine attributes. The mourning play overcomes the melancholic paralysis that affects the disligated subject, the subject that understands the losses inherent to finitude as an expropriation of what (the subjects believes) belongs to it. If we owe psychoanalysis anything, it is—as

---

146 H. Corbin, 'Theology as Antidote to Nihilism', tr. M. Evans-Cockle, paper presented in Tehran, 20 October 1977, during a conference organised by the Iranian Centre for the Study of Civilizations, <https://www.amiscorbin.com/en/>.

147 F. Hölderlin, 'Bread and Wine', in *Poems*, tr. J. Mitchell (San Francisco: Ithuriel's Spear, 2004), 14.

148 'Our destiny is, therefore, to endure or to suffer (*pathein*) mourning for the divine. Or our experience, and this amounts to the same thing, is melancholic.' P. Lacoue-Labarthe, 'Hölderlin's Theatre', in M. de Beistegui and S. Sparks (eds.), *Philosophy and Tragedy* (London: Routledge, 2000), 133.

Alemán puts it—'[h]aving learned to know how to lose. But to know how to lose is always not to identify oneself with what is lost [...]',[149] letting it go. And if we owe Derrida anything, it is having learned that this learning is an infinite task, that the Freudian sharp opposition between mourning and melancholia also has to be sublated, that every loss is necessarily followed by its revenants, that we also have to mourn over the impossibility of an accomplished mourning, that even our capacity to embrace finitude is itself finite, that the 'life of spirit' does not unfold by 'having done with [the negative once and for all], turning away and passing on to something else' but rather 'by looking the negative in the face and tarrying with it',[150] that the mourning play (*Trauerspiel*) is also a mourning work (*Trauerarbeit*) that proceeds patiently, laboriously, accepting the *double bind* of letting go and lingering with the losses. The ungrounded resolution to throw the dice against the melancholic impossibility of fully coming to terms with finitude and loss decides on the religious dilemma *par excellence*, that of being an aboriginal or a foreigner: 'Tupi or not tupi'! The spectral apparitions that haunt the melancholic subject parapeted in his tower are not emanations of the dead Father, but Akasic ripples excited by the vibrations of the mat(t)er's lifestring, 'living emanations'[151] of the plasmic insubstance that broadcast the maternal imperative *par excellence*, that of being there, channelling and modulating in a singular manner the omnipresent living Yes.

The Christian divinisation of the living—the understanding of every living being as an avatar of Yesses—should not be understood as an infinitisation of the living, but rather as a transinsubstantiation of the living into the finite modes of the infinite immanental life. As Hölderlin argues in the short essay 'On Religion', a truly immanental religion—removed from all nostalgia for the everlasting One and the corresponding contempt for the finite embodied in the figure of Empedocles (and endorsed by Hölderlin himself in his 'Frankfurt plan' before his 'native reversal [*die*

149 J. Alemán, *El aprendizaje de saber perder*, <https://redpsicoanalitica.org>.

150 Hegel, *Phenomenology of Spirit*, 19.

151 Pizarnik, *Diarios*.

*mutterländische Umkehr*]')[152]—finds in every lifeworld, in every vital sphere, in the life of every spiritual community, a receptacle in which divine infinity can be expressed singularly, from a certain angle, certainly in a partial and limited manner but nonetheless in its terrible and beautiful majesty: 'Yet even in a restricted life [humans] can exist infinitely, and also the limited representation of a divinity which emerges for [them] from [their] life can be an infinite one.[153] [...] Even here [at the stove (...) in the sphere of the familiar] the [spirits] come to presence.'[154] As Hölderlin argues in his 'Notes on Antigone', the 'native reversal' transmutes 'the striving out of this world into the other into a striving out of' this ontotheological phantasmagoria into the immanental realm of life.[155] The 'native reversal' invites us 'not to give in unrestrainedly to the Empedoclean will, to the dizziness and the dazzling brilliance of the fire [...] to learn measure, lucidity, and also how to subsist steadfastly in this [life]'.[156] However, we shall not understand this native reversal as an infinite distantiation between humans and the gods, but rather as an immanentisation and polytheistisation of the divine: 'Is God unknown? Is [it] manifest like the sky? I rather believe this.'[157] The native does not try to poetically locate the traces of the fugitive gods in order to patiently prepare their return (an option which, by virtue of the distance its puts between the living and the divine, compromises with ontotheology), but lets itself fall freely—letting go, like Poe's character, of the false protections and the false promises of salvation—into the Maelstrom of intra-divine life. 'Only a God can save us', Heidegger warned.[158] But '—a little uterine

152 Cf. Blanchot, 'Hölderlin's Itinerary'.

153 F. Hölderlin, 'On Religion', in *Essays and Letters on Theory*, tr. T. Pfau (New York: State University of New York Press, 1987), 93.

154 Heraclitus, quoted in Heidegger, 'Letter on Humanism', *Basic Writings*, 257–58.

155 Hölderlin, 'Notes on the Antigone', *Essays and Letters*, 328.

156 Blanchot, 'Hölderlin's Itinerary', 270.

157 F. Hölderlin, 'In lieblicher Bläue', in *Sämtliche Werke*, ed. F. Beissner, Stuttgarter Hölderlin-Ausgabe (Stuttgart: W. Kohlhammer Verlag, 3 vols., 1951), vol. 2, 372.

158 M. Heidegger, 'Only a God Can Save Us: Der Spiegel's Interview with Martin Heidegger', *Philosophical and Political Writings*, 38.

question—do we really want to be saved? And if so, for what, why, what is there to save?'[159] What should we save ourselves from? From the uprooting caused by modern technoscience (as Heidegger maintains)? Rather than hoping for 'salvation', we should assume our responsibilities. The capitalist, extractivist and colonising coopting and instrumentalisation of the desire to understand is not the inexorable fate of science as a mode of thought and practice attuned to the *logos*. Rather than mystifying an alleged destinal 'essence of technics' and being terrified by the photographs of the earth taken from the moon, we prefer to take on the responsibility of deciding which interests of reason and which philosophical constellations will orient our commitment to unfold the desire to know, the will to fine-tune our questions, to refine our understanding, to entertain a rational dialogue with nature. From the native and mortal fragility of finite existence (as Promethean transhumanism argues)? To this, both Heidegger and Christianity respond that birth, mortality, and other figures of finitude are the conditions of the possibility of the subjective perspectivist and desiring autonomy, the ultimate link between 'nature' and 'freedom', a necessary moment of the immanental trinitarian procession through which life enhances its self-revelation. Rather than acquiescing to the 'sterilising, self-indulgent and self-fulfilling myths of apocalypse and salvation',[160] we prefer to engage in a religating healing process and assume with dignity and humility—beyond backwards nostalgia, melancholic paralysis, and infinitising hubris—our native and mortal condition. No God will ever save us but—if we dare to go where the danger is—life can cure us, cure itself, of the arche-disease of disligation.

Goddard argues, reading Fichte with Freud, that the tension between the living and life can manifest clinically in two opposite forms, *neurosis* and *psychosis*.[161] The neurotic type denotes a disaffected, apathetic subject,

159 H. Miller, 'The Enormous Womb', in *The Wisdom of the Heart* (New York: New Directions, 1941).

160 Haraway, *Staying With the Trouble*, 35.

161 Cf. S. Freud, 'Neurosis and Psychosis', in *The Standard Edition of the Complete Psychological Works of Sigmund Freud, Volume XIX (1923–1925): The Ego and the Id and*

disligated from the *natura naturans* (what Freud calls the impersonal *id*), stripped of its desiring freedom and its vital spontaneity, reduced to a reified worldly exteriority whose coercive symbolic norms (embodied in the figure of a primordial Father) are interiorised in the form of an unquestioned superego's commands, dispossessed of its capacity to be there—witnessing and channelling the living revelation—to affirm 'I am who I am', to transform the world through its praxis, to be enthralled by phenoumenodelic visions. On the other hand, the psychotic types denotes an autarchic subject, supposedly self-sufficient in its disconnect from reality, unable to cope with any form of real resistance, friction, heat, or noise, incapable of constituting an exterior and intersubjective world by means of an effective symbolisation, deprived of the capacity to embrace its separation, to feel on its transcendental epidermis the caress and pain of its confrontation with the world and with other living beings, to live and be propelled by its finitude, its mortality. The neurotic forecloses the crack in the prevailing umweltic order and might need an analysis in order to induce a hysterisation of its own subjective structure, to challenge the corresponding symbolic norms, to transform the universal taboos into transcendental totems, and to religate with its own exogamic speculative desire. On the contrary, the psychotic denies their own castration and needs to somehow relearn to restrain its own blind spontaneity and hold a receptive space open for the other to come. Whereas the neurotic is completely caught in the net of a reified symbolic pattern without living mat(t)er, the psychotic is fully submerged in a mat(t)er without pattern, in an anomic materialistic dreaminess. Whereas neurosis results from an open fault between the self and the vital ground of desires and drives, thus making possible an 'automation of the tendency to crystallise life into a coercive [super-egoic] system', psychosis operates by means of an 'automation of the tendency toward unlimited activity', of a freedom that is seemingly unrestricted (and therefore merely abstract, without real points of support) enabled by the formation of a fault-line

---

*Other Works*, ed., tr. J. Strachey (London: The Hogarth Press, 1986), 149–53, and the chapter 'Le cercle pathologique' in Goddard, *La philosophie fichtéene de la vie*, in particular 139–41 [§36].

between the self and the material resistance of the exterior intersubjective world.[162] Both of these transcendental pathologies entail an abandonment of the possibility of 'existing life'[163] by means of a worldly and intersubjective effort. Both the neurotic subject dispossessed of its vital desire and the psychotic subject for whom the real—far from manifesting itself as an impasse of the symbolic—only appears in the form of an unlimited drive that blinds the subject with respect to any external constraint are separated from the capacity for 'spiritual' self-transformations of their transcendental types required to place their finite lives in the service of the regulative ideas of reason—truth, beauty, justice, and love. Ultimately, both neurosis and psychosis are particular forms of the one arche-disease, that of disexisting life, of deserting our desiring being-there in the midst of an intersubjective world drifting through the phenoumenodelic pleroma.[164]

In Kantian terms, both neurosis and psychosis result from a dysfunction of the imagination as the transcendental faculty capable of bringing about the synthesis between passivity and activity, between the receptivity proper to a finite, instituted subject, located in an external intersubjective world, and the spontaneity proper to a worlding subject capable of disturbing the *natura naturata* by means of the production of supernatural images. Seen in this light, dogmatic realism and dogmatic idealism are the true philosophical definitions of the transcendental pathologies denoted by neurosis and psychosis respectively.[165] And the transcendental conception of health was clearly outlined by Kant: neither receptivity without spontaneity (dogmatic realism), nor spontaneity without receptivity (dogmatic idealism). Transcendental imagination, as a faculty capable of effecting the

---

162 Goddard, *La philosophie fichtéenne de la vie*, 140.

163 Ibid., 141.

164 In this sense, psychoanalysis can be considered as a religating practice (and therefore as a practice oriented by the idea of love, as Badiou maintains) since it aims to reconnect the neurotic subject with the unconscious ground of drives submerged beneath conscious life and the psychotic subject with everything in the experiential field that obstructs the unfolding of its idealising imperialism.

165 Cf. Goddard, *La philosophie fichtéenne de la vie*, 171–74 [§44].

synthesis between concepts and intuitions, between activity and passivity, between spontaneity and receptivity—the synthesis that defines every finite and desiring subject—is thus the faculty around which both the Kantian system and its Fichtean 'apotheosis' (Novalis) pivot. That is why the healing medicine is received upon the altar of imagination, in those inner depths where the life of the living is rooted in the one life that engenders it, nurtures it, bears it, and transforms it. According to the Fichtean orientation of this perspective, the depths of the living soul are not (as Schelling argues) the site of a disturbing uncanniness (*Unheimlichkeit*) that should remain repressed in the shadows of its extimacy so that the individual can escape the pull of its gravity and emerge into the light of existence, but the portal to the force of imagination that enlivens, to the love that engenders, to the necessarily blessed (*selig*) life.[166] Deep within the human soul, the living can drink the elixir of life that transforms the essentialist inertia (the neurotic inability to self-posit oneself, to channel desire, to feel love as the 'affect of being', to make kin with other lifeforms and ingress into spiritual communities) into the 'vast enlivening' that 'reexists' disligation, into a local vocalisation of the absolute 'I am that I am' as pure 'satisfaction [*Zufriedenheit*] with oneself, joy [*Freud*] in oneself, enjoyment [*Genuss*] of oneself'.[167] The instance to which the cure religates is not a 'dark ground' removed from phenomenalisation, but the living pleroma whose phenoumenalisation overflows every phenomenological horizon, the turbulent infinity of a manifestation that can only be partially experienced by a finite subject thanks to the mediation of transcendental valves that filter, cut down, select, edit, renormalise—protecting the subject from an arche-revelation that would otherwise obliterate its subjective integrity: '[t]he most merciful thing in the [pleroma] is the inability of the human mind to correlate all its contents. We live on a placid island of ignorance in the midst of [phenoumenodelic] seas of infinity', but it was meant that we should voyage far. The sciences, the arts, the spiritual and political

166 Cf. J.-C. Goddard, 'Schelling ou Fichte. L'être comme angoise ou l'être comme Bonheur', in A. Schnell (ed.), *Le bonheur* (Paris: Vrin, 2006).

167 Fichte, *The Way Towards the Blessed Life or, The Doctrine of Religion*, 2.

practices, each straining in its own direction—as well as the philosophical piecing together of these dissociated modes of thought and practice—'open up such beautiful and terrible vistas of [the real] [...] that we shall either go mad from the revelation [and] flee [back] [...] into the peace and safety of a new dark age'[168] or resolutely assume our being-there as finite probes of the pleroma at the service of its infinite manifestation. On the altar of *Einbildungskraft*, the living ask for the strength to withstand the flood of the real, to afford the trance that partially unworlds their existence and experience, to sprout toward new phenomenological horizons, toward new visions: *Gib mir Kraft, gib mir Bilder.*

In terms of the Fichtean distinction between the (finite) *knowledge of* (infinite) *life* and the *life of knowledge*, the knowledge produced by a neurotic subject will necessarily be a devivified knowledge, the knowledge of an uprooted subject, detached from the impersonal and concrete vitality that fuels knowledge as a singular form of desire, the knowledge of a suject that wanders through life as a foreigner, feeling at home nowhere. A devivified knowledge is the product of an essentialised subject fallen into the sheer exteriority of non-glorious mundanity, a subject confronted with an inert, reified, and disenchanted world, a world that presents itself as a mere 'standing reserve' deserted by divinity and offered up to extractivist exploitation. In turn, the life of a psychotic subject will be a life without knowledge, the life of a subject which, denying its finitude, its castration, gives up the desire to accept, face, and confront the real resistances that limit the horizon of its experience. Ventriloquising Fichte, Deleuze explicitly describes medicine—beyond a physiology that reifies the subject and a 'disembodied psychology' abstracted from worldly, material, and intersubjective incarnation—as a practice through which life is reinjected into the knowledge of life: 'Beyond a psychology disincarnated in thought, and a physiology mineralised in matter, mathesis will be fulfilled only in a true medicine where life is defined as knowledge of life, and knowledge

168 H.P. Lovecraft, 'The Call of Cthulhu', in *The Call of Cthulhu and Other Weird Stories* (London: Penguin, 1999), 139–69: 139.

as life of knowledge. Hence the motto, "*Scientia vitae in vita scientiae*"'.[169] On the one hand (and against any psychoticisation of the subject), 'true medicine' makes the life that exists within the living into a knowledge of life, into a process through which the subject can entertain a cognitive relation with a not-I that marks its finitude and offers it a material pivot on which to support its process of spiritual self-transformation, of speculative mediation of its transcendental limits, of practical transformation of its world. On the other (and against any neuroticisation of the subject), 'true medicine' makes all finite knowledge a vital knowledge, a knowledge which is reimplanted in life, that is nothing other than self-knowledge of life. True medicine reimplants every subjective experience into the life of the subject of experience and thus into the impersonal one life that exists locally in that subject. True medicine plugs the subject back into self-affecting (self-knowing, self-perceiving, self-feeling, self-enjoying) living flesh.

To return to the project of German Idealism: How is it possible to synthesise a philosophy that makes every experience relative to a given transcendental type and a philosophy that refuses to yield its desire for the absolute? How can the melancholic neurosis of 'capitalist realism' (Mark Fisher)—in which the subject 'cedes its [vital] desire', ceases to incarnate the Word and to vibrate as a local modulation of the living act, and begins instead to identify with things (and in particular with the things it *has*, with its private property), reifying itself, dessicating itself—be cured? How to cure oneself of the psychotic flight out of the intersubjective world, of the idealistic inability to assume both the real impasses and the effort and frustration inherent to all worldly, intersubjective practice? The solution to these different manifestations of the same arche-pathology, laid out by Fichte, is strictly Christian. Against the thesis that Fichte is a sort of evanescent precursor of Schelling

169 Deleuze, 'Mathesis, Science and Philosophy', 143. We can only be dazzled by the rainbow that arcs between the implicit Fichtean resonances of Deleuze's first text ('Mathesis, Science and Philosophy') and the explicitly Fichtean tone of his last text ('Immanence: A Life').

and Hegel, we could say that Fichte already fully implements what we shall call *the briefest systematic programme of German Idealism*: to sanction a wedding between Spinozist immanentism and Kantian transcendentalism in a Christian ecclesia. The Christian solution to the problem of synthesising Spinozism with Kantianism consists first in affirming that we live, move, and die in the most absolute revelation—that phenoumenodelic insubstance is the kingdom of life, the self-narcotising sacrament—and second, that this immanental absolute self-manifests through its subjective modes, that is, by instituting finite living beings which (as cases of different transcendental types) constitute and thus limit the phenomenological horizons of their experience through their transcendental receptive-imaginative-expressive faculties. The finitude of the living—their birth and mortality, their singular being-there, their desires, their pains and anguish, their one-sideness, their empirical and transcendental perspectivism—is the eye of the needle through which the Christian God—that is, life as such—flows in its own manifestation. The finite selves conform a dynamical network of sieves, valves, and slits through which life refracts and streams into manifold interfusing 'worlds of revelation'.

The Christian nature of the synthesis between Kantian transcendentalism and Spinozist immanentism enriches the relations between science, arts, politics, and philosophy that we have schematised thus far with a new form of practice—religion—and its corresponding regulative idea, love. The inclusion of religion in our discussion of the human modes of thought and practice allows us to revisit one of the main distinctive hallmarks of the modern period, namely the tension between modern science and religion. In its least interesting form, the rationalistic, empiricist, and hypercritical stance of modern science (philosophically enriched by the Kantian exponentiation of the Copernican revolution) was used as a weapon that targeted the dogmatic, fundamentalist, and obscurantist distortion of the religious and intended to ground a new scientifically informed form of atheism. While the deconstruction of forms of the religious that compete with modern science on the latter's own playground (that is, by trying to provide theoretical explanations of what it is) is certainly necessary, the conflation of this deconstruction with a dismissal of the religious as such is an abstract negation based (1) on the incapacity to free the notion of religion from the idea of an ontotheological God and (2) on the incapacity to establish a clear demarcation line between radically different and non-overlapping modes of thought and practice. The theistic defences of religion, the 'new' atheistic attacks, as well as the agnostic stances that proceed by trying to prove, disprove or un(dis)prove the 'existence' of God respectively keep the problem at stake at its lowest possible level. The modern tension between science and religion relies in the last instance on the illegitimate amalgamation of modes of thought and practice that are oriented by different ideas of reason: respectively, truth (the idea that prescribes the expansion of the rational understanding of the experiential field in which we are embedded) and love (the idea that prescribes the trinitarian religation of the finite living with infinite life in its three declensions: impersonal, personal, and transpersonal). The thesis that we are sketching here is that it is possible to unlock new possibilities for modernity beyond the deathtrap of colonial-neoliberal-capitalism (the possibility of becoming an absolute modernity) by undoing this spurious conflation between the proper tasks of science and religion. Far from necessarily being associated with a dismissal of the religious and a progressive secularisation of human existence, the emergence of modern science (as Spinoza had already seen) allows religion to be released from the burden of pretending to dogmatically annunciate truth (a pretension that forces religion into an unnecessary competition with modern science, lost in advance). Religion neither produces theoretical knowledge nor relies on an alleged knowledge: religion (oriented by love, not by truth) is a practice that reconnects, that make kin, that binds together (*Bindung*), that stitches a *Band* that (dis)joints the separate. 'The question is not one of belief—whether these *orishas* exist or not—but rather of experimenting with how these figures operate',[170] of evaluating to what extent these archetypal figures induce practices of religation, disalienation, communitarisation. We shall therefore 'make this chief distinction between religion and superstition,

170 Touam Bona, *Sagesse des lianes*, 96.

that the latter is founded on ignorance, the former [...]'[171] on a clear separation with respect to the scientific organon of rational knowledge. In this sense, an absolutely modern religion—a religion capable of bringing itself into sync with modern science—can depend neither on a theoretical dogma capable of competing with science nor base its devotion on a personal belief removed from common understanding (a religious form, one might say, of private property). The infinite idea that guides religious praxis, as we understand it here, is that of deepening and enhancing the most universal of experiences: the experience of the life that ceaselessly engenders us, the life that we incarnate, the shared life. But both science and religion—as practices ultimately oriented by the desire to empower, from our finite, native, and mortal being-there, revelation—are opposed to capitalism, to the appropriation of the common in all its forms, to the privatisation and control of life, to the psychotic foreclosure of castration.

This unbinding of the epistemic suture between religion (understood as a dogmatic, speculative, or metaphysical theology) and the theoretical interest of reason has to be generalised to the manifold 'sutures' that establish different forms of dependence between religion and other modes of thought and practice, notably the *theologico-political suture* and (what we could call) the *juridical suture*, that is, the understanding of religion as a mode of thought and practice that orbits around the Law. First, modernity has to fail better in its attempt to separate the political and the theological beyond the modern persistence of theologico-political motives—*cf.* Löwith (the understanding of modern progress in terms of Christian eschatology), Voegelin (the immanentisation of the eschaton and the modern pregnancy of a gnostic motif), Schmitt (the understanding of the theory of modern state in terms of 'secularised' theological concepts), Derrida ('mondialatinisation'). This unbinding of the theologico-political knot must be accompanied by a sublation of the juridical conception according to which religion would have the prerogative to fix, in the form of a body of prescriptions, rules

---

171 B. de Spinoza, Letter XXI to Oldenburg, in *The Collected Works of Spinoza* (Princeton, NJ and Oxford: Princeton University Press, 2 vols., 2016), ed. E. Curley, vol. 2, 467–68: 467.

and legal norms, the ultimate coordinates for human behaviour and social relations. Only this dissolution of any form of dependence between religion and other modes of thought and practice makes possible the opening of a space of symphilosophical concertation between them.

In his *Lectures on the Philosophy of Religion*, Hegel distinguishes three moments of the religious. The first moment is the ontotheological moment in which God appears as the abstract concept of the infinitely distant Other ('the religious object appears as something alien and external, an infinite power vis-à-vis the subject. This objective [being] can appear for the subject's knowing as completely other, as completely unknown on this side').[172] The second moment is the subjective moment—'the side Luther called faith'[173]—in which God is the ultimate presupposed term of a purely subjective 'orientation', 'a feeling, speaking, and praying directed toward God above—but [only] toward God, [hence] (a nullity for God, a shooting into the blue)—which accordingly means that we know nothing of God, have no acquaintance with the divine content, essence, and nature [...].'[174] Compared with the infinite power attributed to God, the finite subject 'knows itself to be only an accident [...] something vanishing and transient',[175] infinitely separated from the almighty target of its worship. The sublation of this tension between the infinite and the finite, between the 'objective' Other and the merely subjective belief, characterises the third moment of the religious, namely what Hegel calls the *cultus*. According to Hegel's description, the third moment 'is the sublating of this antithesis of the subject and God, of the separation, this remoteness of the subject from God. Its effect is that as a [living] being one feels and knows God [qua life] internally, in one's own [living] subjectivity, that as this [finite] subject one [embeds in] God, gives oneself the certainty, the pleasure, and the

172 G.W.F. Hegel, *Lectures on the Philosophy of Religion, Volume I: Introduction and the Concept of Religion*, ed. P. C. Hodgson, tr. R.F. Brown, P.C. Hodgson, and J.M. Stewart (Berkeley, CA: University of California Press, 1984), 188.

173 Ibid., 188.

174 Ibid., 192.

175 Ibid., 189.

joyfulness of [being religated to divine life] [...]. This is the cultus.'[176] In the framework of this third moment, religion depends neither on a purely speculative attempt intended to demonstrate the 'existence' of an infinitely distant almighty God (*theologia naturalis*) nor on a purely subjective, one-sided, and private belief. Now, the sublation of these two moments assumes for Hegel the form of a liturgical activity that effectuates this unity, that concretely produces in the intersubjective world of the community this unity—this *Band*—between the infinite (life) and the finite (living), and takes joy in this unity. Beyond theoretical dogmas and subjective beliefs, religion is an experimental performative activity intended to effectuate the 'mat(t)ership connection', that is, to radicalise the immersion of the individual and collective subjects in the immanental vital milieu in order to launch them into the supernatural sky.

In Durkheim's terms, an absolutely modern definition of religion—a definition of religion compatible with the existence of modern science—must comply with (at least) the following three conditions. Firstly, an absolutely modern religion has to be released from the presupposition of any form of meta-physical exception (e.g. miracles, the 'supernatural', the utterly inconceivable and inexpressible) with regards to the 'natural' realm of manifestation, of any instance withdrawn de jure from the domain of (speculatively extended) rational understanding and cognitive discursivity.[177] The supernatural as we shall understand it here does not refer to an unfathomable other-than-natural realm, but rather to the hypertelic prodigality of the *natura naturans*, to the pleromatic exuberance that surpasses the different transcendental-dependent *naturae naturatae*, to the real impasses

---

176 Ibid., 180.

177 'One notion that is generally taken to be characteristic of all that is religious is the notion of the supernatural. By that is meant any order of things that goes beyond our understanding; the supernatural is the world of mystery, the unknowable, or the incomprehensible. Religion would then be a kind of speculation upon all that escapes science, and clear thinking generally. [...] What is certain, in any case, is that this idea appears very late in the history of religions. It is totally alien not only to the peoples called primitive but also to those who have not attained a certain level of intellectual culture.' Durkheim, *The Elementary Forms of Religious Life*, 22–23.

that make holes in every symbolic order, to the 'super-visibility',[178] the super-audibility, the super-conceptuality, the super-affectibility that extends beyond and envelops the different phenomenological horizons. Secondly, it is necessary—as we have already argued—to disentangle the understanding of the phenomenon of religion from the ontotheological idea of God, that is, in particular, from the problem of demonstrating the 'existence' of a hypothetical separated 'God'.[179] If we might continue to use the term 'God' (but we shall rather not), it will always be in a context-dependent manner, that is, within the framework of a precise definition (such as Spinoza's identification of God with immanental substance, the Christian identification of God with life, or Dedalus's definition of God as a 'shout in the street'). God—far from being a hypothetical hypertranscendent *ens realissimum* whose existence would be the object of a supposed demonstration, the *absconditus* term of an endless apophasis, the alleged target of a personal belief, the ultimate dispenser of salvation, or a 'God of the gaps' that would relay the finitude of human understanding—is nothing but a devotional name for the immanental self-revelation of life in all its beauty, its terrible mercilessness, its unbearable strength, its fragility, its outstanding intelligibility, its pleromatic outpouring, and—last but not least—its mystery. More generally, every characterisation of the sacred that distinguishes it from the transient and exuberant realm of individuated and finite life—in the

---

178 Viveiros de Castro, 'The Crystal Forest', 164.

179 '[T]here are great religions from which the idea of gods and spirits is absent, or plays only a secondary and inconspicuous role. This is the case of Buddhism. [...] [The Buddhist is] atheist in the sense that [it] is uninterested in whether gods exist. [...] [M]any rites that are wholly independent of any idea of gods or spiritual beings are found even in deistic religions. [...] In any cult, there are practices that act by themselves, by a virtue that is their own, and without any god's stepping in between the individual who performs the rite and the object sought. [...] Thus there are rites without gods, and indeed rites from which gods derive. Not all religious virtues emanate from divine personalities, and there are cult ties other than those that unite man with a deity. Thus, religion is broader than the idea of gods or spirits and so cannot be defined exclusively in those terms.' Durkheim, *The Elementary Forms of Religious Life*, 28, 32, 33.

form of a hypothetical eternal 'life', of a supposed 'nirvanic' state absolved from (re)birth, suffering, and death, of a *Deus absconditus*, of a Promethean sublation of castration, of an undifferentiated continuity 'heterogeneous' to the realm of individuation—all these versions of the ontotheological 'beyond' only deepens the arche-disease of disligation. Besides releasing itself both from the notion of an ontotheological God (and from the concomitant theistic-atheistic-agnostic debates) and from the theoretical pretensions that perpetuate an unnecessary tension with science, the conception of an absolute modern religion requires the definitive abandonment of the dismissal of finitude and the corresponding promises of 'salvation'. Rather than seeking to neutralise death by promising an afterlife removed from the decay inherent to all forms of life, an absolutely modern religion must fully embrace it and revere life in both its overwhelming power and its fragile delicacy. Finally, it is necessary to define religion as a set of *practices*, to the detriment of its supposed theoretico-speculative dimension. As we have maintained above, the pretension to provide explanations about the origin, nature, and destination of all that exists is the main source of the conflictual relationship between religion and science, and simply obstructs the possibility of raising the conception of the religious to an absolutely modern phase. Science 'classifies the universe and divides it into this being and that, seeks out the reasons for what exists, and deduces the necessity of what is real while spinning the reality of the world and its laws out of itself. Into this realm [...] religion must not venture too far. It must not have the tendency to posit essences and to determine natures, to lose itself in an infinity of reasons and deductions, to seek out final causes, and to proclaim eternal truths.[180] [...] It is essentially [in its practices] that a religion reveals its secret, much better than in any dogmatic exercise.'[181] Rather than expanding our understanding, the sacred is that which heals—*das Heilige ist das, was heilt*. Exploiting the etymology that derives the term 'religion' from the Latin *religare*, we understand religion as a set of religating practices

180 F. Schleiermacher, *On Religion: Speeches to its Cultured Despisers*, tr. R. Crouter (Cambridge and New York: Cambridge University Press, 1996).

181 H. Corbin, *En Islam iranien* (Paris: Gallimard, 4 vols., 1971–1972), vol. 4, 457.

guided by an infinite regulative idea in the Kantian sense of the term, the idea of love. And love—and here we find the truly Christian declension of the religious—is manifest in three ways: as the love of the *impersonal* life, as the love of the finite, autonomous, and singular individual through which life assumes a *first-person* perspective, and as the love of the *transpersonal* community of the living. As we shall understand it here, religion is an a-theological experimental practice oriented by the infinite idea of strengthening and multiplying the ligaments that keep us bound to life in its threefold impersonal, personal, and transpersonal refraction. Only a radical critique of all the deformations, compromises, deviations, crimes and betrayals carried out in the name of religion and of its connivance with oppressive power structures, as well as an understanding of this critique as a determinate negation capable of producing a positive reconceptualisation of religion as a practice of threefold religation oriented by the infinite idea of love, only this can put us on the path to a cure for the illness that afflicts the collective subject that is modern humanity. If the emergence of modern science brought forth the possibility of overcoming 'the old religious vice [...] of deviating into the incomprehensible or the abstruse' one of the most perennial drives of human existence—that of enhancing its capacities for love—the times are ripe to exhumate, resume, deform, and exponentiate the manifold religating practices by means of which human beings tried to deepen, share, and express their 'erotic' devotion to life: '[I]t was impossible that in a religion, even if abandoned since, the race had not put its unknown intimate secret. The time has come, with the necessary detachment, to carry out diggings there in order to exhume ancient and magnificent intentions. [...] When the old religious vice [...] will have been diluted with the waves of the evidence and the day, it will not remain less, that the devotion to [life] [...] in some joy, requires a cult [...] nothing, in spite of the insipid tendency, will show itself exclusively secular, because this word does not precisely elicit any meaning.'[182]

182 S. Mallarmé, 'Offices', in R.G. Cohn, *Mallarmé's Divagations: A Guide and Commentary* (New York: Peter Lang, 1990), 131–32 [translation modified].

As Pasolini contends, in the modern age 'the opposite of religion [is not science but] capitalism'[183] and (we shall argue) only an absolutely immanental religion—that is, one fully removed from the mirages of hypertranscendent ontotheology and released from the understanding of finitude as a flaw to be redeemed, that is, from the rejection of castration—can put a halt to the metastasis of capital. Like a cancer cell, capitalism 'has no destiny, no human purpose beyond endless replication'; 'just dedicated to producing identical replicas on an assembly line', capitalism knows nothing about truth, justice, beauty, and love. 'It has no work to finish and no reason to die.'[184] Capital spreads the illness of appropriating disligation in the body of immanental life, and only life is capable of suturing its wounds, of sewing together a *Band* that restores its self-ligation where the centrifugal forces of individuation tend to rend its vital tissue. As Lacan holds, '[w]hat distinguishes the capitalist discourse is this, *Verwerfung*, rejection from all the fields of symbolic [...] of castration. Every order, every discourse that aligns itself with capitalism leaves aside what we will simply call the matters of love.'[185] The capitalistic hubris rejects castration in all its forms: death, pain, sadness, boredom, anguish, inoperativity, unproductivity—even mourning is now considered as a psychiatric pathology that has to be 'cured'—as well as the patience, frustration, slowness, and restraint proper to every infinite task. Capitalism is a system of the 'uninterrupted production of hyperbolic positivity',[186] of endless acceleration of production and accumulation, of the subordination of every synthesis with alterity to the imperative to extract profits, of the generalised commodification of everything and everyone. Capitalism proceeds by fostering a threefold disligation, a disligation between the people and their lands, their origins, their cultures, their languages, their natures; a disligation between the

---

183 P.P. Pasolini, *Scritti Corsari* (Rome: Garzanti, 1975).

184 W.S. Burroughs, *The Western Lands* (London: Penguin, 1987), 60.

185 J. Lacan, *...or Worse: The Seminar of Jacques Lacan, Book XIX*, tr. A.R. Price (Cambridge: Polity, 2018).

186 J. Baudrillard, *The Transparency of Evil* (London: Verso, 1993), 106.

people and their own self-positing desiring subjectivity, making of them neurotic medicated consumers free to choose between different commodities; capitalism proceeds by isolating people, by teasing communities apart. Capitalism uproots people from their lands and their communities and piles them up in urban agglomerations, thereby obtaining in one and the same gesture lands available for extractivism, an urban workforce to produce commodities, and consumers for these very commodities.[187] Now, the finitude that capitalism forecloses is the condition of possibility for speculative desire, both the desire for truth that drives science and the desire for beauty, justice, and love. Desire is the singular sprouting of infinite life through the finite lifeform and the 'ethics of psychoanalysis' ('[T]he only thing of which one can be guilty is of having given ground relative to one's desire')[188] can be understood as a religating therapethics. Desire is another name for the umbilical thread that connects the finite sieves with the impersonal life that springs through them, that religates the living one to its singular destiny as a unique perspectival source of splashing manifestation.[189] 'Capitalist realism' rejects castration, represses desire, and fosters the idiotic loops of the immediate autarkic jouissance associated with unrestricted consumption: '[O]ne can easily substitute for Kant's "Thou shalt" [follow the orientations provided by the infinite ideas of reason] the Sadean phantasm of jouissance elevated to the level

187 'Modernisation has pushed these people out of the countryside and the forests to become labourers, and now they are crowded into favelas on the outskirts of the metropolises. These people have been torn from their collectives, their places of origin, and have been thrown into this crusher called "humanity". [...] While humanity is being pushed out of its land everywhere, big business [...] is taking over the Earth.' Krenak, *Idées pour retarder la fin du monde*, 22, 26.

188 J. Lacan, *The Ethics of Psychoanalysis. The Seminar of Jacques Lacan. Book VII, 1959–1960*, ed. J.-A. Miller, tr. D. Porter (New York: Norton, 1992), 319.

189 '[D]esire is nothing other than that which supports an unconscious theme, the very articulation of that which roots us in a particular destiny [...] and desire keeps coming back, keeps returning, and situates us once again[—like a sort of inertio-gravitational field—]in a given track, the [geodesic] track of something that is specifically our business.' Ibid., 319.

of an imperative—it is, of course, a pure and almost derisory fantasm, but it does not exclude the possibility of its being elevated to a universal law.'[190] In so doing, in fostering the immediate satisfaction of the vicious circles of drives to the detriment of a desiring-vectorisation of existence, capitalism sanctions the end of the infinite ends of reason: 'As far as that [...] which has to do with desire, with its array and disarray, so to speak, the position of power of any kind in all circumstances and in every case, whether historical or not, has always been the same. The essential point is "Carry on working. Work [and the show] must go on." Which, of course, means: "Let it be clear to everyone that this is on no account the moment to express the least surge of desire." The morality of power, of the service of goods, is as follows: "As far as desires are concerned, come back later. Make them wait."'[191]

If 'only love allows jouissance to condescend to desire',[192] if love alone allows the circuits of the self-centred drives that circulate around the troumatic extimities to be vectorised in the direction of an infinite collective project and the concomitant engendering of new forms of the spirit, then the capitalist denial of desire—the end of ends—is indeed tantamount to the abandonment of 'matters of love'. According to Lacan, the unconditional 'Thou shalt' of Kant's moral imperative does point toward the 'place occupied by desire'.[193] Whereas the symbolic prescriptions commanded by the Name-of-the-Father (e.g., 'Thou shalt no kill') are inscribed on the inner surfaces of the intra-umweltic skies and are deprived of any form of unrestricted (or transtypical) universality, Kant's imperative is intended to provide an unconditional prescription, which means that it should not depend upon any particular symbolic order whatsoever; it should be a prescription beyond transcendental-dependent norms. We could say

190 Ibid., 316.

191 Ibid., 315.

192 J. Lacan, *Anxiety. The Seminar of Jacques Lacan, Book X, 1962–1963*, tr. A.R. Price (Cambridge: Polity, 2014), 179.

193 Lacan, *The Ethics of Psychoanalysis*, 316.

that what Kant called the categorical imperative took different context-dependent formulations, such as for instance the Lacanian 'Thou shalt not cede thy desire', the materialistic imperative 'Thou shalt live!',[194] the Christian pleroma of love beyond the law (intended 'to have done once and for all with the judgement of God'), or the Augustinian precept 'Love, and do what thou wilt.'[195] These declensions of the unconditional imperative overcome 'the cold formal universality' of the Kantian imperative by injecting into it the burning insubstance of desire and love, by directly plugging it into the living mat(t)er: it is no longer an abstract 'you ought to' that orients the subject, but the pleromatic surge of life.[196] In all these formulations, no particular content or behaviour is prescribed, only the commitment to live a life religated to life and to channel the desire that refracts the infinite (far too inhuman) living power through the finite human slits. Whereas capitalism can be understood as the (police-based) 'service of the goods' ('the morality [...] of a human—far too human—power'),[197] psychoanalysis relies on the proposition that '[t]here is no other good than that which may serve to pay the price for access to desire',[198] there is no other good than that which is sacrificed on the pyre of the burning desire to live, to know, to see and hear and touch and taste, to feel and to love. Spiritual sublimation—the upwards unfolding of spirit supported by the downward rooting upon the mat(t)er—is fuelled by the burning of goods; it is an alchemical operation of the transmutation of goods into upraising life. If we understand religion as a practical exploration of the different manners in which a subject can sacrifice goods (its capital, its properties, its essences) in the altar of desire, then psychoanalysis can be understood as a particular religating practice subtracted from the 'service of the goods' and oriented by the infinite idea of love: 'Sublimate as much

---

194 Rozitchner, 'Primero hay que saber vivir', 387.

195 Saint Augustine, Seventh Homily on 1 John 4:4-12, <https://www.ccel.org/ccel/schaff/npnf107.iv.x.html>.

196 Derrida, *Glas*, 68–69.

197 Lacan, *The Ethics of Psychoanalysis*, 314–15.

198 Ibid., 321.

as you like; you have to pay for it with something. And this something is called jouissance [the jouissance of dreadful accumulation and consumption of goods]. I have to pay for that mystical operation with a pound of flesh. That's the object, the good, that one pays for the satisfaction of one's desire. [...] It is, in effect, there that the religious [and the psychoanalytical] operation lies [...]. That good which is sacrificed for desire—and you will note that that means the same thing as that desire which is lost for the good—that pound of flesh is precisely the thing that religion undertakes to [transmute, to existentialise, to resurrect]. That's the single trait which is common to all religions; it is coextensive [...] with the whole meaning of religion.'[199] Religious experience operates the transmutation of the reified subject that possesses goods into the possessed subject that drifts in the *mareaçao*: '[W]hen it is a matter of the practices of those [...] who go crazy through a trance, through religious experience, through passion or through anything else, the value of the catharsis presupposes that, in a way that is either more-or-less directed or wild, the subject enters into the zone described here, and that [its] return involves some gain that will be called possession.'[200] From a religious perspective, the goods have to be sacrificially reintegrated, beyond any form of accumulative conservation, to the living flux. Through this sacrificial expropriation, the subject becomes a possessed that channels the impersonal Dionysiac life through a personal Apollonian form. By means of the alchemical transmutation of goods into desire, the religious potlach fosters in particular what Lacan considers to be the principal site of desire in 'this historical period', the scientific desire to know, the 'most subtle and blindest of passions'.[201] It follows that only

199 Ibid., 322.

200 Ibid., 323.

201 'As far as science is concerned, the kind that is presently occupying the place of desire is quite simply what we commonly call science [...] I think that throughout this historical period the desire of [humans], which has been felt, anesthetised, put to sleep by moralists, domesticated by educators, betrayed by the academies, has quite simply taken refuge or been repressed in that most subtle and blindest of passions, as the story of Oedipus shows, the passion for knowledge.' Lacan, *The Ethics of Psychoanalysis*, 319.

a philosophical concertation between science and an absolutely modern religion—between the uncompromising will to know and the affirmation of life as the highest value (*Scientia vitae in vita scientiae*!)—might allow science to recover itself from its capitalistic cooptation.

How is it that Christianity can be understood as a synthesis *avant la lettre*, deployed in the realm of 'popular philosophy'—what we might call the 'German Idealism of the people'—of Kantian transcendentalism and Spinozist immanentism? We shall begin to explore the landscape opened by this question by moving—inspired and guided by Goddard's seminal reading of Fichte (a reading that operates a gradual process of transmutation in which the scholarly exegesis of the Fichtean corpus turns progressively toward the project of 'Fichteanising' again, as Novalis proposed in his *Logological Fragments*—that is to say, continuing by other means and in another medium—Latin America? Africa?—the philosophical performance whose first essays were the successive versions of Fichte's *Wissenschaftslehre*)—in the direction of a Christianity that is shamanic, other-than-Roman, synchretically umbandaimic, catatauically tropical, alchemically stoned, baroquodelised, narcissistically speculative, idolatrous and iconophilic, ritualistic and performative, animistic and polytheistic, devoted to the Queen of the Forest, calibanistically carnivalesque, bounded to its mineral finitude, synaesthetically sensual, endowed with an entheogenic sacred host—the force of imagination (*Einbildungskraft*)—destined to reactivate visionary outbursts of life within us. Anthropophagically (un)digested, regurgitated, and vomited, the Christian *performance* becomes an initiatory practice of religation with the absolute immanental life in which we exist and move and suffer and think and love and die, a healing potlatch capable of effecting the resurrection of a desiring subject and the institution of spiritual communities out of the ravages of capitalism, a 'reverse anthropology' of the 'people of merchandise',[202] a postcolonial ethnopsychiatry of European

202 Kopenawa and Albert, *The Falling Sky*, 327.

melancholy destined to institute a tribe religated to a land—to make it native and mortal by means of a 'permanent aboriginal revolution'.[203]

The speculative kernel of Christianity as conceptualised within the framework of German Idealism is strictly trinitarian, which means that the Christian God is refracted into three coninsubstantial hypostases. Trinitarianism is opposed to non-trinitarian forms of Christianity, such as those of Arius and Eunomius. According to non-trinitarian positions, there is a hierarchy between the hypostases, such as between the impersonal life and the living one. The living one, far from being coninsubstantial with the impersonal life qua immanent cause, is a mere creature made in time (rather than begotten before all worlds and linear history), a merely human and historical figure subordinated to the first hypostasis. The Arian controversy condenses all the tension between the received monarchic conception of God and the trinitarian conception of a material immanent cause that gives life without ruling over the living ones. Since the living are multiple, finite, and interdependent personae—since being-with is an existentiale of any living being—there cannot be two hypostases, the impersonal life and the personal living ones, without a third one, the 'spiritual' communities of the living. Briefly, there is no impersonal life without personal living ones that belong to transpersonal communities. From a speculative standpoint, the problem of non-trinitarianism is that it subordinates finitude and temporality to a mono-archic instance, thereby reintroducing ontotheology and the motif of an everlasting salvation. We might say in Luther's terms that non-trinitarian stances subordinate *theologia crucis* to *theologia gloriae*, thereby demoting what we consider here to be the principal innovation of Christianity, namely to maintain that finitude is not a flaw to be redeemed, but an integral coninstubstantial moment of divine life. Whereas non-trinitarianism is based on the idea of a 'God's life *in se* [or God in Godself] [...] to the exclusion of God's life [with me and] with us',[204] trinitarian

203 J.-C. Goddard, 'Fichte, ou la révolution aborigène permanente', in G. Marmasse and A. Schnell (eds.), *Comment fonder la philosophie ? L'idéalisme allemand et la question du principe premier* (Paris: CNRS Éditions, 2014).

204 C.M. LaCugna, 'God in Communion with Us: The Trinity', in C.M. LaCugna

orthodoxy tends to eliminate any hierarchical and linear relationship of subordination between hypostases. In trinitarian Christianity, the (one) *life*, the (multiple) *living ones* (the avatars of Yesses), and the (wholly) *tribes* are coninsubstantial hypostases of the triune pleroma, of the pleroma that ceaselessly engenders, reveals, and federates, disseminating the impersonal unity of its one life into separate autonomous and singular individuals and concertating the latter into tribal forms of the spirit.

As for the first hypostasis of triune pleroma, we shall assert that the 'fundamental equation of Christianity is: God is life [...]'.[205] A God separated from worldly multiplicities, hypertranscendent, ontotheologised—far from being, strictly speaking, absolute—would be relative with respect to that from which it is separated. It is therefore necessary that God 'separates [it]self from [its] separation',[206] that it incorporates the multiple so that its dismembering into finite individuals becomes a necessary moment of its intra-divine life. Christianity satisfies this demand by proposing a purely immanental thesis: far from being a hypertranscendent instance which—being beyond all possible experience—can only be the object of a personal belief or a supposed speculative 'demonstration' of its non-evident 'existence', the God of Christianity is the devotional name of life itself. But then what is life? In order to start diving into this abyssal question, we can begin with the thesis that life is the force that begets and bears experiencing beings, the force that excites breathing finite modes of the immanental insubstance endowed with receptive-imaginative-acting capacities, the force that institutes beings that reveal, local operators of the revelation. In this sense, the theozoetic identification God = Life implies the phenoumenodelic definition 'God is essentially self-revelation'.[207] In Spinozist terms, we shall

(ed.), *Freeing Theology: The Essentials of Theology in Feminist Perspective* (New York: HarperCollins, 1993), 94.

205 M. Henry, *C'est moi la Vérité. Pour une philosophie du christianisme* (Paris: Seuil, 1996), 40.

206 Levinas, 'Hegel and the Jews', in *Difficult Freedom*, 235.

207 Hegel, *Lectures on the Philosophy of Religion, Volume I*, 374.

say that life is the immanent and not the transitive cause of all living beings.[208] Life as immanent cause of the living is not separate from that which it generates and it remains the life that irrigates them and bears all subjective experience. According to its primary hypostatic declension, the pleroma is an insubstantial vibrant womb, the primal vortex, the immanental mat(t)er: God qua absolute insubstance is 'not an inert, abstract universal [...] but rather the absolute womb or the infinite fountainhead out of which everything emerges, into which everything returns, and in which it is [transiently] maintained. This basic determination is therefore the definition of God as [living ma(t)ter].'[209]

In Christianity, God ceases to be a stern master, a sovereign father, or a hypertranscendent despot and becomes an immanental living power who cannot but institute local subjective modes, vibrant subjects, breathing excitations of the insubstance.[210] To emphasise this transition from the hypertranscendent God who rules over the created (ex nihilo) to the immanent God who begets the coninsubstantial living, we shall abruptly install in place of the Father in the holy trinity the 'matter, mutter, mother',[211] the riverrunning Anna Livia Plurabelle, the immanental mater that 'tabularases' 'with a dustwhisk' the patriarchal 'obliteration done upon her involucrum',[212] that 'insignificant and inessential exception'[213] that is conspicuous in its

---

208 Cf. Spinoza, *Ethics*, 21 (Book I, Prop. XVIII).

209 Hegel, *Lectures on the Philosophy of Religion, Volume III*, 197.

210 On the relation between monotheism and patriarchy–and the anti-patriarchal potential of trinitarian religion–see L. Boff, *Trinity and Society* (New York: Orbis, 1988).

211 Cf. Haraway, *Staying With the Trouble*, 120.

212 Joyce, *Finnegans Wake*, 50.

213 Derrida, *Glas*, 44. See also L. Rozitchner, *La Cosa y la Cruz. Cristianismo y Capitalismo (en torno a las Confesiones de San Agustín)* (Buenos Aires: Ediciones Biblioteca Nacional, 2015), Appendix II, 449–55. According to the patriarchal Athanasian Creed, the mother only provides the human, worldly, and temporal component in a Christ that is both human and divine: '[O]ur Lord Jesus Christ, the Son of God, is God and Man; God, of the Substance [Essence] of the Father; begotten before the worlds; and Man, of the Substance [Essence] of his Mother, born in the world'.

absence from the speculative family. '[T]o the Jewish idea of God as their Lord [*Gebieter*] and Governor [*Herrs*], Jesus opposes a relationship of God to [humans] like that of a [mat(t)er] to [her] children.[214] [...] Love for and relationship with another [becomes] primary over autonomy, ecstasis over stasis, fecundity over self-sufficiency.'[215] The first hypostasis of the phenoumenodelic conjugation of the Christian trinity is the Virgin Mary—a Rainha da Floresta—Pindorama, Notre-Dame-des-Fleurs, the material daydream, the *natura naturans*, Iemanjá—the Queen of the flowing insubstance—'Mater Virgo—virgin matter or the unploughed soil, [...] the Prima Materia prior to its division [...] into the multiplicity of [begotten] things',[216] 'the untouched plenitude, the virgin continuity of the nonscission',[217] the underlying engendering *Band* that makes of every living being a sibling. Full of grace, the Virgin Ma(t)ter is the Mediatrix of all Graces, the Generatrix of all Figures, 'the Mother of the Living, [...] who is the beginning of all the emanations that [breathe in] th[e] world[s].'[218] The virginity of Mary encodes its immanental self-sufficiency, the causasuiness of the insubstance: the mat(t)er is not a passive primitive chaos waiting for the ordering inscription of a hypertranscendent (S)Word, but a self-organising insubstance endowed with the immanental resources to engender souls, to blow up worlds, to unfold histories, a vibrating immaculate Womb that does not need the insemination of a paternal *logos* in order to engender the living ones, in order to divide its unity and refract its univocity into multiple lifeforms, in order to polarise itself in I/not-I correlations: '[The infinite mat(t)er] gives itself, by [...] self-insemination and self-conception, a finite [child] who has to stand there and incarnate as a child of [life] [...]: "I conceive myself without a father, I am born of myself" [...] I am

214 Hegel, *On Christianity: Early Theological Writings*, 253.

215 LaCugna, 'God in Communion with Us', 86.

216 A. Watts, *Myth and Ritual in Christianity* (New York: Grove Press, 1960), 107.

217 Derrida, *Dissemination*, 302.

218 F. Bermejo Rubio and J. Montserrat Torrents (eds.), *El maniqueismo y textos fuentes* (Madrid: Editorial Trotta, 2009), 157 [*Kephalaion* 29 (82, 1–3): text 1.3.10].

my father, my mother, my [child] and myself.'[219] The thesis that the Virgin Mary is inseminated by a transcendent Holy Spirit fails to think to its ultimate consequences its immanental virginity, its sovereign capacity to spiritualise itself, the coninsubstantiality between the first and the third hypostasis. The notion of spirit denotes nothing but the capacity of mat(t)er to transcend the worldly configurations that locally crystallise in its own immanence, the immanental resource through which mat(t)er absolves itself from the essentialisation of the living ones and the reification of the correlative Umwelten. The spirit supervenes within the mat(t)er but in the last instance '[o]ne does not take [mat(t)erwaters]. She always reforms. She stays. There, even, calm. Intact, impassive, always virgin.'[220]

This substitution of the mat(t)er for the Father allows us to avoid the danger of surreptitiously reintroducing an overarching and vertical hyper-transcendent figure into Christian trinitarianism. For instance, Joachim de Fiore's superimposing of a linear and teleological conception of world history onto the Christian trinity—and in particular the thesis that the first trinitarian hypostasis corresponds to the ruling God of the Old Testament—perpetuates within Christianity the impasses of an ontotheological conception of God. The persistence of the Father in the trinity—together with the thesis that the three hypostasis are coeternal—is, according to Merleau-Ponty, the key to understanding the conservative character of Catholicism, its inability to fully assume the experience of the incarnation in all its immanent radicality.[221] However, Merleau-Ponty persists, in the

219 Derrida, *Glas*, 39, 95.

220 Ibid., 229.

221 '[T]he religion of both the Father and the Son are to be fulfilled in the religion of the Spirit, [...] God is no longer in Heaven but in human society and communication, wherever [human beings] come together in His name. Christ's stay on earth was only the beginning of his presence, which is continued by the Church. Christians [...] should live out the marriage of the Spirit and human history which began with the Incarnation. Catholicism arrests and freezes this development of religion: the Trinity is not a dialectical movement; the Three Persons are co-eternal. The Father is not surpassed by the Spirit; the religion of the Father lives on in the religion of the Spirit, for Love does not eliminate the Law or the fear of God. God is

wake of Joachim de Fiore, in understanding the first hypostasis as a hypertranscendent Father, and limits himself to demanding, against the thesis of coeternality, the Father's dialectical overcoming in the Spirit. The closure of ontotheology would thus take place by means of a kind of dialectical procession which—traversing the various hypostases in order to culminate in the incarnated Spirit—would definitively leave behind the idea of a paternal God in heaven. Here we shall remain faithful to trinitarian orthodoxy by affirming the coninsubstantiality of the hypostases. To do so, we shall banish from the trinity once and for all any form of hypertranscendent, overarching, monarchic figure. So as not to betray the Christian rejection of the Jewish figure of a separate God, the first hypostasis of the trinity must also satisfy the Spinozist demand for immanence. This condition can be fulfilled by identifying the first hypostasis with the impersonal and universal life, the one life within which 'I and not-I, outside and inside no longer mean anything'.[222] The incarnation instantiated in the second hypostasis of the trinity is not a movement through which a hypertranscendent Father would condescend to the world, to history and to finitude, but rather a localisation of immanental life, the excitation of a subjective finite mode within living insubstance.

The mat(t)er is the hypostasis with respect to which the ab-original being of a (singular or collective) subject is defined. That which Fichte, in the seventh *Address to the German Nation*, calls the *primitive* or *aboriginal people* (*Urvolk*) is the community of those who—in contrast to the non-originality or the non-primitivity of the outlanders (*Ausländer*)—are religated to and linger in their origin, in the *mater*, *matter*, *ma-terre* [my land]: 'To be [aboriginal] is to have as a primary reference the relationship with the land where one was born and where one has settled to make one's life. [...]

---

not completely with us. Behind the incarnate Spirit there remains that infinite gaze which strips us of all secrets, but also of our liberty, our desire, and our future, reducing us to visible objects.' M. Merleau-Ponty, 'Faith and Good Faith', in *Sense and Nonsense*, tr. H.L. Dreyfus and P.A. Dreyfus (Evanston, IL: Northwestern University Press, 1964), 177.

222 Deleuze and Guattari, *Anti-Oedipus*, 2.

The [aboriginals] look downwards, toward the Earth from which they are immanent; they draw their strength from the ground. [...] The land that [the aboriginals inhabit] is not their property [...] because they belong to the land, not the other way around. Belonging to the land, rather than owning it, is what defines the [aboriginal]. [...] [T]he [aboriginals] are part of the body of the earth.[223] [...] To "inhabit" is not to "occupy".'[224] The origin of the living cannot be an essence, a fixed and dead being, something 'immutably permanent', but instead is vitality itself, the force that begets and informs and deforms the living forms. The constant nomadic hustle and bustle of the outlanders—their type-centric cosmopolitanism, their touristic curiosity, their colonising drive—conceals a transcendental inertia: their tireless movements across the empirical earth and beyond—their will to extend and impose their type, to discover and conquer new territories and even spacetime itself—only reinforce the foreclosure of their inability to undertake a true 'spiritual' transformation. The outlander, separated in this way from the vital force capable of existentialising its essentialised being, lives in a reified world circumscribed by transcendental limits that are impermeable to the ebb and flow of life. Contrary to this, a subject religated to the mat(t)er is an *ab-origine*, a living being who is there from the origin, where the prefix *ab-*, far from referring to a presumed past, denotes the contemporary primal vortex that is always active, the 'hystorical' event that never ceases enacting its 'mamafestation',[225] the Ur-spring of phenoumenodelic fluxions. In this enduring wellspring the living can sink their roots, anchor their soul, refresh their feet: 'Yes, what used to be abides.[226] [...] The beginning still is. It does not lie behind us, as something that was long ago, but stands before us. As what is [almighty], the beginning has passed in advance over all that is to come and thus already

223 Viveiros de Castro, 'Les involontaires de la patrie', 124–25, 127.

224 Goddard, 'Fichte, où la révolution aborigène permanente'.

225 We borrow the terms 'hystorical' (from the Greek *hysteros*, womb) and 'mamafesta' from Joyce, *Finnegans Wake*, 564 and 104.

226 F. Hölderlin, 'Homecoming', in *Selected Poems and Fragments*, tr. M. Hamburger (London: Penguin, 1998), 165.

over us as well. The beginning has invaded our future. There it stands as the distant command to us to catch up with its [overabundant delicacy].[227] [L]oyalty to the origin is innate to [the aboriginal]. A place of dwelling this near to the source is hard to leave',[228] and yet being an outlander—being separated from the land, from the community, from the body, from one's own desire—seems to be the most widely distributed mode of existence in modern humanity. The mat(t)er is not the lost unity to which one could return in death or mystical ecstasy, but the 'enormous womb' in which the aboriginals live, move, and die, the womb that envelops the aboriginals' continuous gestation and their successive births, deaths, and resurrections. The mat(t)er is 'what is all-encompassing, what is One. [...] The universal here includes everything [that is there] within itself.[229] [...] [T]here is never anything but womb.'[230] The sickness of disligation is a 'loss of soul', a weakening of the appendage that religates the living with the first hypostasis, that plugs the living into the begetting mat(t)er, into its land. In turn, 'the resurrection of the dead' should not be understood as a miracle by means of which the subject would have access to eternal life after dying, but rather as an act of revining–of binding the liana of the living and the dead–that strengthens the connection between the living and dying person and the impersonal realm of life in its manifold manifestations, as an act of binding 'backtowards motherwaters',[231] back into the wombing material dreaminess. 'A dream within a dream within a dream within a dream within a dream within, and at the bottom of the dream of dreams, [the Lady] of the Lights and of the [Forces, Lucifuerza] *rex somniorum*! [...] Soul, go inside yourself. [...] The memorial of wonders does not repeat the show. The soul comes out of the dream into the [constituted] world, [its reality;] the world begins in the [instituted] soul. [...] The abolished self.

227 Heidegger, 'The Self-Assertion of the German University', 5.

228 F. Hölderlin, 'The Migration (*Die Wanderung*)', *Hyperion and Selected Poems*, 203.

229 Hegel, *Lectures on the Philosophy of Religion, Volume III*, 194–5.

230 Miller, 'The Enormous Womb', in *The Wisdom of the Heart*, 40–43: 40.

231 Joyce, *Finnegans Wake*, 84.

Killed by the bug. Blue phenomena in unexplained circumstances. [...] I forgot I was in the world. [...] Colourful dots in the spring water, green eyes from within the green foliage. [...] The world flooded with dreams.'[232] For a revined living being, worldly reality drifts within the oneiric insubstance, within the material dreaminess that bears, enlivens, and disrealises it. The world is not a material prison for the soul from which the latter should be liberated, but a phenomenal bubble suspended in the phenoumenodelic insubstance, an umweltic chalice that collects—'for the joy of the dew on the flower of the fleets on the fields of the foam of the waves of the seas [...]'[233]—some distilled drops of the alchemical theogenesis. The soul is the umbilical thread that channels the living forces of the primal mat(t)er and pushes the living to sublate its circumambient world, to sprout into the supernatural sky. A living one is 'one of those [...] for whom the audible-visible-gnosible-edible [circumambient] world existed. That [it] was only too cognitively conatively cogitabundantly sure of it because, living, loving, breathing and sleeping morphomelosophopancreates, as [it] most significantly did, whenever [it] thought [it] heard [it] saw [it] felt [it] made a bell clipperclipperclipperclipper.'[234] But this subjective constitution of a whole existing reality and the concomitant ego-cognitive certainty about its 'matteroffactness' is in the last instance a dreamlike pattern rhythmically morphing itself in the surface of the solaristic flowing mat(t)er: '*Amor matris*, subjective and objective genitive, may be the only true thing in life. Pat[t]ernity may be a [symbolic hallucination].'[235] The one life that nourishes the aboriginal intoxicates it with its transcendental plasticity and imprints in its existence a process of continuous self-formation (*sich bilden*), a rhythm of *determination* (position of self, affirmation and care for one's own figure, one's own desiring autonomy and subjective integrity) and *indetermination* (deformation of its figure, shamanic mutations, inter-totemic exogamy,

232 Leminski, *Catatau*, 10, 103, 105–6.

233 Joyce, *Finnegans Wake*, 331.

234 Ibid., 88.

235 Joyce, *Ulysses*, 266.

trans-species fluency): a religated existence 'proceeds from the "one and pure" divine life, [...] [from] life as such (*als Leben schlechtweg*), which always remains singular, "one life", without being the life of this or that individual, without being the life of a formed, stable subject, and which consists in the constant rhythmic beating of an opening and a closing, of an *arsis* and a *thesis*, of a determination and an indetermination, through which the continuous formative activity, the infinite *sich bilden* of the aboriginal people is exercised.'[236]

The characterisation of the immanental background from which the living being is 'separated' as one impersonal life, an 'absolute womb' that bears, nourishes, and nurtures the living being diverges from the thesis that the living organism is something like a fluctuation in a purely inorganic field (or that life on Earth is an exception resulting from a highly unlikely convergence of coincidences in a universe that is, for the most part, 'dead'). The 'death drive' introduced by Freud is defined as the inherent tendency in any disturbance of equilibrium toward its restoration, the entropic urge to return to an earlier state by dissolving the living fluctuations back into the inorganic background. This definition of the death drive falls within the framework of what Jonas calls an 'ontology of death',[237] an ontology resulting (according to Jonas) from the image of the world revealed by modern science. According to this ontology of death, organic life emerges locally within an inorganic background ('The living is only a form of what is dead, and a very rare form at that'),[238] and vital functions have no other objective than to resist death (Bichat). Yet this ontology of death is the very opposite of Christianity and its fundamental thesis: God is life. For the purpose of clarifying the tension between the ontology of death and Christianity, it is important to point out that for Freud the death drive is the archetype of the concept of drive, since Freud implicitly presupposes

236 Goddard, 'Fichte, où la révolution aborigène permanente', 197–98.

237 Cf. Jonas, 'First Essay. Life, Death, and the Body in the Theory of Being', in *The Phenomenon of Life*, 7–37.

238 F. Nietzsche, *The Gay Science*, tr. J. Nauckhoff (Cambridge: Cambridge University Press, 2007), 110 [translation modified].

the 'scientific' validity of the ontology of death. But the death drive becomes the archetype of the drive (defined in broad terms as the urge to return to the earlier state) only if we assume that this previous state is defined by inorganicity. Freud explicitly indicates that his definition of the drive could also apply to the drive for life (Eros) if we understood the 'earlier state' as a 'living substance' not yet torn apart by individuation.[239] In a footnote, Freud points out (probably alluding to Aristophanes's speech in Plato's *Symposium*) that the understanding of the 'earlier state' as 'living substance' (which Freud does not endorse) was developed by the 'poets'. Consequently, Freud seems to reach the paradoxical conclusion that one of the 'two basic drives' does not satisfy his own proposed definition of the drive concept. Of course, it is completely legitimate to adopt an ontological framework (in Freud's case, the ontology of death) and to explore its theoretical, clinical, ethical, and political consequences. What is more problematic is the dogmatic assertion that the ontology in question is definitively sanctioned by modern science. The task of science is not so much to provide answers but rather to continuously refine and multiply the questions, to craft our relationship with the unknown with subtler and more sophisticated

239 '[The drives] are of a conservative nature; the state, whatever it may be, which an organism has reached gives rise to a tendency to re-establish that state so soon as it has been abandoned. [...] After long hesitancies and vacillations, we have decided to assume the existence of only two basic instincts, Eros and the destructive instinct. [...] The aim of the first of these basic instincts is to establish ever greater unities and to preserve them thus—in short, to bind [*Bindung*] together; the aim of the second is, on the contrary, to undo connections and so to destroy things. In the case of the destructive instinct we may suppose that its final aim is to lead what is living into an inorganic state. For this reason, we also call it the death instinct. If we assume that living things came later than inanimate ones and arose from them, then the death instinct fits in with the formula we have proposed to the effect that instincts tend towards a return to an earlier state. In the case of Eros (or the love instinct) we cannot apply this formula. To do so would presuppose that living substance was once a unity which had later been torn apart and was now striving towards re-union.' S. Freud, 'An Outline of Psychoanalysis', in *The Standard Edition of the Complete Psychological Works of Sigmund Freud, Volume XXIII (1937–1939)*, tr. J. Strachey, A. Freud, A. Strachey, and A. Tyson (London: The Hogarth Press, 1964), 148–49.

conceptual and technical means.[240] Thanks to physics and astrophysics, thanks to biology, today we can ask theoretical and experimental questions about life and the universe with an unprecedented degree of conceptual, formal, and technological precision. But let us not, in the name of science, give in to the dogmatic temptation to betray the infinite idea of truth that guides scientific endeavour.[241] Theoretical reason can inform practical reason, but never ground it. It is not possible to absolve ourselves of the vertiginous responsibility and the risk inherent in any given existential decision by attempting to ground it on assumed scientific knowledge. All of the objective knowledge provided by modern science does not relieve us of the need to tell stories—to forge myths, as the German Romantics would say—to orient our existences. We cannot disentangle the imaginary from the-symbolic-and-the-real without also untying the latter; we cannot remain faithful to the modern Enlightenment without acknowledging that conscious rationality emerges from and drifts in a collective unconscious ocean. In particular, Christianity as we are trying to rethink it in this work tells a very different story from that of the 'ontology of death'. If we anachronistically reconceptualise Christianity as a synthesis between (phenoumenodelicly suspended) Spinozist immanentism and (speculatively extended) Kantian transcendentalism, then the fundamental Christian thesis can be reformulated as follows: the immanental insubstance in which the living vibrate, in which lifeworlds sprout, and in which images are

240 'Questioning is then no longer merely a preliminary step that is surmounted on the way to the answer and thus to knowing; rather, questioning itself becomes the highest form of knowing.' Heidegger, 'The Self-Assertion of the German University', 6.

241 It might be worth quoting here one of the greatest scientists of modernity: 'I do not know what I may appear to the world; but to myself I seem to have been only like a boy playing on the sea-shore, and diverting myself in now and then finding a smoother pebble or a prettier shell than ordinary, whilst the great ocean of truth lay all undiscovered before me.' I. Newton, in D. Brewster, *Memoirs of Sir Isaac Newton* (Edinburgh and London: Thomas Constable/Hamilton, Adams, 2 vols., 1855), vol. 2, 407. After quoting Newton, Brewster adds the following comment: 'What a lesson to the vanity and presumption of philosophers, —to those specially who have never even found the smoother pebble or the prettier shell' (408).

revealed (and, in particular, the images that compose the *Weltanschauungen* projected by modern science) is life, one life.... 'Self-revelation [...] is what God essentially is',[242] and God self-reveals by throwing living beings to a singular existence freefalling in its own immanental depths. The distinction between the impersonal background and the local saliencies (between the ground state of insubstance and its localised states of excitation) cannot be superimposed onto the distinction between the inorganic and the organic. Both background and local saliencies are in the Christian trinity coninsubstantial hypostases of life: the mat(t)er qua impersonal life that engenders and nourishes and the living qua life incarnate respectively. 'In what we call dead matter there converge at every point, no fewer and no lesser divine forces. [...] We swim in an ocean of [living] omnipotence [...].'[243] In this conceptual framework, a living being cannot be understood as an improbable local exception in an otherwise dead background, but must rather be thought of as a local broadcasting antenna, an appendage, a living probe of omnipresent life. Life is not understood as an accident of death and the projected end of the living is not return to the inorganic. Bergson's criticism of the notion of nothing and his attempt to reveal the presuppositions behind the metaphysical question *Why there is something instead of nothing?* echoes the Christian deconstruction of the ontology of death: whereas in the framework of this ontology life is understood as a conquest over death, in the metaphysics criticised by Bergson 'existence appears [...] as a conquest over nought'.[244] The immanence of the living insubstance proclaimed by Yesses, the Affirmator, should be understood in the most radical manner: any form of negation should be immanentised, understood as a local operation taking place within the living insubstance. The Spinozist thesis that every determination is a negation should be complemented with the reciprocal thesis, namely that every negation is a determination carved out of the pleromatic overabundant life. This implies that the living insubstance

242 Hegel, *Lectures on the Philosophy of Religion, Volume III*, 197.

243 J.G. Herder, *God, Some Conversations*, tr. F.H. Burkhardt (New York: Bobbs-Merrill, 1940), 107.

244 Bergson, *Creative Evolution*, 300.

itself cannot be thought of as an exception to an overall negative ground state given by nothingness or death. In Christianity, death is not the presupposed global background out of which local living fluctuations would eventually arise here and there, but rather the process of decaying to the local vacua spontaneously produced within the immanence of life by the procession through which life ceaselessly diverges from itself ('the living comes out of the living and returns to it').[245] Life is not a local and improbable fluctuation taking time and place before a global inert backdrop, but an omnipresent unfolding process, a vital continuum, that continually produces new forms of equilibrium and institutes transient receptive-expressive modes of the latter. Like the leaves falling onto the fermenting soil of the rainforest or the deer that makes ingression into the living flesh of the jaguar that devours it, these subjective excitations do not decay to a global arche-ground of death, but rather to living local vacua.[246] In Christianity, the living is born out of the living, lives as a local mode of life, and decays into the living background. By making the living and mortal one—the crucified Yesses—the second hypostasis of triune life, Christiânity openly takes up the challenge of thinking and living finitude—and thus death—as a necessary moment in the self-revelation of life.[247]

---

245 Eboussi Boulaga, *Christianisme sans fétiche. Révélation et domination*, 133.

246 As Deleuze and Guattari argue, '[t]he experience of death is the most common of occurrences [...] precisely because it occurs in life and for life, in every passage or becoming, in every intensity as passage or becoming. It is in the very nature of every intensity to invest within itself the zero intensity starting from which it is produced, in one moment, as that which grows or diminishes according to an infinity of degrees. [...] [D]eath is what [...] never ceases and never finishes happening in every becoming—in the becoming-another-sex, the becoming-god, the becoming-a-race, etc., forming zones of intensity on the [pleromatic insubstance]. Every intensity controls within its own life the experience of death, and envelops it.' Deleuze and Guattari, *Anti-Oedipus*, 363.

247 As Saint Aubert states, commenting on a text by Merleau-Ponty on Christianity, it was necessary for Christianity to go to the extreme of conceiving of a God who dies so that humanity could finally accept and mourn its own carnality and mortality: 'God here is no longer an expanded image of our phantasmic positivity (a god

In Christianity, the infinitising hubris of the human is counteracted by the reverse moment: the finitising incarnation of the divine. Birth, death, and the transcendental limitations of experience are understood as moments of finitude. And finitude—the singular determination of the living form—is the eye of the needle through which revelation passes. Far from understanding the unexperienceable background as an inorganic state of equilibrium from which the living depart and to which they must return in death, the impersonal life is understood as an infinite will to reveal channelled by the institution of finite living beings, as a phenoumenodelia of spirit, a negentropic process that continually rises toward new emergent forms of spiritual coherence. The pleromatic exorbitance that exerts pressure on the finite living being is not that of a dead background, but that of an infinite will to live in its manifold forms, the will to know and learn, the will to hear, to see, to touch, to smell, to eat and taste, the will to feel, to enjoy, to love, to share, the will to express, the will to explore and reveal, to be a breathing channel through which life (over)flows in itself. If we accept this Christian-Spinozist reconceptualisation of the background from which the living organism is separated, then the drive par excellence is no longer the death drive but the drive for life (Eros). The will to remain religated to the impersonal life, far from taking the form of a death drive that pulls the individual back to the undifferentiated one, manifests as an erotic desire to engender and to federate the separated living beings into higher form of living unity. Both the centrifugal begetting of separated individuals and the centripetal institution of tribal totalities are manifestations of the same erotic drive for life. The genius of trinitarian Christianity lies in the

---

adorned with the power, wealth assets and knowledge of a [human being] drawn into infinity as a result of being freed from the finitude of our bodily capacities), he becomes, through the Incarnation, a magnified expression of our real negativity. [...] God is thus adorned with a condition that [human beings] cannot recognise and assume. As if it took an incarnate God to teach [human beings] what [they are] and to help [them] to live with this. As if it had taken a carnal God for [human beings themselves] to consent to be flesh.' E. de Saint Aubert, '« L'incarnation change tout »; Merleau-Ponty critique de la « theologie explicative »', *Transversalités* 112 (2009), 152–53.

dialectical logic through which it understands this drive: the drive for life tends to restore the unity of life beyond its dismembering into separated individuals through the institution of collective forms of spirit understood as concrete totalities made up of finite and singular lifeforms. The spirit (the third hypostasis) is the life which recreates its unity not through a mystical regression from the second hypostasis to the first, but through a projection toward a wholly spiritual synthesis of the impersonal unity of life and the multiplicity of the living persona. The speculative role played by death is not that of reintegrating the individual into the undifferentiated one, of diluting the second hypostasis into the first one, but rather that of radicalising the individual's singular localisation, its being-there-and-thus, its irreducible heterogeneity, and, by doing so, that of endowing the living with an irreplaceable perspective in the midst of revelation.

Let us return for a moment to the relationship between the fundamental thesis of Christianity (God is self-revealing life) and modern science. Is not Christian pan-vitalism refuted plain and simple by the image of the world provided by modern cosmology? Isn't 'modern materialism' closer to the Gnostic heresy than to Christianity *strictu senso* in 'proving' that 'the whole world is tomb [...] to the soul or spirit [...]'?[248] A purportedly uncompromising assessment of the existential situation of human beings in the modern era was proposed by Monod in the following terms: '[Our ancestors] did not have the reasons we have today for feeling themselves strangers in the universe upon which they opened their eyes. [...] Thus was the world's strangeness resolved for those early human beings: in reality there exist no inanimate objects. For such a thing would be incomprehensible. In the river's depths, on the mountaintop, more subtle spirits pursue vaster and more impenetrable designs than the transparent ones animating [human beings] and beasts. [...] [human beings] must at last wake out of [their] millenary dream; and in doing so, wake to [their] total solitude, [their] fundamental isolation. Now [do they] at last realise that [...] [they] live on the boundary of an alien world. A world that is deaf to [their] music, just as indifferent to [their] hopes as it is to [their] suffering

248 Jonas, *The Phenomenon of Life*, 14.

or [their] crimes. [...] The ancient [animist] covenant is in pieces; [human beings] know at last that [they are] alone in the universe's unfeeling immensity, out of which [they] emerged only by chance.'[249] In their response to Monod, Prigogine and Stengers argued that Monod's desolate depiction of 'the human place in the cosmos' stems from what they call 'classical science' (in short, Newtonian science). They argue that 'non classical science'—mainly relativity theory, quantum mechanics, non-linear dynamics, and far-from-equilibrium thermodynamics—started suturing the cleavage between humans and the universe and brought forth the possibility of forging a 'new alliance'. Such non-classical science would provide an 'image of the world' that is incompatible with the ontology of death, that is, with the idea that life is an improbable local event in an otherwise dead universe. In particular, we now understand that morphogenesis and self-organisation are as 'natural' as gravitational interaction,[250] and that the pretension 'to describe the world from an external, almost divine point of view'[251] is pre-critical naivety. As Prigogine and Stengers emphasise (and we agree), Monod's conclusions rely on a conflation between a certain state of science (the mechanistic image of the world associated with Newtonian physics) and a supra-historical conception of scientific rationality as such that would overarch its different epochal phases.[252] Now, this important remark is also valid for 'non-classical science'. The relativistic, quantum,

249 J. Monod, *Chance and Necessity: An Essay on the Natural Philosophy of Modern Biology*, tr. A. Wainhouse (New York: Alfred A. Knopf, 1971), 29–30, 172–73, 180.

250 'If we equate life with a phenomenon of self-organisation of matter evolving toward more and more complex states, then, in well-defined circumstances that do not seem to be exceptionally rare, life is predictable in the Universe, and is as "natural" a phenomenon as the fall of heavy bodies.' I. Prigogine and I. Stengers, *La Nouvelle Alliance. Métamorphose de la science* (Paris: Éditions Gallimard, 1979), 193.

251 Prigogine and Stengers, *La Nouvelle Alliance*, 60.

252 'Monod's exhortation, which urges [the human being] to assume his destiny of solitude and to renounce the illusions in which traditional societies took refuge, typically leads to the identification of Western science, as it has developed over the last few centuries, with a rationality that transcends all cultures and all times.' Prigogine and Stengers, *La Nouvelle Alliance*, 38.

and non-linear 'image of the world' is also an 'image' subject to the merciless scrutiny of scientific criticism, and no one can predict how this image will be assessed by the physicists of the future. Hence, any amalgamation between the relativistic, quantum, and non-linear 'image of the world' and a supra-historical conception of scientific rationality as such is as misleading as Monod's canonisation of the mechanistic image provided by classical physics. Of course, the relativistic, quantum, and non-linear 'scientific revolutions' certainly show that we are not condemned to uncritically accept the desolate landscape described by Monod, to resign ourselves to the fact that we are 'strangers in a disenchanted world', and that the 'ring of the old [animist] covenant' is definitively broken. As Prigogine and Stengers eloquently argue, 'science and "disenchantment of the world" are not synonymous'.[253] However, if science can certainly inform our existential decisions and enrich our conceptual schemes and tools, it is certainly not by clinging to the latest scientific 'image of the world' that we shall heal from our disligation. Along the same lines, attempts to ground different forms of religious spirituality (Taoism, Hinduism, Buddhism, aboriginal cosmovisions) on the results of contemporary physics not only improperly mix heterogeneous registers of thought and practice but also foster a contagion of the provisional character of scientific descriptions into a radically different domain, that of religious practices. If for instance we accepted that the current scientific cosmovision converge with that proposed by Buddhism, then are we to consider Buddhism falsified when this scientific cosmovision is superseded by a radically different image? By undoing the suture between science and religion, by uncompromisingly affirming their irreducible sovereignty as heterogeneous modes of thought and practice, it becomes possible to philosophically constellate them and to orient ourselves in existence by means of a new absolutely modern knot between truth and love. In this respect, the difference that is relevant here is not the difference between classical and non-classical science—a difference which is already to a certain extent an abstraction (we could say with Hegel and Schelling that 'scientific revolutions' are historical discontinuities that

253 Ibid., 15.

foreclose a retrospectively discernible underlying continuity)—but rather the difference between a science that hypostasises the 'images of the world' it produces and conflates a particular model of rationality with rationality as such, and a science that submits itself to the hyperbolic hypothesising of any scientific image prescribed by the infinite idea of truth.

It is not by relying on abstract cuts between different historical phases of modern science that we shall forge a 'new alliance' with nature and overcome the contemporary sickness of disligation. It is our disligation with respect to the immanental force of imagination (*Einbildungskraft*) that projected those images into the phenomenological foreground that made possible our fall into the disenchanted world depicted by classical physics. Rather than putting our hopes on the latest scientific 'images of the world', on the brave 'new paradigms', we shall bracket our immersion within any image and try to ground ourselves back in the immanental background, in the living mat(t)er that innervates the scientific desire to produce always new rational images of our existential situation. 'The being of God is existence' and 'existence means manifestation',[254] and manifestation unfolds by engendering and transforming forms of life that exist, that are there in the open, receiving signals, forming images, broadcasting them, dreaming, understanding, feeling, establishing contacts of the *n*th kind. By way of the phenoumenodelic *epoché*, the theoretical theses provided by modern science (on fundamental particles, on the origin of the universe and the genesis of the various stellar bodies, on the evolution of life on Earth, and so on) are suspended, put into a limbic state of flotation. The description of our existential situation in terms of a planet in orbital freefall inhabiting a lost corner of a dead, dark, and silent universe is just an 'image of the world' hovering in the living self-revelation of life. The phenoumenodelicly stoned philosopher floats in living matterfestation, refraining from endowing the 'images' provided by modern science with the prerogative of setting the ultimate coordinates of its existential situation and ethical decisions. All rational understanding of life (that is, all science)

254 M. Henry, *The Essence of Manifestation*, tr. G. Etzkorn (The Hague: Martinus Nijhoff, 1984), 69, 303.

is itself a local form of revelation, a living image of the pleroma; all appearance—and in particular every theoretical construction—takes place in the living specious present of immanental life. In this suspended environment, life is the absolute phenoumenodelic insubstance in which the living are engendered and in which they constitute their lifeworlds, project their cosmovisions, and build up their rational knowledge. The zoom out from the Gaia-and-anthropos-centred description of our existential situation to an heliocentric 'general economy' and from there to the universe described by scientific cosmology cannot stop at the latest scientific *Weltanschauung* (or at any point in the infinite series of its speculative extensions). Our existential situation is a concrete situation and it cannot be faithfully described by clinging to a particular 'image of the world' constructed by using our capacity to tune a particular abstract attribute of the pleroma—the *logos*—to the detriment of the infinite others. Our existential situation is not only informed by the concepts provided by modern science, but also by the percepts, the imaginary landscapes, the affects, the myths, the habits, the sociolepts, the dreams, the practices, the fictions, the semiotic processes, the lifeforms, the rituals that we can tune and channel. This suspension of the scientific 'images of the world' does not mean that we no longer inhabit the expanding universe described by modern cosmology or that we shall not pursue our efforts to improve its understanding. But we can dwell within this image and explore its confines while at the same time remaining anchored in the self-concealing living mat(t)er—our ancestral soil—and projecting ourselves toward the supernatural sky 'beyond' the cosmological sky. The modern 'infinite universe' with its unfathomable spatiotemporal extensions spans the living earth 'below' and the supernatural sky 'above'. It follows that (what Spinoza calls) knowledge of the second kind—the attempt to rationally understand the microscopic, macroscopic, and cosmological quandaries of the 'infinite universe'—cannot have the last word regarding the description of our existential situation and its different (im)possibilities. In particular, only knowledge of the third kind—the religating act by means of which we plug the soul back into the concrete immanental insubstance with its not-only-conceptual infinite attributes and 'conceive [everything] to be contained in

God'[255]—makes possible encounters of the third kind, that is, encounters in which the other is experienced beyond particularities, as another singular vibrating mode of the universal living insubstance.

In his description of Lévi-Strauss's disenchanted experience of the Brazilian rainforest and the supposedly melancholy post-finitude of a certain contemporary 'speculative realism', Goddard suggests that both Lévi-Strauss's anthropology and this putative realism are based on the same ontology of death. In both cases, the immanental life in which we are born, in which we breathe, and in which we die, is subordinated to a supposedly objective and inorganic world within which life, sensibility, and consciousness locally and contingently emerged; a purely objective, inanimate, dead world which would be the unavoidable premise—or so some would have us believe—of all science: 'For the Frenchman driving through it, the rainforest is a world of objects, uninhabited nature [...] [that] exists without us [...] nature without [humans], uninhabited by any species at all, neither [humans], nor plants and beasts, [...] nature in itself. This is taken to be an unavoidable premise of all science. [...] A purely objective, ancestral world, dating back thousands of years before the appearance of the human species, that is to say [...] before the appearance of sensibility—as if there were no sensibility other than that of the erudite human species, and above all as if humanity were a single species. A curious realism: one without experience and without magic, which ruins every encounter and every transcendence in advance and which, to be quite honest, shares with the most absolute idealisms the illusion of having triumphed over finitude, that is, over the reality of life and death, over the jaguar and over blackness, over the death that oppresses and devours you. All of this is characteristic of the melancholic sadness of the European metaphysician, who, unable to bear the shock, the rush of sensation, of that manifestation that summons up existence at the same time as it annihilates it, does everything possible to avoid it. [...] It's hard to believe that the first impression the tropics make on the great French Amerindianist is that of uninhabited nature, without [humans] and without predators. One need not ever have set foot on the

255 Spinoza, *Ethics*, 240 [Book V, Prop. XXVIV, Scholium].

land of the New World to understand it under the auspices of pre-subjective ancestralism, of naked objectivity. Pure speculation. Purely speculative realism, from a Parisian bistro.'[256] The idea of an absolute beginning, of a creation *ex nihilo*; the 'mistake [of thinking] that the painter [or the writer] works on a white and [empty] surface',[257] ('The page is white but it has been written on from time immemorial; it is white through forgetfulness of what has been written, through erasure of the text on which everything that is written is written');[258] the ethnographic projection of a barbarian people without writing, without history, without culture; the hypothesis of an ancestrality without sensibility, without phenomenological givenness; the supposition of a purely objective nature, without language, without thought, without affects; the conception of a cosmos in which life is nothing but an improbable local exception; these are the Euro-geo-anthropo-phallocentric myths *par excellence* 'of a colonial or "modern" power that only operates by wiping out the living forces of the past [and the beyond] [...];'[259] that only functions by producing 'a virgin and homogeneous surface ready to be gouged, scarred, squeezed to the last drop by the faceless conquistadores of globalised capitalism.[260] [...] It is, in the first place, on a white surface that the modern subject, the conquering ego, imposes its will [...]. [A]n indigenous land is covered with a veil of virginity—the innocence of that which has no history—in order to be able to violate it better.' [261] Whereas the whitening operation triggers the urge to transgress the incest taboo,[262] the

256 Goddard, *Un brésilien noir et crasseux*, 33–5.

257 G. Deleuze, *Francis Bacon: The Logic of Sensation*, tr. D.W. Smith (London and New York: Continuum, 2003), 11.

258 Derrida, *Dissemination*, 310.

259 Touam Bona, *Sagesse des lianes*, 1, 36.

260 Ibid., 35.

261 Ibid., 36–37.

262 'As soon as writing, which entails making a liquid flow out of a tube onto a piece of white paper, assumes the significance of copulation, or as soon as walking becomes a symbolic substitute for treading upon the body of mother earth, both writing and walking are stopped because they represent the performance of a forbidden

deconstruction of the myth of the white virginal surface, of a purely objective nature, of a dead background, opens up the possibility of reimplanting one's own lifeline into 'the infinite interweaving of life lines [...] the fine mesh of relationships and memories in which all life is embedded',[263] and, in doing so, performing an exogamous synthesis with the other.

Whereas Christianity as we understand it here relies on the panvitalist thesis that absolutely everything is alive—that is, a local mode of the living insubstance—the ontology of death, of pre-subjective ancestralism, and of naked objectivity, reaches an apogee in the zombie thesis that everything (including ourselves) is always 'already dead'. Bracketing out all supposedly definitive knowledge about 'what is that it is', we find ourselves at this point in a situation where ultimately the only thing that counts is our practical ability to make an existential decision without theoretical guarantees. But we are certainly not compelled by modern science to live as if life were a 'death on credit'. Rather than encrypting life in a burial chamber, we can take the decision to place our lives in the service of the resurrection, the healing, the vast vivification. 'Living and dying together'[264] is fragile, beautiful and terrible—delightful and painful. I am alive, freefalling within the phenoumenodelic living manifestation, and I shall die, attempting to assume and accept the finitude of my transient existence, to endure the corresponding mourning play with dignity and joy, striving to pass from impotence to an existence after finitude (an animic tonality that results from the phantasmatic projection of an ontotheological realm beyond finite life) to the impossible real that never ceases to arrive, insisting, disturbing the transcendental-dependent previsions in the form of local epiphanies, the real that never stops not being written, that always continues to make holes in the symbolic orders;[265] to the recognition that finitude (far from

---

sexual act.' S. Freud, 'Inhibitions, Symptoms, and Anxiety', in *The Standard Edition of the Complete Psychological Works of Sigmund Freud, Volume XX (1925–1926)*, tr. J. Strachey, A. Freud, A. Strachey, and A. Tyson (London: Hogarth, 1953), 90.

263 Touam Bona, *Sagesse des lianes*, 39, 67.

264 Haraway, *Staying with the Trouble*.

265 Cf. J. Lacan, *Autres écrits* (Paris: Éditions du Seuil, 2001), 551.

being a defect in need of being fixed) is precisely the condition of possibility for revelation, that any living and dying perspective on life is a singular channel through which life (over)flows in its own self-revelation.

The impersonal life only refers to the first hypostasis of the triune pleroma: life qua mat(t)er. But there is no one life without multiple living beings, there is no impersonal life without finite persons, nor is there insubstance without the vibratory modes capable of bringing it into existence, invaginating it and deepening it by means of its percepts, affects, concepts, sociolepts. Absolute life absolves itself from its indetermination by engendering determinate persons that channel and potentiate its self-disclosure. The very existence of the living insubstance relies on the finite local modes that express it in unexpected manners from a multiplicity of singular perspectives. It could be said, in a kind of phenoumenodelic declension of the indeterminacy principle, that phenoumenodelic insubstance does not allow for a classical vacuum state. There are always 'undulating unknowns' wandering around, dancing 'on top of the [spiritual] flame [...] as the unicorn drinks from the [source]', oscillatory minstrels drifting across the experiential field, local organs through which 'the unconditioned [life] floods and illuminates [intra-worldly] causality [...] expressing its all-encompassing terrible [immanence]'.[266] A living being born to life is a local subjective mode of the pleroma that breathes, that oscillates through inhalation-retention-exhalation cycles operated by the dimensions of subjectivity that Kant called, respectively, receptivity, imagination, and spontaneity. Life informs, that is, it institutes forms capable of processing information—'differences that make a difference'[267]—by means of breath cycles locally resonating in the living fluxus (the living 'are nothing else but puffs of breath in duration').[268] Life is the modulated Word, i.e. a semiorrhagic process equipped with subjective vortices qua instruments that

266 Cf. J. Lezama Lima, 'Preludio a las eras imaginarias', in *Ensayos barrocos. Imagen y figuras en América latina* (Buenos Aires: Ediciones Colihue, 2014). See also denaKmar naKhabra, 'The Undulating Unknown'.

267 Bateson, *Mind and Nature*, 99.

268 A. Artaud, *Heliogabalus or, the Anarchist Crowned*, tr. A. Lykiard (London: Creation Books, 2003), 55.

modulate—by means of cycles of decoding inhalation, imaginative interpretation, and expressive exhalation—the continuous flux of sangnification.

Every process of immanental institution of a lifeform equipped with particular transcendental capacities and affordances enworlds the pleroma. The institution of a lifeform leads to a singular polarisation of the pleroma through the formation of an opposition between a subjective I and a correlated not-I. The existentialisation of *the absolute life that is* in *a living being that exists there* is concomitant with the emanation of a not-I, a surrounding world, an umweltic aeon constituted by the transcendental faculties of the corresponding subject. In this sense, the act of creation (of a lifeworld) can, in the last instance, be traced back to a process of immanent procreation of the lifeform that constitutes the world, 'an immanent process in which life remains in the living which it generates and never puts out of it. [...] [But life as such] is uncreated. Foreign to creation',[269] being rather the immanental realm within which the 'worlds of revelation' are 'created', in which they drift, coalesce and dissolve. Every opening up of a worldly transcendence correlated to a given transcendental type takes place in the immanence of the absolute life: every world is a world of and in life: '[T]he givenness of [this world] never happens except in the self-givenness of life.[270] [...] [A]ll transcendence is constituted solely in the stream of immanent consciousness proper to the plane. Transcendence is always a product of immanence.'[271] By means of its transcendental valves, the living being makes a cut-out of the pleroma, trimming down an umweltic retort in which, through the sway of its respiration, the subject distils, drop by drop, actions, visions, affections, conceptualisations. The one life engenders living beings within itself that live this impersonal life singularly, in the first person, always from a particular changing viewzone. The main theopractical (rather than theological) problem posited by God qua immanental life is not that of demonstrating (or believing in) its existence, but that of bearing its

269 Henry, *Paroles du Christ*, 107.

270 Henry, 'The Four Principles of Phenomenology', 11.

271 Deleuze, 'Immanence: A Life', 388.

overwhelming and omnipresent theophany, of grinding and polishing the transcendental lenses thanks to which this prodigious phenoumenodelic outburst can be experienced and potentiated by a finite lifeform. From the infinite experiential superabundance that is the self-revealing immanental life, each finite transcendental type—tourmaline, the hydrogen atom, the bee, the human, the black hole, the philodendron—cuts out, selects, and informs the phenomena that scintillate in its Umwelt.

The immanental procession of life is only possible through the institution of finite subjects and the concomitant opening up of their corresponding phenomenological horizons. There is no absolute life without living beings capable of revealing it in their visions, conveying its self-intellection and transforming it by means of their actions. By begetting forms of life, the vital pleroma is awakened to its own spectacle, churns its lactescent foam and probes its own depths, always remaining in the immanent movement—in the ebb and flow—of its self-affection. The second trinitarian hypothesis—that of the finite, native, and mortal living—far from denoting a fall which should be bypassed either through a mystical dissolution into indistinct unity or through a projective infinitisation of the subject, is an (insurmountable) constitutive moment of the divine life: 'To touch, to touch, there's a whole sun calling out for it! / The perfection of making oneself the mortal vehicle / and no longer preaching about the ultra-plane / To be populated with local, tangible fleshes / the blessing of achieving these inhuman, infantile mortalities. / To have arrived here was not a fall but an achievement, / which does not discount'[272] the hypertelic achievement of supernaturalisation. The impersonal life cannot be thought of as independent from its finite and worldly existentialisation, as independent from its coninsubstantial union with the living child who experiences life: '[A]s original and underived as the being of [impersonal life] is [its personal] being-there, [its finite existence,] and the latter is inseparable from the former [...] and this divine being-there in its substance is necessarily

272 Las Señoras del Arcoiris, *Documentos de la Escuela Nocturna* (Buenos Aires: Hekht, 2015), 12.

[experience], and it is only in this [experience] that a world has arisen.'[273] Every living being that is there defines a focal point of experience endowed with a unique perspective on the experiential field, and which is thus a unique source of images and actions—an irreplaceable operator in the self-disclosure of life. There is no self-revelation of life without phenomena; there are no phenomena without finite subjects capable of enworlding the experiential field; there are no subjects without life as the force that institutes subjectivity. The definitions of life as a force begetting transcendental types of subjectivity and as immanental self-revelation reciprocally presuppose one another. In the last instance, 'life is only self-revelation as such',[274] the field of impersonal experience itself in its perpetual self-manifestation, in its dehiscence from itself and toward itself: 'life generates itself to the extent that it is propelled into phenomenality in the form of a self-revelation'.[275] Life reveals itself by 'propelling itself into phenomenality' and for this thrust it requires the institution of finite lifeforms that trim down phenomenological clearings by means of their own transcendental structures: '[F]or Fichte as for Böhme before him, we cannot consider the Divine Being apart from the process whereby it emerges into the light, [the mat(t)er] is indissociable from the [child] whom [it] eternally begets.[276] It is not, therefore, by annihilating [it]self through fusion into the divinity [...] it is not by abandoning that which defines [it] as a [finite] person and instates [it] in being, but it is, on the contrary, by realising what is most personal and deepest in [it] that [the child] fulfils [its] essential function, which is a theophanic function: to express God, to be the *theophore*, the God-bearer.'[277] Life discloses itself by engendering, life is nothing but the manifold ways in which it brings about its existentialisation in finite beings

273 Fichte, *The Way Towards the Blessed Life; Or, The Doctrine of Religion*, 103 [translation modified].

274 Henry, *C'est moi la Vérité*, 39.

275 Ibid., 75.

276 Henry, *The Essence of Manifestation*, 69.

277 Corbin, 'Theology as Antidote to Nihilism' [translation modified].

confronted by material resistances, resistances offered by the mat(t)er in order that these living beings ceaselessly—until their deaths—institute themselves, perpetuate their births, abide in the immediate vicinity of the primal source.

The begetting of individuals introduces differences in perspective, and only a difference in perspective makes a difference in experience. In order to raise the self-experience of life to higher powers, it is not a matter of neutralising the differences between the various perspectives by focusing exclusively on the invariants, but of making the difference in perspective the object of an affirmation capable of excavating a new depth in the extension. In this regard, the multiplicity of transcendental perspectives is 'the matrix of [a phenoumenodelic] extension'[278] which constantly expands the number of its dimensions: 'Oppositions [between different perspectives] are always [unidimensional]; they express on a given [linear interval] only the distorted effect of [a higher dimensional] depth'.[279] Dialecticising oppositions means immersing oneself in this compatibilising depth. When the differences between these perspectives are articulated, combined, integrated, harmonised, synthesised, concerted, what emerges are transpersonal structures, collective patterns, aperspectival narratives, self-referential articulated wholes, new functional capacities, holarchies and super-organisms, new channels and circuits of communication, new grammars, self-organising processes, self-correcting capacities, new modalities of abstraction, new reproductive and self-conservative affordances, unusual *gestalten*, new forms of global coherence which exhibit emergent behaviour.

If the first trinitarian hypostasis refers to the force (*Mariri*) that begets, the second refers to the light (*Chacruna*) which reveals as it propagates through the mundane clearings; if the first hypostasis is the force that informs the eye, the second hypostasis decodes the luminous forms that vibrate in its mundane sphere: 'and what was revealed, in the undulation, if

278 Deleuze, *Difference and Repetition*, 229.

279 Ibid., 236.

not the scintillation of the filament in its jellyfish fineness?'[280] The Spinozist God is a God that necessarily engenders, a material God that brings to life finite subjects capable of inflating new worlds into which its unconcealement can be decanted and raised to new powers, a God that does not allow for a state of phenoumenodelic void—a static, flat insubstance that is no longer stirred up by local subjective modes—a God that is always already traversed by vibrations, reverberations, coruscations. The theopataphysical question *par excellence*, *Can one hear the shape of God?*,[281] can be met with a well-defined answer: God has no other shape than that which can be experienced (heard, felt, conceived) through the integration of its vibrant modes, its insubstantial forms, its context-dependent names, its living icons, through the interweaving of the undulating unknowns' lifelines. There are no experiences, there is no living-through (*erleben*), without life (*leben*); there can be no transcendental phenomenology without immanental vitalism. Intrinsic to the concept of life is both the immanental Spinozist motif—according to which every finite subject is a local fluctuation of the living insubstance—and the Kantian transcendental motif—according to which these fluctuations constitute phenomenological lifeworlds out of phenoumenodelic insubstance. The synthetic circle established by Christianity between Spinozist immanentism and Kantian transcendentalism refers in the first instance to this connection between the first two trinitarian hypostases; the connection between the turbulent infinity of the pleroma and the multiple finite lifeforms; the connection between the absolute (*natura naturans*) and the relative (the spectrum of *naturae naturatae*), of immanental *physis* and transcendental *gnosis*; the connection in the *Einbildungskraft* of the engendering life force (*Kraft*) that performs the immanental self-formation (*sich bilden*) of the insubstance and the 'joint of [iridescent] light'[282] revealed by different lifeforms.

---

280 Perlongher, *Aguas Aéreas*, in *Poemas completos*, 258.

281 Cf. M. Kac, 'Can One Hear the Shape of a Drum?', *American Mathematical Monthly* 73:4.2 (1966): 1–23.

282 R.M. Rilke, *Duino Elegies*, tr. E. Snow (New York: North Point Press, 2000), 339.

The child is eternally begotten since it is coninsubstantial with the mat(t)er. Certainly '[the mat(t)er] is the absolutely pre-given, that which precedes the splitting of individuality in the appearance [...]',[283] but this precedence does not refer to some chronological sequence of the plerophany, in which the child has not yet been begotten. There is no life of the mat(t)er prior to the institution of the finite living beings that pulse the flux and reflux of her Ichor, her sap, prior to the excitation of undulating living forms nourished by the whitish placenta that sprouts out of the roach's belly.[284] 'The [child] is the heart pulsating in the [mat(t)er]' writes Hegel on the philosophy of Böhme in his *Lectures on the History of Philosophy*; 'the kernel in all energies, the cause of the burgeoning joy in all. From eternity the [child of the mat(t)er] is perpetually born, from all the powers of [its "Mater Mary Mercerycordial of the Dripping Nipples"];[285] [it] is the brilliance that shines in the [mat(t)er]; if the [child] did not thus shine in the [mat(t)er], then the [mat(t)er] would be a dark valley, the [mat(t)er's] power would not ascend from [duration to duration], and the divine [existence] could not endure.'[286] The infinite life that begets and the finite begotten that reveals are two coninsubstantial hypostasis in the same intradivine procession. The first hypostasis—impersonal life—is, strictly speaking 'Deipara, God's childbearer':[287] the finite living are no less divine than life because it is impossible to have one without the other. In this sense, this other-than-Roman Christian heresy is a polytheistic religion filled with forest spirits, dancing xapiripë, angels of the odd, fravashis, flying mirrors that potentiate speculation, orishas, suspended 'pollen of the flowering godhead',[288] primordial lights,

283 Fichte, *La doctrine de l'État (1813)*, 213.

284 Cf. Lispector, *The Passion According to G.H.*, 57.

285 Joyce, *Finnegans Wake*, 260.

286 G.W.F. Hegel, *Lectures on the History of Philosophy 1825–6, Volume III: Medieval and Modern Philosophy*, tr. R.F. Brown (Oxford: Clarendon Press, 2009), 50.

287 Lezama Lima, *El reino de la imagen*, 9.

288 Rilke, *Duino Elegies*, 339.

'numinous chants';[289] a religion in which each living being, each breathing mode of the pleroma, is a singular avatar of child Yesses, a finite perspectival expression of life. This animistic declension of Christianity 'recoils in horror from [the] deadly impasse of the [monarchic] OGU [One God Universe]. [The latter] is all-powerful and all-knowing. Because [It] can do everything, [It] can do nothing, since the act of doing demands opposition[, resistance, finitude]. [It] knows everything, so there is nothing for [It] to learn. [It] can't go anywhere, since [It] is already fucking everywhere, like cowshit in Calcutta. The OGU is a [...] flat, thermodynamic[, desireless] universe, since it has no [material] friction by definition.'[290] The refraction of divinity brought forth by finite individuality brings opposition, ignorance, locality, friction, opacity, vulnerability, curvature, heat, angst, anomalies, perspectives, quilombos, vertigo, discrete spectra of vibrations. There is no self-revelation of life without experiences and there is no experience without existence, without native and mortal finitude exposed to a not-I that resists, without the unfolding of dermal, sensitive, vibratile surfaces offered to a worldly transcendence, without an imaginative *Band* between a patience and an agency; there is no experience without transcendental conditions (skin, eyes, petals, brains, wings, categories, antennae, glands, filaments, shells) capable of selecting, from the infinite exuberance of the pleroma, a world among other possible worlds, each correlated to a certain transcendental type of subjectivity. The living are but local modes of the infinite life (which places a limit on all supposed subjective self-sufficiency), a finite pneumatisation of the Word, of the pure activity that enlivens. But at the same time life only reveals itself through such modes, through the delirium of engendering, through the excitation of vibrant modes on the surface of the phenoumenodelic void: 'If God did not exist, nor would I; if I did not exist, nor would [It]',[291] because I am its existence. The Word only expresses itself in the language of birds, stones, elementary particles,

289 N. Perlongher, *Parque Lezama*, in *Poemas Completos*, 187.

290 Burroughs, *The Western Lands*, 113.

291 Eckhart, quoted in Hegel, *Lectures on the Philosophy of Religion, Volume I,* 347–48.

crickets, stars, octopuses and fields. It is only '[w]hen all creatures pronounce [its] Name [by singularly modulating the Word], [that] God comes into [existence]'.[292] Every singular modulation of the universal Word intones a Name of God and the progressive neologenetic coordination of God's names ceaselessly gives rise to new forms of the spirit, to new holobionic modes of God's self-experience, to new pneumatic forms resonating in the 'Pindorama's jaguaresque matrianarchy'.[293]

The thesis that God is not a concealed instance which may or may not reveal itself, but rather is in and for itself a living process of revelation, eliminates the problem of having to prove its 'existence'. God does not exist, but rather *ek-sists*:[294] it ceaselessly comes out of itself in the flux and reflux of its self-manifestation. We could say that the problem regarding the existence of God is not a problem of scarcity (of 'proofs'), but rather a problem of overabundance, a problem that is solved differently by each lifeform and that can be phrased as follows: How can a lifeform filter and channel the surge of revelation so that it will not simply be devastated? How can a finite subject withstand the turmoil and the splendour of God's omnipresent disclosure? In this sense, the subject's transcendental apparatus—far from being an obstacle to the apprehension of the absolute—is what allows the subject to experience it (albeit in a perspective-dependent partial manner). Whereas within the framework of ontotheology God is understood as an *ens supremum*, a super-entity that (by the very definition of entity) is in a superlative manner, in Christianity, God is not distinguishable from the ecstasy of its ek-sistence, of its manifestation, of its insubstantial, purely phenoumenodelic, revelation. In trinitarian Christianity, the existence of God plays out in three ways: by being lived out through the generation of living beings thrown into the pleromatic 'outside', by revealing itself through intramundane images and actions, and by being

---

292 Eckhart, Sermon 12.

293 E. Viveiros de Castro, 'Zénon d'Hiléia', foreword to Goddard, *Un brésilien noir et crasseux*, 13.

294 Cf. J. Lacan, *R.S.I. The Seminar of Jacques Lacan, Book XXII (1973–1974)*, tr. C. Gallagher, <http://www.lacaninireland.com/web/translations/seminars/>.

permeated by the epiphanic real which, through its intrusion into their transcendentally constituted worlds, opens them up to the trans-mundane pleroma. The triune God does not have to be the object of belief or of an 'explicative theology'. It is itself the ultra-evidence, the absolute experiential field that envelops the different worlds correlative to different transcendental types, the Open as 'pure perception' (the Ultra-Vision) and as a pure act (Word) that is refracted into images and actions as it passes through transcendental prisms. It is that which ceaselessly opens up ('The moment of living is a ceaseless, slow creaking of doors continually opening wide'),[295] the absolute revelation that is poured into the panoply of lifeworlds constituted by different lifeforms. 'God is not an abstraction', a hypothesis, or the term for an ungrounded belief, 'but what is utterly concrete',[296] the field of experience considered both in the concrescence of its many attributes (*sensorium*, *affectum*, *logos*, *socius*, *textum*) and in the coalescence of the 'worlds of revelation'. There is only experience *of* God in the double sense of the genitive, and faith is nothing but unconditional surrender ('adherence without reserve') to the experience of the vision, the emotion, the understanding, the act 'of entering body and soul into [the] enigmatic Life'[297] that we incarnate, breathe, and reveal, an unrestrained 'Yes to life' that might assume the form of a 'no to scorning [living beings]', a no to the commodification of the common, 'to exploitation of [life]'.[298] Faith cannot be understood as a belief or as a disposition of the spirit that would come to supply some piece of missing knowledge, or to overcome a hyperbolic doubt. It is a plunge made by the finite living into the abyss of the intradivine life, the maximal opening up (perceptively, emotionally, conceptually, politically, spiritually) to the experience of and in God: 'and yes

295 Lispector, *The Passion According to G.H.*, 75–76.

296 Hegel, *Lectures on the Philosophy of Religion, Volume III,* 215.

297 Merleau-Ponty, 'Faith and Good Faith', in *Sense and Non-Sense*, 175.

298 F. Fanon, *Black Skin, White Masks*, tr. C.L. Markmann (London: Pluto Press, 2008), 173.

I said yes I will Yes'.[299] 'Faith [...] transplants mountains into the sea';[300] it transposes the seemingly most stable configurations into the 'broad and stormy ocean[—Solaris—]the true site of [phenoumenal revelation], where many a fog bank and rapidly melting iceberg pretend to be new lands and, ceaselessly deceiving with empty hopes the voyager looking around for new [unshakable forms of stability], entwine [it] in adventures from which [it] can never escape and yet also never bring to an end';[301] faith leads to an 'elsewhere that can be inhabited beyond *terra firma*: the place of dreams', the site in which the trance suspends the phenomenal worlds, the 'preserved night' of an 'experience in which the cocoon of the human implodes to open up to other unbound visions of life'.[302] Faith suspends existence within the supernatural sky of the 'abundant life'. Faith is the acceptance that the only ground—beyond possessions, identifications, spaceships, arks, fatherlands and power-over—is to be found in the phenoumenodelic Maelstrom of life, in its living vortex: 'Vanoleando, vanolean, lanolean en el limo azul de la maraña: Corazon de la luz.'[303] According to what Fichte calls the true philosophical way of seeing, the life of every living being (as well as the 'conatus by which each thing endeavours to persevere in its own being')[304] is not an end in itself but simply a means to the service of the only end, the self-disclosure of life in the multiplicity of attributes (be they perceptive, affective, conceptual or political) to which the living being has access as a function of its transcendental affordances and its speculative degrees of freedom, the enjoyment and the celebration of 'that which [partially] appears in every life', namely the continuous formation of the image and the sound and the smell and the taste of the pleroma which

---

299 Joyce, *Ulysses*, 933.

300 Silesius, *Cherubinischer Wanderer*, Book I, §221.

301 Kant, *Critique of Pure Reason*, 303 [B295/A236].

302 Krenak, *Idées pour retarder la fin du monde*, 50.

303 'Around they go. Goaroundrolling. Rollingaround they go into the blue slime of the tangle: heart of light.' Perlongher, *Aguas Aéreas*, 277.

304 Spinoza, *Ethics*, 102 [Book III, Prop. VII].

ceaselessly offers itself up (by virtue of and yet beyond all individual life) to its own experience: 'In the true way of seeing, [experience] goes beyond [...] all appearing and temporal life, and aims at what appears in all life and must appear in it, namely [...] the [always changing] image of [the living] God. [Finite existence] is merely the means to this end. [...] Any given form and figure of this life may come to an end, but life itself can never do so. The life of individuals does not belong to [worldly and historical] appearances, it is absolutely [everlasting, *sub specie durationis*], like life itself. [...] [Individual] life and its preservation can never be an end, but only a means.'[305] Placing the individual life in the service of an end that exceeds it is not to detriment of one's capacity for self-determination but rather the opposite: it is through the exercise of one's freedom that individual life becomes a vehicle of revelation: '[I]f [individual] life must be a means to its end, it must necessarily be constituted as follows: it must be free, it must determine itself with absolute autonomy and on its own basis [...].'[306] The resolute affirmation of the autonomy of the human subject is not coeval with the defence of (what Taylor calls) an 'exclusive humanism' based on the affirmation of the absolute primacy of human life and on the sheer rejection of any value or aim beyond the good of 'human flourishing' and the corresponding consideration of suffering and death as 'dangers and enemies to be [unconditionally] avoided or combatted'.[307] Subjective freedom can simply be in the service of life in the widest possible sense of the term, that of a pleromatic life, of an 'abundant life' (John 10:10), of a *natura naturans* that envelops and concertates every possible lifeform and every possible circumambient world. The Christian commitment to such an 'abundant life' brings forth a twofold imperative, that of sacralising finite life as such (which entails the abandonment of both the promise of an 'eternal life' beyond finitude and the dismissal of vulnerability and death as flaws to be fixed) and that of resolutely affirming that life as

305 Fichte, *La doctrine de l'État (1813)*, 96.

306 Ibid., 96.

307 C. Taylor, *A Catholic Modernity: Charles Taylor's Marianist Award Lecture* (Oxford: Oxford University Press, 1999), 24.

such—in its more-than-human character—fixes a value which is higher than the preservation of one's own life at all costs. The maternal imperative *Thou shalt live!* does not mean that the preservation of the individual's life against external dangers fixes the ultimate ethical coordinates, but rather that the individual should commit to placing its resources in the service of the infinite life that it locally embodies and singularly channels. This imperative forces the subject to assume the responsibility of living its life as a finite organ of its 'immanent cause'. The affirmation that the finite (the transient, the fragile, the vulnerable, the limited) is not to be sublated in some form of 'eternal life' absolved from decay and death does not mean that we are closing (what Taylor calls) the 'transcendent window, as though there were nothing beyond'.[308] But what is 'beyond' our finite lives is life itself, the impersonal 'immanent cause' of our finite lives, the open multiplicity of heterogeneous lifeforms, and the transpersonal living communities we are part of. In this sense, the imperative *Thou shalt live!* invites us to keep open what we could call the immanent window.

Every living being is thus summoned by life—in its finitude, in having been born and being mortal, in its singular determination and vocation, in its dependency and in its freedom, in its being-dropped into the primal vortex—to occupy firmly and worthily its place as a child, its being-there in the midst of (and in the service of) revelation. Science, art, politics, philosophy, and religion are human forms of revelation. It is only human beings who sometimes dare to ask themselves, in their arrogance, in their disligated melancholy: Why should we be resolute in the flowering of our own desire if we are condemned to disappear without a trace, if transience is the hallmark of existence, if all human enterprise is already futile, if ultimately nothing will have taken place or time? Long before every biological death, every planetary catastrophe, every cosmic apocalypse, the very formulation of this question is already a symptom of the disease of disligation that desiccates and reifies the individual, that neuroticises it, that separates it from the act of living, from the Word that enlivens.

308 C. Taylor, *A Secular Age* (Cambridge, MA and London: The Belknap Press of Harvard University Press, 2007), 638.

The religating individual—child of life and breathing in life—throws the dice, fights in the Kurukshetra War, and 'brings forth [like the plant, like the star, like the jaguar] its light [and its strength] from itself, as its own self [...] in the blossom [...]',[309] unconcerned with the hypothetical ephemerality of its acts and its works, without demanding guarantees that not only the place will have taken place. Scientific, artistic, political, and philosophical production can be understood as local modulations—channelled by the finite human type—of the pure act, of the pure perception, of the pure intellect, of the pure language. In the wake of the Lutherian subordination of *theologia gloriae* to *theologia crucis*[310] we shall accept that even the glorious halos that surround the works of spirit, far from making possible an overcoming of finitude, are nothing but ephemeral glowing roses on the cross of the present revelation.

'There is only one way to trust[, to have faith in] existence: love.'[311] The religation that heals, that reimplants the individual in absolute life so that its sap can irrigate it again, orients itself along the gravitational gradients of a certain onto-existential affect, *love*. In its ontological dimension, love is the feeling of the life that holds onto itself and carries itself through the differentiation and separation proper to its self-revelation, the centripetal auto-affection thanks to which life can remain connected to itself in the very movement of its coming out of itself, the elastic force that preserves the continuity of the vital fabric in the face of the tensions and deformations stemming from the processes of individuation: 'this sensing of life, a sensing which finds itself again [beyond and through the separation concomitant with individuation] is love [...].[312] [L]ove is [...] the being-affected of being-there by being, that is to say by life'.[313] The 'pure relation of the

309 G.W.F Hegel, *The Philosophy of Nature, vol. 3*, tr. M. J. Petry (London: Allen and Unwin, 1970), 91 [§348].

310 Cf. M. Luther, 'Heidelberg Disputation' (1518), in *Martin Luther's Basic Theological Writings*, ed. T.F. Lull (Minneapolis: Fortress Press, 1989).

311 Labou Tansi, *Encre, sueur, salive et sang*, np.

312 Hegel, 'The Spirit of Christianity and its Fate', 232.

313 Goddard, *1804–1805. La désubjectivation du transcendantal*, 437.

appearance to itself'—its imagining itself, its feeling itself, its desiring itself, its understanding itself—is thus not 'a cold, disinterested [reflexivity]',[314] one that is disaffected, disenchanted: 'Being [*Seyn*] is self-reliant, self-sufficient, self-complete, and needs no being beyond itself. Now let this be felt in absolute self-consciousness; and what arises? Manifestly nothing else than a feeling [*Gefühl*] of this act by which it holds itself together and carries itself [*Sichzusammenhaltens, und Sichtragens*]; hence, a love of this self;—or, as I said, an affection, a being affected by being, precisely therefore a feeling of being as being.'[315]

Love as ontological affect makes it possible to understand more deeply the relationship between characterisations of life as the power to beget on the one hand (the first hypostasis) and as self-revelation on the other (the second hypostasis). How could the one life reveal itself without begetting living beings capable of distilling images into worlds, without localising itself in manifold singular viewpoints on itself? How could life beget things if its arising were not affected by love, if its existence were not a 'joyous [and celebratory] affirmation of a self-enjoying vitality',[316] if being itself were not already a (propositional) copula, *copula mundi*, 'a ligating, binding, ligamentous position',[317] if separate individuals were not always already under the spell of an attraction which brings them together, composes them, federates them, integrates them, reunites them, collectivises them? The love that binds the living together in tribes (a movement guided by the third hypostasis, the Holy Spirit) engenders new forms of subjectivity, thereby inducing new forms of revelation. The love that religates does not eliminate separation and fuse the living together, rather it is the affect which, within the individual, channels the force that institutes subjectivity—the delirium of procreation, the force of living mat(t)er. In this sense,

---

314 Goddard, *Schelling ou Fichte*.

315 Fichte, *The Way Towards the Blessed Life; Or, the Doctrine of Religion*, 133 [translation modified].

316 Goddard, *Schelling ou Fichte*.

317 Derrida, *Glas*, 67.

the love that religates creates new forms of individuation, separation, and determination. The third hypostasis—by reconciling those who are separated from one another—forms living collectivities and thus closes and reopens the trinitarian helicoid: the one life differentiates itself into multiple living beings that reveal it and which, gravitating in love away from the centrifugal tendencies of individuation, form new separate collective subjects, new emerging foci of perceptions, affections, conceptualisations, and actions that will themselves freefall in love. We could say metaphorically that every process of separative individuation is a source of local curvature in the pleroma, a curvature that manifests itself in the form of a 'force of attraction' acting both on the individual (guaranteeing its subjective integrity in the form of self-love) and on their relationship with other individuals. The trinitarian dialectic is not propelled by a hypothetical tension between two opposing drives—Eros and Thanatos—since the unique religating force of love accounts for the two fundamental tendencies: the centripetal tendency toward the concertation of separate individuals (the love that religates) and the concomitant centrifugal institution of new forms of separated individuality (the love that engenders).

According to the Sermon on the Mount, love comes to fulfil and sublate the Law. As a first approximation, the Law can be understood as the symbolic order (natural laws, moral norms) that constitutes and organises a particular communitarian Umwelt. Every subjective form of experience relies on transcendental reducing valves that filter the continuum of the pleroma into discrete significant unities structured by a particular 'symbolic' grammar. Every I/not-I correlation determines certain capacities for abstract judgement, i.e. singular transcendental-dependent forms of separating, distinguishing and attributing properties. But trinitarian love—the religation with the transcendental plasticity of impersonal life, egophanic love for one's own subjective singularity, and fraternal communion with other lifeforms—forces the suspension of any reification of a particular I/not-I polarisation, and (in particular) any attachment to a particular intra-umweltic symbolic order and the concomitant judgemental (separating) modalities. 'Judgement [*Ur-teil*] in the highest and strictest sense, [relies on] the [transcendental] separation of [self and non-self] which are most deeply united in intellectual intuition, that separation through which alone object and subject become possible, the [transcendental] arche-separation.[318] [But] judgement is not an act of the divine [...] the [child] of God does not judge, sunder, or divide, does not hold to an opposite in its opposition. An utterance, or the stirring, of the divine is no lawgiving or legislation, no upholding of the mastery of the law.'[319] It is not possible to have done with the judgement of God since judgement is a transcendental capacity of finite beings.

In this sense we could say that love as an infinite regulative idea has a certain preeminence over other ideas of reason (truth, beauty, justice): if these latter orient the cognitive, aesthetic, and political mediations of a certain world of life respectively, love orients religation with the living force that nourishes and invigorates these mediations, that 'allows jouissance to condescend to desire',[320] that excites oscillations in the fringes of the worldly horizons, that transforms forms, transnorms norms and transcodes codes, that dynamises halted flows, that orgonises neurosis. Since life informs living beings and sparks off worlds, nurturing their dehiscence into the supernatural sky, the love that religates with life has the capacity to inform and deform all intra-worldly law. The speculative freedom made possible by love is a liberation from the pre-critical subjection to all objective law, to all morality. 'In love, every notion of duty is set aside'[321] and the only absolute prescription that remains is (as Rozitchner argues) that of the material imperative par excellence: You will live, you will affirm the life that is incarnated (that is-there) in you by taking care of yourself and your living siblings, by placing your life in the service of the revelation of life in its various trinitarian declensions (impersonal, individuated, and tribal).

---

318 F. Hölderlin, 'Judgement and Being', in *Essays and Letters on Theory*, 37–38: 37.

319 Hegel, *On Christianity: Early Theological Writings*, 262.

320 Lacan, *Anxiety*, 179.

321 Hegel, quoted in Derrida, *Glas*, 69.

We can now consider one of the most unsupportable theses of (speculative Christianity, namely that 'Death [and therefore finitude] is love itself'.[322] There is no centripetal love without the centrifugal dissemination of native and mortal individuals (no love without separated finite lifeforms) and there are no separated finite lifeforms that do not gravitate in love. The second moment of the triune divine nature is given by the finite existence of the individual, death (along with birth) being one of the boundaries of its temporal conjugation (or, in more philosophical terms, one of the existential structures of its being-there). Finitude is the condition of possibility of perspectivism, that is, of the existence of singular breathing sources of unforeseen living actions and new images of life. It follows that finitude (and thereby death) plays a central role in the trinitarian process by means of which life self-reveals. In begetting finite living beings that could channel its self-revelation, life i(nstitute)s death. But far from 'abandoning' the living, life inundates them with a religating affect that retains them within the self-begetting fabric of life. By gravitating in the amoriferal fields, finite beings can afford the highest risk entailed by finite individuation: not the risk of dying but the risk of living and dying in disligation. In this way, the love that heals and raises the life of spirit to new powers by engendering new lifeforms (awakening vortices in the phenoumenodelic whirlpool) blossoms from finitude and death. We can then restate the helicoidal con-insubstantiality of the three hypostases by saying that life is death is love

322 It is worth considering the whole of this paragraph in Hegel's *Lectures on the Philosophy of Religion* here: 'God is the true God, spirit, because [it] is not merely [mat(t)er], and hence closed up within [itself], but because [it] is [child], because [it] becomes the other and sublates this other. This "negation" is intuited as a moment of the divine nature in which all are reconciled. Set against God there are finite [living] beings; [...] the finite, is posited in death itself as a moment of God, and death is what reconciles. Death [that is, the finite] is love itself; in it absolute love is envisaged. The identity of the divine and the [finite] means that God is at home with itself in [...] the finite, and in [its] death this finitude is itself a determination of God. Through death God has reconciled the world and reconciles ["itself"] eternally with [itself]. This coming back again is [its] return to [itself], and through it [it] is spirit. So this third moment is that Christ has risen.' Hegel, *Lectures on the Philosophy of Religion, Volume III*, 219–20.

is life—that is, that life institutes finite (living and dying) lifeforms which, by being affected by love, engender more living beings that enhance life's self-revelation. Life begets living and mortal beings that can be healed from the illness of disligation (that is, resurrected) by falling—following the geodesics of the entheogenic insubstance—in love. These gravitational collapses are gravid with new finite lifeforms.

The love that orients the existence of the religated living being is refracted in the trinitarian prism: love of the mat(t)er, of the child, and of the Holy Spirit; filial love, narcissistic love, fraternal love; love of the impersonal, love of the first person, love of the transpersonal; love as the affect associated with religation with the impersonal life, love as self-love—as love of the very (transcendental and existential) limits that make every living being a sibling of Yesses qua 'temple of God' (Corinthians 3:16)—and finally love of the communitarian life of the spirit, of the intersubjective religations that play out across worlds and histories: concertations, articulations, and consonances in the communities of the living.

Love as religation with the impersonal life is not a kind of mystical fusion to the detriment of one's own determined individuality. In Fichte, this religation is conveyed by an experience that is neither an experience of the phenomenal-objective world (transcendental transcendence) nor a speculative experience of the supernatural sky (speculative transcendence), but an experience—termed 'intellectual intuition' and following on from the Kantian transcendental apperception—of the absolute in me, of the singular and finite life that I am as local incarnation of the one infinite life. It is an experience of the self-awareness that accompanies every representation as local and singular instantiation of the 'I am that I am' of the absolute self-positing and self-experiencing life, an experience of the identity Atman = Brahman (*tat tvam asi*). As Henry argues, every living being is an *Imago Dei* which receives from life the very same reflexive Ipseity that defines it as self-revelation, as self-positing experience of self: '[L]ife [...] "cannot give a little" for it can give nothing but itself, that is, the Ipseity which in its self-giving it eternally engenders in itself as in all living things.'[323]

323 Henry, *Quatre principes de la phénoménologie*, 25–6.

Intellectual intuition is a reflexive apprehension of the (finite, determined and limited) empirical individual in its freedom, in its capacity to (trans) form itself, to absolve itself of every essentialisation of its existence, to be the beginning of an action and the source of a revelation, to be the singular witness of an epiphany. What is singular about intellectual intuition is that this subjective autonomy is absolved of the mystification according to which this freedom would be the prerogative of a supposedly self-sufficient subject, a subject that forecloses its castration. In intellectual intuition, the *potentia* of the self-positing living being is exhibited as a singular instantiation of the 'impersonal and pre-individual'[324] pure activity (*Tathandlung*) of the one life. Intellectual intuition does not provide an intuition of a supposed immortal soul that would precede and succeed finite existence, but of the native and mortal soul that connects the finite living being with the impersonal life, the umbilical appendage that unites the exploratory probe that is the living being with the immanental womb that is living insubstance. It is not a question of calming the vertigo of birth and the anguish of mortality by feeling and demonstrating that 'we are eternal', as Spinoza maintains,[325] but of rooting the finite living being in the biodelic soil—the mat(t)er—so that the impersonal force of the latter allows it to endure its being-thrown-into-risk, the vulnerability of its finite life. Intellectual intuition allows the subject to tune into the Word that breathes vivifying activity, to awake the 'arrested words': 'Intellectual intuition consists in "being in one's own person the absolute and life", that is to say, the Word, in order to apprehend in oneself, through the experience of one's own pure activity, this active and universal presence that is [life].'[326] Intellectual intuition is an experience in which the *I live* (through this or that experience) is apprehended in its underlying immanental neutrality: I live 'in the same way that it rains'.[327] Being alive is not only to live through this or that, 'being alive is [also,

324 Goddard, *La philosophie fichtéenne de la vie*, 67.

325 Spinoza, *Ethics*, 238 [Book V, Prop. 23, Scholium].

326 Goddard, *La philosophie fichtéenne de la vie*, 65.

327 Deleuze, *Logic of Sense*, 152.

beneath every experience] something else', to intuit how one's own soul sinks into the immanent and impersonal one life, to be connected with the force that informs, deforms, and transforms, to breathe in the narcotic pneuma; 'to be alive is inhuman', where 'the nonhuman is the radiating [vortex] of [an impersonal] love in [gravitational] waves'.[328]

Intellectual intuition is an act of conversion by means of which the living being 'turns back to that from which it proceeds',[329] reimplanting its empirical and intentional self within the impersonal life. This conversion is not a regressive dissolution of its determined individuality in the direction of the undifferentiated one, but an apprehension of its finite experiential activity as a local condensation of the original living act. The Fichtean intellectual intuition intends to apprehend 'the precise point where conscious life appears' in order to draw from this point the vivifying elixir,[330] the nectar of transient life—Amrita—that flows from the ocean of milk. In neoplatonic terms, the conversion conveyed by intellectual intuition is an act that potentialises the downstream procession by reimplanting the subject in the upstream source. This does not mean that the primal vortex becomes the objective target of a subjective experience, but rather that the subject becomes permeable to the living influx that emanates from it. '[T]he "conversion" of the Alexandrians [...] is indistinguishable from their "procession", [...] when [human beings], sprung from divinity, succeed in returning to it, [they] perceive that what [they] had at first taken to be two opposed movements of coming and going are in fact a single ["back-towards"] movement.'[331] This Spinozist reading of Plotinus presupposes,

---

328 Lispector, *The Passion According to G.H.*, 182 [translation modified].

329 G. Deleuze, Lecture, 17 March 1987, Vincennes, <https://deleuze.cla.purdue.edu/seminars/leibniz-and-baroque/lecture-13>.

330 J.-C. Goddard, 'Bergson: Une lecture néo-platonicienne de Fichte', *Les Etudes Philosophiques* 4, 'Bergson et l'idéalisme allemand' (2001), 465; *Un brésilien noir et crasseux*, 77.

331 Bergson, *The Creative Mind*, 120. See the insightful critical analysis of this topic in J.-C. Goddard, *Mysticisme et folie. Essai sur la simplicité* (Paris: Desclée de Brouwer, 2002).

nonetheless, an essential shift that substitutes Spinoza's immanent cause (such that its immanate effects remain in it) for Plotinus's emanative cause (which remains transcendent with respect to its emanated effects).[332]

We could say that intellectual intuition is a literally entheogenic experience, an experience of God within—of the impersonal divinity perceiving, feeling, understanding, acting through the finite living being—an apperception of the active principle that is life itself in its singular declension as the subject's own freedom, as the subject's capacity to self-posit, to confront the risk into which life throws it, to keep the life-forming transcendental plasticity that is life itself active within. Through intellectual intuition one accepts the '[ultimate] passivity of our activity': 'new as our initiatives may be, they come to birth at the heart of being [...] supported on the pivots or hinges of "our" life',[333] of a life which does not belong to us but for which we are responsible. Through intellectual intuition the initiate realises that there is absolutely nothing within them but life itself in its uninterrupted act of being born, of (trans)forming itself, 'a life that is not their own in the sense that they neither created it, nor put it there, nor willed it—but which is theirs, irreducibly and forever, for the same reason: namely, that there is nothing in them, not the least experience of the slightest impression which is not the self-experience brought about by life, nor the least parcel of their Self which is not the Self of Life. That is why we say that we are born of Life and that this birth never ceases, because in the self-affection which makes us conscious of ourselves at every instant, there is nothing but the self-affection of Life itself, its Arche-Revelation.'[334]

By virtue of intellectual intuition, the living being understands itself as an avatar of the second trinitarian hypostasis, of Christ qua archetype of the religating subject, coninsubstantial with the impersonal life. As such, the affirmation of the divine character of the separate and finite living

---

332 Regarding the difference between emanative cause and immanent cause see G. Deleuze, *Expressionism in Philosophy: Spinoza*, tr. M. Joughin (New York: Zone Books, 1992), 171–72.

333 Merleau-Ponty, *The Visible and the Invisible*, 221.

334 Henry, *Quatre principes de la phénoménologie*, 25.

being depends neither on regressive nostalgia for the primordial one nor on the foreclosing of castration. Christ does not represent a particular (transcendental) type, but is rather an arche-type of which every living convert (whatever its transcendental type might be) is an avatar, the arche-totem of the speculative clan (the *ecclesia*) of those who strive to remain religated to the vital force of the (re)generation of new types, of those who exist as 'pilots of the living wave',[335] i.e. as local operators of the absolution that dissolves in the insubstantial flow what has been fixed, essentialised, naturalised, reified in the form of a subjective essence or of inert capital. A living being is an avatar of Child Yesses when it remains umbilically religated to the primal mat(t)erial vortex that institutes life, thereby being able to channel in a singular manner the unconditional affirmation of the transient phenoumenodelic splendour that is life. Attaining intellectual intuition is the ultimate aim of the yogic religating practice whereby the living individual, absolving itself of all identification with its thoughts, emotions, properties and possessions, can finally 'abide in its own nature',[336] that of being a finite witnessing probe of the unique living insubstance, a local bioduct of its pure self-positing activity.

The concept of intellectual intuition as a philosophical entheogen in which the finite self intuits the divine in its act of local self-positioning—the Word vocalising itself singularly in each finite living instrument—should definitively shut off the possibility of making that first Fichtean principle ('I am I') the cornerstone of a dogmatic idealism. One of the difficulties of Fichtean philosophy is the state of indiscernibility in which the I that affirms the 'I am I' is held: empirical and finite subjectivity on the one hand, absolute subjectivity of life (i.e. immanental life absolved of every particular empirical I and every correlated Umwelt) on the other. Intellectual intuition experiences the finite self as a local mode of the absolute self, as a singular instance of the original self-reflective act. This indiscernibility operates on both of its two poles: both on the empirical self (making it a

335 DenaKmar naKhabra, 'The Undulating Unknown', 198.

336 *The Yoga Sūtras of Patañjali: A New Edition, Translation and Commentary*, ed., tr. E.F. Bryant (New York: North Point Press, 2009), I.3.

local operator of the absolute self) and on the absolute self (making it—in the framework of a *theologia crucis*—inseparable from the *kenosis* by means of which it condescends to finitude in all its forms). The apprehension of this indiscernibility is precisely the object of that which Fichte calls intellectual intuition. In this sense, 'Intellectual intuition can [...] in no way be interpreted as an act of empowerment of a solitary subjectivity infinitely enjoying its unlimited activity and autarkic unity, robbing God of his glory. [...] The I of the *Doctrine of Science* is not God but [its finite] image, and *for this reason* nonetheless God. [...] [I]t is the Word of John: an immanent and universal power of life, present in all the interior and exterior acts of regenerated humanity [...] The act of returning by which true life is inaugurated [...] first of all humbles [human beings] with regard to [their] illegitimate metaphysical pride by reminding [them] that [they are] only the image of God and [are] not in [themselves their] own light, then elevates [them] by making [them] see that [they] therefore [bear] within [themselves] the imprint of the divinity of which [they are] the living temple[s]'.[337]

The distinction between the conception proper to dogmatic idealism (the infinitising I that forecloses its castration, usurping the place of God and considering itself as the ultimate and self-sufficient source of all worldly order) and the Christian conception of the I (the finite I as singular instantiation of the immanental life) induces a distinction between two forms of narcissism: the egocentric and self-sufficient narcissism of a disligated I that denies its finitude, and the egophanic narcissism of a coninsubstantialised I according to which they who can intuit their own self-awareness as a singular image of the divine 'I am that I am' owe themselves, 'trembling before [their] own majesty', 'a religious respect'. Within the framework of egophanic narcissism, one of the quintessential experiences of the divine is the experience of the finite self, and one of the first devotional acts is the care of this self in its threefold nature—that is, of the soul that religates the subject with the one life, of the phenoumenal body that appears differently in each Umwelt, and of the spirit that

337 Goddard, *La philosophie fichtéenne de la vie*, 59, 185, 203.

ventures into the supernatural sky. Thus the divinisation of humanity (and of every living being)—the understanding of all living existence as instantiation of the trinitarian second person, its becoming Christ as 'icon of the [pleromatic] God'[338]—does not necessarily imply a usurpation of God's place by the human being: instead, every living being occupies a place in God—in its divine trinity—the place of the child of the mat(t)er and the sibling of the rest of the living.

Narcissistic love and care for the self is correlatively love of the worldly not-self: both the self and the not-self are images of God: 'All is the appearance and image of God, and there is no other being-there.'[339] The Fichtean I searches for the divine 'in herbis et lapidibus', i.e. between the plants and the stones, as the Spinozist Goethe wrote in a letter to Jacobi. The establishment of a purported fixed universal boundary between phenomena and noumena and the concomitant pseudo-speculative fascination with the 'Great Outdoors' reactivates an ontotheological and hypertranscendent mystification that obliterates the dynamical dialectical conversion between inside and outside proper to speculative thought and practice. As Benjamin writes in his critique of the tendency (which he characterises as Romantic) to make a radical distinction between (noumenal) 'mystery' and quotidian (phenomenal) life: 'Any serious exploration of occult, surrealistic, phantasmagoric gifts and pheno[u]mena presupposes a dialectical intertwinement to which a Romantic turn of mind is impervious. For histrionic or fanatical emphasis on the [noumenal] side of the mysterious takes us no further; we penetrate the mystery only to the degree that we recognise it in the everyday world, by virtue of a dialectical optic that perceives the everyday as impenetrable, the impenetrable as everyday.'[340] The tasks of the various modes of thought and practice find their points of application within worldly horizons, seeking to deepen experience differentially, to perceive more, to understand more, to feel more, to mediate all supposedly immediate

---

338 Letter of Saint Paul to the Corinthians (1:15–20).

339 Fichte, *Doctrine de la science. Exposé de 1812* (Paris: PUF, 2005), 53.

340 Benjamin, 'Surrealism: The Last Snapshot of the European Intelligentsia', 216.

experience by means of a 'dialectical optic', to suspend all 'natural attitude', to resolve the phenoumenodelic depths foreclosed by the transcendental apparatus, to use the impasses of the associated symbolic structures as pivots for speculative extensions of the corresponding transcendental types. Far from subordinating finitude and its inherent relativity to a supposedly hypertranscendent instance, the Christian stance brings about an 'absolute transfiguration of finitude',[341] a glorification of the tiniest droplet of ephemeral revelation ('The Parousia of the Absolute shines through in the simplest of impressions'),[342] effecting a roseate reconciliation with crucified actuality. In so doing, Christianity sublates the conception of religious practices in which the ultimate goal would be to offer some sort of access to a spiritual realm of eternity and immutability beyond the material turmoil of change, death, and transience: '[T]he true life, the eternal life has been found–it is not just a promise, it exists, it is in *each of* [*us*]: as a life of love, as a love without exceptions or rejections, without distance.[343] [...] The concepts of guilt and punishment are completely missing from the psychology of the "evangel"; so is the concept of reward. "Sin", any distance between [life] and [living beings]: these are abolished,–*this is what the "glad tidings" are all about.* Blessedness is not a promise [...] it is the *only* reality [...][344] the expression "blessed life" has in it something superfluous. To wit: Life is necessarily blessed; for it is blessedness.[345] [...] Everyone is a child of [the living mat(t)er]–[Child Yesses] did not claim any special privileges. [...] The kingdom of [life] is *in each of* [*us and all around us*].[346] [...] Nothing is less Christian than [...] a "kingdom of [life]" that is *yet to come*, a "kingdom

341 Hegel, *Lectures on the Philosophy of Religion, Volume III*, 115.

342 Henry, *Incarnation*, 367.

343 F. Nietzsche, *The Anti-Christ*, in *The Anti-Christ, Ecce Homo, Twilight of the Idols and Other Writings*, tr. J; Norman (Cambridge: Cambridge University Press, 2005), 26 [§29].

344 Ibid., 30 [§ 33].

345 Fichte, *The Way Towards the Blessed Life; Or, the Doctrine of Religion*, 1.

346 Nietzsche, *The Anti-Christ*, 26–27 [§29].

of heaven" in the *beyond.* [...] The "kingdom of [life]" is not something that you wait for; it does not have a yesterday or a day after tomorrow, it will not arrive in a "thousand years"–it is an experience of the heart; it is everywhere and it is nowhere...[347] [...] I'm not going to be able to transcend [the kingdom of life] anymore. [...] Pray for me, [living mat(t)er], since not transcending [thy immanental kingdom] is [healing], and transcending used to be my human effort at salvation. [...] And I will have to stay inside whatever is. [...] I was little by little abandoning my human salvation. [...] [W]hat comes out of the roach's belly is not transcendable [...] what comes out of the roach is [actual revelation,] blessed be the fruit of thy womb—I want [the overwhelming actuality of manifestation] without dressing it up with a future that redeems it, not even with a hope—until now what hope wanted in me was just to conjure away [the pleromatic overabundance of life]. But I want much more than that: I want to find the [cure in this specious present], in the reality that is being, and not in the promise, I want to find joy in this [living] instant—I want [life] in whatever comes out of the roach's belly. [...] [T]ranscending is an exit. [...] [I]n the interstices of primordial [mat(t)er] there is the mysterious, fiery line that is the [life]'s breathing.'[348]

The resolute assumption of finitude—the finitude both of the native and mortal character of all living things and of the transcendentally determined nature of all experience—is a necessary condition for the activation of an absolutely modern conception of the religious. In this respect, both Hegel's tarrying with the negative and Heidegger's 'fundamental ontology' are contributions of paramount importance to the project of establishing a modern definition of religious practices, i.e. to a conception of religion definitively absolved of every promise of salvation and of any hyper-transcendence with respect to the immanental realm of life and death. Christianity is the speculative religion *par excellence*, since it does not shy away from the pain that accompanies every form of finite existence, and does not understand the religious cure (the 'resurrection') as a salvation from finitude and its

347 Ibid., 31–32 [§34].

348 Lispector, *The Passion According to G.H.*, 79–80, 83, 99.

attendant afflictions, while it affirms the absolute divinisation of every form of life, the absolutely necessary role played by finite existence in divine revelation. According to the Hegelian *theologia crucis*, 'death [...] is of all things the most dreadful and to hold fast to what is dead requires the greatest strength. [...] [T]he life of Spirit is not the life that shrinks from death and keeps itself untouched by devastation, but rather the life that endures it and maintains itself in it. It wins its truth only when, in utter dismemberment, it finds itself. [...] Spirit is this power only by looking the negative in the face, and tarrying with it.[349] [...] Affirmation of life-AND-death appears as one. [...] To grant one without the other is [...] a limitation which in the end shuts out all that is infinite. [...] [T]he blood of the mightiest circulation flows through both [spheres]: there is neither a here or a beyond, but the [living and dying immanence].'[350]

The dialectical reconciliation (brought about by the spirit) between the infinite mat(t)er and the finite child does not eliminate the conflicting terms (for example through a dissolution of the separate living individuals into the material solution) but reconciles them through the distinction itself. Given that this reconciliation does not eliminate finitude, nor does it 'save' the individual from the afflictions of being-there (such as anguish in the face of death).[351] The thesis of coninsubstantiality between the first two hypostases of the triune pleroma (stated in particular in the Nicene Creed) signifies that the union of the finite subject with the mat(t)er does not take place 'after' death, so to speak, in a blessed blue yonder, but in the

349 Hegel, *Phenomenology of Spirit*, 19.

350 R. Maria Rilke, Letter to Witold von Hulewicz (November 13, 1925), in *Letters of Rainer Maria Rilke, 1910–1926*.

351 'The suffering of the soul, this infinite anguish, is the witness of the Spirit, inasmuch as spirit is the negativity of finite and infinite, of subjectivity and objectivity being conjoined but still as conflicting elements; if there were no longer any conflict, there would be no anguish. Spirit is the absolute power to endure this anguish, i.e., to unite the two and to be in this way, in this oneness. Thus, the anguish itself verifies the appearance of God.' Hegel, *Lectures on the Philosophy of Religion, Volume III*, 215.

finite and separate existence now understood as the being-there of divine life. The world thus divinised becomes a 'world of revelation',[352] a world in which every phenomenon is epiphanic, a world in which 'particular things are simply affections of God's attributes',[353] a world in which 'the more we understand particular things, the more we understand God',[354] a world in which, therefore, the exact and natural sciences become an endless hermeneutics of the holy scripture. This divinisation of the world is, however, correlative to a relativisation whereby the world—far from being understood in terms of a putatively autonomous in-itself—is nothing more than the mode in which the one life appears and externalises itself in the experience constituted by a certain transcendental type of subjectivity: 'After we find shelter in [immanental life], we do not lose the world either, it only receives another meaning, and becomes, from a being for itself, autonomous [...] simply the appearance and the exteriorisation in [experience] of the hidden [living] essence itself.[355] [...] The world is irreal—not intrinsically—but in relation to something more real, which has the power to make the world plastic.'[356] In our own terminology, every *worldly phenomenon*—everything that appears in a world—is nothing more than an objectivation (correlated to a certain transcendental type) of a *transmundane phenoumenon*, of a phenoumenal appearing that is objectivated differently in each world, that is phenomenalised differently by each transcendental type of subjectivity. Despite being begotten in the premundane life, every living being lives its experiencing life in the circumambient world framed by its transcendental faculties (a world that might change depending on the speculative resources of the subject). Ultimately, however, every living

352 Cf. W. Benjamin, Letter to Florens Christian Tang, December 9, 1923, in *The Correspondence of Walter Benjamin 1910–1940*, 224.

353 Spinoza, *Ethics*, 26 [Book I, Prop. 35, Corollary].

354 Spinoza, *Ethics*, 238 [Book V, Prop. 24].

355 Fichte, *The Way Towards the Blessed Life; Or, the Doctrine of Religion*, 182 [translation modified].

356 P.K. Dick, *The Exegesis of Philip K. Dick*, ed. P. Jackson and J. Lethem (New York: Houghton Mifflin Harcourt, 2011), 11:8.

being can make their own the words of Christ: 'I am not of this world'. Even so, it is not a question of leaving the world to enter God, but of suspending both the world and one's own life in (the phenoumenodelic revelation of) God. To be disligated from life—the arche-disease—is to fall into the world, to cease to be-there in a world rooted in the pre- and transmundane life in order to subsist solely in the constituted world, to transform the world from a particular system of images correlated to a certain transcendental type of consciousness into an autonomous, reified and closed realm. The fall breaks the unity between the first two trinitarian persons, and the individual is no longer recognised as a singular avatar of the child. Thus, 'the [tri]unity of the powers in God by which God's being-out-of-itself was originally brought back to [its] being-in-itself [is broken]. [...] The form of this world abandoned by the divine is nothing more than the lower form of the "being-outside-and-alongside-one-another", of the sad and inorganic extension.'[357] Disligated individuals position themselves and the world 'outside' of God, depriving both themselves and the world of their true theophanic natures. The mundane self is no longer an icon of the pre- and transmundane God, a singular instantiation of the 'I am that I am' that is ceaselessly enacted in the intradivine life. A subject disligated from absolute life falls—a thing among things—into a reified and naturalised world that is no longer a 'world of revelation' suspended and glowing in the supernatural night. On the contrary, the religating cure immerses the world in the transmundane life—transmuting it into a world of life—and converts the subject situated in its world into a living being levitating in life: '[...] God enters into us [...] we ourselves are this immediate life that is [Its]. Of this immediate divine life we certainly know nothing. [...] [I]n consciousness we cannot apprehend more than the being-there [...] that belongs to us, this being that is ours *in God.* [...] We know nothing of this immediate divine life [...] since, from the first stirring of consciousness, it metamorphoses into a [constituted] world. [...] It may well always be God [itself] who lives behind all these figures, but we do not see [It], we never see [It] except in [Its] wrappings; we see [It] as stone, grass, animal—we

357 Goddard, *La philosophie fichtéenne de la vie*, 206.

see [It], if we go higher, as a law of nature, as a moral law, and yet all this is never [It]. Always, for us, the [phenomenal] form envelops the [living] essence. [...] To you who complain, I say: just rise to the standpoint of religion and all the wrappings will [be suspended]; [...] and divinity itself will enter you again, in its first and original form, as life, as your own life, that which you must live. [...] [L]ook no further than the clouds; you can find it everywhere you are.'[358] As we argued above, Fichte suspends—an *epoché avant la lettre*—Spinozist substance, turning it into a purely phenoumenodelic insubstance in which every phenomenon is an image of God. Far from being betrayed by the multiple images in which it is refracted, the one life is iconophilic. It constantly engenders new transcendental types capable of constituting, by means of the transcendental structures proper to them, surrounding worlds-kaleidoscopes of unique images by means of which life ceaselessly raises its self-manifestation to higher powers. Self-love, glorification of the living flesh and love of the world thus take on a devotional character: 'True Christian faith, therefore, distances us both from depreciation of self, celebrating in our clearly affirmed autonomy the existential act of God, and from contempt for the world, whose value it affirms and renews. Ultimately, only by loving ourselves enough and loving the world enough do we love God.[359] [...] The [human being] is defined as the possibility [...] of being a sibling of Christ. The [human being] possesses this fraternity in the flesh, for it is in the humility of the flesh that the God who extraverts [*extrapose*] itself can be actualised without being lost and manifest its glory. To be [human] is not to exile oneself in this pure interiority of the I and to desolate the body and the world [...] but to participate in [pro]creation, to realise it in its own immediate reality. [...] To disown the flesh, to dissolve corporeality into the sufficiency of the singular Self, means both to deprive God of [Its] radiance, to tarnish the beauty of the world and to disown the [human being].'[360]

358 Fichte, *The Way Towards the Blessed Life; Or, the Doctrine of Religion*, 90 [translation modified].

359 Goddard, *La philosophie fichtéenne de la vie*, 98.

360 Goddard, *Le corps*, 156.

Now, what are the concrete effects of the religation of the living with life? We could say, in Fichtean style, that the living force of imagination bifurcates along the fork I/not-I, thereby becoming a force of spiritual transformation of the I and a force of speculative mediation of the not-I. There is no religation without a concomitant practice of self- and hetero-transformation. 'The effective and true religiosity is not content merely to consider and contemplate, it is not content to ruminate over devout thoughts, it is on the contrary necessarily active. It consists [...] in the deep awareness that God, within us, currently lives, is active and accomplishes [its] work. [...] [I]t is the living activity that distinguishes the true religion from this [mystic] exultation.[361] [...] Christians are not characterised by their "faith": Christians act, they are characterised by a different way of acting. [...] [T]he practice of life is the only thing that can make you feel "divine", "blessed", "evangelic", like a "child of [life]" at all times. "Atonement" and "praying for forgiveness" are *not* the way to [life]: *only the practice* leads to [life], in fact it *is* "[life]". [...] A new way of life, *not* a new faith....'[362] The transcendental correlation between each living individual and its Umwelt implies that spiritual self-transformation—the continuous formation of self (the 'celestial battle')—is indissociable from practical activity exercised in the world, from the task of suspending and subverting all assumed naturalness (the 'worldly battle'). The existence of the Fichtean I has the character of a 'permanent aboriginal revolution'.[363] This can be understood in the twofold sense of (a) a 'continuous movement of self-formation' beyond any humanism depending on a presumed essence of the human and (b) as a practical activity (*Tätigkeit*) that aims to overcome the worldly reification of the given. The 'permanent aboriginal revolution' is an exploration of the supernatural sky that periodically returns to the material origin, that is, to the vital force of formation that irrigates both the spiritual transformations of the subjective I and the mediations of the worldly not-I: 'no one

361 Fichte, *The Way Towards the Blessed Life; Or, the Doctrine of Religion*, 92–93 [translation modified].

362 Nietzsche, *The Anti-Christ*, 30–31 [§33].

363 Cf. Goddard, 'Fichte, ou la révolution aborigène permanente'.

can transmute [the worldly substance] unless they transmute themselves' (Paracelsus) and no one can transmute themselves without changing the worldly horizon of their existence. Ultimately, an aboriginal 'people is only realised when it traces the [Caravaca] Cross in its [transient] sphere. The Cross has [three crossbeams]: how does a people trace them? With the [patient] march of [their activity of mediation of the transcendental limits of their aesthetic, emotional, conceptual, and political experience] below (such is the horizontal) and the [freefalling] levitation of their [absolunauts] above [and below]' (such is the vertical)'.[364] The roseate crucifixion of Christ thus schematises the two dimensions of his archetype, the existential conversion of the I along the vertical crossbeam ('Come. The spirit breathes out of the [subjective essence]') and the transformation of the not-I across the horizontal one ('Come. The spirit breathes out of the [world]'):[365] subjective self-formation and objective de-reification. In turn, the second horizontal crossbeam on the Caravaca cross represents the second coming, which begins with the conception of the body of Christ as entheogenic sacrament (already prefigured in the Christian host) brewed up in the *feitio* from the alchemical union of strength (*Mariri*) and light (*Chacruna*). The second coming is triggered by the alchemical concoction of the 'universal medicine', first as 'magical substances, [spices,] nectars and ambrosias',[366] then—substance being suspended—as purely phenoumenodelic insubstance. Thanks to the universal *pharmakon*, the Christic arche-totem can be reborn in every living person, making each one a unique case of the child Yesses, an inhabitant of the immanental kingdom of life. 'The Virgin I must be and bring God forth from me.'[367]

---

364 L. Marechal, *Didáctica de la Patria*, in *Heptamerón* (Buenos Aires: Sudamericana, 1974).

365 A. Artaud, 'À Table', *La Révolution Surrealiste* 3 (15 April 1925).

366 Lezama Lima, 'Introducción a un sistema poético', in *El reino de la imagen* (Caracas: Biblioteca Ayachuco, 1981), 258–79: 259.

367 Silesius, *Cherubinischer Wanderer*, Book I, §23 [tr. M. Shrady, *The Cherubinic Wanderer* (New York: Paulist Press), 40].

The question of Christ on the cross, 'Mother, can't you see that I am burning?',[368] touches upon a real that is so overwhelming—the finite being-there in life, without possible salvation, beautiful and terrible—that the preservation of subjective integrity in the face of this true pleromancy sometimes requires 'waking up' to 'reality' and placing oneself unilaterally in the reified world. 'God is unconscious'[369] since both the mat(t)er (who institutes the living being that constitutes the world) and the Holy Spirit (in whom living beings are brought into concert in supra-individual subjective structures) overflow the worldly consciousness of the living being, its mundane reality. To interlace the hypostases—to circulate in the trinitarian helicoid—requires an awakening of 'reality': both to let oneself be infused by the force of the spiritual transformation of one's own subjective structure and to suspend the world constituted by the transcendental apparatus in the phenoumenodelic pleroma, to inhabit it in a form of *daydreaming*. Whereas in the real daydream there is always—when what is revealed in the unconscious God becomes unbearable—the possibility of waking up to worldly reality, reality can in turn then be suspended (the *epoché*). This suspension maintains an 'analytic' space (sometimes referred to as the shrink's couch) in which it becomes possible to pay the requisite attention to the real impasses that might set off a process of the speculative mediation of worldly reality. In this sense, 'ontological psychoanalysis' deploys a kind of operation that is the converse to 'waking up' to 'reality', in that it transforms worldly reality itself into a kind of daydream, one open to epiphanic ingressions and speculative extensions, a flowing daydream into which ICHTYS, the Christ-Fish, plunges.

Love of the first trinitarian person—i.e., of the impersonal life qua mat(t)er, of the originary life-giving activity, of the life-breathing Word (the resonating tuning in to 'a non-historical and non-grammatical Word

368 See J. Lacan, *The Seminar of Jacques Lacan, Book XI: The Four Fundamental Concepts of Psychoanalysis*, tr. A. Sheridan, ed. J.-A. Miller (New York and London: Norton, 1998), 59–60.

369 Ibid., 59.

that telegraphs toward a border of the Real')[370]—and love of the second person—of oneself as an avatar of the arche-typical child, of the reexisting aboriginal, of the breathing, beating, and desiring being-there of life—religating love also acquires, as love of other living beings, an eschatological projection oriented by the third hypostasis of the triune pleroma: that of the Holy Spirit as a religious community of the living: 'All these apostles of [Yesses] [...] so intimately united and forming One heart and One soul, had once been totally alien to one another [...]. Here they are now united in the depths of themselves. [...] The souls of all were but One soul, they were united by the bonds of sweetest harmony [*Übereinstimmung*]. [...] "We are [siblings]"[371] [...] In this harmony their many-sided consciousness chimes in with one spirit and their many different lives with one life [...] and the same living spirit animates the different beings, who therefore are no longer merely similar but one; they make up not a collection but a [community], since they are unified not in a universal [...] but through life and through love. [...] In the Kingdom of [Life] what is common to all is life in [Life]. This is not the common character which a concept expresses, but is love, a living bond which unites the [religated ones]; it is this feeling of unity of life [...][372] This order recognises in principle only one mat(t)er [the all-powerful, self-begetting life], so that all living beings are its [children] and the only real relationship that remains [...] is that of brothers and sisters.'[373]

The coninsubstantiality between the first two hypostases—the *homoousion* creed—implies that every transcendent and intentional experience of a finite subject is in the last instance an immanent and reflexive experience of the impersonal life of which the subject is a local probe. Every experience (*erleben*) is channelled by an individual living (*leben*) as a local act of the

370 Las Señoras del Arcoiris, *Documentos de la Escuela Nocturna*, 20.

371 J.G. Fichte, 'Prédication sur Luc', in *Querelle de l'atheisme suivie de Divers textes sur la religion*, 241–42.

372 Hegel, *On Christianity: Early Theological Writings*, 277–78.

373 Henry, *Paroles de Christ*, 48.

impersonal life (*das Leben*). Life engenders finite beings, and experiences the lives of these beings as its own life. The third hypostasis of the triune pleroma enriches this characterisation of life as immanental self-experience channelled by lifeforms by spanning a new spiritual dimension along which life raises itself to collective forms of spirit. The Holy Spirit is the hypostasis of the triune pleroma that prescribes a progressive harmonisation of local subjectivities into global subjects, minds-at-large, vast active living intelligence systems, swarm-forms of intelligence, global patterns endowed with patience and agency, tiny superorganisms, wandering holobions, spiritual communities. Rather than understanding redemption as a path of return capable of dissolving the living who have 'fallen' into the multiple in the original undifferentiated unity (which would amount to denying the divinity of the Incarnation)—the communitarian whole of the spirit articulates them, brings them together, concerts them, composes, them, federates them as determined individuals in a concrete living unity. While the first hypostasis—the mat(t)er—encodes the begetting unity of life that underlies multiple individuals, the third hypostasis—the pattern—denotes the overarching structured wholes of harmonies, counter-points, holarchies and global forms of coherence that emerge from the connections between separated individuals. The finite living beings (second person) are interconnected both by the underlying mat(t)er (first imperson) and the overarching patterns (third transperson).

In this way, the Holy Spirit is the name for the life processes by means of which separated individuals are incorporated, integrated, connected, concerted, amalgamated, mutualised, federated into new subjectivated wholes such as, for instance, particles, atoms, molecules, cells, organisms, nexuses, couples, clans, families, flocks, hordes, tribes, networks, teams, lodges, villages, bodies, holarchies, swarms, institutions, gangs, churches, clubs, galaxies, communities, ecosystems, societies, sects, clusters, bands, structures, assemblies, mutualisms, tissues, federations, and universes. These integrations result from a panoply of forms of connectivity such as symbiosis, predation, weddings, messenger pigeons, covenants, physical interactions like gravitation or electromagnetism, cooperation, coordination, solidarity, miscegenation and exogamy, empathic resonance, seclusion, letters, synergies, translations and transports, choreographies, networking, natural and social contractual links, phone calls, rules, communicating vessels, kin-making, pathways and bridges, rituals and ceremonies, knots and braids, erotic practices, and so on and so forth. These different forms of intersubjective connectivity trigger self-organising processes, make it possible for global forms of coherence, ordered patterns, and systemic behaviour to emerge, and foster the sublation of the juxtapositional 'being-outside-and-alongside-one-another' and the expanded interiorisation of the corresponding forms of mutual exteriority. The Holy Spirit raises life's force of engenderment and mutation to a new hybridising power: rooted in the impersonal life that nourishes them, taking care of themselves and asserting their desiring autonomy, the various forms of life—the cricket, the datura, the human, the crystal, the jaguar—can also compose themselves, federate, enter into symbiotic relations, institute new emergent subjective types, make active ingressions into the unfolding life of the spirit. The emerging patterns (this 'involved delicacy of organisation [...] "ferns sprouting ferns sprouting ferns in multidimensional spaces"')[374] supervene as higher order structures out of the living matter. The concertation of different forms of life into an inter-type tribe correlatively determines a coalescence of their surrounding worlds: the umweltic bubbles constituted by different transcendental types coalesce into a unique world of superior phenomenological depth, into a new lifeworld traversed by percepts, affects, and concepts that only the resulting emergent collective subject will be able to perceive, feel and think.

The Christian doctrine of the trinity endowed the speculative philosophy of German Idealism with its fundamental schema, whereby the abstract unity of the mat(t)er and the multiplicity of different living beings is dialecticised into the concrete unity of unity and difference which is the Holy Spirit as the communities of finite spirits.[375] If impersonal life is the

374 Watts, *The Joyous Cosmology*, 55–56.

375 In Fichte's words: '[T]he [Mat(t)er] is the absolutely pre-given, that which precedes the excision of individuality in the appearance; the [Child] is the absolute elevation of this appearance to the intuition of the Kingdom of [Life], and the Spirit

hypostasis of the triune pleroma corresponding to the category of the one and if the child instantiates the category of the multiple, the Holy Spirit incorporates the category of the wholly in the trinity. The Holy Spirit is the hypostasis that orients the overcoming of the opposition between the one of preindividual life and the multiplicity of singular living beings into a whole understood as an articulated community of singular individuals. The abstract unity of the one life is diversified by becoming incarnate and the diverse is driven toward concrete unity by becoming totalised, thus passing from the indistinct one to a one articulated by determined and separate (albeit not unlinked) individualities. The circulation between

---

is the reunion of the two [...].' Fichte, *La doctrine de l'État (1813)*, 213. For Hegel, 'God is the Trinity, i.e., [it] is the course of life that consists in being the universal that has being in and for itself, or in differentiating itself and then in setting itself over against itself, yet in so doing, being identical with itself—in a word, it consists in being this syllogism' (Hegel, *Lectures on the Philosophy of Religion, Volume III*, 369). In his *Lectures on the Philosophy of World History*, Hegel maintains that it is 'this doctrine of the Trinity which raises Christianity above the other religions. [...] The Trinity is the speculative part of Christianity, and it is through it that philosophy can discover the Idea of reason in the Christian religion too.' G.W.F. Hegel, *Lectures on the Philosophy of World History: Introduction*, tr. H.B. Nisbet (New York: Cambridge University Press, 1998), 51. Finally, we encounter a similar use of the Christian Trinity in Schelling, for example in *The Ages of the World:* 'But here where the initially concealed unity of unity and opposition steps forth as something actual, unity as such constitutes the highest principle and subordinates the two conflicting systems to it. The Christian doctrine that regards both of the initial principles as different personalities but as belonging to one and the same nature [*Wesen*] unites duality in the most complete and perfect way possible to unity. For even the unity that was first only potential until it has become real in the Spirit can by no means be regarded as nullifying the duality. It too is again only a personality of God. Thus unity, duality, and the unity of both all appear as independent for themselves. That dualism is the highest, in which dualism and pantheism, the dyad and the monad, have re-emerged as opposites. It is impossible to think of a more complete resolution of the conflict between all human systems than the one that has already long been revealed in the concept of the three-in-oneness of the divine nature.' F.W.J. von Schelling, *The Ages of the World (1811)*, tr. J.P. Lawrence (New York: SUNY Press, 2019), 152–53.

the three hypostases gives rise to the restless continuity of life, always instituting new local lifeforms which unfold themselves by circumventing material obstructions, unravelling their tentacles into the open, connecting to other lifeforms and weaving global patterns, broadcasting their chants, vacuolising breathing clearings like eyes in the pleroma, multi-ocularising their visions. Maintaining the trinitarian balance between the different hypostases—the Borromean knot between the illegible and invisible real of material life always already partially foreclosed by its transcendental enworlding, the imaginary of individual existence in its specular correlation with the circumambient world and the semiotic amalgrammation of transcendental-dependent languages into the vast single semiotic process that is life–defines what we could call the art of living of the saintomatic religator, the heresiarch. This art consists in linking together in the singularity of an individuated life (a) a religation with the impersonal flow of the intra-divine life (being rooted in the infra-sensible soil, the probing of unconsciousness, the immersion of existence in the material womb, the daydreaming), (b) the affirmation of one's own determination and voca(lisa)tion, of one's own desiring and self-positing autonomy, and, finally, (c) the placing of this singular being-there into the service of the life of the spirit, of the holobionic tribes. By knotting togethers the three hypostases, the religator defines an *axis mundi* for the particular alignment of the infra-sensible engendering soil, of the revealing lifeworlds, and of the supernatural sky. If the 'conquest of space' is concomitant with the extractivist devastation of the earth, the spiritual exploration of the supernatural sky is only possible from a rootedness in the infra-sensible earth that irrigates the living with the immanental force that models new probes *of* life in the double sense of the genitive.

In a religious schema endowed with only two hypostases—the undifferentiated one and the differentiated many (such as sacred continuity and profane discontinuity in Bataille, for example)—the restitution of unity can only take place by means of the inverse movement of engendering, either in the form of the (sacrificial) death of the individual, or by means of near-death ecstatic experiences of approach to the underlying continuity, or by any other retro-Romantic protocol for retreating into a prior fusion[376] or into a fetishised 'noble savage' state prior to the nature/culture or human/nonhuman divide. In other words, the restitution of the primordial one through the dissolution of discontinuity is a regressive movement that conflates individualising differentiation with pathological disligation. According to the trinitarian dialectic, the risk of disligation that accompanies individualising differentiation cannot be dealt with through regression to an undifferentiated state (or to any other supposed previous golden age), but only by means of a further propulsion of the phenoumenodelic unfolding of subjective forms of experience. In trinitarian Christianity as understood here, the reconstitution of unity relies on a communal 'delirium of engendering' new forms of life, on collective experimentation in new forms of living, perceiving, feeling, thinking, sharing, acting, chanting, and dying together. In this sense, trinitarian religiosity makes it possible to circumvent the regressive tendencies (the 'exultation of dissolution')[377] inherent in the abstract opposition between the one and the multiple.

Rather than understanding itself as a finite probe of life in the double sense of the genitive, a fallen individual understands life as its private property. The notion of the fall does not refer to the incarnation of life in a separate individuality, but to the disligation of the finite, determined, and separate individual, to the breaking point where the self-sufficiency of the individual tears apart the continuous fabric of life. Therefore, the cure can be understood neither as redemption from finite incarnation

---

376 It is worth quoting here Wilber's description of what he calls the *pre/trans fallacy*: '[The retro-Romantic approach] [...] simply confuses differentiation and dissociation [what we have here called *disligation*]. [...] Thus, whenever evolution produces a new differentiation, and that differentiation happens to go into pathological dissociation, then this approach seeks to permanently turn back the pages of emergent history to a time prior to the differentiation. [...] That will indeed get rid of the new pathology, at the cost of getting rid of the new depth, the new creativity, the new consciousness. By that retro-Romantic logic, the only way to really get rid of pathology is to get rid of differentiation altogether.' K. Wilber, *Sex, Ecology, Spirituality: The Spirit of Evolution* (Boston and London: Shambhala, 2000), 111.

377 Land, *The Thirst for Annihilation*, 103.

nor as a mystical dissolution of separation into the indeterminacy of the primordial one, nor as a 'retro-Romantic' return to any supposedly pristine state whatsoever, nor as an act of transcendence with respect to the material dimension of existence, nor as 'salvation' with respect to the world and to history. Besides relying on a strengthening of the religation with the impersonal material life, the cure depends on a spiritual process driven by the fraternal love between finite, determinate, separate individuals. In dialectical terms, being thrown into the hazards of separation, of division, and of desiring autonomy can be understood as a negation of the underlying impersonal life that makes the fraternal connection possible as a negation of that first negation: 'The Absolute [...] is the eternally fertile ground of life [...] the abstract unity which will divide itself in order to become the concrete, organic and living unity of a reunited multiplicity. We can even say that it always aspires to this division by means of which it can be reunited. [...] The Absolute is never absolutely in itself; in itself, it is essentially desire for manifestation, i.e. determination–a living God.'[378] Far from reconstituting the indistinct original unity that subtends the multiple individuals, the spiritual negation of the individuating negation raises that impersonal unity of life to a tribal phase in which individuation is preserved and reinforced. According to the orientation provided by the Holy Spirit, each emerging collective subject must articulate and preserve the singularity of its members as unique experiencing modes through which life manifests itself: 'The heterogeneous remain, indeed, but knotted, attached, enveloped in each other in the most intimate way.'[379]

Trinitarian religation is not intended to absolve life of death, but to understand and live finitude as a necessary moment—between the impersonal ma(t)ter and the transpersonal pattern—in the immanental dehiscence of life. The fact that the reconciliation of the mat(t)er and the child in the spirit takes place 'after' death means that this reconciliation requires the assumption of death, its incorporation within life and the endurance of the corresponding mourning play. Just as speculation does not do away

378 Goddard, *Le corps*, 159.

379 Derrida, *Glas*, 80.

with finitude, spiritual reconciliation does not eliminate death. As Clarice Labou Tansi maintains, it is not death that is opposed to life, the opposite of life is the disease of disligated self-sufficiency which corrupts both life and death: '"Good is living"... she stammered. "Bad is..." "Is...?" "Bad is not living..." "Dying?" he asked. "No, no..." she groaned. [...] "Bad is not living, that's all. Dying is something else."[380] [...] [W]e are killing life. Death does not kill life—we also kill death.'[381] Reconciliation preserves death as the vital moment in which the arche-disease that manifests in the attempt to appropriate life is called into question. In this sense, going through the experience of death—of the ultimate dispossession—is a necessary initiatory phase in the process of healing the disease that affects life. To exist in the sense of living by absolving oneself of all supposed 'natural' essence and of all private property is to be-for-death. The life of the spirit can be understood—in Hegel's terms—as a sublation of 'nature'—that is, of any essentialisation of the corresponding transcendental type and any reification of the correlative 'natural' order of things. By taking on existence-beyond-essence, by taking on the death that turns into derision every gesture of appropriation, by lingering with the negative and embracing the absolution, the living being becomes spiritualised, it brings about in its own flesh the reconciliation between the transcendental plasticity of the infinite life and the singular determination of its finite life.

The bringing together of separate individuals into a community is in turn to be understood as institution of subjects at a higher degree. Hegel characterises the Holy Spirit that overcomes the dialectical tension between mat(t)er and child as the (emerging) spirit of the people (*Volkgeist*), understood as a collective and individuated form of subjectivity.[382]

---

380 C. Lispector, *Near to the Wild Heart*, tr. A. Entrekin (London: Penguin, 2014), 45.

381 Labou Tansi, *Encre, sueur, salive et sang*, np.

382 'The essence of spirit [...] is self-consciousness. [...] [B]ut in the field of world history, we are not concerned with particulars and need not confine ourselves to individual instances or attempt to trace everything back to them. The spirit in history is an individual which is both universal in nature and at the same time determinate: in short, it is the [people] in general, and the spirit we are concerned with is the spirit of the [people].' Hegel, *Lectures on the Philosophy of World History*, 51.

As 'self-consciousness', the spirit of a people—its determinate and distinct subjectivity—expresses itself concretely, according to Hegel, in their culture, i.e. in their customs, law, religion, arts, economy, sciences, philosophy, technology, and practices, in their forms of individual and collective self-care (in cuisine, medicine, clothing, eroticism), in their myths and rituals, in the rhythm of their collective breath, in their transcendental plasticity, in the external exchanges and relations with alterity (such as other communities) that it can bring about.[383] The spirit of the people should however be distinguished from a mere superstructure defined by a certain number of 'cultural' forms or productions as exchangeable commodities. Every true culture is infused with the subterranean, chthonic forces of the first hypostasis; every true culture sinks its roots in the infra-sensible soil from which it draws its strength, its sap, its pulse, its trans-formative plasticity; every true culture—far from any mere accumulation of cultural goods, of knowledge, of meaning, of values—is a singular form of the spirit through which life reveals, probes and transforms itself: 'Real culture helps to probe life.[384] [...] Culture is a movement of the spirit that goes from [mat(t)er] to forms and from forms to [mat(t)er], to [living mat(t)er] as to death. To be cultivated is to burn forms, to burn forms to gain life. It means learning to stand upright in the ceaseless movement of [transient] forms [...].'[385]

Since the gathering of separated individuals into a community also engenders a new form of (collective) subjectivity, we can say that the Holy Spirit also engenders (like the mat(t)er). By virtue of the third hypostasis, the trinity is helicoidally opened. But this means that the whole that dialecticises the relationship between the one and the multiple is conjugated in the plural, namely in the form of communal totalities of the living qua collective emergent subjects, which are also multiple, capable of entering themselves into totalisation of higher orders (communities of communities of communities...). Every living being totalises the individuals that make

383 Ibid., 52.

384 A. Artaud, *Œuvres, Messages révolutionnaires* (Paris: Gallimard, 2004), 692.

385 A. Artaud, 'El teatro y los dioses', in *Mexico y Viaje al pais de los tarahumaras* (Mexico: Fondo de Cultura Económica, 1984).

it up and is at the same time capable of entering—by combining itself with other individuals—into subjectivating processes of higher orders: '[*t*]*he many* [individuals] *become one* [community], *and are increased by one* [namely, the community as another (collective) individual].[386] [...] And if we discover such a totality [...] it is added to [its parts] as a new part fabricated separately.'[387] Both the infra-society that the individual envelops or totalises and the supra-societies of which it is a local component might be beyond the thresholds that define the individual's conscious window. We use the term *holobion*[388] (enveloping the notions of wholeness, particle—as in proton or neutron—and living entity) to designate the Janus-like nature of individuals which are both self-positing wholes (super-organisms) with respect to the sub-individuals they totalise, and parts with respect to the higher-order structures they are part of. While the narcissistic 'self-assertive tendency [oriented by the second hypostasis] is the dynamic expression of the [holobion]'s wholeness', the 'integrative tendency' oriented by the Holy Spirit is 'the dynamic expression of its partness'.[389] Since every community is itself a finite individual endowed with transcendental affordances and confronting a correlated non-self, the wholly spiritual tendency to integrate individuals should not be understood as a process by means of which the individualising tendencies of the second hypostasis would be left behind. The relation between the three hypostases is not that of a linear progression by means of which each hypostasis would absolve itself of the previous one. The three hypostases coexist—are coninsubstantial—within the pleromatic life.

*Spirit rising*—emerging dialectically from the tension and interplay between the self-positing tendencies that preserve the separation of the individual as a well-determined local and finite mode of life against the

---

386 Whitehead, *Process and Reality*, 21.

387 Deleuze and Guattari, *Anti-Oedipus*, 42.

388 The term 'holobion' is a variant of the term 'holobiont' used in L. Margulis, *Symbiosis as a Source of Evolutionary Innovation* (Cambridge, MA: MIT Press, 2016).

389 Koestler, *The Ghost in the Machine*, 56.

backdrop of the pleromatic exorbitance and the social tendency to constitute resonating communities. This last tendency is at least one of the sources of the novelty required to propel the self-revelation of life. The neo-Darwinist stance according to which the evolution of life is exclusively driven by the accumulation of random mutations favoured or discarded by natural (individual or kin) selection transforms what is a mere constraint (fitness) into a source of novelty. As Margulis argued, if Darwin's natural selection is the eliminator, symbiosis is the innovator:[390] 'the outside is converted into an expanded inside. [...] Bodies of different origins and proclivities joined to form vibrant communities that become new units of life, new "individuals" at larger, more inclusive levels of organisation.'[391] The life of spirit is a permanent renegotiation of the limits between interiority and exteriority, between the individual and the environment, between the living part (*-bion*) and the emerging whole (*holo-*), oriented in the direction of an increasing integration of separated individuals into vaster holobions endowed with higher computational, perceptual, affective, conceptual, and practical capacities. The emergent distributed forms of the spirit redefine the demarcation line between interior and exterior and are themselves equipped with higher-order transcendental structures that regulate the reception-imagination-expression relations of breath between the redefined (collective) individual and the correlated environment. As more subjects from the 'outside' are literally incorporated into the collective body, intersubjective relations become reflexive relations of the collective subject. These processes of incorporation into higher-order organisms ceaselessly call the assumed boundary between living and nonliving entities into question: 'The planet Pluto may be nonliving when it is considered as a

---

390 Cf. L. Margulis and D. Teresi, 'Discover Interview: Lynn Margulis Says She's Not Controversial, She's Right'. *Discover Magazine*, 17 June 2011, <https://www.discovermagazine.com/the-sciences/discover-interview-lynn-margulis-says-shes-not-controversial-shes-right>.

391 L. Hall and L. Margulis, 'From Movement to Sensation', in L. Margulis, C.A. Asikainen, and W.E. Krumbein (eds.), *Chimeras and Consciousness* (Cambridge, MA: MIT Press, 2011), 161.

separate entity. But if there is interaction between Pluto and "me", it is legitimate to examine the characteristics of a larger whole of which Pluto and "I" are parts. This larger whole will have "life" because a component part, "me", is living, just as the whole that I call "me" has nonliving components, like teeth or blood serum.'[392] These processes of the integration of local and transcendent experiences into reflexive experiences defined with respect to wider localities are oriented toward an ideal pole at infinity—an omega point or the immanental insubstance qua absolute subject at the end of time—defined by a purely immanental and reflexive (rather than transcendental and intentional) experience in which there is no longer an outside. However, as previously stated, the wholly spiritual procession never effectively leaves behind the second hypostasis, which means that there is no final whole that would not define a new perspectival individuation (a new avatar of the child), a new focus for new revelations, a new local part to incorporate into higher-order integrations. There is no whole that is not there, that is not itself in confrontation with an outside. Like the regulative ideas that orient the different modes of thought and practice (science, arts, politics), the ideal pole at infinity defined by the Holy Spirit does not denote a final accomplishment, a definitive halt, of the corresponding process of expansion and potentialisation of the forms of experience but—quite on the contrary—the impossibility of such an actual culmination.

In this way, the eschatological projection oriented by the Holy Spirit progressively realises the abstract unity of the impersonal life in concrete transpersonal communities as holobions of higher orders. The properly political question that orients the tasks of religation prescribed by the third hypostasis is that 'of knowing whether relations (and which ones?) can compound directly to form a new, more "extensive" relation, or whether capacities can compound directly to constitute a more "intense" capacity or power. It is no longer a matter of utilisations or captures, but of sociabilities and communities. How do individuals enter into composition with one another in order to form a higher individual, ad infinitum?'[393] The regulative

392 Bateson and Bateson, *Angels Fear*, 132.

393 Deleuze, *Spinoza: Practical Philosophy,* 126.

infinity proper to the third hypostasis demands that these composites be raised to increasingly higher degrees: from the microphysical interactions to the symbiogenesis that gives rise to cellular organisms, passing through the nexus of cells that make up plant, animal, human individuals and the concertations of individuals into trans-species peoples, to the alliances of peoples, intergalactic confederations, and multiversal clubs. The triune pleroma is the 'fullest and most intense Individual, with [living modes] that vary [and resonate] in an infinity of ways',[394] integrating the experiences of every finite subject into a single self-experience and effecting within itself the harmonic coalescence of their phenomenological horizons. The absolute consciousness of the one life—far from being always already given—is thus the result of a continuous birth, the Holy Spirit being the hypostasis that guides the gradual and progressive integration of relative forms of self-awareness into an absolute consciousness. If within the disease there is no *Band* ('no hay Banda'), the cure that surmounts the tension between the one mat(t)er and the multiple lifeforms necessarily takes the form of a concertation: there is no cure that is not collective, that is not collectivising. The integrated unity of a society of the living is no longer the abstract unity of pre-individual, impersonal life as the vital generative background from which they emerge, but their political orchestration, their becoming tribe as the establishment of a singular collective subject. While the love of the first person roots the individual in a new ground given by the impersonal life, and the love of self affirms, nurtures, and tempers the individual's own singularity, the love of other living beings federates a tribe.

The inter-type concertation of different individuals is not the only way in which the Holy Spirit can institute new transcendental types. As we have argued above, a living being religated to the morphogenetic power of life can activate shamanic degrees of freedom in the transcendental landscape of types, thereby being able to enter—through predatory, mimetic, exogamic, or symbiogenetic practices—into inter-type, trans-species, crossbreed mutations. By definition, a shaman is a lifeform that can move through the transcendental landscape of types, integrate the multiple visions associated

394 Ibid., 126.

with different transcendental perspectives into single trans-species visions endowed with a higher degree of experiential depth, and sing Icaros in the language of the angels. For instance, a shaman might be able to integrate the visions of a human being and the visions of the uncle jaguar into single visions associated with a wider transcendental viewzone that we could call the humjaguar. This integration of different transcendental types does not result from the concertation of numerically different individuals qua tokens of different transcendental types, but from the integration of the visions associated with the different states of a single shamanic parallaxis, a shamanic stroll through the transcendental landscape. In the same way that the different profiles of an object can be experienced either by a collective subject composed of multiple subjects located in different empirical positions or by a single subject moving around the object, different objectivations of the same phenoumenon can be experienced either by a community of subjects of different transcendental types or by a single subject in a shamanic process of speculative variation between corresponding locations in the transcendental landscape.

According to the (détourned) liturgical embodiment of the trinitarian formula—In the names of the begetting mat(t)er, and of the free living beings, and of the Holy Spiritual communities—the hand of the religating individual first retraces the 'ascending-differentiating' movement of the incarnation, from pre-individual life—the mat(t)er at the level of the womb—to the determined and free living being—the child at the level of the head (the site of individual awakened consciousness). Standing upright in its circumambient world between the infra-sensible soil and the supernatural sky, the child is there, thrown into its singular and finite existence, (con)templating itself in its self-positing affirmation, tensing its existential bow, thrown into the risk of disligation. The material ground state locally contracts into a vertex qua tuning antenna broadcasting new images and actions: each living being rises like an orgonic pyramid in the univocal desert of Shyr, the mat(t)ership. The living individual is partially disengaged and disentangled from the 'natural' realm within which it was instituted in order to be able to blow bubbles of decisional autonomy and construct causally-disconnected black boxes, to transform material inputs into spiritual outputs, to pick up on other attributes of the insubstance and tune into the pink beams that bridge the umweltic viewzones, to activate new degrees of freedom and gain access to other realms of experience, to build theoretical spaces of reasons, juridical palaces of ethical norms, and domes of sensorial splendour. The relative detachment that makes such dimensional enrichments of the experiential field possible curves its fabric in such a way that it increases the risk of reaching singular breaking points. This danger plays out in two different ways: in the form of a psychotic affirmation of the self-sufficiency of the individual which forecloses its castration, its finitude, its entanglement with the immanental texture of material life, or in the neurotic form of a reification of the counterposed restricted 'natural world' to the detriment of the new (conceptual, aesthetic, ethico-political) dimensions opened up by subjective speculative self-positioning. Before reaching the limit of the disligating rupture—the limit beyond which ascending-differentiating would become an astralising 'fall' out of the gravitational attraction of the mat(t)er—the hand descends and expands into horizontality at heart level, thereby summoning the concrete communion between siblings, the tribal concertations through which life can unfold as spirit. '[I]n order for the [phenoumenodelic] possibilities of the [mat(t)er] to reveal themselves, it is necessary that [its] inner Word, the [child Yesses, the affirmator], "pronounces" them distinctly[, as actions and visions and concepts and feelings] and makes them [ascend] to the existential planes[—the phenomenological worlds of revelation—]where they are to manifest themselves. [...] [I]n naming the [child], [the initiate] trace[s] a vertical [ascent] from [its navel] to [its forehead], traversing all the horizontal [sexuses,] plexuses [and nexuses] of [its finite existence]. The [blessing] will be consummated as soon as the Holy Spirit, in generative movement [of collective forms of subjectivity], develops it according to the horizontal of the [communitarian] "expansion".'[395] By resuming the cycle of individualising contractions and collectivising expansions, this wholly spiritual process of the federation of experience institutes collective individuals and asserts their singularity and autonomy, their capacity

395 Marechal, *Megafón o la Guerra*, 138.

to separate and position themselves, thus resuming the ascent into those places where the danger of disligation lurks.

The singularity of a collective subject follows the same principles as that of the individual: every people in its being-there owes itself an egophanic narcissistic devotion that venerates, cares for, and tempers in the singularity of its existence a unique and irreplaceable image of the living God. The second trinitarian hypostasis entails an ethical prescription that is valid for individuals as well as for peoples: you shall not cede your desire, in the determination-vocation-vocalisation—*(Be)stimmung*—that characterises your singular modulation of the Word. Every people must therefore resist any attempt at uniformising annexation under the aegis of a 'universal monarchy' (represented in Fichte's case by the Napoleonic invasion) that would tend to hypostasise a single form of life or to impose a single transcendental type. The invader will not simply be rejected (How could one miss such an opportunity to perform a 'radical synthesis of alterity'?) but will be submitted to baroquodelicising anthropophagy, catatauically projected into a space striated by 'discoordinated artisans', swollen and numb, digested and metabolised, détourned, ventriloquised, fermented in the tropical heat, smoked, interpreted, adorned with garlands of fireflies ('apoplectic in the entropic tangled exuberances of the tropics'),[396] painted, disguised, and somewhat drugged, crossbred, academically respected (and even admired!), skinned and dismembered—rotting among flies and suckers ('torrid nature perpetually *naturans* drives all analytic geometry mad'),[397] translated, quoted, and commented upon, inebriated, counter-conquered, awakened to a lush daydream, maddened, chewed, reflected and diffracted, oriented through a barbarian disoccidentalisation, dialectised, 'stung forty times by forty thousand fire-ants',[398] stammered, stunned, imitated, shaved with

396 P. Leminski, 'Descoordenadas artesianas. Un libro y su historia, 23 años después', in *Catatau*, 249.

397 Viveiros de Castro, 'Zénon d'Hiléia', 13.

398 M. de Andrade, *Macunaíma. El héroe sin ningún caracter*, tr. J. Benedetto (Buenos Aires: Mansalva, 2022), 72.

Ogum's razor, entropicodelicised, voraciously diluted in that 'incorporeal protoplasm',[399] gnawed at, bestialised, subjected to 'tantalising tortures', ridiculed, deprived of all redundancy ('only receives new information: frustrated expectation'),[400] disassembled, disjointed, kneaded and spiced, discussed and insightfully criticised, induced, deduced and abducted ('The shaman versus the philosopher, oneirism [...] versus the onanism of the concept'),[401] transinsubstantiated in the concoction that boils in Caliban's pot. This care for the subjective singularity of a people should not be understood as a vindication and defence of a supposed 'essence'. The Fichtean *Urvolk*—the 'native, aboriginal people' as Goddard translates it[402]—practices a 'permanent aboriginal revolution' as 'continuous self-formation' aimed at spiritually dissolving all essentialist inertia and orbitally dissolving all worldly reification. An aboriginal people is a collective subject that lives, thinks, and acts rooted in the infra-soil, nourished by its transcendental plasticity, absolved from any identification with its essences and possessions. 'I am [sick] because I have no desire / I have no desire because I think I possess, / I think I possess because I do not try to give. / Trying to give, one sees that one *has* nothing, / Seeing that one has nothing, one tries to give oneself, / Trying to give oneself, one sees one *is* nothing, / Seeing one is nothing, one desires [...]; Desiring [...], one lives.'[403]

The communitarian gathering of lifeforms of different transcendental types and the correlative coalescence of their Umwelten rely on transtypical semiotic processes that integrate different transcendental-dependent languages (the language of birds, the language of stones, the language of pulsars) and different kinds of semiotic process (indexical, iconic, symbolic, etc.). Communication between subjects that instantiate different

399 J. Lezama Lima, *La expresión americana* (Mexico, D.F.: Fondo de Cultura Económica, 1993), 177.

400 P. Leminski, *Quince puntos en las íes*, in *Catatau*, 253.

401 Viveiros de Castro, 'Zénon d'Hiléia', 16.

402 Cf. Goddard, 'Fichte, ou la révolution aborigène permanente'.

403 René Daumal, May 1943. My thanks to Laurent Prost for having brought this text to my attention.

transcendental types (e.g. a human being and a dog) is just a sheer, persistent fact, a fact that indicates the existence of a trans-transcendental semiotic regime beyond the multiplicity of intra-umweltic grammars. The living semiosis that structures the unfolding of the Holy Spirit is an absolute language that integrates the intra-umweltic languages associated with the different transcendental types, a language of angels—of those who can navigate the *intermundias*—a vast conversation that flows through communicating vessels between different lifeforms, the unique vibration modulated locally—in each Umwelt—by the corresponding living instruments. Against the postmodern division of experience into irreducible, incommensurable, and untranslatable language games, against the various forms of multicultural and multinatural relativism, the Holy Spirit urges us to draw together the various language games, to perform transnatural and transcultural concertations, to philosophically constellate the infinite regulative ideas that orient the different interests of reason, to forge new channels of communication between heterogeneous lifeforms, to conceive of a cosmopolitanism that does not dissolve the irreducible singularity of each form of life in an abstract universality, that does not abstract out the transcendental perspectivism associated with every form of expression, to inscribe every local linguistic structure into the vast global semiosis.

Whereas by definition it is not possible for an individual of a well-defined transcendental type to experience that which exceeds their perceptual, affective, linguistic and conceptual resources, there is no legislative limitation that can circumscribe a priori the type of experiences that speculative subjects or collective subjects can have. We cannot overcome the phenomenal realm constituted by our transcendental faculties, but we can enter into morphogenetic processes involving different integrated transcendental types, either by performing speculative variations of our own transcendental structures or by making ingression into inter-type collective subjects. By surrendering 'to the belief that [our finite experience] is a small part of a wider integrated [experience] that knits the entire [plero]sphere',[404] we can bypass transcendental claustrophobia and participate in broader

404 Bateson, *Mind and Nature*, 88.

inter-transcendental regimes of experience, engaging animal, vegetal, mineral, and extraterrestrial actors. As Kohn writes, '[i]t is because thought extends beyond the human that we can think beyond the human'.[405] We cannot experience beyond the limits fixed by the transcendental type that we instantiate, but we can place our perceptual, emotional, conceptual, and aesthetic resources in the service of 'a vortex of intelligence extending as [an inter-umweltic] field, involving humans but not limited to them, drawing objects and processes into a coherency which it arranges into information. A FLUX of purposeful arrangement of living information, both human & extra-human, tending to grow & incorporate its environment as a unitary complex of subsumations.[406] [...] [Such a Vast Active Living Intelligence System] is a vortex of Brahman which has passed over to wakefulness, which is to say to consciousness and purpose, as a super lifeform subsuming such lower lifeforms as individual humans.'[407] Rather than being defined once and for all by a set of well-determined transcendental faculties, this evolving 'Mind-at-Large' is fed into all the way up by the living force of the institution of new lifeforms, and continually mutates by integrating new transcendental types. Mind-at-Large continuously emerges from the network of inter-umweltic pathways of communication that entangles every living subsystem: 'The individual mind is immanent, but not only in the body. It is immanent also in pathways and messages outside the body; and there is a larger Mind, of which the individual is only a subsystem. This larger Mind is comparable to [the Holy Spirit].'[408]

The fact that the marriage between Spinozism and Kantianism takes place in a Christian *ecclesia* has two main consequences: first, the reactivation of a regulative idea (*love*) which—by orienting the tasks of religion—meta-orients

405 E. Kohn, *How Forests Think: Toward an Anthropology Beyond the Human* (Berkeley and Los Angeles, CA: University of California Press, 2013), 22.

406 P.K. Dick, in L. Sutin (ed.), *In Pursuit of Valis: Selections from the Exegesis* (Novato, CA: Underwood-Miller, 1991), 72.

407 Dick, *The Exegesis of Philip K. Dick*, 9:36.

408 Bateson, *Steps to an Ecology of Mind*, 461.

the infinite tasks of science, arts, politics, and philosophy; and second, the introduction of a trinitarian or speculative logic that refracts the healing process oriented by love along three dimensions. Regarding the last point, and in order to remain faithful to the phenoumenodelic suspension of Spinozist substance fostered by Fichte and endorsed here, we shall not understand the Christian trinity in metaphysical or ontotheological terms, that is, as the 'object' of some form of scholastic speculation about the ultimate triune nature of a hypothetical 'God in Godself'. We shall not understand the trinity as (in Rahner's terms) an 'immanent trinity'.[409] We thus circumvent the Kantian criticism according to which any speculation about the triune nature of God would constitute a case of pre-critical dogmatism.[410] Rather, we shall assume that the three hypostases of the phenoumenodelicly suspended 'economic trinity' (Rahner) describe helicoidally entangled (impersonal, personal, and transpersonal) dimensions or strata of experience that are relative to the phenoumenodelic first-person actuality of a given subject and orient the subject's threefold healing process. Every living being refracts the open continuum of life threefold, in a way that admits—as we shall now see—multiple conjugations, such as a temporal conjugation (the origin, the actuality, the eschaton) or a spatial conjugation (the earth, the worlds, and the sky). The Christian trinity will be decomposed into a series of resonant and partially overlapping trinities, each of which is signalled by a certain key that emphasises a different sense of the same trinitarian referent. We shall then refract the Christian trinity in an Indra's net of trinities, each of which partially and unfaithfully reflects all the others. The dialectical logic that interlaces the three hypostases is analogous in all the nodes of the network:

---

409 Cf. K. Rahner, *The Trinity*, tr. J. Donceel (New York: Continuum, 2001).

410 As Kant writes in *Religion within the Boundaries of Mere Reason*: 'But, if this very faith (in a divine Trinity) were to be regarded not just as the representation of a practical idea, but as a faith that ought to represent what God is in [it]self, it would be a mystery surpassing all human concepts, hence unsuited to a revelation humanly comprehensible, and could only be declared in this respect as mystery.' I. Kant, *Religion within the Boundaries of Mere Reason And Other Writings*, tr., ed. A. Wood and G di Giovanni (Cambridge: Cambridge University Press, 1998), 143.

far from any regressive nostalgia, the tension between the first two hypostases is not resolved by means of a relapse or regression from the second to the first, but rather through a potentiation of the first hypostasis propelled by the second. The regressive path—that of reintegrating the primordial One of living matter at the expense of one's own individuation—is the extreme form of what Wilber calls retro-Romanticism, which can be conjugated in a whole range of forms associated with the different operative modes of what he calls the 'Way Back Machine' or the 'Regress Express': a regression to the ancient Greeks, a return to 'nature', a regression to horticultural or foraging societies, the confection of 'noble savage'-type phantasmic landscapes, neo-Luddite and anarcho-primitivist activism, as well as regressions to different forms of pre-rational, pre-cultural, pre-industrial, or pre-modern modes of experience (such as, for instance, the nostalgia for the world of the peasant in Heidegger). In this sense, the intrinsically eschatological nature of Christianity (in which the reconnection with the first hypostasis is put at the service of a propulsion toward the eschaton) might help to understand why the German idealists used the Christian trinitarian logic to resist—in an absolutely modern manner—the (retro-)Romantic tendencies of their time.

As the Indra's net of trinities displays in myriad ways, the trinitarian inner logic of Christianity succeeds in enveloping in a unique conception of religion the different terms of a threefold alternative associated with the possible 'positions' occupied by the 'absolute' with respect to the intentional subject-object correlation: either on this side of the subject, or in the correlation itself, or beyond the object. In other words, one might try to define an uncorrelated 'absolute' by absolving the I from its intentional correlation with the not-I, by absolutising the correlation itself, or by absolving the not-I of its transcendental constitution, that is, by leaping over the subject's transcendental shadow toward the 'thing in itself'.[411]

411 Laruelle describes this threefold alternative in terms of three conceptual characters, the Jew that worships the infinite Other, the (critical) philosopher that abides in the transcendental correlation between the I and the not-I, and the non-philosopher that intends to step back from the world accessible through representation into a radical form of pre-wordly immanence: 'The thinkers of extreme transcend-

According to the first conception, the act of religation is understood as an inward conversion toward a non-ekstatic mode of appearing that absolves the subject from its intentional fall into the external world, as an upstream run to a 'radical immanence' withdrawn from the objective transcendence of the world. This motif unfolds through a sequence of progressive radicalisations that starts with Descartes's discovery of a dimension of subjectity that is prior with respect to the representational relation with an objective world, and proceeds through Schopenhauer, Freud and Husserl up to Henry's self-affective immanence, withdrawn from any external worldly horizon of light. According to the second this-worldly or pantheistic conception, the divine is exhausted by the revelations conveyed by the actual world. According to the third otherworldly conception, religion is a practice eschatologically oriented by a hypertranscendent and otherwise-than-being Omega Kingdom placed beyond this world (John 18:36) (e.g. ontotheology, gnosticism, etc.).[412] Confronted by this threefold fork, Christian religation as understood here first engages in a simultaneous operation that envelops in a unique pleromatic insubstance these pre-worldly, worldly, and otherworldly instances. First, we have a conversion toward the immanental realm of impersonal life which we came from (the unifying *Band* beneath every I/not-I polarisation), a turnaround by means of which the living plugs back into the living source. Secondly, Christian religation engages

ence and radical immanence, the Jew and the non-philosopher, are thus opposed to the [critical] philosopher.' Whereas for the Jew 'the Real is the infinite [hypertranscendence] of God or the Other', for the non-philosopher (or for the 'philosopher' that is Henry) the Real is on the side of the 'intrinsic radical finitude' of the living in so far as the latter is considered to be an inhabitant of the immanental kingdom of life. Both are 'foreclosed to [intentional] representation [...]. The radical transcendence of the infinite [Other], the radical immanence of [life], this radicality separates Transcendence and Immanence from the world.' F. Laruelle, 'Les effets-Levinas. Lettre non-philosophique du 30 Mai 2006', Organisation Non-Philosophique Internationale.

412 Regarding the opposition between the 'ascending' *otherworldly* and the 'descending' *this-worldly* conceptions of religion see A. Lovejoy, *The Great Chain of Being* (Cambridge, MA: Harvard University Press, 2001).

in a glorification of both finite subjects and their correlative worlds, i.e. a 'total transfiguration of all [phenomena] (blessedness)'.[413] The living being senses itself as a finite being-there of life—as a local instance of its existence conveying singular forms of its self-revelation—and senses the world around it as a transcendental-dependent bubble hovering in the kingdom of life. Finally, the Christian religation engages—through its wholly spiritual tendencies—speculative variations of the relevant transcendental structures intended to mediate the transcendental limits of experience. In this way, the Christian religation to the pleromatic life is refracted into a conversion to the pre-subjective life that engenders and enworlds, a self-positing glorification of every I/not-I correlation, and an eschatological projection to an otherworldly transcendence.

According to Cusanus's trinity (oneness-equality-connection or *unitas-aequalitas-nexus*), the one life provides the underlying impersonal *unity*, the multiple living the *equal* modal excitations of such an univocal insubstance, and the Holy Spirit realises its effective *connection* in the form of *totalities* by means of which the multiple concretely realises the presupposed abstract unity:[414] 'In the [mat(t)er] is [the underlying] unity, in the [different living ones] equality, in the Holy Spirit the [connecting] harmony of unity and equality.'[415]

According to the pneumatological declension of this trinity (vibration-modulation-concertation), the first hypostasis is given by the vibrating Word (*pneuma* or *pranava*), the reverberation of Gabriel's wing, the 'unique [humming] Breath'[416] that insufflates life. The second hypostasis is given by the pneumatics, the living instruments—'breath[s] within the [whirling]

---

413 Nietzsche, *The Anti-Christ*, 32 [§24].

414 Nicolas of Cusa, *On Learned Ignorance*, tr. J. Hopkins (Minneapolis: The Arthur J. Banning Press, 1990), I, 7–9. Strictly speaking, Cusa understands the third hypostasis as the union in Love of the Father and the Child.

415 St. Augustine, *On Christian Doctrine*, Book I, Chapter 5.

416 P. Klossowski, *The Baphomet*, tr. S. Hawkes and S. Sartarelli (Hygiene, CO: Eridianos Press, 1988), 64.

Breath',[417] 'fluctuations forming figures on the crests of waves',[418] whirlwinds existing as transient forms of insubsistence—that modulate singularly the primeval sound. And the third hypostasis is given by the flying noetic Arkestras that concert the breaths, synthesise grains of sound out of pure tones, sample the undulating unknowns, compose rhythmic patterns, harmonise the spheres, and orchestrate the croaks, the whistles, the chirps, the quacks, the chuckles, the buzzes.

According to Rosenzweig's starry trinity (beget-reveal-redeem), the mat(t)er begets (in-forms the living forms), the child reveals the images that appear as a function of its transcendental affordances, and the Holy Spirit, by incorporating the singular living into a community of siblings, redeems the subject from its isolation and delivers its correlative world from reification. In order to manifest itself the pleroma has to engender individuals that constitute worldly retorts in which to distil the revelation, image by image. But this act of individuation triggers the danger of disligation, of isolation. And this danger brings forth the necessity of a 'redemptive' cure that raises the first hypostasis to new powers by begetting collective forms of subjectivity.

According to the daimic trinity (Mariri, Chacruna, Daime), the Mariri is the enlivening strength that—acting in the immanental background—asserts its impersonal sovereignty over the living and triggers the vineal trance, the *Lyannaj* whose function is 'to unite and rally, to bind, link and relay everything that has become disassociated';[419] the Chacruna is the light that is revealed locally in visions projected in the phenomenological foreground of the living; and the Daime—concocted in the sylvan Athanor out of the wedding of the Mariri and the Chacruna—the entheogenic sacrament that makes possible the Second Coming, that is, the rebirth of the firstborn in

417 Ibid., 82.

418 Deleuze, *Logic of Sense*, 297.

419 E. Breleur, P. Chamoiseau, G. Delver, S. Domi, E. Glissant, G. Pigeard de Gurbert, O. Portecop, O. Pulvar, and J.-C. William, *Manifeste pour les "produits" de haute nécessité* (Éditions Galaade/Institut du Tout-Monde, 2009).

every living person: 'Soy la embajada divina, / soy de la naturaleza / una especia de marquesa / de la marca celestial: / *mi poder no tiene igual.*'[420]

According to the subjective trinity (soul, body, spirit), the body is the dimension of the subject that appears in a world, the experienceable or phenomenal part of the subject, that which can be seen, touched, heard, emphatically felt, conceptually understood, socially related to. It follows that an individual has as many bodies as Umwelten in which it appears: whereas a snake appears in the world constituted by a spider in the form of a particular phenomenal body, it makes ingression into the Umwelt of the owl clad in a radically different bodily appearance. In particular, a subject is there in the world constituted by its own transcendental faculties, which give rise to what Metzinger calls the phenomenal self-model. The spectrum of the subject's different phenomenal bodies (one for each Umwelt in which it appears) defines what we could call its phenoumenal body. The soul is the umbilical chord that connects the individual to the impersonal mat(t)er, to the immanental soil, to the one life of which the subject is a local emanation, a breathing dehiscence, a finite experiencing mode. The soul channels the living forces that irrigate the native and mortal subject and fuel its desire to live, to experience, to love, to think, to self-transform and to mediate its circumambient world. Losing the soul—the shamanic definition of sickness[421]—is tantamount to 'falling' into the world, identifying oneself with the phenomenal self-model, being trapped in a transcendental-dependent I/not-I correlation, existing in the form of an essentialised subject dwelling in a reified world, living a life deprived of epiphanies. 'It is not the [phenomenal] ego that is the [illness], but its mutilation compensated by a sickly inflation, in brief by its [fall]

420 'I am the divine embassy, / I am of nature / a type of marquis / of the celestial mark: / my power has no equal.' N. Perlongher, 'Autosacramental del Santo Daime', *Revista de poesía Tsé-Tsé* 9/10 (2001).

421 '[It] is in shamanism that the interpretation of sickness as a flight of the soul to the land of the dead acquires clarity.' M. Eliade, 'Le problème du chamanisme', *Revue de l'histoire des religions* 131:1–3 (1946): 13.

into this world'[422] of phenomena. The spirit is the subject in so far as it engages in spiritual process of self-transformation, in so far as it inhabits a fuzzy world whose transcendental limits are constantly fluctuating, in so far as it makes kin with other lifeforms and places its transcendental and speculative resources in the service of collective forms of vital coherence. A subject is certainly there in many circumambient worlds. But its mundane localisation is only a section of its lifeline, which also sinks into the impersonal living soil and springs up into the supernatural sky. A subject endowed with a soul, a body, and a spirit is like a feathered black box which—nonchalantly perched on an arboreal axis mundi—transmutes seeds into spherical harmonies.

According to the structuralist trinity (différance, difference, differonça), différance is the force that differs and defers, that spatialises worlds and temporalises histories, that polarises the pleroma into I/not-I correlations, the generative force that engenders totemic differences between different transcendental types, 'the movement that produces [subjects and objects] [...] the unfolding of difference',[423] the living force as an 'origin' which was never present and which disappropriates every present, which prevents the constitution of a stable, fixed, lasting presence, trivially identical to itself, 'referring only to itself'.[424] The concept of difference makes reference to the synchronic dimension associated with the transcendental landscape of discontinuous types, to the system of intervals and relations between the products or the effects constituted by différance. The concept of difference encodes the structuralist thesis that the individuation of a node in structure does not require the presumption of any form of 'bare substantial particular' beneath the relational properties that define the nodes. Finally, the concept of odontological differonça proposed by Viveiros de Castro encodes the speculative, shamanic, teratological or inter-species processes of continuous transformations thanks to which a subject can de-type itself

---

422 Corbin, 'Apophatic Theology as Antidote to Nihilism'.

423 J. Derrida, *Positions*, tr. A. Bass (Chicago: University of Chicago Press, 1981), 9–10.

424 Ibid., 26.

and become a bastard, a mestizo, an outcast with respect to the limited combinatorial of discontinuous positions defined by the structure.[425] By means of different kinds of rituals, the living being can remove itself from the restricted space of discontinuous possibilities defined by the mythical exemplarity.[426] Whereas the space of paradigmatic myths is structured like a linguistic 'tissue of differences', the enaction of rituals of transformation is like the stuttered vocalisation of a 'lanjaguar' destructured by a continuous system of differonças.[427]

According to the trinity of forms of violence (immanental institution, transcendental conservation, speculative mediation), the immanental mat(t)er denotes the anomic force, the founding violence (*die rechtsetzende Gewalt*) that institutes each singular nomos 'by which a tribe [...] becomes settled, i.e., by which it becomes historically situated [in a circumambient world] and turns a part of the [insubstance]'s surface into the force-field of a particular order'.[428] The second hypostasis, the law-preserving violence

425 Concerning the properly *odontological* scope of the notion of *differonça*, Viveiros de Castro writes: '[I]n America the indigenous people did not have ontology but odontology, and the odontological problem was: (what) are we going to eat? To say that the problem is odontological is to say that it is onçological, because the jaguar's problem is to find meat to sink its teeth into. It's a problem that concerns us rather closely, since one of the solutions is precisely to eat people.' Viveiros de Castro, 'Rosa e Clarice, a fera e o fora', 26.

426 Regarding the relation between *myth* and *type* see P. Lacoue-Labarthe and J.-L. Nancy, 'The Nazi Myth', tr. B. Holmes, *Critical Inquiry* 16:2 (Winter, 1990), 291–312 ('[T]heir specific function [that of myths] is, in fact, that of exemplarity. Myth is a fiction, in the strong, active sense of "fashioning," or, as Plato says, of "plastic art": it is, therefore, a fictioning, whose role is to propose, if not to impose, models or types [...] in imitation of which an individual, or a city, or an entire people, can grasp themselves and identify themselves. [...] [T]he nature and the finality of myth [...] is to incarnate itself in a figure, or in a type. Myth and type are indissociable' [297, 306]). Regarding the difference between *rites* and *myths*, see the final chapter of C. Lévi-Strauss, *The Naked Man: Introduction to a Science of Mythology, Vol. 4*, tr. J. and D. Weightman (New York: Harper & Row, 1981).

427 Viveiros de Castro, 'Rosa e Clarice, a fera e o fora', 26.

428 C. Schmitt, *The Nomos of the Earth*, tr. G.L. Ulmen (New York: Telos, 2006), 70.

(*die rechtserhaltende Gewalt*), denotes the *conatus ese conservandi* that takes care of this nomos, the effort to conserve it and develop its finite form organically, without calling its transcendental limits into question ('Position is already iterability, a call for self-conserving repetition').[429] The third hypostasis denotes the violence conveyed by the speculative mediation of transcendental limits. This speculative violence is oriented by the infinite ideas, that is, by the truth that calls any finite configuration of knowledge into question and dissolves any dogmatic crystallisation of the will to know, by the beauty that overflows any particular 'distribution of the sensible' and exposes the subject to the terrible splendour of the pleromatic revelation, by a justice that cannot be faithfully embodied in any particular juridical framework ('a justice beyond the law').[430] In his text on the notion of violence, Benjamin yields to the 'Romantic turn of mind' he earlier criticised by establishing a clear-cut distinction between (what he calls) the mythic order given by the magic circle of the forms of law that follow one another through the oscillation between 'foundational violence' (maintained by the law preserving violence) and 'hostile counter-violence', and a new historical era in which this circle would be definitively broken and would give way to a stateless regime beyond the law.[431] We cannot help but recognise here an instance of the ontotheological motif that establishes a radical separation between the divine—in this case effective in the form of the 'divine violence'—and the sublunar realm of human jurisdiction. Now, the Christian trinitarian framework revisited here induces us to substitute a 'dialectical intertwinement' between the different forms of violence for

429 J. Derrida, 'Force of Law: The "Mystical Foundation of Authority"', tr. M. Quaintance, *Cardozo Law Review* 11: 5/6 (1990), 920–1045: 997.

430 Ibid., 1035.

431 'This lasts until either new forces of those earlier suppressed triumph over the hitherto lawmaking violence and thus found a new law, destined in its turn to decay. On the breaking of this cycle maintained by mythic forms of law, on the suspension of law with all the forces on which it depends as they depend on it, finally therefore on the abolition of state power, a new historical epoch is founded.' Benjamin, 'Critique of Violence', *Selected Writings, Vol. 1,* 251–52.

Benjamin's sharp opposition between foundational-conservative mythic violence and divine-revolutionary violence:[432] all these forms of 'violence' are hypostases of the same 'divine violence' of sovereign life, a founding violence that engenders and institutes, a conservative violence that preserves the finite form as a singular manifestation of life, and at the same time a speculative violence that induces mediations of every particular nomos. The revolutionary force by means of which life asserts its absolute sovereignty over all relative worlds cannot by definition be grounded on any particular intra-umweltic system of norms. However, this anomic force is channelled by the subjects that enact the corresponding speculative mediations. The speculative force that propels the phenoumenodelics of the spirit beyond every constituted world is an orbital return to the anomic flux that institutes subjects endowed with transcendental and speculative capacities. What we might call the divine force of life is refracted threefold in the immanental force that institutes a nomos, the transcendental force that preserves it, and the speculative force that mediates its transcendental limits.

According to the trinity of services, that of labour sustains the very material existence of a tribe: cultivating, hunting, cleaning, gathering, producing, caring, healing, designing, building, repairing, cooking, knitting. The defence service preserves the self-positioning autonomy of the collective subject and guards the boundaries that protect it from attempts to reduce its singular determination—the auric radiance of its *hic et nunc*—to the homogeneity of an atonal world order based on a type-centric form of universality. The mission of the defence service is to prevent the 'decline of the aura', to resist the colonising and extractivist forces that try to 'pry the [tribe] from its shell', from its halo.[433] The spiritual service pursues the work of self-formation—the continuous birth of the tribe as a collective

---

432 'Just as in all spheres God opposes myth, mythic violence is confronted by the divine. And the latter constitutes its antithesis in all respects. If mythic violence is lawmaking, divine violence is law-destroying; if the former sets boundaries, the latter boundlessly destroys them; if mythic violence brings at once guilt and retribution, divine power only expiates [...].' Ibid., 238.

433 Benjamin, *Illuminations: Essays and Reflections*, 187, 223.

subject—beyond all essentialisation in a determinate form. Thanks to the spiritual service, the aura of the tribe flickers as a fragile flying lifeform giving to light its light 'in the midst of the overwhelming power of' the forest. The radiance of the aura imprints the *res conquerans* of the enforested Renatius Cartesius—completely 'lost in this labyrinth of delightful deceptions'[434]—with indelible impressions, providing him with a sharp response to the sound question elicited by his Byzantine curiosity: 'Who the hell turned on the light in the back of the firefly?'[435]

According to the different interrelated trinities proposed by Wilber (Dharma-Buddha-Shanga, respect-rights-responsibility, ground value-intrinsic value-extrinsic value), all living modes of formless impersonal insubstance (Dharma) deserve unconditional respect as 'expressions of the absolute' endowed with 'an equal Ground value'.[436] Secondly, each living mode is a singular avatar of the Buddha endowed with an 'intrinsic value', a free and autonomous self equipped with the right to exist and express life in a singular manner. Finally, the collective Shanga prescribes an ethic of service to the community and of responsibility in relation to the different totalities of which the living being is a part. According to the Trikaya of Mahayana Buddhism, the first body (kāya) of Buddha–the Dharmakāya–encodes the ultimate insubstantiality of all things; the second body of Buddha–the Nirmānakāya–denotes the body of a living and dying being in so far as it appears in a spatiotemporal phenomenological horizon; the third body of Buddha–the Sambhogakāya–is the celestial body, the rainbow body, the enjoyment-body, the body of bliss, the phenoumenal body that transcends the limits of the phenomenal world and unfolds in the supernatural sky or Pure Lands.[437]

According to the revolutionary trinity (equality, liberty, fraternity), the first hypostasis is the one life that guarantees the equality or univocity of

434 Leminski, *Catatau*, 21.

435 Ibid., 44.

436 Wilber, *A Brief History of Everything*, 301.

437 Cf. Nagao Gadjin and Hirano Umeyo, 'On the Theory of Buddha-Body (*Buddha-kāya*)', *The Eastern Buddhist* 6:1 (May 1973), 25–53.

living modes, the second hypostasis, the finite child, assumes the responsibility of liberty (the autonomy of the being capable of saying I am, I breathe, I desire, I act, I think, I determine and transform myself, I am a witness, I love), and the third hypostasis denotes the fraternity-sorority, the siblinghood of the living, their integration into a collective body, their tribalisation. The revolutionary device encodes the transition from biodelic unity to subjective autonomy to fraternal wholeness.

According to the interpretation of the trinity proposed by Taylor (sameness, singularity, complementarity), all living beings share a thread of commonality given by the fact that they are all finite incarnations of the same life, that they are all instituted in God's image (*imago Dei*). This sameness qua living beings entails their singularity qua individuals, since their singularity as probes of life grounds the necessary role that incarnation plays in revelation. All living beings share the condition of participating in the living force that singularises them as unique forms of life. These unsurpassable differences between individuals (even between individuals of the same transcendental type) bring forth the possibility of a kind of unity between them that is not a 'unity-through-identity' (embodied in the first hypostasis) but rather 'unity-across-difference', which takes the form of what Taylor characterises as complementarity: 'Redemption [...] brings reconciliation, a kind of oneness. This is the oneness of diverse beings who come to see that they cannot attain wholeness alone, that their complementarity is essential, rather than of beings who come to accept that they are ultimately identical. [...] Our great historical temptation has been to forget the complementarity, to go straight for the sameness [...]. [W]e need to complement our own partiality, on our road to wholeness [...].'[438]

According to the philosophical trinity (immanental, transcendental, speculative), the first hypostasis is the immanental insubstance in which every living being is instituted, undulates, and dies. The second hypostasis is the local operator of the transcendental constitution of experience; the framer, the editor, the renormaliser, the decoder of the pleroma. The Holy Spirit is the hypostasis that potentiates finite experience by means of

438 Taylor, *A Catholic Modernity*, 14.

speculative variations of transcendental types and inter-typical integrations. The transcendentally determined experience of the finite subject is bordered by the pre-subjective realm of the immanental life that flows beneath the subject and by the trans-objective 'beyond' defined by that which overflows the phenomenological horizon of its experience. What is in excess with respect to a certain Umwelt is not only that which surpasses the corresponding phenomenological horizon, but also the immanental force that institutes and supports the experiencing subject. Objective experience can thus be the triple target of an 'ontological psychoanalysis' intended to religate the subject's life to the immanental life, of a transcendental reflection focused on the transcendental framing that defines the subject's phenomenological horizon, and of a speculative transgression of this framing.

In the trinity given by the formless infinity, the finite form, and the transfinite transformations, the first hypostasis denotes the 'infinite turbulence' of the formless pleroma that informs every salient form. The second hypostasis encodes the finite form of native and mortal existence and its transcendental-dependent experience. The third hypostasis defines the horizon of horizons in which the transfinite living beings transform themselves. According to the perichoretic circulation between the three hypostases, 'the formless threatens [the living forms it had previously informed] with deformities that are [speculative] anamorphoses'.[439]

In the Hindu trinity or Trimurti (Brahma, Vishnu, Shiva), the first hypostasis is Brahma, the lactescent ocean, the procreator of the living forms; the second hypostasis is Vishnu, the preserver of the form, the deity who wears the divine jewel that radiates the resplendence of finite consciousness; and the third hypostasis is Shiva, the destroyer of the fixed form, the transformer, the de-reifier of worlds, the disappropriater, the regenerator, the vomiter.[440]

---

439 R. Jimenez, Introduction to Leminski, *Catatau*, 11.

440 Regarding the relation between the Christian trinity and the Hinduist Trimurti, see F.X. Clooney, 'Trinity and Hinduism', in P.C. Pahn (ed.), *The Cambridge Companion to the Trinity* (Cambridge: Cambridge University Press, 2011), 309–24.

In the Borromean trinity (real, semiotic, imaginary), the mat(t)er is associated with the register of the foreclosed real that engenders new subjective types by appearing as a material impasse of intra-mundane structures. The child who looks at itself in the mirror stages the register of the imaginary, that is, the register in which the 'images' that compose the subject's experience reflect back to the subject the features of its own transcendental type. In particular, the subject appears in its own phenomenological horizon in the form of a 'phenomenal self-model'. The Holy Spirit encodes the register of the semiotic, that is, the flow of information between lifeforms that instantiate different transcendental types, the phenoumenodelic unfolding of an inter-typical Mind-at-Large 'structured like an angelical language'.

According to the psychoanalytical trinity (impersonal unconscious, personal consciousness, transpersonal supra-consciousness), the mat(t)er is the impersonal unconscious background that supports the conscious experience of the living. The child represents the conscious being intentionally opened up to the corresponding world, the transformer of material drives into spiritual desire. The Holy Spirit is the supra-consciousness that emerges from the different forms of transpersonal collectivisation of experience. The conscious life of the individual is bounded by the impersonal unconscious below the threshold of its conscious resolving power and the transpersonal supra-conscious of which it is—like a neuron in a brain or an eye in a multi-ocular optical system—merely a local component. In this sense, the psychoanalytic motif can be understood as a symmetrical completion of the speculative motif: while the latter establishes the existence of a phenoumenal 'beyond' of intentional consciousness, psychoanalysis establishes the existence of an unconscious realm 'beneath' it.

According to the Hegelian trinity (universal, particular, singular), the universal is the univocal insubstance of which the different lifeforms are local vibrating modes, the particular is the living being qua instantiation of a species, of a totemic clan, of a transcendental type of subjectivity, and the singular is the living being in so far as it removes itself from any transcendental taxonomy, pilots its own morphogenetic process of institution beyond the given types, engages in symbiogenetic process of inter-species kin-making, mediates its surrounding world, and reaffirms its belonging to the universal life by existing it in a singular manner.

According to the Spinozist trinity (*natura naturans, natura natura*, supernatural), *natura naturans* denotes univocal insubstance qua power to institute lifeforms. The avatars of the child are the subjective modes of the insubstance that constitute, through their transcendental faculties, the spectrum of *naturae naturatae*.[441] The Holy Spirit defines the supernatural milieu to which these multiple *naturae naturatae* open up when their transcendental limits are speculatively mediated. These three conjugations of nature are coupled through the visionary force (*Einbildungskraft*): the *natura naturans* itself, circulating in the blood of the narcotised being, forces it to produce phenoumenodelic visions that might overflow the correlative *natura naturata*, thereby pouring into the supernatural realm: 'What is the supernatural? It is created by the penetration of the [vision] into [*natura naturata*]. [...] [F]aced with the determinism of [the latter], the [human being] responds with the [unforeseeable character] of the [speculative vision]. [...] It's an unknown space and a wandering time that does not dwell [within the Umwelt]. However, we walk in this here and we pass in this now, and we manage to reconstruct [a vision beyond the umweltic horizon]. It is the supernatural [...] [which] never loses that primordiality [of *natura naturans*] from which it is derived.'[442]

According to the pronominal trinity (it, I, we), the *it* denotes the impersonal field out of which finite subjectivity (the *I*) is instituted and the *we* denotes the trans-type community of *I*s. It is worth emphasising that the

---

441 Regarding the identifications of *natura naturans* and *natura naturata* with the mat(t)er and the child of the Christian trinity, see the following fragment by Jacobi: '[T]he deity must be absolutely devoid of reality, which can only find expression in determinate individuality. The latter [...] is therefore based on *natura naturata* (the [Child] from all eternity), just as the former–i.e. [...] the substantial being of the infinite [...]–is based on *natura naturans* (the [Mat(t)er]).' F.H. Jacobi, 'Recollections of Conversations with Lessing in July and August 1780' (1785), in G.E. Lessing, *Philosophical and Theological Writings*, tr. H.B. Nisbet (Cambridge: Cambridge University Press, 2005), 255–56.

442 Lezama Lima, *El reino de la imagen*, 358–59.

distinction between the *it* and the *I* does not coincide with the distinction between objective and subjective domains, since it is only through the institution of an *I* that a particular horizon of objectivity is transcendentally constituted out of the pre-subjective and pre-objective *it*. Since the different *I*s in a given *we* might instantiate different transcendental types, the *we* that we are describing here might be a trans-umweltic and trans-historical community. Another *I* in a community is a *Thou* which—far from being an object in the *I*'s Umwelt (a mere he or she)—breathes the phenoumenodelic insubstance through its own umweltic helmet.[443]

The trinity that results from the encounter between Rozitchner and Levinas is composed of (a) a living field that we can characterise—in the wake of Rozitchner—as an enchanted materiality, a maternal daydream, the uterine realm of the living there-is-ness; (b) the instituted subjects and the constituted worldly 'totalities', the realm of the thisness and suchness; and (c) the infinity in which the worlds sprout, the realm of otherness.[444]

443 We find similar versions of this pronominal trinity (albeit with essential differences) in Viveiros de Castro in the form of the triad *natura* ('*the impersonal it of nature*', the Other qua corporeal bodies)-*culture* (the reflexive I)-*supernatural* (the Other qua subject); See E. Viveiros de Castro, 'Cosmological Deixis and Amerindian Perspectivism', *Journal of the Royal Anthropological Institute* 4:3 (September 1998), 469–88, in Wilber in the form of the triad *it* (external value-free objectivity)-*I* (interior subjective awareness),-*we* (cultural or intersubjective world view), see K. Wilber, *A Brief Theory of Everything* (Boston: Shambhala, 2000), 120–26, and in Popper and Habermas in the form of the objective, subjective, and cultural 'worlds'. In particular, Wilber relates these three pronominal realms to the three transcendentals *Truth* (associated with the objective *it*), *Beauty* (associated with the perspectival *I*), and *Good* (associated with the intersubjective *we*) and to Habermas's different 'validity claims' (truth, sincerity, and normative rightness). In the framework proposed in this work, we have not associated the three transcendentals with the three pronominal realms (*it*, *I*, *we*), but rather with the Kantian regulative ideas that orient the mediation of the transcendental limitations of experience associated with a given Umwelt along different attributes (namely, the *logos*, the *sensorium-affectum*, and the *socius*).

444 A similar analysis of the trinity has been proposed in O. del Barco, *Exceso y Donación. La busqueda del Dios sin Dios* (Buenos Aires: Biblioteca Internacional Martin Heidegger, 2003), 43–45.

The living material field takes the place of what Levinas describes as the neutral and impersonal there-is-ness (*il y a*, *es gibt*, *hay*) of the anonymous Being without beings.[445] The German term *es gibt* highlights the fact that this dimension can be understood as a donation that precedes every subjective constitution of a correlative world: 'Givenness is prior to [transcendental] constitution. Constitution needs the given. The [human being] is not the constituent of the given in an ontological sense'.[446] What Levinas does not seem to have acknowledged is that every subjective constitution of an objective world presupposes the corresponding institution of the constituting subject, that every creation relies on a prior procreation, that every form of experience presupposes the life of the experiencing subject, that every intraworldly phenomenological appearing relies on a pre-worldly kind of appearing, that of the immanental life. The *es gibt* gives birth, gives life. Levinas perpetuates the modern 'ontology of death', that of conceiving the institution of living subjects as a sort of contingent event taking place and time before a dead backdrop that can only elicit anguish, horror, and despair ("The negation of every qualifiable thing allows the impersonal there is to arise again. [...] The silence of infinite spaces is terrifying').[447] In the wake of Heidegger, Levinas does not describe the living subject as being engendered in a living womb, but rather as being thrown before a dead background. However, far from being a 'hypostasis' that would miraculously introduce a crack in the anonymous there-is-ness (as Levinas understands it), the subject is engendered in the entrails of the living mat(t)er. From this generation, the subject retains the maternal imperative par excellence: *Thou shalt live and reveal!* (Rozitchner).

The immanental institution of an *I* within the living mat(t)er frames a phenomenological 'totality' (the transcendental-dependent world) accessible

---

445 See in particular E. Levinas, *Time and the Other*, tr. R.A. Cohen (Pittsburgh, PA: Duquesne University Press, 1987) and E. Levinas, *Existence and Existents*, tr. A. Lingis (The Hague: Martinus Nijhoff, 1978).

446 Del Barco, *Exceso y Donación*, 17.

447 E. Levinas, *Totality and Infinity*, tr. A. Lingis (Pittsburgh, PA: Duquesne University Press, 1979), 190.

through the lenses of intentional representation. Far from being completely impermeable with respect to the pleromatic infiltrations, the integrity of this totality might be put into question by the speculative encounter with the Other, an encounter that by definition can not be reduced to a worldly phenomenon. The notion of religion assumes in Levinas the form of a rel(ig)ation that bypasses the limits of the transcendental-dependent intensional representation, that transcends the totality toward a Wholly Other than cannot be represented or inscribed within a mundane co-presence: 'We propose to call "religion" the bond that is established between the same and the other without constituting a totality.[448] [...] It is a relation or religion that is not structured like knowing—that is, an intentionality',[449] a relation without relation, a diachronic relation without co-presence. According to the trinitarian framework that we are distorting here, the Levinasian notion of religion only encodes one dimension of the Christian religation, the wholly spiritual. The non-intentional relation between the 'same' (the totality) and the 'other' (the infinity)—the living relation between and *I* and a *Thou* in Buber's terms—only encodes the Christian religation between the second and the third persons of the Christian trinity. Briefly, the relation *I–Thou* (and the concomitant institution of a communitarian *we*) is enriched in a Christian framework by the relations *I–I* (religation with the second person) and I–*it* (religation with the first [im]person). It is not only through the *Thou* that infinity makes ingression into the worldly totality constituted by the *I*. First, trinitarian religion includes a religation with the second hypostasis, which can be understood as an existential assumption of the fact that the individual living being is an avatar of the firstborn, a native and mortal incarnation of life destined to refract it in a singular manner. Second, trinitarian religion also includes a religation with the first hypostasis, with the impersonal *it*. Here the *it* does not denote the objective and reified side of the worldly totalities (as it is the case in Buber), but rather the living material background wherein the subjects are instituted and the worlds constituted. The *it*, far from being a dead

448 Ibid., 40.

449 Levinas, *Time and the Other*, 30–31.

background, denotes the impersonal vital ma(t)ter that informs our eyes, irrigates us with its strength, and bears us above the flood.

The Levinasian duality between phenomenological totality (the world) and phenoumenodelic infinity (the supernatural sky) ignores the immanental field, the living arche-soil. This foreclosure is consistent with the conspicuous absence of a maternal figure in Levinas's writings. Levinas does address the fecundity of the paternal subject, but forecloses (at least until *Otherwise Than Being, or Beyond Essence*) the ab-original maternal institution of separated subjectivity. As Rozitchner argues, the Levinasian there-is-ness is a meta-physical stance that conceals the fecund mater-iality, the *physis*, the *natura naturans*, that effectively engenders and carries lifeforms: 'His approach to the "il y a" comes out of metaphysics [...]. The birth of the existent is metaphysical, not maternal. Strangely Levinas speaks of the woman as the object of erotic love [...] but when he speaks of the child, he speaks only of paternity: of being a father. [...] [H]e finds the woman too late, having evicted the mother from the origin of being [...].'[450] Levinas recognises the necessity of presupposing a background for the 'hypostasis' of a subject to take place (what he calls the anonymous there-is-ness), but he fails to acknowledge the material capability of such a background, namely that of engendering. Hence, Levinas can only understand the emergence of a subject as a contingent event that cannot be derived from the anonymity of the impersonal there-is-ness: 'Obviously I will not be able to explain why this [the hypostasis of the subject] takes place. There is no physics in metaphysics.'[451] Levinas's phrasing could not be more accurate: the hypostasis of the subject is for him a meta-physical stance that forecloses the instance of the *physis*, of the *natura naturans* that engenders lifeforms which transcendentally constitute *naturae naturatae* qua phenomenological totalities and can then break through these totalities into infinity. The materialistic imperative *Thou shalt live!* grounds both every living act of transcendental constitution of a particular nomological order ('foundational

450 L. Rozitchner, *Levinas o la filosofía de la consolación* (Buenos Aires: Biblioteca Nacional, 2013), 124.

451 Levinas, *Time and the Other*, 51.

violence') and every speculative mediation of such an order ('revolutionary violence'). In the last instance, the love *of* life in the two senses of the genitive institutes, conserves, and sublates any particular nomos. It is love that 'demands the *Aufhebung* of the right that is born of a separation (*Trennung*); [...] love demands reconciliation (*Versöhnung*)'[452] before and beyond the law. Even 'the responsibility for the Other'—that is, the capacity to respond to the trans-worldly call arriving from the infinite—presupposes the subjective capacity to remain connected to the immanental realm of life within which both the *I* and the *Thou* are instituted and borne as singular probes of life.

According to the Schellingian trinity (philosophy of nature, transcendental philosophy, philosophy of identity), the immanental mat(t)er that institutes individuals is addressed by the philosophy of nature, the conditions of possibility of the subject's experience are addressed by transcendental philosophy, and the circular entanglement between the natural institution of the subject and the subjective constitution of nature is addressed by the philosophy of identity.[453] While in transcendental philosophy the subject is the source of the operations that constitute objectivity, in the philosophy of nature the subject is merely a result: where the philosophy of nature ends (in the institution of the subjective modes of insubstance) transcendental philosophy begins. However—as argued above—the relationship between transcendental philosophy and philosophy of nature cannot be unidirectional, that is, it cannot rely on a unilateral foundation given either by the former or by the latter. Far from being able to define itself independently of all transcendental reflection, philosophy of nature as we understand it here depends on a concept of nature—*natura naturans*—that cannot be identified with the objective nature—*natura naturata*—of pre-critical modern science. Strictly speaking, the institution of a transcendental type of subjectivity and the constitution of the correlative *natura naturata* are the two sides of the

---

452 Quoted in Derrida, *Glas*, 43.

453 With respect to the relation between transcendental philosophy and philosophy of nature in Schelling, see for example F.W.J. Schelling, 'On the True Concept of Philosophy of Nature and the Correct Way of Solving its Problems', tr. D. Whistler and J. Kahl, *Pli: The Warwick Journal of Philosophy* 26 (2014), 24–45.

same I/not-I dualisation of the pleroma: 'Nature and the spirit world arise, always uniformly, out of the common middle point of one and the same original unity. Through one act of eternal splitting into two [*Dualisirung*], they arise simultaneously with one another.'[454] Philosophy of nature and transcendental philosophy constitute two sections of the virtuous circle of speculation—of the 'philosophy of identity' in Schelling's terms—which cannot but presuppose, correct, and enhance one another. As we have argued above, the circular complementation of transcendental philosophy and philosophy of nature naturally leads to a speculative stance: if the naturalised transcendental types are dynamical–the partial products of a 'natural' process of institution of subjectivity–then the phenomena-noumena demarcation line is also dynamic and the thesis that the transcendental limits of experience cannot be mediated appears completely unjustified.

According to the Fichtean trinity (life of experience, experience of life, absolute experience), the mat(t)er denotes the immanental life of experience (the life that bears the living being who experiences), the child constitutes and lives the subjective experience of life, and the Holy Spirit denotes the absolute experience in which the life of experience and the experience of life are intertwined in the infinite circle of self-experiencing life.

According to the Nietzschean trinity (Dionysian force, Apollonian form, tragic synthesis of force and form), Dionysus incarnates the ancestral '[in] substantial force, [...] the primal Force of all sources',[455] the 'overflowing fertility' of the 'primordial One', the 'metamorferocious Dionissances'[456] of the vibrating mat(t)er, 'eternally [pro]creative beneath the surface of incessantly changing appearances, eternally forcing life into existence'.[457] Apollo embodies the realm of appearances governed by the *principium individuationis*, the 'divinisation of individuation', and the perspectivism

454 Schelling, *The Ages of the World (1811)*, 122.

455 Herder, *God, Some Conversations*.

456 Leminski, *Catatau*, 242.

457 F. Nietzsche, *Birth of Tragedy and Other Writings*, tr. R. Speirs (Cambridge: Cambridge University Press, 2007), 80.

that comes with this. From the whirlwinds of Force are abstracted the folds of Form, 'swirling forms, full of voluptuous whisps that fill the topaz of a void',[458] 'rippling the waters' ever anew.[459] While the primordial One condescends to take on finite forms by limiting itself ('Dionysus speaks the language of Apollo'), forms are in turn deformed and transformed by the primal force ('Apollo who speaks that of Dionysus').[460] Tragic existence, far from giving in to infinitising hubris, accepts 'that everything which comes into being must be prepared [to disappear]';[461] it accepts finitude as that which makes possible the vocation of every singular life, the revelation of life through the condensation of Dionysian forces into forms, images, and actions. In tragic existence, the form (individual, finite, determined) is not detached from the force that continues to inform and transform it: 'The cause was [...] a force; the effect was the form [...] but was the form the extinction of the cause? [...] Or, perhaps, once the form was found, another numinous causal series was engendered anew, as if it were plunging back into the generatrix of becoming.'[462] The synthesis of the Dionysian force that engenders and the Apollonian image that represents results in an imaginative force (*Einbildungskraft*) channelled into existence by pneumatic living forms. The synthesis of the (noumenal) will and (phenomenal) representation does not take the form of a quietist and ascetic denial of the will-to-live intent on saving the individual from suffering, but rather that of a reimplantation of the personal self-positing will into the impersonal realm of life's will to live and reveal. This reinscription does not save the individual from the pains of existence but rather cures it from the illness of disligation in its manifold forms (like egotistical self-sufficiency, the will to conquer, to dominate and to possess, the denial of death). In the trinitarian model, the individuation of the self and the correlative

---

458 Perlongher, *Caribe Transplatino*, 93–94.

459 Lezama Lima, *La expresión americana*, 182.

460 Nietzsche, *Birth of Tragedy and Other Writings*, 104.

461 Ibid., 80.

462 Lezama Lima, 'Preludio a las eras imaginarias', 153.

constitution of worlds of experience are not mere illusions from which we should awaken, but rather are necessary phases of the divine procession. The (Spinozist) 'consciousness of the identity of one's own inner [insubstance] with that of all things'[463] does not necessarily mean that individual existence is intrinsically guilty and that redemption can only take place by means of a denial of one's own self and a 'decided opposition to [constituted] nature'. The Spinozist consciousness of the underlying impersonal unity of life can also foster an ethic of solidarity, cooperation, kindness, compassion, and empathy for other lifeforms and prescribe practices of attunement, inter-species communication, and concertation based on the recognition and respect of their singular individuality. Taking away the veil of Maya here means embedding the phenomenal world (always correlative to a certain transcendental type) into the phenoumenal pleroma, submerging the worldly manifestation in a pleromatic revelation that no world or history can fully contain.

According that the trident brandished by the 'Indian dressed as senator of the Empire' (calibanise, cannibalise, carnivalise), calibanisation refers to the resolution to be rooted in the mat(t)er, to become ab-original, autochthonous (sprung from the Pure Land itself), rejecting the prosperity of that appropriation which endows citizenship by uprooting, by making foreign: 'Tupi or not Tupi, that is the question:[464] to be indigenous is to have as a primordial point of reference the relationship with the land where you were born and where you settled to make your life. [...] It means being part of a community linked to a specific place, i.e. being part of a people. To be a citizen on the contrary is to be part of a population controlled (both "defended" and attacked at the same time) by a [transcendent] State. The native looks downwards, toward the Earth which they are immanent to; they draw strength from the soil. The citizen [...] receives [its] rights from above [...]. The land [the indigenous peoples] occupy is not their property [...] because it is they who belong to the land, not the inverse.

463 A. Schopenhauer, *The World as Will and Representation*, tr. E.F.J. Payne (New York: Dover, 2 vols., 1969), vol. 2, 613.

464 Andrade, *Cannibalist Manifesto*, 38.

Belonging to the land, rather than owning it, is what defines the indigenous. [...] Separating the Indians (and all other indigenous peoples) from their organic, political, social and vital relationship with the land and from their communities which live off the land—this separation has always been seen as a necessary condition for turning the Indian into a citizen. [...] The earth is the body of the Indians, the Indians make up a part of the body of the Earth. [...] The separation between the community and the land has as its reverse [...] the separation between people and their bodies, another operation carried out by the State which is indispensable for the creation of administrated populations.'[465] Cannibalisation denotes the anticolonial act of anthropophagic self-positing that removes one from the Romantic position of the *noble savage* ('All the charms of Sycorax—toads, beetles, bats—light on you [...]. You taught me language and my profit on't / Is, I know how to curse. / The red plague rid you / For learning me your language!') devouring the deserving invader in order to incorporate, transmute, transculturate and redirect its force, and, in particular, to pervert and junglise its Christianity. Finally, carnivalisation expresses the teratological celebration of miscegenation, of the hybridisation of worlds, of inter-species mimesis, of loves against *natura naturata*; a carnival ('the concretist-anti-speculative image par excellence') in which 'the hypotheses in which the German masters indulge vanish: eu-cosmos ou cosmos-eu, Eu é tudo ou Tudo é eu, Eu-Tudo ou Tudo-Eu, Tudo-Tudo ou Eu-Eu, Meu-Tu-Tu ou Tu-Meu-Teu, Eu-Teu-Teu ou Tu-Eu-Teu. And other nonsense'.[466]

In Merleau-Ponty's trinity (invisible, visible, flesh), the first hypostasis refers to the invisible insubstance that begets and underlies any transcendental constitution of an I/not-I correlation,[467] the ultimate 'formative

465 Viveiros de Castro, 'Les involontaires de la patrie', 124–27.

466 Goddard, *Un brésilien noir et crasseux*, 40.

467 '*What* it does not see it does not see for reasons of principle, it is because it is consciousness that it does not see. *What* it does not see is what in it prepares the vision of the rest (as the retina is blind at the point where the fibres that will permit the vision spread out into it). *What* it does not see is what makes it see, is its tie to Being, is its corporeity, are the existentials by which the world becomes visible, is

medium of [both] the object and the subject',[468] the underlying blind spot out of which the transcendental conditions of the possibility of vision are materially generated, the pre-worldly life that 'forever lies in wait about each one of us in all its abundance, but veiled from view, deep down, invisible, far off',[469] the life that 'inhabits [every] world, sustains it, and renders it visible, its own and interior possibility, the Being of this [existence]'.[470] The second hypostasis refers to the visible images that scintillate within that horizon of visibility constituted by the finite consciousness. The flesh enacts the panspsychic-oriented reversibility between the I and the not-I, 'the whole cycle' of 'the sensible in the twofold sense of what one senses (the sensible world = the correlated of my active body) and what senses (the body that experiences)',[471] the generalised awakening of material insubstance in which the subjective hand that touches an object of its Umwelt is in turn a hand that is touched as an object of another Umwelt, in which all supposed 'naked objectivity' is always already subjectivated, in which every *it* is a *you* in an inter-typical *we*. The notion of flesh underscores the fact that the intentional relations between the I and the not-I are in the last instance forms of the self-affection of life, an inter-umweltic dynamics through which the sentient hand can leave behind the transcendental limits of its world and make ingression into the night of another world, taking the form of an unknown visitation dreamt by the sleeper. Whereas the invisible refers to the insubstance's capability to engender visionary beings, the notion of flesh points toward the self-affectability of an insubstance already inhabited by such mutually experiencing living vortices.

---

the [living insubstance] wherein the [subject-object correlation] is born.' Merleau-Ponty, *The Visible and the Invisible*, 248.

468 Ibid., 147.

469 F. Kafka, *The Diaries of Franz Kafka, Volume Two, 1914–1923*, ed. M. Brod, tr. M. Greenberg and H. Arendt (New York: Secker and Warburg, 1949), 18 October 1921.

470 Merleau-Ponty, *The Visible and the Invisible*, 151.

471 Ibid., 259–60.

According to the temporal conjugation of the trinity (the originary, the actuality, the eschaton), the mat(t)er corresponds to the originary or pre-historical era—the past that was never present—of impersonal, pre-individual and pre-mundane life; the child defines the era which we shall call actuality (the aeon in which worlds spring forth and in which histories are decanted, an aeon in which the chronological past, present and future define the different ages of the world), and the Holy Spirit defines the eschaton, the era of transworldly and transhistorical concertation in which the phenoumenodelics of the spirit unfolds. Far from succeeding one another, the three eras coexist within the pleroma: every living being is born from and lives in the originary, unfolds its transcendental-dependent experience within the historical and worldly horizons of actuality, and explores (performing spiritual variations of its own transcendental structures, communicating with lifeforms that instantiate other transcendental types) the eschaton. The abstract opposition between a 'conservative' attachment to the past and to tradition (which would appear to imply a closure with respect to the openness of the future) and the 'revolutionary' radicality that claims to open onto the future by asserting a supposedly unconditioned freedom is overcome by means of the trinitarian idea that only a rooting in the originary vortex of impersonal life allows the present to open itself freely onto an unforeseen future. Merely abstract freedom (the freedom to decide from a given selection of options in an unconditional manner) gives way to a concrete conception of freedom: a subject can act in revolutionary manner upon a concrete world-historical situation only when it allows itself to be infused with the living forces that underlie and inform both the historical world in question and its own subjectivity.

According to the phenoumenodelic trinity (the pre-worldly, worldly, and trans-worldly realms), 'classical' phenomenology (phenomenology in its Husserlian and Heideggerian versions) is constructed on the basis of the Greek notion of phenomenon, that is, on the thesis that manifestation is exhausted by that which appears within the worldly horizons of visibility. Both Husserl's phenomenology (based on the intentional correlation between subjects and objects) and Heidegger's 'ek-static truth of being' (defined with respect to a Dasein that is always already there in a world) presuppose that experience necessarily takes place within a worldly horizon. However, worldly phenomenology does not exhaust the notion of manifestation. First, the sequence that started with Descartes's hyperbolic doubt concerning the existence of the external world, continued through Schopenhauer's other-than-worldly-representation will and Freud's discovery of the life of the unconscious, and culminated with Henry's radical immanence, brought to the phenomenological attention the existence of a pre-worldly kind of manifestation.[472] Now, the Cartesian project was partially hindered by the thesis that the last instance which we cannot doubt is a personal cogito (always already transcendentally correlated to a world) rather than an impersonal realm (called *natura naturans*, will, Dionysus, and life by Spinoza, Schopenhauer, Nietzsche, and Henry respectively) endowed with the capacity to institute living beings. Beyond the Cartesian ego, Husserl's absolute subjectivity, and Freud's personal unconscious, the Cartesian motif culminates in the recognition of an impersonal form of manifestation that can be acceded to by performing an *epoché* of the world. According to Henry's variation of the Cartesian motif, '[t]here is Life and the proof is given by Life itself. That which experiences itself is indisputable. You can criticise everything [...] [but there is always] this unshakeable ground that no one can question. That is why all the criticisms of the cogito by modern thought [...] simply did not see what it was all about.[473] [...][This Life] is the infinite Life that surpasses me, is actualised and lives in lives such as mine. [...] That which transcends the self is not [only] a kind of [phenoumenal] transcendent, [...] that which transcends the self is [also] that which comes before it and in which it comes, which is therefore deeper than it and from which it arises at every moment[474] [...] [namely,] this life, which is not primarily in the world, which is not an *in der Welt sein*.'[475] On the other side, the speculative extension of transcendental

472 Regarding this shift from the Cartesian cogito to Henry's phenomenology of life, see M. Henry, *Généalogie de la psychanalyse. Le commencement perdu* (Paris: PUF, 2003).

473 M. Henry, *Entretiens* (Arles: Sulliver, 2005), 70.

474 Ibid., 68.

475 Ibid., 71.

philosophy we have advocated here implies that the phenomenological horizon of visibility constituted by a given transcendental type of subjectivity can always be deformed and expanded in a trans-worldly horizon of horizons. This trans-worldly supra-horizon encodes the 'spiritual' fact that the horizon of possibilities defined by a given world is open to inter-species kins, to shamanic variations, to 'domain extensions', to transcendentally unforeseen possibilities, to the ingression of spiritual epiphanies conveyed by phenoumenal pigeons, angels of mediation, ghostly visitations. According to the phenoumenodelic trinity, every circumambient world is always subjected to a perichoretic dynamics that keeps it open to the influence of the other two coninsubstantial hypostases: every world is irrigated and kept alive by a pre-worldly life and every world is suspended in a trans-worldly supra-horizon alongside other worlds. The phenomenological horizon constituted by the subject of experience is not only bounded by a phenoumenal beyond 'above' as Kant maintained, but also but a living soil below. The Christian trinity encodes the two portals that open the life of the child 'beneath' and 'beyond' the transcendental horizon of possibilities defined by its transcendental type. In this sense, Schleiermacher's attempt to identity the Spinozist *natura naturans* with the Kantian noumena into a single non-phenomenal instance does not take into account the fact that any I/not-I correlation is bounded by two different hypostasis: the instituting life beneath the I and the supernatural sky beyond the not-I.[476]

In the framework of the spatial schematisation of the trinity (the infra-sensible soil, the worlds of revelation, the supernatural sky), the infra-sensible soil is the Pure Land 'begotten before all worlds',[477] the presupposed vital background that supports the living and flows through them with its force while remaining itself undisclosed, the underlying

476 According to Schleiermacher, 'the world of noumena is the cause of the sense-world in precisely the same way that Spinoza's infinite substance is the cause of finite things.' (Schleiermacher, 'Kurze Darstellung des Spinozistischen Systems', quoted and translated in J.A. Lamm, 'Schleiermacher's Post-Kantian Spinozism: The Early Essays on Spinoza, 1793–94', *The Journal of Religion* 74:4 [1994], 476–505: 486).

477 Watts, *The Joyous Cosmology*, 47.

living soil in which living beings sink their souls. The child inflates with its breath the worldly vessels into which revelation is poured image by image. In these lifeworlds the being-there of life—its existence—takes time and place, the *there* in question denoting not only a spatial localisation but also a temporal one: the lifeworlds are the realms of natives and mortals. The Holy Spirit is spatially schematised in the form of the supernatural sky, the 'preserved night' in which worlds are hatched, 'the dreaming Serpent which surrounds the [constituted] World[s].'[478] The four cardinal points are indeed three: above and below (Huidobro): each worldly clearing—the phenomenological horizon of possible experiences of an individual—is circumscribed by the infra-sensible soil 'below' and by the supernatural sky 'above'. Being 'beneath' and 'beyond' the experiential window of the subject, neither the infra-sensible soil nor the supernatural sky appears as such. Only the phenomena (e.g. the planet Earth and the celestial bodies that travel through the sky) appear, and they always do so on the horizon of a lifeworld.

The infra-sensible soil harbours the impenetrability of the forest, the nurturing hummus in which the insect burrows, the density of the bush, the impervious rock, the opacity of material resistance, the rhythmic base that ascends from the chthonic depths, the generative 'infra-syntax'. The infra-sensible soil is the arche-ground on which it is possible to live an ab-original existence, an existence that remains connected to the force that—foreclosing itself in its unconsciousness—informs existence and infuses it with its transcendental exuberance. In this sense, Husserl's and Heidegger's attempts to disentangle the notion of an 'immobile' self-secluding earth that generates every phenomenological revelation from the astronomical notion of a planet that freefalls in the astrophysical extension can be integrated into the Christian threefold: we can accept and endure the Copernikantian launching of humanity while at the same time radicalising our aboriginal condition, that of belonging to an 'historical people' that rests upon a 'self-closing ground', the living soil. 'Early on, the Greeks called this coming forth and rising up in itself and in all things *physis*. At the same time *physis*

---

478 Pynchon, *Gravity's Rainbow*, 412.

lights up that on which [humans base their] dwelling. We call this the earth. What this word means here is far removed from the idea of a mass of matter and from the merely astronomical idea of a planet. [...] [The earth] first comes forth as homeland [...]. The earth is the unforced coming forth of the continually self-closing [...] [that] shatters every attempt to penetrate it [...]. The [essential] self-seclusion of the earth is, however, no uniform, inflexible staying-in-the-dark [*Verhangenbleiben*], but unfolds, rather, into an inexhaustible richness of simple modes and shapes.[479] [...] [F]or it is in the symphonic sweep of crickets, spiders and batrachians, if stretched along their own pneumatic curve, that the angelic diagonals of the Earth intersing, acousmatic, where the stellar intensities wink at us in [their own] language [...].'[480] The infra-sensible life only mediately reveals itself by instituting finite forms of subjectivity as instances of various transcendental types (mineral, vegetable, animal, human, cybernetic, extraterrestrial), forms that induce the dehiscence of phenomenological clearings, the hatching of phenomenological worlds as alembics in which life distils unique visions of itself. Engendering the living, the self-secluding Earth opens up different lifeworlds ('each time unique, the beginning, the blossoming, and the end of a world') and these worlds—thanks to the transcendental plasticity of life—deform and intermingle with other worlds, the supernatural sky being the realm in which this *Harmonices mundi* unfolds.

The supernatural sky is the pleromatic night in which the clearings light up ('a light in each globule'),[481] the 'preserved night' in which 'worlds of revelation' hatch and float, the extra-worldly horizon of the worldly horizons. 'The Heavens mean the supernatural, that which does not appear in any way [...]'.[482] But its supernatural character does not refer to an outside of manifestation: the obscurity of the heavens is as of a blinding

479 Heidegger, 'The Origin of the Work of Art', in *Off the Beaten Track*, 21–42.

480 Lady Hélène Fluxor, 'Documentos de Recienvenidas: Circulaciones a la Etcétera', in Las Señoras del Arcoiris, *Documentos de la Escuela Nocturna*, 51–52.

481 Perlongher, *Aguas Aéreas*, 258.

482 Fichte, *La doctrine de l'État (1813)*, 197.

light (Olber's evidence). Its supernaturality is not that which—as with the self-occluding force of the earth—is removed from its manifestation, but instead denotes a phenoumenal arche-manifestation whose pleromatic infinity cannot be contained in any given phenomenological horizon, in any transcendentally determined form of manifestation: all sensible manifestation is a finite trimming down—a selection—of this infinite suprasensibility, of the hyperabundance of the phenoumenodelic donation, a selection that depends on the individuals perceptual, conceptual, emotional and social thresholds. The transcendental frames, filters, and valves project a 'sheltering sky' that preserves the subjective integrity of the corresponding living being from an otherwise unbearable revelation, from the 'Hellish power' of an insubstance that 'is wholly alive'.[483] As the Ladies of the Rainbow instruct us, 'the heavens are not above us but where the grammas of our song nictilate, emitting their constellations. [...] [I]t is not this hard or planetary zodiac that we instantiate, but a soft one [...] immediately influenceable and plastic, which provides the strength and the means to go further and further through the *influx* [...] "The star is all of a sudden half a metre away! / through the emitting cosmichain / the stellar [*estelado*] and this side of things [*este lado*] are touching, / rising and falling through the parliament of the bugs" poeticises the moon-man of Iguazú.'[484] In the night the emergent wisps of the spirit dehisce and scatter; in the night life raises its self-manifestation to higher powers, through the big banging of new worlds, the triggering of new historical timelines, the institution of new mutant, mongrel, inter-species types of subjectivity as radiant foci for new actions and visions, as fragile living icons of its overwhelming power. When night falls you can hear the 'joyful buzzing in unison (beating wings) of the swarms of bees (bits of life)' that together make up the vast living organism, the 'cloud of gnats floating, singing hymns of worship joyfully to Brahman'.[485] At night the crystal tinkling that rises from the 'mythical

483 Lispector, *The Passion According to G.H.*

484 Las Señoras del Arcoiris, *Documentos de la escuela nocturna*, 17.

485 Dick, *Exegesis*, 23:133.

riverrun of fluent metamorphosis'[486] becomes perceptible: 'It darkles, (tinct, tint) all this our funnaminal world. Yon marshpond by ruodmark verge is visited by the tide. Alvemmarea! We are circumveiloped by obscuritads. [Humans] and belves frieren.'[487]

According to the trinity dreamt by Lezama Lima, the prebreath and the ultrachaos intersect their shadows all throughout the scintillations—leaves and light—of the Hanga Songa.[488] The prebreath is the impersonal realm of the vibrating pneuma, the Word that has not been vocalised and modulated by the living ones yet ('no proper name exists for the [hypertelic pre]breath that is my own').[489] The ultrachaos denotes the fulminant order in which all transcendental perspectives become compatible, 'a region where the overabundance cancels the countersense',[490] the chaosmic profusion that infilters the worldly totalities under the form of epiphanies, visitations, and impasses. Hanga Songa is the name of the forest, 'the exalted garden'[491] that hosts the clearings wherein revelation takes place and time. By preventing the collusion of the first and the third hypostasis—by preventing the supernatural sky from falling—the trees hinder the catastrophic collapse of the worldly clearings. If we destroy the forest, if we forget that revelations always take place in a singular living milieu, then subjective integrity will implode under the phenoumenodelic pressure of the ultrachaos: 'If you destroy the forest, the [ultrachaos will be unleashed] and [the sky] will fall on the earth again! [The white people] do not pay any attention to them, for they do not drink the yãkoana. Yet their skill with machines will not allow them to hold up the falling sky and repair the spoiled forest. [...] But if we peoples of the forest are no longer, the white people will never be able to replace us there, living on the old traces of our houses and abandoned

486 Viveiros de Castro, 'The Crystal Forest', 159.

487 Joyce, *Finnegans Wake*, 244

488 Cf. J. Lezama Lima, *Paradiso* (Madrid: Ediciones Cátedra, 1997), 298.

489 Klossowski, *The Baphomet*, 9.

490 Lezama Lima, *La dignidad de la poesía*, 294–312: 295.

491 Cf. H. Michaux, *Le jardin exalté* (Montpellier: Fata Morgana, 1983).

gardens. They will perish in their turn, crushed by the falling sky. Nothing will remain. It is so. As long as there are shamans alive, their xapiri will be able to quiet the sky when it threatens to come apart and hold back its fall. If all the shamans die, the sky will break apart for good, and no one will be able to do anything. That is why, for us, what the white people call "future" is to protect the sky from the xawara epidemic fumes to keep it healthy and strongly fastened above us.'[492] In the dreamspacetime of the suspended forest, the trees stand like Jacob's ladders for the selenite frogs and golden toads. The humming of the leaves refracts the monstrous moonshine into resonating patterns propagating along the dew-pearled webs, igniting the nocturnal take-off of the onoahiric Ark: 'Nor yet through starland that silver sash. What era's o'ering? Lang gong late. Say long, scielo! Sillume, see lo! Selene, sail O! Amune! Ark!? Noh?! Nought stirs in spinney. The swayful pathways of the dragonfly spider stay still in reedery. Quiet takes back her folded fields. Tranquille thanks. Adew.[493] [...] Our pontiffs are the crickets with their tiny ladders. [...] Their action consists in lifting the fourth and fifth lotus in the ascent of the Shiva-Langa. [...] It is just what crickets and batrachians do with their gurgling concerts: they lift up this planet and its creatures during the nights, stretching the weightless ropes for the somnambulists who find them hanging on the way.'[494] The pleromatic night is not the dwelling place of the gods, but neither is it the terrifying night of Pascal or the silent night that elicits the Fermi paradox.

Following Elie During, we can establish a parallel between the so-called Fermi paradox and the existential and cosmological condition outlined by Pascal when he described the frightening 'eternal silence' of the 'infinite spaces'.[495] Pascal's wager relies on a particular ontotheological (gnostic) thesis, namely, that of a *Deus absconditus*, of a God that is both 'infinitely incomprehensible' and uncompromisingly absent from the material universe.

492 Kopenawa and Albert, *The Falling Sky*, 406–7.

493 Joyce, *Finnegans Wake*, 244.

494 Las Señoras del Arco Iris, *Documentos de la Escuela Nocturna*, 20, 24, 27.

495 Cf. E. During, Bruno Latour et les 'Extraterrestres', *Critique* 78 (August–September 2022): 903–904.

This is why Pascal's God can only be the object of a wager that cannot be grounded on any rational argument or worldly experience: only 'by faith we know His existence'.[496] On the contrary, we can try to 'give full force to the notion of cosmic life', we can patiently work to give shape to 'an intuition for an extended concept of "life" of which we still have only sketches', and attempt to 'reintroduce to the empty [...] scene described by Pascal a link, however tenuous, that snatches us from our planetary solitude and attaches us to a notion of extraterrestrial life that might minimally matter to us.'[497] The 'objective description' of our existential condition in the midst of the spatiotemporal extensions of the physical universe changes completely when we assume that there is no experience that is not always already a filtered, partial, and perspectival experience of a pleromatic immanent 'God', that there is no experience that is not a living experience *of* life in the double sense of the genitive. Rather than 'believing' in what we cannot comprehend, we can try to tune in—rationally, emotionally, perceptually—to as many attributes of the living insubstance as possible and do not cede our desire to mediate the transcendental limits of our experience. 'The real wager is that one can feel *embarked*'[498] in a life that is everywhere revealing itself in all its sensorial, emotional and conceptual splendour, navigating through a living ocean of 'sangnifiance'. As Cabrol (cited by During) writes, '[t]he search for life beyond Earth is not so much a search anymore if everything we are, we live on, interact with and observe is alive. Rather, it becomes an exploration of life's expression of diversity and complexity—not *in* the universe but *by* the universe, and a search on how to *connect* and *exchange information* with it.[499] [...] The great thing about [life] is it doesn't require belief.'[500] We are not 'engulfed in the infinite immensity of spaces',[501] drifting in

496 Pascal, *Thoughts, Letters and Minor Works*, 84 [§233].

497 During, Bruno Latour et les 'Extraterrestres', 666.

498 Ibid.

499 N.A. Cabrol, 'The Quantum of Life?', *Scientific American*, September 2019.

500 T. MacKenna, 'Countdown into Complexity', Lecture, March 1996.

501 Pascal, *Thoughts, Letters and Minor Works*, 78 [§205].

solitude through a silent darkness; we are embedded into and probing the depths of an omnipresent pleromatic life in which there is no experience that is not always already a contact of an unknown kind, a reception of signals broadcast by the most extravagant living forms. In the 'dark night of the phosphene', noctilucas and moths—'threading iridiscences in the ethereal sulphing'[502]—arrive as visitations from other shores: 'I saw the night as if something had fallen to the earth, a descent. [...] For me, the night was that territory where you could recognise the hand. [...] Stretch out your hand and you will see how there is the night and its unknown hand. [...] I was slowly moving my hand forward, like an anxious person wandering through the desert, until I found the other hand, the Other. [...] There will always be the night when the other hand will come. [...] Knowing that for a moment something comes to complete them, and that by expanding the breath a universal rhythm is found. Breathing in and breathing out is a universal rhythm. What is hidden is what completes us and is the plenitude in the length of the wave.'[503] The pleromatic night provides the stage for a radical synthesis of outsiders and insiders that is not restricted to taking place and time in a fixed transcendental framework, it provides the horizon of horizons for transumweltic migrations, the interzone where the law is suspended and where life is an experimental practice of love for interzonal forms of experience. The supernatural sky is the playground for symbioses, hybridisations, and crossbreeding, for inter-species practices of love, for the blurring of any fixed ego-alien divide. From the pleromatic night come the hands of the others and in the night we depart for encounters of the *n*th kind, with those who come from other tribes, with those who communicate with other *grammas*, the Martians and the Venusians, the neighbours, the intergalactic, the multiversal, the caboclos and the orishas, those creeping around in other Umwelten, those extending into other dimensions, the *xapiri*, those who broadcast from other scales, those who exist in other epochs (the dead, the unborn, those who will never be) or in other modalities (merely possible beings, necessary beings, chimaeras), those who can

502 Perlongher, *Aguas Aéreas*, 247.

503 Lezama Lima, *El reino de la imagen*, 356.

tune into attributes of the pleroma other than the finite set available to human experience (the *logos*, the *sensorium*, the *affectum*, the *socius*), those that pulsate in other durations, those that excite other void states, that radiate outward from our own nested extimities, the machine elves that 'stop in front of you and vibrate [...] singing structures into existence [...] like the toys that are scattered around the nursery inside a U.F.O',[504] those we devour and that come to live in and with us, the gnomic cabiri that 'work below the threshold of consciousness',[505] the extended immanent minds that transmit to their local and lower-order neural components, our different (past or future) selves that communicate with our present self either broadcasting forward from the past or backward from the future, those who visit us in dreams, those that speak to us in the 'language of leaves', those that we ourselves already are—'I is another'—in the specious present of a speculative transmutation.

To the capitalist devastation of the earth and the conquest of space we oppose an absolutely modern aboriginal life, rooted in the infra-sensible earth—'I am not white, I am Indian, I am from my mother's family, my uncle is a jaguar'[506]—and projected (shamanic probe) into the supernatural sky: Dionysus-Christ-Apollo mission, navigating the pleroma, 'walking on the aerial waters of Deep Space',[507] arriving at the shores of other worlds, humanoid appendage of the arche-soil sprouting out of its world, probing the supernatural night.

---

504 T. McKenna, *Take the Third Hit*, <https://www.youtube.com/watch?v=BvTG8wEjtzA>.

505 C.G. Jung, 'A Psychological Approach to the Dogma of the Trinity', in *Psychology and Religion: West and East* (Princeton, NJ: Princeton University Press, 1958), 164.

506 J. Guimaraes Rosa, 'Meu tio o Iauaretê', quoted in Viveiros de Castro, 'Rosa e Clarice, a fera e o fora', 27.

507 R. Bradbury, 'Christus Apollo—Cantata Celebrating the Eight Day of Creation and Promise of the Ninth', in *I Sing the Body Electric* (New York: Knopf, 1969).

# CONCLUSION

In our modern era, philosophy can no longer maintain the naive pretension of trying to build a new all-encompassing philosophical system, provide the pillars of any brave new ontology or demonstrate any ultimate truth whatsoever. Let the sciences patiently and painstakingly—'Science with patience / The ordeal is certain'[1]—pursue their infinite probing of the *logos* that makes the experiential field intelligible. According to the state of suspension that we have adopted here, we have tried to sketch a phenoumenodelic description of the existential situation in which we find ourselves, that of being finite living subjects embedded in a worldly realm wherein we can perceive, feel, and think the phenoumena offered to experience according to different subject-dependent transcendental capacities that can be speculatively mediated. In particular, such a description should be able to accommodate the particular 'image of the world' provided by modern science. Even the most sophisticated scientific narratives—such as the modelisation of the life and death of the different observed astrophysical structures (planets, stars, galaxies, black holes, up to the whole universe itself)—is (like the fatherhouse floating in a cloud-like structure at the very end of *Solaris*) an image suspended in the phenoumenodelic insubstance of appearing, an image that partially depends in a nontrivial manner on the transcendental perspective of modern humanity (for instance, on the current state of theoretical physics, on the available technological resources for astrophysical observations, and on the distance and energy scales to which we have experimental access). Moreover, such an 'image of the world' is a scientific image obtained by abstracting out the other attributes of the concrete experiential field and thereby of aesthetic, ethical, and religious values.

1 Rimbaud, *Complete Works, Selected Letters*, 189 [translation modified].

According to this line of reasoning, the description proposed here is finally surprisingly close to Husserl's claim that the Copernicanism of modern science can be phenoumenodelically reduced: every form of revelation—including those provided by modern science—is like an aurora borealis hovering somewhere in between the infra-sensible 'arche-Earth that [unlike our freefalling planet] does not move' and the supernatural sky in which lifeworlds are born, shine out, live, and die. The world of the capitalist subject—unfolding between the devastation of the earth and the 'conquest of space'—is only one world among others, a sick world that—having lost its collective soul—becomes more and more detached from the living forces of the arche-soil. The terrifying image of the current 'human place in the cosmos'—that of a wasted planet freefalling into the darkness of a unfathomably vast, silent, cold, and seemingly lifeless universe ruled by people with extreme forms of dementia who have decisional control over nuclear weapons, global warming, and natural resources—is simply overwhelming. In order to cope with this situation, there is always the possibility (for those 'who are unable to endure the fate of the age') to make an 'intellectual sacrifice' and 'return to the welcoming and merciful embrace of the old churches',[2] to pull back existence to a premodern landscape or to indulge in different forms of obscurantist superstition or 'speculative' dogmatism. Or alternatively, we can recognise that this image of our current situation is still an abstract image that depends upon the perspective defined by our available transcendental resources. We can acknowledge that the ultimate source of this image is the specious living present of life, the immanental force that institutes living things that constitute worlds and infuses them with the desire to perform speculative mediations of those worlds. It is at this moment that it becomes more necessary than ever to adhere to the phenoumenodelic, speculative, and concretist directives: to bracket the naturalisation of every image, to index them to the transcendental regimes that make them possible and to explore the horizon of possible deformations of these regimes, to reinsert every abstract image

---

2 M. Weber, 'Science as a Vocation', in *The Vocation Lectures*, tr. R. Livingstone (Indianapolis and Cambridge: Hackett, 2004), 30.

in the multimodal concreteness of the experiential field, to deploy dermal surfaces sensitive to other affects, other percepts, other concepts, to enter into symbiogenetic transformations and make kin with other lifeforms,[3] to educate ourselves in schools of other worlds. There are other valves, other filters, other resolutions, other scales, other sieves, other categories, other bodies, other languages by means of which it is possible to constitute—from the same phenoumenal data—other phenomenal realities, other objective descriptions. This does mean that the problems that appear in the abstract 'image of the world' we have described above are not 'real' and do not require concrete theoretical, aesthetical, and political interventions. A transcendental-dependent description of our existential situation is certainly partial and limited, but not for that reason erroneous. The only mistake we must guard against is falling prey to the pre-critical fallacy of misplaced universality. The actions of resistance elicited by the aforementioned abstract image of the current 'human place in the cosmos' need not submit to the pre-critical naturalisation of the image in question or restrict themselves to using the political, aesthetic, and conceptual weapons available in such a world. Pulling back the veil of Maya—suspending the reification of the worlds and bracketing the canonisation of particular historical timelines, embedding them in the transworldly and transhistorical pleroma—does not mean that the dice should not be thrown, that the Kurukshetra War should not be fought.

With these caveats in place, let us recapitulate the main concepts sampled above. We have called pleroma the suspended phenoumenodelic insubstance within which we and our environing world are embedded, what James called the 'primal stuff'[4] of impersonal experience. We have stated in a Spinozist manner that this concrete insubstance is endowed with different attributes, elements, or abstract sections, such as, for instance (as far as human experience goes), the incandescent *sensorium*, the liquid *affectum*, the metallic *logos*, and the aerial *socius*. The *sensorium* is the attribute of the pleroma throughout which visions, sounds, tastes, haptic sensations,

3 Cf. Haraway, *Staying With the Trouble*.

4 James, 'Does "Consciousness" Exist?', in *Essays in Radical Empiricism*, 2.

and smells are propagated. The *affectum* denotes the 'aerial waters' whose propagating and pulsating waves affect the living in joy, fear, anguish, and love, the attribute in which the 'reasons of the heart' vibrate and resonate. The *logos* is the attribute that expresses the intelligible structure of the pleroma, its symmetries, its regularity, its harmony, its predictability, the attribute along which geometric, algebraic, arithmetic, statistical, and logical structures make ingression. The *socius* is the attribute in which the possible forms of being-together, of being-with, the modes of intersubjective relationality are embodied, organised, structured, transformed, woven and unwoven—the *Mitwelt* in Binswanger's terms. The concrescence—the concrete coalescence—of the different attributes makes it possible to image pleroma as 'carnal tissue' made up of the phenoumenodelic insubstantiality of appearing, a sensitive (perceptive, affective, intellective) breathing flesh in which every local mode offers itself to experience (is touched) and experiences (touches), a rubber dripping with illuminations,[5] a plastic arche-element spellbound by its own narcotic virtues, awakened by the internal propagation of daydreams.

The transcendentalisation of (a phenoumenodelically suspended) Spinozism amounts to stating that the insubstance is equipped with local subjective modes qua world-constituting instantiations of different transcendental types. The pleroma can be both refracted into different attributes and mundanised by local subjective modes. Being atonal, lacking a global vacuum state = 0 (a single fundamental state toward which local excitations would decay), the living flesh is always pulsed by local patterns, propagating waves of a 'narcotic calm'[6] whose vibratory circles scan the experiential field across diverse spatial and temporal scales. A subject is a vortex of the insubstance endowed with patience and agency, a local pattern that is 'responsive to difference.'[7] These subjective excitations of the pneumatic flesh contract the iridescent vibrations into perceived qualities

5 Cf. Perlongher, *Hule* and '*Chorreo' de las iluminaciones*, 127–31.

6 S. Mallarmé, 'Igitur ou la Folie d'Elbehnon', in *Igitur, Divagations, Un coup de dès*, 61.

7 Bateson and Bateson, *Angels Fear*, 135.

(receptive inspiration), incorporate and transmute the resulting rhythmic duration (temporal retention), and radiate dehiscent information (expressive expiration). The pneumatic flesh is an autotelic element capable of locally supporting the expressive ebb and flow of its self-experience: to be-there in the midst of the flesh is to breathe, to support the rhythmic conversion—mediated by the force of imagination—between receptivity and spontaneity. The specious insubstantiality of the experiential field is narcotising and the living modes are entranced, cyclically pulsed by the affective waves that propagate through the ethereal solution, forced to become visionaries by the rising tides.

Depending on its transcendental and speculative affordances, a subject can attune itself to the different abstract attributes of the concrete pleroma and endeavour to mediate the transcendental limits of experience along these different sections. The mediation of the limits of the subject's capacity to tune in to the *logos*, to perceive and feel, and to live-and-die-together defines the regulative tasks of science, art, and politics respectively. This means that the always already concrete experience of the subject can be cut into abstract sections whose modes are percepts, affects, concepts, and sociolepts, and that each of these attributes can be the object of a focused practice of speculative mediation. The infinite ideas of truth, beauty, and justice that orient these modes of thought and practice 'shine only in the night of nature' because they prescribe a mediation of the 'worlds of revelation', because they show that, beyond the 'sun of revelation' which illuminates and enlivens our worldly clearing, there are other lifeworlds that we can explore if we allow ourselves to be irrigated by the transcendental plasticity of life.[8] The strict 'differentiation of value spheres' or interests of reason in accord with the different attributes of the pleroma constitute the 'dignity of modernity' since 'now questions of truth, of justice, and of taste can be worked out and unfolded in accord with their own proper logics'

8 Cf. W. Benjamin, Letter to Florens Christian Tang, December 9, 1923, in *The Correspondence of Walter Benjamin 1910–1940*, 224.

and 'validity claims'.[9] However, this essential step beyond the pre-modern indifferentiation between the different interests of reason carries a risk: that of forgetting that these spheres of value were abstracted from a concrete field of experience. Such a risk cannot be bypassed by relapsing into a premodern conflation between science, arts, politics, and religion, but rather by introducing a particular mode of thought and practice—which we have here and elsewhere called philosophy—intended to compose these abstract modes of thought and practice and to constellate the corresponding ideas of reason. Whereas abstract modes of thought and practice astralise out of the concrete, philosophy pleromatises 'towards the concrete'.[10] By projecting dynamical constellations of reason, the symphilosophical organon synthesises the abstract vectors of (theoretical, aesthetical, and political) mediation into concrete mediators of the transcendental limits of experience. According to this (re)definition, the 'philosophy' of a community is given by the particular manner according to which it composes its conceptual, perceptual, affective, and social capacities to exist life, by the continuously transforming concrete form of its collective subjectivity.

Now, why should humans engage in the abstract and concrete practices of mediation of their Umwelten? We can become artists, scientists, militants, philosophers, and successfully perform effective differential mediations of our Umwelt just for the sake of distraction and entertainment, obtaining power-over, nurturing our narcissism, accumulating different forms of capital, or perpetuating and enhancing the prevailing forms of domination and inequality. All of these forms of thought and practice can be (and indeed to a large extent are) placed in the service of the sickness of disligation. It is here that we have assumed the necessity of the mode of thought and practice called religion. According to the characterisation of it that we have proposed, religion orients finite existence by means of an infinite regulative idea—the idea of love—which meta-orients the other

---

9 Cf. J. Habermas, *The Philosophical Discourse of Modernity: Twelve Lectures*, tr. F.G. Lawrence (Cambridge, MA: MIT Press, 1998).

10 Cf. J. Wahl, *Vers le concret. Etudes d'histoire de la philosophie contemporaine (William James, Whitehead, Gabriel Marcel)* (Paris: Vrin, 2015).

ideas of reason as well as their philosophical constellations. As the Gospel of Matthew states, the greatest of Christian commandments is: thou shalt love the (triune) pleromatic life with all your heart, with all your senses, with all your mind, with all your faculties and capacities, placing every wisp of your breath in the service of life (Matthew 22:37). Love is the love *of* life in the double sense of the genitive, and this living love of life refracts into three modalities that we have described as love of the impersonal ma(t)ter, egophanic love of the personal self, and the love of the emerging transpersonal patterns. This 'meta-idea' of reason orients the triple religation of the finite living with life, its healing with respect to the permanent threat of a rupture, a weakening of the vital tissue, a disconnection, a conflation between individualising differentiation and the pathological severance of the self with respect to biodelic immanence. By means of the trinitarian refraction of love, the triangulation of the virtuous circle of speculation, the 'original unity' between infinite life and finite living beings, between impersonal being and local existence, between immanental insubstance and transcendental experience, between the absolute pleroma and the relative lifeworlds, between *physis* and *gnosis*, is unceasingly concretely realised. The subject whose life is oriented by love is a subject that does not cede its desire to be religated to life, a subject irrigated by the vital drive *par excellence*, that of engendering (new living beings, new transcendental forms of experience, new holobionic tribes) in order to reveal. In this sense we can affirm, with Augustine, that 'the deeds of humans are only discerned by the root of [Love]. [...] Once for all, then, a short precept is given thee: Love, and do what thou wilt:[11] They war loving, they love laughing, they laugh weeping, they weep smelling, they smell smiling, they smile hating, they hate thinking, they think feeling, they feel tempting, they tempt daring, they dare waiting, they wait taking, they take thanking, they thank seeking [...].'[12]

11 Cf. Seventh Homily on 1 John 4: 4–12 (#8), <https://www.ccel.org/ccel/schaff/npnf107.iv.x.html>.

12 Joyce, *Finnegans Wake*, 142.

# Coda

In this primordial scene—'far from everything, Nature [between the constellations and the sea] prepares her Theatre'—the *Maître* enacts 'the Play *par excellence*': methodically 'mad on the outside and flagellated by the [speculative] demands of [eidetic] duty',[1] he is inwardly 'the character who, believing in the existence of the sole Absolute, imagines he is everywhere in a daydream. He acts from the Absolute point of view'.[2] Among other visitations, the iridescent flesh assumes the shape of a siren. Before dissolving back into the insubstance, the visitor suddenly dispels in mist, undulating its tail, the mirage of a solid ground capable of 'imposing a limit on infinity'.[3] The *Maître* remains faithful to the foolhardy task passed down to him by the haunting spectres of his ancestors: that of being tempered by the sinking of his interzonal vessel, 'standing firm in the storm' as a transmitting and receiving antenna. To exist is to tune in while breathing in a state of pneumatic suspension: 'Turn on, tune in, drop out.'

1 S. Mallarmé, 'Hamlet', in *Igitur, Divagations, Un coup de dès*, 194–99.

2 S. Mallarmé, 'Igitur ou la Folie d'Elbehnon', in *Igitur, Divagations, Un coup de dès*, 32.

3 Mallarmé, 'A Throw of the Dice', 138.

# Bibliography

Anonymous. *The Yoga Sūtras of Patañjali: A New Edition, Translation and Commentary*, ed., tr. E.F. Bryant. New York: North Point Press, 2009.

Agamben, Giorgio, and Andrea Pensotti. 'Where is Science Going? An Interview with Professor Giorgio Agamben.' *Organisms. Journal of Biological Sciences* 4:2 (2020), 105–109.

—— *Where Are We Now? The Epidemic as Politics*, tr. V. Dani. Lanham, MA: Rowman and Littlefield, 2021.

Alemán Lavigne, Jorge. *El aprendizaje de saber perder*, <https://redpsicoanalitica.org>.

Althusser, Louis. *The Future Lasts Forever: A Memoir*, tr. R. Veasey. New York: The New Press, 1992.

—— 'Lenin and Philosophy', in *Lenin and Philosophy and Other Essays*, tr. B. Brewster, 23–70: New York and London: Monthly Review Press, 2001.

Angelus Silesius. *Cherubinischer Wandersmann*, ed. L. Gnädinger. Stuttgart: Reclam, 2006.

Arasse, Daniel. *L'Annonciacion italienne. Une histoire de perspective*. Paris: Éditions Hazan, 2010.

Arendt, Hannah. *The Human Condition*. Chicago: The University of Chicago Press, 1998.

Artaud, Antonin. 'À Table', *La Révolution Surrealiste* 3 (15 April 1925).

—— *Le Theatre et les dieux*. Paris: Aubry-Rueff, 1966.

—— *Les Tarahumaras*. Paris: Gallimard, 1971.

—— *Heliogabalus or, the Anarchist Crowned*, tr. A. Lykiard. London: Creation Books, 2003.

—— *Œuvres, Messages révolutionnaires*. Paris: Quarto Gallimard, 2004.

—— 'To Have Done With the Judgement of God', in *Selected Writings*, tr. H. Weaver, ed. S. Sontag. New York: Farrar, Straus and Giroux, 1976, 555–571.

Assmann, Jan. *The Price of Monotheism*, tr. R. Savage. Stanford, CA: Stanford University Press, 2010.

Auden, W.H. *Selected Poems*, ed. E. Mendelson. New York: Vintage, 1979.

Augustine, Saint. *On Christian Doctrine*. New York: Dover, 2009.

Awodey, Steve. *Category Theory*. Oxford: Clarendon Press, 2006.

Badiou, Alain. *Manifesto for Philosophy*, tr. N. Madarasz. Albany, NY: SUNY Press, 1999.

—— *Saint Paul: The Foundation of Universalism*, tr. R. Brassier. Stanford, CA: Stanford University Press, 2003.

— *Le Séminaire, Heidegger L'être 3 – Figure du retrait 1986–1987*. Paris: Fayard, 2015.

Bakker, R. Scott, and David Roden. 'Interview with David Roden'. *Figure/Ground*, 2015, <http://figureground.org/interview-with-david-roden/>.

Balibar, Etienne. 'Foucault's Point of Heresy: "Quasi-Transcendentals" and the Transdisciplinary Function of the Episteme', *Theory, Culture & Society* 32:5–6 (2015), 45–77.

Barbaras, Renaud. *Dynamique de la manifestation*. Paris: Vrin, 2013.

— *La vie lacunaire*. Paris: Vrin, 2011.

— *Introduction à une phénoménologie de la vie*. Paris: Vrin, 2008.

Barbour, Julian B. *The Discovery of Dynamics. A Study from a Machian Point of View of the Discovery and Structure of Dynamical Theories*. New York: Oxford University Press, 2001.

Barr, Michael, and Colin McLarty and Charles Wells. *Variable Set Theory*, 1986, <http://www.math.mcgill.ca/barr/papers/vst.pdf>.

Barth, Karl. *Church Dogmatics, Vol. 1.1. The Doctrine of the Word of God*, tr. G.W. Bromiley, G.T. Thomson, and H. Knight. London: T&T Clark, 2009.

Bataille, Georges. *Le Coupable, Œuvres completes V*. Paris: Gallimard, 1973.

— 'The Psychological Structure of Fascism', tr. C.R. Lovitt, *New German Critique* 16 (Winter 1979), 64–87.

— *Eroticism: Death and Sensuality*, tr. M. Dalwood. San Francisco: City Lights Books, 1986.

— 'La guerre et la philosophie du sacré', in *Oeuvres Complètes XII. Articles II 1950–1961*, 47–57. Paris: Gallimard, 1988.

Bateson, Gregory. *Mind and Nature: A Necessary Unit*. New York: E.P. Dutton, 1979.

— *Steps to an Ecology of Mind*. Chicago: University of Chicago Press, 2000.

— and M.C. Bateson, *Angels Fear: Towards an Epistemology of the Sacred*. New York, Bantam Books, 1988.

Baudrillard, Jean. *The Transparency of Evil*. London: Verso, 1993.

Benjamin, Walter. 'Theses on the Philosophy of History', in *Illuminations. Essays and Reflections*, tr. H. Zohn, 254–264. New York: Shocken, 1969.

— *The Correspondence of Walter Benjamin, 1910–1940*, ed. G. Scholem and T.W. Adorno, tr. M.R. Jacobson and E.M. Jacobson. Chicago: The University of Chicago Press, 1994.

— *The Arcades Project*, tr. H. Eiland and K. McLaughlin. Cambridge, MA: The Belknap Press of Harvard University Press, 1999.

— 'Outline of the Psychophysical Problem', in M. Bullock and M.W. Jennings (eds.), *Selected Writings, Volume 1, 1913–1926*, 393–401. London and Cambridge, MA: Belknap Press, 2002.

—— 'Surrealism: The Last Snapshot of the European Intelligentsia', tr. E. Jephcott, *Selected Writings Volume 2, part 1, 1927–1930*. Cambridge, MA: The Belknap Press of Harvard University Press, 2005.

—— 'The Task of the Translator', in H. Arendt (ed.), *Illuminations: Essays and Reflections*, tr. H. Zohn. New York: Schocken, 2007.

—— 'To the Planetarium,' in M.W. Jennings et al. (eds.), *The Work of Art in the Age of Its Technological Reproducibility, and Other Writings on Media*, 58–59. Cambridge, MA and London: The Belknap Press of Harvard University Press, 2008.

Benveniste, Émile. *Dictionary of Indo-European Concepts and Society*. Chicago: Hau Books, 2016.

Berardi, Franco. 'Desire, Pleasure, Senility, and Evolution', *e-flux journal* 106 (February 2020), <https://www.e-flux.com/journal/106/312516/desire-pleasure-senility-and-evolution/>.

Bergson, Henri. *Creative Evolution*, tr. A. Mitchell. New York: Random House, 1944.

—— *Matter and Memory*, tr. N.M. Paul and W.S. Palmer. New York: Zone, 1991.

—— *The Creative Mind. An Introduction to Metaphysics*, tr. by M.L. Andison. New York: Dover, 2007.

Berman, Antoine. *L'épreuve de l'étranger*. Paris: Gallimard, 1984.

Bermejo Rubio, F., and J. Montserrat Torrents (eds.). *El maniqueismo y textos fuentes*. Madrid: Editorial Trotta, 2009.

Bernays, Paul. *Abhandlungen zur Philosophie der Mathematik*. Darmstadt: Wissenschaftliche Buchgesellschaft, 1976.

Bishop, John. *Joyce's Book of the Dark*. Madison, WI: The University of Winsconsin Press, 1986.

Blake, William. 'Auguries of Innoncence', in *The Complete Poetry and Prose of William Blake*, ed. D.V. Erdman. New York: Anchor Books, 1988.

Blanchot, Maurice. *The Space of Literature*, tr. A. Smock. Lincoln, NE: University of Nebraska Press, 1982.

—— 'The Conquest of Space', tr. C.C. Stevens, in M. Holland (ed.), *The Blanchot Reader*. 269–271. Oxford: Blackwell, 1995.

—— *The Writing of the Disaster*, tr. A. Smock. Lincoln, NE: University of Nebraska Press, 1995.

Blumemberg, Hans. *The Legitimacy of the Modern Age*. Cambridge, MA and London: MIT Press, 1999.

Boff, Loenardo. *Trinity and Society*. New York: Orbis, 1988.

Bohm, David. *Wholeness and the Implicate Order*. London and New York: Routledge, 2005.

Bonilla, Oiaro, Jean-Christophe Goddard and Guillaume Sibertin-Blanc. 'L'autre-mental de Pierre Déléage. Figure de l'anthropologue made in France en polygraphe réactionnaire', *lundimatin* 254 (14 September 2020), <https://lundi.am/L-autre-mental-de-Pierre-Deleage>.

Borges, Jorge Luis. 'Funes, His Memory', in *Collected Fictions*, 131–137. New York: Penguin Books, 1999.

Bourdieu, Pierre. *The Logic of Practice*, tr. R. Nice. Stanford, CA: Stanford University Press, 1990.

— 'The Political Field, The Social Science Field and The Journalistic Field', in R. Benson and E. Neveu (eds.), *Bourdieu and The Journalistic Field*, 29–47. Cambridge: Polity, 2005.

Bradbury, Ray. 'Christus Appolo—Cantata Celebrating the Eight Day of Creation and Promise of the Ninth', in *I Sing the Body Electric!* New York: Knopf, 1969.

Brassier, Ray. *Nihil Unbound: Enlightenment and Extinction*. Basingstoke: Palgrave Macmillan, 2007.

— 'The View from Nowhere,' *Identities: Journal for Politics, Gender and Culture* 8:2 (2011), 7–23.

— 'Prometheanism and its Critics,' in R. Mackay and A. Avanessian (eds.), *#accelerate: The Accelerationist Reader*, 467–487. Falmouth: Urbanomic, 2014.

— and Marcin Rychter. 'I Am a Nihilist Because I Still Believe in Truth', *Kronos*, 16:1 (2011).

Brecht, Bertholt. *Galileo*. New York: Grove Press 1966.

Breleur, Ernest, Patrick Chamoiseau, Gérard Delver, Serge Domi, Édouard Glissant, Guillaume Pigeard de Gurbert, Olivier Portecop, Olivier Pulvar, and Jean-Claude William. *Manifeste pour les "produits" de haute nécessité*. Paris: Éditions Galaade/Institut du Tout-Monde, 2009.

Brewster, David. *Memoirs of the Life, Writings, and Discoveries of Sir Isaac Newton*. Edinburgh and London: Thomas Constable/Hamilton, Adam, 2 vols, 1855.

Bueno, Wilson. *Mar paraguayo*. Buenos Aires: Interzona, 2020.

Burroughs, William S. *The Western Lands*. London: Penguin, 1988.

Calonne, David Stephen (ed.). *Conversations with Gary Snyder*. Jackson, MS: University Press of Mississippi, 2017.

Carel, Havi, and David Meacham (eds.). *Phenomenology and Naturalism: Examining the Relationship between Human Experience and Nature*. Cambridge: Cambridge University Press, 2013.

Carnap, Rudolf. 'Empiricism, Semantics, and Ontology', *Revue Internationale de Philosophie* 4 (1950), 40–50.

Cassirer, Ernst. *Philosophy of Symbolic Forms. Volume Three: The Phenomenology of Knowledge*, tr. R. Manheim. New Haven, CT: Yale University Press, 1957.

— *Substance and Function* and *Einstein's Theory of Relativity*, tr. W.C. Swabey and M.C. Swabey. Chicago and London: Open Court, 1923.

Catren, Gabriel. 'La tâche du philosophe. Variation à partir de *Die Aufgabe des Ubersetzers* de Walter Benjamin', *Philo-Fictions. La Revue des non-philosophies* 3 (2010).

— 'Outland Empire: Prolegomena to Speculative Absolutism', in L. Bryant, N. Srnicek, and H. Harman (eds.), *The Speculative Turn: Continental Materialism and Realism*. Melbourne: Re.press, 2011.

— and F. Cukierman, 'Grothendieck's Theory of Schemes and the Algebra-Geometry Duality', *Synthese* 200:3 (2022).

Cavaillès, Jean. '*Transfini et continu*', in *Œuvres Completès de Philosophie des Sciences*, 271–274. Paris: Hermann, 1994.

Celan, Paul. *Collected Prose,* tr. R. Waldrop. New York: Sheep Meadow Press, 1986.

Césaire, Aimé. *Discourse on Colonialism*, tr. J. Pinkham. New York: Monthly Review Press.

Clarke, Arthur C. *Profiles of the Future. An Inquiry into the Limits of the Possible.* New York: MacMillan, 1973.

Cleland, Carol E. *The Quest for a Universal Theory of Life. Searching for Life as We Don't Know It*. Cambridge: Cambridge University Press, 2019.

Clooney, Francis X. 'Trinity and Hinduism', in P.C. Pahn (ed.), *The Cambridge Companion to the Trinity*. Cambridge: Cambridge University Press, 2011.

Corbin, Henry. 'A propos de Luther', *Le Semeur* (1 March 1932): 289.

— 'Theology as Antidote to Nihilism', tr. M. Evans-Cockle, paper presented in Tehran 20th October 1977 during a conference organised by the Iranian Centre for the Study of Civilizations, <https://www.amiscorbin.com/en/>.

— *En Islam iranien*, Vol.IV. Paris: Gallimard, 1971–1972.

— 'Conférence de M. Henry Corbin', *École pratique des hautes études, Section des sciences religieuses, Annuaire* 84 (1975–1976), 273–78.

— and Philippe Nemo. 'From Heidegger to Suhravardi : An Interview with Philippe Nemo,' 1976, tr. M. Evans-Cockle, <http://amiscorbin.com/en/biography/from-heidegger-to-suhravardi/>.

Cuvier, Georges Baron. *Animal Kingdom, Arranged According to its Organization, Forming the Basis for a Natural History of Animals, and An Introduction to Comparative Anatomy*. London: E. Henderson, 1833.

Daston, Lorraine, and Peter Galison. *Objectivity*. New York: Zone, 2007.

De Andrade, Oswald. 'A crise da filosofia messiânica', in *Obras Completas VI. Do Pau-Brasil à Antropofagia e às Utopias. Manifestos, teses de concursos e ensaios*. Rio de Janeiro: Civilição Brasileira, 1978.

— 'Cannibalistic Manifesto', tr. L. Bary, *Latin American Literary Review*, 19:38 (1991), 38–47.

— *Macunaíma. El héroe sin ningún caracter*, tr. J. Benedetto. Buenos Aires: Mansalva, 2022.

De Saint Aubert, Emmanuel. *Maurice Merleau-Ponty*. Paris: Hermann, 2008.

— '« L'incarnation change tout »; Merleau-Ponty critique de la « theologie explicative »', *Transversalités* 112 (2009), 152–53.

Debs, Talal, and Michael Redhead. *Objectivity, Invariance, and Convention: Symmetry in Physics*. Cambridge, MA: Harvard University Press, 2007.

Del Barco, Oscar. *Exceso y Donación. La busqueda del Dios sin Dios*. Buenos Aires: Biblioteca Internacional Martin Heidegger, 2003.

Deleuze, Gilles. 'Leibniz and the Baroque (17 March 1987)', *The Deleuze Seminars*, <https://deleuze.cla.purdue.edu/seminars/leibniz-and-baroque/lecture-13>.

— *Spinoza: Practical Philosophy,* tr. R. Hurley. San Francisco, CA: City Lights Books, 1988.

— *The Logic of Sense*, tr. M. Lester with C. Stivale. New York: Columbia University Press, 1990.

— *Expressionism in Philosophy: Spinoza*, tr. M. Joughin. New York: Zone Books, 1992.

— *The Fold: Leibniz and the Baroque,* tr. T. Conley. London: The Athlone Press, 1993.

— *Difference and Repetition,* tr. P. Patton. New York: Columbia University Press, 1994.

— *Bergsonism,* tr. H. Tomlinson and B. Habberjam. New York: Zone, 1997.

— 'Immanence: A Life', in *Pure Immanence: Essays on a Life*, tr. A. Boyman, 25–33. New York: Zone Books, 2001.

— *Francis Bacon: The Logic of Sensation*, tr. D.W. Smith. London and New York: Continuum, 2003.

— *Foucault*, tr. S Hand. London and New York: Continuum, 2006.

— 'Mathesis, Science and Philosophy', tr. R. Mackay, in R. Mackay (ed.), *Collapse III: Unknown Deleuze*. Falmouth: Urbanomic, 2007.

— and Félix Guattari. *A Thousand Plateaus. Capitalism and Schizophrenia*, tr. B. Massumi. Minneapolis: University of Minnesota Press, 1987.

— and Félix Guattari. *Anti-Oedipus,* tr. R. Hurley, M. Seem, and Helen R. Lane. London: Continuum, 2004.

— and Félix Guattari. *What is Philosophy?* tr. H. Tomlinson and G. Burchell. New York: Columbia University Press, 1994.

DenaKmar naKhabra. 'The Undulating Unknown', in J. Ramey and M. Harr Farris (eds.), *The Enigmatic Absolute: Heresy, Gnosis and Speculation in Continental Philosophy of Religion*. London: Rowman and Littlefield International, 2016.

Dennett, Daniel C. *Consciousness Explained*. London: Penguin, 1991.

Depraz, Natalie. 'Le statut phénoménologique du monde dans la gnose: du dualisme à la non-dualité', *Laval théologique et philosophique* 52:3 (October 1996), 625–47.

Derrida, Jacques. *Glas*. Paris: Éditions Galilée, 1974.

— 'Economimesis', tr. R. Klein, *Diacritics* 2:11 (1981), 2–25.

— *Positions*, tr. A. Bass. Chicago: University of Chicago Press, 1981.

— *Dissemination*, tr. B. Johnson. London: Athlone Press, 1981.

— *Edmund Husserl's Origin of Geometry: An Introduction*. Lincoln, NE and London: University of Nebraska Press: 1989.

— 'Force of Law: The "Mystical Foundation of Authority"', tr. M. Quaintance, *Cardozo Law Review* 11: 5/6 (1990), 920–1045.

— 'Faith and Knowledge: The Two Sources of "Religion" at the Limits of Reason Alone', in G. Anidjar (ed.), *Acts of Religion*, 70–73. London: Routledge, 2002.

— *Who's Afraid of Philosophy. Right to Philosophy 1*, tr. J. Plug. Stanford, CA: Stanford University Press, 2002.

— and D. Birnbaum and A. Olsson. 'An Interview with Jacques Derrida on the Limits of Digestion', *e-flux journal* 2 (January 2009), <https://www.e-flux.com/journal/02/68495/an-interview-with-jacques-derrida-on-the-limits-of-digestion/>.

Despret, Vinciane. 'It Is an Entire World That Has Disappeared', in D. Bird Rose, T. van Dooren, and M. Chrulew (eds.), *Extinction Studies. Stories of Time, Death, and Generation*, 219–21. New York: Columbia University Press, 2017.

Dick, Philip K. *In Pursuit of Valis: Selections from the Exegesis*, ed. L. Sutin. Novato, CA: Underwood-Miller, 1991.

— *The Exegesis of Philip K. Dick*, ed. P. Jackson and J. Lethem. New York: Houghton Mifflin Harcourt, 2011.

During, Elie. 'Présence et répétition: Bergson chez les phénoménologues', *Critique* 678:11 (2003), 848–64.

— Bruno Latour et les 'Extraterrestres', *Critique* 78 (August–September 2022): 903–904.

— and A. Bublex. *Glenn Gould*. Paris: Philharmonie de Paris Éditions, 2021.

Durkheim, Émile. *The Elementary Forms of Religious Life*, tr. K.E. Fields. New York: The Free Press, 1995.

Dussel, Enrique. *Philosophy of Liberation*. New York: Orbis Books, 1985.

Eboussi Boulaga, Fabien. *Christianisme sans fétiche. Révélation et domination*. Paris: Éditions Présence Africaine, 1981.

Eddington, Arthur. *Space, Time and Gravitation*. Cambridge: Cambridge University Press, 1921.

Eliade, Mircea. 'Le problème du chamanisme', *Revue de l'histoire des religions* 131:1–3 (1946), 5–52.

Eliot, T.S. *The Waste Land. Authoritative Text. Contexts. Criticism*, ed. M. North. New York: Norton, 2001.

Emerson, Ralph Waldo. 'The Over-Soul', in *The Complete Essays and Other Writings of Ralph Waldo Emerson*, 261–78. New York: Random House, 1950.

Fanon, Franz. *Black Skin, White Masks*, tr. C.L. Markmann. London: Pluto Press, 2008.

Fichte, Johannn Gottlieb. *The Vocation of Man*, tr. W. Smith. London: John Chapman, 1846.

— *The Way Towards the Blessed Life; Or, The Doctrine of Religion*, tr. W. Smith. London: John Chapman, 1849.

— 'Second introduction à la Doctrine de la Science', in *Œuvres choisies de philosophie première (1794–1797)*, tr. A. Philolenko. Paris: Vrin, 1972.

— *Doctrine de la science 1801–1802 et textes annexes*, tr. A. Philolenko. Paris: Vrin, 1987.

—— 'Concerning Human Dignity', in *Fichte: Early Philosophical Writings*, ed., tr. D. Breazeale. New York: Cornell University Press, 1988.

—— *The Science of Knowledge*, tr. P. Heath and J. Lachs. Cambridge: Cambridge University Press, 1991.

—— *Doctrine de la science. Exposé de 1812*, tr. I. Thomas Fogiel. Paris: Presses Universitaires de France, 2005.

—— *The Science of Knowing: J.G. Fichte's 1804 Lectures on the Wissenschaftslehre*, tr. W.E. Wright. Albany, NY: State University of New York Press, 2005.

—— *La doctrine de l'État (1813). Leçons sur des contenus variés de philosophie pratique*, tr., ed. J.-C. Goddard. Paris: Vrin, 2006.

—— *Addresses to the German Nation*, ed. G. Moore. Cambridge: Cambridge University Press, 2009.

—— 'On the Ground of Our Belief in a Divine World-Governance', in Y. Estes and C. Bowman (eds.), *J.G. Fichte and the Atheism Dispute (1798–1800)*, 17–30. London: Routledge, 2010.

FISCHBACH, FRANCK. '"Possession" versus "expression": Marx, Hess et Fichte', in E. Renault (ed.), *Lire les Manuscrits de 1844*. Paris: PUF, 2008.

FOUCAULT, MICHEL. 'What is Enlightenment?', tr. C. Porter, in P. Rabinow (ed.), *The Foucault Reader*. New York: Pantheon, 1984.

—— *Hermeneutics of the Subject. Lectures at the Collège de France 1981–1982*, ed. F. Gros, tr. G. Burchell. New York: Palgrave Macmillan, 2005.

—— and G. Preti, 'An Historian of Culture', in S. Lotringer (ed.), *Foucault Live: Collected Interviews, 1961–1984*, 95–104. New York: Semiotext(e), 1996.

—— *The Order of Things*. London and New York: Routledge, 1996.

FREUD, SIGMUND. 'An Outline of Psychoanalysis', in *The Standard Edition of the Complete Psychological Works of Sigmund Freud, Volume XXIII (1937–1939)*, tr. J. Strachey, A. Freud, A. Strachey, and A. Tyson, 148–49. London: The Hogarth Press, 1964.

—— 'Inhibitions, Symptoms, and Anxiety', in *The Standard Edition of the Complete Psychological Works of Sigmund Freud, Volume XX (1925–1926)*, tr. J. Strachey, A. Freud, A. Strachey, and A. Tyson, 75–176. London: The Hogarth Press, 1959.

—— 'Neurosis and Psychosis', in *The Standard Edition of the Complete Psychological Works of Sigmund Freud, Volume XIX (1923–1925). The Ego and the Id and Other Works*, ed., tr. J. Strachey, 149–153. London: The Hogarth Press, 1986.

—— *Beyond the Pleasure Principle*, tr. J. Strachey. New York: Norton, 1961.

—— 'Totem and Taboo', in *The Standard Edition of the Complete Psychological Works of Sigmund Freud, Volume XIII (1913–1914). Totem and Taboo and Other Works*, ed., tr. J. Strachey. London: The Hogarth Press, 1981.

Friedman, Michael. *Reconsidering Logical Positivism*. Cambridge: Cambridge University Press, 1999.

—— *Dynamics of Reason*. Stanford, CA: Stanford University Press, 2001.

Fulcanelli. *The Dwellings of the Philosophers, and Hermetic Symbolism in Relationship with Sacred Art and the Esoterism of Grand Work, Volumes One and Two*, tr. D. Bernardo. Sojourner Books, 2021.

Gadjin, Nagao, and Hirano Umeyo. 'On the Theory of Buddha-Body (*Buddha-kāya*)', *The Eastern Buddhist* 6:1 (May 1973), 25–53.

Ginsberg, Alan, and William Burroughs. *The Yage Letters*. San Francisco: City Lights Books, 1975.

Gironi, Fabio. 'What Has Kant Ever Done for Us? Speculative Realism and Dynamic Kantianism', in S. de Sanctis and A. Longo (eds.), *Breaking the Spell. Contemporary Realism under Discussion*, 89–113. Mimesis International, 2015.

Goddard, Jean-Christophe. *La Querelle de l'athéisme*. Paris: Vrin, 1993.

—— *La philosophie fichtéene de la vie. Le transcendental et le pathologique*. Paris: Vrin, 1999.

—— 'Bergson: Une lecture néo-platonicienne de Fichte', *Les Etudes Philosophiques* 4, 'Bergson et l'idéalisme allemand' (2001), 465–77.

—— 'Croyance et intelligence dans la *Staatslehre* de Fichte', *Carnets du Centre de Philosophie du Droit* 99 (2002).

—— 'Autonomie, réduction et réflexivité: la philosophie naturelle de Francisco J. Varela et le projet transcendental', *Intellectica. Revue de l'Association pour la Recherche Cognitive* 36–37 (2003), 205–25.

—— 'Dans quelle mesure Fichte est-il spinoziste?', in C. Bouton (ed.), *Dieu et la nature. La question du panthéisme dans l'idéalisme allemand*. Zurich: Olms, 2005.

—— 'Idéalisme et Spinozisme chez Fichte dans les Doctrines de la science de 1811 et 1812', in K.S. Ong Van Cung (ed.), *Idée et Idéalisme: Études sur l'idéalisme et le romantisme allemand II*, 149–65. Paris: Vrin, 2005.

—— 'Incarnation et philosophie dans l'idealisme allemand (Schelling, Hegel)', in J.-C. Goddard (ed.), *Le corps*. Paris: Vrin, 2005.

—— 'Schelling ou Fichte. L'être comme angoise ou l'être comme Bonheur', in A. Schnell (ed.), *Le bonheur*. Paris: Vrin, 2006.

— '1804–1805. La désubjectivation du transcendantal', *Archives de Philosophie* 72:3 (2009), 423–41.

— 'Fichte, ou la révolution aborigène permanente', in G. Marmasse and A. Schnell (eds.), *Comment fonder la philosophie ? L'idéalisme allemand et la question du principe premier*. Paris: CNRS Éditions, 2014.

— 'Fichte. Le hêtre et le palmier,' in J.-C. Lemaitre (ed.), *Jean-Marie Vaysse: cartographies de la pensée à la fin de la metaphysique*, 254–55. Hildesheim: Georg Olms Verlag, 2015.

— 'La non-existence de l'Occident. Graeber décolonial', *Anthropologie décoloniale*, 2021, <https://anthropodeco.hypotheses.org>.

— *Un brésilien noir et crasseux*. São Paulo: n-1 edições, 2017.

— and Alberto Rangel. *A Scabby Black Brazilian/Verdant Inferno*, tr. T. Murphy. Falmouth: Urbanomic, 2023.

Goldschmidt, Victor. 'Cours sur le premier chapitre de *Matière et Mémoire* (1960)', in F. Worms (ed.), *Annales bergsoniennes, I. Bergson dans le siècle*, 69–128. Paris: PUF, 2002.

Graeber, David. 'Radical Alterity is Just Another Way of Saying "Reality." A Reply to Eduardo Viveiros de Castro', *Hau: Journal of Ethnographic Theory* 5:2 (2015), 1–41.

Grothendieck, Alexander. *Recoltes et Semailles (English translation),* tr. R. Lisker, <https://uberty.org/wp-content/uploads/2015/12/RS-grothendeick1.pdf>.

— 'Allons-nous continuer la recherche scientifique?', *Écologie & politique* 52 (2016), 159–69.

— *Recoltes et Semailles I. Reflection et temoignage sur un passé de mathematicien*. Paris: Gallimard, 2022.

— and J.A. Dieudonné. *Éléments de Géométrie Algébrique I*. Berlin and Heidelberg: Springer-Verlag, 1971.

Grush, Rick. 'Self, World and Space: The Meaning and Mechanisms of Ego- and Allocentric Spatial Representation'. *Brain and Mind* 1 (2000), 59–92.

Habermas, Jürgen. *The Philosophical Discourse of Modernity: Twelve Lectures*, tr. F.G. Lawrence. Cambridge, MA: The MIT Press, 1998.

Hägglund, Martin. *This Life: Secular Faith and Spiritual Freedom*. New York: Pantheon Books, 2019.

Hall, John L., and L. Margulis. 'From Movement to Sensation', in L. Margulis, C.A. Asikainen, and W.E. Krumbein (eds.), *Chimeras and Consciousness*. Cambridge, MA: MIT Press, 2011.

Haraway, Donna. 'Situated Knowledges: The Science Question in Feminism and the Privilege of Partial Perspective', *Feminist Studies* 14:3 (1988), 575–99.

— *Staying With the Trouble: Making Kin in the Chthulucene*. Durham, NC and London: Duke University Press, 2016.

— 'A Cyborg Manifesto: Science, Technology, and Socialist-feminism in the Late Twentieth Century', in R. Latham (ed.), *Science Fiction Criticism. An Antology of Essential Writings*, 306–29. New York: Bloomsbury Academic, 2017.

Harman, Graham. 'Zero-person and the Psyche', in D. Skribina (ed.), *Mind that Abides: Panpsychism in the New Millennium*, 253–82. Amsterdam and Philadelphia: John Benjamins, 2009.

— *Object-Oriented Ontology: A New Theory of Everything*. London: Penguin Random House, 2017.

Harris, Michael. *Mathematics without Apologies: Portrait of a Problematic Vocation*. Princeton, NJ: Princeton University Press, 2015.

Hegel, Georg Wilhelm Friedrich. *On Christianity: Early Theological Writings*, tr. T.M. Knox. New York: Harper & Brothers, 1961.

— 'Who Thinks Abstractly?', in W. Kaufmann (ed.), *Hegel: Texts and Commentary*, 113–18. Garden City, NY: Anchor Books, 1966.

— *The Philosophy of Nature III,* tr. M. J. Petry. London: Allen and Unwin, 1970.

— *Phenomenology of Spirit*, tr. A.V. Miller. Oxford: Oxford University Press, 1977.

— *The Difference Between Fichte and Schelling's Philosophy*, tr. H.S. Harris and W. Cerf. Albany, NY: State University of New York Press, 1977.

— *Lectures on the Philosophy of Religion, Volume I: Introduction and the Concept of Religion*, ed. P. C. Hodgson, tr. R.F. Brown, P.C. Hodgson, and J.M. Stewart. Berkeley, CA: University of California Press, 1984.

— *Lectures on the Philosophy of World History. Introduction*, tr. H.B. Nisbet. New York: Cambridge University Press, 1998.

— *Philosophy of Right*, tr. S.W. Dyde. Kitchener, ON: Batoche Books, 2001.

— *Lectures on the Philosophy of Religion, Volume III, The Consummate Religion*, ed. P.C. Hodgson, tr. R.F. Brown, P.C. Hodgson, and J.M. Stewart. Oxford: Clarendon Press, 2007.

— *Lectures on the History of Philosophy 1825–6, Volume III: Medieval and Modern Philosophy*, tr. R.F. Brown. Oxford: Clarendon Press, 2009.

— *Encyclopedia of the Philosophical Sciences in Basic Outline Part I: Science of Logic*, tr. K. Brinkmann and D.O. Dahlstrom. Cambridge and New York: Cambridge University Press, 2010.

— *Philosophy of Mind*, tr. W. Wallace and A.V. Miller. Oxford: Clarendon Press, 2007.

HEIDEGGER, MARTIN. *Being and Time*, tr. J. Macquarrie and E. Robinson. Oxford: Blackwell, 1962.

— *What Is a Thing?*, tr. W.B. Barton, Jr. and V. Deutsch. Indianapolis: Gateway Editions, 1967.

— *Identity and Difference*. New York, Evanston, IL, and London: Harper & Row, 1969.

— *Schelling's Treatise on the Essence of Human Freedom*, tr. J. Stambaugh. Athens, OH: Ohio University Press, 1985.

— 'Letter on Humanism', in D.F. Krell (ed.), *Basic Writings*, 217–65. New York: HarperCollins, 1993.

— *Introduction to Metaphysics*, tr. G. Fried and R. Polt. New Haven, CT and London: Yale University Press, 2000.

— 'Why Poets?', in *Off the Beaten Track*, 200–241. Cambridge: Cambridge University Press, 2002.

— 'The Self-Assertion of the German University', tr. K Harries, in *Philosophical and Political Writings*, ed. M. Satssen, 2–11. New York: Continuum, 2003.

— 'Only a God Can Save Us: Der Spiegel's Interview with Martin Heidegger (September 23, 1966)', tr. M.P. Alter and J.D. Caputo, in *Philosophical and Political Writings*, ed. M. Satssen, 24–48. New York: Continuum, 2006.

HENRY, MICHEL. *L'amour les yeux fermés*. Paris: Editions Gallimard, 1976.

— *The Essence of Manifestation*, tr. G. Etzkorn. The Hague: Martinus Nijhoff, 1984.

— *Phénoménologie matérielle*. Paris: Presses Universitaire de France, 1990.

— *C'est moi la Vérité. Pour une philosophie du christianisme*. Paris: Seuil, 1996.

— *Paroles de Christ*. Paris: Seuil, 2002.

— *Généalogie de la psychanalyse. Le commencement perdu*. Paris: Presses Universitaires de France, 2003.

— *La barbarie*. Paris: Presses Universitaires de France, 2004.

— *Le bonheur de Spinoza*. Paris: Presses Universitaires de France, 2004.

— *Entretiens*. Arles: Sulliver, 2005.

— 'The Four Principles of Phenomenology', tr. J. Rivera and G.E. Faithful, *Continental Philosophy Review* 48 (2015), 1–21.

— and Caruana, Virginie. 'Entretien avec Michel Henry', *Philosophique* 3 (2000), 69–80, <http://journals.openedition.org/philosophique/230>.

Herbert, Frank. *Dune*. London: Penguin, 2003.

Herder, Johann Gottlieb. *God, Some Conversations*, tr. F.H. Burkhardt. Indianapolis: Bobbs-Merrill, 1940.

Hess, Moses. 'The Philosophy of the Act', in A. Fried and R. Sanders (eds.), *Socialist Thought: A Documentary History*, 260–70. Chicago: Aldine, 1964.

Hilbert, David. 'Die Rolle von idealen Gebilden', in D. Rowe (ed.), *Natur und mathematisches Erkennen*, 90–101. Basel: Birkhäuser, 1992.

— 'Über das Unendliche', *Matematische Annalen* 95 (1926), 161–90.

— 'On the Infinite', in P. Benacerraf and H. Putnam (eds.), *Philosophy of Mathematics: Selected Readings*, 183–201. Cambridge: Cambridge University Press, 1984.

Hiller, Daniel Rudy. 'La dernière crise gnostique: Pascal et le gnosticisme ad hominem', *Philosophiques* 45:1 (2018), 3–20.

Hölderlin, Friedrich. 'Bread and Wine', in *Poems*, tr. J. Mitchell, 14. San Francisco: Ithuriel's Spear, 2004.

— 'Homecoming', in *Selected Poems and Fragments*, tr. M. Hamburger. London: Penguin, 1998.

— 'In lieblicher Bläue', in *Sämtliche Werke*, éd. F. Beissner, vol. 2, 372. Stuttgart: W. Kohlhammer Verlag, 1951.

— 'On Religion', 'Judgement and Being', in *Essays and Letters on Theory*, tr. T. Pfau. New York: State University of New York Press, 1987.

— 'Remarks on the Oedipus', in *Essays and Letters,* tr. J. Adler and C. Louth. London: Penguin, 2009.

— *Hyperion & Selected Poems*, tr. W.R. Trask. New York: Continuum, 1990.

— *The Death of Empedocles. A Mourning Play*, tr. D.F. Krell. New York: SUNY Press, 2008.

Husserl, Edmund. 'Philosophy as a Strict Science', tr. Q. Lauer, *CrossCurrents* 6:3 (1956), 227–46.

— *Cartesian Meditations. An Introduction to Phenomenology*, tr. D. Cairns. The Hague: Martinus Nijhoff, 1960.

— *Experience and Judgment: Investigations in a Genealogy of Logic*, tr. J.S. Churchill and K. Ameriks. Evanston, IL: Northwestern University Press, 1973.

—— *Ideas Pertaining to a Pure Phenomenology and to a Phenomenological Philosophy. First Book: General Introduction to a Pure Phenomenology*, tr. F. Kersten. The Hague: Martinus Nijhoff, 1983.

—— *Ideas Pertaining to a Pure Phenomenology and to a Phenomenological Philosophy: Second Book: Studies in the Phenomenology of Constitution*, tr. R. Rojcewicz and A. Schuwer. Dordrecht: Kluwer, 1989.

—— *The Crisis of European Sciences and Transcendental Phenomenology*. Evanston, IL: Northwestern University Press, 1978.

—— *Die Lebenswelt. Auslegungen der vorgegebenen Welt und ihrer Konstitution. Texte aus dem Nachlass (1916–1937), Gesameltte Werke, Band XXXIX*, ed. R. Sowa. Dordrecht: Springer, 2008.

Huxley, Aldous. *The Doors of Perception and Heaven and Hell.* New York: Harper and Row, 1954.

Hyppolite, Jean. 'L'idée fichtéenne de la doctrine de la science et le projet husserlien', in *Figures de la pensée philosophique, I*, 22–31. Paris: PUF, 1971.

Illich, Ivan. 'The Institutional Construction of a New Fetish: Human Life', in *In the Mirror of the Past: Lectures and Addresses, 1978–1990*, 218–32. London: Marion Boyars, 1992.

Infeld, Leopold. 'From Copernicus to Einstein', in B. Bienkowska and Z. Kopal (eds.), *The Scientific World of Copernicus: On the Occasion of the 500th Anniversary of his Birth 1473–1973*, 66–83. Dordrecht: D. Reidel, 1973.

Jackson, Michael. 'Knowledge of the Body', in *Paths Towards a Clearing: Radical Empiricism and Ethnographic Inquiry*, 119–36. Bloomington and Indianapolis: Indiana University Press, 1989.

—— 'Persons and Types', in *As Wide as the World is Wise: Reinventing Philosophical Anthropology*, 137–52. New York: Columbia University Press, 2016.

Jacobi, Friedrich Heinrich. *Main Philosophical Writings and the Novel Allwill*, tr. G. di Giovanni. Montreal: McGill-Queen's University Press, 1994.

James, William. 'Does "Consciousness" Exist?,' 'How Two Minds Can Know One Thing', in *Essays in Radical Empiricism*. Lincoln, NE: University of Nebraska Press, 1996.

—— *The Meaning of Truth.* New York: Longman Green and Co., 1911.

Jiménez, Reynaldo. 'Del endés y su demasiada', in P. Leminski, *Catatau*, tr. R. Jiménez. Madrid: Libros de la Resistencia, 2019.

Jonas, Hans. *The Phenomenon of Life: Towards a Philosophical Biology*. Evanston, IL: Northwestern University Press, 2001.

— *The Imperative of Responsibility: In Search of Ethics for the Technological Age*, tr. H. Jonas and D. Herr. Chicago, IL: University of Chicago Press, 1984.

JOYCE, JAMES. *A Portrait of the Artist as a Young Man*. Oxford: Oxford University Press, 2000.

— *Finnegans Wake*. Oxford: Oxford University Press, 2012.

— *Ulysses*. London: Penguin, 2000.

JUNG, CARL GUSTAV. 'A Psychological Approach to the Dogma of the Trinity', in *Psychology and Religion: West and East*. Princeton, NJ: Princeton University Press, 1958.

— 'Psychotherapists or the Clergy?', in *Modern Man in Search of a Soul*, tr. W.S. Dell and C.F. Baynes. New York: Harcourt, 1933.

KAC, MARK. 'Can One Hear the Shape of a Drum?', *American Mathematical Monthly* 73:4.2 (1966), 1–23.

KAFKA, FRANZ. *The Diaries of Franz Kafka, Volume Two, 1914–1923*, ed. M. Brod, tr. M. Greenberg and H. Arendt. New York: Secker and Warburg, 1949.

KANT, IMMANUEL. 'What Does it Mean to Orient Oneself in Thinking?', in *Religion and Rational Theology*, tr. A.W. Wood. Cambridge: Cambridge University Press 1996.

— *Critique of Pure Reason*, tr. P. Guyer and A.W. Wood. Cambridge and New York: Cambridge University Press, 2000.

— *Opus Postumum*, tr. E. Förster and M. Rosen. Cambridge: Cambridge University Press, 1993.

— *Philosophical Correspondence, 1759*–1799, ed. A. Zweig. Chicago: University of Chicago Press, 1967.

— *Prolegomena to Any Future Metaphysics That Will Be Able to Come Forward as Science*, tr. G. Hatfield. Cambridge and New York: Cambridge University Press, 2004.

— *Religion within the Boundaries of Mere Reason And Other Writings*, tr. and ed. A. Wood and G di Giovanni. Cambridge: Cambridge University Press, 1998.

KLOSSOWSKI, PIERRE. *The Baphomet*, tr. S. Hawkes and S. Sartarelli. Hygiene, CO: Eridianos Press, 1988.

KOESTLER, ARTHUR. *The Ghost in the Machine*. London: Pan, 1970.

KOHN, EDUARDO. *How Forests Think: Toward an Anthopology Beyond the Human*. Berkeley and Los Angeles, CA: University of California Press, 2013.

KOPENAWA, DAVI, AND BRUCE ALBERT. *The Falling Sky: Words of a Yanomami Shaman*, tr. N. Elliott and A. Dundy. Cambridge, MA: The Belknap Press of Harvard University Press, 2013.

Krakauer, David, Nils Bertschinger, Eckehard Olbrich, Nihat Ay and Jessica C. Flack, 'The Information Theory of Individuality', *Theory in Biosciences* 139 (2020), 209–23.

Kuhn, Thomas. *The Road Since Structure: Philosophical Essays, 1970–1993, with an Autobiographical Interview*, ed. J. Conant and J. Haugeland. Chicago and London: University of Chicago Press, 2000.

Labou Tansi, Sony. *Encre, sueur, salive et sang*. Paris: Seuil, 2015.

Lacan, Jacques. *Autres écrits*. Paris: Éditions du Seuil, 2001.

— *The Seminar of Jacques Lacan, Book XX: Encore 1972–1973, On Feminine Sexuality, The Limits of Love and Knowledge*, tr. B. Fink, ed. J.-A. Miller. New York and London: Norton.

— *R.S.I. The Seminar of Jacques Lacan, Book XXII (1973–1974)*, tr. C. Gallagher, <http://www.lacaninireland.com/web/translations/seminars/>, undated.

— *The Ethics of Psychoanalysis. The Seminar of Jacques Lacan. Book VII, 1959–1960*, ed. J.-A. Miller, tr. D. Porter. New York: Norton, 1992.

— *The Seminar of Jacques Lacan, Book XI: The Four Fundamental Concepts of Psychoanalysis*, tr. A. Sheridan, ed. J.-A. Miller. New York and London: Norton, 1998.

— *Anxiety. The Seminar of Jacques Lacan, Book X (1962–1963)*, tr. A.R. Price. Cambridge: Polity, 2014.

— *...or Worse: The Seminar of Jacques Lacan, Book XIX*, tr. A.R. Price. Cambridge: Polity, 2018.

Lacoste, Jean-Yves. *Expérience et Absolu*. Paris: Presses Universitaires de France, 1994.

Lacoue-Labarthe, Philippe. 'Hölderlin's Theatre', in M. de Beistegui and S. Sparks (eds.), *Philosophy and Tragedy*, 117–36. London: Routledge, 2000.

— *Typography: Mimesis, Philosophy, Politics*. Cambridge, MA: Harvard University Press, 1989.

LaCugna, Catherine Mowry. 'God in Communion with Us—The Trinity—', in C.M. LaCugna (ed.), *Freeing Theology: The Essentials of Theology in Feminist Perspective*. New York: HarperCollins, 1993.

Lamm, Julia A. 'Schleiermacher's Post-Kantian Spinozism: The Early Essays on Spinoza, 1793–94', *The Journal of Religion* 74:4 (1994), 476–505.

Land, Nick. *The Thirst for Annihilation: Georges Bataille and Virulent Nihilism*. London: Routledge, 1992.

— *Fanged Noumena: Collected Writings 1987–2007*. Falmouth and New York: Urbanomic/ Sequence Press, 2011.

Laruelle, François. 'Les effets-Levinas. Lettre non-philosophique du 30 Mai 2006', Organisation Non-Philosophique Internationale.

Las Señoras del Arcoiris. *Documentos de la Escuela Nocturna*. Buenos Aires: Hekht, 2015.

Lautréamont, Comte de. *Maldoror*, tr. P. Knight. London: Penguin Classics, 1978.

Lawrence, D.H. 'Apocalypse', in M. Kalnins (ed.), *Apocalypse and the Writings on Revelation*. Cambridge: Cambridge University Press, 1980.

Leary, Timothy. *Start Your Own Religion*. Berkeley, CA: Ronin Publishing, 2005.

Leminski, Paulo. *Catatau*. São Paulo: Editora Iluminuras, 2010.

— *Catatau*, tr. R. Jiménez. Madrid: Libros de la Resistencia, 2019.

Lessing, Gotthold Ephraim. *Philosophical and Theological Writings*, tr. H.B. Nisbet. Cambridge: Cambridge University Press, 2005.

Levinas, Emmanuel. 'God and Onto-Theo-Logy', in *God, Death and Time*, tr. B. Bergo, 121–224. Stanford, CA: Stanford University Press, 2000.

— 'Heidegger, Gagarin and Us', in *Difficult Freedom: Essays on Judaism*, tr. S. Hand, 231–34. Baltimore, MD: The Johns Hopkins University Press, 1990.

— *Existence and Existents*, tr. A. Lingis. The Hague: Martinus Nijhoff, 1978.

— *Time and the Other*, tr. R.A. Cohen. Pittsburgh, PA: Duquesne University Press, 1987.

— *Totality and Infinity*, tr. A. Lingis. Pittsburgh, PA: Duquesne University Press, 1979.

Lévi-Strauss, Claude. *Introduction to the Work of Marcel Mauss*, tr. F. Baker. London: Routledge & Kegan Paul, 1987.

— *The Naked Man. Introduction to a Science of Mythology, Vol. 4*, tr. J. and D. Weightman. New York: Harper & Row, 1981.

Lewis, Clarence Irving. *Mind and the World-Order: Outline of a Theory of Knowledge*. New York: Dover, 1956.

Lezama Lima, José. 'Preludio a las eras imaginarias', in *Ensayos barrocos. Imagen y figuras en América latina*. Buenos Aires: Ediciones Colihue, 2014.

— *El reino de la imagen*. Caracas: Biblioteca Ayacucho, 1981.

— *La dignidad de la poesía*, in *Tratados de la Habana*. Buenos Aires: Ediciones de la Flor, 1969.

— *La expresión americana*. Mexico, D.F.: Fondo de Cultura Económica, 1993.

— *Paradiso*. Madrid: Ediciones Cátedra, 1997.

LICHTENBERG, GEORG CHRISTOPH. *Philosophical Writings*, tr. S. Tester. Albany, NY: SUNY Press, 2012.

LISPECTOR, CLARICE. *Agua Viva*, tr. S. Tobler. New York: New Directions, 2012.

— *Near to the Wild Heart*, tr. A. Entrekin. London: Penguin, 2014.

— *The Passion According to G.H.*, tr. I. Novey. New York: New Directions, 2012.

LORENZ, KONRAD. 'Kant's Doctrine of the A Priori in the Light of Contemporary Biology', in M. Ruse (ed.), *Philosophy after Darwin. Classical and Contemporary Readings*, 231–47. Princeton, NJ: Princeton University Press, 2009.

LOVECRAFT, HOWARD PHILIPS. *The Call of Cthulhu and Other Weird Stories*. London: Penguin, 2012.

LOVEJOY, ARTHUR. *The Great Chain of Being*. Cambridge, MA: Harvard University Press, 2001.

LUTHER, MARTIN. 'Heidelberg Disputation' (1518), in *Martin Luther's Basic Theological Writings*, ed. T.F. Lull. Minneapolis: Fortress Press, 1989.

LYOTARD, JEAN-FRANÇOIS. *The Postmodern Explained. Correspondence 1982–1985*, tr. B. Don et al. Minneapolis: University Of Minnesota Press, 1992.

— *Moralités postmodernes*. Paris: Galilée, 1993.

— *The Inhuman: Reflections on Time*. Stanford, CA: Stanford University Press, 1991.

MAC LANE, SAUNDERS, and IEKE MOERDIJK. *Sheaves in Geometry and Logic. A First Introduction to Topos Theory*. New York: Springer-Verlag, 1992.

MALABOU, CATHERINE. 'Can We Relinquish the Transcendental?', *Journal of Speculative Philosophy* 28:3 (2014), 242–255.

MALLARMÉ, STÉPHANE. *Correspondance complète 1862–1871. Lettres sur la poésie 1872–1898*, ed. B. Marchal. Paris: Gallimard, 1995.

— *'A Throw of the Dice'*, in *Collected Poems*, tr. H. Weinfield. Berkeley and Los Angeles: University of California Press, 1994.

— 'Notes sur le Langage', in B. Marchal (ed.), *Igitur, Divagations, un coup de dés*. Paris: Éditions Gallimard, 2003.

— 'Offices', in R.G. Cohn, *Mallarmé's Divagations: A Guide and Commentary*. New York: Peter Lang, 1990.

— *Divagations*, tr. B. Johnson. Cambridge, MA and London: Belknap Press, 2007.

MARECHAL, LEOPOLDO. 'Didáctica de la Patria', in *Heptamerón*. Buenos Aires: Sudamericana, 1974.

— *Megafón o la guerra*. Barcelona: Seix Barral, 2014.

MARGULIS, LYNN. *Symbiosis as a Source of Evolutionary Innovation*. Cambridge, MA: MIT Press, 2016.

— and DICK TERESI. 'Discover Interview: Lynn Margulis Says She's Not Controversial, She's Right', *Discover Magazine*, 17 June 2011, <https://www.discovermagazine.com/the-sciences/discover-interview-lynn-margulis-says-shes-not-controversial-shes-right>.

MARION, JEAN-LUC. *God Without Being*. Chicago: University of Chicago Press, 1991.

— 'The Reduction and the "Fourth Principle"', *Analecta Hermeneutica* 8 (2016), 41–63.

— *Reduction and Givenness: Investigations of Husserl, Heidegger, and Phenomenology*, tr. T.A. Carlson. Evanston, IL: Northwestern University Press, 1998.

MARX, KARL. *Capital: A Critique of Political Economy, Volume One,* tr. B. Fowkes. London: Penguin, 1990.

— *Economic and Philosophical Manuscripts*, tr. M. Milligan. New York, Prometheus Books, 1988.

— and F. ENGELS. *The German Ideology*. New York: Prometheus Books, 1998.

MCLARTY, COLIN. '"There is No Ontology Here": Visual and Structural Geometry in Arithmetic', in P. Mancosu (ed.), *The Philosophy of Mathematical Practice*, 370–406. Oxford: Oxford University Press, 2008.

MEILLASSOUX, QUENTIN. *After Finitude. An Essay on the Necessity of Contingency*, tr. R. Brassier. London: Continuum, 2008.

— *The Number and the Siren*, tr. R. Mackay. Falmouth and New York: Urbanomic/Sequence Press, 2012.

MERLEAU-PONTY, MAURICE. 'Faith and Good Faith', in *Sense and Nonsense*, tr. H.L. Dreyfus and P.A. Dreyfus. Evanston, IL: Northwestern University Press, 1964.

— *Husserl at the Limits of Phenomenology. Including Texts by Edmund Husserl*, eds. L. Lawlor and B. Bergo. Evanston, IL: Northwestern University Press, 2002.

— *The Primacy of Perception*. Evanston, IL: Northwestern University Press, 1964.

— *The Visible and the Invisible. Followed by Working Notes*, ed. C. Lefort, tr. A. Lingis. Evanston, IL: Northwestern University Press, 1968.

MESTRANO, NICOLE, and CARLOS SIMPSON. 'Stacks,' in M. Anel and G. Catren (eds.), *New Spaces in Mathematics: Formal and Conceptual Reflections*, 462–504. Cambridge: Cambridge University Press, 2021.

METZINGER, THOMAS. *Being No One: The Self-Model Theory of Subjectivity*. Cambridge, MA: MIT Press, 2003.

MICHAUX, HENRI. *Le jardin exalté*. Montpellier: Fata Morgana, 1983.

MILLER, HENRY. 'The Enormous Womb', in Henry Miller and Arnold S. Miller, *The Wisdom of the Heart*. New York: New Directions, 1941.

—— *Hamlet's Letters*, ed. M. Hargraves. Santa Barbara, CA: Capra Press, 1988.

MONOD, JACQUES. *Chance and Necessity: An Essay on the Natural Philosophy of Modern Biology*, tr. A. Wainhouse. New York: Alfred A. Knopf, 1971.

MORRISON, JIM. 'The Lords', in F. Lisciandro (ed.), *The Collected Works of Jim Morrison. Poetry, Journals, Transcripts, and Lyrics*. London and New York: Harper Design, 2021.

NAGEL, THOMAS. *The View From Nowhere*. Oxford: Oxford University Press, 1986.

NAKH AB RA, 'Breve Diccionario de Brujería Portátil', in J. Salzano (ed.), *Nosotros, los brujos. Apuntes de arte, poesía y brujería*. Buenos Aires: Santiago Arcos, 2008.

NANCY, JEAN-LUC. *The Inoperative Community*, tr. P. Connor et al. Minneapolis and Oxford: University of Minnesota Press, 1991.

NEGARESTANI, REZA. 'The Corpse Bride. Thinking with Nigredo', in R. Mackay (ed.), *Collapse IV: Concept-Horror*, 129–61. Falmouth: Urbanomic, 2012.

—— 'Globe of Revolution: An Afterthought on Geophilosophical Realism', *Identities: Journal for Politics, Gender and Culture* 8:2 (2011), 25–54.

NEGRI, ANTONIO. *The Savage Anomaly. The Power of Spinoza's Metaphysics and Politics*, tr. M. Hardt. Minneapolis: University of Minnesota Press, 1991.

NERVAL, GÉRARD DE. *Selected Writings*. London: Penguin, 1999.

NICOLAS OF CUSA, *On Learned Ignorance*, tr. J. Hopkin. Minneapolis: The Arthur J. Banning Press, 1990.

NIETZSCHE, FRIEDRICH. 'On Truth and Lying in an Extra-Moral Sense', in *On Rhetoric and Language,* tr. S.L. Gilman, C. Blair and D.J. Parent, 246–67. Oxford: Oxford University Press, 1989.

—— 'The Anti-Christ', in *The Anti-Christ, Ecce Homo, Twilight of the Idols and Other Writings*, tr. J. Norman. Cambridge: Cambridge University Press, 2005.

—— *Birth of Tragedy and Other Writings*, tr. R. Speirs. Cambridge: Cambridge University Press, 2007.

—— *The Gay Science*, tr. J. Nauckhoff. Cambridge: Cambridge University Press, 2007.

NODARI, ALEXANDRE. '"A transformação do Tabu em totem": notas sobre (um)a fórmula antropofágica', *Das Questões* 2:2 (2015), <https://periodicos.unb.br/index.php/dasquestoes/article/view/18320>.

NOVALIS. *Fragmente und Studien 1799/1800*. Paderborn, Munich, Vienna and Zurich: Ferdinand Schöningh, 1987.

—— *Schriften, Dritter Band*. Stuttgart: Kohlhammer Verlag, 1968.

Nozick, Robert. 'Invariance and Objectivity', *Proceedings and Addresses of the American Philosophical Association* 72:2 (1998), 21–48.

Ogden, C.K. *Basic English: A General Introduction with Rules and Grammar*, 3rd ed. London: Kegan Paul, Trench, Trubner & Company, 1932.

Panofsky, Erwin. *Perspective as Symbolic Form*, tr. C. Wood. New York: Zone, 1991.

Pascal, Blaise. *Thoughts, Letters and Minor Works*, tr. W.F. Trotter. New York: P.F. Collier & Son, 1910.

Pasolini, Pier Paolo. *Palabras de corsario*. Madrid: Editorial Círculo de Bellas Artes, 2005.

—— *Heretical Empiricism*, tr. B. Lawton and L.K. Barnett. Washington, DC: New Academia Publishing, 2005.

Pasquinelli, Matteo. 'Machines that Morph Logic: Neural Networks and the Distorted Automation of Intelligence as Statistical Inference', *Glass Bead* 1 (2017), < https://www.glass-bead.org/article/machines-that-morph-logic/>.

Patočka, Jan. *Le monde naturel et le mouvement de l'existence humaine*. Dordrecht: Kluwer, 1988.

Pendell, Dale. *Pharmako/Gnosis: Plant Teachers and the Poison Path*. Berkeley, CA: North Atlantic Books, 2009.

Perlongher, Néstor. 'Autosacramental del Santo Daime', *Revista de poesía Tsé-Tsé* 9/10 (2001).

—— 'Caribe Transplatino', in *Prosa Plebeya. Ensayos 1980–1992*, 96. Buenos Aires: Colihue, 2008.

—— 'Aguas Aéreas' in *Poemas completos*. Buenos Aires: La Flauta Mágica, 2002.

—— 'Chorreo de las iluminaciones', in *Poemas completos*. Buenos Aires: La Flauta Mágica, 2002.

—— 'Sopa Paraguaya', in W. Bueno, *Mar paraguayo*, 9. Buenos Aires: Interzona, 2020.

Petitot, Jean, and Francisco J. Varela, Bernard Pachoud, and Jean-Michel Roy (eds.). *Naturaliser la phénoménologie. Essais sur la phénoménologie contemporaine et les sciences cognitives*. Paris: CNRS Editions, 2002.

Philipps, Steven. 'Going Beyond the Data as the Patching (Sheaving) of Local Knowledge', *Frontiers in Psychology* 9 (2008).

Piaget, Jean. 'Piaget's Theory', in B. Inhelder and H.H. Chipman (eds.), *Piaget and his School. A Reader in Developmental Psychology*. New York: Springer-Verlag, 1976.

PIPER, ADRIAN M.S. 'Xenophobia and Kantian Rationalism', *Philosophical Forum* 24:1–3 (1992–93), 188–232.

PIZARNIK, ALEJANDRA. *Diarios*, ed. A. Becciú. Barcelona: Lumen, 2013.

PLANTINGA, ALVIN. *Warrant and Proper Function*. New York: Oxford University Press, 1993.

PRADO JR., BENTO. *Présence et champ transcendental. Conscience et négativité dans la philosophie de Bergson*, tr. R. Barbaras. Paris: Olms, 2002.

PRIGOGINE, ILYA, and ISABELLE STENGERS. *La Nouvelle Alliance. Métamorphose de la science*. Paris: Éditions Gallimard, 1979.

PUTNAM, HILARY. 'There Is At Least One *A Priori* Truth', in *Realism and Reason: Philosophical Papers, Volume 3*, 98–114. Cambridge: Cambridge University Press, 1983.

PYNCHON, THOMAS. *Against the Day*. New York: Penguin Books, 2007.

— *Gravity's Rainbow*. New York: Viking, 1973.

— *Mason & Dixon*. New York: Henry Holt, 1997.

QUINE, WILLARD VAN ORMAN. 'Two Dogmas of Empiricism', in *From a Logical Point of View*, 20–46. New York: Harper & Row, 1963.

RAHNER, KARL. *The Trinity*, tr. J. Donceel. New York: Continuum, 2001.

REICHENBACH, HANS. *Selected Writings 1909–1953: Volume One*, ed. E.H. Schneewind et al. Dordrecht: Springer, 1978.

— *The Philosophy of Space and Time*. New York: Dover, 1958.

RICHTER, HENDRIK AND ANDREAS P. ENGELBRECHT (eds.). *Recent Advances in the Theory and Application of Fitness Landscapes*. Berlin and Heidelberg: Springer-Verlag, 2014.

RICHTER, JEAN-PAUL. 'Speech of the Dead Christ from the Universe that There Is No God', in *Jean Paul: A Reader*, tr. E. Casey, 179–83. Baltimore, MD: Johns Hopkins University Press, 1992.

— *Sämmtliche Werke*. Paris: Tétot Frères, 65 vols., 1837.

RICHTER-GEBERT, JÜRGEN. *Perspectives on Projective Geometry: A Guided Tour Through Real and Complex Geometry*. Berlin and Heidelberg: Springer-Verlag, 2011.

RILKE, RAINER MARIA. *Duino Elegies*, tr. E. Snow. New York: North Point Press, 2000.

— *Letters of Rainer Maria Rilke 1910–1926*, tr. J.B. Greene and M.D. Herter Norton. New York: The Norton Library, 1947.

RIMBAUD, ARTHUR. *Complete Works, Selected Letters*, tr. W. Fowlie. Chicago: The University of Chicago Press, 2005.

ROLLAND, ROMAIN. *L'éclair de Spinoza*. Paris: Éditions Manucius, 2014.

ROSENBLATT, FRANK. *Principles of Neurodynamics: Perceptrons and the Theory of Brain Mechanisms*. Buffalo, NY: Cornell Aeronautical Laboratory, 1961.

ROUSSEAU, JEAN-JACQUES. *The Social Contract and Other Later Political Essays*. Cambridge: Cambridge University Press, 1997.

ROVELLI, CARLO. *Quantum Gravity*. Cambridge: Cambridge University Press, 2004.

ROZITCHNER, LÉON. 'Primero hay que saber vivir', *El Ojo Mocho. Revista de crítica política y cultural* 20 (2006).

— *No matar. Sobre la responsabilidad*. Cordoba: La intemperie, 2007.

— *La Cosa y la Cruz. Cristianismo y Capitalismo (en torno a las Confesiones de San Agustín)*. Buenos Aires: Ediciones Biblioteca Nacional, 2015.

— *Levinas o la filosofía de la consolación*. Buenos Aires: Biblioteca Nacional, 2013.

— *Materialismo ensoñado*. Buenos Aires: Tinta Limón Ediciones, 2011.

RUSHDIE, SALMAN. *Haroun and The Sea of Stories*. London: Puffin, 2012.

SAILER, S.S. 'Universalizing Languages: "Finnegans Wake" Meets Basic English', *James Joyce Quarterly* 36:4 (Summer 1999), 853–68.

SAMBIN, GIOVANNI AND SILVIO VALENTINI. 'Building up a Toolbox for Martin-Lof's Type Theory: Subset Theory,' in G. Sambin and J.M. Smith (eds.), *Twenty-five Years of Constructive Type Theory: Proceedings of a Congress Held in Venice, October 1995*. Oxford: Oxford University Press, 1998.

SARTRE, JEAN-PAUL. 'Intentionality: A Fundamental Idea of Husserl's Phenomenology', in D. Moran and T. Mooney (eds.), *The Phenomenology Reader*, 382–84. London: Routledge, 2002.

— *Being and Nothingness*, tr. H.E. Barnes. New York: Washington Square Press, 1984.

— *The Transcendence of the Ego*, tr. A. Brown. London and New York: Routledge, 2004.

SCHAUL, TOM, and JÜRGEN SCHMIDHUBER. 'Metalearning', *Scholarpedia* 5(6): 4650 (2010), <http://www.scholarpedia.org/article/Metalearning>.

SCHELLING, FRIEDRICH WILHELM JOSEPH. 'Presentation of My System of Philosophy',' tr. M. Vater, *The Philosophical Forum* 32:4 (Winter 2001), 339–71.

— *First Outline of a System of the Philosophy of Nature*, tr. K.R. Peterson. Albany, NY: State University of New York Press, 2004.

— *On the History of Modern Philosophy*, tr. A. Bowie. Cambridge: Cambridge University Press, 1994.

— *Philosophical Investigations into the Essence of Human Freedom*, tr. J. Love and J. Schmidt. Albany, NY: State University of New York Press, 2006.

— 'On the True Concept of Philosophy of Nature and the Correct Way of Solving its Problems', tr. D. Whistler and J. Kahl, *Pli: The Warwick Journal of Philosophy* 26 (2014), 24–45.

— *The Ages of the World (1811)*, tr. J.P. Lawrence. New York: SUNY Press, 2019.

SCHLEGEL, FRIEDRICH. *Characteristiken und Kritiken I (1796–1801)*. Munich: Ferdinand Schöningh, 1967.

SCHLEIERMACHER, FRIEDRICH. *On Religion: Speeches to its Cultured Despisers*, tr. R. Crouter. Cambridge and New York: Cambridge University Press, 1996.

SCHMIDHUBER, JÜRGEN. *Evolutionary Principles in Self-Referential Learning*, Diploma Thesis, Tech. Univ. Munich, 1987.

SCHMITT, CARL. *The Nomos of the Earth in the International Law of the Jus Publicum Europaeum*, tr. G.L. Ulmen. New York: Telos, 2006.

SCHOPENHAUER, ARTHUR. *The World as Will and Representation*, tr. E.F.J. Payne. New York: Dover, 2 vols., 1969.

SHELLEY, MARY. *Frankenstein; or, The Modern Prometheus*. Project Gutenberg, <https://www.gutenberg.org/ebooks/84>.

SHELLEY, PERCY BYSSE. *Prometheus Unbound*. London, 1821.

SIMPSON, CARLOS T. 'Descent', in L. Schneps (ed.), *Alexandre Grothendieck: A Mathematical Portrait*, 83–141. Somerville, MA: International Press, 2014.

SOLÉ, JIMENA (ed.). *Jacobi, Mendelssohn, Wizenmann, Kant, Goethe, Herder. El ocaso de la ilustración. La polémica del Spinozismo*. Bernal and Buenos Aires: Universidad Nacional de Quilmes Editorial/Prometeo 3010, 2013.

SPINOZA, BARUCH. *Ethics: Proved in Geometrical Order*, tr. M. Silverthorne and M.J. Kisner. Cambridge: Cambridge University Press, 2018.

— *Theological-Political Treatise*, tr. M. Silverthorne and J. Israel. New York: Cambridge University Press, 2007.

STJERNFELT, FREDERIK. *Diagrammatology: An Investigation on the Borderlines of Phenomenology, Ontology, and Semiotics*. Dordrecht: Springer, 2007.

STRAWSON, GALEN. 'Realistic Monism: Why Physicalism Entails Panpsychism', in D. Skribina (ed.), *Mind that Abides: Panpsychism in the New Millennium*. Amsterdam and Philadelphia, PA: John Benjamins Publishing Company, 2009.

STROGATZ, STEVEN H. *Nonlinear Dynamics and Chaos: With Applications to Physics, Biology, Chemistry, and Engineering*. New York: Perseus Books, 1994.

Sun Ra, *The Immeasurable Equation: The Collected Poetry and Prose*, ed. J.L. Wolf and H. Geerken. Norderstedt: Waitawhile, 2005.

Taylor, Charles. *A Catholic Modernity: Charles Taylor's Marianist Award Lecture*. Oxford: Oxford University Press, 1999.

— *A Secular Age*. Cambridge, MA and London: The Belknap Press of Harvard University Press, 2007.

Teilhard de Chardin, Pierre. *Hymn of the Universe*, tr. Gerald Vann. London: Collins, 1970.

— *The Human Phenomenon*. London: Harper Perennial, 1958.

Thom, René. *Semio Physics: A Sketch*, tr. V. Meyer. Boston: Addison-Wesley, 1990.

Touam Bona, Dénètem. *Sagesse des lianes. Cosmopoétique du refuge, 1. Post-éditions*, 2021.

Valéry, Paul. 'The Crisis of the Mind', tr. D. Folliot and J. Matthews, in *Paul Valéry, An Anthology*, 94. London: Routledge, 1977.

— 'Variation sur une Pensée', in *Variété I et II*, 118. Paris: Gallimard, 1930.

— *Œuvres Complètes*. Paris: Gallimard, 2 vols., 1960.

Vallier, Robert. 'Être Sauvage and the Barbaric Principle: Merleau-Ponty's Reading of Schelling', in J.M. Wirth and P. Burke (eds.), *The Barbarian Principle: Merleau-Ponty, Schelling, and the Question of Nature*. New York: State University of New York Press, 2013.

Vaquié, Michel. 'Sheaves and Functors of Points', in M. Anel and G. Catren (eds.), *New Spaces in Mathematics. Formal and Conceptual Reflections*, 407–61. Cambridge: Cambridge University Press, 2021.

Varela, Francisco J. 'Neurophenomenology: A Methodological Remedy for the Hard Problem', *Journal of Consciousness Studies* 3:4 (1996), 330–49.

Vaysse, Jean-Marie. *Totalité et Finitude. Spinoza et Heidegger*. Paris: Vrin, 2004.

Verne, Jules. *Twenty Thousand Leagues Under the Sea*, <https://www.gutenberg.org/ebooks/164>.

Viveiros de Castro, Eduardo. 'Cosmological Deixis and Amerindian Perspectivism', *Journal of the Royal Anthropological Institute* 4:3 (September 1998), 469–88.

— 'Les involontaires de la patrie', *Multitudes* 69 (2017), 123–28.

— 'Perspectival Anthropology and the Method of Controlled Equivocation', *Tipití: Journal of the Society for the Anthropology of Lowland South America* 2:1 (2004), 3–22.

— 'The Crystal Forest: Notes on the Ontology of Amazonian Spirits', *Inner Asia* 9:2 (2007), 153–72.

—— 'Zénon d'Hiléia', Foreword to Jean-Christophe Goddard, *Un brésilien noir et crasseux*. São Paulo: n-1 edições, 2017.

—— *Cannibal Metaphysics,* tr. P. Skafish. Minneapolis: Univocal, 2014.

—— 'Le monde a commence sans l'homme et s'achèvera sans lui', Postface to Ailton Krenak, *Idées pour retarder la fin du monde*, 55–56. France: Éditions Dehors, 2020.

—— 'Metaphysics as Mitophysics. Or, Why I Have Always Been an Anthropologist', in P. Charbonnier, G. Salmon, and P. Skafish (eds.), *Comparative Metaphysics: Ontology After Anthropology*. New York: Rowman & Littlefield, 2017.

—— 'Rosa e Clarice, a fera e o fora/Rosa and Clarice, the Beast and the Outside', *Revista Letras, Curitiba, UPFR* 98 (2018), 9–30.

—— and Yuk Hui. 'For a Strategic Primitivism: A Dialogue between Eduardo Viveiros de Castro and Yuk Hui', *Philosophy Today*, 20 April 2021.

Von Balthasar, Hans Urs. *The Glory of the Lord: A Theological Aesthetics. I. Seeing the Form*, tr. E. Leiva-Merikakis. San Francisco: Ignatius Press, 2009.

Von Foerster, Heinz. 'Notes on an Epistemology for Living Things', 'Perception of the Future and the Future of Perception', in *Understanding Understanding: Essays in Cybernetics and Cognition*. Berlin: Springer, 2010.

Von Uexküll, Jakob Johann. *A Foray into the Worlds of Animals and Humans with a Theory of Meaning*, tr. J.D. O'Neil. Minneapolis and London: University of Minnesota Press, 2010.

—— *Biologische Briefe an eine Dame*. Berlin: Verlag von Gebrüder Paetel, 1920.

—— *Theoretical Biology*. London: Kegan Paul, Trench, Trubner and co., 1926.

Wagner, Roy. 'The Reciprocity of Perspectives', *Social Anthropology* 26:4 (November 2018), 502–10.

—— *The Invention of Culture*. Chicago: University of Chicago Press, 1981.

Wahl, Jean. *Vers le concret. Etudes d'histoire de la philosophie contemporaine, William James, Whitehead, Gabriel Marcel*. Paris: Vrin, 2015.

Watts, Alan W. *Myth and Ritual in Christianity*. New York: Grove Press, 1960.

—— *The Joyous Cosmology*. Novato, CA: New World Library, 2013.

Weber, Max. 'Science as a Vocation', in *The Vocation Lectures*, tr. R. Livingstone. Indianapolis and Cambridge: Hackett, 2004.

Weil, Simone. *Intimations of Christianity Among the Greeks*. London: Routledge, 1998.

Westhelle, Vitor. *Eschatology and Space: The Lost Dimension of Theology Past and Present*. New York: Palgrave MacMillan, 2012.

Whitehead, Alfred North. *Adventures of Ideas*. New York: The Free Press, 1967.

— *Process and Reality*. New York: The Free Press, 1978.

— *Modes of Thought*. Cambridge: Cambridge University Press, 1938.

— *Science and the Modern World*. London: MacMillan, 1925.

— *The Concept of Nature*. New York: Dover, 2004.

Wilber, Ken. *Sex, Ecology, Spirituality: The Spirit of Evolution*. Boston & London: Shambhala, 2000.

Williams, Bernard. *Descartes: The Project of Pure Enquiry*. Oxford: Routledge, 2005.

Wilson, Robert Anton. 'Creative Agnosticism', *The Journal of Cognitive Liberties* 2:1 (2000), 61–84.

— Introduction to Israel Regardie, *The Eye in the Triangle: An Interpretation of Aleister Crowley*. Tempe, AZ: New Falcon Publications, 1997.

— *Prometheus Rising*. Grand Junction, CO: Hilaritas Press, 2006.

Youngquist, Paul. *A Pure Solar World: Sun Ra and the Birth of Afrofuturism*. Austin: University of Texas Press, 2016.

Zalamea, Fernando. *Modelos en haces para el pensamiento matématico*. Bogota: Editorial Universidad Nacional de Colombia, 2021.

Zubiri, Xavier. *Naturaleza, Historia, Dios*. Madrid: Alianza Editorial, 1971.

# Index of Names

## T



## U



## V



## W



## Y



## Z

# Index of Subjects

## A

## D

## E

## F

## I

**O**



**P**

## Q



## R

## S

## T